THE FORMS OF THE OLD TESTAMENT LITERATURE

Editors

ROLF P. KNIERIM • GENE M. TUCKER • MARVIN A. SWEENEY

*I	Genesis; with an Introduction to Narrative Literature	George W. Coats
*IIA	Exodus 1–18	George W. Coats
IIB	Exodus 19–40; with an Introduction to Legal Genres	Rolf P. Knierim
III	Leviticus	Rodney R. Hutton
*IV	Numbers	Rolf P. Knierim & George W. Coats
V	Deuteronomy	Frederick G. Tiffany
VIA	Joshua	Robert L. Hubbard, Jr.
VIB	Judges	Serge Frolov
*VII	1 Samuel	Antony F. Campbell
VIII	2 Samuel	Antony F. Campbell
*IX	1 Kings; with an Introduction to Historical Literature	Burke O. Long
*X	2 Kings	Burke O. Long
*XI	1 and 2 Chronicles	Simon J. De Vries
XII	Ezra, Nehemiah	Kent Richards
*XIII	Ruth, Esther, Job, Proverbs, Ecclesiastes, Canticles; with an Introduction to Wisdom Literature	Roland E. Murphy
*XIV	Psalms, Part 1; with an Introduction to Cultic Poetry	Erhard S. Gerstenberger
*XV	Psalms, Part 2; Lamentations	Erhard S. Gerstenberger
*XVI	Isaiah 1–39; with an Introduction to Prophetic Literature	Marvin A. Sweeney
XVII	Isaiah 40–66	Roy F. Melugin
XVIII	Jeremiah	Richard D. Weis
*XIX	Ezekiel	Ronald M. Hals
*XX	Daniel; with an Introduction to Apocalyptic Literature	John J. Collins
XXIA	Minor Prophets, Part 1	Ehud Ben Zvi & Gene M. Tucker
*XXIB	Micah	Ehud Ben Zvi
*XXII	Minor Prophets, Part 2	Michael H. Floyd
XXIII	Glossary of Genre Terms	Rolf P. Knierim & Gene M. Tucker
XXIV	Indices	Rolf P. Knierim & Gene M. Tucker

*Published

NUMBERS

ROLF P. KNIERIM
and
GEORGE W. COATS

The Forms of the Old Testament Literature

VOLUME IV

WILLIAM B. EERDMANS PUBLISHING COMPANY
GRAND RAPIDS, MICHIGAN / CAMBRIDGE, U.K.

Wm. B. Eerdmans Publishing Co.
255 Jefferson Ave. S.E., Grand Rapids, Michigan 49503 /
P.O. Box 163, Cambridge CB3 9PU U.K.

Printed in the United States of America

10 09 08 07 06 05   7 6 5 4 3 2 1

ISBN 0-8028-2231-2

www.eerdmans.com

CONTENTS

Abbreviations and Symbols   vi

Editors' Foreword   xi

NUMBERS

Chapter 1: The Book of Numbers: The Saga of the Migratory
Campaign (1:1–36:13)   3

Chapter 2: The Legend of the Organization of the
Sanctuary Campaign (1:1–10:10)   27

Chapter 3: The Individual Units (1:1–10:10) 42

Chapter 4: The Saga of the Campaign Itself (10:11–36:13) 135

Chapter 5: The Individual Units (10:11–36:13) 148

Appendix   332

Glossary   337

ABBREVIATIONS AND SYMBOLS

I. Miscellaneous Abbreviations and Symbols

ANE	Ancient Near East
Aufl.	Auflage
B.C.E.	before common era
cf.	compare
ch(s).	chapter(s)
cs.	construct
D	Deuteronomist source
Dec.	December
Diss.	Dissertation
Dtn	Deuteronomic
Dtr	Deuteronomistic; Deuteronomist
DtrH	Deuteronomistic historian
DtrR	Deuteronomistic redactor
E	Elohistic source
ed.	editor(s), edited by; edition
e.g.	for example
Eng.	English
Eng. tr.	English translation
esp.	especially
et al.	*et alii* (and others)
f(f).	following
Fest.	*Festschrift*
Hebr.	Hebrew
heraus.	herausgegeben
hiph.	hiphʿil
idem	the same
i.e.	*id est* (that is [to say])
impf.	imperfect
impv.	imperative

inf.	infinitive
J	Yahwistic source
LXX	Septuagint
masc.	masculine
MS(S)	manuscript(s)
MT	Masoretic Text
n.	note
niph.	niph'al
NT	New Testament
Num	Numbers
OT	Old Testament
P	Priestly source
p(p).	page(s)
par.	parallel (of words or phrases set in parallel)
part.	participle
pers.	person
Pg	original Priestly narrative
pi.	pi'el
pl.	plural
PN	Proper noun
repr.	reprint
rev. ed.	revised edition
RJE	Jehovistic combination of Yahwistic and Elohist sources
Rjep	redactor of Yahwistic, Elohistic, and Priestly sources
Sam Pent	Samaritan Pentateuch
sg.	singular
Syr	Syriac
Tiq Soph	Tiqqun Sopherim
tr.	translator(s), translated by
v(v).	verse(s)
vol(s).	volume(s)
vs.	versus
Vul	Vulgate
→	the arrow indicates a reference either to another section of the commentary, to another commentary, or to another biblical text
//	parallel

II. Publications

AB	Anchor Bible
ABLA	H. W. Wolff, ed., *Aufsätze zur biblischen Landes- und Altertumskunde* (Neukirchen: Neukirchener, 1971)
AJBI	*Annual of the Japanese Biblical Institute*
AnBib	Analecta biblica
ANEP	J. B. Pritchard, *The Ancient Near East in Pictures Relating to*

	the Old Testament (2nd ed. with supplement; Princeton: Princeton University Press, 1969)
ANET	J. B. Pritchard, ed., *Ancient Near Eastern Texts Relating to the Old Testament* (3rd ed.; Princeton: Princeton University Press, 1969)
AOAT	Alter Orient und Altes Testament
ARE	J. H. Breasted, ed., *Ancient Records of Egypt* (5 vols.; Chicago: University of Chicago Press, 1906-1907)
ASTI	*Annual of the Swedish Theological Institute*
ATANT	Abhandlungen zur Theologie des Alten und Neuen Testaments
BA	*Biblical Archaeologist*
BBB	Bonner Biblische Beiträge
BDB	F. Brown, S. R. Driver, and C. A. Briggs, *A Hebrew and English Lexicon of the Old Testament* (Oxford: Clarendon Press, 1968)
BFPLUL	Bibliothèque de la Faculté de Philosophie et Lettres de l'Université de Liège
Bibl	Biblica
BJS	Brown Judaic Studies
BK	*Bibel und Kirche*
BKAT	Biblischer Kommentar: Altes Testament
BN	Biblische Notizen
BR	*Biblical Research*
BT	*Bible Translator*
BTB	*Biblical Theology Bulletin*
BWANT	Beiträge zur Wissenschaft vom Alten und Neuen Testament
BZ	*Biblische Zeitschrift*
BZ NF	*Biblische Zeitschrift Neue Folge*
BZAW	Beihefte zur Zeitschrift für die alttestamentliche Wissenschaft
CBQ	*Catholic Biblical Quarterly*
CBQMS	Catholic Biblical Quarterly Monograph Series
CHAL	W. L. Holladay, *A Concise Hebrew and Aramaic Lexicon of the Old Testament* (Grand Rapids: Eerdmans, 1971)
CNEB	Cambridge Bible Commentary on the New English Bible
DD	*Dor le Dor*
EKL	*Evangelisches Kirchenlexikon*
EncJud	*Encyclopaedia Judaica* (Jerusalem: The Macmillan Company, 1971-72)
EOTHR	A. Alt, *Essays on Old Testament History and Religion* (tr. R. A. Wilson; Garden City: Doubleday, 1967)
ErIs	*Eretz Israel*
FOTL	The Forms of the Old Testament Literature
FRLANT	Forschungen zur Religion und Literatur des Alten und Neuen Testaments
HALAT	L. H. Köhler and W. Baumgartner, *Hebräisches und aramäisches Lexikon zum Alten Testament* (3 vols.; Leiden: E. J. Brill, 1967 [I], 1974 [II], 1983 [III])

HTR	*Harvard Theological Review*
HTS	*Hervormde Theological Review*
HUC	*Hebrew Union College Jubilee Volume*
HUCA	*Hebrew Union College Annual*
ICC	International Critical Commentary
IDB	*Interpreter's Dictionary of the Bible*
IDBSup	Supplementary volume to *Interpreter's Dictionary of the Bible*
Int	*Interpretation*
JAOS	*Journal of the American Oriental Society*
JBL	*Journal of Biblical Literature*
JEA	*Journal of Egyptian Archeology*
JPOS	*Journal of the Palestine Oriental Society*
JPS	Jewish Publication Society
JQR	*The Jewish Quarterly Review*
JSOT	*Journal for the Study of the Old Testament*
JSOTSup	*Journal for the Study of the Old Testament Supplement Series*
JTS	*Journal of Theological Studies*
JTVI	*Journal of Transactions of the Victoria Institute*
KHC	Kurzer Hand-Commentar zum Alten Testament
KK	Kurzgefasster Kommentar zu den heiligen Schriften Alten und Neuen Testaments
KS	*Kleine Schriften zur Geschichte des Volkes Israel*
LAS	Leipziger ägyptische Studien
LCL	The Loeb Classical Library
MTS	Mass. Text Stuttgartensia
NCB	The Century Bible. New Edition
NICOT	New International Commentary on the Old Testament
NRSV	New Revised Standard Version
OTL	Old Testament Library
PEQ	*Palestine Exploration Quarterly*
Pers	*Perspectives in Religious Studies*
PJ	*Palästina Jahrbuch*
PSB	*The Princeton Seminary Bulletin*
QD	Quaestiones Disputatae
RB	*Revue biblique*
RevExp	*Review & Expositor*
RGG3	*Die Religion in Geschichte und Gegenwart* (3rd ed.; 7 vols.; Tübingen: Mohr, 1957-65)
RSV	Revised Standard Version
SANT	*Studien zum Alten und Neuen Testament*
SB	Sources bibliques
SBL	Society of Biblical Literature
SBLASP	Society of Biblical Literature Abstracts and Seminar Papers
SBT	Studies in Biblical Theology
SJLA	Studies in Judaism in Late Antiquity
SJT	*Scottish Journal of Theology*
TBü	Theologische Bücherei

TDNT	G. Kittel and G. Friedrich, eds., *Theological Dictionary of the New Testament* (tr. and ed. G. Bromiley; 10 vols.; Grand Rapids: Eerdmans, 1964-76)
TDOT	G. J. Botterweck and H. Ringgren, eds., *Theological Dictionary of the Old Testament* (Eng. tr.; 12 vols.; Grand Rapids: Eerdmans, 1974-)
THAT	E. Jenni, ed., *Theologisches Handwörterbuch zum Alten Testament* (2 vols.; Munich: Chr. Kaiser, 1971, 1976)
ThPQ	*Theologisch-praktische Quartalschrift*
TRE	G. Müller, ed., *Theologische Realenzyklopädie* (Berlin/New York: W. de Gruyter, 1994-)
TWAT	G. J. Botterweck und H. Ringgren, eds., *Theologisches Wörterbuch zum Alten Testament* (Stuttgart: Kohlhammer, 1970-)
TynB	*Tyndale Bulletin*
TZ	*Theologische Zeitschrift*
UF	*Ugarit-Forschungen*
VT	*Vetus Testamentum*
WBC	Word Biblical Commentary
WMANT	Wissenschaftliche Monographien zum Alten und Neuen Testament
YNER	Yale Near Eastern Researches
ZAW	*Zeitschrift für die alttestmentliche Wissenschaft*
ZDPV	*Zeitschrift des deutschen Palästinavereins*

Editors' Foreword

The work for the present volume IV, on Numbers, continues to follow the basic design for the entire FOTL series. While discussion of its guidelines is found in the volumes published thus far — in volumes I, IIA, IV, VII, IX, X, XI, XIII, XIV, XV, XVI, XIX, XX, XXIB, and XXII — the reader's particular attention is directed to the Editors' Updated Foreword to volume IIA of the series on Exodus 1–18 by Professor George W. Coats. In that Foreword reference is made to the particular conditions under which the process of the production and editing of volume IIA evolved. The work on the present volume had to proceed under the same, only much more complicated conditions as the years have gone by.

The volume was originally designed by a division of authorial labor in which everything belonging to Num 1:1–10:10 was to be done by R. P. Knierim and everything belonging to Num 10:11–36:13 by G. W. Coats. In fact the prevailing developments necessitated that Chapters 1, 2, 3, but also Chapter 4 and the unit Num 10:11-36 in Chapter 5 as well were done by R. P. Knierim. Num 11:1–36:13 of Chapter 5 was originally submitted by G. W. Coats. It was especially technically thoroughly updated by the former research associates to the FOTL project, Ms. Mignon Jacobs and — after her — Mr. David Palmer, both now Ph.D's from Claremont Graduate University (CGU). They also set the stage for the organization of the Glossary. Their work deserves decisive credit for upgrading the shape of these parts of the volume. For processing the readiness of the volume towards final redactional work the level and quality of Mr. Palmer's efforts deserve more praise than words can express. Ms. Janice Bakke, current senior Ph.D. student in the department of Hebrew Bible at CGU, deserves gratitude for contributing to the final organization of the Glossary and for superb technical and substantive assistance across the volume. The continuing home of the project at, and its support by the Institute for Antiquity and Christianity, cannot be highly enough appreciated. The grant by its Research Council of the stipend for Ms. Bakke is the most direct evidence. But gratefully acknowledged must also be the constructive support of the Institute by the members of its Board of Trustees, and particularly through the leadership of its active and circumspect chairperson, the Hon. Rafael Chodos, including his personal commitment also to FOTL.

It must be repeated that the foremost interest in the design of the FOTL project is its application of form-critical work first of all to the literature of the biblical books as we have it before us, including attention to the discernible strata that belong to the history of the development of this literature. Before everything else the project focuses on the work of these biblical writers, on the perspectives from which they structured their large and individual units, on the genres by which those structures were influenced, and on the traditions of those genres. It focuses on the writers' own settings rather than on the question of the "historical situations" — often misleadingly called "settings" — situations to which the texts refer and which in part antedate the conditions of the writers who depicted them by almost a millennium. To interpret these writers' intention amounts as is generally known to nothing more than the interpreter's attempt to keep the writers connected with their texts and to imagine with better rather than weaker arguments their meaning and purpose for their readers as far as their texts themselves allow.

The reader will recognize that next to the presentation of the conceptualized structure of each unit the explanation of this structure takes most of the space in the commentary. Together with the discovery of the structure itself it represents the exegete's predominant workload. First and above all else the structures reveal to those seriously interested in the study of the biblical texts that these texts are conceptualized entities, works of literature ordered systemically and which demand admiration for the intellectual efforts of their writers the longer one studies them. With this focus the FOTL project remains to this day a unique contribution to the work of exegesis without parallel in any of the existing commentaries. Although what Professor Coats was able to accomplish declined over the course of the years, his discussions of the individual units of Num 11:1–36:13 remain irreplaceable and a testament to his brilliance and productivity. Bibliographical reference does thereby not always include the latest entries on Numbers. But it is in principle also not required to be universal; it can be confined to those publications that are relevant for the focus on this kind of form-critical work.

Finally it is time to announce that Professor Gene M. Tucker decided some years ago to relinquish his position as one of the two co-editors of the FOTL series and that Professor Marvin A. Sweeney has taken Professor Tucker's place since 1997. Professor Sweeney joins Rolf P. Knierim at this time in expressing profound appreciation to Professor Tucker for his hard work throughout the decades and for his exemplary role in the design and launching of this project. Professor Tucker still remains responsible for writing the commentary on Amos — a part of volume XXIA — and, along with this authorial task, also for co-editing the very same volume.

ROLF P. KNIERIM
MARVIN A. SWEENEY

NUMBERS

Chapter 1

THE BOOK OF NUMBERS

Bibliography

W. F. Albright, "The Administrative Divisions of Israel and Judah," *JPOS* 5 (1925) 17-54; A. Alt, "Beiträge zur historischen Geographie und Topographie des Negeb," *KS* III, 382-459; "Die Staatenbildung der Israeliten in Palästina," *KS* II, 1-65 (Eng. tr. "The Formation of the Israelite State in Palestine," *EOTHR,* 223-309); H. Alterman, *Counting People: The Census in History* (New York: Harcourt, Brace and World, 1969); T. A. Ashley, *The Book of Numbers* (NICOT; Grand Rapids: Eerdmans, 1993); R. Bach, *Die Aufforderungen zur Flucht und zum Kampf im alttestamentlichen Prophetenspruch* (WMANT 9; Neukirchen: Neukirchener, 1962); B. Baentsch, *Exodus-Leviticus-Numeri* (Göttingen: Vandenhoeck & Ruprecht, 1903); M. Barnouin, "Les recensements du livre des Nombres et l'astronomie babylonienne," *VT* 27 (1977) 280-303; "Remarques sur les tableaux numériques du livre des Nombres," *RB* 76 (1969) 351-64; J. R. Bartlett, "Zadok and His Successors at Jerusalem," *JTS* 19 (1968) 1-18; R. A. Bascom, "Prolegomena to the Study of the Itinerary Genre in the Old Testament and Beyond" (Diss., Claremont Graduate School, 1986); A. Bentzen, *Introduction to the Old Testament* (5th ed., 2 vols. in 1; Copenhagen: G. E. C. Gad, 1959); E. Blum, *Studien zur Komposition des Pentateuch* (BZAW 189; Berlin/New York: Walter de Gruyter, 1990); J. H. Breasted, "Building Inscription [of Ahmos I]," *ARE* II, 33-37; "The Building Inscription of the Temple of Heliopolis," *ARE* I, 498-506; "The Reign of Thutmose III: The Annals II: The First Campaign (Year 23)," *ARE* II, 408-43; M. Buber, *Moses: The Revelation and the Covenant* (New York: Harper Torchbooks, 1958); P. J. Budd, *Numbers* (WBC V; Waco: Word, 1984); J. Calvin, *Calvin's Commentaries* (Vol. III; Grand Rapids: Baker Book House, 1979); A. F. Campbell & M. A. O'Brien, *Sources of the Pentateuch* (Minneapolis: Fortress, 1993); U. Cassuto, *A Commentary on the Book of Exodus* (tr. Israel Abrahams; 2nd ed.; Jerusalem: Magnes, 1974); H. Cazelles, *Les Nombres* (Paris: Editions du Cerf, 1952); B. S. Childs, *An Introduction to the Old Testament as Scripture* (Philadelphia: Fortress, 1979); R. E. D. Clark, "The Large Numbers of the Old Testament — Especially in Connexion with the Exodus," *JTVI* 87 (1955) 82-92; D. J. A. Clines, *The Theme of the Pentateuch* (JSOTSup 10; Sheffield: JSOT, 1978); G. W. Coats, *From Canaan to Egypt: Structural and Theological Context for the Joseph Story*

(CBQMS 4; Washington: Catholic Biblical Association of America, 1976); idem, *Genesis: With an Introduction to Narrative Literature* (FOTL I; Grand Rapids: Eerdmans, 1983); idem, *Exodus 1–18* (FOTL IIA; Grand Rapids: Eerdmans, 1999); idem, *Rebellion in the Wilderness: The Murmuring Motif in the Wilderness Traditions of the Old Testament* (Nashville: Abingdon Press, 1968); G. W. Coats, ed., *Saga, Legend, Tale, Novella, Fable: Narrative Forms in Old Testament Literature* (JSOTSup 35; Sheffield: JSOT, 1985); M. A. Cohen, "The Role of the Shilonite Priesthood in the United Monarchy of Ancient Israel," *HUCA* 36 (1965) 59-98; F. M. Cross, *Canaanite Myth and Hebrew Epic* (Cambridge: Harvard, 1973); G. I. Davis, *Numbers* (The New Century Bible Commentary; Grand Rapids: Eerdmans, 1995); idem, "The Wilderness Itineraries: A Comparative Study," *TynB* 25 (1974) 46-81; S. J. De Vries, *1-2 Chronicles* (FOTL XI; Grand Rapids: Eerdmans, 1988); O. Eissfeldt, *The Old Testament: An Introduction* (tr. Peter R. Ackroyd; New York: Harper & Row, 1965); H.-J. Fabry, *"nēs,"* *TWAT* V, 468-73; G. Fohrer, *Introduction to the Old Testament* (Nashville: Abingdon, 1968); V. Fritz, *Tempel und Zelt: Studien zum Tempelbau in Israel und zu dem Zeltheiligtum der Priesterschrift* (WMANT 47; Neukirchen: Neukirchener, 1977); Sir A. H. Gardiner, "The Defeat of the Hyksos by Kamose: The Carnarvon Tablet, No. I," *JEA* 3 (1916) 95-110; Sir A. H. Gardiner, ed., *Ancient Egyptian Onomastica* (3 vols.; London: Oxford, 1968); T. H. Gaster, *Myth, Legend and Custom in the Old Testament* (New York: Harper & Row, 1969); W. H. Gispen, *Het Boek Numeri* (2 vols.; Kampen: J. H. Kok, 1959, 1964); M. Görg, *Das Zelt der Begegnung* (BBB 27; Bonn: Hanstein, 1967); N. K. Gottwald, *The Hebrew Bible: A Socio-Literary Introduction* (Philadelphia: Fortress, 1985); idem, *The Tribes of Yahweh: A Sociology of the Religion of Liberated Israel, 1250-1050 B.C.E.* (Maryknoll: Orbis, 1979); idem, "War, Holy," *IDBSup;* G. B. Gray, *A Critical and Exegetical Commentary on Numbers* (ICC; New York: Charles Scribner's Sons, 1903); H. Gressmann, *Mose und seine Zeit: Ein Kommentar zu den Mose-Sagen* (FRLANT 18; Göttingen: Vandenhoeck & Ruprecht, 1913); idem, *Die Heilige Schrift des Alten und des Neuen Testaments* (Zürich: Zwingli-Bibel, 1980); R. K. Harrison, *Numbers* (Wycliffe; Grand Rapids: Baker, 1992); K. J. Heinisch, ed., *Kaiser Friedrich II, in Briefen und Berichten seiner Zeit* (Darmstadt: Wissenschaftliche Buchgesellschaft, 1968); H. W. Helck, *Historisch-Biographische Texte der 2. Zwischenzeit und neue Texte der 18. Dynastie* (Wiesbaden: Harrassowitz, 1975); F. J. Helfmeyer, *Die Nachfolge Gottes im Alten Testament* (BBB 29; Bonn: Hanstein, 1968); *"ḥānâ, maḥaneh,"* *TDOT* V, 4-19; A. Hermann, *Die ägyptische Königsnovelle* (LAS 10; Glückstadt: J. J. Augustin, 1938); H. A. Hoffner, *"bayith,"* *TDOT* II, 107-16; H. Holzinger, *Numeri* (KHC IV; Tübingen: J. C. B. Mohr, 1903); Homer, *The Iliad* (LCL; tr. A. T. Murray; Cambridge: Harvard University, 1965-67); B. Jacob, *Der Pentateuch: Exegetisch-kritische Forschungen* (Leipzig: von Veit, 1905); E. Jenni, *"bájit, Haus,"* *THAT* I, 308-13; M. Z. Kaddari, *"nāsa',"* *TWAT* V, 493-97; Y. Kaufmann, *The Religion of Israel: From Its Beginnings to the Babylonian Exile* (tr. and abridged by M. Greenberg; Chicago: University of Chicago Press, 1960); D. Kellermann, *Die Priesterschrift von Numeri 1,1 bis 10,10: Literarkritisch und traditionsgeschichtlich untersucht* (BZAW 120; Berlin: Walter de Gruyter, 1970); R. W. Klein, "How Many in a Thousand?" (paper presented at the annual meeting of SBL, New York, Dec. 1982); R. P. Knierim, "The Composition of the Pentateuch" (SBLASP 24; Atlanta: Scholars, 1985) 393-415; idem, *Exodus 19–40: With an Introduction to Legal Genres* (FOTL IIB; Grand Rapids: Eerdmans, forthcoming); K. Koch, *"ʼōhel, ʼāhal,"* *TDOT* I, 118-30; J. R.

Kupper, *Les nomades en Mésopotamie au temps des rois de Mari* (BFPLUL 142; Paris: Société d'Édition "Les Belles Lettres," 1957); idem, "Le recensement dans les textes de Mari," *Studia Mariana* (ed. A. Parrot; Leiden: E. J. Brill, 1950) 99-110; W. W. Lee, "Punishment and Forgiveness in Israel's Migratory Campaign: The Macrostructure of Numbers 10:11–36:13" (Diss., Claremont Graduate University, 1998); B. A. Levine, "Numbers, Book of," *IDBSup;* idem, "Priestly Writers," *IDBSup;* idem, *Numbers 1–20* (AB 4A; New York/London: Doubleday, 1993); J. Liver, "The Half-Shekel Offering in Biblical and Post-Biblical Literature," *HTR* 56 (1963) 173-98; B. O. Long, *I Kings: With an Introduction to Old Testament Historical Literature* (FOTL IX; Grand Rapids: Eerdmans, 1984); A. Lucas, "The Number of Israelites at the Exodus," *PEQ* 76 (1944) 164-68; G. Maier, *Das vierte Buch Mose* (Wuppertal: Brockhaus, 1989); Y. Margowsky, "War and Warfare: To the Destruction of the First Temple," *EncJud* 16, 266-78; A. D. H. Mayes, *Israel in the Period of the Judges* (SBT II, 29; Naperville: A. R. Allenson, 1974); G. E. Mendenhall, "The Census Lists of Numbers 1 and 26," *JBL* 77 (1958) 52-66; idem, "The Hebrew Conquest of Palestine," *BA* 25 (1962) 66-87; idem, "Social Organization in Early Israel," in *Magnalia Dei: The Mighty Acts of God (Fest.* G. E. Wright; ed. F. M. Cross et al.; Garden City: Doubleday, 1976) 132-51; J. Milgrom, *Numbers* (JPS; Philadelphia/NewYork: Jewish Publication Society, 1990); idem, *Studies in Cultic Theology and Terminology* (SJLA 36; Leiden: E. J. Brill, 1983); K. Möhlenbrink, "Die levitischen Überlieferungen des Alten Testaments," *ZAW* 52 (1934) 184-231; M. Noth, *A History of Pentateuchal Traditions* (tr. B. W. Anderson; Chico: Scholars, 1981); idem, *Die israelitischen Personennamen im Rahmen der gemeinsemitischen Namengebung* (BWANT III, 10; Hildesheim: G. Olms, 1980); idem, *Numbers: A Commentary* (OTL; tr. J. D. Martin; Philadelphia: Westminster, 1968); idem, *Das System der zwölf Stämme Israels* (Darmstadt: Wissenschaftliche Buchgesellschaft, 1966); idem, "Die Topographie Palästinas und Syriens im Licht ägyptischer Quellen," *ABLA* II, 1-132; idem, "Der Wallfahrtsweg zum Sinai (Nu 33)," *ABLA* I, 55-74; idem, "Zur Geschichte und Topographie einzelner Stämme Israels," *ABLA* I, 157-343; D. T. Olson, *The Death of the Old and the Birth of the New: The Framework of the Book of Numbers and the Pentateuch* (BJS 71; Chico: Scholars, 1985); Sir W. M. Flinders Petrie, *Egypt and Israel* (New York: Macmillan, 1923); idem, *Researches in Sinai* (New York: E. P. Dutton, 1906); T. Pola, *Die ursprüngliche Priesterschrift* (WMANT 70; Neukirchen: Neukirchener, 1995); G. von Rad, *Genesis: A Commentary* (OTL; tr. J. H. Marks; rev. ed.; Philadelphia: Westminster, 1973); M. Razin, *Census Lists and Genealogies and Their Historical Implications for the Times of Saul and David* (Hebr.; 2nd ed.; ed. S. Bendor; Haifa: The School of Education of the Kibbutz Movement, 1977); M. D. Rehm, "Zadok the Priest," *IDBSup;* R. Rendtorff, *The Old Testament: An Introduction* (tr. J. Bowden; Philadelphia: Fortress, 1986); E. Rivkin, "Aaron, Aaronides," *IDBSup;* idem, "Ben Sira: The Bridge Between the Aaronide and Pharisaic Revolutions," *ErIs* 12 (1975) 95-103; idem, *The Shaping of Jewish History: A Radical New Interpretation* (New York: Scribner, 1971); J. A. Sanders, "Census," *IDB* I, 547; J. M. Sasson, "A Genealogical 'Convention' in Biblical Chronography?" *ZAW* 90 (1978) 171-85; C. Schedl, "Biblische Zahlen — unglaubwürdig?" *ThPQ* 107 (1959) 58-62; W. H. Schmidt, J. Bergman and H. Lutzmann, *"dābhar, dābhār,"* *TDOT* III, 84-125; H. Seebass, *Numeri* (BKAT, IV/1ff.; Neukirchen: Neukirchener, 1993ff.); J. Skinner, *A Critical and Exegetical Commentary on Genesis* (ICC; 2nd ed.; Edinburgh: T&T Clark, 1930); N. H. Snaith, *Leviticus and Numbers* (NCB; Greenwood: Attic Press, 1967); B. D. Sommer,

"Reflecting on Moses: The Redaction of Numbers 11," JBL 118/4 (1999) 601-24; A. J. Spalinger, *Aspects of the Military Documents of the Ancient Egyptians* (YNER 9; New Haven: Yale, 1982); E. A. Speiser, "The Alalakh Tablets," *JAOS* 74 (1954) 18-25; idem, *Genesis* (AB I; Garden City: Doubleday, 1964); H. L. Strack, *Die Bücher Genesis, Exodus, Leviticus und Numeri* (KK; Nördlingen: C. H. Beck, 1894); J. Sturdy, *Numbers* (CNEB; Cambridge: Cambridge University Press, 1976); S. Talmon, "Ezra and Nehemiah (Books and Men)," *IDBSup;* J. de Vaux, *Les Nombres* (SB; Paris: J. Gabalda, 1972); R. de Vaux, *Ancient Israel: Its Life and Institutions* (tr. John McHugh; 2 vols.; New York: McGraw-Hill, 1961); M. Weippert, *The Settlement of the Israelite Tribes in Palestine* (SBT II, 21; Naperville: Alec R. Allenson, 1971); J. Wellhausen, *Die Composition des Hexateuchs und der historischen Bücher des Alten Testaments* (4th ed.; Berlin: Walter de Gruyter, 1963); idem, *Prolegomena to the History of Ancient Israel* (1883; repr. Gloucester, MA: Peter Smith, 1973); idem, *Der Text der Bücher Samuelis untersucht* (Göttingen: Vandenhoeck & Ruprecht, 1871); J. W. Wenham, "Large Numbers in the Old Testament," *TynB* 18 (1967) 19-53; R. R. Wilson, "The Old Testament Genealogies in Recent Research," *JBL* 94 (1975) 169-89; idem, "Between 'Azel' and 'Azel': Interpreting the Biblical Genealogies," *BA* 42 (1979) 11-22; R. Wischnitzer, "Ark," *EncJud* 3, 450-58; D. J. Wiseman, *The Alalakh Tablets* (Occasional Publications 2; London: British Institute of Archaeology at Ankara, 1953); Y. Yadin et al., "Temple," *EncJud* 15, 942-87.

Prolegomena

The book of Numbers is a part of the Pentateuchal narrative, and many signs in it point to its place between the books of Leviticus and Deuteronomy in the flow of that narrative. However, its own shape does not easily reveal a coherent and homogeneous literary work. Numbers is a literary composite: it is cast in different styles; it contains a respectable diversity of genres; it betrays in its individual units a variety of aspects whose relationship among one another and place in the composition of the whole are not self-evident.

The multifaceted shape of Numbers has been recognized to be the result of a complex growth process which extended throughout several centuries, during which individual traditions and new concerns were committed to texts and increasingly woven together. Cf. the commentaries, OT introductions, and the articles on Numbers, Pentateuch, literary criticism et al. in, among others, *EncJud, EKL, IDB, IDBSup, RGG3*. The growth process of Numbers is part of the growth process of the entire Pentateuch. It is the result of a specific kind of history for which generations of experts were accountable. These experts were on the one hand the collectors and interpreters of tradition — especially the traditions of Israel's religion — and on the other hand the persons involved in or responsible for the ongoing shape of Israel's societal life, especially the life of its religious institutions. The close study of these texts has convincingly shown that the assumption of their origin by the hand of one writer or in one generation is ultimately alien to the convictions of the many generations who accounted for these works, and to the specifically theological nature of the works themselves.

It is possible that in some instances the literary texts were preceded by oral traditions. The existence of such traditions can only be postulated hypothetically from case to case. The hypothetical nature of the assumption of oral traditions is inevitable. What can be observed in Numbers is primarily a development on the written, literary level and of a literary nature. None of its texts can automatically be assumed to belong to what is called oral literature. In the transition of texts from oral to written stages, transformation is always possible. In many literary types, in prose and especially in larger corpora, it is the rule. Wherever the literary units in Numbers suggest an oral background — a background which we do not possess — specific indications are necessary for such an assumption. Finally, we will have to account for the fact that certain texts represent *ad hoc,* genuinely literary creations without an oral tradition behind them. We have to distinguish between oral and genuinely written literature.

The evidence indicates that by far most of the individual text-units presently contained in Numbers, and especially their coordination, belong to the literary level. The literary history which they indicate is complicated and in part still and perhaps forever obscure. There is justifiable reason to assume the existence of the source strata found in Genesis, Exodus, and Leviticus: the Yahwist (J) and perhaps the Elohist (E), the Yahwistic combination of both (RJE), and especially the Priestly writings (P). The expression "Priestly writings" refers much more to a history of ongoing priestly traditions rather than to a uni-level source, as in the case of J or E. In this priestly history, which lasted about as long as the entire growth of the Pentateuch and which had its setting in the continuous history of the Israelite — especially Jerusalemite — priesthood, a great variety of traditions was adapted and amalgamated. The inherited corpora which we no longer possess were successively expanded in new editions throughout the generations. The book of Numbers reflects a part of this history of the Israelite priesthood. It is a part of the ongoing literary activity generated by this setting, the office of these priests, and the basically theological priestly interests emanating from this setting. Childs correctly speaks of the sacerdotal perspective in Numbers (pp. 195-98).

However, not all the text-units can be explained in terms of sources. Many of them, especially in the Priestly writings, are in their entirety or in part the result of accretions to or expansions of older units. And in some cases we have to account for the incorporation of independent traditions. These aspects will be discussed where necessary at their places below.

Under the guidelines of the FOTL series, the primary task of this commentary is not to reconstruct the historical growth of the book of Numbers itself. That process is in any case interdependent in a bilateral sense with the books of Genesis-Leviticus and the deuteronomic/deuteronomistic literature. For a comprehensive discussion of these problems, cf. the essays on "Numbers" and "Priestly Writers" in the *IDBSup* by B. Levine, and for a meticulous analysis of the literary-historical development in Num 1:1–10:10 cf. the work of D. Kellermann. In this commentary, the growth process is presupposed in principle, but referred to in specifics with restraint; restraint not only because it is difficult to establish the diachronic and synchronic stages definitively but especially because the commentary focuses on the sociological aspects of the literature, its individual and generic structures, and its genres and settings in that history. These aspects can be determined even if we do not always know their specific historical moment. But it is nonetheless important for us to be aware of the fact that they represent distinct developments in Israel's history. Like most of the OT literature, Numbers did not and could not emerge at any time and from any people in the history of humanity. Numbers reflects its own time and the setting of its own people in that time.

Such awareness is of fundamental importance also for the form-critical interpretation. It reveals the active involvement of many generations of Israelite narrators and writers in the ongoing adaptation of their most important ancient story, and their conceptualization of its significance for their own and for future generations. It points to the ongoing living communities to whom we owe our texts and without whom we would have nothing. The texts are the work of people, and reflect the realities and interests of these people.

This fact also constitutes the reason why the form-critical interpretation focuses on the texts themselves, and not on the question of the historicity of the events related in the texts. The times and societal settings of the writers of the texts are in principle different from the times and settings of the events which they narrated. Whether the modern reader realizes it or not, when one reads these texts, one encounters the generations who authored these texts. The events of which the texts speak are encountered only in the sense in which those generations understood the events and themselves. This distinction, often not accounted for, between the times and settings of the texts themselves on the one hand, and the times and settings of events narrated in the texts on the other, is inevitable and programmatic, especially for the so-called historical literature of the OT.

The texts and their growth processes reveal in many ways that the generations who transmitted their ancient traditions were not preoccupied with the modern historiographical question as to what really and exactly happened in the past. This modern question aims at reconstructing the past on its own terms, in a critical review of the transmitted traditions about it, and in distinction from its meaning for the modern time. This modernistic study of history was alien to our authors, and so would be our reading of their texts governed by this question. Instead of researching for the sake of the knowledge of what had happened in the past, these narrators and writers adapted from generation to generation the traditions about the past, and shaped them in view of their importance for their own time. In their emerging narratives, traditional memory and new interpretation were interwoven. This fact is decisive for the form-critical understanding of the entire Pentateuch, including Numbers, and of much of the rest of the so-called historical literature in the OT. Strictly speaking, this literature belongs at best to the genre of history writing in the ancient sense before Thucydides (at least), but not in the modern sense of the word. And in that sense, ancient history may be called more appropriately Hermeneutics of History. It is an interpretation of the present in the form of that past which reflects the present conditions and is considered constitutive for them. It is, therefore, entirely consistent with the function and intention of this Hermeneutics of History that the Pentateuch as a whole, and with it Numbers, came to be understood and called Torah: Instruction, Teaching.

In view of the fact that the Book of Numbers represents primarily a literary history, form-critical interpretation must above all come to grips with the literary nature of the structures, genres, settings, and functions or intentions of its individual units and its composition as a whole. In this respect, it seems helpful to distinguish between older traditions which antedate the texts, and upon which the texts rest, and conditions contemporaneous with or underneath the texts, conditions in certain settings that generated the texts whether these conditions were traditional or not. We may distinguish between form-history and form-sociology. At the same time, the concerns and contents of these units, or their themes, cannot be neglected. Form criticism is not formalism criticism that would subtract what is said from the formal aspects of the texts. Indeed, many individual and generic text structures are organized conceptually. They represent semantic systems which cannot be understood without accounting for the concepts that generated them. This fact is also relevant for Numbers, which is eminently governed by the theological interests and concepts of its writers. These essentially theological concepts are part of Israel's history of religion. The form-critical interpretation must not fail to account for them.

Finally, but in fact to begin with, attention must be paid to the mainly final outcome of the long growth process of Numbers, the shape of its final redaction in its Masoretic form. Cf. on this point also the FOTL volumes on Genesis and Exodus. For too long, this task has been left aside, in part because of the seemingly incoherent organization of the work, and only recently has explicit attention to it been called for. The chapters in this commentary on the structure of the work as whole and its major parts represent a step in that direction.

The Saga of the Migratory Campaign (1:1–36:13)

Structure

I. The Legend of the Organization of the Sanctuary Campaign	1:1–10:10
II. The Saga of the Campaign Itself	10:11–36:13

The twofold subdivision of Numbers focuses on the super- or macro-structure of the entire book at the highest level. This subdivision is not self-evident. Numbers offers a variety of structural signals, but it is not explicit about their relevance for the various structural layers in the book. Exegetes have been puzzled by this problem: Gray said that Numbers "possesses no unity of subject" (p. xxiv); Noth spoke of "the confusion and lack of order in its contents" (*Numbers,* 4); Levine referred to its "tenuous literary structure" ("Numbers," 631) and to Numbers as "the least coherent of all the Torah books" ("Numbers," 634); Childs said that the scholarly disagreement "confirms the impression that there are no clear indications within the text of how the editors wished to divide the material at this juncture" and that "although geographical features are significant, their importance in establishing a structure should not be exaggerated. The biblical editors seem less concerned with this literary problem than are modern commentators" (195). And most recently, Rendtorff said that "of all the books in the Pentateuch, the Book of Numbers is the hardest to survey. It is even difficult to decide how to divide it" (*Introduction,* 147). The authors just mentioned are representative. For a comprehensive review of the history of scholarship, cf. Olson, 9-40.

Nevertheless, almost every exegete attempts to recognize some subdivisions in Numbers, mostly three, and these basically on geographical grounds. Yet they differ on the specifics, e.g.: 1:1–10:10; 10:11–21:9; 21:10–36:13 (Gray, xxvi-xxix); 1:1–10:10; 10:11–20:13; 20:14–36:13 (Snaith, 180, 222, 276; Rendtorff, *Introduction,* 147-50); 1:1–10:10; 10:11–22:1; 22:2–36:13 (de Vaux, 10-13; Childs, 195-99); 1:1–9:14; 9:15–25:18; 26:1–35:34 plus appendix (Budd, xvii); 1:1–10:36; 11:1–20:13; 20:14–36:13 (Noth, *Numbers,* vii-viii; cf. Coats, *Genesis,* 17).

Olson's work deserves special attention as the first programmatic attempt to determine the superstructure of Numbers in its present form. According to Olson, Numbers is a separate literary unit in the Pentateuch which consists of two parts, chs. 1–25 and 26-36. This main subdivision is based on the thematic aspect of the transition from the old generation to the new generation. The difference between the two generations is signaled structurally by the two census reports in chs. 1 and 26. Several formal and thematic aspects support the main signal.

Olson's focus on a thematically based structure, on the difference between both generations, and on the two census reports is without doubt important. Whether it suffices to sustain his thesis is a different question.

Olson's criteria prove little. They may just as much support a different thesis once it is assumed. His obvious concentration on the two generations has prevented Olson from carefully analyzing alternative structural options suggested by the material itself. Such options appear both within Numbers and in the context of the Pentateuch.

The thesis itself raises major questions. The motif of the two generations would have to be compared with other factors, including the tradition of the thirty-eight or forty years of "wandering in the wilderness," the reasons given for that period and its territory, and the evidence within that tradition for structurally identifiable blocks.

The position of Numbers 1 in the Sinai pericope and in Num 1:1–10:10 is discussed insufficiently. This deficit affects a proper understanding of the relationship of "census" and camp order in Numbers 1 and 2, the relationship of the twelve tribes and the Levites in Numbers 1–2 and 3–4, the function of Numbers 1 within Num 1:1–10:10 and within the Sinai pericope (Yahweh begins to speak from the tent of meeting from Leviticus 1 and not from Numbers 1 on!), and consequently, the relationship between Numbers 1 and 26. The results of such considerations raise serious doubts about the correlation of Numbers 1 and 26 on the highest structural level.

Numbers 1 and 2 speak about the new formation of the twelve tribes (without Levi) at the Sinai camp on a certain date — the old generation is of interest — after the exodus and before the impending migratory campaign. In this context the "census" in Numbers 1 stands neither for the beginning nor for the failure nor obedience of the old generation. Numbers 26 while assuming the same formation — not a new one (Olson) — focuses on the "census" of the new generation for a specific reason: the failure of the old generation. This failure, however, is narrated only from Numbers 11 on. It has nothing to do with Numbers 1–10 and the function of Numbers 1 therein. In its context the "census" in Numbers 26 represents the beginning of the new generation because of the death of the old generation due to its failure. In their respective contexts, Numbers 1 and Numbers 26 do not have the same function, and Numbers 26 appears to be one of the major subdivisions within Num 10:11–36:13 only. Num 26:63-65 confirms this contextual limitation even as it refers to the first census. The relationship of the second census to the first is referential in nature, but it does not indicate two structurally equal narrative parts, neither on genealogical nor on theological grounds.

The Levites as a tribe must be exempted from Olson's argument about the failure of the old generation. They are everywhere set apart from the twelve tribes, also in the tribal pattern of Numbers 13–14. Korah, Aaron, and Miriam do not affect the tribe. And despite a contextual tension with Num 26:63-65, their inclusion in the second census (Num 26:57-62) rests on the genealogical transition, not on any failure of the tribe of Levi.

The difference between the old and the new, according to Olson, does not rest only on the failure of the old generation and the less clear obedience of the new; it also rests on the priestly genealogical pattern *(tôlēdôt)* around which the texts are grouped in the Tetrateuch. In this pattern, however, the failure of one generation is certainly not constitutive for the emergence of a new one. And on the basis of this pattern, Olson's structural subdivision of the five-fold Pentateuch (114) and with it of the function of Numbers 1 is indefensible. His old generation would encompass a unit such as Exodus 7–Numbers 25, and his new generation a unit such as Numbers 26–Joshua 24 (Hexateuch!). In such a genealogical pattern, Numbers 1 marks neither the failure nor the beginning of the old generation, and cannot be considered as the substantive and structural opposite of Numbers 26.

Olson's major thesis is not persuasive. But it is nonetheless valuable because it significantly advances our critical attention to the factors that constitute larger texts, and our methods for their interpretation. The interpretation in this commentary differs from Olson's interpretation, yet both share the same question. They represent a beginning which awaits further study. As for Numbers, it may be that at some points the structural signals are not sufficiently clear for a definitive solution. But it may also be that we have not yet been able to distinguish sufficiently the dominant from the subordinate structural signals. The superstructure presented above depends not on those structural signals that indicate subordinate levels; it depends only on those of the highest structural level.

Numbers has fifty-five individual literary units. It is immediately clear that these units are composed in larger blocks which are distinguished from other multi-unit blocks. The super-structure of Numbers does not consist of a list of fifty-five parts associated on the same level.

It is equally clear that Numbers is not organized on the basis of the identifiable literary strata J, E, and P. The book certainly owes its basic structure to the priestly writers who incorporated the J/E strata within its second part from ch. 11 on. But in that part, all literary strata are interwoven in the coordination of units and even within individual units themselves. This interweaving of the literary strata shows that aspects other than the literary-historical ones were responsible for the formation of the book, including its two main parts. The absence of J/E material in Num 1:1–10:36 means only that J/E had no traditions pertinent to that section, not that the priestly writers wanted to present their own traditions first and the Yahwistic traditions second.

Nor is the occurrence of Moses' name a signal for the structure of the book. This name occurs in fifty-one units (exceptions: 21:1-3, 21-31; 22:1–24:25; and 36:13). It unites all units of the final narrative under the aspect of the biography of Moses (cf. Knierim, "Composition," 406-15; Coats, *Genesis,* 14-26; Coats, ed., *Saga-Legend,* 33-44), and it does not provide the criterion for subdividing that narrative. On the traditio-historical penetration of Moses' name into these units cf., among others, Noth's *History of Pentateuchal Traditions,* 156-75, and Anderson's report on the subsequent discussion in his introduction to Noth's work (*Pentateuchal Traditions,* xiii-xxxii).

What has been said so far is also true for the frequent reports of Yahweh speeches that pervade Numbers, sixty-six altogether. These speeches are introduced by the two narrative formulae *wayyĕdabbēr yhwh ʼel . . .* (and Yahweh spoke to . . .; forty-four times) and *wayyōʼmer yhwh ʼel . . .* (and Yahweh said to . . .; twenty-two times). With few exceptions (Num 11:16, 23, 25; 12:4, 14; 14:11, 20; 21:8, 34; 25:4, 10, 16) they belong to the P tradition throughout its development. The reasons for the alternation between both introductory forms are not yet clear (cf. Schmidt, Bergman, and Lutzmann, 100). Both forms almost always introduce a direct Yahweh speech to Moses, only occasionally a speech to Moses and Aaron (Num 19:1; cf. Lev 11:1; 13:1; 14:33; 15:1), to Moses, Aaron, and Miriam (Num 12:4), or to Aaron alone (Num 18:8; cf. Lev 10:8). Cf. Schmidt, Bergman, and Lutzmann, 102.

Important for the discussion of structure is the fact that in twenty-six out of sixty-six cases, the speech formula opens a literary unit itself: Num 1:1; 2:1; 3:5, 11, 14, 40, 44; 5:1, 5, 11; 6:1, 22; 8:1, 5, 23; 10:1; 15:1, 17, 37; 17:16; 19:1; 27:12; 28:1; 31:1; 35:1, 9. In the majority of cases, however, the formula opens Yahweh speeches within literary units. The latter situation shows that the Yahweh speeches are subordinate to those units and play no role in the structural correlation of those units, let alone in the superstructure of Numbers. But in the former case, too, the references referred to show clearly that the Yahweh speech reports representing the twenty-six literary units are themselves parts of larger conceptual units within which they constitute subordinate units that must be accounted for.

Childs is correct when he says (p. 195) that the chronological indicators in Num 1:1; 7:1; 10:11; 33:38 are an unlikely basis for the formation of the book. They support in certain respects the structural and generic aspects of the entire Moses-Israel narrative, but they do not constitute the decisive criteria. Cf. Knierim, *Exodus 19–40*. For Gray already, the threefold subdivision of Numbers was primarily based on the geographical "scenes" and only secondarily on the chronological "periods" of the scenes (pp. xxvi-xxix). The chronology is subordinate to the geography. Gray's interpretation implies that Numbers is organized according to a systematized conceptualization of the migration and not simply by the step-by-step listing of localities as in ONOMASTICA of localities or in ITINERARIES. Cf. Numbers 33.

The geographical and topographical aspects are indeed important because the references to them pervade the book and indicate the ongoing movement of the Israelites. They represent a sort of plot according to which many individual units are directly arranged. And even those units that are not explicitly linked to certain localities must be understood in the formation of the book as related to the localities mentioned in their context. Yet here the problem begins. It involves the structural function of the geographical and topographical aspects in Numbers, specifically, the question whether these aspects represent the superstructure of the book.

There is a difference between geographical and topographical texts (cf., e.g., Alt, "Beiträge," 382-459; Noth, "Die Topographie Palästinas," 1-132, and "Zur Geschichte und Topographie," 157-343). Geographical texts reflect more inclusive aspects. They focus on regions and countries such as "the wilderness of Sinai" or "the land of Egypt." Topographical texts focus on the names of specific localities. They are characteristic for ONOMASTICA, LISTS, among others, of local names, e.g., cities within a territory or of territorial boundaries, and for ITINERARIES as well. The interpretation of Numbers, or any literary work which involves both aspects, will have to ask which one supersedes the other as a structuring factor. But it will also have to ask whether a work that uses geographical and topographical data includes additional aspects which may play a role in the structure of the work and which may either serve or dominate the geographical-topographical factors.

The ITINERARY is a case in point. An itinerary is a subtype of the ONOMASTICON. It is a list of place names that is organized according to the sequence of the stations from which and to which movements of groups or individuals such as MARCH, MIGRATION, CAMPAIGN, JOURNEY, PROCESSION, and PILGRIMAGE proceed. Generally, it reflects an established route, a pattern. But it may also be particular. Its elementary focus and form are topographical. But it may also involve overarching aspects under which series of stations are united and distinguished from one another, as in the combination of topographical and geographical data. An overarching aspect which might influence the pattern of the straight list is the greater than normal importance of special places. That which makes such places special may differ. They may involve special events, intermediate objectives of a campaign, or the need for resupply and longer rest after the rapid sequence of stations passed. The name of a chain of hotels in Southern California, La Quinta, was chosen as a reminder of the early Spanish travelers (and no doubt as an invitation to modern travelers to do likewise) who on every fifth day of a long journey used to put in a longer rest after four consecutive days of travel.

The influence of overarching aspects already shows that conceptual factors other than the topographical or geographical ones may be at work in the incorporation of the itinerary into narratives about movements such as migrations, campaigns, pilgrimages, and so on. The structures of such narratives may very well be governed by the overall patterns of such operations that involve more than the itinerary, and of which the itinerary is only a subordinate part.

The influence of the itinerary in Numbers is indisputable. Yet its function in the overall structure of the book, and especially its relationship to other conceptual factors, must be clarified. An approach to this clarification demands close attention to the language in which the itinerary is couched.

In its rudimentary form, the itinerary is a list of nothing but place names. Such a list does not exist in Numbers. Characteristic for the narrative next to the place names in Numbers is the terminology for the movement itself. This terminology consists overwhelmingly of the two verbs *nāsaʿ* (to pull out, set out, start out) and *ḥānâ* (to pitch a camp, encamp). *nāsaʿ* occurs ninety-two times, forty-two times in ch. 33 alone (Kaddari, 493-97), whereas *ḥānâ* occurs seventy-nine times, forty-nine times in ch. 33. Related to *ḥānâ* is *maḥăneh* (camp), about thirty times; it means either the group as camp or the camp of the group (cf. Helfmeyer, "*ḥānâ*," 4-20). This noun is important for the discussion of the nature of the march, but not for the structure of Numbers. Other terms used infrequently are *bôʾ* (to go into, Num 20:1; 21:1; 33:9, 40; in Exod 19:1-2, *bôʾ* and *yāṣāʾ* [to come out, march out] appear as the opposite pair to *ḥānâ* and *nāsaʿ*); *šûb* (to return, Num 33:7); *ʿābar* (to pass through, Num 20:17-21; 21:22, 23; 32:7, 21, 27, 29, 30, 32; 33:8, 51. All except 33:8 refer to the march indirectly); and *hālak* (to go, walk, directly referring to the march only in Num 33:8); the nouns *massaʿ* (breaking camp, departure, Num 10:2, 6, 12, 28; 33:2) and *môṣāʾ* (going out, Num 33:2).

The following is important: first, the narrative repertoire for the movement consists almost exclusively, and certainly stereotypically, of the verbs *nāsaʿ* (to set out) and *ḥānâ* (to encamp). These verbs belong to standardized language. They represent the formulae for the decampment and encampment. The rest of the terminology is insignificant for the narrative of the process of the movement. Second, both verbs are frequently related to one another in the same units, especially in chs. 1–2; 9:17-23; 12:15, 16; 21:10-20; and consistently in ch. 33. Third, both verbs are with few exceptions (part. form in 10:29, 33b, 34, 35) used in the narrative form, with morphological variations depending on the subject noun to which they are related. Fourth, in these narrative elements, the following aspects are important:

(a) Whether they are used together or not, both verbs are related as two aspects of one contextually understood stage of the march from one station to another.

(b) They presuppose the unity of the march in terms of its beginning, the breaking of tents (cf. Kaddari, 494), and of its end in the encampment. But they do not narrate or describe the march itself. It is striking that verbs describing the march itself, or its nature (such as *ʾāraḥ* [to be on the way, wander], *hālak* [to go, walk], *ʿābar* [to pass through], *dārak* [to tread], *ʾādâ* [to walk], *pāśaʿ* [to step forth], *ṣāʿâ* [to walk, step], *ʾālâ* [to go up, ascend]) are not constitutive for the narrative.

14

(c) The two constitutive verbs are more specific than the general verbs *yāṣā'* (to go forth, leave) and *bô'* (to come, come to, arrive at) which are predominant in the deuteronomic language. They are specifically rooted in the idea of a moving (tent) camp, and emphasize the alternation between the beginnings of the marching from and the beginning of the staying in camp places. They are generated by those aspects which reflect the two basic experiences of the breaks of the ongoing movement, and not by what happens during either the march or the encampment. They presuppose the unity of a longer movement in many stages, and focus on the essential alternation between decampment and encampment that constitutes the process. Relative to the view of the movement is the fact that the sequence in which both verbs are related changes: the individual units usually begin by reporting the start and end by reporting the encampment, whereas summary statements such as Num 2:17, 34; 9:20, 23; 21:10-13 say that the Israelites "encamped and set out" (Kaddari, 495).

(d) The twofold focus on decampment and encampment is also the basis of the description of the two different orders in Numbers 2, the encampment and the marching order.

(e) Finally, this focus attracts the names of the localities from which and to which a march moves. It attracts the primarily topographically oriented itinerary. Taken together, these two components, the typical word pair and the itinerary list, constitute the basic elements of NARRATIVE of a journey, migration, campaign, pilgrimage.

The individual forms of these narratives vary. The most elementary form is found in Numbers 33 where "they set out from . . . and encamped at . . ." represents virtually the entire text. A variation is found in Num 21:10-20 where the pattern occurs in its elementary and a slightly expanded form. In the rest of Numbers, the pattern is in principle opened to make room for the inclusion of many materials, especially at places of encampment.

The flexible usage of the movement narrative pattern shows that aspects other than its pure, topographically oriented form account for the structures of the individual units and of the whole of Numbers. There is a difference between that stereotypical form in Numbers (and elsewhere) and the narrative structure of Numbers which avails itself of that pattern under the influence of its own aspects. This difference is strikingly evident in the comparison of the structure of Numbers 33 with that of the book. The superstructure of Numbers, or of the entire wandering narrative from Exodus on, is not based (as is Numbers 33) on the sequence of the locations of the movement (cf. Noth, "Der Wallfahrtsweg zum Sinai," 55-56). It is based on organizing aspects that supersede the narrative pattern of movement, quite apart from the fact that the itineraries of both differ.

What, then, are the aspects that govern the structure of Numbers? Factors such as the length of the marching or staying periods, the distances traveled, or resting and dwelling (*ḥānâ*, "to encamp," does not focus on rest as does *nûaḥ-měnûḥâ*, and those marching do not "dwell" [*yāšab*]) play either a subordinate role or no role at all. The geographical clustering of the topographical narrative data is, as correctly observed, a major organizing factor. Unresolved is the question of the structural role of narrative expansions connected with specific, important, topographically identified campsites. This aspect is different from the geographical aspect of a cluster of sites, and the relationship of both aspects is an open question.

Which aspects determine the first major block of Numbers? Noth and Coats end the first major unit at 10:36, apparently on the literary-critical distinction between the P and the J/E sources which begins at Num 11:1. But the fact that P extends to the end of ch. 10 does not mean that literary criticism was for P the basis for dividing the narrative. This argument has already been set aside. Budd refers to "three important geographical references which help . . . to shape the structure of the book" (xvii) given in 1:1; 10:12; 22:1 par. 36:13. He says that the "work is on the whole well ordered, and falls into three major sections" (xvii). But his sections, mentioned earlier, depart from the geographical references said to be important for the structure of the book. Budd's first section ("A. Constituting the community at Sinai") ends with 9:14, whereas his second section ("B. The Journey . . .") "begins with the means of guidance — the cloud and the trumpets (9:15–10:10)." But the narrative about the resumption of the "Journey" after the narrative about the encampment begins in its typical language in 10:11, 12, which clearly refers to Exod 19:1, 2. And "the means of guidance" while looking forward to the march like everything else in 1:1–10:10 belongs to the narrative of the encampment, and not to the narrative of the march. The unit about the cloud in 9:15-23 could be understood as the beginning of the narrative of the movement. But this pericope is a summary statement about the cloud over the tabernacle from "the day that the tabernacle was set up," i.e., it extends from Exodus 40 — and not from Num 1:1 only — throughout the entire movement and not only throughout the second section of Numbers. It belongs to the section before the resumption of the journey, just as much as the following unit about the trumpets in 10:1-10. We must conclude, with the majority of the interpreters, that Num 1:1–10:10 represents the first major section of the book. This conclusion rests on two criteria: the combination of topographical-geographical and typical movement narrative language which connects this passage solidly with the entire Sinai narrative, and the conceptual aspect of the preparatory organization of the following movement which distinguishes it from the narrative of that movement itself.

What is the relationship of the rest of Numbers to its first section? Decisive for this question is the distinction between the preparatory organization of the march and the march itself. This organization has in view the subsequent march in its entirety to the border of the promised land, including all stations and regions, and including the instructions at the end of Numbers from ch. 26 on. Compared to the aspect of preparatory organization, the rest of Numbers appears to be united conceptually under the aspect of the execution of the preparation. All topographical and geographical — let alone chronological — aspects and the aspects of the ongoing encampment-decampment movement are subordinate. The entirety of the march itself is specifically implied in 10:13 by the word *bāri'šōnâ*, "they set out *for the first time*. . . ." The superstructure of Numbers consists, therefore, of two parts. These parts are related to one another as preparation or organization and implementation or execution, and united in the conceptuality of those genres which narrate, among others, migration, campaign, pilgrimage. The structure of Numbers is constituted by the basic aspects of such types or genres of narratives. It reflects a conceptual unity in its own right, notwithstanding the fact that its first part also belongs to the Sinai narrative. The result is indirectly supported by the fact that Num 1:1–10:10 is logically, but not necessarily, placed at the end of the Sinai pericope. It is further supported by the fact that 1:1–10:10 was added to the Sinai pericope by the priestly writers in the first place. It has no precedent in the other literary traditions and must have been incorporated at its place because of the difference between the nature of Israel's migration before and after Sinai, and in view of the older migration tradition from Numbers 11 which did not make this difference clear enough, not even in the priestly materials Exodus 25–Leviticus 27. Before Sinai, Israel migrated as the liberated community. Now, it is organized and supposed to march as a sacral congregation, an *ʿēdâ*.

The twofold place of Num 1:1–10:10, in the Sinai pericope and in the book of Numbers, is lastly the result of two overlapping principles of organization. In the structure of the entire Moses narrative (cf. Coats and Knierim, *Exodus*), Num 1:1–10:10 belongs to the encampment at Sinai. In the structure of Numbers, it belongs to the campaign-pilgrimage narrative from Sinai on. And it is more than arbitrary that Numbers was established as a distinct book within the Pentateuch when the Pentateuch was divided into five parts.

Genre

Whether or not the superstructure of Numbers reflects a genre depends on two questions. First, it must be decided what kind of wandering narrative Numbers represents specifically. So far we have used generic terms loosely. We must now be specific. Involved is a large group *en route* in stages in a process of translocation from the holy mountain to the promised land. It is led by Yahweh directly and through Yahweh's representative Moses, and strictly organized as a military-sacral community. (On the connection of this part with the theme of the Pentateuch, cf. Clines, esp. 53-60.)

It is immediately clear that terms for generic narratives of (business) TRIP, (private, tourist) JOURNEY, or TRAVEL, or WANDERING, are not accurate enough for characterizing what is typical for the genre of this narrative. The word MARCH covers some aspects. The term MIGRATION covers the aspect of the ongoing translocation but not the specific kind of this migration. Numbers does not portray any and every type of migration. Its dominating aspects, the military and sacral-cultic, and the destination of this definitive, once and for all time migration require a more specific definition of the genre of this narrative. Also, a more specific choice will have to be made as to the type of the narrative itself. This subtype of the narrative form must be defined on the basis of the dominating typical features of the text.

From the narrative genres, types such as STORY, FAIRY TALE, FABLE, and MYTH must be set aside. History is an element, but Numbers is not similar to the more specifically historical works in the OT or in the Ancient Near East, either in form or in function. ACCOUNT, close to REPORT, is primarily matter-of-fact oriented, and both are shorter forms used in history-writing. EPOS is too much oriented on the heroic element of individuals or groups, which is not the case in Numbers. LEGEND and SAGA come closest generally, legend because of its clearly edifying intention as in (etiological) cult-legends, and saga, basically — and across its subtypes — because of its drawn-out length, its presentation of a total picture, and the composite nature of many elements involved.

None of these terms covers the typical in Numbers exclusively. SAGA comes closer than LEGEND if one accounts for its subtype of "communal saga," more appropriately so-called, rather than "national saga," in this case; if one allows for the inclusion in saga of the traits, or parts, of legend; but nonetheless for the strong, if not predominant, emphasis on the community's human factor, especially its fallacy in light of its vocation and legendary divine guidance.

The word TORAH is unsuitable for the definition of the genre of Numbers because it does not identify the specific kind of instruction which the book represents.

From the genres of movement narratives, those of MIGRATION, CAMPAIGN, PROCESSION and PILGRIMAGE represent the narrower pool for determination. The term procession is least preferable because it does not connote the migratory translocation of those involved and because it presupposes a confined territory and may also connote a circular movement as in Joshua 6 or presumably in Ps 24:7-10. The term migration plays a role because of the typically migratory traits of the saga. It must be an element of the genre of Numbers. Specifically pertinent are the genres pilgrimage and campaign. Neither of them involves migration *a priori*. Both involve series of events in successive stages over a larger territorial distance and a longer duration. They include more than a local procession or battle. Either one may or may not involve a cultic or military escort, respectively, as is documented throughout history, and especially in the ANE and OT. Yet both are different in nature. A PILGRIMAGE is an essentially cultic event to which a military escort, should it exist, is subservient. It is governed by the cultic conditions, arrangements, and objectives of the march themselves: usually along sacred stations, and its destination: a sacred place. Its itinerary is determined by those stations. Its essential personnel consists of pilgrims who perform an act of religious devotion which is fulfilled in the pilgrimage itself. The objective of a march along and to sacred places lies in the pilgrimage itself, and not in the creation of a sacred place or the destruction of hostile places and the defeat of enemies.

A CAMPAIGN is an essentially military event of which a cultic escort, should it exist, is supportive. It is governed by military strategy, logistics, and objectives of the march, usually towards places demanding military encounters. Its itinerary is determined by the search for the enemy. Its essential personnel consist of soldiers who perform military duty (with or without religious devotion). The duty is fulfilled in the defeat of enemies, and in the conquest of their cities and countries. The objective of a march to hostile places lies in the destruction of enemies and their fortresses, and not in the *modus operandi* of the campaign even where this objective is considered to be an act of religious devotion.

Next to the aspect of migration, the two specific and different aspects of pilgrimage and campaign are interwoven in all literary strata of Numbers.

18

THE BOOK OF NUMBERS

Numbers does not reflect a development from a non-cultic military campaign in the Yahwistic traditions to a non-military cultic pilgrimage in the priestly traditions. The combination of all three generic factors is germane to the entire growth process in Numbers. The difference in this respect lies in the relationship of pilgrimage and campaign, and not in the difference between a military aspect in the older traditions and a cultic aspect in the later traditions.

The migratory traits have been mentioned. The campaign aspect is expressed in Num 1:2-3, which explains the census for this purpose, in the understanding of the units of the outer tribal encampment in Numbers 1f., and in part in Num 10:1-10. It is pervasive in the second part of Numbers where from the outset the ark is the cultic symbol of the military campaign (10:35-36), and where Israel frequently has to contend with enemies (13–14; 20:14-21; 21:1-3, 14-15, 21-25; 22-24; 26:1-3 [par. 1:2-3]; 31; 32; 33:50-56). None of the particular military encounters is isolated. All are parts of an ongoing campaign. It seems, however, that the objective of the campaign is the conquest of the promised land both east and west of the Jordan, and the defeat of the enemies between Sinai and Moab only to the extent to which they stand in the way of that objective. We must distinguish between the primary or proper and the secondary, supporting objectives. The narrative of the former begins in Numbers 32 and extends through Deuteronomy into Joshua 1-12. The latter is contained in Num 10:11–31:54. It serves the primary objective. Despite their difference, however, both objectives reflect the totality of a military campaign.

The campaign aspect is not the only one that is constitutive for Numbers. Not all the materials of the book are related to it. The cultic aspect must be considered equally because it may point to pilgrimage rather than campaign, even in texts displaying the military side. The organization of the tribes around the sanctuary in ch. 2 shows the campaign at least also as a cultic event. The reservation of the Levites in Numbers 3–4 for the service at the sanctuary may point to a sanctuary pilgrimage with a military escort. As the inner circle of the camp they belong more to the sanctuary than to the tribes. The same is even truer for the Aaronides. And the sanctuary is not only and always a military symbol. It is no longer the ancient ark only. The same is true for the cloud over the sanctuary. Num 9:15-23 depicts the migration as a cultic event in which the sanctuary and Israel set out and encamp wherever and whenever the cloud moved and settled, and "at the command of Yahweh by Moses," from station to station and for whatever duration, but not from battle to battle.

Num 10:1-10 defines the function of trumpets as for war (v. 9) and for times of gladness and appointed feasts (v. 10). The trumpets are meant not only for the campaign but also for the life in the land in times of war and peace. The alarm *(těrûʿâ)* blown by the trumpets (v. 5, during the campaign; v. 9, in the land) calls to war in v. 9, but in vv. 1-8 it calls the congregation *(ʿēdâ)* together at "the tent of meeting" and — again — to set out for the march, and not for battle (cf. Kellermann, *Numeri,* 140-47). The trumpets are essentially cultic instruments administered by the Aaronide priests "throughout your generations" (v. 8), i.e., the hierarchy of the cultic personnel, not even the Levites in general. Besides many other priestly units, Num 10:1-10 shows that the aspect of the military campaign, especially as it refers to the historical event, is not everywhere dominant or even present. The same is true for many passages concerning cultic instruction.

Of particular interest in this connection are the various traditions about the sanctuary in all literary layers of Numbers. The centrality of the sanctuary in 1:1–10:10 is self-evident. Involved in the second part of Numbers are the ark (*'ărôn*) in 10:33-35; 14:44; the tent (*'ōhel*) very frequently in chs. 11; 12; 14; 16; 17; 18; 19; 20; 25; 27; 31; the tabernacle *(miškān)* in chs. 10; 16; 17; 19; 24; 31; and the sanctuary *(miqdāš)* in 10:21; 18:1; 19:20; cf. also the cloud *(he'ānān)* in 9:15-21; 10:12; 12:10; 14:14 with fire; 16:42. Implicit is further the assumption in all texts that Yahweh speaks to Moses always from the tent/tabernacle.

The camp in Numbers has been called a combination of war and pilgrimage camp (Helfmeyer, *"ḥānâ,"* 10). This definition may imply that cultic elements on the one hand and military ones on the other point to the respectively different genres of pilgrimage and campaign. Such an *a priori* implication is unwarranted. The question is whether the cult, especially the sanctuary in Numbers, is an element of the military campaign, or whether the military camp escorts a lastly epiphanic pilgrimage in which the pilgrim is Yahweh migrating from Sinai to the promised land. Is Numbers based on a migratory military pilgrimage, or on a cultic campaign? In the first instance, the generically constitutive pilgrimage would be specified through the military component. In the second instance, the cultic component would specify the nature of the campaign. In either case, Numbers would reflect the genre of one type of camp only, and not a combination of two different types of camp. The question remains in need of further study. In the meantime, it seems that the objective of the migration, namely, the conquest of the promised land by the sanctuary host preceded by encounters with hostile powers rather than a pilgrimage to an already established sanctuary in the land along sacred stations, is the basic perspective by which Numbers is governed. This perspective receives its sharpest focus in the sanctuary tradition itself in which the sanctuary itself is the subject of the campaign. The interpretation of Num 1:1–10:10 will reinforce this view. Numbers is the SAGA of the Migratory Campaign.

Second, we must ask whether the twofold superstructure of Numbers is typical for genres such as CAMPAIGN, MIGRATION, PILGRIMAGE, and PROCESSION–NARRATIVES/ACCOUNTS/REPORTS and in what sense it is related to any or all of them. For a proper focus, a few methodological clarifications are necessary. First, the question focuses on narratives about such events, and not on events themselves. Second, what is fundamental for the bipolarity of the narrative is the distinction between the preparation and the execution of the preparation. To this distinction, a great variety of aspects in each of the two parts are subordinate. Third, the bipartite narrative structure is not confined to narratives of movement; it is also used for other kinds of operations, especially for construction reports. Fourth, we must distinguish in texts (prose or poetry, oral or written literature) between formal references to the fact of preparatory and executing events and narratives that relate the contents of such operations. Fifth, the variability of aspects and contents in each of the two constitutive parts depends on the specific circumstances of the individual texts, but it does not relativize the stability of the text-pattern. And sixth, the evidence points out that narratives relate sometimes only the preparation, sometimes only the execution of the preparation, and sometimes both. Whatever the reason(s) for the report of only one part of an operation, the texts imply the other part as well, unless there are indications that either a preparation or its execution did not take place. A preparation or execution report points in principle to the other part because a preparation looks forward to the execution and an execution presupposes the decision or preparation. Each part is only an element of a larger whole. And where a whole operation is narrated, the narrative represents the full pattern, whereas the narrative of one part represents the pattern only in part.

In view of the fact that the tradition history of this form is not at all sufficiently researched, the classifications just mentioned and a sample of examples alluded to in the following are tentative. Documentation of formal references to preparatory events or to the execution of preparations is not given at this time. They are numerous.

Narratives of a preparatory nature alone which are not directly followed by statements or narratives about the execution of a preparation are found in various forms, e.g., in Ps 2:1-3, 4-9; Isa 7:5-9; 40:3-5; Jer 23:18-22; Ezek 40–48; Num 13:1-33 (vv. 1-2, 3-20, 21-33); 33:50-56 (cf. Joshua 1–12); 34:1-15 (cf. Joshua 13–19); 35 (cf. Joshua 20–21). In a sense, all of Deuteronomy belongs to the preparation for the conquest. But the preparatory texts in Num 33:50–35:34 are closer to those in Joshua than the deuteronomic text.

The close relationship between the narratives of preparation and its execution in Numbers and Joshua has already pointed to those narratives in which both elements form literary units. The result is surprising. The relationship of Exodus 25–31 and 35–39(40) is known. Josh 7:2-3 and 4-5 speak about the preparation and execution of the campaign against Ai. Josh 8:1-2 and 3-29; Judg 7:1-18 and 19-25 repeat this pattern. The same is true for Judg 20:1-18 and 19-48; 2 Sam 17:1-14 and 17:24–18:18; 1 Kgs 5:1-9 and 10ff. (cf. Long, *1 Kings*); 1 Kgs 12:6-11 and 13-15; 22:5-28 and 29-40. The book of Chronicles is of particular interest. 1 Chr 13:1-4; 15:16-24; 16:4-6 report the plan to return the ark, and 13:5-14; 15:1-15, 25-29; 16:1-3, 7-43 report the execution of the plan. David's plan for the building of the temple is recorded in 1 Chr 22:1–29:9, and Solomon's execution of the plan in 2 Chr 2–6 (cf. De Vries, *1-2 Chronicles*). Cf. also Ezra 3:7-9 and 10-13 and more, and Neh 2:17-20; 3:1–4:23; 12:27-47. Cf. also the Joseph novella.

Narratives that relate the execution of plans only and not the preceding preparations are too numerous to be listed here. They represent the largest of the three groups.

Similar observations can be made in the extra-biblical literature, in Herodotus, Thucydides, and Homer's *Iliad.* Emperor Frederick II (1194-1250) is known to have sent letters to the Pope in which he reported the progress of his preparations for the crusades (Heinisch, 125, 149). Closer to the biblical material is the information from ancient Egypt and Mesopotamia. The Egyptian accounts about campaigns and the construction of temples and tombs, mainly contained in the Royal Novellas, frequently consist of two parts, one about the preparation, especially the deliberation in Pharaoh's council, and the other about the actual execution of the campaign or construction (cf. *ANET,* 232-57; *ARE* I, 14-16; *ARE* II, 175-90, 240-45; A. H. Gardiner, "Defeat," 95-110). By contrast, Mesopotamian records seem to have contained the actual campaign reports only (cf. *ANET,* 265-317).

We may summarize. Together with other literatures the OT contains a form of narrative or description, in prose and poetry, which focuses on the two typical stages of major (royal) operations, their preparation and implementation. The contents change from case to case. Most prominent are narratives about campaigns and building projects. This literary form is typical, and not the property of individual authors. It represents a pattern. The ideal form is bipartite. It is explicit in the bipartite narratives. But it is also implied where only one of the two parts is narrated. The reasons for the usage either of the full form or of only one of its two parts seem to depend on the individuality of the report or the reporter's aspect, possibly also on a certain tradition as in Mesopotamia. These reasons have to be determined from case to case.

The alternations in the typical form reflect the emphasis on specific aspects of an operation. Narratives relating only the second part (as in the Yahwistic materials of Numbers 11–36) emphasize the execution while implying its preparations *e silentio.* Narratives relating only the first part emphasize the existence of the preparation, especially a plan or a decision, while implying or saying that the execution is yet to take place or failed to take place. The emphasis in narratives that relate both parts is of a different nature. These narratives are interested in highlighting not only that a preparation was executed but also that an execution was prepared. The shifting reasons for the combination of these two emphases can be seen exemplarily in the priestly blocks Exodus 25–31 and 35–39(40) and in Num 1:1–10:10 and 10:11–36:13. Exodus 35–39(40) represents essentially a secondary accretion of equal length to Exodus 25–31. The reason for this accretion was apparently to emphasize that Moses executed Yahweh's detailed instructions just as specifically as he had received them, and not just summarily. The accretions emphasize Moses' meticulous obedience and the correspondence of the built sanctuary to its revealed blueprint. This emphasis triggered the emergence of the full form of the narrative. In Numbers 1–36, the process is reversed. The older tradition in 11–36 had no material analogous to the material in 1–10. And the accretion of 1–10 emphasized that the campaign was prepared by Yahweh through Moses and organized as a sanctuary campaign. This emphasis reveals again that from Sinai on, a fundamentally new situation existed which was not sufficiently expressed in the older traditions. In view of this new situation, the (following) actual campaign had to be understood in a new light. It is no longer a narrative about Yahweh's guidance despite Israel's failure if even in a more radical sense; it now represents a problematic period of Israel's past which is no basis for Israel's future. The basis for the future is laid out in the remaining validity of the program in Num 1:1–10:10, the priestly program of the *'ēdâ* congregation.

The typical form of the preparation-execution narratives undoubtedly had a tradition history that awaits further study. In the process of its tradition history, the form developed into ever larger proportions and played a prominent role in the priestly writings and in the chronistic work. Cf. De Vries, *1-2 Chron-*

icles. This development indicates that the priestly layers representing the expanded form belong to the later stages in the historical emergence not only of the Pentateuch but also of the priestly writings themselves. And their emphasis on the Aaronide priesthood in contrast to the subordinate position of the Levites seems to put them into the exilic-postexilic time, after Deuteronomy and on the way to Chronicles (cf. De Vries, *1-2 Chronicles*).

The twofold structure of Numbers is a typical literary form. How is this form related to the already determined genre of Numbers? The form is used for the genre, but it is not constitutive for this genre alone because it can also be used for other genres, e.g., especially building reports. The genre of Numbers is constituted by the nature of the narrated operation. But the typical narrative form supports the genre by portraying its picture in full.

It is interesting that in its narratives about the sanctuary (Exodus 25–31; 35–40) and the campaign (Numbers 1–36), P contains the two main genres for which the combination of preparation and execution is constitutive, and both in their full forms. And the two narratives are closely related: the construction of the sanctuary awaits the sanctuary campaign while the sanctuary campaign presupposes the established sanctuary.

Setting

The discussion of setting must distinguish between the typical setting of the events themselves, the typical setting of narratives about such operations, and the specific setting of a particular narrative such as Numbers.

The typical settings of events such as building constructions, military campaigns, migrations, cultic pilgrimages or processions, and similar operations, reflect the realities of major organized operations undertaken by societies throughout the history of civilization. Such operations involve in every case the totality of all elements necessary for any operation in all its steps, and in by far most of the cases more than what the records about them report. In the ancient world they involve decision makers, normally the kings or as in Greece the representatives of the cities, counselors, a composite staff of experts for planning and execution, commanders or supervisors, supply systems for materials and food for the masses, and their personnel, work forces, or recruited armies whose hundreds or thousands of individuals perform the task, and so on. And depending on the nature of the operation — military, cultic, civil — the system of organization varies, and so does the set of those involved.

We possess no records at all from ancient history that would accurately describe the totality of any such operation in all its details. All records, the Bible included, report at best the operations in part only and, hence, from a setting that is in principle different from that of the operation itself. Especially different from the setting of the persons involved in an operation is the setting of its recorders, primarily scribes at royal courts or at sanctuaries, but also poets or narrators associated with groups or institutions whose operations they narrate. Any description of the persons, materials, and steps involved in the totality of an operation is very different from the description of the elements involved in its narration. The total recording process is an operation that reflects a setting of its own kind.

While the recording settings are typical, they are also variable. They may represent the group or institution of the operation, but also any other group not associated with the operation or even opposed to it. The recording settings and their diversity must be assumed because the records themselves mostly do not mention them directly and because the evidence indicates that not all the records about operations originated in the settings closely associated with certain operations. We must guard against the *e silentio* assumption that the setting of a recording is in each case coordinate with the setting that controls an operation. Not every narrative about Israel's monarchy originated in the royal court. Finally, the historical distance of the narrating setting from that of the operation narrated must be taken into account. Such a distance may be short or long; it always exists. Many indicators in the records demonstrate it — in most cases directly.

The discussion of the typical settings of narratives about major campaign, migration, pilgrimage, building, and similar operations shows that the variety of possibilities necessitates the attempt to determine the setting of any such narrative or report as much as possible specifically. This specific determination depends mostly on indirect evidence, which must be gained from the texts themselves. It is inevitably hypothetical, but necessary if any explanation is given at all for the fact of the existence of a narrative.

The fact that Numbers is part of the Pentateuch, which according to our best insights owes its extant shape to priestly writers, means that Numbers, too, reflects the settings of the activities of these priestly writers. Specifically, it is the result of a particular group of priests from among several priestly denominations in Israel's cultic history: the Aaronides. The priestly writings in Exodus-Numbers leave no doubt as to the sole and supreme control of Israel's entire Yahweh-cult forever by "Aaron and his sons," to the exclusion of all other (priestly) groups such as Korah, Dathan, and Abiram (Numbers 16–17); David's Abiathar; the Levites; the Zadokites of Ezek 44:15-24; and also the Yahwistic-deuteronomistic Aaron himself (Deut 9:20). Cf. Rivkin, "Aaron," 1-3; Fritz, 155-57. Historically, this priestly dynasty was in control of the Second Temple institution from the end of the fifth century on until the Hasmonean revolt around 180 B.C.E. Cf. Sir 50:1-21. By that time, however, the Pentateuch had been completed, basically as the product of the Aaronide ancestors of those who were later in actual control. Those ancestors responsible for the Pentateuch were themselves at no time in control of Israel's central cult. Within the history of the Aaronide priesthood we must therefore distinguish between those late generations in actual institutional control and the earlier generations who were already in control of the final formation of the Pentateuch and claimed the control of the central cultic institution which only their successors achieved.

These earlier generations of Aaronide priests represent the setting for the emergence of the Pentateuch, of the Moses story, and certainly also of Numbers in their final form. Little is known about the history of this priestly denomination and about the specific nature of its setting, e.g., how it was related to the actual institutional history. Nevertheless, a few hypothetical assumptions seem preferable. These Aaronides must have represented an identified priestly group setting that was distinct from the settings of other groups, at times polemically. Their connection with the finalization of the Pentateuch, especially in the program of Exodus 25–Numbers 10, and their recourse to their Sinaitic-Mosaic authorization — the foundation of Israel's cultic institutions, which set aside all other authorizations from the time of Joshua on and was in blatant contrast to the Yahwistic-deuteronomistic traditions about Aaron — relate the emergence of this priestly dynasty into prominence to the time from 587 through the early Second Temple period. Symptomatic for this setting is the fact that these priests were writing and teaching or instructing and law-giving priests, and not only (and at times not at all) cultically officiating priests. Their laws and instruction proclaim a program of what is to be, much more — if at all — than a report of what exists. This instructing and law-giving function, also about their own cultic officiating, is reflected in their literary work. It reveals a particular setting in which the Aaronides operated. That this setting itself had a history is sufficiently evidenced by the discernible literary priestly strata.

Intention

Numbers does not state its intention explicitly. Its intention must be derived by interpretation. Any such interpretation is approximate and subject to correction and improvement. Several factors must be kept in mind: the twofold superstructure and generic nature of Numbers; substantively, the newness of Israel as a camp at Sinai in its organization around the tabernacle, including the concern for the purity of the camp, and Israel's failure to adhere to this newness; the goal towards which the campaign points; and the recourse by the "sons of Aaron" to the unquestionably authoritative beginnings, not only to their progenitor Aaron but to the Mosaic inauguration of the total sacral organization of Israel with Aaron at the top. The "sons of Aaron" do not legitimize themselves with Aaron. They legitimize Aaron with Moses. Aaron's authority neither replaces nor equals Moses' authority. It is derived from Moses. The intent is clear: in a competition of priestly dynasties, Aaron himself is — and was — subject to challenge unless his exclusive authority can be claimed as conveyed by the one authority which was uncontestable among all the priestly families.

But more is at stake. Important as the authorization of the Aaronides is in P, it stands in the service of a larger goal: the organization of Israel as a cultic-military campaign community around the central sanctuary from Sinai on. Only with respect to that organization are Aaron and his sons relevant. The recourse to Sinai reveals again the intent: in a competition of several blueprints from the deuteronomic time on for Israel's new beginning, none of the programs devised during Israel's existence in the land could claim the authority of the Sinai revelation before the occupation of the land. The intent was not to provide a program, but to legitimize the supremacy of this priestly program by casting it back into the foundational Sinai-Moses event. In this intent, the deuteronomic and the priestly programs coincide. But it may be more than coincidental that in the late postexilic time the representatives of the Aaronides prevailed over those of the deuteronomists. The Aaronide program was strictly cultic-hierocratic whereas the deuteronomic-deuteronomistic program was, conceptually and historically, compromised through its connection with the monarchy. The deuteronomic program could be integrated, but only as the "second law."

Next to the intentions just mentioned Numbers indicates some specific intentions of its program. One of them is revealed in the fact that the campaign camp organized in 1:1–10:10 represents a specific formation of the new Sinaitic community. Against this organization, the narrative about the actual pilgrimage appears to be a reminder of the failure of the first generation in the wilderness, and a warning for the readers not to repeat that failure. The narrative about the wilderness campaign itself reflects the qualified past, whereas the priestly program of the camp transcends the past. By portraying its Sinai camp the priestly program claims that the new beginning in its own time is to be based on a radical newness. It points out that the foundational preparation and its obedient execution are essential for Israel's new way towards its life in the promised land — ending the exile. And it emphasizes that it is itself divinely ordained. The proximity to the exilic time of Ezekiel and Deutero-Isaiah cannot be overlooked.

Finally, the specifications of the campaign genre in terms of migration and sanctuary-camp organization are telling. These specifications may not be as unique as one might suspect. Traditio-historically, they are in the older layers at least prepared, a fact that points to a continuity regarding the basic aspect in the transmission of the tradition, a continuity in which the priestly tradents also remained. Yet there are also shifts in perspective within the specified genre, especially in the priestly layers. One is the addition of 1:1–10:10 to the available saga; another is the specific view of the campaign camp; a third is the creation of a mixture between narrative about the past and instructions that quite obviously presuppose and envision conditions of later times — to mention but the more important shifts. → the interpretation of Num 1:1–10:10 in Chapter 2 and of the individual units in Chapter 3.

Both together, their loyalty to the continuity of the tradition and their freedom for shifting interpretations point once more to the intentions of the priestly writers: to submit in and with their portrayal of the foundational past their own theological program for the true congregation, together with the warning against the repetition of the failure of the original generations.

Chapter 2

THE LEGEND OF THE ORGANIZATION OF THE SANCTUARY CAMPAIGN (NUMBERS 1:1–10:10)

Structure

I.	The organization of the sanctuary camp	1:1–4:49
	A. The outer camp: the militia of the twelve tribes	1:1–2:34
	1. Report of the military conscription: preparation for the mobilization	1:1-54
	a. The leaders and their tribes	1:1-47
	b. Addendum: the Levites excepted	1:48-54
	2. Report of the mobilization	2:1-34
	B. The inner camp: the sanctuary personnel	3:1–4:49
	1. Genealogical list of the Aaronides	3:1-4
	2. Report of the conscription and mobilization of the Levites	3:5–4:49
II.	Expansion of the organization report	5:1–10:10
	A. Concerning Israel's outer camp	5:1–6:27
	1. Report about the unclean	5:1-4
	2. Instruction about restitution	5:5-10
	3. Instruction about the ritual of jealousy	5:11-31
	4. Instruction about the Nazirites	6:1-21
	5. Instruction about the Aaronide blessing	6:22-27
	B. Concerning Israel's inner camp	7:1–10:10

The first part of Numbers belongs exclusively to the tradition of the priestly writers. Its structure depends first of all on the final composition of the entire Sinai pericope by these writers, of which it is the conclusion. But it also depends on the function of this conclusion: to narrate the preparatory organization at Sinai for the impending campaign from Sinai to Moab and beyond. At the same time, the structural arrangement of the units within Num 1:1–10:10 appears to be the result of a growth process in which two influences interacted: the ongoing expansion and addition of individual units, and their ongoing conceptual coordination. It seems that the structural outcome of this interaction was determined at times by the conceptual coordination of units, and at times by the chronological sequence of new accretions, and not everywhere by the definitive prevalence of one of the two influences over the other.

Num 1:1–10:10 consists of two main parts: 1:1–4:49 and 5:1–10:10. All identifiable individual units in 1:1–10:10 are subordinate to this twofold division.

In I. (1:1–4:49), at least four units (1:1-47 [48-54]; 2:1-34; 3:1-4; 3:5–4:49) — more if one subdivides further — are tightly knit together. They are related under the influence of a concept according to which the entire part unfolds in successive order and in which each subsection — except 1:48-54 — has received its proper place. This concept is in itself complete, and highly systemic. The structure of part I. reflects and reveals this concept. It is concerned with the organization of the congregation ('ēdâ) for the sanctuary campaign. This definition indicates that part I. focuses on both the sanctuary and the impending campaign as well as on the camp of the Israelites. It also focuses on the process of the organization of both the encampment and the marching order in successive steps.

Part I. (1:1–4:49) consists of two main sections. The first, I.A. (1:1–2:34) focuses first of all on the organization of the outer camp: the militia of the twelve tribes of Israel. It distinguishes primarily between two successive steps in this organization: I.A.1. (1:1-54) the recruitment of the leaders and the military conscription of the members of the tribes, and I.A.2. (2:1-34) the mobilization of the conscripted through the establishment of their encampment and marching formations under their tribal leaders. In this sequence, the conscription report I.A.1. (1:1-54) must not be understood in isolation from its context I.A.2. (2:1-34). The military conscription of the males functions as the direct pre-stage — and only that — of their mobilization in the newly created outer camp which is the goal of the whole section I.A. (1:1–2:34).

The organization of the outer camp is followed by the organization of the inner camp, which is reported in I.B. (3:1–4:49). This section distinguishes between two groups, I.B.1. (3:1-4) the Aaronide priests first and I.B.2. (3:5–4:49) the Levites. Both groups belong together as the cultic personnel of the inner camp, in distinction to the tribes and their leaders in the outer camp. The structural arrangement of the units I.B.1. (3:1-4) and I.B.2. (3:5–4:49) points to the hierarchical order within the cultic personnel in which the Aaronides alone are the priests. They are placed in front of the sanctuary, and privileged with the administration of the cult. The Levites are the clerical servants charged with serving the priests and the Israelites in maintaining and transporting the sanctuary.

The texts about the tribal leaders and the tribes in I.A. (1:1–2:34) and about the priests and Levites in I.B. (3:1–4:49) are very uneven in length. They also differ generically. In I.A.1.a. (1:1-47) a short genealogically oriented list of twelve tribal leaders in 1:4-16 is followed in 1:17-46 by a long report about the conscription of the twelve tribes, and in I.A.2. (2:1-34) by a long report about their mobilization in the outer camp. Similarly, the Aaronides are in I.B.1. (3:1-

28

4) introduced by a short genealogical list which in I.B.2. (3:5–4:49) is followed by a long report about the conscription and the mobilization of the Levites in the inner camp. For both camps, the texts, even in their sequential arrangement, reflect an analogous leadership structure in which a small group of leaders commands a great majority of subordinates. In both cases, the individuals of the tribal units must be conscripted and mobilized. Whereas the individuals of the leadership are either chosen, without the need for conscription and mobilization because of their genealogical identity and societal status (so the tribal leaders), or — except Aaron himself — not chosen at all let alone registered and organized because of their identity established in the genealogical priestly register. The difference in rank between commander and soldier in the outer military camp corresponds to the difference in rank between the priests and Levites in the inner hierarchic camp.

The total camp consists exclusively of male persons of serviceable age for the functions of the two camps. The conscription reports in I.A.1. (1:1-54) and I.B.2. (3:5–4:49) stipulate this condition already, and the mobilization reports confirm it. The tribal units serve military purposes, the priests and Levites serve cultic purposes. Conscriptions may serve more than these purposes. The specific conscriptions in the text are clearly subservient to the narrative of this specific campaign camp organization. The tribal leaders, too, have in the outer encampment a military function. Only in Numbers 7, outside Numbers 1–4, do these leaders appear in a non-military function providing (at least) the original supplies for the newly dedicated sanctuary.

The different functions of the military and hierarchic personnel are also revealed in their separate locations. The priests and Levites are with the sanctuary and oriented toward it. They bear no arms. The extent to which they — especially the priests — are involved in military operations of the total camp (cf. Num 10:1-10) depends on the role of the sanctuary itself in such operations, not on the role of the cultic personnel as soldiers. Indeed, the numerous Levites (8,580 between thirty and fifty years of age!) are excused from military duty. They are the substitutes for the male firstborn of the tribes at the sanctuary. They belong to Yahweh. By contrast, the tribal army is located at the outer perimeter of the total camp, not coincidentally.

The text does not explain why the process of organization moves from the outer to the inner camp, i.e., why I.A. (1:1–2:34) precedes I.B. (3:1–4:49). The opposite movement would also have been possible. This structure may depend on older traditions or on the growth process of the text within the priestly tradition itself. But it seems to have a programmatic meaning which is based on the nature of the campaign itself and which is presupposed in the text and in its context.

The campaign alternates between encampment and march. Accordingly, the total camp alternates between its encampment formation and marching formation. Both formations are again conceived from the aspect of the narrative about the campaign. However, the two formations are not identical. During encampment, both camps are situated around the erected sanctuary in an outer and inner quadrangle. During the march, the quadrangular formation converts into a linear formation. For specifics → Num 2:1-34; 10:14-28.

29

The different formations during encampment and march reveal two different functions especially of the tribal militia. During encampment, the quadrangular formation no doubt serves a defensive purpose. The tribal units protect the sanctuary and its hierarchic personnel on all sides against enemies from outside. This defensive function is not relativized by the fact that the camp is at rest. This campaign camp is never in the situation of the rest *(měnûḥâ)* envisioned in Deuteronomy. The rest during the campaign does not necessitate a change from the linear to the quadrangular formation, just as the sanctuary by virtue of its centrality or holiness does not require the quadrangular formation during the march. The change in formation documents that during the periods of encampment the camp takes on a defensive posture.

The linear marching formation could not fulfill the same defensive function because the flanks of the sanctuary would remain unprotected. It has a different function altogether. It is organized offensively. This offensive function could not be accomplished by the quadrangular formation. The offensive formation with sanctuary and cultic personnel in the middle may be questionable under ancient and modern aspects of offensive strategy. Josh 3:11-17 portrays a different picture. Yet Josh 6:1-9 confirms the same linear formation for offensive purposes. On the formation of march and attack in Ramesses' II campaign at Kadesh-Orontes cf. Yadin, *Warfare,* vol. I., 103-10, 236-37; also 292-93. Cf. also Kuentz, plates 32, 33, 43, 39, 42; and discussion by Kellermann, *Numeri,* 22.

The military camp order in Numbers 2 serves both purposes: defense during encampment, and offense during the march. In the alternation between both situations, Numbers 1–4 reflects Israel's situation on the campaign to the land but not yet settled in the land. Under the aspect of this situation, however, the encampment conditions with defensive posture are transitional. They are part of the basic forward movement of the campaign and reflect the overall plot of the book of Numbers in its present text and its older traditions of the campaign from Sinai to Moab and beyond.

The importance of the alternating formations for the military aspects is also indicated by the fact that the alternation is made explicit repeatedly in I.A.2. (2:1-34), while prescribing its quadrangular formation apparently assumes the same alternation based on 2:17. Cf. also 10:17, 21. But it only vaguely indicates it in 4:15, despite the fact that it is frequently aware of the march, too, and not only of the encampment.

However, the distinctly different locations and functions of both camps cannot mean that they are unrelated, and that the sanctuary would be related to the inner camp only and not also to the outer camp. The societal picture in Numbers 1–4 is scarcely one of two separate societies in which a non-cultic military has nothing to do with a non-military cult. The Levites by substituting for the male firstborn represent the tribes at the sanctuary. The tribal military formation, by guarding the sanctuary and its hierarchy, serves the cultic institution. It does not serve a political or military interest apart from the goals of that institution. The cultic institution does not pursue its non-military tasks exclusively, and the tabernacle is not exclusively a non-military sanctuary. While on the march, and according to Num 10:1-10 even while encamped or in final settlement, it also serves the purpose of war. This picture is quite traditional, and the priestly writers share it. It is presupposed in Numbers 1–4, especially in the formation of the offensive aspect of the march. This march points to the formation of a military campaign of a specifically cultic nature, the sanctuary campaign.

The role of the sanctuary itself in the organization of the campaign must come into focus. The total camp does not consist only of the two Israelite formations. It also consists of the sanctuary, which is different from either formation. In its original layer already (Pg), Numbers 1–4 presupposes the story of the creation of the sanctuary in Exodus 25–31 and 35–40. It narrates the progress of the events from the creation of the sanctuary via the ordination of the priests in Leviticus 8–10 to the establishment of Israel's camp formations. It assumes that the existing and erected sanctuary is already in place while the two camps are organized, and that these camps are placed around the central sanctuary and not around a vacuum. The two camps neither exist without nor precede nor determine the sanctuary. They follow and are determined by it in terms of location and function. Strictly speaking, the sanctuary is not in Israel's midst, but Israel's camps are organized around the sanctuary. The sanctuary is central because the camps are laid out from this center, and not because the center is determined by the camp.

The total camp has three local dimensions. This layout is not compromised in the marching order where the distance between the disassembled sanctuary and the Levites carrying it and its vessels is collapsed. However, more important than the threefold layout is the difference between the sanctuary on the one hand and the inner and outer camps on the other. These camps are established because of and for the sanctuary. The total camp consists of two parts: the sanctuary and its twofold escort. It is a *sanctuary* camp, and the campaign from which it cannot be separated is a sanctuary campaign.

The relationship between the sanctuary *(miqdāš)* and the specific twofold formation of the Israelite congregation *('ēdâ)* is under discussion. The exclusion of the non-military and non-hierarchic Israelites from the camp in Numbers 1–4 cannot mean that they are suddenly forgotten or non-existent; it only means that they are not representative of the nature of this specific campaign. Their absence points once more to the specifically military nature of the sanctuary campaign. In this campaign, the sanctuary does not only, not even primarily, function as the place for the atonement cult. It could do so only during the intermittent encampments. It functions primarily as the center of the military campaign. Through this function, the military campaign itself becomes a cultic campaign. And the hierarchic personnel as well as the tribal host are its escorts.

In its respective contexts (Exodus 25–31; 35–40; and Numbers 3–4), the sanctuary *(miqdāš)* is more than the tent *('ōhel)* or tabernacle *(miškān)*. It is both the structure and its vessels, especially the ark and the mercy seat *(kappōret)*.

We may summarize the discussion of I.A. (1:1–2:34) and I.B. (3:1–4:49). The unit Numbers 1–4 is based on the concept of the organization of a sanctuary campaign for Israel's migration from Sinai to the promised land. The placement and personnel of the outer and inner camps have different functions. Both camps and their functions are elements of the unit of the entire organization. This unity is constituted by the sanctuary from which the organization is laid out and which the camps serve.

The sanctuary has both military and non-military functions, which are reflected in the different functions of the two camps serving it and in the difference between the encampment formation and marching formation. In the encampment formation it serves the operation of the Yahweh-cult. In the marching formation it is the reason for the offensive movement of the military camp.

The alternation between encampment and march is based on the ongoing movement for which the marching formation is the primary aspect, whereas the encampment formation reflects the periodic breaks during the march. In this respect, the organization at the Sinai encampment reflects the preparation for the march before its beginning. It is the Sinaitic organization embedded in the entire Sinai-pericope. But it is also a program for the protection of the non-military function of the sanctuary cult during the periods of encampment.

Nevertheless, as long as the march continues, the periods of encampment and the non-military function of the tabernacle during those periods are restricted by the march, and depend on military protection. They become possible through the military nature of the march that identifies the migration as a campaign. Its military nature is documented by the conscription of all males falling within the age of service, by their mobilization into camp order, by the offensive and defensive functions of that order, and in the involvement of the sanctuary in the military operation. Numbers 1–4 narrates the process of the military-cultic and hierarchic organization of Israel in preparation of its migrating sanctuary campaign.

The clear structure of the process of the narrative is interrupted only by the unit I.A.1.b. (1:48-54), which summarily describes the task of the Levites. This unit is an addendum to Num 1:47, a concluding statement about the exception of the Levites from the tribal census. The addendum is a variation of the large report about the Levites in I.B.2. (3:5–4:49), and its appearance in the present text is premature. It must have been in this place before Numbers 3f. reached its final form. Its explanatory relation to 1:47 indicates, however, that this unit cannot offset the twofold structural division of Numbers 1 and 2.

Part II. (Num 5:1–10:10) is set apart from part I. (1:1–4:49) because it is no longer concerned with the organization of the total camp as is part I. From 5:1 on the narrative is no longer governed by a process of successive steps. Part II. consists of twelve units which cover a diversity of aspects and presuppose different contexts. The relationship of these units to one another is anything but self-evident. All attempts at discerning an organizing principle have been either tentative or insufficiently substantiated.

The camp *(maḥăneh)* is only mentioned in 5:1-4; 10:6. And in all twelve units it is no longer the military hierarchic camp of Numbers 1–4 only. The camp refers to Israel's total camp. The aspect of purity *(ṭāhōr)* and its opposite *(ṭāmēʾ)* play a role in 5:1-4, 11-31; 6:1-21; 8:5-22; 9:1-14. This aspect is not confined to the campaign camp. The tent of meeting *(ʾōhel môʿēd)* is mentioned in 6:10-18; 7:5-9; 8:9-26; 9:15, 17; and the tabernacle *(miškān)* in 5:17. The evidence does not suggest a uniting principle based on any of these aspects. The structural problem is further complicated by the fact that seven out of the twelve units are not related at all to Numbers 1–4. They are supplements to contexts outside part I. And their own sequential arrangement in Num 5:1–10:10 does not follow the sequence of the texts which they supplement. Thus, Num 5:1-4 belongs with Leviticus 12-15, Num 5:5-10 with Lev 6:1-7, Num 7:1-89 with Exodus 40, Num 8:1-4 with Exodus 25, Num 9:1-14 with Exodus 12, Num 9:15-23 with Exodus 40, and Num 8:23-26 with Num 8:5-22, which is the only supplement to a text within Numbers 1–4, namely, 3:5–4:49.

Only four units are not of supplementary nature. Of these 5:11-31 refers to defilement without mentioning the camp, and rightly so: the unit involves women. Num 6:1-21 mentions defilement, but the Nazirites play no role in the camp of Numbers 1–4 either. Num 6:22-27 is concerned with the Aaronide blessing of Israel and with none of the other aspects mentioned. Only Num 10:1-10, the instruction about the priestly trumpets, is concerned with the camp, too, if not only so. For further observations on the relationship of individual units cf. the comments to those units.

Only in one aspect are the eleven units united. Except for 5:1-4 the priests are mentioned everywhere. They play a role in all parts of the camp which is not the case in Numbers 1–4, and which clearly indicates the claim to hierarchic predominance over the total camp and also points to the authors of these units. And Num 5:1-4 belongs to the same aspect even though it does not mention the priests directly.

The best explanation for the diverse aspects and the uncoordinated relationship of the units in 5:1–10:10 is that this part in its present structure reflects to a large extent the history of the growth of the text in successive accretions in which, from situation to situation, new units involving important aspects were added.

In view of this picture, it is a legitimate question whether Num 5:1–10:10 is not actually a supplement to the entire Sinai pericope rather than to Numbers 1–4 only. Whichever interpretation is preferred, the placement of this unit at the end of both the Sinai pericope and narrative about the organization of the camp represents a structural tension. The reason why most of the units in 5:1–10:10 were not placed at their appropriate contexts in Exodus, Leviticus, and Numbers is neither given nor easily discernible.

It nevertheless seems that the units in 5:1–10:10 were clustered as much as the growth process allowed in accordance with the division of the two camps on which the structure of Num 1:1–4:49 rests. The first five units in 5:1–6:27 address affairs of the Israelites of the outer realm, including 6:22-27 which — significantly — concludes this section. By contrast, the following seven units in 7:1–10:10 focus on the inner realm, including 7:1-89, and possibly also the instruction concerning the Passover in 9:1-14 because of its specifically cultic nature, although this unit deals with the purity of the outer realm.

The clustered arrangement in part II. reflects a division of that part into two sections, II.A. (5:1–6:27) and II.B. (7:1–10:10), which correspond sequentially to I.A. (1:1–2:34) and I.B. (3:1–4:49). The structure of part II. appears to follow the literary structure of part I. in which the order of the total camp is implied. In this regard, part II. is an expansion of the organization report in part I. Not coincidentally, this expansion is introduced in 5:1-4 by the instruction to remove the unclean from the camp — which camp? — and is concluded in 10:1-10 by the instruction about the role of the trumpets for the camp.

The structure of the present text of Num 1:1–10:10 represents the final outcome of a literary-historical process within the priestly tradition. There is agreement that the final text must have had pre-stages of different shapes. But a major consensus on the identification of the different layers has remained elusive. Kellermann's latest attempt assigns only portions of chs. 1, 2, and 4 to Pg (*Numeri,* 147), and the rest of the material to several stages of expansions between this oldest and the final layers. In view of the task of this commentary, the form-critical interpretation of the successive layers pervading all pertinent units is ill advised as long as no sufficient consensus exists. Where significant, the commentary pays attention to this problem in the discussion of the individual units. However, even Kellermann's minimal determination of the oldest layer suggests that already in its earliest stage the text contained the structurally significant division between the outer and inner camp formations that still governs the final text. This structural continuity shows that the aspect of the organization of the sanctuary camp remained throughout the redaction-historical development of Num 1:1–10:10 and was the fundamental aspect to which all successive accretions were subordinated. This aspect is decisive for the structure of the entire narrative about the preparation of the campaign, and for its generic nature, its setting, and its intention as well.

Genre

Num 1:1–10:10 belongs to the SAGA of the migrating sanctuary campaign. More specifically, it narrates its preparatory organization. Constitutive for its generic identity is Numbers 1–4. Num 5:1–10:10 is generically not homogeneous and at best organized in analogy to I.A. (1:1–2:34) and I.B. (3:1–4:49) in Numbers 1–4.

The definition of the camp for the sanctuary campaign in Numbers 1–4 provides the basis for the discussion of the genre of this text.

Even in its earliest layer (Pg), the text about the camp formation cannot be isolated from the priestly narrative about the migration with its alternation between encampment and decampment. Should Num 2:9b, 16b, 24b, 31b be from a secondary hand (cf. Kellermann, *Numeri,* 20-22), they would reflect only an extension and not a modification of the original view. The priestly camp is a migratory camp in both march and encampment, and not a camp at a sedentary local sanctuary. It is a camp intended for a campaign with both military and cultic participants, and not for a pilgrimage. Both aspects militate against the assumption that in the background of Numbers 1–4 stands the tradition of the encampment of pilgrims at a festival of a sedentary local sanctuary. They also militate against the assumption of a fictitious literary combination of the two genuinely separate traditions of war and pilgrimage camps, a combination that is not grounded in reality. (For a reflex of this widespread view cf.

Helfmeyer, *"ḥānâ,"* 4-20.) They point instead to the campaign camps in the tradition history of Israel's warfare.

Despite the exegetical consensus about the military nature of Numbers 1–2, the unit Numbers 1–4 has played no role in the discussion on warfare in the OT. In the latest study by Lind, the text is nowhere mentioned. Even less considered under this aspect is Numbers 3–4, although Deuteronomy and 1 Chr 26:20-27 document the relation of the Levites to the military organization. The assumption of a non-military orientation of the priestly writings is highly doubtful. With respect to the military, the sociology of P appears to be basically in line with, rather than in contrast to, the sociology of the jehovistic and deuteronomic traditions.

Numbers 1–4 is based on the tradition history of Israel's holy wars in which Yahweh and Israel participate together in battles and campaigns, and which is also evident in the jehovistic layers in Num 10:11–36:13. It is probably not coincidental that in the context of the older campaign saga, Numbers 1–4 portrays Yahweh's campaign escorted by Israel rather than Israel's campaign supported by Yahweh. Deutero-Isaiah offers an even stronger variant of this aspect (Isa 40:1-11). On holy war and especially the relationship between Yahweh and Israel in war cf., among others: Fredriksson; von Rad, *Heiliger Krieg;* Smend; Glock; Stolz, *Kriege;* Weippert, "Heiliger Krieg"; Lohfink; L. Schmidt; Craigie, "Man of Wars," *Problem of War;* Gottwald, "Holy War"; Helfmeyer, *"ḥānâ";* Lind; and Preuss with up-to-date bibliography.

The older holy war traditions know of no transportable sanctuary of the kind portrayed in P. They know only of the ark, the transportable shrine of ancient Israel's holy wars; cf. Num 10:33-36; 14:39-45; Joshua 3-6; 1 Sam 4–6. The older traditions also know of a transportable tent (cf. Kutsch, "Lade Jahwes," 197-99; "Zelt," 1893-94; Kellermann, *"miškān";* Quellette, "Temple of Solomon"; Aharoni, "Temples, Semitic"; Zobel, *"ărôn"*). The reference to "prefabricated structures" in ancient Egypt such as the "splendid, prefabricated portable bed-canopy of Queen Hedep-heres I" (Kitchen, 8) is beside the point because these structures are indeed portable. The priestly sanctuary is said to have been served and carried by 8,580 Levites (Num 4:48-49), and not on the back of a camel. The portability and movability of the tremendous size of this sanctuary is under discussion, and not its obviously prefabricated structure. The elaborate and heavy structure of the priestly sanctuary reflects the tradition of sedentary local sanctuaries, not a tradition of such sanctuaries used in migrations, let alone in campaigns. In the literary history of the Sinai campaign narrative, the transportable campaign ark of the jehovistic tradition was replaced in the priestly tradition by the transportable campaign sanctuary, a combination of tent and house or palace.

How was it possible — indeed, necessary — for the essentially non-transportable priestly tabernacle to replace the transportable jehovistic ark, thereby transforming an ark campaign saga into a LEGEND of the sanctuary campaign? The answer to this question does not lie in the fantasies of the priestly writers. It lies in the combination of the ark and temples in Israel's history in the land. In that history, the older transportable holy war shrine had been placed in a non-transportable temple, first in Shiloh, then in Jerusalem. And as time passed, it lost its original function and especially its independence over against the sanctuary, and became a part, however important, of the sanctuary itself. The house of Yahweh *(bêt yhwh* or *hêkāl yhwh)* replaced the ark of Yahweh, and the sedentary local temple became the permanent home for the migratory ark. This process in Israel's institutional history was at least originally contested, and always in need of legitimation. In this tension between ark and temple, it was the temple that was in need of legitimation, and not the ark regardless how its function was understood. While the temple of Shiloh was discarded, the ark was not despite its defeat by the Philistines. The Jerusalem temple was and remained contested. The ark was scarcely ever contested, even as its significance seems to have more and more receded behind the predominance of the temple.

The integration of the ark into, and its increasing replacement by the temple in, Israel's institutional history represents an exact analogy to the replacement of the jehovistic campaign ark by the priestly campaign sanctuary in the literary history of the Pentateuch. This analogy cannot be coincidental. One must assume that the portrait of the sanctuary in the priestly writings is the priestly response to the need for the legitimation of the temple in Israel's institutional history. Especially for the priests, this need was fundamental unless they wanted to disclaim their own relationship to the temple. And the most fundamental way to legitimize the temple sanctuary was for them to anchor it in the indisputable Sinaitic constitution, the centerpiece of their theology, and not in Jerusalem — let alone in Shiloh — because the temple in Jerusalem was itself in need of legitimization.

It is, therefore, understandable that the P sanctuary is no copy of the Solomonic temple, but a special blueprint even as it reflects with discernment the reality of this temple and probably its predecessor, the tent-house at Shiloh (cf. Fritz, 147-49). It is also understandable that the priestly desert sanctuary is nowhere recorded to have been transported into the promised land. It was never supposed to be the temple at Shiloh. And neither the Solomonic temple nor the temple of 515 B.C.E. was meant to be the norm for the priestly desert sanctuary. Rather, the desert sanctuary was meant to be the critical prototype for any pan-Israelite temple in Jerusalem, past and future. It was nothing but the unique sanctuary of the unique desert campaign. Most importantly, it was the tradition of the ancient campaign ark in the temple itself that made the implantation of the temple tradition into the priestly Sinai campaign narrative possible, because it provided the link to the transportable ark in the jehovistic narrative, the forerunner of the sanctuary in P. Yet under the influence of that institutional history in which the temple remained in need of authentication despite its actual control over the ark, the sanctuary of the priestly writers, which reflects the same control over its ark, could and had to replace the jehovistic ark in the literary history. It is not without irony: in the institutional tradition history and in the reaction to it in the literary tradition history, the ark, in providing the legitimation for the temple sanctuary, also provided the ground for the demise of its own independence and predominance.

The implantation of the temple tradition into the Sinai campaign narrative explains why the originally sedentary and non-transportable temple had to become a transportable sanctuary. If the desert shrine had to be a sanctuary, its migratory and transportable nature was inevitable in the context of the P narrative and its predecessors. In this context it had to become the sanctuary of the campaign. The priestly sanctuary took over the role of the holy shrine of the campaign from the jehovistic ark. The nature of the transportable priestly campaign sanctuary was determined by the narrative context about the unique, one-time event of Israel's campaign from Sinai to the border of the promised land. Its nature is, therefore, just as unique as the context that generated it. And unless one assumes that the original priestly narrative (Pg) contained no chapter at all on the migration from Sinai on, the conclusion seems once again inevitable that its sanctuary was from the outset meant to be the migratory and transportable holy shrine of the campaign.

For good reason, there are no accounts of holy campaigns involving transportable temples. The genre of the narrative about the sanctuary campaign can therefore not rest on the ground that the transportable shrine of Numbers 1–4 is a temple-sanctuary. But it does rest on the genres of ACCOUNT of military campaign in general, and of ACCOUNT of holy war or campaign specifically. It represents a unique variation of the traditional genre of narratives about holy war campaigns. This variation was generated by the acute need of the priestly writers for superimposing their sanctuary on the ark of the jehovistic saga, which they did in their own expansion of that saga in Exodus 25–31; 35–40; and Numbers 1–4 (5–10). Through this expansion, the older ark campaign saga became a sanctuary campaign narrative. Yet despite this shift in focus, the priestly narrative remained within the genre of the older narrative about a holy war campaign. It belongs to this genre because it depends on its tradition.

In only one respect, the genre of the older narrative changed in P: from SAGA to LEGEND. The transportable desert sanctuary is unique and incomparable, and so is the narrative about it. This narrative intersects with the genre of SANCTUARY LEGENDS, but only in part because of its portrayal of the sanctuary as a campaign sanctuary, and because the uniqueness of the sanctuary is matched by the unique narrative of the formation of the campaign camp in preparation for a unique migration. The uniqueness of the total narrative is not coincidental. It portrays not only an ideal (cf. Childs, 196) but a miraculous event. This kind of narrative belongs to a particular narrative genre which is distinguished from REPORT or ACCOUNT or SAGA by its overall concern for the miraculous and ideal in events. It belongs to the narrative genre of LEGEND.

A LEGEND is not an untrue story. It is neither unrelated to past or existing realities nor an altogether incorrect rendering of facts. However, it is not governed by a critical historical reconstruction of events. It highlights instead the unique aspects of traditions in order to point out their miraculous and ideal nature, and thus their programmatic or at least edifying function for its hearers and readers in the present. The legend does not merely report. It interprets with a specific concern when reporting.

The legendary nature of Numbers 1–4 is evident in two additional factors. Lind has correctly shown that the emphasis on the miraculous belongs to the entire tradition history of Israel's holy wars. With its own emphasis on the miraculous, the sanctuary campaign legend of Numbers 1–4 is part of that tradition history. This emphasis has found its specific expression in the form of the preparation of the campaign, the exclusively priestly addition to the older saga. The picture of this preparation is distinctly different from the picture of the executed campaign in the jehovistic saga. It is the picture of an unblemished miraculous event. It contrasts the ideal miracle at the Sinai encampment with the contested miracle on the campaign, the preparation and program with their execution, the legend with the saga.

Two factors are constitutive for "The Legend of the Organization of the Sanctuary Campaign": The "Organization of the Sanctuary Campaign" is the particular generic issue of this "Legend," and the "Legend" expresses the particular generic function of this narrative. But in the total narrative about the sanctuary campaign in Numbers, the legend is a part of the saga, not only because the saga is longer and a part of the entire biography of Moses, but also because in the campaign itself, the legend of the valid ideal is overshadowed by the saga of its imperfect execution.

Setting

The setting of Num 1:1–10:10 is identical with the setting of the priestly redactors of the Pentateuch. → Chapter 1, Setting. Especially Num 5:1–10:10 but also Numbers 1–4 show the hands of successive generations at work in a probably uninterrupted history of priests, especially Aaronide priests stretching over some two hundred years, from 600 to 400 B.C.E. It is possible that the local settings of these generations changed. Their traditional home seems to have been Bethel (cf. Gunneweg, 90-93; Fritz, 155-57), rather than Anathoth (cf. Fretheim, 317) or Shiloh (cf. Haran, 14-24) or the southland (cf. Noth, *Pentateuchal Traditions,* 178-82). Whether the history of their work began in Mesopotamia and continued in Palestine or whether it took place in Palestine alone remains a question. It did not take place in Jerusalem, however. In this regard, the setting of the priestly writers is different from the setting of their Aaronide successors in Jerusalem. This fact may help to explain why their work is not unequivocably obligated to the existing realities of the first and second temple.

While the local and historical aspects of the setting of the Aaronide authors cannot be ignored, the societal aspects are especially important. These priests must have been institutionalized. They belonged to a genealogically identified priestly family which not only set itself apart from other priestly families but also claimed a priestly class-status in distinction from the inferior Levites, who in Dtn times were recognized as priests at the central sanctuary. They were not in charge of the Jerusalem temple at their time. But they were nonetheless professional priests with profoundly theological and educational interests, which may have been heightened precisely because they were not in the driver's seat. Despite their local and/or temporary distance from the Jerusalem temple, the mirroring of this temple in their work demonstrates their preeminent interest in the cultic institution.

It is this specific setting that provided the interpretive needs and possibilities for the legend of the organization of the sanctuary campaign just as much as for the entire priestly work. It provided the contemporary historical and institutional context, the normative ancient Sinai tradition, and the Israelite traditions for reshaping the Sinai tradition in light of the present needs. It especially generated the preeminent focus on the sanctuary. Through this focus, the ancient saga of the holy war campaign received a distinct expansion, concentration, and reevaluation. Whatever their program for the present and future was, it was above all executed through a recasting of the story of the past.

In portraying the organization of the camp for the impending campaign, the priests remained within the genre of Israel's holy war tradition of which they especially emphasized the typical element of the organization of such campaigns. For this traditional genre and its long history, however, we cannot assume only one setting. The genre was expressed in poetry and prose, and was used by prophetic circles, by poets, by historians, and by priests as well. And it was expressed in varying aspects (cf. L. Schmidt, 235). The different sources, forms of expression, and interpretive aspects suggest a history of different settings in which the holy war tradition was transmitted and interpreted, much more than one group only (L. Schmidt, 236) whose setting cannot be clearly determined. A similar history of settings must be assumed for the genre of legend, which was also employed by the priestly narrators. The priestly authors represent one more setting in the histories of these genres.

Finally, the mobilization of the conscripted into the camp around the campaign sanctuary points, despite the uniqueness of the sanctuary, to the traditional setting of actual organizations of cultic-military campaigns themselves in which cultic shrines play a role besides the military. The fact is sufficiently documented religio-historically (cf. Stolz, *Kriege*). Yahweh's ark with its priests was a cultic object in Israel's actual ancient wars, and not an abstract idea. The perception of Yahweh's representation through cultic shrines, personnel, and rituals in campaigns was at home in campaigns themselves, and not only in the theories of narrators or writers about campaigns. The texts that reflect this perception, whether in terms of historical campaigns or in terms of a more articulate theological awareness, represent the linguistic complement to the institutional setting of religious warfare.

In view of the cultic nature of warfare itself, the assumption of a basic dichotomy between actual secular warfare and its secondary theological spiritualization appears to be alien to the ancient world-view. Theology and spirituality are intrinsic to the setting of warfare itself, even in modern times. They are the matrix for cultic warfare. The priestly legend of the organization of the sanctuary campaign camp reflects the history of that institutional setting, and not a fiction unrelated to historical and societal realities. In applying its Sinai sanctuary to the historical institution of cultic warfare, it regarded this prototypical sanctuary as representative of that institution, and the institution as an integral extension of Israel's ideal and miraculous sanctuary.

Intention

The adaptation of the full, twofold form of the genre of campaign narratives through the addition of the legend of the organization of the sanctuary camp to the older campaign saga indicates an emphasis on the particular kind of campaign from Sinai on. This campaign was to be understood as the specifically organized *sanctuary* campaign of the Sinai covenant community, and no longer as the campaign of the Sinai covenant community only — so at least the combination of the jehovistic and priestly tradition. The emphasis is expressed in the legend in which, at Sinai, the campaign host above all is miraculously and ideally organized around the sanctuary through Yahweh's instruction and its obedient execution. The preparation narrative intends to show the uniqueness of the Sinai event for the organization of pan-Israel for its impending future, and the importance of the preparation itself for that future. (Cf. the analogous function of Deuteronomy as the extensive programmatic preparation in Moab for the impending conquest of the promised land.) It is in the preparation, and not in the execution, that the pure picture and the program can be seen. It is the preparation in the beginning that remains foundational. The legendary nature of this picture cannot be surprising. Any miracle, ideal, or program is in tension with reality. If anything, it is not the tension that renders the program contestable.

The legend narrates a unique event at Sinai as an event of the past. But unless one assumes that it was written for the sake of historical reminiscence — an understanding alien to the Hebrew concept of remembrance — one has to notice that the legend intends to be a message to its receivers. It does not deflect the attention from their present situation. Quite the contrary. Its way of addressing the unresolved present situation is to focus on a situation ideally resolved in a particular past event. Under this aspect, the legend of the preparation for the sanctuary campaign suggests a specific focus on an analogous situation confronting its receivers. Such a situation would be characterized by Israel not being in possession of the land, perhaps in exile and having to move towards the land, and intending to return and preparing for the return, especially to Jerusalem. In such a situation, the legend of the campaign preparation would be programmatic, especially as it takes the involved generation back to the one event that exceeded all other traditions in significance and from which the new campaign had to be devised.

However, since the date of at least the original priestly work (Pg) is still debated, the specific historical situation remains a relatively open question. In view of successive priestly generations at work, the programmatic intention of their work must have been valid for more than one generation only. It must have been valid for the generation of Cyrus and even for the generation of 520-515 B.C.E. (cf. Fritz, 159). If Fritz is — with good arguments — correct in assuming for Pg a time shortly after 587 B.C.E. (p. 157), the nucleus of Numbers 1–4 would project the vision of a return to the land by way of an epiphanic sanctuary campaign accompanied by the Yahweh-host, not unmilitary in nature. The program would be in line with the Dtr program a generation earlier, though in distinct variation, and not unlike the prophetic program of Deutero-Isaiah a generation later (Isa 40:1-11). Indeed, Pg could have originated in parallel to the Dtr program during Josiah's time. Whether there is sufficient evidence for Haran's thesis of the time of Ahaz and Hezekiah (*Temples*, 228) is even more in question than the possibilities just mentioned.

Bibliography

Y. Aharoni, "Temples, Semitic," *IDBSup;* B. S. Childs, *An Introduction to the Old Testament as Scripture* (Philadelphia: Fortress, 1979); P. C. Craigie, "Yahweh Is a Man of Wars," *SJT* 22 (1969) 183-88; idem, *The Problem of War in the Old Testament* (Grand Rapids: Eerdmans, 1978); H. Fredriksson, *Jahwe als Krieger* (Lund: C. W. K. Gleerup, 1945); T. E. Fretheim, "The Priestly Document: Anti-Temple?" *VT* 18 (1968) 313-29; V. Fritz, *Tempel und Zelt: Studien zum Tempelbau in Israel und zu dem Zeltheiligtum der Priesterschrift* (WMANT 47; Neukirchen: Neukirchener, 1977); A. E. Glock, "Warfare in Mari and Early Israel" (Diss., University of Michigan, 1968); N. K. Gottwald, "'Holy War' in Deuteronomy: Analysis and Critique," *RevExp* 61 (1964) 296-310; A. H. J. Gunneweg, *Leviten und Priester* (FRLANT 89; Göttingen: Vandenhoeck & Ruprecht, 1965); M. Haran, *Temples and Temple-Service in Ancient Israel: An Inquiry into the Character of Cult Phenomena and the Historical Setting of the Priestly School* (Oxford: Clarendon, 1978); F. J. Helfmeyer, *"ḥānâ; maḥaneh," TDOT;* D. Kellermann, *"miškān," TWAT; Die Priesterschrift von Numeri 1,1 bis 10,10: Literarkritisch und traditionsgeschichtlich untersucht* (BZAW 120; Berlin: Walter de Gruyter, 1970); K. A. Kitchen, "Some Egyptian Background to the Old Testament," *TynB* 5-6 (1960) 4-18; C. Kuentz, *La Bataille de Qadech* (Cairo: L'Institut Français d'archéologie orientale, 1928); E. Kutsch, "Lade Jahwes," *RGG3;* "Zelt," *RGG3;* M. Lind, *Yahweh is a Warrior: The Theology of Warfare in Ancient Israel* (Scottdale: Herald Press, 1980); N. Lohfink, "Die Schichten des Pentateuch und der Krieg," in E. Haag et al., *Gewalt und Gewaltlosigkeit im Alten Testament* (QD 96; Freiburg: Herder, 1983) 51-110; M. Noth, *A History of Pentateuchal Traditions* (tr. B. W. Anderson; Chico: Scholars, 1981); H. D. Preuss, *"milḥāmāh," TWAT;* J. Quellette, "Temple of Solomon," *IDBSup;* G. von Rad, *Der Heilige Krieg im alten Israel* (3. Aufl.; ATANT 20; Gottingen: Vandenhoeck & Ruprecht, 1958); L. Schmidt, *Menschlicher Erfolg und Jahwes Initiative* (WMANT 38; Neukirchen: Neukirchener, 1970); R. Smend, *Yahweh War and Tribal Confederation: Reflections upon Israel's Earliest History* (tr. M. G. Rogers; Nashville: Abingdon, 1970); F. Stolz, *Jahwes und Israels Kriege* (ATANT 60; Zurich: Theologischer, 1972); M. Weippert, "'Heiliger Krieg' in Israel und Assyrien," *ZAW* 84 (1972) 460-93; Y. Yadin, *The Art of Warfare in Biblical Lands: In the Light of Archaeological Study* (2 vols.; tr. M. Pearlman; New York: McGraw-Hill, 1963); H.-J. Zobel, *"ărôn," TDOT.*

Chapter 3

THE INDIVIDUAL UNITS
(NUMBERS 1:1–10:10)

The Report of the Military Conscription (1:1-54)

Structure

I. The conscription of the twelve tribes	1:1-47
A. The Yahweh command to Moses	1:1-16
1. Reporter's introductory statement	1:1
2. The command proper	1:2-16
a. Concerning the conscription	1:2-3
b. Concerning the tribal leaders	1:4-16
B. The compliance	1:17-47
1. Compliance report proper	1:17-19
2. The protocol of the result	1:20-47
a. According to the tribal catalogue	1:20-43
b. According to the Israelite total	1:44-47
1) Concerning the twelve tribes	1:44-46
2) Concerning the exempted Levites	1:47
II. Supplement: report about the exemption of the Levites	1:48-54
A. The Yahweh order to Moses	1:48-53
1. Reporter's introductory statement	1:48
2. The order proper	1:49-53
a. Prohibition	1:49
b. Command	1:50-53
B. = I.B. + II. The compliance	1:54

The unit is a composition in which different elements are combined under the aspect of a military conscription. It is a report in which the content and the essential process for its implementation are narrated in brief, recording style.

The report focuses in its major part (I., vv. 1-47) on those conscripted for, and in its smaller parts [I.B.2.b.2), v. 47, and II., vv. 48-54] on those exempted from military duty. It includes the two typical categories in a society-wide mandatory military conscription. And it presupposes the pan-Israelite perspective by combining all of the tribes and the Levites. In both respects the report is guided by the concept of "all the congregation of the people of Israel," the *'ēdâ* (vv. 2, 45), which is in this text the totality of draftable males.

The conscription of the members of the tribes in part I. is reported in two sections: Yahweh's command to Moses, I.A. (vv. 1-16), and Moses' and Aaron's (and the leaders', v. 44) compliance in I.B. (vv. 17-47). The combination of command and compliance, typical for the tradition and especially for P, points to the importance of the relationship of the two aspects: Moses' conscription of the *'ēdâ* originated in Yahweh's commanding speech, and Yahweh's command was promptly obeyed by Moses. But it also reflects the basic pattern of conscription itself. No conscription is executed automatically. It is always preceded by an authoritative decision — in antiquity normally a royal decree — which includes the determination of administrative mechanisms such as the selection and designation of officials just as much as the definition(s) of the objective. Numbers 1 reflects the two basic steps of this pattern. In adopting this pattern the priestly writers replaced the royal by the divine overlord, the king's decree by Yahweh's command, and the royal palace by the tent of meeting in the desert of Sinai (v. 1).

Section I.A. (vv. 1-16), the report of the Yahweh command, consists of the narrator's introductory statement (I.A.1., v. 1) and his quotation of the command (I.A.2., vv. 2-16). The introductory statement at the beginning of the Book of Numbers is the most extensive used by P (cf. 1:48; 3:5, 11, 40, 44, et al.; 2:1; 4:1, 17; 3:14; 9:1). It consists of the standard formula for the report of an address, "And Yahweh spoke to Moses," with two expansions that define the twofold locale and the time of Yahweh's speaking. Both expansions connect the unit with the priestly Exodus and Sinai narrative.

The subunit I.A.2. (vv. 2-16) is based on Yahweh's address to Moses. Its form is a COMMAND. What is commanded is the conscription of the *'ēdâ* (I.A.2.a., vv. 2-3) and the selection of the tribal officers for the conscription (I.A.2.b., vv. 4-16). Here as elsewhere, the words and grammatical forms for the command vary (cf. vv. 2a, 3b, 4a, 5a), but they have in common the positive charge in direct address to do something or have something happen in a specific situation.

The command concerning the conscription (I.A.2.a., vv. 2-3) is structured as follows:

1) Expressed in demographic terms	2
a) Corporately	2a
(1) Basic command	2aα
(2) Specifications: clans and families	2aβ
b) Individually	2b
(1) Number of names of all males	2bα-bβ_1
(2) Specification: individually	2bβ_2

2) Expressed in military terms   3
  a) Specifications   3a
    (1) Age   3aα
    (2) Fitness for war   3aβ
  b) Basic command proper   3b
    (1) Command   3bα₁
    (2) Specifications   3bα₂-β
      (a) Concerning the military units   3bα₂
      (b) Concerning the chief registrar   3bβ

In a partly chiastic arrangement the structure reflects an attention to the demographic and military aspects of a military conscription, and to procedural steps as well. Demographically, the individuals of the total *ʿēdâ* are to be counted (*śěʾû ʾet-rōʾš*, v. 2aα). The counting involves the "number of the names" *(běmispar šēmôt)* of the heads or "skulls" of all males in Israel listed according to their clans *(mišpěḥōtām),* and their paternal houses *(bêt ʾăbōtām).* The reference to the "number of the names" (v. 2bα) indicates that procedurally the count is thought of as based on a (written) list of names rather than on the physical presence of those counted. Militarily, the totality of those fit as soldiers *(terminus technicus kol-yōṣēʾ ṣābāʾ),* from twenty years on, are to be appointed *(tipqědû)* by Moses and Aaron (according) to or into their military units *(lěṣibʾōtām).* Cf. Schottroff, 472-73; Preuss, 799.

The combination of the demographic and military criteria makes it clear that the commanded operation is not a society-wide census, a *Volkszählung.* It is a military conscription in the service of which the demographically based procedures also stand. The anticipated military units do not consist of professional soldiers and generals. They are the subunits of the genealogically based Israelite militia and their leaders. Except for the Levites, no exemption is granted for any male who is capable of going to war. In this subunit, the tribal aspect that governs vv. 4-16 and 20-47 is absent. The subunit is a typical element of a decree or command for a military conscription.

The command concerning the tribal leaders (I.A.2.b., vv. 4-16) is structured as follows:

1) The basic command   4
2) Explication   5-16
  a) Introduction   5a
  b) The list of tribal and individual names   5b-15
  c) Conclusion   16

The text maintains the form of a Yahweh address to Moses understood as a command (cf. v. 19a). Only v. 16 does not have this form. In I.A.2.b.1), the text opens with a basic command to Moses to have a man from each tribe who is the head of his paternal house with himself and Aaron (cf. v. 3b). In I.A.2.b.2), the basic command is unfolded by a short introduction, the list, and a conclusion which defines those to be selected under three aspects: they are the called ones of the *ʿēdâ,* the leaders *(něśîʾîm)* of the tribes of their fathers, and the heads of the thousands of Israel *(rā'šê 'alpê yiśrā'ēl)*. In this complex definition, they are more than only the helpers in the conscription process.

In the introduction [2)a), v. 5a], the address form "who shall stand with you" continues vv. 3b-4. It is combined with the form of a superscription, "These are the names of the men." The merger of these two forms suggests that an originally independent list was integrated into the Yahweh-speech report. The observation is supported by v. 16, a subscription, in form analogous to the superscription. It is also supported by the fact that vv. 4-16 are governed by the tribal and not by the clan perspective as are vv. 2-3.

The list of the tribal leaders [I.A.2.b.2)b), vv. 5b-15] rests on the correlation of their names and the names of the twelve tribes. (On the sequential order of the tribes, cf. Wilson, 184, 187; Olson, 56-81.) The twelve "men" *('ănāšîm,* vv. 5a, 17) are "leaders" *(nĕśî'îm)* by virtue of their function on the tribal level. They are the leaders of the tribes; cf. 1:4a, 16a, 17-47 (cf. Niehr, 651-54; Stolz, *"nś',"* 115-16; Kellermann, *Numeri,* 5-7, 155-59). The list focuses on the selection of these persons because of their position, but not on their role, in contrast to the clear expression of their role in Num 2:3-31; 10:14-27 (military); and 7:1-88 (economical). Only by its context (vv. 2-3, 4, 5a, 17) is their role uniquely defined as assistants for the conscription. This definition contrasts with v. 16 which agrees essentially with 2:3-31 and 10:14-27. Together with v. 16, vv. 5b-15 show no signs of the Yahweh speech form. In several respects, the list of the tribal leaders is not self-evidently an intrinsic part of the conscription report. How did it come into existence, and why was it inserted into the context of the Yahweh command for the conscription?

The undefined role of the leaders in the list together with their defined role in its context (vv. 2-5a, 17) suggests that originally they had nothing to do with the conscription, and that either an originally independent list became the basis for their presence in the other three texts (2:3-31; 10:14-27; 7:1-88), or this list was created from those texts for the purpose of the conscription report. The latter assumption is more difficult because one cannot sufficiently explain why the subscription (v. 16) was not used as the superscription of the list in the first place. Indeed, v. 16 seems to be the slightly modified text of the original superscription to the list which was — not for the first time in redactional techniques — transposed to its end because it did not lend itself clearly enough to the context of the conscription and had to be replaced by the smoother and more general formulation of v. 5a. The original text of this former superscription and present subscription can still be discerned (priestly additions in parentheses): *'ēlleh (qĕrû'ê [Q] hā'ēdâ) nĕśî'ê maṭṭôt ('ăbôtām) rā'šê* (or: *śārê?*) *'alpê yiśrā'ēl,* "These are (the called of the congregation) *the leaders of the tribes* (of their fathers), *the heads* (or: the officers?) *of the thousands of Israel."*

We assume that an original list consisted of a superscription that defined the subsequently named leaders of the individual tribes as the heads of the largest, the tribal units of Israel's militia. This list was used for the conscription report that then became the basis for its application in the other three passages. The age of the list is unknown. However, if it refers to real and not invented (Kellermann, *Numeri,* 6) leaders, it must have belonged to a particular generation in which the pan-Israelite militia was organized on the basis of a twelve-tribal system under the leadership of these persons, and before the time of the priestly writers. How should the writers have been able to place known contemporary leaders back into the desert time! Also, the age of the list involves both the particular order of the tribal system and the individual names of its leaders — unless one assumes that an original list of tribes without personal names was secondarily combined with the names of those persons. If real, the list's origin would have to be sought in a central administrative setting in which Israel's militia was organized under the system of the twelve tribes, not yet understood as *ʿēdâ,* and in which the leaders of the established tribal divisions were selected from their respective clans.

Except for the context of the list in Numbers 1, none of the four texts explains how the leaders came into their office. The tradition history of the *nĕśîʾîm* and the priestly writers know that they were automatically the heads of their clans and paternal families by virtue of their genealogical status. The same automatic status cannot be assumed for them in the tribes. They must have been chosen somehow, most probably through acts of the military administration. This mechanism for their selection must have been problematic for the priestly writers, especially in view of their persistent emphasis on Israel's constitution as the result of Yahweh's explicit initiatives. And the priestly inclusion of the original list into their report of Yahweh's command for the military conscription responds to this problem. At the outset of the total process they were selected by Yahweh as helpers without being named "helpers," in addition to being recognized as established leaders. Accordingly, Moses complies with Yahweh's command, v. 17. Thus, the leaders of a particular generation of Israel's militia became Moses' (and Aaron's) assistants in the conscription at Sinai.

The list of the tribal leaders was inserted into its context for specific reasons. At the same time, the selection of such high-level administrators and their role in the process of society-wide military conscriptions are no unique literary construct. In terms of military just as of other society-wide administration, the text reflects the typical setting of such processes (cf. Exod 18:13-27; 2 Sam 24:1-9; 1 Kgs 4:1-19; 2 Chr 19:4-11). It must be considered to be a generic element of such processes and their recording.

The compliance report, I.B. (vv. 17-47), consists of two parts: the compliance proper, I.B.1., and the protocol about its result, I.B.2. The two parts reflect different forms. The compliance report proper narrates the event, whereas the protocol documents the results in formulaic language. However, both parts belong together as compliance vis-à-vis the Yahweh command in I.A. The protocol in vv. 20-47 is not a third part of the vv. 1-16 and 17-19. It is stylistically and logically firmly connected with the preceding unit.

Part I.B.1. (vv. 17-19) is structured as follows:

a. The induction of the designated persons	17
b. The conscription of the congregation	18-19
1) The assembling	18aα
a) Basic statement	18aα$_1$
b) Calendric specification (cf. v. 1)	18aα$_2$

46

2) The following conscription: registration and
  appointment   18aβ-19
  a) Registration   18aβ-19a
    (1) Registration proper   18aβ-b
      (a) Basic statement   18aβ$_1$
      (b) Specifications   18aβ$_2$-b
      α. Genealogically:
          clans and families   18aβ$_2$-aβ$_3$
      β. Individually: names and age   18b
    (2) Reference to Yahweh command (cf. vv. 2-3)   19a
  b) Appointment in desert of Sinai   19b

The passage reports Moses' and Aaron's compliance with the total
Yahweh command in I.A. on the same day (v. 18aα$_1$; cf. v. 1). Here as elsewhere, the inclusion of Aaron belongs to a secondary layer of the text, whereas
originally Moses was not only the one receiving the command but also the
only one complying. In its first part (I.B.1.a.) the text basically refers to
I.A.2.b. (vv. 4-16). Its second part (I.B.1.b.) refers to I.A.2.a. (vv. 1-3). In only
one instance do the organizers do more than had been commanded: before the
actual conscription they assemble the congregation [I.B.1.b.1)] obviously at
the tent of meeting (v. 1, sic!) where or whence everything that follows is to
take place. After the assembling, the members of the ʿēdâ, from twenty years
on, are in I.B.1.b.2) said to have themselves registered *(wayyityalĕdû)* upon
their clans according to their paternal house, in the number of names — as
Yahweh had commanded. Subsequently (?, Impf. cs.) Moses appointed them in
the desert of Sinai.

    The short report bears the marks of its literary context. It is nevertheless a
typical element of the genre of protocols about military conscriptions that reflect the history and settings of such events as executions of decrees about conscriptions (cf. the discussion at the end of the next unit).

    The protocol, I.B.2. (vv. 20-47) is structured as follows:

a. Stated distributively: the individual tribes   20-43
  1) Reuben   20-21
    a) Identification   20-21a
      (1) Tribal name and origin   20aα
      (2) Twofold genealogical explication   20aβ-21a
        (a) First: expressed specifically   20aβ-b
        α. Formal reference to genealogy
          (tôlĕdōtām)   20aβ$_1$
        β. Twofold expansion   20aβ$_2$-b
        aa. Corporately: clans and paternal
           house(s)   20aβ$_2$-aβ$_3$
        bb. Individually   20b
          α) Number of names of heads
            individually   20bα
          β) Militarily   20bβ

aa) Gender and age	$20b\beta_1$
bb) Military qualification	$20b\beta_2$
(b) Second: expressed summarily	21a
b) The number	21b

This structure basically reoccurs in the following:

2) Simeon, vv. 22-23;
3) Gad, vv. 24-25;
4) Judah, vv. 26-27;
5) Issachar, vv. 28-29;
6) Zebulun, vv. 30-31;
7) (Joseph) Ephraim, vv. 32-33;
8) Manasseh, vv. 34-35;
9) Benjamin, vv. 36-37;
10) Dan, vv. 38-39;
11) Asher, vv. 40-41;
12) Naphtali, vv. 42-43.

b. Stated inclusively: the tribal totality	44-47
1) The total of those conscripted	44-46
a) Superscription	44
b) The total proper	45-46
2) Report of those exempted: the Levites	47

The second subunit of the compliance report (I.B.2.) states the result of the executed conscription. The first of its two parts (I.B.2.a. [vv. 20-43]) documents the result distributively, and the second (I.B.2.b. [vv. 44-47]) inclusively. Each tribe receives special and equal attention and space, yet only because it is a part of the *'ēdâ*. Accordingly, the numbers for each tribe, indicative as they are individually, are primarily relevant as the basis for the sum of all the conscripted.

With minimal variations, the text is formulaic. Throughout the twelve sections about the tribes it consists of concise, virtually identical nominal constructions whose interdependence is signaled by prepositional phrases, appositions, and suffixes. The formulaic nature and stylistic precision of the text document that the varying numbers of the individual tribes were ascertained through the same system of criteria and procedures. They document the equality of all tribes in the conscription, and above all else the sum totals themselves of the conscripted "appointed" *(pĕqudîm)* at the end of each segment. The statistical documentation of the numbers, distributively and inclusively, is the dominant element of the text. However, the documentation also includes in great detail the references to the genealogies *(tôlĕdōtām)*, catalogues in which at least the names and age of the individual men were registered, and perhaps also their military qualification.

The text combines the dominant statements of the number with those references in its parts a) and b) of each segment, and again in I.B.2.b.1)b) [vv. 45-

46]. It therefore distinguishes between the final result of the conscription and the sources, the criteria, and the process through which this result was ascertained. Together with its context in Numbers 1 and 2, it was apparently generated by a conceptual understanding of the total system of such conscriptions that in its essential elements can be approximately reconstructed from several distinctive signals. The reconstruction is necessary for a better understanding of the nature of the text itself.

The expressions "and they had their names entered" *(wayyityalĕdû)* in v. 18aβ$_1$ and "their genealogies" *(tôlĕdōtām)* in vv. 20aβ$_1$, et al., belong etymologically together. They point to individuals who *register themselves* by entering their names *(šēmôt,* v. 2bα, et al.) in written, genealogically based catalogues. This step must be different from "lift(ing) the heads" *(nāśā' 'et-rō'š)* in v. 2aα which results "in the number of (the) names" *(bĕmispar šēmôt),* v. 2bα; cf. 3:40b: to lift the number of the names.

The verb "to lift" *(nāśā')* the heads of people and the noun "the number" *(hammispār)* belong together in the sense that the actual number is regarded as the sum of the process of additive counting. The expression "to lift the head(s)" is synonymous with the verb "to count" *(sāpar)* from which the noun "the number" *(hammispār)* stems. The men are to be counted, and the numbers of the counts are protocolled in vv. 20-47.

However, the counting "in the number of (the) names" indicates that the numbers themselves are ascertained on the basis of the names entered in written registers, and not on the basis of persons present (cf. Ps 87:6). A count of persons present is a head-count, literally a counting (or lifting) of the "heads" *(rō'š)* or "skulls" *(gulgōlet),* but not a count of names. A count of registered persons who are personally absent establishes their number *(mispār)* on the basis of their names, not on the basis of their heads. The text alludes to a distinction between the two types of counting, but seems to assume that its count is based on the counting of names in written registers organized as catalogues.

The text also distinguishes between the registration of the individuals, and their count and its registered results. In this distinction, the persons are the subject of the action when registering; but they are the object of the process when being counted and summed up. And the lists of registration are not the same as the lists that contain the sums of the count.

"And he appointed them" (Impf. cs. *wayyipqĕdēm),* v. 19b, (according) to their military units *(lĕṣib'ōtām),* v. 3b. (The military units [*ṣĕbā'ôt*] are themselves the totals of the appointed ones. They are in a service assigned to and imposed upon them by a higher authority; cf. van der Woude, 500.) Cf. Buber: *"Er ordnete sie ein."* They are not "numbered." Nobody receives a number, an I.D. tag. Lexicographically, neither the verb *pāqad* nor any of its nominal derivatives refer to "numbering" or to "numbers." The verb means, among other things, to call up, to entrust with, to commission, to appoint, to arrange. Unless 1:49a is a tautology one has to translate: "do not appoint *and* do not count their heads." In 4:27, Moses is to appoint the vessels or the burden, not people; he is to appoint the vessels to the people, and the vessels are neither counted nor numbered. In 3:15-21, the Levites are to be arranged according to their families, not numbered. In 4:34-36, et al., they were appointed to the service at the tent of meeting, not numbered. "And (the number from the count of) those appointed according to their clan was . . ." in Num 3:36 refers to the appointment to the charge, not to its numbering.

In 1:21, et al., *pĕqudîm* does not mean "the number" of the tribes as in Gray, NRSV, Budd, and Noth, *Numbers,* in the English translation (versus *ihre Gemusterten* in the German original). The word refers to persons, not to an abstract "number" for which the writers use the abstract noun *mispār.* These persons are the appointed ones. In numerical statements, the noun *kol,* "(the) total(ity)," is used by metonomy, as a substitute for the noun *hammispār,* "the number." Instead of saying "the number of cities (was) ten," Josh 21:26 formulates: "the total of the cities (was) ten" *(kol-'ārîm 'eśer).* And in this construction, the genitive *(nomen rectum)* refers to the kind of objects being counted, in this case, the cities. Num 1:46 is an identical kind of numerical statement: "The total of the appointed (was) . . . 603,550" *(kol-pĕqudîm . . . ;* cf. 1:45, et al.). "The total" is substituted for "the number." One has to say that 603,550 is a total, but not that it is a number! Nor does one have to say, pleonastically or redundantly, that the 603,550 were counted. Instead, *pĕqudîm* refers to the *kind* of persons counted, the appointed ones. Num 1:45, 46 do not say: "The total of the numbered."

In 3:22, 34, "their appointed ones in/by the number of all males" means: those appointed to their — or as clerical units which consist of the number of their names counted from their — clan and family registers. Accordingly, the formulation in 1:21 means: *the number (hammispār,* v. 20) *for the tribe of Reuben of their* (i.e., the sons of Reuben, v. 20) *appointed ones* — the sum total based on all specifications given in v. 20 — was 46,500. The title of the Book of Numbers refers to the number of the Israelites, not to *pāqad* as numbering. Cf. also 2:9, et al.: "The total (number) of the appointed to the camp of Judah was . . ."; and 2:32b: "The total (number) of the appointed of the camps (according) to their units was . . ."

The English translation of *pāqad* with "to muster" — analogous to the German *mustern* — in the same passages conflicts with that of "to number." The two English words are not interchangeable, and one of the two is wrong. "Mustering" carries a military notion, but it includes registering as well as numbering, counting, and appointing or assigning. The word *pāqad,* however, points to the specific assignment or appointment of registered individuals to military or clerical units.

The text I.B.2. (vv. 20-47) speaks about the result of a unique military conscription. It was the commanded, and therefore compulsory, registration, count, and induction of all draftable men to military units. Their numbers are explicitly documented, and the documentation is based on the count either of the members of the units themselves or of the genealogical catalogues of those registered. The process of the conscription up to the completion of the count of the conscripted provided the presupposition for the encampment of the units that is narrated in Numbers 2.

The text is above all interested in the numerical strength of the whole army and its twelve divisions. But it also refers to the sources, procedures, and levels from which, through which, and at which the numbers were ascertained.

The counts were tabulated at least "by Moses," i.e., at the central office of the 'ēdâ, but possibly earlier at the tribal level by the tribal registrars, and perhaps still earlier at the level of the clan genealogies. With all these references and allusions, the text reveals more than an isolated event. It reveals an understanding of the typical pattern of such military conscriptions that was applied to the narrative of this specific event.

When determining the genre of this text one has to notice the difference between its emphases and its references. It refers to but does not list by name the individuals, families, and clans. It is therefore neither a genealogical catalogue nor merely a census list or muster roll. (On genealogy, cf. Wilson, *Genealogy and History,* esp. 183-202.) Nor is it a tally-sheet listing numbers only statistically. It presupposes and includes these genres. In its formulaic language, and its combination of numbers and references to their origin, this text is a PROTOCOL which officially documents the numerical result of a particular conscription of the Israelite militia.

The discussion about the age of the protocol, and about its historical or fictitious background, is undecided (cf. Olson, 55-81, and the commentaries). Form-critically it is important that the protocol belongs to a genre in which the results of conscriptions, military and otherwise, were documented in Israel just as much as elsewhere. These conscriptions took place. They were official administrative acts of central governments. And at least their statistical results, the census lists, were submitted to the administrations and taken to protocol (cf. Exod 30:11-16; Numbers 3–4; 26:1-51; 2 Sam 24:1-9 [par. 1 Chr 21:1-6]; Luke 2:1-5; Acts 5:37). The forms of these protocols may have varied; certainly their contents did. A protocol always documents a specific event. But it represents a generic administrative tradition, normally in preparation of subsequent governmental operations such as mobilization for warfare or other service, or for the collection of taxes. Num 1:20-47 adopted this genre for its narrative of the scenario at Sinai.

The appendix in v. 47 notes that the Levites were not appointed to military service "in their midst." This appendix sets the stage for Num 1:48-54; 3–4. More importantly, after the whole report about the conscription of the militia, the stage is set for the report of its encampment in Numbers 2.

The second part, II. (vv. 48-54), is structured as follows:

A. Report of Yahweh speech: the order	48-53
1. Introductory formula	48
2. The order proper	49-53
a. Twofold prohibition	49
b. Command and instructions	50-53
1) Concerning the Levites and the foreigner	50-52
a) The Levites	50-51a
(1) Basic command — emphatic	50aα
(2) Instructions	50aβ-51a
(a) To carry tabernacle and vessels	50aβ_1
(b) To serve it	50ab$_2$
(c) To camp around it	50b

(d) To erect it and bring it down	51a
b) The foreigner: death penalty law	51b
2) Instruction concerning Israelites	52
c. Instruction about Levites repeated	53
B. = I.B. + II. Inclusive statement of compliance	54

This unit is a self-contained report about the exemption of the Levites from military conscription. It reports the Yahweh-order, II.A. (vv. 48-53), and the compliance with it, II.B (v. 54). The introductory address formula (II.A.1., v. 48) points out an extra Yahweh-speech, and the following content makes clear why a new Yahweh-speech was necessary. After v. 47 had stated the exemption of the Levites, it had to be made certain that this exemption was also an act of compliance with an order of Yahweh, and not a dangerously autonomous act on Moses' or the Israelites' part. Accordingly, the emphasis lies on the Yahweh-order (II.A.2., vv. 49-53) and the text is a supplement to v. 47 by a later writer whose different hand is also discernible stylistically and terminologically.

The ORDER (II.A.2.a., v. 49, and II.A.2.b., vv. 50-53) is a combination of a prohibition and a command or *vice versa*. It is a rhetorical device to make certain that both sides of a charge are considered, that one side expressed is not misunderstood by the silence on the other side. In our text, the prohibition precedes the command because v. 47 must be explained. As if to approve of v. 47 explicitly it is introduced emphatically by *'ak* "indeed," and prohibits Moses from appointing and counting the Levites. The following command [II.A.2.b.1)a)(1), v. 50aα], again introduced emphatically, complements the prohibition. It clarifies that the exemption of the Levites does not mean that they have no appointment. They are appointed to the tabernacle and its vessels. The command is explicated by a number of instructions concerning the Levites. The instructions are interrupted by a restriction of the access by foreigners to the tabernacle in form of DEATH PENALTY LAW, and by an instruction of the Israelite camp in distinction from the levitic camp. The interruptions reinforce the statements about the position and function of the Levites in the tabernacle camp.

The command concerning the Levites says in advance what is reported in Numbers 3–4. But the composition of the text as well as its position in the context show that the text functions as a midrash to v. 47 although it is not yet explicitly introduced as such.

Genre

The genres of the subunits of Num 1:1-47 (48-54) function as generic elements of the entire unit. This unit is a REPORT about a society-wide military CONSCRIPTION. Its typical elements are its reporting form, and the basic aspects and procedures of a conscription: the command/decree and its compliance/execution. With variations, all parts refer to the involved personnel and its line of authority (from Yahweh to Moses to the leaders, and, lastly, to the recruits), to the steps in the conscription (first, registration; second, count; and third, appointment), and to its results. The results are presented as a PROTOCOL, which is organized distributively and inclusively, and which refers besides the given numbers to the sources on which the numbers rest.

The unit reflects the typology of actual conscriptions. On this basis, it reflects a genre. As a particular report it is analogous to similar reports, although their individual structures vary. Numbers 1 is most representative for the genre because it reflects the typical elements of the setting of such conscriptions from their beginning to their completion.

By applying this genre to the Sinai narrative the priestly writers achieved the transformation of the Exodus-Sinai community in the older traditions into a militarily conscripted army.

Setting

The setting of the event of a military conscription involves the application of the pattern of society-wide activities of central — in the Ancient Near East normally royal — administrations, and of the totality of those affected.

The setting of such events must be distinguished from the setting of official reports about them. This setting involves the identity and activity of particular recorders and narrators. It presupposes the settings in which decrees are issued and their results protocolled, but it is not necessarily identical with the settings of such administrative recording offices. The report about a conscription represents in principle the setting of its narrators — whatever that setting is.

The report in Numbers 1 points to the setting of the priestly writers which cannot be assumed to have been the office of a central Israelite administration. In this setting, the narrators made their report about the conscription at Sinai understandable by using the genre and also specific data (names and numbers) from the known settings of actual conscriptions. They applied the genre more clearly than any known narrator of such events. The origins of their specific data are unknown. The fundamental difference between their report and other conscription reports is that in the setting of the Sinai conscription, the overlord of the conscription is not a king but — strictly theocratically — Yahweh himself.

Intention

The conscription report intends to show that at Sinai, Israel's formation as a militia was commanded by Yahweh himself, and promptly and fully executed by his chief representative Moses who was assisted by his designated and installed helpers and — in a secondary layer — by the chief priest Aaron. It especially emphasizes the results of the conscription in terms of the militia's total numerical strength, but with particular attention to the strength of the individual tribes. Finally, it wants to make clear that the presupposition is completed for the actual mobilization of the militia in its encampment, in anticipation of the campaign.

Bibliography

M. Buber, *[Die Schrift] Verdeutscht von Martin Buber* (4 vols.; Koln: Jakob Hegner, 1954-62); H. Niehr, *"nāśî'," TWAT;* D. T. Olson, *The Death of the Old and the Birth of the New: The Framework of the Book of Numbers and the Pentateuch* (BJS 71; Chico: Scholars, 1985); W. Schottroff, *"pqd,* heimsuchen," *THAT;* F. Stolz, *Jahwes und Israels Kriege* (ATANT 60; Zurich: Theologischer, 1972); idem, *"nś',* aufheben, tragen," *THAT;* A. S. van der Woude, *"ṣābā', Heer," THAT;* R. R. Wilson, *Genealogy and History in the Biblical World* (New Haven: Yale University, 1977).

The Report of the Mobilization of the Militia — The Outer Camp (2:1-34)

Structure

I. The Yahweh command 1-31
  A. Introductory formula 1
  B. The command to encamp 2-31
   1. Expressed basically 2
    a. Regarding the banners 2a
    b. Regarding the tent of meeting 2b
   2. Expressed specifically: the protocol 3-31
    a. The front guard: two banner divisions 3-16
     1) The division east: Judah 3-9
      a) Location and identification 3a
      b) The tribal units 3b-8
       (1) The primary tribe: Judah 3b-4
        (a) Its leader 3b
        (b) Its/his tribal unit and its number 4
       (2) Two associated tribes 5-8
        (a) Locative introduction 5aα
        (b) Locative distribution 5aβ-8
         α. Issachar 5aβ-6
          aa. Tribal identification 5aβ
          bb. Its leader and unit 5b-6
           α) The leader 5b
           β) The unit 6
            aa) The unit and its adjoined 6a
            bb) The number 6b
         β. Zebulun 7-8
      c) The number of the division Judah 9
     2) The division south: Reuben 10-16
    b. The tent, the Levites, and the marching order 17
    c. The rear guard: two banner divisions 18-31
     1) The division west: Ephraim 18-24

2) The division north: Dan · 25-31
II. The conclusion · 32-34
  A. The sum total · 32
  B. Report statement about the Levites · 33
  C. Report statement about compliance · 34

The structure of this unit rests on the extant text. The unit is framed by narrative language in vv. 1, 33, 34, and kept in concise style. It is a REPORT. What is reported is a Yahweh command (I., vv. 1-31) and a conclusion (II., vv. 32-34), which includes in v. 34 the compliance with the command. After the introductory report formula (I.A., v. 1), the command (I.B., vv. 2-31) covers the bulk of the text. Indicative of this extent are vv. 2, 9b, 16b, 17, 24b, and 31b which reflect the continuation of the Yahweh speech. By contrast, vv. 33-34 report what was done "as Yahweh had commanded Moses." On syntactical grounds, v. 32 should be considered to precede v. 34 and to belong to the conclusion. Stylistic and other observations in vv. 32-33 and elsewhere show that aspects other than those of command and compliance are at work in the formation of the text. Nevertheless, these two aspects are dominant even as they at times appear to be superimposed on the other aspects.

The command is expressed basically in I.B.1. (v. 2). Each man is to encamp by his banner *(degel),* by the signs *('ōtōt)* of their paternal house(s), I.B.1.a. (v. 2a), opposite the tent of meeting — as perceived from it *(minneged)* — all around *(sābîb),* I.B.1.b. (v. 2b). The "signs" which are mentioned only here are distinguished from the banners which play a major role in the following.

The encampment, I.B.2. (vv. 3-31), is to proceed according to a specific plan. Those encamping *(hahōnîm)* are to be positioned in four divisions either *around* the tent (so perhaps the Pg layer of this text) or *alongside* the *rectangular* tabernacle *(miškān)* (so under the influence of the tabernacle concept in the priestly context). The two different concepts are not reconciled. The question remains open whether, as in the case of the tabernacle, the camp order is also rectangular, or quadrangular. The banner of Judah, placed along one of the two short sides of the tabernacle, its eastern front, represents by far the strongest division: 186,400, versus 108,100 for Ephraim on the west side, 151,450 for Reuben, and 157,550 for Dan on the southern and northern sides, respectively. Judah's position scarcely allows for the idea of a rectangular camp. However, it does allow for the idea that during the march, the stronger divisions in the front guard and the rear guard form the point and the end of the column, that the front guard (337,850) is much stronger than the rear guard (265,650), and that the strongest of all divisions spearheads the campaign (cf. I.B.2.a. [vv. 3-16], b. [v. 17], c. [vv. 18-31], and → Num 10:14-28 where the tribal sequence is the same as in Numbers 2 although the marching order is different: first, Judah with the structure of the tabernacle carried by Gershon and Merari; second, Reuben with the vessels of the tabernacle carried by Kohath; third, Ephraim; and fourth, Dan).

Each of the four divisions consists of three tribes which are united under one banner *(degel),* the banner of their primary tribe. It consists of a banner tribe and two associated tribes. The banner tribes are: Judah, v. 3a; Reuben, v. 10a; Ephraim, v. 18a; and Dan, v. 25a. The structure of the text reflects this fourfold division in its subdivisions: I.B.2.a.1) [vv. 3-9]; I.B.2.a.2) [vv. 10-16]; I.B.2.c.1) [vv. 18-24]; and I.B.2.c.2) [vv. 25-31].

The structures of the description of each of the four divisions are essentially identical. As demonstrated for Judah, the text first of all identifies the location of the division according to the point of compass [I.B.2.a.1)a), v. 3a] and proceeds to identify the locations of its tribal units [I.B.2.a.1)b), vv. 3b-8]. Of those, the position of the banner tribe with its own units is mentioned first, with reference to its leader and the number of his/its host [ṣĕbā'ô, b)(1), vv. 3b-4]. "The ones camping next to it" (2)(a), v. 5aα, are — distributively — the two associated tribes, (2)(b), vv. 5aβ-8: Issachar [(b)α., vv. 5aβ-6] and Zebulun [(b)β., vv. 7-8; note the asyndetic construction]. Their detailed description follows that of Judah's, and the pattern throughout.

The fact that the associated tribes are said to be "next to" Judah, which is supported by their asyndetic juxtaposition, can only mean that Judah camps in the middle, with Issachar on the one side of Judah and Zebulun on the other. Accordingly, Simeon and Gad, respectively, camp on the two sides of Reuben (vv. 12-15), Manasseh and Benjamin next to Ephraim (vv. 20-23), and Asher and Naphtali next to Dan (vv. 27-30). As in 2.a.1)c), v. 9a, each of the four subdivisions of the text states the numerical strength of its total banner division.

Except for the conclusions in vv. 9b, 16b, 24b, and 31b, the language of the four subunits vv. 3-9a, 10-16a, 18-24a, and 25-31a consists of nominal sentences. It does not report what happened or is to happen; it describes what is taking place: "the ones encamping," vv. 3, 5, 12, and 27. Taken in isolation these units reflect more a parallel to the protocol of compliance in Num 1:20-47 than an element of a Yahweh command. (They were possibly a part of a compliance report at an earlier stage.) This may indicate a shift in redactional emphasis in which the command as such was considered to be more important than a description of the process and order of an encampment. In either case, however, the text points to more than the description of an encamped militia only. It also, and perhaps first of all, points to the process, the sequence in which the units are encamping.

The part. form "the ones encamping" (vv. 3, 5, 12, 27) expresses the act of encampment as a process. The sequence in which the encampment is described is scarcely accidental. The Judah division, which in Num 1:5b-15, 20-43 ranks in positions 3-5 and 4-6, respectively, appears in Num 2:3-9 in positions 1-3. Apparently as the most important division it is encamped before the entrance of the tent, and it also spearheads the march as the strongest division. At the same time, one has to assume that Judah encamps first, just as it is listed first in the text.

Therefore, one also has to assume that the sequence in which the text lists the encampment of the four divisions reflects the order of their successive encampment: clockwise from east to south to west to north. The same visualization must be assumed for the encamping sequence of the three tribes in each division. The positioning of the associated tribes depends on the prior positioning of their banner tribe, just as the text describes. The banner tribe does not move into the vacuum between the two other tribes. By virtue of its position vis-à-vis the cosmologically positioned sanctuary — tent or tabernacle — the banner tribe's own cosmologically defined place — east, etc. — corresponds to the compass point correctly, and not to a place "beside the point." The middle position of the banner tribe is constituted by the sanctuary, and the positions of the associated tribes are derived from that position. That position must therefore be taken first, and afterward the associated tribes take their positions simultaneously, just as the syntax of the text indicates.

Both the command in and the context of Numbers 2 presuppose that as of this moment the militia is not yet encamped, and that it is to be encamped after the command. Numbers 2 presupposes the preceding report about the conscription of the militia, and relates the next necessary step about its encampment, itself in successive steps. Numbers 2 is the second part of the priestly report about the organization of the outer quadrangle of the campaign camp in two main steps. In this report, the two parts are intrinsically related already in its oldest recognizable layer. Any assessment of Numbers 2 in isolation from Numbers 1 would have to show evidence that a text in Numbers 2 can be reconstructed that would not be connected with Numbers 1 and would be older than the priestly narrative.

Such evidence is hard to come by. Indeed, Numbers 2 is connected with Numbers 1 in other respects as well. Except for the different positions of Judah's division already mentioned, the sequence of the twelve tribes in 1:20-43 and 2:3-31 is identical, and so are their numbers, the names of their leaders, and the overall style and terminology. Only the list of the leaders in 1:5b-15 may reflect a tradition adopted by the priestly writers. Numbers 2 is the conceptually based continuation of the conscription report in Numbers 1. This continuation introduces the next important step in the process by reference to a new Yahweh command that initiates this next step. It refers substantively to what now must be done and how it must happen. The conclusion in II. (vv. 32-34), clearly of composite literary nature, is also connected with Numbers 1. Num 2:32-33 reflects 1:44-47, and 2:34 reflects 1:54.

The connection of Numbers 2 with Numbers 1 shows that its description of the encampment order and process cannot be isolated from the priestly narrative about the campaign. The campaign aspect, however, means that the alternation between encampment and march is itself an intrinsic element of the process and the order of encampment. According to the extant text, the two aspects of march and encampment interpenetrate. The passages referring to the march, vv. 9b, 16b, 17, 24b, and 31b, may belong to a secondary layer (Kellermann, *Numeri,* 17-25). But they only explicate what the layout of the four divisions already indicates. They say that these divisions shall break camp in the sequence in which they encamp. Indeed, they point out that the sequence of the divisions is listed because they are to march in this sequence. As in vv. 1-2, this language complements the descriptive language.

In one respect only, the explicit references to the marching order change the structure of vv. 3-31. By saying in v. 17a that "the tent of meeting, the camp of the Levites" shall break "in the midst of the camp," the text, besides suggesting even a quadrangular — or circular — marching order rather than a linear one, splits the marching order into two divisions for the front and two divisions for the rear of the tent of meeting. Thus, the structure of the text is split into

I.B.2.a. (vv. 3-16) referring to the front guard, I.B.2.b. (v. 17a) referring to the tent and Levites in the middle, and I.B.2.c. (vv. 18-31) referring to the rear guard. Verse 17b is again different, and is not well-positioned. It says summarily, in accordance with vv. 9b, 16b, 24b, and 31b, but not in accordance with v. 17a, that the Israelites shall break camp as they encamp, i.e., first, second, third, and fourth. It is at least an open question whether the transitions from the encampment to the marching order visualized in all parts of the text are functional in the reality of military strategy. Just as in the case of the possibly circular, rectangular, or quadrangular camp order, the scarcely realistic assumption of these transitions suggests that the priestly writers were not professional military strategists more than it suggests a need for literary critical operations.

Genre

Four aspects are essential for determining the genre of Numbers 2. First, despite the descriptive and protocol style for most of it, the unit is a narrative report that emphasizes the Yahweh command, and the compliance only in a short, general conclusion. Second, the report does not describe the existing camp order of an encamped army. It rather narrates the command to encamp the militia including the instructions about the process of its encamping through which the camp order was to come and came into existence and the camp itself became established. Third, the camp order is perceived as a campaign order. It already reflects the alternation of encampment and march in the campaign. Not coincidentally, the divisions and their tribes start in Num 10:14-28 in exactly the same sequence in which they go into camp in Numbers 2. Indeed, Numbers 2 should be understood to instruct about the encampment order and its process *whenever* the militia pitches camp, and not only about its first-time encampment at Sinai. Fourth, the encampment report cannot be isolated from its context. It stands between the preceding report about the conscription and — after its expansion in Num 3:1–10:10 — the following narrative about the beginning of the campaign in Num 10:11-36. In this context, it refers to the first encampment of the just conscripted militia, immediately — twenty days at most! — before and for the beginning of the campaign. It is, therefore, a constitutive element of an overall report of a campaign that reflects the reality of such campaigns including their preparatory organization.

The genre of Numbers 2 is determined by the report of the encampment of the conscripted members of the militia for the purpose of its impending campaign. Such an encampment is a specific, necessary, and typical procedure. It represents the last step in a preparatory organization of a campaign, namely, the actual mobilization of the militia through its encampment in the field. The report reflects this step. Numbers 2 is the REPORT of a MOBILIZATION of the militia. Through its mobilization, the militia is set for the campaign, and after its completion (including the organization of the inner quadrangle and of some logistical problems) the campaign can begin.

The militia does not consist of professional soldiers. Professional soldiers are neither subject to nationwide conscription nor in need of a special encampment. By contrast, the members of the militia may be subject to permanent registration, but they are subject to encampment only in view of an impending campaign. This purpose of their encampment represents their mobilization.

The mobilization report in Numbers 2 is written from the writers' position after the completed mobilization, v. 34. But it overwhelmingly focuses on Yahweh's command to mobilize, and on the instructions for the establishment of the camp order. This focus in the extant text may be the result of a shift from traditional reports of actual mobilizations to a report of a command and instruction to mobilize. Even so, this focus is neither unrealistic, nor atypical, nor undocumented. The issue of mobilization has not received the necessary attention in research. But passages such as Judges 7; 20; 1 Samuel 4; 13; 2 Samuel 18; 20; 2 Kings 8; 13; 14; 2 Chronicles 10; 25; et al. document a tradition history not only of implementations but also of the plans for the implementation of mobilizations. The texts also point to the acts of demobilization. The forms in which the texts refer to these events vary. But the attention to the plans, decrees, or commands reveals a tradition history in which supreme commanders, mostly kings, define in their headquarters the strategy for a campaign and decree it for implementation to their chiefs of staff and through them to their major commanding officers. The tradition sees not only kings in this role but also Yahweh himself. It is therefore quite typical and generic when Numbers 2 depicts Yahweh in the role of the — royal? — supreme strategist who from his headquarters already established in the field, the tent of meeting, commands his chief of staff Moses to mobilize the militia, and reveals to him his plan for the implementation of the mobilization. The priestly writers depicted this traditional scenario in its typical, generic form.

Such records belonged to international practice. Homer's "Catalogue of ships" (*Iliad,* II, 1) mentions the population group, the leaders by name and patronym, their towns, and the number of their ships. The Homeric catalogues represent orders of battle for overseas expeditions (cf. Lorimer, 46; Page, 120, 154, 168; Kirk, 154-55, 223-24; and Bowra, 69, 111).

Interestingly, the command begins in v. 2a with the basic call "each to his banner" (*ʾîš ʿal-diglô*) which looks like an oral formula by which a call to mobilize is opened, or in which it may even exist. This call is the opposite of the call to demobilize, or the references to demobilization as in "each to his tents" (*ʾîš lěʾōhālāyw),* or similar; cf. Judg 7:8; 20:8; 1 Sam 4:10; 13:2; 2 Sam 18:17; 19:9; 20:1, 22; et al.; and Koch, *ʾōhel* (130-31). Another formula which may have belonged to the oath taking by the mobilized militia in a Yahweh war was "a hand upon the banner of Yahweh" (*yād ʿal-kēs yāh,* Exod 17:16).

Setting

Numbers 2 belongs first of all to the immediate setting of the priestly writers and their own tradition history from the earliest identifiable layer on (Pg). The exact identification of this layer in Numbers 2 continues to be a matter of debate (cf., e.g., Kellermann, *Numeri,* 18-32, and Budd, 21-23).

To be distinguished from the priestly setting of Numbers 2 are the settings of such mobilization records in the tradition history of warfare in the OT and the ancient world. These settings obviously vary just as much as the forms and intentions of the records produced by them. They can only be determined from case to case. The settings of accounts about Yahweh's mobilization of the militia are certainly different from the setting of a protocol about a royal mobilization in the royal administration. However, one should assume that the royal administrations represented the settings for such recordings that were most directly connected with the events themselves.

The tradition history of such records behind Numbers 2 also involves the questions whether they describe existing military camps or camps of cultic festivals (Kraus, 152-53), or whether they record the mobilization of the militia or a work force. Particularly, it involves the questions of the presence in the camp of the tent or the ark, or of both, and of any reference to the camp's order (Kuschke), and to the age of such traditions (Cross, "Tabernacle"). It is obvious that the report in Numbers 2 rests on several of these traditions, but also that it is unique and must be distinguished from them. Attempts to reconstruct from Numbers 2 a text older than the priestly narrative are futile. One tradition on which the priests also depend — probably specifically here as elsewhere in their work — is the theological tradition in which Yahweh himself is not only the divine warrior but also the designer of his campaign. It is the tradition about Yahweh's plans.

Finally, the records about mobilization point to the settings of actual mobilizations themselves, including their planning stages and including those for holy wars. The records have their origin in the historical reality of warfare. It is from that history, and from the tradition history of its records, that the priests visualized the ideal mobilization of Israel's militia at Sinai.

Intention

The report in Numbers 2 intends to show that — and how — the conscripted militia was mobilized and therefore ideally set for the campaign from Sinai on. It especially emphasizes that the executed mobilization originated in Yahweh's own design. This specific intention is a part of the overall intention of the entire narrative about the organization of the sanctuary campaign. The question is legitimate as to what the priestly writers were trying to communicate specifically to their own and to future generations. The answer to this question lies in principle within the trajectory of the content of the text and its design of reality. For a specific answer, we would just as much have to know how its original readers perceived the text specifically, as we can detect its own essence.

Bibliography

C. M. Bowra, *Tradition and Design in the Iliad* (Oxford: Clarendon, 1930); F. M. Cross, "The Tabernacle: A Study from an Archaeological and Historical Approach," in *Biblical*

Archaeologist Reader 1 (ed. G. E. Wright and D. N. Freedman; Garden City: Doubleday, 1961) 201-28 (repr. from *BA* 10 [1947] 45-68); G. S. Kirk, *The Songs of Homer* (Cambridge: Cambridge University Press, 1962); H.-J. Kraus, *Worship in Israel: A Cultic History of the Old Testament* (tr. G. Buswell; Richmond: John Knox, 1965); A. Kuschke, "Die Lagervorstellung der priesterschriftlichen Erzählung: Eine überlieferungsgeschichtliche Studie," *ZAW* 63 (1951) 74-105; H. L. Lorimer, *Homer and the Monuments* (London: Macmillan, 1950); D. L. Page, *History and the Homeric Iliad* (Berkeley: University of California Press, 1959).

The Report of the Conscription and Mobilization of the Sanctuary Personnel — The Inner Camp (3:1–4:49)

Structure

I. The genealogy of Aaron	3:1-4
II. The mobilization of the Levites	3:5–4:49
A. Two programmatic Yahweh speeches to Moses	3:5-13
1. A command concerning their service to Aaron	5-10
2. A declaration concerning their situation for Israel	11-13
B. The unfolding of the speeches	3:14–4:49
1. Concerning the substitution for Israel's male firstborn	3:14-51
a. The substitution	14-43
1) The Levites	14-39
a) Yahweh command	14-15
b) Compliance	16-39
2) The Israelites	40-43
a) Yahweh command	40-41
b) Compliance	42-43
b. The ransom	44-51
1) Yahweh command	44-48
2) Compliance	49-51
2. Concerning the adult Levites	4:1-49
a. The Yahweh commands	1-33
b. Compliance	34-49

Numbers 3–4 is set apart from Numbers 1–2 and 5:1–10:10 through its focus on the conscription and mobilization of the cultic personnel in the inner camp. The unit represents the second part of the report about the organization of the sanctuary camp in Numbers 1–4 (→ Chapter 2, Structure).

Numbers 3–4 is not structured in analogy to Numbers 1–2 where the two major subdivisions of the text coincide with the division of the two biblical chapters. In our Bibles, the total of one hundred verses is conveniently subdivided into two chapters of equal length. This division has some basis in the division of the two subunits 3:14-51 and 4:1-49, but it obscures the fact that the major subdivisions in the text consist of 3:1-4 and 3:5–4:49, and subsequently between 3:5-13 and 3:14–4:49. In order to show how the various parts of 3:5–4:49 are related, we best proceed inductively.

The unit contains eight Yahweh speeches introduced each time by the typical speech report formula: 3:5-10, 11-13, 14-15, 40-41, 44-48; 4:1-16, 17-20, 21-33. Of these speeches, four are followed by reports about Moses' (and Aaron's) compliance: 3:16-39, 42-43, 49-51; 4:34-49. We have therefore four subunits each of which consists of two parts, the reports of a Yahweh command and its immediate obedient execution: 3:14-39, 40-43, 44-51; and 4:1-49. In 4:1-49, the compliance report (vv. 34-49) responds — for reasons explained below — to all three Yahweh speeches, vv. 1-16, 17-20, 21-33, and not to only one of them. Besides substantive reasons, this conclusion is already supported by the fact that the three speeches follow one another directly. 4:1-33 is one literary subunit combining three speeches. This unit as a whole is concluded by the compliance report, vv. 34-49.

What is true for 4:1-33 is not true for the three successive Yahweh speeches in 3:5-10, 11-13, 14-15. The compliance report in 3:16-39 responds to vv. 14-15 only, while vv. 5-10 and 11-13 stand in front of the entire unit 3:5–4:49. The two speeches in vv. 5-13 are an introduction to the larger unit 3:14–4:49 with its already identified four subunits 3:14-39, 40-43, 44-51; and 4:1-49. How are the four units in 3:5–4:49 related, and how is this large unit related to its introduction?

The subunit 4:1-49 is clearly distinguished from 3:14-51 by the appointment of the male levitic adults to the Aaronides for the work at the sanctuary. So also Milgrom, *'ăbōdâ,* 22. By contrast, 3:14-51 is concerned with the appointment of all male Levites from the age of one month on to be the substitutes for the male firstborn of the Israelites who normally belong to Yahweh and therefore to "the duty of the sanctuary." The difference is somewhat obscured because 3:25, 28, 31, 32, and 36 speak already of the "duty" *(mišmeret)* of the Levites, and 3:26, 31, and 36 even of their "work" *('ăbōdâ),* as if 3:14-51 were already speaking about the levitic adults. However, it is quite clear that the appointment of all Levites to "the duty of the sanctuary" *(mišmeret haqqōdeš,* 3:28, 32; *mišmeret hammiqdāš,* 3:38) is neither the dominant aspect in 3:14-51 nor the same aspect as the one that governs 4:1-49.

The terminological distinction between *mišmeret,* "custody, obligation, duty, (service)," and *'ăbōdâ,* "forced labor, work, (service)," is indicative of the difference between 3:14-51 and 4:1-49. The two words are related but not synonymous. *mišmeret* refers to the work as duty, whereas *'ăbōdâ* refers to the duty as work. While also mentioned in 4:27, 28, 31, and 32 the word duty *(mišmeret)* belongs essentially to 3:14-51 where it refers in vv. 25, 28, 31, 32, 36, and 38 to the appointment in principle of all male Levites to the duty of the sanctuary. Their appointment to this duty happens by virtue of their genealogical identity, and is different from the mobilization of their adults between age thirty and fifty for the actual work at the sanctuary. This "work" *('ăbōdâ)* is addressed in 4:1-49. For the discussion of the age for entry to work → Num 8:23-26. While also mentioned in 3:26, 31, and 36 the word overwhelmingly governs the description of their actual work assignments in 4:4, 19, 23, 24, 26, 27, 28, 30, 31, 32, 33, 35, 39, 43, 47, and 49. The analogous verbs do not change this picture.

Also, the noun *maśśā'*, "carrying, burden," and its verb *nāśā'*, "to carry," are connected with "work" and used only in 4:1-49; cf. vv. 15, 19, 24, 27, 31, 32, 47, 49, and vv. 15, 25. The same is true for the noun *ṣābā'*, "army," here: "work force," cf. vv. 3, 23, 30, 35, 39, and 43. Cf. also the verbs for work used in 4:5-15: *nātan*, "to give, put" (v. 6a); *pāraś*, "to spread" (v. 6a); *śîm*, "to put" (v. 6b); *lāqaḥ*, "to take" (v. 9a); and *kissâ*, "to cover" (v. 9a).

The numbers given set 3:14-51 apart from 4:1-49 as well. They also show that the three passages 3:14-39, 40-43, and 44-51 belong together as three sub-units of the unit 3:14-51, which stands opposite the unit 4:1-49. According to 4:36, 40, 44, and 48, the total of the work force is 8,580. The total of all male Levites according to 3:22, 28, 34, and 39 is 22,000, whereas the total of the male Israelite firstborn is 22,273 (v. 43).

With respect to the age groups, their numbers, and the description of their function, the two units 3:14-51 and 4:1-49 complement one another, yet they are fundamentally different. The difference exists in an even more important respect. In 4:1-49, the Levites mobilized for work are related to Aaron their supervisor (and his sons), vv. 5-16, 27, 28, and 33, whereas in 3:14-51, except for v. 32, all male Levites are related to the Israelites as the substitutes for the Israelite firstborn. The entire unit 3:14–4:49 is, therefore, concerned with the conscription and mobilization of the tribe of Levi (3:6) which is unfolded in two subunits under two conceptual aspects: the conscription of all its males as substitution for the male Israelite firstborn regarding the duty of the sanctuary (3:14-51), and the mobilization of its adults for the actual work at the sanctuary (4:1-49).

The two units 3:14-51 and 4:1-49 are related, and not juxtaposed. Chronologically, the events in 4:1-49 are meant to follow those in 3:14-51, and to be based on them logically. They represent the consequence of the events in 3:14-51, and the goal of the entire unit. For the actual mobilization of the adult work force, 3:14-51 reports the presupposition for a specific reason. What had to be explained was not so much the provision of the total and permanent pool of people from which to recruit (and replenish) the adult workers, but the fact that this work force consisted of Levites and not of the Israelite firstborn. For the tradition history of the Levites, their connection with the sanctuary was nothing new. In need of explanation was the possible conflict between Yahweh's claim to the Israelite firstborn and Yahweh's requisition of the adult Levites for the same purpose. This conflict between two claims of Yahweh to his property is resolved through 3:14-51: in the organization of the whole camp at Sinai, the actual work force for the sanctuary had to be recruited from the Levites, and not from the Israelites, because the male Levites had been predetermined *in toto* for that work, as substitution for the Israelites.

The two passages 3:5-10 and 11-13 address the two aspects in 3:14-51 and 4:1-49, each in a separate Yahweh speech. The first speech appoints the tribe of Levi to the service of Aaron (and his sons), vv. 6 and 9, while the Aaronides attend to the priesthood. To be sure, vv. 7-8 when speaking of their "duty" *(mišmeret)* to Aaron refer to this aspect also in 3:14-51. However, this duty is immediately defined as "to perform the work of the tabernacle" *(la'ăbōd 'et-'ăbōdat hammiškān),* vv. 7b and 8b, even as they "keep" *(šāmĕrû)* its vessels, v. 8a. While not ignoring the aspect of "duty" the expressions in vv. 7b and 8b anticipate the work with the vessels under Aaron's supervision in 4:1-49. By contrast, 3:11-13 anticipates the unit 3:14-51 exclusively by declaring the substitution (*taḥat,* "instead of") of the Levites for the consecration (hiph. *qādaš,* v. 13) of the male Israelite firstborn which had been declared from the exodus on. This unit, vv. 11-13, is not a command. It is a declaration by Yahweh of his privileged right *(Privilegrechtliche Deklaration),* specifically of the right to his property. It is concluded by the SELF-Revelation or HOLINESS formula "I am Yahweh." The two Yahweh speeches in 3:5-10 and 11-13 open the entire unit 3:5–4:49 programmatically. The first anticipates 4:1-49, and the second, 3:14-51. 3:5–4:49 consists of two parts: a twofold programmatic introduction, 3:5-13, and its twofold unfolding, 3:14–4:49. The sections of the introduction and the unfolding are related in chiastic order.

We can now refer to the structure presented initially. The unit 3:5–4:49 (II.) is the second part of the report of the organization of the inner camp. Its first part (I., 3:1-4) presents the genealogy of Aaron. In II., the twofold introduction (II.A.) is unfolded (II.B.) in two major units. The first of these units, II.B.1. (3:14-51) addresses the substitution for Israel's firstborn. Unfolding II.A.2. (3:11-13) it reports in II.B.1.a. (vv. 14-43) the substitution itself, and in II.B.1.b. (vv. 44-51) the role of ransom or redemption. The report about the substitution is developed in II.B.1.a.1) [vv. 14-39] with regard to the Levites, and in II.B.1.a.2) [vv. 40-43] with regard to the Israelites.

The passage about the Levites is introduced by a Yahweh command [II.B.1.a.1)a), vv. 14-15] according to which all male Levites from a month old and upward are to be appointed on the basis of their genealogical affiliation. The following compliance report [II.B.1.a.1)b), vv. 16-39] amounts specifically to a PROTOCOL. It consists of a short narrative statement about the compliance itself, v. 16, and of a long formulaic description of its result in vv. 17-39 in which the genre of REGISTER is dominant (→ Num 1:17-19, 20-43). This description is based on the genealogy of Levi in such a way that the sons of Levi — Gershon, Kohath, and Merari — and their sons, respectively, are listed first and summarily, vv. 17-20. Thereafter, basic information under identical aspects is given in three subsections about the Gershonites, vv. 21-26, the Kohathites, vv. 27-32, and the Merarites, vv. 33-37. For each of the three groups, reference is made to its clans, its total number, the site of its encampment, its head, and its duty. The fact that the three groups are said to be encamped west, south, and north of the tabernacle prompts the statement (v. 38) about the encampment of Moses and the Aaronides on its east side. Verse 39 concludes by stating the total of all male Levites, derived from the summation of the three sums given in vv. 22, 28, and 34: 22,000. The summation is not correct.

The unit about the Levites is more than a census report only. It is even less a census list. It gives numbers only summarily. It is a report about the appointment or conscription of all male Levites of which the data about the results of their registration or census constitute only a part. This particular unit represents a parallel to the report of the conscription of the members of the militia in Num 1:17-54. Here as elsewhere, only males are appointed, and the given numbers include males only.

The text distinguishes between the appointment and its function. The appointment or conscription, expressed as in Numbers 1–2 by *pāqad,* is either to the duty of the sanctuary or to the work at it. The function of the appointment of the Levites consists of their substitution for the male Israelite firstborn who are in principle also appointed, vv. 11-13 and 40-43. Those firstborn are set aside from all other Israelites in registers of their individual names, v. 40, and the entering of their names into these registers apparently constitutes — or is thought to constitute — an official act of their appointment. That such appointment or designation may happen to children already, and is in principle different from the following mobilization or installation, is just as much true for the priestly tradition as it is known for the royal and prophetic traditions. Without this distinction, the difference between 3:14-51 and 4:1-49 can scarcely be understood. The details of the duties of the firstborn need not be mentioned because they are mentioned where it matters, in the texts about the appointment of the Levites.

However, the function of the levitic appointees as substitutes for the Israelite firstborn requires the text's attention to and comparison of the numbers. This requirement is the reason for the additional subunits II.B.1.a.2) [vv. 40-43] and II.B.1.b. [vv. 44-51]. The text presupposes that the substitution of one group for the other involves an exact numerical *quid pro quo.* Hence, after the total of 22,000 Levites is established, the total of 22,273 firstborn is established, vv. 40-43, and with it an excess amount for which there are no Levites! The deficit in the substitution of person for person calls for the ransom (*happidyōm,* v. 49) of the excess firstborn by money (vv. 44-51), whereby v. 45 repeats the command of substitution, and applies it even to cattle. The economic aspect is involved, and not only the aspect of personal duty and work. The payment for each firstborn not covered amounts to five shekels, currency of the sanctuary, for a total of 1,365 shekels. Again, the text distinguishes between the duty, now in terms of ransom and those to be ransomed, and the amount, now in terms of shekels. The report about the ransom consists of the rule of ransom that is couched in the forms of command and compliance.

The report about the mobilization of the levitic adults (II.B.2., 4:1-49) focuses in the Yahweh command (II.B.2.a., vv. 1-33) first on the Kohathites (vv. 1-15, 16, and 17-20), then on the Gershonites and on the Merarites (vv. 21-28 and 29-33). The Kohathites, in 3:27-32 mentioned in second place, are now mentioned first because of their special work assignment. They have to carry the most holy vessels (vv. 4b and 15b). Their special status is also indicated by the fact that the text reserves for them a separate Yahweh speech, and that an additional Yahweh speech secures their permanent existence in their appointment. Verse 16, a notice about Eleazar's duty, is apparently added to vv. 5-15 because of the liturgical materials associated with the vessels, and because the Kohathites are assigned to Eleazar who is at the same time the chief supervisor of the entire sanctuary.

In their work assignment, the Kohathites are restricted from touching the holy vessels (v. 15aβ2). To that effect, the Yahweh instruction about them is expanded by an extensive and detailed instruction for the Aaronides themselves, vv. 5-15a. When(ever) the camp sets out and the sanctuary must be disassembled, they have to perform all the specific types of actions necessary for the proper packaging of all the vessels. After that is done (*wĕ'ahărê-kēn*, v. 15aβ₁), the Kohathites shall come to carry but not touch them lest they die.

The appointment of the Gershonites and the Merarites is combined in only one Yahweh speech, vv. 22-33. Both groups have to carry the sanctuary itself, the former its curtains and covers, the latter its structure. They work together under Ithamar.

Apart from vv. 5-15aβ₂, the mobilization of each of the three levitic groups is commanded — with some variations — in the following pattern: the call to the appointment, the definition of the work, and the identification of the priestly supervisor.

The compliance report (II.B.2.b., 4:34-49) consists again of sections about the Kohathites (vv. 34-37), the Gershonites (vv. 38-41), and the Merarites (vv. 42-45). In its usual formulaic language, each section refers in detail to the identity of the appointed group (*kol-habbā' lassābā'*, vv. 35, 39, and 43), lists its number (vv. 36, 40, and 44), and concludes with a summary subscription (vv. 37, 41, and 45). A final summary (vv. 46-49) applies the pattern to all male Levites, and lists their number: 8,580.

The genealogy of Aaron (I., 3:1-4) is a composite text. It consists of a superscription, v. 1, and the genealogical REGISTER itself in vv. 2-4. The superscription has in v. 1a the typical form, except that the name of Moses is added and in v. 1b presumably the reason for this addition. In its present form, the superscription apparently wants to make sure that Aaron's genealogy is linked to Moses and the time when Yahweh spoke at Sinai. The genealogical statement itself consists first of the list of Aaron's four sons and the notice that they had been appointed as priests, vv. 2-3. It concludes with a report statement about the childless death of Nadab and Abihu (cf. Lev 10:1-7), so that Eleazar and Ithamar, appearing in 4:16, 28, and 33, were the only priests left during their father's lifetime. In the present context, the installation of the Aaronides is presupposed, and so is their register. Only their encampment and their assignment for specific work in 4:5-15a and as supervisors belong to the organization of the camp, but not their registration. And the genealogical statement in 3:1-4 does not report a step in the organization of the camp. It rather points to the existence already of the basis for the conscription of the Levites. On this basis, the Levites become related to the Aaronides, in terms of location (3:38), in terms of assignment, and in terms of their restriction from the deadly prerogatives of the Aaronides (4:15, 20). The structural relationship of units I. and II. signals this chronological and systemic order in its proper sequence. In the plot of 3:1–4:49, Num 3:1-4 is positioned properly.

Numbers 3–4 belongs to the plot of the total report about the organization of the sanctuary campaign. It relates the step following the organization of the outer camp. And it relates in successive order the steps of the mobilization of the inner camp by referring in I. to what already exists, and in II. to what has to be organized. The unfolding of the plot in II. is based on narrative language according to which each event is followed by another one until the process is complete. On this basis, the report consists of a chain of twelve units that reflects a chain of twelve successive events 3:5-10, 11-13, 14-15, 16-39, 40-41, 42-43, 44-48, 49-51; 4:1-16, 17-20, 21-33, and 34-49.

However, Numbers 3–4 does not simply report the organization of the inner camp as a chain of twelve successive events. It reports this succession as a systematic organization in which the progression is ordered according to a hierarchy of five conceptual aspects. The aspect above the chain consists of the combination of Yahweh speech and compliance in the four sections 3:14-39, 40-43, 44-51; and 4:1-49. On this level, Yahweh's command does not only initiate the process each time and trigger the following action, but each new command also opens a new concern and therefore moves the entire process forward from aspect to aspect: from the Levites to the Israelites to the ransom to the levitic adults. Yahweh does not only speak; he also thinks, and expedites the organization systematically. Without that activity, nothing would happen. On the next higher level, the plot distinguishes in 3:14-51, again systematically, between substitution and ransom. Again on a higher level, it distinguishes in 3:14–4:49 between the conscription of all Levites for the duty of the sanctuary and subsequently the mobilization of their adults for the actual work at the sanctuary. Finally, it distinguishes on the highest level between the priests and the Levites.

The plot is highly systemic and is organized systematically. It reflects the intellectual effort *(Geistesbeschäftigung)* of the priestly writers and their understanding of order in history when its organizer is Yahweh himself and those addressed are obedient. Last but not least, the systematized plot shows that the extant text of Numbers 3–4 is no collection of disparate pieces more or less loosely or fittingly juxtaposed. It represents a coherently conceptualized literary unity in which each part addresses a different aspect, is chronologically and logically related to the other parts, and is in its proper place. And to whatever extent the extant text is the result of a literary growth process, we will have to be prepared for the probability that this systematized plot was inherent in its earlier layers already, and not only in the final redaction.

The interpretation of the structure of the extant text does not prejudge the question of the probable literary history behind the text. The answer to this question depends on the greater degree of evidence when all arguments are balanced against each other. A consensus on the problem of literary strata has not been reached, as the latest representative publications by Noth *(Numbers)*, Kellermann *(Numeri)*, de Vaux, and Budd show. There is sufficient philological and substantive reason for assuming a literary history in principle and not an *ad hoc* creation by one writer. To a large extent the text, just as the units in Num 5:1–10:10, presupposes the already existing text of the books of Exodus and Leviticus. The existence of this context proves only that the extant text of Numbers 3–4 cannot be older than the latest time of this context. But it proves nothing about the probable literary history of that context, about its own history, and about the interdependence of both in historical growth. It seems, however, that the discernment of literary strata may receive additional help if the insights gained from the study of the extant text would also be considered. In view of the absence of a sufficient literary critical consensus, and in view of the fact that the extant text has received no form-critical attention, the form-critical discussion is for the time being confined to the extant text.

Genre

Whether or not Numbers 3–4 belongs to a typical structure and a genre of narrative is an unresolved question. Narrated is an event in which all males of a specific group, "the tribe of Levi," are conscripted as substitutes for the male firstborn of an entire society, the twelve tribes of Israel, to the duty of the only sanctuary of that society. They are encamped around the sanctuary, and subsequently given their different work assignments to be performed under the supervision of its priests. Numbers 3–4 is a report about the organization of the service personnel for the sanctuary of an entire society. The goal of this organization consists in the preparation for the work at this sanctuary, especially its transport.

The discussion of genre has to focus on the nature of this text primarily, and on the historical question only to the extent to which the genre reflects the historical conditions of the text. The REPORT reflects a number of traditional elements. The genres of PROTOCOL and REGISTER employed by the priestly writers are typical for the tradition of such records. References to the recruitment of labor forces for public projects are attested. And although references to their groupings, encampments, numbers, and assignments are harder to come by, the fact of these elements in the organization of such work forces can scarcely be denied. The same is true, at least in the history of Yahwism, for the early designation, even from childhood on, of specific groups such as priests, Levites, Rechabites, or of individuals for specific functions possibly to be activated later. The aspects of substitution and ransom are also traditional, and no creation of the priestly writers. Even the specific aspect of the organization of the Levites for service at sanctuaries or the central sanctuary, and their role as priests or in relation to priests reflects the actual tradition history of the Levites (cf. Gunneweg; Fohrer, "Levi").

Some of these traditional elements, especially those found in Numbers 4, point to the reality of such mobilizations of work and service forces, to the decree and the process of their execution, the principles for their selection, their actual draft, the organization of their encampment, and their momentary or permanent assignment. They represent a parallel to the reality of military mobilizations that stand behind the generic reports in Numbers 1–2. To the extent that the actual societal reality of the mobilization of work and service forces must be assumed, Numbers 3–4 reflects on this basis already a report about the mobilization of such a force.

However, passages such as Ezek 44:10-14; Ezra 3:8-9; 1 Chr 9:14-34; 23:2-32, besides others, show that the mobilizations of such forces, or the plans for them, particularly from among the Levites, were also reported literarily. The structures of these reports vary. They may be short and general or long and specific. Also variable are the references to their essential elements and aspects, including the difference between momentary and permanent assignments, and among different kinds of assignments as well. The focus on the mobilization of the Levites in these reports comes as no surprise because it reflects the reality especially of that group as the most prominent, and in Numbers 3–4 as the sole group among all others organized for the work and particularly for the permanent service at the postexilic temple.

Numbers 3–4 is, therefore, a REPORT about the MOBILIZATION of a Work and Service Force, specifically of the Levites for their service at the central sanctuary. Decisive for this determination of the genre of Numbers 3–4 is the distinction between reports about the initial organization of service forces before the beginning of their work and/or service and reports about their actual work or service after their initial organization as, e.g., in Nehemiah 3. Only the first type of report is relevant for Numbers 3–4. It includes reference to phases such as authoritative decree or command and their execution in conscription and various elements of mobilization. It may involve either certain contingents for a particular (construction) project which dissolve when their project is completed, or different contingents for the ongoing maintenance of an existing institutional operation or a completed project. The aspect of organization is presumed in both types of reports, and also for both types of reported service: the completion of a work project or the ongoing institutional duty.

Numbers 3–4 focuses on the permanent service force for the already completed sanctuary, and not on the different force for its construction. Even so, it reports about the initial organization of that force, generated by Yahweh's command and implemented through conscription and mobilization. And in as much as it implies the process of continuous recruitment of at least the Levites, it still focuses on the initial organization of that process. But it is no report about the actual performance of their permanent service. It belongs to reports about the — initial — mobilization of maintenance forces.

The report Numbers 3–4 is an extension, both contextually and conceptually, of the report of the mobilization of the militia in Numbers 2 for which Numbers 1 reports the preparation. Both reports belong together under the aspect of the mobilization of the total camp, in its two quadrangles around the sanctuary and in its two parties essential for the sanctuary: the militia and the maintenance personnel.

Nevertheless, the uniqueness of the composition of Numbers 3–4 must not be overlooked. Those parts of it that report about the substitution of the Levites for the Israelite firstborn are foreign to the pattern of mobilization reports. They are concerned with the Levites as substitution and with money as ransom for the Israelites, but not with their role in the mobilization. And they emphasize the appointment of all Levites from early childhood on, in contrast to their mobilization as adults. This aspect reveals an interest in the *reason* for the mobilization of the Levites, and in the permanent institutionalization of that reason.

As cultic personnel, the Levites belonged, together with the priests, to the sanctuary. And their responsibilities were clearly not profane. But nowhere are they more set apart from and subordinated to the priests than here and in the respective passages in Ezekiel, Ezra, and Chronicles. Those passages provide the closest context to Numbers 3–4, including their references to the location of the Levites in Jerusalem. They show that Numbers 3–4 reflects the vantage point of the Aaronide priests about the Levites in a specific historical situation, a viewpoint that is different from the rest of the levitic tradition history.

It is, therefore, relevant substantively that the function of the Levites is portrayed in the genre of their mobilization as nothing more than work and service personnel, and that the special component of the appointment of all Levites from early childhood on as substitutes for Israel's firstborn reinforces that aspect of the genre by placing them on the side of the Israelites, vis-à-vis the priests.

Setting

The report of Numbers 3–4 owes its unique composition to the setting of the Aaronide writers in their particular historical situation. The original setting of the genre of such reports must be sought in institutions in which the mobilization of such work forces, their recruitment, organization, and assignments, were recorded. Those institutional settings of recording stand behind the biblical narrative reports. They reflect the various types of operations themselves, and were probably closely related to them. And certainly the mobilization and organization of the cultic personnel, both priestly and clerical, must have been a prominent factor in the ongoing life especially of the first and second temples; and it was recorded, most probably by scribes associated with the administrations of these two temples. Those records themselves are no longer available, and the narrative-reports in the historical writings, except perhaps Ezra's, do not belong to these settings of the temple administrations. But they are based on the genre of recording in those settings and seem to have in part drawn from such records. It is on the basis of this traditional setting and its generic reporting that Numbers 3–4 reports the mobilization of the first inner camp at Sinai. In this sense, Numbers 3–4 reflects institutional reality, and by no means something fictitious.

Intention

Numbers 3–4 intends above all to portray the Sinaitic ideal of the organization of the entire levitical community as clerical personnel under the supervision of the Aaronide priests. For this purpose, it must refer to names, numbers, and the overall situation at Sinai in contradistinction to all other possibly available data, especially those from the time of the writers themselves. But it must lay out the basic elements of this ideal organization: the principles of substitution and ransom, their relationship to and work at the sanctuary, the numbers of available people, and their clear subordination to the priests.

However, since we possess more information from the postexilic time about the levitical situation than we possess about the organization of the militia, it is possible to say something more about the intention of Numbers 3–4 for the writers' own time. With authoritative claim, the text presents an ideal design for the place and the role of "the tribes of Levi" in Israel which is just as much a program for the future as it is a corrective for its past history. This design coincided with the time of the emergence or the existence of the institution of the second temple. And it leaves no doubt as to who controlled this program. How the program was fulfilled specifically during the second temple period, we do not know. That it was fulfilled in principle, is a historical fact.

Bibliography

A. Cody, *A History of Old Testament Priesthood* (AnBib 35; Rome: Pontifical Biblical Institute, 1969); G. Fohrer, "Levi und Leviten," *RGG*3; H. Freedman, "Levi," *EncJud;* A. H. J. Gunneweg, *Leviten und Priester* (FRLANT 89; Gottingen: Vandenhoeck & Ruprecht, 1965); D. Kellermann, *"lēwî," TWAT;* J. Milgrom, "The Term *'Aboda*," in *Studies in Cultic Theology and Terminology* (SJLA 36; Leiden: E. J. Brill, 1983) 18-46.

Report of the Exclusion of the Unclean (5:1-4)

Structure

I. The Yahweh command to Moses	1-3
A. Introductory speech report formula	1
B. The command	2-3
1. Introduction: command the Israelite	2aα
2. The content	2aβ-3
a. Basic	2aβ-b
b. Specifications and substantiation	3
1) Specifications in terms of location	3a
2) Substantiation	3b
II. The compliance by the Israelites	4

This unit reports a Yahweh command and the compliance by the Israelites. Its first part (I., vv. 1-3) consists of the usual report formula (I.A., v. 1) and of the content of Yahweh's speech (I.B., vv. 2-3). The speech opens in I.B.1. (v. 2aα) with an impv. form *ṣaw*, "command!", which defines the entire Yahweh speech to Moses as a command. The content of the same word, *ṣiwwâ*, "to command," indicates what Moses is commanded to do: he himself must give a command to the Israelites. Yahweh's command to Moses must be passed on as Moses' command to the Israelites.

I.B.2. (vv. 2aβ-3) contains the content of the command. Basically (I.B.2.a., v. 2aβ-b) they (3rd pers. pl.) are to send out of the camp (1) all having a skin disease, (2) all having a discharge, and (3) all being unclean through (contact with) a corpse (cf. Num 19:13, 20). Specifically (I.B.2.b., v. 3) you (2nd pers. pl.) are to send the unclean "from the male to the female" outside the camp so that they do not defile "their camp in which I am dwelling in their midst" — "their camp" apparently referring to the camps in the outer quadrangle.

In a cadence of three short sentences, part II. (v. 4) states that the Israelites did what Yahweh had commanded to Moses. What is presupposed, but not said, in the statement of compliance is that Moses himself had commanded the Israelites what to do. The text takes Moses' obedience for granted and focuses instead on the obedience of the Israelites.

Genre

The text is a short report about an event: the exclusion by the Israelites of all unclean persons from the sanctuary camp at Yahweh's command. It presupposes the laws in Leviticus 12–15 and summarily narrates that these laws were implemented at Sinai in conjunction with the organization of the camp. The text is neither a law nor a comment on the laws of Leviticus 12–15. It is in part a report of a Yahweh command to be executed immediately. But it also reports Israel's compliance. At issue in both parts is the treatment of all unclean persons, now both male and female, in the camp. And the correlation of command and compliance indicates that Yahweh's command concerning this issue demanded Israel's immediate obedience, and that Israel's action was not arbitrary but grounded in Yahweh's explicit command.

In the background of this report stand the extensive traditions of priestly laws and instructions concerning purity and impurity, of priestly decisions of such cases, and most probably the fact that such instructions and decisions were executed in and by the Israelite community. This background was institutionalized, and the present text reflects its reality. Num 5:1-4 is a REPORT about the ADMINISTRATION OF IMPURE PERSONS. But we do not yet know whether or not this text belongs to a literary genre of such reports.

Setting

The text owes its present position to the concerns emerging at this juncture in the context of the priestly work. It belongs to the later setting of those priestly writers who in view of the already existing text in Leviticus 12–15 added an aspect to Numbers 1–4 that had played no role in that narrative. This setting is to be distinguished from the settings in which the laws of purity originated, in which cases of impurity were administered, and from the legendary setting at Sinai in which such administration took place for the first time. While generated by the priestly writers the text says nothing about the involvement of priests in the Sinaitic event.

Intention

The report clarifies that the Sinai camp, now including the female gender, was subject also to the laws of ritual purity, and that those given laws were carried out at Sinai already in conjunction with the organization of the camp with respect to all unclean persons. It confronts its readers with the validity and viability of the strict claims to purity on the ground that the Sinai community had already fulfilled this claim. It shows the ideal fulfillment of the purity of the *'ēdâ* which is the prototype of the fulfillment expected by its descendants.

For this purpose, the text selects a few aspects from the broad priestly tradition history on purity and impurity. It is interested in a typical picture, and neither in all aspects of the tradition nor in possibly being at variance with some of its aspects. For example, it is not always the case that impure persons have to be separated from the community. Indeed, the separation of these persons from the camp is the main thrust in the text. Their impurity not only separates them from the cult; it separates them from the pure persons in the camp, and from the camp itself. The sanctuary camp at Sinai consisted of — and is the prototype for — the community of the pure only.

The unclean were sent *(šālaḥ)* outside the camp for the duration of their affliction, not forever. They were neither expelled nor cut off.

The text explains why unclean persons must be excluded from the camp. They pollute their camp in which Yahweh dwells in their midst. But the text does not explain why the distinction between purity and impurity is fundamental for Yahweh. Nor does it explain why persons afflicted with physical impurity are unacceptable in the presence of Yahweh. It presupposes the profound claim that Yahweh more than anything else represents the sphere of unpolluted life. At the same time, it translates the fundamental physiological distinction between purity and impurity into the law and ethical command for a societal separation of the unclean from God and the clean.

Bibliography

G. André and H. Ringgren, *"ṭāmē',"* *TDOT;* F. Hauck, *"μιαίνω,"* *TDNT;* "Purity and Impurity, Ritual," *EncJud;* F. Maass, *"ṭm', unrein sein,"* *THAT;* L. E. Toombs, "Clean and Unclean," *IDB.*

Legal Instruction about Restitution (5:5-10)

Structure

I. Introductory speech report formula	5
II. The Yahweh speech to Moses	6-10
A. The command to Moses (Commission formula)	6aα
B. The content of the command	6aβ-10
1. A case law	6aβ-8
a. Protasis: the legal case	6aβ-b
b. Apodosis: the legal consequence	7-8
1) Stated basically	7
a) Confession	7aα
b) Restitution	7aβ-b
2) The exception	8
a) The case	8aα
b) The consequence	8aβ-b
(1) Restitution proper	8aβ
(2) The addition: a ram of atonement	8b
2. A regulation concerning contributions to the priest	9-10

This unit reports a Yahweh speech. It is introduced by the redactor's report formula (I., v. 5), which is followed by the speech itself (II., vv. 6-10). Moses is in the commission formula commanded to speak to the Israelites (II.A., v. 6aα) and given the content of the command (II.B., vv. 6aβ-10). A compliance is not reported. The unit is at best indirectly concerned with the Sinai camp. It does not address an acute case to be resolved immediately. It aims at permanence.

The main part of the content consists of a case law which Moses must promulgate to the Israelites (II.B.1., vv. 6aβ-8; cf. "Introduction to Legal Genres," Knierim, *Exodus 19–40*). In typical fashion, the case law presents first the legal case (II.B.1.a., v. 6aβ-b) and then the legal consequence (II.B.1.b., vv. 7-8). The form by which the case is introduced, a noun (or two) followed by a conditional clause, is typical for the priestly literature. It is one of the forms for introducing a case law in the OT (cf. Liedke, 19-31). The case is stated summarily and most generally. It refers to any sin (*ḥaṭṭā't,* in the end result a failure) by humans — man or woman — which is also a breach of trust *(mā'al)* against Yahweh, and by which they became liable for their guilt *('āšām)* resulting itself from that sin.

The stipulation of the legal consequence in II.B.1.b. (vv. 7-8) reaffirms in its basic statement II.B.1.b.1) [v. 7] and in II.B.1.b.2)b)(2) [v. 8b] what is said in Lev 5:20-26 (*NRSV* 6:1-7): The culprit has to confess *(wĕhitwaddû),* to pay his/her liability in full *(hēšîb 'et-'ăšāmô bĕrō'šô),* to add one fifth — obviously in money — as a penalty, to give it to the violated person, and to offer a ram of atonement for his/her breach of trust against Yahweh.

The sub-case in II.B.1.b.2) [v. 8] refers to the exception, which is not envisioned in Leviticus 5: If neither — so the implication — the original recipient of the guilt payment nor a redeeming substitute recipient *(gō'ēl),* a next of kin, is available [II. B.1.b.2)a), v. 8aα], the restitution shall go to the priest, in addition to the ram by which the priest effects Yahweh's atonement for the culprit.

In an appendix (II.B.2., vv. 9-10) caused by the sub-case of the law, instruction is given that every contribution concerning holy things given to the priest shall belong to the — same — priest.

Genre

The unit is a REPORT of the PRONOUNCEMENT or PROCLAMATION OF LAW. It presupposes the redactor/reporter, and says that the law pronounced by Yahweh has to be passed on to the Israelites by an intermediary, Moses. It distinguishes between the case law itself and the report about its source in Yahweh's pronouncement. The law has to be spoken to Israel, which is what the text itself does instead of Moses. The text itself communicates to Israel a law pronounced by Yahweh. It functions as presently occurring instruction about a law, or as LEGAL INSTRUCTION, in which the pronouncement of the law and the reference to its author are combined. The form of the report and its function complement one another. The form points to the lawgiver, and its function to the recipient.

In its specifically priestly form including its formulaic language, the law adopts the traditional genre of CASE LAW. Its legal nature is constituted by the fact that it defines an anticipated case of conflict and prescribes the consequences necessary for its resolution. In the present unit, the case law genre was applied to the substantive issue of liability for guilt *('āšām)*. In as much as this issue represents a particular legal category, the present text belongs to specific laws of LIABILITY FOR GUILT, or *'āšām* LAWS, which regulate such situations substantively and procedurally.

The question is not yet resolved whether the frequent form of pronouncements of law by Yahweh (to Moses for Israel), the reports about such pronouncements, and their function as legal instruction are only literary, redactional devices by which to historicize these laws, or whether they reflect generic forms of such pronouncements and instructional reports about them from the history of Israelite — and Ancient Near Eastern — legal and cultic institutions. While the literary nature of the text is indisputable, the question of the institutional background of its form remains open.

Setting

The text belongs to the instructional setting of the priestly writers that includes legal instruction, apparently during the postexilic time. Its particular emphasis in v. 8 suggests typical situations in which people could be tempted to keep misappropriated property because its original owner or his next of kin was unavailable. For such situations, the text establishes the law, and not only an ethical obligation, that restitution must be made nevertheless, now to Yahweh and hence to the priest, because the misappropriation of human property is also a breach of trust against Yahweh. The priestly institution becomes under this condition the legal recipient of liable restitution. And vv. 9-10 suggest a specific situation within the priesthood itself in which specific priests may be deprived of donations *(tĕrûmâ)* given to them.

Intention

The legal instruction is a supplement to the law in Lev 5:20-26 (*NRSV* 6:1-7). It neither replaces nor relativizes that law, but rather reaffirms its specific formulations summarily. By adding what was not discussed in the former law it wants first of all to make sure that a guilt incurred by misappropriated property is liable to be corrected under any circumstance. The addition closes a loophole in the former law. By designating the priests as the receivers of the restitution it wants, second, to secure the livelihood of the priests. Finally, by prescribing both the confession and the restitution, it offers the culprit the opportunity of restoring his/her ethical integrity through compliance with the law.

Bibliography

D. Kellermann, *"'āshām," TDOT;* R. P. Knierim, *Exodus: With an Introduction to Legal Genres* (FOTL IIB; Grand Rapids: Eerdmans, forthcoming); idem, *"ḥṭ', sich verfehlen," THAT;* idem, *m'l, treulos sein," THAT;* idem, *"'āšam, Schuldverpflichtung," THAT;* idem, "Sünde II. Altes Testament," TRE; K. Koch, *"chāṭā'," TDOT;* B. Lang, *"kippær," TWAT;* G. Liedke, *Gestalt und Bezeichnung alttestamentlicher Rechtssätze: Eine formgeschichtlich-terminologische Studie* (WMANT 39; Neukirchen: Neukirchener, 1971); F. Maass, *"kpr, pi. sühnen," THAT;* J. Milgrom, "The Priestly Doctrine of Repentance," in *Studies in Cultic Theology and Terminology* (SJLA 36; Leiden: E. J. Brill, 1983) 47-66; "Sin-Offering or Purification-Offering?" in *Studies in Cultic Theology and Terminology* (SJLA 36; Leiden: E. J. Brill, 1983) 67-69; "Two Kinds of *ḥaṭṭā't,"* in *Studies in Cultic Theology and Terminology* (SJLA 36; Leiden: E. J. Brill, 1983) 70-74; R. Rendtorff, *Studien zur Geschichte des Opfers im Alten Israel* (WMANT 24; Neukirchen: Neukirchener, 1967); H. Ringgren, *"mā'al," TWAT.*

Legal Instruction about the Trial of Jealousy (5:11-31)

Structure

I. Introductory speech report formula	11
II. The instruction: the Yahweh speech to Moses	12-31
A. The command (conveyance command formula)	12a
B. The law for the trial: the content	12b-31
1. Protasis: the legal case	12b-14
a. A wife's (possible) adultery	12b-13
1) Her action	12b
a) Expressed actually: going astray	12bα
b) Expressed morally: breach of trust	12bβ
2) Her lover — a man	13aα
a) His action: lies with her sexually	13aα
b) Non-detection by husband	13aβ1
3) Her situation	13aβ2-aβ3
a) Remains undetected	13aβ2
b) State: defiled	13aβ3
4) Fourth party	13b
a) No witness	13bα
b) She is not caught in the act	13bβ
b. Her husband's jealousy	14
1) Assuming her defilement	14a
a) Statement about the jealousy	14aα
(1) Expressed passively: befallen by spirit	14aα1
(2) Expressed actively: he generates . . .	14aα2
b) Statement about the case of defilement	14aβ
2) Assuming her purity	14b

    a) Statement about the jealousy   14bα

      (1) Expressed passively   14bα$_1$

      (2) Expressed actively   14bα$_2$

    b) Statement about non-defilement   14bβ

2. Apodosis: the prescription of the judicial ritual   15-26

  a. The opening part: husband's actions   15

    1) Bring his wife to the priest   15aα

    2) Bring her offering   15aβ-b

      a) Expressed positively: basic and specific   15aβ

      b) Twofold prohibition and reasons   15b

  b. The main part: the actions of the priest   16-26

    1) First stage: concerning her approach   16

      a) Make her approach   16a

      b) Make her stand before Yahweh   16b

    2) Second stage: mixing of water and dust   17

      a) Take holy water   17a

      b) Take dust from floor of tabernacle   17bα

      c) Put dust into water   17bβ

    3) Third stage: the filling of hands   18

      a) The woman's hands   18a

        (1) Make her stand before Yahweh (v. 16b) 18aα

        (2) Unbind (the hair of) her head   18aβ$_1$

        (3) Put memorial/jealousy offering in her

            hands (v. 15aβ-b)   18aβ$_2$-aβ$_3$

      b) The priest's hands: waters of bitterness

        (v. 17)   18b

    4) Fourth stage: administration of the oath   19-22

      a) Introductory statement   19aα$_1$

      b) The oath and its process   19aα$_2$-22

        (1) The priest's part: addressing the woman 19aα$_2$-22a

          (a) For the case of innocence (v. 14b) 19aα$_2$-b

             α. Twofold statement of case   19aα$_2$-β

                aa. Concerning a lover   19aα$_2$

                bb. Concerning straying to

                    defilement   19aβ

             β. The consequence: declaration

                of immunity   19b

          (b) For the case of guilt (v. 14a)   20-22a

             α. Statement of case   20

                aa. Basically: in factual and moral

                    terms   20a

                bb. Specifically: lain with other man 20b

             β. The consequence   21-22a

                aa. Introductory statement

                    repeated (v. 19aα$_1$)   21aα-aβ$_1$

                bb. The pronouncement of

                    the curse   21aβ$_2$-22a

α) Expressed theologically 21aβ₂-b

β) Expressed dynamistically 22a

(2) The woman's affirmation 22b

(a) Introductory statement 22bα

(b) Formula of affirmation: Amen, Amen 22bβ

5) Fifth stage: the curses and the water

(vv. 17, 18b, 21-22) 23-24

a) The priest's part 23

(1) Write curses in scroll 23a

(2) Wash them off into water (v. 18b) 23b

b) The woman's part: cause her to drink 24

(1) Action proper 24a

(2) Result 24b

6) Sixth stage: the offering (v. 18a) 25

a) The priest's part 25a-bα

(1) Take it from her hands 25a

(2) Wave it before Yahweh 25bα

b) The woman's part: make her approach 25bβ

7) Seventh stage: the 'azkārâ and the drinking

(vv. 15b, 18a, 25a-b, 23-24) 26

a) The priest's part 26a

(1) Take the 'azkārâ from offering 26aα

(2) Burn it on the altar 26aβ

b) The woman's part: make her drink 26b

1.-2. Concluding prognosis 27-28

a. For the case of her defilement 27

b. For the case of her purity 28

3. Summary of instruction: the tôrâ concerning jealousy 29-31

The structure of the extant text represents a systematized instruction about the approach to a husband's jealous suspicion against his wife. It is based on the sequence of the events and steps to be taken, but also on several conceptual aspects under which the sequence is organized.

After the usual redactional introduction in I. (v. 11) and II.A. (v. 12a), the text relates in II.B. (vv. 12b-31) the law (for the trial) of jealousy (tôrat haqqĕnā'ōt, v. 29a). This law consists of the protasis, the definition of the legal case (II.B.1., vv. 12b-14), and of the apodosis, the prescription for the administration of the case (II.B.2., vv. 15-26). Its structure conforms to the structure of the case laws.

The definition of the case involves two aspects: a wife's possible act of adultery (II.B.1.a., vv. 12b-13) and her husband's jealous suspicion of such an act (II.B.1.b., v. 14). The act of adultery (tiśṭeh, "she goes astray," v. 12bα) is analyzed under the aspect of its possibility for which, however, no proof can be ascertained. For such a situation the analysis meticulously defines four pertinent aspects each of which consists of two complementary aspects, and all of which together constitute the first part of the legal case. See the structure. The case is a legal one because it is rooted in a legal perception of both marriage and adultery. The language in vv. 12b-13 and elsewhere in the law gives the impression that the woman had in fact committed the act, is presumed guilty, and that only the proof of her guilt is lacking. However, the context shows that whether she has committed the act or not is an open question. The case presumes only the possibility of her act, and not her guilt. Accordingly, the following trial is based on her being a suspect, and not on the presumption of either her guilt or her innocence. On the presumption of the suspicion alone, the trial aims at establishing either her guilt or her innocence.

The suspicion becomes legally relevant in her husband's passion or jealousy *(qin'â)* to which the second aspect in the definition of the case refers (II.B.1.b., v. 14). In this aspect, the definition of the case again distinguishes with precise specifications between the possibilities of either her defilement [II.B.1.b.1), v. 14α] or her purity [II.B.1.b.2), v. 14b] and the husband's jealousy in either case. See the → Structure above. This definition protects his wife by clarifying that her husband's jealousy proves nothing as to her guilt or innocence. But it also acknowledges the fact of the husband's jealousy as a legal ground for a trial and for the law itself. It is not her act or non-act but his jealousy that triggers the judicial process. Without the husband's jealousy, neither a trial nor the law for it would be necessary. The law is therefore concerned with the case of a husband's jealousy about a possible adulterous act by his wife, and not with the case of a wife's adultery. It is a law concerning jealous suspicion, and not a law concerning adultery. It accommodates the husband.

The usage of the words *qanā'/qin'â,* "to be envious, jealous/passion, jealousy" (v. 14a, et al.) must be understood from the context because they could also mean jealousy about an actual and evident adulterous act and breach of trust *(mā'al,* v. 12b). It is therefore correct to interpret this word as suspicion (Budd), or jealous suspicion. The same contextual interpretation is necessary for the forms of the root *ṭāmē',* "unclean," v. 13aβ3, et al., because "uncleanness, defilement," as in the sexual sphere, refer also to natural processes that are not criminal.

The definition in the legal case of a husband's actual suspicion about his wife's possible adultery establishes the situation before a trial as the legal basis for a trial. The basis consists of three factors: the recognition of the fact and severity of the husband's suspicion, the inadmissibility of this suspicion as evidence, and the impossibility of resolving the necessary case through regular, i.e., civil, judicial procedure. This legally established case requires a trial through the instrumentality of an exceptional, revelatory procedure. The logical relationship between the nature of the case and the nature of the trial corresponds to the chronological relationship between the two parts of the legal process: the pretrial and the trial phase.

Prescribed in the apodosis (II.B.2., vv. 15-26) is the trial procedure. This part of the law belongs to the category of procedural law and represents its most explicit example in the OT. And since the procedure involves a revelatory adjudication, it belongs to the specific category of cultic judicial rituals. The application of procedural law and cultic judicial ritual in the law is not coincidental. It is grounded in the nature of the case, the problem of which can only be solved through the ritual process itself. It is the performance of the ritual that brings the truth to light. The meticulous attention in the instruction to the specifics of the ritual procedure reflects not the subjective literary idiosyncrasies of the writers but the indispensable necessities of the precise ritual performance by which the deity himself can discern the alternatives of the case and the truth.

The prescription includes the husband, his wife, the priest, and Yahweh. It requires a variety of relevant materials such as a gift offering (*qorbān,* v. 15), which in v. 15b is defined as a "cereal offering of jealousy" *(minḥat qĕnā'ōt)* and as a "memorial offering causing remembrance of guilt" *(minḥat zikkārôn mazkeret 'āwōn),* holy water *(mayim qĕdōšîm),* dust *('āpār,* v. 17bα) from the floor of the tabernacle *(hammiškān),* a scroll *(sēper,* v. 23a), and the *'azkārâ* (v. 26aα), a part from the offering to be burnt on the altar probably together with an invocation of Yahweh. It requires an oath administered by the priest which takes place "before Yahweh" and at the altar. Above all it is prescribed as a series of actions to be performed in consecutive order. However, the sequence of these actions rests not on a simple step-by-step enumeration but on a systemic understanding of the procedure. See the Structure above.

The prescription distinguishes first of all between the opening part, the actions of the husband (II.B.2.a., v. 15), and the main part, the ritual proper conducted by the priest (II.B.2.b., vv. 16-26). The husband brings his wife and the gift offering on her behalf to the priest. Thereafter the husband recedes and the priest, who is presumed to be informed, conducts the ritual.

The priest's actions consist of seven stages each of which involves some steps which he partly takes himself and partly makes the woman take. Except for vv. 17b, 18b, and 21a 1+2, the beginning of each stage is indicated by the grammatical subject "the priest" *(hakkōhēn,* cf. vv. 16a, 17a, 18a, 19a, 23a, 25a, and 26). The first three stages [II.B.2.b.1), v. 16; 2.b.2), v. 17; 2.b.3), v. 18] are preparatory in nature. The priest in 2.b.1) [v. 16] motions the woman before Yahweh (place not clear). He mixes the holy water with dust from the floor of the sanctuary into an earthen vessel, whereby the water (vv. 17b, 26b, and 27aα$_1$) or "holy water" becomes "bitter water" [*mê hammārîm,* v. 23b; 2.b.2), v. 17]. After taking her (again) before Yahweh and unbinding her hair, he fills her hands with the offering and his own hands with the "curse-producing bitter water" [*mê hammārîm hamĕ'ārărîm,* vv. 18b, 19b, 24a, also 22a; 2.b.3), v. 18]. After this preparation, the two human participants are ready for the decisive part of the ritual, which is prescribed in stages four through seven.

Stages four and five prescribe the rite of the curse water. It is introduced in II.B.2.b.4) [vv. 19-22] by a twofold oath spoken by the priest to the woman in which her possible guilt or innocence is conjured together with the respective consequences. Each formulation describes the possible case once again. In the case of her innocence she will be free from the curse produced through the water, i.e., she will be fertile. But she must take a self-curse *(šĕbu'at hā'ālâ)* upon herself for the case of her guilt which Yahweh and the water she is to drink will make effective as infertility branding her publicly as a cursed person. Subsequently, the woman submits to the condition of the twofold oath by saying "Amen, Amen"; cf. v. 19aα$_1$, *wĕhišbîa' 'ōtāh hakkōhēn.*

In stage five [II.B.2.b.5), vv. 23-24] the spoken words of the curse are transformed into physical substance. They are written on a scroll, and the writing is washed into the bitter water whereby this water becomes the "curse-bringing bitter water" or the "curse-bringing water for bitterness" (*hammayim hamě'ărărîm lěmārîm,* vv. 24b and 27aβ₁). The woman has to drink this water, thereby taking the potential curse into her body physically.

Finally, stages six and seven prescribe the rite of the *'azkārâ* from the offering which has from stage three on been in the woman's hands. First, the priest takes the offering from her hands, waves it before Yahweh, and makes her come to the altar [II.B.2.b.6), v. 25]. The waving *(těnûpâ)* is "a ritual of raising or lifting intended to dedicate the offering to God"; Milgrom, *Hattěnûpâ,* 158. It is not a special sacrifice. Then he takes the *'azkārâ* from the offering, burns it on the altar, and makes the woman drink. According to the extant text, the woman drinks the curse water twice, once in conjunction with the curse and again with the *'azkārâ* taken from the offering of jealousy, possibly with respect to herself and her husband.

II.B.1.-2. (vv. 27-28) concludes with a prognosis by the law of the results of the ritual, quite appropriately because these results are expected after the ritual has ended. Depending on her defilement or purity the woman will apparently either be infertile or fertile. And depending on the physical outcome, her infertility will reveal or *de facto* amount to a verdict of guilt and to punishment, whereas her fertility will reveal or amount to a verdict of innocence. No further judicial action is involved.

II.B.3. (vv. 29-31) provide a summary of the instruction. It defines, among others, the type of this specific instruction *(tôrâ),* and says that the husband is in any case free of guilt *('āwōn).*

Despite problems, the clearly structured instruction reflects a prescription for an actual ritual performance. The generally accepted fact that it reveals pre-stages of a differently structured ritual points only to its traditional nature and its currently more composite edition, but not to an anarchy of incompatible elements. Reconstructions of the pre-stages remain tentative; cf. the more recent discussions in Noth, *Numbers;* de Vaux; Kellermann, *Numeri;* Frymer; and Budd. Nevertheless, the text indicates uneven points. It repeatedly speaks about the guilt of the woman while also saying that neither her guilt nor her innocence is presumed. Her second drinking after the *'azkārâ* is suspicious. Twice she is brought before Yahweh (vv. 16, 18aα), and she is also brought to the altar (v. 25bβ). Her affirmation in v. 22b may originally have referred to the curse only in case of her guilt. The function of her husband's offering which is at the same time a donation *(qorbān)* for the priest and a cereal offering for jealousy including the special part of the *'azkārâ* is not self-evident. The correlation of the spoken oath and the drinking of the water may not be original although such correlation of word and action in ritual or symbolic performances is quite traditional. Also, the correlation of Yahweh's role (v. 21aβ₂-b) and the self-efficaciousness of the curse (vv. 22a, 24, and 27) may but does not necessarily indicate a secondary combination of two originally separate versions. This correlation of theological and dynamistic expression is quite normal, not late, and certainly points to a ritual by a Yahweh priest. Verses 20-22 are in 21aα-aβ₁ interrupted by an anacoluthon, a redactional repetition of v. 19aα₁. There are terminological variations, especially in technical terms; cf. vv. 15, 16, 18, 19b, and 21-27. Some words are evidently late; some depend on the priestly context. The reference to "the priest" reflects the original tradition, whereas vv. 11 and 12a reflect its inclusion into the priestly narrative.

Genre

The unit is a LEGAL INSTRUCTION → Num 5:5-10, Genre. The report as pronounced by Yahweh, with the command to convey the pronouncement, is a CASE LAW. This law belongs to the subgenre PROCEDURAL LAW. Prescribed is the procedure of a TRIAL BY ORDEAL, a ritual which is both cultic and judicial. The total text aims at this LAW ABOUT A TRIAL BY ORDEAL.

The ORDEAL is a specific mode of trial in customary judicial systems. Trial by ordeal is the necessary adjudication by revelatory divine judgment through a specific, ritually performed test, of the guilt or innocence of persons suspect of a crime, in cases that cannot be decided by human agencies. Constitutive for the ordeal is the invoked divine presence in the procedure by which the procedure becomes an efficacious tool of the divine agent and which renders the result of the trial valid. Intrinsic to the procedure are therefore the places and words that identify and invoke the deity, and the procedural actions as well. The water to be drunk in Numbers 5 is not poisonous but made potent by Yahweh. From several types of ordeals, Num 5:11-31 belongs to the ORDEAL BY WATER, especially to ordeals of drinking of bitter water, which is not poisonous. It is actually a harmless water of testing, and not an instrument of execution for a convicted person as in the case of Socrates. Accordingly, the divine judgment of this specific ordeal is revealed through the consequences following the ritual, and is neither revealed in the procedure itself nor pronounced in addition to it.

Setting

The unit belongs to the instructional setting of the priestly writers. They adopted an older prescription of the ritual, perhaps already couched in the form of a case law. Its origin and age are unknown. The total law contains instruction for both the husband and the priest, and is not coincidentally defined as TORAH, v. 29a. But since the case of jealousy is administered by a priest and not by a civil court, and since the law prescribes in detail the priestly ritual, the law containing the procedural prescription must from the outset have originated in a priestly setting. The extant text reflects the unbroken continuity of this setting. It belongs to a legal tradition in which the law giving and the adjudication of certain cases were reserved for the representatives of the cultic institution, and not in the hands of civil authorities. This tradition existed beside the civil authorities and does not necessarily reflect their replacement through a hierocratic constitution.

The practice of ordeals throughout history is an established fact. But records about the practice of the ordeal prescribed in Numbers 5 exist only for the postbiblical time (Frymer). The absence of such records for the biblical time does not mean either that the ordeal was not practiced or that the instruction was not intended to be practiced. It may be sought in the specific circumstances under which this ordeal is said to be performed: in the secluded place at the altar of the sanctuary, in the presence of only three involved persons (a married couple and a priest), at a specifically scheduled performance in private, and without subsequent public judicial actions. Under such circumstances, records about the practice of the ritual are not likely to be expected, if at all. But the practice should not be denied in principle. It would be a parallel to the rituals for the COMPLAINTS of the individuals which were performed under similar circumstances; cf. Gerstenberger, *Der bittende Mensch,* and his "Introduction to Cultic Poetry" in *Psalms,* vol. XIV.

Intention

The text intends to instruct about the legal obligation for the trial by ordeal of a woman in the case of her husband's suspicion of an act of adultery on her part, and about the ritual of the ordeal. The ordeal itself intends to produce the evidence for the woman's purity or impurity, or guilt or innocence, in the subsequent outcome of her fertility or infertility. For the case of her resulting infertility which retroactively proves her adultery, the law is noticeably different from laws such as Lev 20:10; Deut 22:22 which prescribe the death penalty.

Most probably, this particular traditional law was included in the present context because the priestly writers considered such cases of jealousy as indications of potentially hidden cases of impurity in the community which were critically dangerous and in need of divine revelation and elimination through their own cultic judicial control. This interest is reflected in the text in the control of the ritual by the presiding priest. And the critical importance of the case for the priests is reflected in the text's reference to purity or impurity more than to guilt or innocence.

Bibliography

P. Blackman, "Tractate Sotah," in *Mishnayoth: Vol. III, Order Nashim* (2nd ed.; New York: Judaica Press, 1963); H. L. Bosman, "Adultery and Tradition: An Historical Investigation of Pronouncements on Adultery in the Old Testament, with Special Reference to the Decalogue" ([Afrikaans] Diss., University of Pretoria, 1984); H. C. Brichto, "The Case of the *śōṭā* and a Reconsideration of Biblical 'Law,'" *HUCA* 46 (1975) 55-70; H. Eising, *"zākhar," TDOT;* M. Fishbane, "Accusations of Adultery: A Study of Law and Scribal Practice in Numbers 5:11-31," *HUCA* 45 (1974) 25-45; T. S. Frymer, "Ordeal, Judicial," *IDBSup;* T. Frymer-Kensky, "The Strange Case of the Suspected Sotah (Numbers V:11-31)," *VT* 34 (1984) 11-26; E. Gerstenberger, *Der bittende Mensch: Bittritual und Klagelied des Einzelnen im Alten Testament* (WMANT 51; Neukirchen: Neukirchener, 1980); idem, *The Psalms* (FOTL XIV and XV; Grand Rapids: Eerdmans, 1987/2001); C. A. Keller, *"'ālā,* Verfluchung," *THAT;* "'*rr,* verfluchen," *THAT;* Wm.

McKane, "Poison, Trial by Ordeal and the Cup of Wrath," *VT* 30 (1980) 474-92; J. Milgrom, "The Alleged Wave-Offering in Israel and the Ancient Near East," in *Studies in Cultic Theology and Terminology* (SJLA 36; Leiden: E. J. Brill, 1983) 133-38; J. Morgenstern, "Trial by Ordeal among the Semites and in Ancient Israel," *HUC Jubilee Vol.* (1875-1925) 113-43; H. Nottarp and E. Kutsch, "Gottesurteil," *RGG*3; A. Phillips, "Another Look at Adultery," *JSOT* 20 (1981) 3-25; R. Press, "Das Ordal im alten Israel," *ZAW* 51 (1933) 121-40 (Part I) and 227-55 (Part II); R. Rendtorff, *Studien zur Geschichte des Opfers im Alten Israel* (WMANT 24; Neukirchen: Neukirchener, 1967); J. M. Sasson, "Numbers 5 and the 'Waters of Judgement'," *BZ NF* 16 (1972) 249-51; J. Scharbert, *"'ālāh," TDOT; "'rr," TDOT;* W. Schottroff, *"Gedenken" im Alten Orient und im Alten Testament* (2nd ed.; WMANT 15; Neukirchen: Neukirchener, 1967); idem, *Der altisraelitische Fluchspruch* (WMANT 30; Neukirchen: Neukirchener, 1969); idem, *"zkr,* gedenken," *THAT.*

Report about the Law for the Nazirites (6:1-21)

Structure

I. Introductory speech report formula   1
II. The Yahweh speech to Moses   2-20 (21)
    A. The command (conveyance command formula)   2a
    B. The instruction for the Israelites: the law of the
      temporary nazirate   2b-20 (21)
      1. The conditions for the duration of the vow   2b-12
        a. The basic instruction   2b-8
          1) The case of the vow   2b
          2) The prescription: form of the order   3-8
            a) Abstinence from everything from the grapevine   3-4
              (1) Drinking of alcoholic types   3a
                (a) (fermented) and fermenting wine   3aα
                (b) wine vinegar and vinegar from
                  fermenting wine   3aβ
              (2) Drinking and also eating of
                non-alcoholic types   3b-4
                (a) Drinking of any (unfermented)
                  grape-juice   3bα
                (b) Eating   3bβ-4
                  α. of grapes — fresh or dried   3bβ
                  β. repeated summarily and more
                    specifically   4
            b) Abstinence from head-hair cutting   5
              (1) Expressed negatively (with temporal qualifier)   5a
              (2) Expressed positively (with temporal qualifier)   5b
                (a) Concerning status: holy   5bα
                (b) Concerning treatment of hair   5bβ

c) Abstinence from the dead — 6-7
  (1) The principle (prohibition; with temporal qualifier) — 6
  (2) Specifications — 7
    (a) Specifications proper: regarding family — 7a
    (b) The reason — 7b
a)-c) Concluding declaratory statement (with temporal qualifier) — 8
b. The exception: the broken nazirate — 9-12
  1) The case [regarding II.B.1.a.2)c), vv. 6-7] — 9a
    a) Proximity to suddenly dead corpse — 9aα
    b) The consequence: defilement — 9aβ
  2) The prescription for termination and renewal — 9b-12
    a) Termination of the invalidated nazirate on the seventh day — 9b
    b) Procedure for renewal on the eighth day — 10-12
      (1) Pre-ritual action: Bringing an offering — 10
      (2) The ritual order — 11-12
        (a) Two actions of the priest — 11a
          α. Actions proper: ḥaṭṭā't and 'ōlâ — 11aα
          β. Actions interpreted — 11aβ+γ
            aa. Function: atonement — 11aβ
            bb. Reason: State of incurred sin — 11aγ
        (b) Three actions of the Nazirite — 11b-12a
          α. Reconsecration of head — 11b
          β. Rededication of the time — 12aα
          γ. A guilt-obligation offering — 12aβ
        (a)+(b) Concluding declaratory statement — 12b
2. For the termination of the nazirate — 13-20
  a. Superscription — 13a
  b. Procedure — 13b-20
    1) The condition: Period of vow completed — 13bα
    2) The actions prescribed — 13bβ-20a
      a) Preparation by the Nazirite — 13b-15
        (1) Coming to tent (MT emended) — 13b
        (2) Presenting the offerings — 14-15
          (a) Expressed basically: the qorbān — 14aα1
          (b) Expressed specifically — 14aα2-15
            α. The sacrificial animals — 14aα2-b
            β. The accompanying produce — 15
      b) The ritual performed by priest and Nazirite — 16-20
        (1) Actions of the priest — 16-17
          (a) Priest steps before Yahweh — 16a
          (b) Priest makes the sacrificial offerings — 16b-17
            α. The animals — 16b-17a
            β. The produce — 17b

(2) Three actions of the Nazirite: shaving-taking-
   burning of hair   18
(3) Actions of priest   19-20a
   (a) Taking a part of the offerings   19a
   (b) Putting it/them in Nazirite's hands (including
       procedural remark)   19b
   (c) Waving/elevating them before Yahweh   20a
       α. Waving   20aα₁
       β. Purpose: donation for priest   20aα₂-β
   3) Declaratory statement: permission to drink wine   20b
   c. Subscription   21

After the redactors' introductory speech report formula and Yahweh's conveyance command (I., v. 1, and II.A., v. 2a; → Num 5:11-12a), the text contains the law for the temporary nazirate (II.B., vv. 2b-20[21]). This law is organized under the two aspects of the conditions for the duration (II.B.1., vv. 2b-12) and for the termination (II.B.2., vv. 13-20) of the nazirate vow. The part about the duration focuses on the nazirate basically (II.B.1.a., vv. 2b-8), and on the exceptional situation of the de- and reactivation of the vow (II.B.1.b., vv. 9-12). The arrangement of sections a. (vv. 2b-8) and b. (vv. 9-12) within II.B.1. (vv. 2b-12) is analogous to structures in legal texts or corpora where basic or dominant aspects are directly followed by exceptions to or specifications for them.

The basic instruction is cast in the traditional form of the case laws that in two parts describe a case and prescribe its consequences. The description of the case [II.B.1.a.1), v. 2b] follows again the syntax typical for the priestly litera-ture (→ Num 5:5-10) and is condensed in short, precise technical terminology: "A man or a woman when *(kî)* he/she commits the marvel" *(yapli',* cf. Lev 27:2) — i.e., the conspicuously marvelous thing — "to vow the vow of a Nazirite *(lindōr neder nāzîr)* to become dedicated to Yahweh *(lĕhazzîr lĕyhwh).*" The vow, a solemn promise made by a man or a woman, is the result of a person's own decision (contrast Judg 11:29-40; 13:2-7; 1 Sam 1:21-28). Its formulation is not quoted but assumed. Among many types of vows it expresses a special dedication to Yahweh through a specific kind of life. The subsequent prescrip-tion shows that the vow is in this case made for a limited duration (cf. vv. 4, 5a, 5b, 6, 8, [9b], 13-20), and not for life. The text focuses on the fact of the vow and on the conditions for its fulfillment.

The legal prescription [II.B.1.a.2), vv. 3-8] responds to the description of the vow. The relationship between the description of the case and the prescrip-tion of its consequences in the text corresponds to the relationship between an actual vow and the imposition of stipulations for its fulfillment. One should en-vision that the prescriptions are implemented as an individualized instruction after a person has declared such a vow and before it is fulfilled. And those — in our case the priests — who instruct the individuals, do so on the basis of the es-tablished written law.

Prescribed are three kinds of abstinence: from alcoholic beverages and pre-alcoholic products from the grapevine in terms of both drinking and eating

[II.B.1.a.2)a), vv. 3-4], from cutting the hair of one's head [II.B.1.a.2)b), v. 5], and from polluting contact with dead bodies including those of close relatives [II.B.1.a.2)c), vv. 6-7]. All prescriptions are formulated as *lō'* followed by the 3rd pers. impf. form. They are indirect prohibitions, or indirect prohibitive pre-scriptions.

In the entire basic instruction (B.1.a., vv. 2b-8), however, there is an im-portant correlation between prohibitive and positive expressions and the posi-tive as well as the negative aspects in these expressions. The vow (v. 2b) is a positive act, however expressed orally. A vow for the Nazirite (v. 2b) — such as, e.g., "I will be a *nāzîr*" — is an act for a positive stance expressed positively; cf. the statement of its function: "to be holy to Yahweh," v. 8. However, since the nazirate predominantly focuses on the negative aspect of abstaining from, rather than on the positive aspect of doing, something, the prescriptions for it are basically expressed as prohibitions. The positive stance for the nazirate is essentially characterized by its negative aspect of abstention, the object of which is spelled out in the prohibitions. The prohibitions determine the positive stance of the nazirate and its negative aspect of abstention.

Of the three kinds of prohibited practice, especially the first (vv. 3-4) is tightly systematized. Apparently, the text proceeds according to the descending order — not of importance but — of commonly assumed degrees of obvious-ness of what must be prohibited.

The prohibited objects are expressed as types, without specifications. Most obvious is the difference between alcoholic (v. 3) and non-alcoholic types (vv. 3b-4). Alcoholic types can be consumed only by drinking the products from the grapevine, whereas the non-alcoholic types can be consumed by drinking such product but also by eating the produce of the grapevine. The as-pects of drinking and eating and also of the difference between product and produce are therefore structurally subordinate to the governing distinction of alcoholic and non-alcoholic.

Among the alcoholic types (v. 3a), the more obvious are fermented and fermenting wines. ("Perhaps *šēkār* is new wine," Levine, 220. This semanti-cally based preference is supported by the fact that vv. 3-4 focus on the grape-vine exclusively.) Less obvious, and therefore following, are vinegar produced from either wine or fermenting wine.

Still less obvious are the following non-alcoholic types, among which the unfermented grape juice, which is also drunk, comes first, v. 3bα. Only then does the text refer to the eating of either fresh or dried grapes, an instruction summarily reinforced and specifically extended to the seeds and skins of the grapes, vv. 3bβ-4.

To some extent, the descending order of the obvious in the text's arrange-ment represents an inversion of the sequence in which produce and products of the grapevine are available for consumption: from eating grapes to drinking un-fermented grape juice to drinking fermenting and finally fermented wine. Only the aspect of the vinegar stands outside this sequence.

The common denominator of the entire instruction in vv. 3-4 is every-thing that comes from the grapevine. The total abstinence from everything from the grapevine may to some extent reflect a nomadic ideal — which was never a reality for Israel — in contrast to agrarian existence that was basic in Israel's settlement as the gift of Yahweh. More important, however, if not decisive for this kind of abstinence is the separation from any, even the least suspicious cultural influence on the sphere of Yahweh's holiness, on being a Nazirite "for Yahweh" exclusively (v. 2b) and on being holy oneself (vv. 5bα, 8) during the time of the vow. The vow to be a temporary Nazirite is radical because of its meaning: to be holy for Yahweh.

The second prescription (v. 5) includes the prohibition against cutting the hair, and two positive formulations: a declaratory formula explaining the person's expected status ("to Yahweh he/she shall be holy") and an indirect command to let (*gaddēl,* pi. inf.) the loose hair of his/her head grow long.

The third prescription (vv. 6-7) starts with the principal prohibition (v. 6) of defilement through dead family members specifically (v. 7a), and concludes again with the reason (v. 7b; cf. v. 5bα). All three prescriptions are concluded in v. 8 with the declaratory statement that "he/she is holy to Yahweh" *(qādōš hû' lĕyhwh).*

II.B.1.b. (vv. 9-12) addresses a special situation in which the vow for the temporal nazirate is invalidated through the violation of one of the conditions for it. The case described in II.B.1.b.1) [v. 9a] is not a sub-case of the vow described in v. 2b. It is not introduced by *wĕ'îm* but by *wĕkî,* and refers to a case in which the immediately preceding prescription in vv. 6-7 is (unintentionally) violated through a Nazirite's contaminating proximity to a suddenly dead corpse. This proximity causes impurity and suspends or ends the efficacy of the vow by invalidating the period for it thus far observed.

The prescription for reactivating the vow [II.B.1.b.2), vv. 9b-12] addresses the two aspects for its suspension: the official termination of both, the invalidated period of the vow and the subsequent period of uncleanness, through the cutting of the hair on the seventh day after contamination (v. 9b), and the reactivation of observance on the eighth day (vv. 10-12).

The reactivation of observance requires a ritual procedure for which the Nazirite must take the preparatory steps. He/she must from her/his respective locale, where the contamination may be assumed to have happened, bring two turtledoves or two young pigeons to the priest at the entrance of the tent of meeting (v. 10). Note that the translation of the pronoun with "they" as, e.g., in NRSV, is ambiguous. An individual, a "he" or a "she," not a combination of acting persons, is always meant.

The following ritual involves first two actions of the priest (v. 11a), and then three actions of the Nazirite (vv. 11b-12a). The priest offers first one from a kind of the two animals brought as a sin-offering *(ḥaṭṭā't)* for the violation, and then the other as a burnt-offering *('ōlâ)* aiming at the deity's acceptance (v. 11aα). Through both offerings, the priest mediates atonement *(kipper)* for the event and the state of the sin incurred (v. 11aβ+γ). These priestly actions ascertain the invalidation of the period thus far of the person's nazirate.

Now, the Nazirite can reactivate her/his vow her/himself by reconsecrating — the hair of — her/his head, rededicating its period to Yahweh, and by offering a male lamb as a guilt-obligation *('āšām),* vv. 11b-12a. The first two of these acts are non-sacrificial (Milgrom, 47), but nonetheless parts of the total ritual in which the Nazirite's last act, the *'āšām,* requires also the sacrificial participation of the priest. In contrast to the original activation of a Nazirite's vow, which happens without a priestly sacrificial ritual and without the sanctuary, its reactivation after defilement requires a ritual at, and controlled by, the sanctuary, in which the Nazirite's two own actions (vv. 11b+12aα) are surrounded and validated by the sacrificial actions of the priest.

After the ritual is completed, the former days of the nazirate are declared to be deactivated, i.e., "they fall" *(yippĕlû),* v. 12b.

The second part of the law (II.B.2., vv. 13-20) prescribes the procedure for the termination of the vowed nazirate. It is highlighted by its superscription [II.B.2.a., v. 13a] and its subscription [II.B.2.c., v. 21] as a special instruction *(tôrâ)* which emphasizes that the predetermined end of a nazirate does not quietly fade away but is subject to an official, ritually performed termination. The prescription belongs to the sub-genre of procedural law. In detail, the prescribed ritual involves three consecutive stages of actions of the Nazirite and sacrificial actions of the priest, before Yahweh at "the tent of meeting" [II.B.2.b.1)-3); see the → Structure and the biblical text]. Involved in this procedure are the donation *(qorbān),* brought to the priest and administered by him, of another set of specified animals for a burnt offering, a sin offering, and a peace offering *(šĕlāmîm),* together with unleavened bread and wafers, a cereal offering *(minḥâ)* and a drink offering *(nesek)* — in reference to the eating and drinking prohibition — as well.

After this procedure, the Nazirite shaves, takes, and burns his (her?) hair under the fire of the peace-offering, apparently because it belongs to Yahweh and to prevent its desecration. The ritual is concluded by a wave-offering ceremony *(tĕnûpâ)* through which the priest receives his own holy portion, apparently from Yahweh out of the hands of the former Nazirite. After all is done, the person may drink wine.

Genre

The unit is again a REPORT of LEGAL INSTRUCTION (→ Num 5:5-10, Genre; → 5:11-31, Genre). Reported as pronounced by Yahweh, with the command to Moses to convey the pronouncement, is a composition of three instructions which is from its beginning to its end organized as the stages of the case unfold. The first two instructions correspond to the CASE LAW pattern outright, whereas the third is a variation of that pattern because its reference to the case ("When the time of his nazirate has been completed") is integrated into the superscription rather than formulated as usual as a temporal or conditioned clause.

The LEGAL PRESCRIPTIONS consist of indirect PROHIBITIONS and COMMANDS that describe the actions not to be or to be taken. The case law form, the promulgating authorities referred to (Yahweh) and presumed (Moses), the instruction responding to a vow, and the contents of the instruction make it clear that these prescriptions are legal, and not only moral or ethical in nature. Because of various aspects that apply to the (or this kind of) nazirate, the instruction resorts to the sub-genres of SUBSTANTIVE LAW and of PROCEDURAL LAW. The basic prescription (vv. 3-8) responding to a vow requires the substantive definition of the obligations of the prospective Nazirite, whereas the abortion or termination of an existing nazirate requires the definition of ritual procedures along with substantive prescriptions for its reinstatement or termination. The employment of both sub-genres is necessitated by the specific situations of the nazirate. It is not the result of the subjective preferences of the law-giving authors.

The subject of the nazirate addressed in the law, its obligations, and the administrative priestly control over its rituals makes it clear that this legal instruction belongs to the domain of CULTIC LAW, especially RITUAL LAW which regulates matters of cultic concern, also when they pertain to the realm outside the sanctuary precinct. The cultic nature of this instructed law is particularly evident in its formulaic expressions found in vv. 2b, 5bα, 5bβ, 8b, 11a, 12b, and in the references to the various types of offerings and sacrifices in vv. 11, 12, 14-16, and 20.

Setting

This text is the only instruction of its kind in the Pentateuch. The setting of this instruction about the Nazirites must be distinguished from the setting of the individual Nazirites themselves in Israel's society and history, and also from the settings of narratives about them. The extant text reflects without doubt the setting of the priestly writers at a later date in their own tradition history, certainly not before the second temple period, possibly during the first half of the fifth century B.C.E. (cf. Mayer, 332-33). It is generally agreed that it presupposes the already late priestly contexts of Exod 29:2-3 and of Leviticus 1–15. It represents a new edition in part containing older stipulations from the long Israelite tradition history of the nazirate institution (cf. Jenni, "Nasiraer"; Keller, "ndr"; Kaiser; Mayer; Rylaarsdam, "Nazirite"; et al.).

The text itself consists essentially of an earlier priestly part found in vv. 2b-8, 9, and 12b, to which were added later vv. 9b-11, 12a, 13-20, and the framework (cf. Kellermann, 83-95).

Intention

The intention of this instruction can be seen against the relatively known background of the tradition history of the nazirate. The older traditions know that Nazirites were individuals especially predestined or raised as charismatics by Yahweh (Judges 13-16; Amos 2:11-12) or dedicated to Yahweh (1 Sam 1:21-28) for the duration of their lives. The distinctive marks of their consecratedness were above all their life-long uncut hair (Judg 13:5; 16:17; 1 Sam 1:11; but cf. Num 6:5a), and later their abstinence from alcohol (Amos 2:11-12; though scarcely Samson, and Samuel only according to LXX of 1 Sam 1:11). These marks, especially the hair, were visible signs of the marvelous presence

90

of Yahweh in such persons (Jenni, "Nasiraer," 1309; Rylaarsdam, "Nazirite," 526), and no expression of human dedication to asceticism.

The following elements also seem to be traditional (though of uncertain age): the vow to be a Nazirite made by a person himself; the person's determination of the limited duration of the nazirate; the abstinence from dead bodies and unclean food (Judg 13:4, 7, 14), and probably a temporary nazirate of barren women (Weisman, 207-20).

Numbers 6:1-21 adapts most of these traditional notions, yet with critically important shifts and some new notions. While not excluding traditional alternatives the law focuses on two conditions under which persons become and are Nazirites: by their personal vow, and for a limited time. Under this aspect, the "marvel" lies in the vow (v. 2b) and not in the sign of the Nazirite's appearance. The reason and purpose for the vow are not mentioned (on the variety of reasons for vows cf. Jenni, "Nasiraer," 1309; Mayer, 333). However, the sin-offerings, guilt-offerings, and peace-offerings which are not documented for the traditional nazirate but which are required for its termination in the present law (vv. 14, 16) may indicate that the cause for the vow was an incurred sin or guilt. They point not just to the termination of the nazirate but to the ritual solution and termination through the nazirate of an especially deficient situation in a person's life which prompted the particular kind of vow for, and the submission to, the nazirate in the first place. This indication dovetails with the fact that a vow was always made for a certain reason and purpose. Should the reason for the vow be incurred sin and guilt, this kind of nazirate would be anything but a meritorious work. It might as well be an act of penitence.

The law intends, therefore, first and foremost to focus on the specific case of someone submitting to the nazirate by vow for a limited time, and to clarify precisely what is substantively and procedurally involved in such a case. For this case, the law applies to any man and — in its final edition (Kellermann, *Numeri,* 83, 95) — any woman, and not only to those elected by Yahweh. Its traditional stipulation concerning alcohol is radicalized through specifications and expansions. The same is true for the defilement of the hair through contact with the dead where the present law is even stricter than the law for the priests in Lev 21:1-4; Ezek 44:25, and through the drinking of wine, v. 20b after v. 18! Above all, while a presumable ritual initiating the nazirate is not mentioned — it is probably implied in the ritual declaration of the vow — the cases of its possible defilement and its actual termination are now strictly subject to cultic rituals performed and supervised by the priest. And at least its termination involves costly material offerings.

The fact that the present law on the nazirate is the only one in the Pentateuch, is the most comprehensive one in the OT, most probably had no predecessor of its kind, and represents amalgamation of traditional and new elements means little. What matters is the question whether this law is an updated edition that intends to cover the Nazirite phenomenon comprehensively by updating and in part replacing its traditional nature and the traditional prescriptions for it, or whether it focuses on one specific aspect only, namely the nazirate by vow for a limited duration (later, in the Mishnah Nazir 1:3; 6:3; cf. 1 Macc 3:49 just 30 days). In the first case, the priestly law would reflect a basically new religio-historical situation in which this specific type of nazirate was the only one left, replacing the older types, and in which the nazirate as a whole was to fall under the exclusive priestly jurisdiction and cultic ritual administration. In the latter case, the priestly law would reflect a supplement to the traditional prescriptions devised for only such persons whose nazirate was prompted by a particularly deficient situation which for its solution allowed as one of the required avenues the special vow for, and submission to, a limited nazirate. Because of the reason for the vow, removal of sin and guilt, this kind of nazirate would be just as much subject to cultic ritual prescriptions and procedures, especially those in vv. 9-12 and 13-20, as any other removal of sin and guilt. And the law would not only presuppose the literary context of the laws in Leviticus 1–15; it would add just another case to which those laws apply.

The question may for the time being remain open. Caution is in order against an assumption that the notion of Yahweh's freedom to raise Nazirites, even for life, was for the priests a matter of the past and had in their theology been replaced by the control of Yahweh through the cultic apparatus. Nevertheless, where a person's own decision to submit to the nazirate was involved, the law intends to define the legitimacy of this Yahweh-phenomenon among laypersons. In doing so it brings this phenomenon substantively and procedurally under the effective control of the Yahweh cult and its priests (Mayer, 333). And it wants to make sure that laypersons devoting themselves to being "holy to Yahweh" take their initiative seriously from the beginning to the end of their status (Keller, *"ndr,"* 40; Kaiser, 274). The prescriptions, old and new ones combined, aim at the radical and complete fulfillment of this exceptional vow to this exceptional kind of nazirate.

Finally, the incorporation of this law into the report of the Yahweh revelation at Sinai, after the law of jealousy, is not coincidental. It points to the critical importance of this exceptional case, too, for the Yahweh community envisioned by the priestly writers.

Bibliography

E. Gerstenberger, *Wesen und Herkunft des "apodiktischen Rechts"* (WMANT 20; Neukirchen: Neukirchener, 1965); E. Jenni, "Nasiraer," *RGG*3; O. Kaiser, *"nādar,"* *TWAT;* C. A. Keller, *"ndr,* geloben," *THAT;* J. Kühlewein, *"nāzîr,* Geweihter," *THAT;* G. Mayer, *"nzr,"* *TWAT;* J. Milgrom, "Nazirite," *EncJud;* W. Richter, *Recht und Ethos: Versuch einer Ortung des weisheitlichen Mahnspruches* (SANT 15; Munich: Kösel, 1966); J. C. Rylaarsdam, "Nazirite," *IDB;* Z. Weisman, "The Biblical Nazarite: Its Types and Roots," *Tarbiz* 36 (1967) 207-20 (Heb., Eng. summary, p. i).

Instruction about the Aaronide Blessing (6:22-27)

Structure

I. Introductory speech report formula 22
II. The instruction: the Yahweh speech to Moses 23-27
    A. The command (conveyance command formula) 23aα
    B. The content: the commission to bless 23aβ-27
        1. The commission proper 23aβ-26
            a. Commissioning formula 23aβ-b
            b. The formula of blessing 24-26
                1) Blessing and protection 24
                2) Countenance and grace 25
                3) Countenance and peace 26
        2. The commission interpreted 27

Again, the unit is a Yahweh speech report. After the introductory formula (I., v. 22), the Yahweh speech to Moses (II., vv. 23-27) covers the rest of the unit. It consists of the usual command to Moses to convey the instruction, here to the Aaronides (II.A., v. 23aα), and of the instruction itself (II.B., vv. 23aβ-27). The latter consists of a commission proper which addresses the Aaronides directly in the 2nd pers. pl. form (II.B.1., vv. 23aβ-26), and of a concluding interpretation of the commission concerning the Aaronides (II.B.2., v. 27). The commission proper is introduced by the commissioning formula "thus you shall bless . . ." (II.B.1.a., v. 23aβ-b), and then dictates the content, the formula of blessing, which the Aaronides are to speak when blessing Israel (II.B.1.b., vv. 24-26).

The formula of blessing consists of a series of three concisely formulated sentences of three, five, and seven words, respectively. It is based on the poetic form of parallelism which in this case is expanded to three complementary cola, a liturgical expression of comprehensiveness or completeness which itself is possibly caused by the threefold exclamation of Yahweh's name in the blessing. It is obviously formed for rhythmic, oral recitation. The different lengths of the three cola may well be understood as an ascending symmetry rather than as an asymmetric composition in need of reconstruction (cf. Fishbane, "Form and Reformulation," 115; Seybold, 18-23).

Each of the three sentences contains two verbal clauses whereby the second, shorter clause is always connected to the first with *wĕ,* "and," presupposing the subject expressed in the first clause after its opening verb: Yahweh, who is to grant the blessing. The verbs of all six clauses are generally assumed to be in the jussive form (exception: Jagersma) which points to the optative nature of the clauses, to wishes. The relationship of the two syndetically joined clauses in each sentence or colon is not self-evident. The clauses are not synonymous, and the sentences do not belong to the hendiadys type. Compared with Yahweh's act mentioned in each first clause, the second clause in each sentence refers either to a specific aspect already implied in the first act or to a different act in addition to the act mentioned first regardless whether such additional acts represent logical or chronological consequences of or complementations to the first acts. Passages such as Ps 67:2-3; Psalm 4; and Mal 1:6–2:9 which seem to depend directly on Num 6:24-26 (27) suggest an understanding of six, or three times two, different acts (cf. Fishbane, "Form and Reformulation," 116-19).

The content of the clauses underscores the reading of six different acts. For the closest translations cf. Fishbane, "Form and Reformulation," 115; and Freedman, "Aaronitic Benediction," 36. The wishes say first that Yahweh may bless *(bārak)* and protect *(šāmar)*. They refer to the granting of life and well-being, and to the protection in or from danger, or to Yahweh's blessing and saving acts (Westermann, 32-33; Miller, 247-48; Seybold, 49-51). They include the two situations of the ongoing life and its crises. The first colon seems to represent the basic statement in two aspects spanning the totality of sustained human life. Over against it, the following two sentences seem to belong together as a parallelistic expression which indicates how blessing and protection are given: "May Yahweh brighten his face toward you, and may he grant you grace/favor," and "May Yahweh raise his face toward you, and may he establish for you peace." The first clauses in both sentences are almost synonymous. Yahweh's face *(pānāyw)*, brightened and raised rather than sinister and lowered, turned toward the receivers *('ēlêkā)* rather than away from them, constitutes the presupposition for the second clauses. Its implication or consequence is that Yahweh offers grace and peace rather than judgment and wrath extending from the personal encounter into the receivers' sphere of life. In the total formula, the gifts of grace and peace appear to be the foci in which blessing and protection materialize.

The formula involves three identities: the speaking priest, Israel, and Yahweh. In addressing Israel (in 2nd pers. sing. form) the priest, by reciting the wish, defers to Yahweh who may grant to Israel what the formula says. The priest is the reciting agent, Yahweh the blessing agent.

The conclusion (II.B.2., v. 27), still spoken to Moses, interprets the formula as the laying of Yahweh's name upon Israel rather than as the gift of his blessing. And it promises Yahweh's blessing as the consequence of the exclamation of his name. The interpretive shift is unmistakable. Yet the conclusion confirms what the grammatical and rhetorical nature of the formula makes clear: that the blessing is exclusively Yahweh's reserve, that it is wished, and that its actualization is promised under the condition of the threefold enunciation of his name.

Genre

The unit is a Yahweh INSTRUCTION for the Aaronide priests about their blessing of Israel. Its redactional elements indicate that this priestly blessing is to be the recitation of a prescribed formula, and not a variable or impromptu formulation. This kind of formulaic nature of the Aaronide blessing is unique among all other forms of blessing in the history of Israel. The priests are to bless because and as they are instructed, and not autonomously. The text belongs to the genre of professional INSTRUCTION for priests, the genre of PRIESTLY DAʿAT. The

Yahweh instruction also indicates that not only the gift but also the formula of blessing itself is Yahweh's reserve.

The instructed recitation of the formula further indicates, besides its tight formal and substantive coherence, that the formula is the canonic blessing in which all forms of Israel's liturgical blessing culminate and from which they derive their validity. It represents the theological criterion for the tradition history of blessing in Israel. The formula itself is a unique systematic condensation of various elements from that tradition history, in Israel and the Ancient Near East. With the exception of its last clause, all other clauses are in essence found throughout the tradition history of blessing (cf. Keller and Wehmeier; Scharbert, "brk"; Seybold; Fishbane, "Form and Reformulation"; Miller; et al.).

The formula is a BLESSING WISH, or WISH FOR BLESSING, in which the speaker wishes to the hearer that a third party, in this case the deity, may fulfill the wish. As a wish, it is a particular form of statements about BLESSING, such as statements/reports about a blessing given or about a blessing promised as in v. 27.

The wish for blessing is no powerful or magic word through the recitation of which its content would be presently actualized or enacted, neither by the deity let alone by the speaker (Keller and Wehmeier, 372; et al.). Nor does the wish describe or define the past or present situation of the receivers, as in PRAISE SPEECHES or in the BLESSING *(bārûk)* FORMULA (Keller and Wehmeier, 355). It anticipates events and conditions henceforth, for the future. Its future fulfillment depends entirely on the independence of the divine giver of the blessing. Its recital does not enact the reality but defers it to the future enactment by Yahweh by whose instruction it is authorized, which it will have to execute, and whose promise for the fulfillment of the wish it trusts.

The BLESSING WISH may be addressed to Yahweh, as in PRAYER or PETITION, or, as in this case, to Israel, as a request for a gift of Yahweh on its behalf. The wish depends on its confinement as a wish, not on who is addressed. However, it must be distinguished from PROMISE and PREDICTION. While the wish itself leaves the certainty of its fulfillment open, this certainty is granted through Yahweh's promise that he will fulfill the wish whenever the priests put his name on Israel — which is separately added (v. 27) to the instruction.

In view of the proximity of the blessing to the function of powerful and magic words, and in view of the exceptional status of the Aaronide priests in the cult, it is remarkable that where the performance of their role offered the greatest temptation to enact the divine blessing themselves, they had to reserve the actualization of the blessing for Yahweh alone, thereby defining their own function as not more than conveyors of Yahweh's commission, and moreover as not more than expressing the commission as a wish the fulfillment of which depends just as much on Yahweh alone as its commission. Compared to the Israelites, the hierocratic position of the Aaronide priests is eminent. But compared to Yahweh, their hierocratic role is, though clearly authorized, subject to the theocratic authority.

Setting

Wishes for blessing belong to a variety of traditional settings (Keller and Wehmeier, 362-63; Scharbert, *"brk,"* 288-93; W. Schottroff, 163-98). They are not confined to the cult. But they have nevertheless an eminent setting in the history of Israel's worship, and in this setting they belonged to the tasks of the priests. In this setting, the widespread tradition of the wish for goodness was adapted and related to the exclamation of the name of Yahweh, which identified the source of all blessing. Yahweh's blessing of Israel through the priests was itself an institution (Westermann, 46-47).

The setting of the blessing in Num 6:24-26 must be sought at the conclusion and culmination of communal worship, together with a theophanic event, and before the worshiping pilgrims were sent on their way home. The key text for this understanding is Lev 9:22-24 (cf. Seybold, 55-62; Miller, 242; Fishbane, "Form and Reformulation," 116. About its subsequent history in the Jewish and Christian liturgies and literatures, cf. Fishbane, "Form and Reformulation," 118-21; Seybold, 9-17; including further references there).

The historical origin of this blessing is not known. It was certainly used in the liturgy of the — late — second temple period; cf. Ps 67:2-3. Several factors indicate, however, that it is older than the priestly work and was adopted by the priestly writers as an existing and probably already paradigmatic liturgical formula, integrated into their work at its present place in the Sinai pericope, and reserved for the Aaronide priests: Israel is in it addressed in the 2nd pers. sing. form, compared with the 2nd pers. pl. form in the redactional context; its formulaic language is "completely alien to the vocabulary of the Priestly Code" (Ruger, 332; also Kellermann, *Numeri*, 95). Its interpretation in v. 27 shifts the emphasis from Yahweh's work to Yahweh's name. The 2nd pers. sg. form in which the recipient is addressed may further indicate that this blessing wish was in its original setting at least also spoken to individuals, and not only to the community.

In the context of the priestly work, the Aaronide blessing belongs to the string of texts that emphasize the importance of the divine blessing for the world and Israel from Genesis 1 on (cf. Miller, 246, with general reference to Brueggeman). In this context, it may not be coincidental that the position of the text at the end of Numbers 6 (→ Chapter 2, Structure) reflects the place of the blessing at the end of the liturgy in worship.

Intention

By referring to the Sinaitic Yahweh command to Moses the instruction intends to establish that the formula of blessing recited by the Aaronide priests represents the most authentic blessing in Israel's liturgy and their privileged commission and prerogative.

The blessing wish itself intends to assure the assembled congregation, corporately and individually, of Yahweh's promise and its own hope that the contents of the formula already experienced in the sanctuary worship will extend into its ongoing life after the worship. The blessing wish in Num 6:24-26 marks the transition for pilgrims from their experience of Yahweh's blessing and name in the sanctuary to the same experience in their daily lives — culminating in peace.

Bibliography

P. A. H. de Boer, "Numbers vi,27," *VT* 32 (1982) 3-13; E. L. Ehrlich, "Ueber den Priestersegen," *Tradition und Erneuerung* 34 (1972) 6-9; M. Fishbane, "Form and Reformulation of the Biblical Priestly Blessing," *JAOS* 103 (1983) 115-21; D. N. Freedman, "The Aaronic Benediction (Numbers 6:24-26)," in *No Famine in the Land* (*Fest.* J. L. McKenzie; ed. J. W. Flanagan et al.; Missoula: Scholars, 1975) 35-48; H. Jagersma, "Some Remarks on the Jussive in Numbers 6,24-26," in *Von Kanaan bis Kerala* (*Fest.* J. P. M. van der Ploeg; ed. W. C. Delsman et al.; AOAT 211; Neukirchen: Neukirchener, 1982) 131-36; C. A. Keller and G. Wehmeier, "*brk,* pi. segnen," *THAT;* O. Loretz, "Altorientalischer Hintergrund sowie inner- und nachbiblische Entwicklung des aaronitischen Segens (Num 6,24-26)," *UF* 10 (1978) 115-19; P. D. Miller, "The Blessing of God: An Interpretation of Numbers 6:22-27," *Int* 29 (1975) 240-51; H. P. Ruger, "Some Remarks on the Priestly Blessing," *BT* 28 (1977) 332-35; J. Scharbert, "*brk,*" *TDOT;* W. Schottroff, *Der altisraelitische Fluchspruch* (WMANT 30; Neukirchen: Neukirchener, 1969); K. Seybold, *Der aaronitische Segen: Studien zu Numeri 6,22-27* (Neukirchen: Neukirchener, 1977); H.-J. Stoebe, "Der aaronitische Segen, 4 Mose 6:22-27," *Evangelisches Missions-Magazin,* vol. 113 (Basel: Basileia Verlag, 1969) 24-26 and 50-53; C. Westerman, *Der Segen in der Bibel und im Handeln der Kirche* (Munich: Chr. Kaiser Verlag, 1968) 32-33.

Report of the Gifts of the Tribal Leaders (7:1-89)

Structure

I. Moses' actions	1
A. Circumstance: the tabernacle erected	1aα₁
B. Anointment and consecration of tabernacle and altar	1aα₂-b
1. Expressed specifically: two actions and objects	1aα₂-aβ
2. Expressed summarily	1b
II. The leaders' subsequent gifts	2-88
A. For the tabernacle	2-9
1. The gifts brought	2-3
a. Definition of the leaders	2
b. Definition of the offerings	3
2. Distribution of the gifts through Moses	4-9
a. The Yahweh command	4-5
b. Moses' compliance	6-9
B. For the initiation of the altar	10-88
1. The initial approach: all gifts on one day	10

2. Its modification: gifts on twelve days   11-83
  a. The Yahweh instruction to Moses   11
  b. The compliance by the leaders   12-83
    1) Day 1: Nahshon of Judah   12-17
    2) Day 2: Nethanel of Issachar   18-23
    3) Day 3: Eliab of Zebulun   24-29
    4) Day 4: Elizur of Reuben   30-35
    5) Day 5: Shelumiel of Simeon   36-41
    6) Day 6: Eliasaph of Gad   42-47
    7) Day 7: Elishama of Ephraim   48-53
    8) Day 8: Gamaliel of Manasseh   54-59
    9) Day 9: Abidan of Benjamin   60-65
    10) Day 10: Ahiezer of Dan   66-71
    11) Day 11: Pagiel of Asher   72-77
    12) Day 12: Ahira of Naphtali   78-83
1. and 2. Summary statement   84-88
  a. Introductory definition (superscription)   84a
  b. The totals of the specified offerings   84b-88a
    1) Metals, partly with incense   84b-86
    2) For the burnt-offering *('ōlâ)*   87aα-aβ1
    3) For the cereal offering *(minḥâ)*   87aβ2
    4) For the purification offering *(ḥaṭṭā't)*   87b
    5) For the peace offering *(zebaḥ haššĕlāmîm)*   88a
  c. Concluding definition (subscription)   88b
III. Statement about theophanic event: the voice   89

The structural division between I. (v. 1) and II. (vv. 2-88) rests on a translation of v. 1 that differs from most of the traditional translations and agrees with LXX and de Vaux. Instead of reading all of v. 1 as a circumstantial introduction to the main report from v. 2 on, it considers the circumstantial clause confined to v. 1aα1 and reads: "On the day when Moses had finished erecting the tabernacle, he anointed and consecrated it." Syntactically, either translation is possible. The preference for the revised translation rests above all on the fact that Numbers 7 reports about events that were not reported in Exodus 40. Exod 40:16-33 fails to report that Moses had anointed and consecrated the tabernacle and the altar, despite a Yahweh command to do so (Exod 40:9-10). This omission in the text implies Moses' potentially serious twofold violation of obedience and of the sacrificial usage of the altar (v. 29) without its prior anointment and consecration! In the traditional translation of Num 7:1aα2-b, the text is assumed to say that Moses had executed Yahweh's command even though it was not reported. In the revised translation the text is assumed to refer in v. 1aα1 to what had been reported in Exod 40:18-28, and to update Exod 40:16-33 by supplementing in v. 1aα2-b important information not given in that text. Num 7:1aα2-b presently reports that Moses did anoint and consecrate the tabernacle and the altar "on the day of completing the erecting of the tabernacle." This report constitutes the first part of Numbers 7. It is set apart from and precedes its second part which reports about the subsequent events, until v. 12 also on that day.

The main part (II., vv. 2-88) shifts from Moses' actions to those of the twelve tribal leaders. In two sections it reports about their gifts for the same two objects just anointed and consecrated: the tabernacle (II.A., vv. 2-9), and the altar (II.B., vv. 10-88).

The first section (II.A., vv. 2-9) distinguishes between the bringing of the gifts (II.A.1., vv. 2-3) and their subsequent distribution through Moses among the Levites at Yahweh's command (II.A.2., vv. 4-9). The leaders are summarily reintroduced (→ Numbers 1–2), and their gift reported, also summarily: "six covered wagons and twelve oxen, a wagon for every two of the leaders, and for each one an ox." The distributive statement emphasizes that each leader contributed an equal share, despite the different sizes of the tribes (→ Numbers 1). These gifts for the tabernacle were placed before Yahweh and before the tabernacle (v. 3). With perfect consistency, Yahweh assigns their acceptance and distribution to Moses (II.A.2.a., vv. 4-5), with instructions concerning their purpose and their recipients, the Levites. In turn, Moses complies (II.A.2.b., vv. 6-9), in v. 6 literally with the instruction from vv. 4-5, and in vv. 7-9 under specific consideration of the assignments of the three levitical families already reported in → Num 4:1-33. The section vv. 2-9 once again supplements relevant information not given in Exodus 40. As soon as the establishment of the tabernacle is complete, the equipment for its transport is provided. The section is once again generated by the concept of the alternation between encampment and march (→ Numbers 2; → Numbers 3–4).

While section II.A. (vv. 2-9) is short, section II.B. (vv. 10-88) pays enormous attention to the gifts for the initiation of the altar (cf. Exod 27:1-8; 38:1-7; 40:29; Num 7:1aα₂-b). It supplements information not given but necessarily presupposed for Exod 40:29 already, and even more so for Leviticus 1–9. In view of this context it had to connect also this event with the events reported in Exodus 40, which it does outright in v. 10.

This section distinguishes between what in hindsight appears to be the original approach (II.B.1., v. 10), its immediate modification (II.B.2., vv. 11-83), and a summary (II.B.1.+2., vv. 84-88), which lists the sum total of the materials specifically listed in vv. 11-83 but links up with the date given in v. 10 as if the dates given in vv. 11-83 were nonexistent. Whether the entire text comes from the hand of the same writer (Kellermann, *Numeri,* 110) may remain open. It is possible that an older statement v. 10 was secondarily expanded by vv. 11-83, based on the list of the tribal leaders in → Numbers 1–2.

In the extant text, the leaders referred to in v. 2 bring also their gifts for the initiation of the altar (*ḥănukkat hammizbēaḥ,* v. 10) on the day of its anointment and consecration. Just as the gifts for the tabernacle were placed before the tabernacle, so the gifts for the altar were placed before the altar (v. 10). As in vv. 4-5, Yahweh answers with an instruction (v. 11). In contrast to vv. 4-5, however, where the Yahweh command causes the processing of the gifts via Moses to the Levites, the instruction in v. 11 intervenes in the process by demanding that the twelve leaders bring their gifts individually on twelve consecutive days. It stops the original approach by starting in II.B.2.a. (v. 11) a modified approach the compliance to which is then reported in II.B.2.b. (vv. 12-83). It is a matter of conjecture why Yahweh wants the transformation from a one-day to a twelve-day event. Yahweh's intervention is certainly no expression of protest against the leaders' uncalled-for initiative. Yahweh accepts their initiative, and only modifies the procedure. The reason for this modified procedure may point to more than the contextual aspect of the distributive presentation of the tribes and their leaders in Numbers 1–2. It may reflect a traditio-historical reality according to which Israel's tribal leaders were known to present their gifts to the central sanctuary, particularly on special occasions. The most direct reason, however, seems to lie in the text itself, namely, in the unusually large amount of all gifts which created a logistical problem that had to be solved by a day-by-day procedure.

The compliance report II.B.2.b. (vv. 12-83) consists of twelve passages, in principle identically formulated except for the names of the leaders and their tribes. Because of the consecutively receding narrative introductions from v. 12 via v. 18 to v. 24, the case of the third day may serve as a basis for the discussion of the patterned structure of all twelve passages. After the introductory statement about the day and the leader, in this case Eliab of Zebulun [II.B.2.b.3)a), v. 24], the CATALOGUE of the gifts follows [II.B.2.b.3)b), vv. 25-29a]. After a short formal reference to "his gift" [qorbānô, II.B.2.b.3)b)(1), v. 25aα$_1$] the catalogue is organized in II.B.2.b.3)b)(2) [vv. 25aα$_2$-29a] according to five types of offerings, basically for sacrifices: (a) for the cereal offering (minḥâ): listing two silver plates and their weight, together with flour and oil, and with a statement of their purpose, v. 25aα$_2$-b; (b) incense (qeṭōret): a golden dish filled with incense, v. 26; (c) for the burnt-offering ('ōlâ): listing three animal objects and their purpose, v. 27; (d) for the purification offering (ḥaṭṭā't): listing one animal object and its purpose, v. 28; (e) for the peace offering (zebaḥ haššĕlāmîm): listing the purpose and four types of animal objects. The passage concludes with a subscription in v. 29b.

Again, as in vv. 2-3, each leader gives the same types and amount of gifts. The aspect of a possibly different economic basis among the leaders or their tribes plays no role. They offer what corresponds to their equal status at the altar, and not what their economic potential allows individually. The picture is probably abstract and idealized.

The gifts themselves, as those in vv. 2-3, are brought in response to a pre-determined need, and not at random. In distinction from the materials elicited in Exod 25:2-7; 35:4-9; and brought in Exod 35:10-29 for the construction of the tabernacle and its vessels, the gifts in Num 7:10-88 consist of the objects for the initiation of the sacrificial cult. Except for the objects for the cereal offering and the incense, which is not a sacrificial offering but is connected with the cereal offering, all objects given are sacrificial animals. The unit II.B. (vv. 10-88) presupposes the need for the previously unreported provision of the materials for the initiation of the sacrificial system at Sinai, and reports the complete delivery of that provision.

Mentioned are the essential types of sacrifices, whereas supplementary sacrifices such as drink offerings (nesek), wave offerings (tĕnûpâ), or consecration offerings (millu'îm) are left out. Also unmentioned is the guilt offering ('āšām) which plays a role in, among others, → Num 5:11-31 and → 6:1-21. The types of sacrifices mentioned represent the core of the tradition history of

Israel's sacrificial system (cf. Milgrom, "Sacrifices," *IDBSup,* 763-71). The sequence in which the gifts are listed reflects a late stage in that tradition history, albeit not the latest one in which the sin or purification offering *(ḥaṭṭā't)* stands at the beginning. The sequence in the extant text is a singular variation of the second latest stage in which the burnt offering ranks before the cereal offering (cf. Rendtorff, *Studien,* 6-37, esp. 31-37). The reason for this singular reversal is not quite clear. It may have been caused by the contextual view of the impending march in which the plates (v. 25) had to be carried by the Kohathites (v. 9) in front of the sanctuary (Rendtorff, *Studien,* 19), but also as in vv. 84-88 by the distinction between metallic vessels and their weight and between animals which allowed for the juxtaposition of the animal objects in one block. The aspect of the impending march is problematic if the gifts are for the initiation of the altar before the march. Finally, the types of animals for the *'ōlâ* (v. 27) and the *zebaḥ haššĕlāmîm* (v. 29a) are apparently listed in the order of their size, from the biggest to the smallest. The text is carefully organized according to an established system of classifications of animals. It is based on the CATALOGUE form.

Section II.B.1.+2. (vv. 84-88) summarizes the totals of the specified types of offerings. This subunit not only combines the information about a one-day event in v. 10 with the amounts given during twelve days in vv. 12-88; it also lists the cereal offering after the burnt offering, contrary to the pattern in vv. 12-83. Indeed, it appends the cereal offering to the burnt offering, thereby disassociating the materials for it from its vessels, also contrary to vv. 12-83. And it summarizes at the outset (vv. 84b-86) the catalogue of the vessels alone, which turns out to be longer than the catalogue of the animals in vv. 87-88a. It is difficult to assume that vv. 84-88 come from the same hand that accounts for vv. 11-83. The summary corresponds to the types of summaries found in → 1:44-46; 2:32-33; 3:39, 43; and 4:46-49.

The entire report is in III. (v. 89) concluded by a statement which reflects the tradition of theophanic language. Rather than belonging to the next unit (Budd) the statement seems to be a signal by which the writer indicates once more that the events just reported belong specifically to the events reported in Exod 40:1-33, and by which he updates Exod 40:35 by emphasizing that Moses indeed went into the tent of meeting where the voice spoke to him. However, rather than being a criticism of the older version in Exod 40:35, the later updating in 7:89 seems to be based on a reason. When understanding Exod 40:16-35 from the perspective of Num 7:1 it appeared that Moses could not yet enter the tabernacle because it had only been erected but not yet anointed and consecrated. Indeed, Yahweh's own theophany without the sanctuary's dedication must have appeared problematic from that perspective. Thus, Exod 40:35, seen from Num 7:1, appeared to state a logical consequence from Moses' omission, and no longer Moses' principal inability to meet Yahweh's theophanic presence as in the original Exodus text. However, after Moses was said in Num 7:1 to have dedicated the tabernacle, not only could Yahweh speak but Moses could also speak to Yahweh and hear his voice "in the tent of meeting." Finally, the statement must belong to that layer of the priestly Sinai pericope, programmatically represented by Lev 1:1, according to which after the erection and now also the anointment and consecration of the tabernacle/tent of meeting Yahweh spoke to Moses from this place and no longer from the mountain.

Genre

The unit is a haggadic supplement to the report of the erection of the tabernacle in Exodus 40. It reports about events uniquely related to that situation. All signals indicate that the unit focuses on that one-time event, its moment, situation, and need, and not on patterns of permanent cultic customs. The composition ties the unit together through its focus on the needs for the tabernacle and the altar at Sinai. And Moses' consecration of both in part I. (v. 1) corresponds to the leaders' subsequent (v. 88: "after") gifts for both in part II. (vv. 2-88). Even so, the composition is a literary creation. Its major components of vv. 2-3, 4-9, 10-88, and 89 do not inherently belong together.

The composite literary nature shows that the unit as a whole does not belong to a particular narrative genre. The question is not sufficiently researched as to what extent its components belong to narrative genres. This question must be distinguished from the possibility that the reported actions reflect known customs of actual events or institutionalized procedures related to the cult, i.e., actual settings rather than generic narratives about them.

Verse 1 reflects the actual widespread tradition of the anointment and consecration of persons and objects for cultic services, certainly also of sanctuaries and altars. To this extent, v. 1 projects the institutional realities back into the Sinai event. Such events were certainly important. But a type of narrative specifically describing such procedures is hard to come by. Lev 8:10-11 is a parallel to Num 7:1 from a different context. If such a type or genre of anointment and consecration reports existed, the two references would represent a form of abstract summaries derived from such reports.

Generic narratives about gifts for the transport of an entire sanctuary — its vessels are carried on the shoulders — are even less to be expected. 2 Samuel 6 provides an example for the ark being driven by a new cart (vv. 3-4) pulled by oxen which stumbled (v. 6). But nothing is said as to who provided that cart, quite apart from the fact that the ark is in that chapter and elsewhere also borne by human carriers (vv. 13, 17). On the question of the transport of the entire sanctuary cf. → Numbers 3–4.

The section about the gifts for the initiation of the altar in vv. 10-88 may be different. For a precise focus, it is necessary to state that the text reports about the gifts for, and not about the act of the initiation of, the altar. It relates an event that precedes the initiation and makes it possible. This event is non-cultic and pre-cultic. All gifts are given for the first operation of the altar. The translation of *ḥanukkat hammizbēaḥ* in v. 10 "dedication of the altar" (NRSV et al.) is at least unclear if not misleading. "Dedication" may refer to a ceremony before the first sacrificial operation, as in Num 7:1. The chapter, and v. 88b explicitly, makes it clear that anointment and consecration of the altar precede the gifts for its *ḥannukâ,* which itself can take place only after the gifts were given, at least twelve days later! As in many late texts, *ḥannukâ* in

Num 7:10, 11, 84, and 88 refers therefore to the initiation, i.e., the first usage of the altar (cf. Deut 20:5; 1 Kgs 8:62-64; 2 Chr 7:4-7, 9; Ezra 6:16-19; 1 Macc 4:56; 2 Macc 10:1-9).

However, since the text is a report about the gifst for such an initiation and not about the initiation itself, its generic nature, if any, must be sought in the tradition of such gifts and reports about them. This specification is confirmed by the fact that vv. 10-88 place the event after the events related in Exodus 40 but before the events related in Leviticus 1–7 and especially in Leviticus 8–9. The report reflects neither a compulsory tax nor a support system for the ongoing sacrificial operation. It does not even presuppose a Yahweh command. It presupposes the leaders' own voluntary initiative for a special type of occasion: the initiation of the sacrificial altar as the beginning of the sacrificial cult. It is a variation of the tradition of the free-will offering *(nĕdābâ)* which is frequently mentioned in the OT and which represents one-time events. It varies from such offerings, e.g., the vow offering *(neder),* in which the offerers determine the kind and amount of their gifts themselves. By contrast, the leaders in Numbers 7 offer voluntarily what is needed for the initiation of the altar. They respond to that need in kind and amount, and equally. Such free-will offerings for one-time, major, pan-Israelite events were obviously not expected often. But when they were needed, they were important because of the historical importance of the event, and as signs of support by the tribes as the Yahweh community, and not of especially imposed taxation. Haggai illustrates the need for such free-will contributions, their impediments, the inability of the priests to enforce them by way of taxation, and their eventual prophetically inspired charismatic happening. The extent to which Num 7:10-88 reflects the settings of such gifts for the needs of the initiation *(ḥannukâ)* of such major institutions, especially cultic ones, points to the history of real institutional events. It is analogous to Exod 35:10-29, and is a variation of the overall genre of REPORTS or records of FREE-WILL VOWS or FREE-WILL GIFTS. Specifically, it belongs to a sub-genre of records of DEDICATION GIFTS or OFFERINGS or INITIATION GIFTS or OFFERINGS *(Einweihungsopfer).* Num 7:10-88 portrays one of the two prototypes of such gifts at Sinai.

Setting

The unit owes its existence to those late priestly writers who had the text at least of Exodus 25–Leviticus 9 before them, and who supplemented it with information about events not reported in it but which were felt to be necessary for a complete understanding of the coherence of the events.

The writers drew on some actual settings from traditions all of which belong to rites or acts at or before the assumption of a cultic operation.

The report about the gifts for the initiation of the altar reveals unique elements that must be attributed to the writers' configuration of the unique Sinai scenario. But it also reveals typical elements the most important of which is the catalogue form for the systematized registration of the gifts needed for the sacrificial system. This form was most probably used for the management of ongoing operations as well as for one-time events, and for taxes as well as for free-will contributions especially from groups. It listed the identity of the givers, and in accordance with the system of the setting in which the gifts were used it systematically ordered the kinds and amounts of their contributions. It represents the managerial link between the (cultic) operation and the supporters of its needs. Its settings must be sought in the administrations or managements of such operations. The tradition of this form is known from innumerable "lists" of deposits in the Ancient Near East. The pan-Israelite aspect in Numbers 7 suggests that such gifts or contributions must have been used in the administration especially of the Jerusalem temple. And the monotonous repetitiveness of this catalogue points above all else to the usage of this traditional form, and not to the stylistic individuality of the priestly writers.

Finally, by using traditional elements from various settings the writers augmented the view of the typical events in the Sinai setting itself. That singular setting was paradigmatic because it was the foundation of all subsequent settings.

Intention

The unit intends first of all to give necessary supplementary information to the preceding context. It intends to update the existing text. In doing so it intends, second, to make explicit Moses' scrupulous obedience to a Yahweh command (and his attention to cultic requirements!), and especially to highlight the autogenous responsibility of the tribal leaders, their initiative born out of their free decision. At the same time, it intends to highlight their own knowledge of the immediate specific needs of the tabernacle and its altar, a knowledge not dictated by the priests.

In meticulously listing the same gifts by all leaders it intends, third, to point to their and their tribes' equal status before the tabernacle and altar, regardless of their different economic potential and political influence. In summarizing the totality of the gifts it intends, fourth, to show the sufficiency of the gifts for the transport of the tabernacle and especially their abundance for the initiation of the altar. This abundance considerably exceeds the number of animals said in Leviticus 8–9 to have been used. Also, the text may by its emphasis especially on the gifts for the altar imply how important the sacrificial cult was considered by the laity for their own benefit. Finally, the report intends to show the gifts for the Sinai tabernacle and its altar as the ideal paradigm for such support, specifically at similar occasions, but by implication also for their ongoing operation.

Report about the Lamps of the Lampstand (8:1-4)

Structure

I. Concerning the correct position of the lamps	1-3
A. The Yahweh command to Moses	1-2
1. Introductory speech report formula	1
2. The command to instruct Aaron	2
a. Conveyance command formula	2a
b. The content	2b
B. Aaron's compliance	3
1. Compliance report formula	3aα
2. Report proper with compliance correspondence formula	3aβ-b
II. Appendix: a summary repetition concerning the making of the lampstand	4

The unit is composite. Its first part (I., vv. 1-3) reports about the correct positioning of the seven lamps *(hannērōt)* upon the lampstand *(hammĕnôrâ)*. It opens with a Yahweh command to Moses (I.A., vv. 1-2), which is introduced with the usual speech report formula. Moses is to instruct Aaron to cause the lamps — metonymy for their light(s); cf. *mā'ôr* in Exod 27:20a; Lev 24:2a — to shine toward the front side of the lampstand when "lifting" them. "Lifting" *(ha'ălōt)* is used in synecdoche for two related actions: when literally lifting the lamps one by one and putting each upon one of the seven arms of the lampstand Aaron must set them so as to incline them toward the hall of the tent, and not upright or toward its wall.

The first part concludes with the compliance report (I.B., v. 3), which begins in I.B.1. (v. 3aα) with the formal statement in the compliance report formula. This statement is followed by the substantive explication (I.B.2., v. 3aβ-b), which is concluded by the reference to the correspondence of the compliance with Yahweh's command to Moses (compliance correspondence formula).

Part II. (v. 4) is an appendix caused by the reference in the first part to the lampstand and to Aaron's action. It is a summary repetition of the execution report about the lampstand in Exod 37:17-24.

Genre

Numbers 8:1-3 is a short REPORT about a specific element of a LITURGICAL PROCEDURE. This procedure is different from clerical work. It involves one of the consecrated vessels, is ceremoniously performed in a sevenfold act, and is reserved for the priests alone to whose liturgical tasks it belongs. The report documents the initiation of this procedure through its first-time execution by Aaron in direct compliance with Yahweh's instruction to Moses. It constitutes the normative basis for the permanent observance of this procedure in conjunction with the permanent liturgical requirements for the entire lampstand and its lamps (cf. Exod 27:20-21; Lev 24:1-4).

Setting

The report belongs to the setting of the Aaronide priestly writers. And the reported procedure is connected with either the projected or the already existing lampstand (and its seven lamps) of the second temple. Cf. Zech 4:2, in contrast to the ten lampstands with presumably one lamp for each in 1 Kgs 7:49. In the latter, more likely case, the report would point to the normative prototype for the priests of the second temple concerning their correct positioning of the lamps of its lampstand with respect to both Yahweh's instruction and its literal execution.

Intention

In contrast to v. 4, to Exod 25:31-36, and (in part) to Exod 27:20-21 and Lev 24:1-4, Num 8:1-3 is not concerned with the lampstand *(měnôrâ)*. Nor is it concerned with the oil and wicks for the lamps (Exod 27:20; Lev 24:2), nor with the lifting of a continual lamp (Exod 27:20b; Lev 24:2b) or the lifting of the lamps as such, nor with keeping the lamp(s) in order from evening to morning *('ārak;* Exod 27:21; Lev 24:3-4; NRSV: "tend").

Verses 1-3 are concerned with one aspect only: the correct positioning of the seven lamps *(šib'at hannērôt)* when Aaron lifts them *(běha'ălōtkā)* upon the lampstand so that they shine *(yā'îrû)* toward the front side of the lampstand *('el-mûl pĕnê hammĕnôrâ)*.

This concern apparently presupposes the differences among (1) the erection of the lampstand together with the erection *(hēqîm)* of the tabernacle and its vessels, cf. Exod 40:16-33; (2) the lifting *(ha'ălōt)* of the seven lamps upon the arms of the lampstand; and (3) the ongoing keeping *('ārak)* of the lights of the lamps through their — daily — resupply with oil and wicks by the priests. And it focuses on a specific act that is related to the second presupposition. This specific aspect further presupposes that the lamps can be individually removed from the lampstand and are not affixed to it permanently.

The text is not explicit on whether it refers to a one-time lifting for the permanent positioning of the lamps, or to their repeated lifting in the sense of "when*ever* you lift," v. 2bα. The alternative depends on whether the lamps are refilled while in permanent position, or whether they are taken down whenever being refilled. Should the latter procedure be the case, specific attention to their ever new correct positioning would be necessary. The aspect of such a possibly daily reoccurring procedure would help to explain why this particular instruction was important enough to be included in the Sinai pericope.

The text assigns this task only to Aaron, and not to his sons as in Exod 27:20-21 and Lev 24:1-4. It does not refer to "a permanent statute" *(ḥuqqat 'ôlām)* as those passages do. It seems that it envisions the lifting and positioning either as a one-time act by Aaron, or as the beginning by Aaron of a continual order. In either case, the lifting of the lamps upon the lampstand cannot be understood as a part of the erection of the vessels and their tabernacle. It is reserved for the priest Aaron, whereas the tabernacle is erected by Moses and then the Levites. It points to a particular liturgical act that presupposes that the tabernacle and its vessels already stand and are anointed and consecrated. It is preferable to assume that in addressing Aaron alone the text refers to the initial liturgical act of Aaron's correct positioning of the lamps. Exod 27:20-21 and Lev 24:1-4 would then reflect, among others, the extension of this task to the Aaronides. This meaning would explain why Num 8:1-3, 4 follows Numbers 7 which is also concerned with — the preparation for — an initiation, the initiation of the altar in the court.

The text does not explain why the lamps must shine "toward the front" of the lampstand. The lampstand was placed on the south side of the tabernacle (Exod 40:24). The lights apparently had to throw light at the hall, and especially at the golden altar in its center before the veil (Exod 40:26).

Most important, however, is the fact that Num 8:1-3 focuses on the two aspects that were not covered in the previous texts about the lampstand and its lamps. The compliance report in 8:3 finally states what was not, and for good reasons could not, be reported in Exod 37:23-24, namely, that Aaron *executed* what Yahweh had in Exod 25:37b commanded to be done. This compliance report was generated by the as yet unfulfilled Yahweh command of Exod 25:37b.

The Yahweh command for *Aaron* in Num 8:2 clarifies or changes what had not even been said in the previous Yahweh command in Exod 25:37b itself. That text relates either an impersonal instruction (MT; NRSV; et al.) or an instruction for Moses (LXX, et al.), but not for Aaron. Depending on the textual version of Exod 25:37b, Num 8:2 either clarifies that impersonal instruction or it changes an original instruction for Moses to an instruction for Aaron. The lack of clarity in the previous instruction is in either case the reason for a new Yahweh command.

Both the elements of the new Yahweh command for Aaron and of his compliance in Num 8:1-3 were generated with respect to Exod 25:37b which thus far had left two problems open. The combination of both aspects in the one report of Num 8:1-3 is the result of the writers' scrupulous attention to the text at their hands, and is not coincidental.

Num 8:1-3 specifically intends at least to supplement, and possibly to replace in part, the content of Exod 25:37b. Num 8:4, the summary repetition of Exod 37:17-24, is appended to v. 3, probably to show that Aaron's compliance is an extension into the liturgical application of the making of the entire lampstand already completed by Moses.

The Report about the Installation of the Levites (8:5-22)

Structure

I. The Yahweh speech to Moses   5-19
  A. Introductory speech report formula   5
  B. The command concerning the Levites   6-19
    1. The prescription for their installation   6-13

      a. Their purification   6-12

1) Expressed basically   6

2) Expressed specifically: the ritual   7-12

a) Formal charge as to procedure   7aα

b) The procedure prescribed   7aβ-12

(1) The water ceremony   7aβ-b

(a) Moses: To sprinkle water of purification   7aβ

(b) The Levites: to shave, wash clothes and
themselves   7b

(2) The sacrificial ceremony   8-12

(a) To take the materials   8

α. The Levites: a young bull and its
minḥâ   8a

β. Moses: a young bull for purification
offering   8b

(b) To lay the hands upon Levites   9-10

α. Preparation by Moses   9-10a

aa. To bring Levites before tent   9a

bb. To assemble congregation   9b

cc. To bring Levites before Yahweh   10a

β. Israelites to lay hands upon Levites   10b

(c) Aaron: to dedicate Levites before Yahweh   11

(d) The sacrifices   12

α. Levites: to put hands on bulls   12a

β. Moses: to sacrifice them   12b

     b. The ritual of their dedication by Moses   13

1) Presentation by Moses to Aaron   13a

2) Dedication to Yahweh   13b

   2. Concluding interpretation   14-19

     a. Concerning the previous actions   14-15

1) Moses to separate Levites from Israelites for
Yahweh   14

2) Levites to work at tent of meeting after
purification and dedication   15

     b. The salvation-historical reason   16-19

1) Status of Levites   16

2) Reason for the status   17-19

a) Basic statement   17a

b) The historical etiology   17b-19

II. The compliance   20-22

  A. Expressed basically   20

  B. Expressed specifically   21-22

   1. Concerning their installation (vv. 6-13)   21

     a. By the Levites (v. 7b)   21aα

     b. By Aaron (v. 13b)   21aβ

     c. By Aaron (v. 12b)   21b

   2. Concerning the beginning of work (v. 15)   22

Num 8:5-22 is in structure and content distinguished from the following unit, 8:23-26. The two units are separate.

The extant text of 8:5-22 is a report in two parts, a Yahweh speech to Moses (I., vv. 5-19), and the compliance (II., vv. 20-22). Their combination is influenced by the context. It expresses the Sinaitic ideal. Yet while the compliance report is short and summary, the disproportionate length of the text belongs to the Yahweh speech to Moses. Moses' compliance is an event at its time; Yahweh's command given once in the initial situation reaches beyond this situation into the generations of the writers. The entire text reports a new event not related before.

After the reporter's introduction (I.A., v. 5), Yahweh gives Moses a command concerning the Levites (I.B., vv. 6-19). The command contains the prescription for the procedure of their installation (I.B.1., vv. 6-13), and a concluding interpretation (I.B.2., vv. 14-19). The prescribed installation consists of two parts: the long ritual of purification (I.B.1.a., vv. 6-12) and the short ritual of dedication of the purified Levites (I.B.1.b., v. 13). Their purification is prescribed basically [I.B.1.a.1), v. 6], i.e., "take . . . and purify" the Levites *(qaḥ . . . wĕṭihartā),* and specifically [I.B.1.a.2), vv. 7-12].

The specific prescription is again introduced by a formal reference to the commanded procedure [I.B.1.a.2)a), v. 7aα], and the procedure is finally unfolded in I.B.1.a.2)b) [vv. 7aβ-12]. It consists of two major parts. In a preparatory water ceremony [I.B.1.a.2)b)(1), v. 7aβ-b], Moses is first to sprinkle "the water of purification" *(mê ḥaṭṭā't)* on them, and the Levites have to shave their bodies and to wash their clothes and themselves. It is not clear whether Moses' sprinkling precedes the following separate washing or whether he keeps sprinkling as the Levites wash. It is a known tradition among the Arabs to wash at least their hands under running and not in standing water, which becomes dirty.

The water ceremony is followed by the main sacrificial ceremony [I.B.1.a.2)b)(2), vv. 8-12]. It consists in the extant text of four steps: the bringing of specified sacrificial materials by the Levites and by Moses [(a), v. 8], the laying of hands upon the Levites by the Israelites [(b), vv. 9-10], the dedication of the Levites before Yahweh by Aaron [(c), v. 11], and the sacrifices of the young bulls previously brought for a purification offering and a burnt offering, to effect atonement for the Levites — again by Moses [(d), v. 12]. The two sacrifices are introduced by the Levites who put *(sāmak)* their hands on each bull.

In the total procedure, Moses and the Levites interact in the water ceremony (v. 7aβ-b) and also in the first and fourth steps of the sacrificial ceremony (vv. 8, 12), whereas the actors in its second step (vv. 9-10) are Moses and the Israelites, and in its third step (v. 11), Aaron alone.

After their purification, Moses is first to present the Levites *(wĕha'ămadtā)* to the Aaronides [I.B.1.b.1), v. 13a], and then to dedicate them to Yahweh [wĕhēnaptā 'ōtām tĕnûpâ lĕyhwh, I.B.1.b.2), v. 13b].

The following section I.B.2. (vv. 14-19) is a concluding interpretation of the preceding prescription, in part still under the form of the Yahweh command to Moses. It reviews the previous procedure, including v. 15b (Kellermann, *Numeri,* 118), with regard to its two major functions: Moses is to separate the Levites from the Israelites, and the Levites are to go to work at the tent of meeting (I.B.2.a., vv. 14-15). It concludes with a theological motivation, a salvation-historical etiology, most of which repeats → Num 3:11-13.

The compliance report (II., vv. 20-22) states basically that Moses, Aaron, and all the congregation of Israel did as Yahweh had commanded (expanded compliance report formula; II.A., v. 20). In a specified listing of their actions it combines aspects from the installation text (vv. 6-13) and the concluding interpretation (vv. 14-19). But it proceeds selectively, summarily, and with some changes.

Despite its steady forward movement and considerable coherence the text shows signs of a literary growth process that at points has led to internal conflicts. In addition to what has already been said about the varying participants, the following must be pointed out: in vv. 10-13, Yahweh is referred to in the 3rd pers., whereas he (v. 5) refers in vv. 14-19 to himself in the 1st pers. In v. 9a, the Levites are to be brought before the tent of meeting, and in v. 10a before Yahweh. Also, when Aaron is introduced in v. 11 as the alternate to Moses, the dedication of the Levites takes place twice, in v. 11a before the sacrifices by Aaron, and in v. 13b after their presentation to Aaron by Moses. Furthermore, while the Levites are in v. 11 the gift from the Israelites for Yahweh, and while the sacrifices in v. 12 are to effect atonement for the Levites, the Levites of v. 19aβ$_2$-b are to effect atonement for the Israelites when those come near the tent of meeting and draw a plague, a notion unique in the OT (Kellermann, *Numeri,* 119). Finally, the compliance in vv. 20-22 conflicts with Yahweh's command on several points, apart from its summary nature: in v. 21a, Aaron instead of Moses dedicates the Levites, v. 13b; in v. 21b, Aaron effects atonement instead of Moses, v. 12b; and vv. 21a and 21b invert the prescribed sequence in vv. 12b and 13b.

There are good reasons for assuming with Kellermann (*Numeri,* 115-24) that the extant text is the expanded version of a nucleus still contained in vv. 5-9a, 12-16 (21). The nuclear text already spoke of both, the purification and the dedication of the Levites — by Moses. Its expansion added in vv. 9b-10b the participation of the Israelites, and in v. 11 the dedication of the Levites by Aaron and the explication of their function. Through the expansion, there are by now two rites of putting on of hands *(sāmak):* not only by the Levites on the bulls (v. 12a) but also by the Israelites on the Levites (v. 10b); and there are two rites of the dedication of the Levites themselves: not only by Moses after their purification (v. 13b) but also by Aaron before it (v. 11a). On the "putting on of hands," cf. Stolz, *"smk,"* 161; Peter, 52-53; Fabry/Milgrom/Wright, 884-87.

Genre

The unit is the REPORT about a specific event in which the command and its immediate execution are correlated. This correlation is the major reason why the Yahweh speech is a command and not, at least not primarily, a law. The combination of command and compliance report belongs to the typology of such reports (→ Chapter 1, Genre).

The genre of this report about the commanded and executed event is based on the other combination of the ritual purification and the dedication of the Levites. The two elements are distinct, and together constitute the unity of the event. Exegetes have defined the passage in terms of the purification of the Levites (e.g., Budd, 94; Snaith, 215), their consecration (e.g., de Vaux, 117: Consecration), their ordination (Kellermann, *Numeri,* 115: Levitenweihe; 121-22: Ordination), or in terms of an "offering" (Noth, *Numbers,* 67: Opfer). Generically, these definitions differ. "Consecration" is least likely. The Levites are not anointed and consecrated as are the priests and the sanctuary with its vessels (cf. Leviticus 8; → Num 7:1-2; Snaith, 215). "Purification" is insufficient because it either covers only the purification ritual of vv. 7-12, or incorrectly understands the *těnûpâ* ceremony in v. 13 as a concluding element of the purification ceremony.

Milgrom has shown that the *těnûpâ* is a "ritual of dedication which is performed in the sanctuary, by means of which the offering is removed from the domain of the owners and transferred to the domain of God" (*Studies,* 145), and that in Num 8:13-15 "the purpose of the *těnûpâ* is clear: it separates them [i.e., the Levites] from the Israelites and transfers them to the Lord's domain" (146). The *těnûpâ* is a specific ceremony of dedication. The verb *hēnîp,* normally translated by "to wave," means actually "to lift, to raise" (Milgrom, *Studies,* 156-57), and the expression *hēnîp těnûpâ* means "to make a dedication" or "to offer as dedication." The words belong to the technical terminology for cultic-ritual dedication. Num 8:5-22 supports this understanding in several respects: First, the expression is used three times in subsequently receding formulations, vv. 11a, 13b, 15b. The repetitions emphasize the writers' particular attention to this act. Second, the act of dedication in v. 13b is preceded in v. 13a by another act in which Moses is to "make the Levites stand *(wěha'ămadtā)* before Aaron and his sons." Verse 13a refers to the formal act of their presentation to the priests which is followed by the formal act of their dedication to Yahweh (cf. Noth, *Numbers,* 68-69; Kellermann, *Numeri,* 118, 122-23). Third, by being — thus, i.e., through their dedication to Yahweh, v. 13b — separated from among the Israelites (v. 14a) the Levites "belong to me" (v. 14b) and "after that they go . . . to work" (v. 15a). Their dedication to Yahweh after their presentation before Aaron is the special act before the start of their work. Neither act is a part of their purification ceremony; cf. → Num 3:6.

Fourth, v. 15 clearly distinguishes between three acts: entering for work (v. 15a); purifying (v. 15bα); and dedication (v. 15bβ). The sequence of the passages does not reflect the sequence of the envisioned events. Were one to read v. 15a after v. 15bα and β, the text would refer to the sequence of the three different events correctly. Fifth, the motivation in vv. 16-19 explains why the Levites belong to Yahweh. Their predestination explains their presently expected dedication, but not the need for their purification, which has a different reason. They must be purified because they work at the tent of meeting. In an unpurified state, they would provoke a plague, as would the unpurified Israelites were they to come to the tent. The different definitions of the work and the predestination of the Levites point again to the two distinct rituals, of their purification and their dedication.

And sixth, the prescription in v. 11 of the extant text for their dedication by Aaron *before* the two sacrifices in v. 12 creates a ritual in which these sacrifices are surrounded by two acts of dedication in vv. 11 and 13. Both dedications would be accompanying elements to the climactic part of the purification ritual, in contrast to the place and function of the dedication indicated otherwise. Specifically, the Levites would be dedicated to Yahweh in an unpurified state, before their purification, a difficult scenario. Verse 11 appears again secondarily interposed to emphasize their dedication "before" *(lipnê)* and not just "to" *(lě)* Yahweh, by Aaron and not by Moses. The emphasis distorts the procedural distinctions, but it is understandable: who else but the Aaronides should at the time of the writers replace Moses in dedicating the Levites!

The definition of the genre must be based on the report about the two distinct consecutive ceremonies of the purification and the presentation-dedication of the Levites (cf. Noth, *Numbers,* 68). Both ceremonies reflect one event in two different functions: their *purification prepares* them for their work at the tent of meeting, and their *dedication transfers* them to it. In the relationship of both ceremonies, the purification represents the precondition for the dedication, and the dedication represents the goal of the procedure and of the report about it. The report narrates the event of their "transfer" (Milgrom, *Studies,* 146) from Israel to Yahweh. This ritual, ceremonial event may be called "ordination." But "ordination" may also be understood to mean "consecration," which is not the case here. The Levites are transferred to clerical work *('ābad).* Num 8:5-22 is an INSTALLATION REPORT, in this case the specific installation for a clerical function at the sanctuary.

The genre of this installation report combines two specific ceremonies because of the installation to work at the sanctuary. In different contexts, each of these ceremonies may appear either independently or in relation to different genres and settings.

Setting

The unit belongs above all to the priestly REPORT about the organization of the inner encampment in → Numbers 3–4, to which it is a direct supplement. In this context, it further develops the legend of the foundational events in the ideal Sinai setting with particular attention to the clerical sanctuary personnel. It reports for that setting the specific liturgical event of the installation of the Levites before they assume their work at the tent of meeting. In its original version, the installation was said to be presided over by Moses who had to perform the purification ritual (vv. 5-9a, 12), to present the Levites to Aaron and to dedicate them to Yahweh (v. 13). In the extant text, the setting of the later Aaronide writers moved Aaron more strongly into the foreground.

The setting of the writing priests suggests that their report either proposes the creation or reflects the existence of an institution for the liturgical installation of the Levites. It also suggests the development of such an institution — in idea or reality — from ceremonies without the presence of the congregation to ceremonies with the congregation's presence and participation (Kellermann, *Numeri,* 122-23). The participation of the congregation by the laying of its hands on the Levites is no farfetched fantasy when one remembers Num 3:11-13, 14-51: each male firstborn Israelite adult had to have a substituting counterpart in an individual Levite.

It may finally be noted that the unit is perhaps not coincidentally positioned behind Num 7:1-89 and 8:1-4. It is again concerned with initiation, and focuses on the Levites while its preceding short unit 8:1-4 focuses on the Aaronides (cf. → Num 3:1-4 and → 3:5–4:49).

Intention

Num 8:5-22 intends first of all to report a new event that was considered necessary and had not been reported before (Noth, *Numbers,* 67). It intends to supplement especially Numbers 4. In pointing to the installation of the Levites it further intends to emphasize that the beginning of the actual work of the Levites, their "transfer" from their "encampment" to the sanctuary, in Numbers 4 at age thirty, was marked by an official institutional cultic act. They did not and could not randomly and covertly slip into their work at the sanctuary. This precondition points to the intention of the two elements of the ritual for their installation. Their purification intended to make sure that the sanctuary was not defiled and the Israelites not struck by plagues. Their presentation to Aaron and dedication to Yahweh intended to assign for them visibly their position in the sanctuary institution. This position was officially recognized and honored: as installation to their work; no more and no less.

Finally, the disproportionate length of the report about Yahweh's command, together with the writers' interest in their own cultic institution and their relationship to the Levites, indicates that their report about the event at Sinai intended to show the authentic paradigm for the levitic installation in their own time, and Moses' compliance as the supreme paradigm for their own equally immediate compliance.

Bibliography

H.-J. Fabry, J. Milgrom, and D. P. Wright, *"sāmak," TWAT;* J. Milgrom, *"Hattĕnûpâ," Studies in Cultic Theology and Terminology* (SJLA 36; Leiden: E. J. Brill, 1983) 139-58; R. Peter, "L'imposition des mains dans l'Ancien Testament," *VT* 27 (1977) 48-55; F. Stolz, *"smk,* stützen," *THAT.*

Legal Instruction about the Levitic Appointees (8:23-26)

Structure

I. Introductory speech report formula	23
II. The Yahweh instruction to Moses	24-26

A. The pronouncement of a law   24-26a
  1. Introductory reference   24a
  2. The law: the ages and kinds of appointment   24b-26a
    a. From 25 years on: to work   24b
      1) Definition of age of entry   24bα
      2) Prescription of appointment   24bβ
    b. From 50 years on: no work, but service   25-26a
      1) Definition of age   25aα
      2) Prescription of appointment   25aβ-26a
        a) Twofold prescription of termination   25aβ-b
          (1) Positively: he returns   25aβ
          (2) Prohibitively: he no longer works   25b
        b) Allowance or prescription of duty   26a
          (1) Prescription proper   26aα
          (2) Clarification: prohibition repeated   26aβ
B. The command to Moses   26b

Through its new Yahweh speech introduction and its different subject, the unit is clearly set apart from the preceding unit, which is itself concluded by a compliance report. After the usual introduction (I., v. 23), the unit relates a Yahweh speech to Moses (II., vv. 24-26). The carefully organized short speech consists of the pronouncement of a law concerning the levitic adults (II.A., vv. 24-26a), and the command to Moses to administer them accordingly (II.B., v. 26b).

After a uniquely formulated reference which reminds of superscriptions (II.A.1., v. 24a), the law pronounced in the speech prescribes the ages and kinds of appointment of the adult Levites (II.A.2., vv. 24b-26a). The law is prescribed in 3rd pers. sing. form for the individual Levites. It is not commanded to them in the 2nd pers. form. Before the prescriptions proper (apodoses), the cases (protases) are in this law stated by prepositional phrases functioning nominally rather than the usual conjunctional verbal clauses because they involve the definition of age, the primary reason for this law.

The law determines two ages from which the assignments of the Levites begin: from twenty-five and upward [mibben . . . wāmaʿĕlâ; II.A.2.a.1), v. 24bα], and from fifty on [mibben; II.A.2.b.1), v. 25aα]. And it prescribes the different kinds of assignment for each of the two groups from its beginning age on. From twenty-five years and upward "he enters to do labor in the work of the tent of meeting" [II.A.2.a.2), v. 24bβ]. From fifty (without "and upward") he is in a twofold status. Its first mode is expressed twice, positively: he returns (yāšûb) from the labor or work force (ṣābā'), and prohibitively: he no longer works (lōʾ yaʿăbōd ʿôd). The two statements are related synthetically; they reinforce one another. No doubt must remain about either prescription! The second mode of his status determines: "but he serves (šērēt) his brethren in/at the tent of meeting in doing duty" [mišmeret; II.A.2.b.2)b)(1), v. 26aα]. And to make sure again that this positive assignment is not misunderstood either, it is also followed by the previous prohibition of work.

In II.B. (v. 26b), Moses is charged or commanded (in 2nd pers. sing. Qal) to administer the duties of the Levites in accordance with this law. No compliance is reported.

Genre

Couched in the Yahweh speech report are a PRONOUNCEMENT OF LAW and a COMMAND to Moses to administer the Levites accordingly. The combination of pronouncement and command in the Yahweh speech amounts once again to a LEGAL INSTRUCTION. Specific elements of this instruction are the PRESCRIPTIONS concerning the Levites, with their particular emphasis on the PROHIBITIONS.

Setting

The unit belongs to a generation of priestly writers who wrote after the authors of → Numbers 4 and with direct reference to it. The terminology in general is derived from that context. More important is a specific comparison between the present unit and Num 4:3; cf. also 4:23, 30, 35, 39, 43, and 47. Num 4:3 had said: "From thirty years and upward and up to fifty years all shall enter (bāʾ) the force (ṣābāʾ)." By giving the two delimiting numbers of thirty and fifty it had in one sentence defined the age period for entry only to work. With reference to those two numbers and their function in that sentence, Num 8:24b-26a stipulates two substantive changes. It does so by formulating two sentences, each of which deals with one of the previously mentioned numbers separately. The first, shorter sentence (v. 24b) repeats the first part of Num 4:3 but changes the time for entry from thirty to twenty-five years of age. The second and longer sentence (vv. 25-26a) addresses a considerable problem created by the second part of Num 4:3. By saying "and up to fifty years (wěʿad ben-ḥămiššîm) all shall go to the force," Num 4:3 had referred to "fifty" only from the aspect of setting the upper limit for entering the force. It had actually demanded that the force had to be entered even at age fifty! Nothing explicit was said about leaving the work force at that or any age. By contrast, Num 8:24b-26a, while still determining the entry age "from (now) twenty-five years and upward," then determines what shall happen "from the age of fifty years on" (mibben ḥămiššîm) instead of "up to fifty" (wěʿad ben-ḥămiššîm). Thus, it addresses in two distinct statements the question of the beginnings of two different entries marked by the ages of twenty-five and upward and of fifty, but not the question of the lower and upper age limit for entering the work force as Num 4:3 et al. did. And while the change at the lower age was easy, the change of the meaning of the identical upper age demanded a specific effort as the structure of vv. 25-26a shows. Num 8:23-26 owes its literary origin to priests who in their administration of the Levites had to change and in effect had to invalidate the older definitions in Numbers 4.

The later date of Num 8:23-26 suggests also a societal setting in which the historical change of the situation of the Levites had to be taken into account. Ezra 3:8, and by implication also the time of Chronicles (cf. 1 Chr 23:24, 27;

2 Chr 31:17; cf. De Vries, *1-2 Chronicles*), set the age for the Levites' entry "from twenty on and upward." None of these passages says what happens at age fifty. It is best to assume a development in which the age of entry was lowered from thirty to twenty-five to twenty, and in which Num 8:23-26, with its additional and unique stipulations about the situation "from fifty years on," reflects conditions after those of Numbers 4 but before those of Ezra or of Chronicles.

Intention

Num 8:23-26 intends first of all to change the pertinent stipulations in Numbers 4, which had to be done by the report of a new authoritative Yahweh pronouncement at Sinai, a new text in its own right which was not an appendix to the previous text. The clarification of the meaning of the age of fifty was necessary because Num 4:3 et al., the only text where that age is mentioned for the Levites, had defined that age as the last time for entry rather than as the time of exit. It had thereby contributed to a possibly actual development in which Levites worked, and were expected to work, beyond that age. To such an understanding and possible or actual development, Num 8:25-26a prescribed a decisive *non licet* while at the same time either allowing for those from fifty years of age or assigning them to continuing service to their active brethren, to a sort of semi-retirement. Together with Num 7:1-89 and 8:1-4 and 8:5-22, the unit is another example of the scrupulous reading of the preceding texts.

Inasmuch as the unit intends to respond to actual levitic conditions, one has to consider both aspects addressed in it, and not only the lowering of the age for entry. The determination of an upper age limit for the termination of active work may therefore in part have been the reason for lowering the entry limit by creating a compensation in the lower age group for the loss of Levites actually working after the age of fifty. Or, the lowering of the entry age may have been the reason for terminating active work at age fifty.

The law may but does not necessarily respond to a demographic problem, namely, the lack of a numerically sufficient levitic work force (Noth, *Numbers,* 69; Kellermann, *Numeri,* 121-22; idem, *"lēwî,"* 517). In view of the demographic problem, the strict termination at age fifty is scarcely a persuasive policy. Nor is the economic argument that the law intends to provide a more secure economic basis (Kellermann, *Numeri,* 122) compelling. While providing such a basis for the younger generation the law would at the same time deprive those above the age of fifty at least in part of the same, if not of even greater need. In a sociological perspective, our understanding of this law may still have to remain open. In the meantime, the biological option should also be considered in view of the fact that the total span of the Levites' active work was adjusted downward while the participation of the older Levites was also adjusted, according to their physical abilities.

Finally, the unit was added behind Num 8:5-22 because it too is concerned with the Levites in the inner encampment and relates to Numbers 4 as 8:5-22 does. Moreover, its statement about the Levites' entry to work coincides with their entry to work in Num 8:15 after their installation in 8:6-13. In this respect, the text about entry in 8:24b is a follow-up text to the text about the preceding installation in 8:5-22. However, Num 8:23-26 addresses a problem in Numbers 4 that is different from the one addressed there by 8:5-22; and it is more than a supplement to Numbers 4, which 8:5-22 is. Thus, it addresses neither the issue of installation in 8:5-22 nor the issue of entry to work alone. It also and especially speaks about the situation at age fifty, an aspect that plays no role in Num 8:5-22 at all.

Bibliography

D. Kellermann, *"lēwî," TWAT;* S. J. De Vries, *1-2 Chronicles* (FOTL 11; Grand Rapids: Eerdmans, 1988).

The Report about the Passover at Sinai (9:1-14)

Structure

I. The Yahweh command for the Israelites	1-4
A. The instruction to Moses	1-3
1. Expanded introductory speech report formula	1
2. The command for the Israelites	2-3
a. Basic: expressed indirectly	2
b. Specifications: expressed directly	3
1) Concerning the appointed time	3a
2) Concerning all statutes and ordinances	3b
B. Moses' compliance: reported formally	4
II. Israel's compliance	5-14
A. The basic fact	5
1. According to time and place	5a
2. According to statutes and ordinances	5b
B. The exceptional case and its regulation	6-14
1. The case: a precedent	6-8
a. Introductory report statement	6a
b. The dialogue between the unclean and Moses	6b-8
1) The cultic inquiry by the unclean	6b-7
a) Statement about their approach	6b-7aα
b) The inquiry proper	7aβ-b
(1) Statement of fact	7aβ
(2) The question	7b
2) Moses' response: announcement of an oracular inquiry	8
2. The Yahweh response: a legal pronouncement	9-14
a. Introductory speech report formula	9
b. The Yahweh oracle to Moses	10-14

1) The command to convey the speech	10a
2) The content of the commandment	10b-14
a) The basic law	10b-13
(1) Concerning the exceptional conditions	10b-12
(a) The cases	10bα
(b) The regulation	10bβ-12
α. Expressed basically	10bβ
β. Expressed specifically	11-12
aa. Concerning the appointed time	11a
bb. Concerning the accompanying diet	11b
cc. Two prohibitions	12a
aa.-cc. Concluding reference	12b
(2) Concerning the violation	13
(a) The conditions for violation	13aα
(b) The regulation and its reason	13aβ-b
b) The appended law concerning the alien	14
(1) The case	14aα
(2) The regulation	14aβ
(1)+(2) Pronouncement of statutory law	14b

The report consists of two major parts, the Yahweh command for the Israelites and its conveyance through Moses (I., vv. 1-4) and their compliance (II., vv. 5-14). This twofold subdivision is based on the synopsis of calendric and chronological data stated by the text itself and implied from its preceding context, especially Exod 12:3, 6, 18; 40:17; Num 1:1; 9:1; but also Lev 8:10, 33-35; 9:1. According to this synopsis, the reported Passover at Sinai on the fourteenth day of the first month in the second year (9:1, 3, 5a, 6a + b) took place two weeks after the erection of the tabernacle (Exod 40:17), six days after the end of the following eight-day-long consecration of the Aaronides (Lev 8:10, 33-35; 9:1), at the end of the four-day preparation from the tenth of the month on for the Passover itself (Exod 12:3), and two weeks before the start of the organization of the camp (Num 1:1), or about one week before that starts if one accounts for the feast of unleavened bread from days fourteen to twenty-one (Exod 12:18). Num 9:1 and 4 reveal neither when Yahweh spoke to Moses nor when Moses spoke to Israel. But the presupposed context of Exod 12:3-6 shows that not only Yahweh's but also Moses' instruction to the Israelites had to allow for the four-day period of preparation from the tenth to the fourteenth of the month. Thus, while the text dates the Passover on the fourteenth, it implies that the two instructions were given before or on the tenth of the month. It implies a four-day lapse of time between vv. 4 and 5, and a direct chronological coherence between vv. 1-3 and 4. And it distinguishes on this basis between the command for the Israelites and their compliance.

The command (cf. v. 5: "Yahweh commanded," [ṣiwwâ] and the jussive verb forms) is initiated by Yahweh to Moses (I.A., vv. 1-3) and conveyed by Moses to Israel (I.B., v. 4). Its context is quoted in the Yahweh speech, and presupposed in the formal statement about Moses' conveyance. After the reporter's expanded introduction (I.A.1., v. 1) Yahweh's speech contains a basic command expressed indirectly (3rd pers. pl., I.A.2.a., v. 2), which is followed by two specifications expressed directly (2nd pers. pl., I.A.2.b., v. 3a + b). The Israelites are to keep ("to do," *'āśâ*) the Passover at its appointed time, and according to all its statutes and all its ordinances. The statutes *(ḥuqqîm)* and ordinances *(mišpāṭîm)* are assumed to be known, especially from Exodus 12. The structure of part I. is quite patterned.

Part II., vv. 5-14, reports in its entirety Israel's compliance. But it distinguishes between the basic fact of compliance in accordance with the previously given command (II.A., v. 5) and the exceptional case of the vitally desired but prevented compliance by unclean men (II.B., vv. 6-14). The exceptional case is reported as a case adjudication story that functions as a precedent. It claims the major portion of the entire unit.

The story presents first the case itself (II.B.1., vv. 6-8), beginning with a narrative statement about the specifics of the case (II.B.1.a., v. 6a). It continues with the dialogue between the unclean and Moses (II.B.1.b., vv. 6b-8) which is opened by the cultic inquiry of the unclean [II.B.1.b.1), vv. 6b-7] and concluded by Moses' answer [II.B.1.b.2), v. 8]. After approaching Moses and Aaron (!) on that day (v. 6) the unclean state the fact of their impurity and its reason, and ask why they are reduced so as not to bring Yahweh's gift *(qorbān)* at its appointed time in the midst of the Israelites (vv. 7aβ-b).

Instead of giving a priestly decision, Moses has to command them to stand by while he listens to "what Yahweh will command for you," a Yahweh oracle [II.B.1.b.2), v. 8]. He announces an oracular inquiry that is, however, not reported. Reported is Yahweh's response (II.B.2., vv. 9-14) introduced by the speech report formula (II.B.2.a., v. 9) and the conveyance command formula [II.B.2.b.1), v. 10a; → Num 5:12a]. Yahweh commands Moses to pronounce the following law [II.B.2.b.2), vv. 10b-14]. The commanded law represents again a legal instruction that at the same time functions as a ruling for the case at hand. It consists of a basic and an appended law, vv. 10b-13 and 14. The basic law responds first to the exceptional conditions presented in the question. In priestly style, it mentions not only one but two cases "for you or your descendants" (v. 10bα) and rules basically: "he shall do the Passover to Yahweh" (v. 10bβ). Specifications, two prohibitions, and a compliance correspondence formula to the statute of the Passover *(ḥuqqat happesaḥ)* follow, vv. 11-12.

In its conclusion (v. 13) the basic law confirms the exception by stipulating the extirpation of the clean not *en route* who fail to keep the regular Passover (cf. the extirpation formula, v. 13aα; Kutsch, *"krt,"* 858; Hasel, 362-63). It adds the reason for this punishment (v. 13bα; cf. v. 7b) and repeats the stipulation of punishment by the threat of punishment (v. 13bβ). Finally, the appended law in v. 14 stipulates that the alien *(gēr)* must also keep the Passover according to its statute (cf. v. 12b); and it concludes with a statutory pronouncement.

Genre

As a whole, the unit is a REPORT about a specifically dated event at a specific place, about Israel's Passover at Sinai on the first anniversary of the exodus

Passover, and about the second most important of all of Israel's Passovers. The unit is a PASSOVER REPORT. This report has parallels in the reports or notes about similarly important Passovers under Joshua (Josh 5:10-12), Hezekiah (2 Chr 30:1-27), Josiah (2 Kgs 23:12-23; 2 Chr 35:1-19), and after the inauguration of the second temple (Ezra 6:19-22). Common to all these reports is that the festival was celebrated as a communal festival either at the temple in Jerusalem or in the camp around the sanctuary or the ark, in the actual or intended presence of all Israelites, and, except for Josh 5:10-12, after the immediately preceding initiation or re-initiation of the sanctuary. They were especially recorded major historical festivals of the cultic community. Num 9:1-14 reflects this genre.

The various elements in Num 9:1-14 are above all determined by the contextual aspects of the Sinai pericope. This fact applies to the Yahweh command in vv. 1-3, to Moses' conveyance (v. 4), to Israel's basic compliance (v. 5), and also to the exceptional case in vv. 6-14 with its legal instruction through a new legal pronouncement by Yahweh.

These elements rest, however, on generic traditions. The case of the unclean men is not narrated in the developed form of a case law story. Num 9:6-14 lacks the identification of the persons and the reference to them in the pronounced law and at the conclusion. Its transition from vv. 8 to 9 is not developed. And unlike the self-contained case law story it is bound into its context vv. 1-5. These factors show that vv. 6-8 (the story part) function only in relation to vv. 9-14, and both in relation to vv. 1-5 or as a whole (cf. Lev 24:10-23; → Num 15:32-36; 27:1-11; 36:1-12). Nevertheless, vv. 6-8 reflect the genre of stories or records that report the adjudication of such cases. Specifically, they reflect the genre of stories about CULTIC INQUIRIES.

Moses' reply in v. 8 reflects the genre of an ORACULAR INQUIRY, but not of a PRIESTLY DECISION. And Yahweh's response reflects in its context the genre of DIVINE ORACLE, and in its various forms in vv. 10b-12, 13, 14 the genres of the traditional CASE LAW, and of COMMANDS and PROHIBITIONS, including the DECLARATORY FORMULAE in vv. 13aβ, 13bα, and 13bβ. All legal elements belong to the STATUTE OF PASSOVER, vv. 12b, 14aβ.

The generic variety in the text reflects the variety of the cultic and legal institutions in Israel's history at an advanced time.

Setting

Several signals indicate that the text was composed by a writer whose own hand is essentially found in vv. 1-10a, and who included an already existing law in vv. 10b-12. Verses 13 and 14 are probably later accretions. I agree in principle with Kellermann's analysis (*Numeri*, 124-33), whose results also bear out — as do those of others — that the law in vv. 10b-12 presupposes the final outcome of the growth of Exodus 12 and that it is therefore later than that text, so that Num 9:1-12 — let alone vv. 13-14 — must be later still, indeed late in the transmission of the priestly writings.

What generated the unit as a whole, and how and why are its parts, especially vv. 1-5, 6-8, 10b-12, related? Verse 1 says clearly that the event took place after the dates given in Exodus 40 and Leviticus 8–9 and before the date of Num 1:1, and not "as the immediate prelude to the journey from Sinai to the land" (Budd, 99). The report presupposes the preceding text Exodus 40– Numbers 1, and explicitly supplements it by saying that the Passover not re- ported there had indeed taken place. It is a supplement to Leviticus 8–10. It is *based on* Exodus 12, but is not an "Appendix to the Passover Legislation" (Noth, *Numbers,* 70). The reason, if any, for this supplement is clear and impor- tant enough. Israel appeared in the preceding text to have failed to celebrate the Passover and, hence, to have violated one of the most fundamental ceremonial laws, and that at Sinai (!) and at the first anniversary after the law had been given and the Passover celebrated. Num 9:1-14 removes that suspicion. Once again, one can see how scrupulously these writers studied not only what their texts had reported but also what they had not reported.

The scene in vv. 1-5 was generated by its preceding context, and not by vv. 10b-12 (Kellermann, *Numeri,* 131) to which it does not respond and which does not speak about the Passover at Sinai explicitly. The law of vv. 10b-12 was for specific reasons adopted into the contextual report of vv. 1-5, together with vv. 6-8, 9-10a. Thus, the short report in v. 5 of the Israelites' compliance on the fourteenth day, which concluded the report about their instruction four or five days earlier, was expanded by the report in vv. 6-12, 13, 14 about the excep- tional case on the same day, obviously for specific reasons.

The sections vv. 1-5 and 6-8 are entirely and apodictically interested in one requirement: that the Israelites are to keep and kept Passover "at its ap- pointed time" *(bĕmô'ădô,* vv. 2, 3aβ, 7bα, 13bα), "on the fourteenth day in *this* month" *(baḥōdeš hazzeh,* v. 3a; cf. v. 5), "on that day" *(bayyôm hahû',* v. 6a + b); and that Passover indeed be *kept* (now! vv. 5-12, 13, 14) while a few unclean were against their will prevented from doing so.

In view of this emphasis that was already satisfied by vv. 1-5, why was it important to add the following report with its two parts? First, the law of vv. 10b-12 for the second month *presupposes,* together with vv. 1-8, the local to- getherness of Israel's community including the unclean, in contrast to → Num 5:1-4. And taken by itself this adopted law also *presupposes* that this Passover was kept in the homes, in accordance with Exodus 12, especially vv. 43-49. However, what does that law *say* on this basis? Does it say that men unclean by contact with a dead person must not, and men on a distant route cannot, keep the Passover in the first month because and as long as they are in their respec- tive conditions? Or does it say that both kinds of men must not keep it in the first month because and as long as they are separate from the Israelite commu- nity? Under the first question, no man would be allowed to celebrate while un- clean, not even in his home where he lives separately from the community and could celebrate separately. No celebration in case of impurity even when sepa- rate! This is established law. However, why should a man *en route* not celebrate in the first month at his momentary place, just in obedience to the existing law? Is he not prevented from celebrating for one reason only, his separation from his homeland *(hā'āreṣ,* v. 14b), specifically from the community in his home- land?

These questions may not be reflected in the text. But at its face value it seems that the common denominator for both cases in vv. 10b and 13a is the issue of separation from the community, within and without, the consequence of impurity or absence, and neither absence nor impurity as such and the validity of the impurity laws.

This possibility is supported by the line of argument in vv. 6-7. It is an open question whether these verses are merely a technical device for introducing the following law regardless of how and what they argue, or whether their author, the author of vv. 1-8, expresses an argument in them to which the available law in vv. 10b-12 lent itself and for which he appropriated it. The verses must be considered in their own right.

Verse 6a says that there were men who were unclean and could not keep Passover. It does not say that they could not keep Passover because they were unclean. And when presenting their case they first state that they are unclean, and after that statement ask the question: "Why are we reduced ('cut off,' 'separated,' Fishbane, *Biblical Interpretation,* 99) to not to bring the gift of Yahweh at its appointed time in the midst of the Israelites?" (v. 7).

The question seems strange. If the men assume that the reason for their exclusion is impurity, they must know that their unclean status is defined and enforced on the basis (Fishbane, *Biblical Interpretation,* 99) of the impurity laws. Why do they ask after having stated the fact themselves? Their question is unnecessary because the answer is self-evident. And they should be the first to know it. And why does Moses resort to an oracular inquiry? Does he not realize that their exclusion is nothing but the enforcement of the laws of purity? Does he not know these laws which should enable him to render his own (priestly) decision as the priests do in Hag 2:10-13, or even to let them give the obvious answer themselves? After all, they had asked *why (lāmmâ)* they were excluded, and not whether there was an exception for their exclusion.

If vv. 6-7 are concerned with their exclusion on the ground of their impurity, at best a simple priestly explanation of the existing law was necessary, not even a decision because that decision had already been cultically enforced, but no amendment to the existing purity laws by a divine oracle. Are vv. 6-7, then, indeed only a device for introducing vv. 10-12, and substantively irrelevant? And should their author have been unconcerned about the striking discrepancy between the inherent answer required by their content and their function for vv. 10-12 regardless of that answer? But what do vv. 6-7 say? Which law is already enforced that they do not understand, a law that was so far not recorded in the purity laws, which, however inexplicit, remained in force, and which needed not so much an explanation as a new legal amendment that could indeed be authorized only by a Yahweh oracle?

Verses 6-12, 13 incontestably involve the threat to the loss of the men's "ethnic status" (Fishbane, *Biblical Interpretation,* 99). Unclear is whether the law in vv. 10b-12 is the response to that *threat,* or whether it is the response to their exclusion and its reasons in the first place, a response that would also preserve their status. The men do not ask: "Is our status not threatened by our exclusion from the scheduled Passover?" They ask: "*Why* are we reduced . . . ?" They refer to the reason for their exclusion, not to its consequences, and thus to

122

the possibility that vv. 10b-12 respond to this exclusion and its reason itself and not, at least not primarily, to its consequences concerning their status. As long as the problem exists, the basis on which vv. 6-7 and 10-12 are coordinated is unclear.

First, v. 6b: "And they drew near *(wayyiqrĕbû)* before Moses and before Aaron." They are in the camp and approach Moses and Aaron who must be at the tabernacle. Second, v. 7bα₁: in their question they state that they are "reduced ('cut off,' 'separated') so as not to bring the gift of Yahweh. . . ." They are reduced or cut off *from the Israelites,* not from their gift. Third, v. 7bα₂: "to bring" *(haqrîb)* means generally and especially always in the priestly sacrificial texts the bringing from one place to another. From where to where? As in v. 6b, from their camp to Moses and Aaron at the sanctuary, as the Israelites do. Fourth, v. 7bα₃: to bring "the gift of Yahweh" *('et-qorban yhwh). qorbān* is a sacrificial gift, and in this sense exclusively used some eighty times in the priestly literature. Num 9:7b can be no exception. This gift is without exception brought near (mostly *hiqrîb;* sometimes *hēbî')* to the priest, to the altar, to the sanctuary. In most of the texts it is called "the gift *for* Yahweh" *(qorban lĕyhwh),* whereas only in Num 9:7, 13; 31:50 is it called "the gift *of* Yahweh" *(qorban yhwh).* Cf. also Num 28:2; Lev 23:14, and de Vaux's translation "l'offrande de Yayweh" (sic!), vs. his interpretation "une offrande à Yahweh," 124, 126. The expression Num 9:7 reflects the latest texts in the Pentateuch. But it is clear that it reflects the gift *for* Yahweh, too.

We can summarize: the text clearly means that at the appointed time and together with the Israelites, these men are excluded from bringing their sacrificial gift for Yahweh to Moses, to the priest(s), to the altar, at the sanctuary. It presupposes a communal Passover at the central sanctuary, and the unclean men are barred from it and ask why this is so.

The idea of a communal Passover coincides with the priestly context of the Sinai camp, and clarifies the nature of the Passover assumed in vv. 1-5 at its first anniversary. This festival was a community Passover at the just erected tabernacle, and not the kind of domestic Passover prescribed in Exodus 12.

The communal Passover at the sanctuary is also assumed in Lev 23:4-8. Not only is there required a "holy convocation" *(miqrā' qōdeš)* twice, on the first and seventh day; there shall also be brought *(wĕhiqrabtem)* "the fire sacrifice for Yahweh" *('iššeh lĕyhwh),* here as always at the sanctuary. Deut 16:1-8 commands the offering of the doubtless communal Passover sacrifice at the place Yahweh will choose, and explicitly forbids to offer it in any of the towns, and that annually and quite beyond the special Passovers in the temple recorded in 2 Kgs 23:12-23; 2 Chr 30:1-27; 35:1-19; Ezra 6:19-22; cf. Josh 5:10-12. But it should be evident that the parallel of the genre of the PASSOVER REPORT in Num 9:1-14 to these other reports is not coincidental.

Moreover, Fishbane has shown that the report in 2 Chronicles 30 is based on a legal exegesis of the provisions of Num 9:6, 9-11, 14 *(Biblical Interpretation,* 154-59). One has to ask whether 2 Chronicles 30 resorts to Numbers 9 only because of its allowance for the second month, and not also and perhaps first of all because Numbers 9 provided the focus on the communal festival at the sanctuary. 2 Chronicles 30 would then not generalize Numbers 9 from a private to a public matter (Fishbane, *Biblical Interpretation,* 157); it would recognize the public matter in Numbers 9 from the outset. And quite remarkably, 2 Chr 30:17-18 say that "the Levites had to kill the Passover lamb for every one who was not clean, to make it holy to the LORD. For a multitude of the people" from the various, listed tribes "had not cleansed themselves, yet they ate Passover otherwise than as prescribed" — and that at the temple and even in the second month! That text is exactly concerned with the problem of impurity at Passover at the sanctuary because of which the men in Num 9:6-7 are excluded from the sanctuary Passover in the first month.

All this cannot mean that the unclean of Num 9:6-7 were allowed to eat the Passover in the first month at home. The laws of purity apparently applied to Passover so self-evidently that the application never had to be made explicit legislatively. It only means that these existing laws were also enforced for the communal Passovers at the sanctuary. When the men ask why they are (irreversibly) excluded, the most likely answer is: at the sanctuary just as much as at home. Interestingly, the text speaks only about their impurity through contact with a dead person, and not about impurity in general. That may be a special example by which the general case is stated. But it may also refute an assumption as if such a contact *at home* may not affect their participation at the sanctuary, or not even be recognized. Enforced is in any case that the contact with a dead person excludes just as much as any other impurity.

It seems that Num 9:10b-12 permits and even commands (v. 10b) as a standard policy the exceptional Passover for all men, including those *en route,* who must not and cannot participate in the communal sanctuary Passover "at its appointed time in the midst of the Israelites," and in direct response to that situation. In the second month, they may celebrate it at home, in accordance with Exodus 12. The existing law that already had stipulated the exception to the law of Exodus 12 for the domestic festival was now adopted for the exception to the communal Passover, too. This law did not make a communal Passover in the second month impossible, especially in an emergency case such as 2 Chronicles 30; but it certainly did not require it. The exceptional Passover is basically kept at home. The motivation for this exceptional provision in response to the exclusion from the communal Passover was that the Israelites' communal status had to be protected. That was certainly the case in any local community in their homeland, too.

Num 9:6-14 points to a problem in the tradition history of the Passover institution. This problem appears in the intersection of special and/or regular communal Passovers at the central sanctuary, on the one hand, and of the domestic Passovers in the homes, on the other hand. The former tradition assumed for Num 9:1-8 is both reported in Josh 5:10-12; 2 Kgs 23:12-23; 2 Chr 30:1-27; 35:1-19; Ezra 6:19-22 and commanded in Lev 23:4-8; Deut 16:1-8. And the latter is commanded in Exodus 12. The two different types are known in the deuteronomic-deuteronomistic, the priestly, and the chronistic literature. The emerging problem of their relationship should come as no surprise. It arises in the priestly text Numbers 9 and focuses on the cases of men (!) temporarily unclean through contact with a dead person. This problem was specific and apparently required for the *communal* Passover in the context of Num 9:1-5 a new, heretofore inexplicit regulation through a Yahweh oracle even as an existing regulation for the domestic Passover was adopted. The Sinai setting provided that context, originally for its own camp, but also for "your descendants" (v. 10b). But the nature of the problem addressed in this priestly text points to a setting in which the deuteronomic and the priestly legislations about both traditions converged, and in which the priests were specifically interested in the purity of Passovers at the sanctuary. It points to a particular moment in the late history of the Pentateuchal text.

Intention

The unit presupposes in all its parts that the Passover must be kept by all Israelites at its appointed time according to the statute of Passover. It is the law of the land, which also includes the alien.

On this basis, the unit has two intentions: it intends to supplement the preceding Sinai narrative in order to make clear that Israel had not missed the Passover at its first anniversary at Sinai — if only through an explicit command by Yahweh. It further intends to make explicit allowance for two kinds of men who each for a specific reason are not allowed to or are unable to keep Passover in the first month, especially the communal Passover among the Israelites in the sanctuary. These men are permitted to celebrate it nevertheless, precisely one month later, and in their homes. Verse 13 reinforces the limitation of this allowance by threatening the extirpation from Israel's community for each person who fails to keep the regular Passover when not falling under the exception.

Bibliography

H.-J. Fabry, D. N. Freedman, and B. E. Willoughby, *"nāśā'," TWAT;* M. Fishbane, *Biblical Interpretation in Ancient Israel* (Oxford: Clarendon Press, 1985); H. Haag, *Vom alten zum neuen Pascha: Geschichte und Theologie des Osterfestes* (Stuttgarter Bibelstudien 49; Stuttgart: Katholische Bibelwerke, 1971); G. F. Hasel, *"kārat," TWAT;* R. Knierim, *"ḥṭ', sich verfehlen," THAT;* K. Koch, *"ḥāṭā'," TDOT;* E. Kutsch, "Feste und Feiern II: In Israel," *RGG3;* idem, *"krt,* abschneiden," *THAT;* J. W. McKay, "The Date of Passover and Its Significance," *ZAW* 84 (1972) 435-47; R. Martin-Achard, *Essai biblique sur les fêtes d'Israel* (Geneva: Labor et Fides, 1974); J. C. Rylaarsdam, "Feasts and Fasts," *IDB;* "Passover and Feast of Unleavened Bread," *IDB;* "Unleavened Bread," *IDB;* H. R. Stroes, "Does the Day Begin in the Evening or Morning?" *VT* 16 (1966) 460-75; S. J. deVries, "Calendar," *IDB;* M. Weippert, "Kalender und Zeitrechnung," *Biblisches Reallexikon* (2nd ed.; K. Galling, ed.; Tübingen: Mohr, 1977).

The Report about the Theophanic March (9:15-23)

Structure

I. The presupposition for the march: the covering cloud   15-16
  A. On day and night one   15
  B. Continually   16
II. The conditions during the march: the moving cloud   17-23
  A. The basic condition   17-18
    1. Expressed phenomenologically   17
      a. For decampment   17a
      b. For encampment   17b
    2. Expressed theologically   18a
      a. For decampment   18aα
      b. For encampment   18aβ
    1.+2. Summary: expressed temporally and phenomenologically   18b
  B. Specifications   19-22
    1. For many days of encampment   19
    2. For a number of days of encampment   20
    3. For decampment after a night's camp   21a
    4. For decampment after a full day's camp   21b
    5. For encampment of two days, a month, or (many) days   22
  C. The basic condition   23

In its main clauses, the unit speaks in vv. 15-16 about the cloud, and in vv. 17-23 about the Israelites. The cloud covered the tabernacle on the day of its erection, "and in the evening it was upon the tabernacle like the appearance of fire until the morning" (v. 15). "So it was continually: the cloud covered it, and the appearance of fire at night" (v. 16). Verses 17-23 no longer use the verb "to cover" *(kissā)*. They speak instead of the reaction of the Israelites when the cloud was being "taken up" *(hēʿālōt,* niph., v. 17aα; *naʿălâ,* niph., v. 21aβ) and "settling down" *(yiškān,* v. 17b) or "extending" (its stay; *haʾărîk,* vv. 19a, 22a) or just "being" *(yihyeh,* vv. 20aα, 21aα), i.e., temporarily settled.

The text seems to distinguish between the continual "coverage" of the tabernacle by the cloud, vv. 16-17, and the cloud's up and down movements during that coverage, vv. 17-23, "up from" *(mēʿal,* v. 17a) the tabernacle, and down "there" *(šām),* at the "place" *(māqôm,* v. 17b). This distinction coincides with the fact that "the cloud" and its correlatives occur in vv. 16-17 in the main clauses, and in vv. 17-23 in the subordinate clauses. The unit consists of two parts. Its first part reports the presupposition for the Israelites' march from before its beginning (I., vv. 15-16), and its second part reports the conditions during their march which were determined by the cloud that continually covered the sanctuary (II., vv. 17-23).

The alternating decampment and encampment of the Israelites is the subject of vv. 17-23. However, these alternations depended on the vertically alternating movements of the cloud. The text speaks neither of the horizontal movement of the cloud nor of the march of the Israelites as such (cf. → Numbers 2;

however, cf. Deut 1:33). The Israelites follow the temporally different up and down movements of the cloud. The text focuses therefore on the cloud's movements, and its structure is based on the aspects evolving from this focus. These aspects are organized systematically.

The major subdivision distinguishes between two aspects: the basic condition during the march (II.A., vv. 17-18, and II.C., v. 23) and typical specifications (II.B., vv. 19-22). The basic condition for encampment as well as decampment is expressed phenomenologically (II.A.1., v. 17) and theologically (II.A.2., v. 18a) with a concluding statement in v. 18b. The two expressions are complementary: the cloud conceals the presence of Yahweh, and "the mouth of Yahweh" *(pî yhwh)* identifies the theophanic nature of the cloud and the speaking of the authority in the cloud.

The specifications of the cloud's vertical alternations are organized chiastically under the aspect of typically different durations of the encampments or decampments. The text moves from "many days" (II.B.1., v. 19) via "a number of days" (II.B.2., v. 20) to a night (II.B.3., v. 21a) and back via a full day (II.B.4., v. 21b) to "two days, a month, or (many) days" (II.B.5., v. 22). And when referring to two days or more (vv. 19, 20, 22) it focuses on *en*campment, whereas it focuses on *de*campment when referring to the short periods of one day or less (v. 21a + b).

Aspects other than those mentioned have their place in subordinate relations. This is especially true for the statements about decampment and encampment or vice versa, but also about the Israelites' observance (Kellermann, *Numeri,* 138) of Yahweh's guidance (scarcely of "service to Yahweh," Budd, 101) in vv. 19b, 23b. Except for the local terms "place" *(māqôm)* and "there" *(šām)* in v. 17b, the text speaks for clear reasons about the movements of the cloud in the temporal terms of day or days (vv. 15a, 18bα, 19a, 20aα, 22aα), of evening and morning (v. 21aα; cf. v. 15b), or of day and night (v. 21bα). But it speaks neither calendrically nor chronologically. And it is not based on guidance along an itinerary.

Genre

The unit is a REPORT about the nature of the march of the Israelites. This nature was throughout the time of the march determined by the cloud covering the tabernacle, and by the irregular intervals of the cloud's vertical movements which determined the intervals of Israel's campaign. The report is characterized by the combination of the cloud (that is, the theophanic form of Yahweh's presence) and of Israel's march.

This combination reflects the merger of two traditions that can be observed in Exodus-Deuteronomy and elsewhere. On the one hand is the exodus tradition in which Israel's march is led by the pillar of fire and cloud; cf. Exod 13:21-22; 14:19-20, 24; 16:10; 33:9, 10; Deut 1:32-33; Ps 78:14; 99:7; 105:39; and Neh 9:12, 19. On the other hand is the Sinai tradition in which Yahweh speaks to Moses out of the cloud on the mountain and then from the tent of meeting; cf. Exod 19:9, 16; 24:15-16, 18; 34:5; 40:34-38; Lev 16:2, 13; Num

11:25; 17:7 (*NRSV* 16:42); Deut 4:11; 5:22; 1 Kgs 8:10-11; 2 Chr 5:13-14; Ezek 1:4; and 10:3-4 (cf. Jenni, *"ānān,"* 351-53; Jeremias, 896-98). The Sinai tradition is reflected in the cultic theophanies in the Jerusalem temple. And it seems as if the merger of the cloud on Sinai and in the temple is the basis on which in the priestly tradition the cloud on Sinai moved down upon the sanctuary and was from Exod 40:34-38 on combined with the cloud of Israel's march from the exodus on. Num 9:15-23 belongs to this final combination in the tradition history of the cloud and of the Pentateuch (cf. Exod 40:34-38; Num 10:11-12, 34 [with the ark]; 12:5, 10; 14:14; and Deut 31:15).

Num 9:15-23 is the REPORT about a THEOPHANIC MARCH, i.e., Israel's march led by Yahweh's theophany (cf. Isa 40:3-5). It is not yet clear whether the combination of sanctuary theophany and march represents a narrative genre in its own right. But the twofold background of the report, without which it could scarcely have been conceived, is doubtless generic.

Setting

The unit is reminiscent of Exod 40:34-38. For stylistic and terminological reasons, however, the question remains at least open whether there is a literary dependence of one of the two passages on the other (cf. Kellermann, *Numeri,* 134-36). They seem to have come from different hands, each of which reported in its own way the alternation of Israel's encampments and decampments from Sinai on under the temporal guidance by the theophanic cloud over the tent of meeting or tabernacle. And each embraced in reporting style the total march, in a contextual position in which the march had not even begun, as if it had been completed. The best explanation for this tension between the report about the completed march and its position in the text before the beginning of the march is the reference to the setting of the late writers. From a vantage point retrospective of the whole march, both writers positioned their typically summarizing reports before Num 10:11, in appropriate contexts, and at any rate not at the end of Numbers or even later.

Apart from the question of literary dependence, Num 9:15-23 functions in relationship to Exod 40:34-38 and → Numbers 2 in a contextual setting. In view of Numbers 2 and the same aspects in the book of Numbers, it connects with the emphasis on the encampment order and marching order, and on encampment and decampment, however, without their military motion (→ Chapters 1 and 2). In view of Exod 40:34-38, it specifically expounds the diversity and, hence, the unpredictability of the schedule according to which the cloud rose and settled. This interest, besides others, points again to a very late setting of Num 9:15-23 in the history of the priestly writers.

Intention

The unit intends first of all to summarize the unique, miraculous nature of Israel's tabernacle march guided by the theophanic cloud that covered the tabernacle *(miškān)* or tent *('ōhel)* or tent of the testimony *('ōhel hā'ēdut)* from the day of its erection and initiation on (cf. vv. 15 [3 times], 16, 18b, 19a, 22a). In depicting the tabernacle as continually covered by Yahweh's cloud, it points to Yahweh's close relationship to the tabernacle, though above it only and not identical with it (cf. Ezek 1; 10; 43:1-5).

Through its position, the unit further intends to inform the reader summarily about how the following report about the entire campaign should be understood. This understanding contrasts sharply with the picture from Numbers 11 on. It claims that in view of Yahweh's cloud and voice over the tabernacle, the schedule of Israel's march is determined by Yahweh alone, totally and exclusively, regardless how Israel appears otherwise. For this exclusively theocratic claim, the cloud over the Sinai tabernacle was the unique paradigm.

Specifically, the unit intends to point out that Yahweh's schedule was diverse and therefore unpredictable, not because of Israel's undoings but because of Yahweh's own choosing. It reveals a theological insight that says that the times of Yahweh's community, while on its way, were, and therefore are, Yahweh's.

Bibliography

J. Dus, "Herabfahrung Jahwes auf die Lade und Entziehung der Feuerwolke," *VT* 19 (1969) 290-311; E. Jenni, *"'ānān,* Wolke," *THAT;* J. Jeremias, "Theophany in the Old Testament," *IDBSup;* L. Sabourin, "The Biblical Cloud. Terminology and Traditions," *BTB* 4 (1974) 290-311; W. Schmidt, "פשׂכָן als Aüsdrück Jerüsalemer Kültsprache," ZAW 75 (1963) 91-92.

The Instruction about the Two Trumpets (10:1-10)

Structure

I. Introductory speech report formula	1
II. The instruction	2-10
A. For the campaign from Sinai on	2-8
1. Expressed basically	2
a. The command to Moses to make two trumpets	2a
b. The declaration of their two functions	2b
1) For congregating the congregation	2bα
2) For breaking the camps	2bβ
2. The specific prescription of their twofold purpose	3-8
a. Concerning congregating	3-4
1) Of the congregation to Moses and the tent	3
2) Of the commanding leaders to Moses	4
b. Concerning the breaking of the camps	5-6
1) Of those encamped east	5

2) Of those encamped south	6
a.+b. Two clarifications	7-8
1) Concerning vv. 3a and 6a	7
2) Concerning vv. 3-7 or 3-4, 7	8
B. For the future in the land	9-10
1. Concerning war	9
a. Going to battle	9a
b. Being remembered and saved	9b
2. Concerning the sacrifices at festivals	10
a. Two sacrifices	10a
b. Being remembered — with grace formula	10b

The unit is a report about a Yahweh speech to Moses that includes a command to Moses and prescriptions for the Aaronide priests. It consists of the typical reporter's introductory formula (I., v. 1) and the speech itself (II., vv. 2-10). A compliance is not reported.

The Yahweh speech contains the instruction about the trumpets. Its structure is in the extant text based on two foci: the usage of these trumpets for the campaign from Sinai on (II.A., vv. 2-8) and for Israel's future in the land (II.B., vv. 9-10). In a basic instruction (II.A.1., v. 2) Yahweh commands Moses to make two hammered silver trumpets and declares their twofold purpose. They shall serve him for congregating the congregation ('ēdâ) and for breaking the camps. Verse 2 refers to the Sinai camp.

The two purposes of the trumpets are in II.A.2. (vv. 3-8) prescribed specifically by unfolding the aspects mentioned in v. 2b concerning congregating (II.A.2.a., vv. 3-4), the breaking of the camps (II.A.2.b., vv. 5-6), and clarifications of problems arising from vv. 3-6 (II.A.2.a.+b., vv. 7-8). Verses 3-8 envision the situation of the impending march from Sinai, as does v. 2. However, their prescriptions vary in several respects.

Verses 3-4 distinguish between the trumpet signals for gathering the entire congregation to Moses and the tent of meeting (v. 3) and for gathering the leaders, the heads of the thousands of Israel, to him (v. 4). The first kind of gathering will happen when "they blow with *them*" (*wĕtāqĕ'û bāhēn*), and the second "when with *one* they blow" (*wĕ'im-bĕ'aḥat yitqā'û*). Blowing "with *them*" presupposes in the context of v. 2a blowing "with *both*," although v. 3a does not say so. Verse 2a contains the only explicit reference to "*two* hammered silver trumpets" (*šĕtê ḥăṣôṣĕrōt kesep miqšâ . . .*) in the OT. It is not clear whether blowing "with them" happens simultaneously or successively. Nor is it said who and how many those are who blow "them." And while the text distinguishes in vv. 3 and 4 between the number of trumpets blown, it does not speak about the number of blowings, i.e., of possibly short staccato thrusts as indicated by the verb *tāqa'*, "to push," "to thrust," versus a blowing in long drawn legato tones (cf. Kellermann, *Numeri*, 141).

Verses 5-6 speak of "blowing alarm" (*tāqa' tĕrû'â*), a different kind of blowing. And for the successive decampment of the four camps of which only the first two are mentioned, they assume the same signals successively. Those encamped east will decamp "when you [2nd pers. pl.] blow alarm" (v. 5) and those encamped south "when you blow alarm a second time" (v. 6). The type of blowing, alarm, is the same for all camps; but one alarm for each camp is blown at a time, and each camp has to recognize its signal from the order of their succession. Again, the text does not say who those are who now in direct address are instructed to blow. It does not say how many trumpets are blown. Verse 6b concludes: "they blow alarm for their decampments." Moses and the tent are no longer mentioned.

In v. 7, a plurality of trumpeters is again addressed directly. But now, "you shall blow but not sound *(titqĕʿû wĕloʾ tārîʿû)* when assembling the assembly *(bĕhaqhîl ʾet-haqqāhāl)*." The text speaks about the assembling of the assembly and not the congregating of the congregation as in vv. 3-4. The terminology is singular in P (Kellermann, *Numeri,* 141). For that purpose they are — only — to "blow" but not to "sound." In order to avoid any misunderstanding of vv. 3-6 where "blowing" is used for both the congregating and the decampment, v. 7b replaces the expression "to blow alarm" used in vv. 5-6 by the word "to sound" *(rûʿa,* hiph.), a word mostly used in connection with battle. The signal for assembling the assembly is no call to war. In view of vv. 3-4 and 5-6, v. 7 wants to prevent the accident that the units start marching into war when instead the assembly is called together. The verse may even see another misunderstanding of unspecified aspects in vv. 3-4 and 5-6. Verse 3a spoke of *both* trumpets *blown* without saying whether they blow simultaneously or successively. Verse 6aα spoke about two successive alarm blowings one at a time, but without saying whether both trumpets were involved or only one. The blowing of two trumpets in v. 3a could be misunderstood as a blowing *twice,* v. 6aα. Verse 7 wants to clarify the relationship between vv. 3-4 and 5-6.

Verse 8 finally says who the trumpeters are: the sons of Aaron, the priests. They are to "blow" the trumpets. The text speaks neither about "two" trumpets, nor about "blowing alarm" or "sounding" (alarm). But the context suggests otherwise. In vv. 3-4, "they" call to the tent of meeting where they are, together with Moses; cf. → Numbers 3–4, especially 3:38. In vv. 5-6, "you [pl.] blow the alarm" for the decampment of the units encamped around the sanctuary according to → Num 2:9b, 16b, and also vv. 24b, 31b, again from the center of the camp in front of the sanctuary. In v. 7, they are the same priests. They are certainly also meant in v. 10, and therefore also in v. 9. Verse 8b is a subscription to the entire section vv. 2-8. Cf. Lev 17:7, and Kellermann, 142. It is a FORMULA OF STATUTORY LAW.

In II.B. (vv. 9-10) the text prescribes the usage of the trumpets "in your [pl.] land," for war (II.B.1., v. 9) and for the sacrifices at apparently special communal occasions of joy, and the regular seasonal and monthly convocations (II.B.2., v. 10). Following v. 7b, the trumpets are "sounded" (for war) and "blown" (for the sacrifices). And in addition to their signal function for Israel, they have a signal function for Yahweh. Israel will through their acoustic effect be remembered before Yahweh (vv. 9b, 10b). The formula of grace in v. 10b supports this promise, and probably concludes the entire Yahweh speech. Finally, it appears that vv. 3-4, 5-6 and 9, 10 are chiastically correlated: from congregating to decamping, and from going to war to the sacrifices at the sanctuary festivals.

In terms of style, syntax, terminology, and content, the unit is by no means homogeneous. The Yahweh speech form embracing it is not everywhere equally evident, if at all as in vv. 9b, 10b. The literary relationship of vv. 1-2, 3-4, 5-6, 7, 8, 9, and 10 is problematic. Much more than a creation by the same hand, it suggests the composition of some diverse literary elements by a writer, and even a growth of that composition up to the extant text; cf. Kellermann, *Numeri,* 140-47. This understanding is easier even as opinions on the specifics of that process may differ, and even though the origin of some elements — e.g., vv. 3-4 and 5-6 — remains elusive. In particular, evidence that most elements originally spoke of two trumpets only and that the combination of Sinai and the land was implied in each element is lacking. The question is, therefore, decisive as to what generated the focus on the two trumpets and the composition of the extant text, and what the nature of this text is.

Genre

The unit must have been generated above all by the motif of the two silver trumpets. This motif is explicit in v. 2 only, but it preempts the meaning of the trumpets in the rest of the text, of their function and of the priests who are to use them. For the sake of this focus, the text was composed from various elements as a Yahweh instruction for the Aaronide priests. These two factors constitute the generic identity of the text. The text belongs to the genre of PRIESTLY DAAT, PROFESSIONAL INSTRUCTION FOR PRIESTS. Cf. Rendtorff, *Gesetze.*

Setting

The composition of the text is unique. It is influenced by factors from Israel's tradition history even more than by its literary history. The focus on the two trumpets coincides with the focus on the two most critical types of events in Israel's existence. Each of the two foci reflects a programmatic condensation of their respective traditions, a condensation intensified by their combination in this text. For Israel as a community, two types of existence stand out as most critical: the historical situation of war, offensively as well as defensively, and the continual convocation at the sanctuary — specifically here for the sacrifices of burnt offerings and peace offerings (v. 10a). For these types of existence, the two trumpets provide the distinct signals, in distinction from all other trumpets and instruments used throughout Israel's history. The two hammered silver trumpets have for these events replaced the ancient horn *(šôpār),* cf. Exod 19:16, 19; 20:18; Josh 6:4-20; Judg 3:27; 6:34; 7:18-20; 1 Sam 13:3; Ezek 33:3-6; et al. They are exceptional when compared with other trumpets frequently mentioned, mostly but not always used by priests, cf. Hos 5:8; 2 Kgs 11:14; 12:14; Ps 98:6; Ezra 3:10; Neh 12:35, 41; and often in the books of Chronicles. The function of horns or trumpets calling to the sanctuary or to war, also by priests, is quite traditional, cf. Josh 6:13, 16; 2 Chr 13:12, 14. But nowhere except in Num 10:1-10 and 31:6 (for war!) are these two primary functions fulfilled by two silver trumpets in the hands of the Aaronide priests. These trumpets existed in the second temple. Cf. Gressmann, *Altorientalische Texte und Bilder,* 41-42; Pritchard, *ANEP,* 116, 289. They are not attested for older times. The text and its genre point to a setting in which the usage of the two trumpets — whether existing or proposed — as the prime cultic signal instruments under the exclusive control by the Aaronides had to be claimed or defended against other traditional signal instruments and other parties. The date of that situation, especially of the origin of the two trumpets, cannot yet be determined exactly. And in view of the fact that they are only mentioned twice, and that Chronicles provides a different picture, the extent to which the claim was realized is not certain.

Intention

The composition of the unit provides the clues to the definition of its intention. Most striking is the correspondence between the two purposes of the trumpets for the impending march from Sinai and for the future in the land. The correspondence between their blowing to the tent and to the sacrifices is self-evident. The same is also true for their sounding to decampment and to war. The call to decampment is a call to the sanctuary campaign. → Chapter 2, and → Numbers 1; → Numbers 2. Indeed, the summons of "the leaders, the heads of the thousands of Israel" to Moses (v. 4) may be understood as the call to a military staff meeting in preparation of the decampment launched by "blowing alarm" (vv. 5-6).

At the campaign and in the land, the two trumpets are used only for important cultic events and for the extraordinary situations of military campaigns. They are not used for any and all events. They are just as exceptional as are the situations for their use. These situations are signaled by the Aaronide priests. The control of the signal instruments as well as the announcement of the situations through the instruments reflect the intentionality of the hierocratic guidance of the community.

The most important intention, however, is indicated by the correspondence of the situations for the campaign and for the land. The report about the origin of the two trumpets at Sinai, commanded by Yahweh, intends to authenticate the claims to their priority in the land forever. Moreover, vv. 9b and 10b affirm that whenever in the land Israel finds herself in situations analogous to those from Sinai on and these trumpets are "blown" and "sounded," Yahweh himself will remember the original ideal situations and reenact them. In war, he will save them from their invading oppressors (v. 9) as he led their offensive during the campaign. And at the sacrifices (v. 10), he will be present as he was present when the trumpets called them to his tent of meeting.

Num 10:1-10 is a unique supplement to the Sinai pericope, and quite appropriately positioned. Its special context is → Numbers 2 and → 3:38. But it is different from Num 9:15-23. It speaks of decampment, and not of both, decampment and encampment. It speaks of signals for campaign and war, which Num 9:15-23 does not, at least not explicitly. It speaks about the land, again unparalleled. Above all, it relativizes the immediacy of Israel's response to Yahweh's theophanic cloud and voice by either offsetting it through the priestly calls to meetings or by delaying it through intermediary priestly signals. Num 10:1-10 is hierocratic, Num 9:15-23 theocratic. Juxtaposed texts imply neither by definition nor always that they are complementary. Sometimes, as in this case, they stand in tension against each other.

Bibliography

H. Gressmann, *Altorientalische Texte und Bilder zum Alten Testament* (Tübingen: J. C. B. Mohr, 1909); R. Rendtorff, *Die Gesetze in der Priesterschrift: Eine gattungsgeschichtliche Untersuchung* (FRLANT 62; Göttingen: Vandenhoeck & Ruprecht, 1954).

Chapter 4

The Saga of the Campaign Itself (Numbers 10:11–36:13)

Editorial Note: The following Macrostructure of Num 10:11–36:13 is based on the 1998 Dissertation of Won W. Lee at Claremont Graduate University, "Punishment and Forgiveness in Israel's Migratory Campaign: The Macrostructure of Numbers 10:10–36:13." Lee has superscribed it as: The narrative of Israel's forty-year campaign in the wilderness, p. 322. It is presented here in full, together with the summary of its explanation. For explanation, see the section → Setting in this chapter.

Structure

I. Event: failed campaign to enter the promised land from the south	10:11–14:45
A. Programmatic departure	10:11-36
B. Distrust of Yahweh's ability to fulfill the promise	11:1–14:45
1. General example	11:1-3
2. Specific examples	11:4–14:45
a. People's rebellion against Moses' leadership	11:4-34
b. Miriam and Aaron's rebellion against Moses' authority	11:35–12:16
c. People's rebellion against Yahweh's leadership	13:1–14:45
II. Consequence: entrance into the promised land delayed by forty years	15:1–36:13
A. Completion of Yahweh's punishment of all the Exodus generation: the death of the Exodus generation	15:1–20:29
1. Reaffirmation of leadership	15:1–18:32
a. Yahweh	15:1-41
b. The human leaders	16:1–18:32
1) Moses	16:1–17:15

2) Aaron 17:16-26
3) The priests and the Levites 17:27–18:32
2. Transition: purification from contamination
by corpse 19:1-22
3. The end of the Exodus generation 20:1-29
a. Denial of the prophetic leadership of Moses
and Aaron 20:1-13
b. Specific examples 20:14-29
1) Retreat from Edom 20:14-21
2) Death of the high priest Aaron 20:22-29
B. Actualization of Yahweh's forgiveness of the Exodus
generation: the call of the new generation as the new
carrier of the divine land promise 21:1–36:13
1. Successful conquest of the promised land:
turning point 21:1-3
2. The wilderness experience of the new generation:
at the end of the forty-year campaign 21:4–36:13
a. Preliminary to matters of the land:
characters of the new generation 21:4-25-18
1) Rebellion: food 21:4-9
2) Migration to the plains of Moab 21:10-20
3) Triumphs over the Transjordan peoples 21:21–24:25
a) Directly: successful possession of
their lands 21:21-35
b) Indirectly: Yahweh's providence over
the new generation 22:1–24:25
4) Rebellion: religious loyalty 25:1-18
b. Matters of the land proper: goal of the new
generation's campaign 25:19–36:13
1) Yahweh's instructions 25:19–36:12
a) Introductory instructions 25:19–32:42
(1) Census for the purpose of the
distribution of the land 25:19–26:65
(2) Various concerns relating to the land 27:1–30:17
(a) Heiresses' right to inherit the land 27:1-11
(b) Joshua — the one who will conquer
the land — the successor of Moses 27:12-23
(c) Cultic regulations of public offerings 28:1–30:1
(d) The male responsibility for the
validity of vows 30:2-17
(3) Distribution of the land 31:1–32:42
(a) Sharing the booty after conquering
the Midianites 31:1-54
(b) The allotment of the Transjordan land 32:1-42
b) Instructions concerning the promised land 33:1–36:12
(1) Summary of Israel's campaign
(from the Exodus to the plains of Moab) 33:1-49

(2) Instructions proper		33:50–36:12
(a) The division of the land of Canaan		33:50–34:29
(b) Apportionment of the Levites		35:1-8
(c) The cities of refuge for involuntary homicide		35:9-34
(d) Legislation of the inheritance of heiresses		36:1-12
2) Subscription		36:13

The macrostructure just shown includes thirty-six distinguishable literary units each of which Lee has identified, structurally presented, and interpreted, 134-231. The units are listed by Lee as follows (134-35):

1) 10:11-36	Report of Israel's departure from the wilderness of Sinai
2) 11:1-3	Taberah etiology: Israel's rebellion against Yahweh regarding the people's misfortunes
3) 11:4-34	Kibroth-hattaavah etiology: Israel's rebellion against Yahweh regarding the lack of meat
4) 11:35–12:16	Rebellion narrative of the event at Hazeroth: Miriam and Aaron challenge Moses' authority
5) 13:1–14:45	Historical narrative concerning Israel's failure to enter the promised land from the south
6) 15:1-16	Yahweh speech: instructions about cultic regulations for the accompanying aspects of an offering by fire
7) 15:17-31	Yahweh speech: instructions about the dedication of the first dough
8) 15:32-36	Report about the wood gatherer on the Sabbath
9) 15:37-41	Yahweh speech: instructions about tassels
10) 16:1–17:15 [NRSV 16:1-50]	Report about Korah's rebellion against Moses and Aaron
11) 17:16-26 [NRSV 17:1-11]	Report about Aaron's budding staff
12) 17:27–18:32 [NRSV 17:12–18:32]	Yahweh speech: instruction about the duties of the priests and Levites
13) 19:1-22	Yahweh speech: instructions about purification from contamination by a corpse
14) 20:1-13	Report about Yahweh's denial of Moses' and Aaron's prophetic leadership
15) 20:14-21	Report of Israel's conflicting encounter with Edom
16) 20:22-29	Report of event at Mount Hor: the death of Aaron
17) 21:1-3	Hormah etiology: Israel's victory over the Canaanites
18) 21:4-9	Rebellion narrative of the event on the way to Oboth: the serpent scourge

19) 21:10-20		Itinerary report: from Mount Hor to the valley near Pisgah in Moab
20) 21:21-31		Report of Israel's campaign against the land of the Amorites
21) 21:32-35		Report of Israel's campaign against the land of Bashan
22) 22:1–24:25		Story of Balak and Balaam: Yahweh's blessing on Israel through the foreign prophet: Balaam
23) 25:1-18		Rebellion narrative of the event at Shittim: Israel's apostasy to Baal of Peor because of their sexual behavior
24) 25:19–26:65	[NRSV 26:1-65]	Census report: preparation for the allotment of the land
25) 27:1-11		Report about the daughters of Zelophehad: heiresses' right to inherit the land
26) 27:12-23		Yahweh speech: instructions about the commissioning of Joshua as Moses' successor
27) 28:1–30:1	[NRSV 28:1–29:40]	Yahweh speech: instructions about various public offerings
28) 30:2-17	[NRSV 30:1-16]	Report about male responsibility for the validity of vows
29) 31:1-54		Report of Israel's holy war against Midian
30) 32:1-42		Historical narrative concerning the allotment of land in Transjordan for the Reubenites, the Gadites, and the half-tribe of Manasseh
31) 33:1-49		Itinerary report: from Rameses to the plains of Moab
32) 33:50–34:29		Yahweh speech: instructions about the division of the land of Canaan
33) 35:1-8		Yahweh speech: instructions about the apportionment of the Levites
34) 35:9-34		Yahweh speech: instructions about the cities of refuge for involuntary homicide
35) 36:1-12		Report of legislation concerning the inheritance of heiresses
36) 36:13		Subscription

The list of these units is very different from the structure of the total text to which they belong. Both, list and structure, are contained in the total volume of the same text, which is throughout cast as a narrative. Yet while the list points out nothing more than the clearly distinguishable individual units and their position in the sequential arrangement of the narrative's surface, the structure points out the aspects according to which the total narrative appears to be conceptualized as a coherent literary work rather than as an accumulation, more or less incidental and fitting, of separate heterogeneous elements. Whether or not the narrative is such a literary work depends therefore on the question of its structure. (For the individual units, → Chapter 5).

The circumference of the narrative Num 10:11–36:13 is predetermined by the concept — and genre — of the book of Numbers, the saga of the migratory sanctuary campaign. In the structure of the whole book, 10:11–36:13 represents the second part of its two-part subdivision, the saga of the execution of the campaign, following its first part in Num 1:1–10:10, about the preparation of the campaign. The sequential order of these two parts is thereby not the result of a discretionary choice for their placement in the — at any rate inevitably — successive literary arrangement of a larger corpus. It is irreversible, conceptualized in accordance with the irreversible sequential order of the preparation and execution in the reality of such campaigns themselves. See → Chapter 1, Structure, and Lee, 75-131.

The execution of the campaign is united under the aspect of Israel's way from its departure at Sinai until its arrival at the plains of Moab and the events there — as far as they are narrated in the book of Numbers and apart from those narrated in the book of Deuteronomy. All units are integrated in the aspect of this way. However, neither this unifying aspect nor the aspects of the individual units reveal the decisive perspectives from which the narrative of this way is conceptualized. These perspectives are imbedded in the structure of the narrative. This structure is not self-evident. It is indicated by a variety of signals, which are discernible in the text throughout its units. These signals point to the conceptual aspects on which the narrative rests, by which it is directed and controlled, and without which its meaning would not be sufficiently understood.

The variety of structural signals has been a crux in the exegesis particularly of the second part of the book of Numbers. All signals appear in the surface text as juxtaposed. However, their juxtaposition does not mean at the outset that they would conflict or compete for predominance. Nor does it mean that any of them would be invalid. It means first of all that they may belong, respectively, to different structural levels in a structurally, possibly multiply, stratified system of the narrative, in which smaller conceptual units are subordinate parts of larger ones on descending structural levels.

The discernment of the structurally relevant signals prompts the question of their relationship, the question of which of them belong to structurally higher levels, and especially of which reflect the macrostructure of Num 10:11–36:13 on its highest level. Since the total structural system depends on its highest structural level, it is foremost important to determine that level, which happens through the comparison of the structural signals of the text. Said in Lee's words:

"The macrostructure reveals the various levels of its [the text's] infrastructure indicating the locations and arrangements of its individual units. This conceptual system is comprised of conceptualities, the information that the text itself provides, which are located underneath the surface of the text. This infratextual conceptual system . . . is responsible for the organization of the extant text in its linguistic-semantic aspects, and without it the extant text in its present content and form would not exist. It determines the relationships of the parts of the text, and thus creates meaning. In other words, by reconstructing the system of the underlying concepts, however hypothetical such reconstruction may be, the exegete does more than restate the explicit surface meaning of the text. He/she explains why the text says the obvious on the surface. Thus, the task of reconstructing the conceptual system of the text stands ultimately in the service of understanding the text properly" (54).

Lee's macrostructure shown above is the result of this investigation. According to it, the signals, such as indicated in the structured units 2, 3, 4, 16, 17, 18, and 23 of his list, do not lend themselves to identifying the higher structural divisions, let alone the highest one. The same is true for the sum totals of all stations of the migration in the reports in Num 21:10-20: from Mount Hor to the valley near Pisgah in Moab (unit 19) — which covers only the text of units 16-19; and in Num 33:1-49: from Rameses to the plains of Moab (unit 31) — which covers the entire narrative from the Exodus until Moab, and before the units 32-36. Within themselves, these itineraries focus on the sequential topographical and geographical order of Israel's way, but they indicate no aspect according to which the literary corpus, to whichever of its extents, is organized.

Likewise, the signals, if units 1 (Sinai), 15 (Edom), 20 (land of the Amorites), 21 (land of Bashan), 29 (Midian), and 30 (land in Transjordan) were considered as the main literary connections, are not decisive for the macrostructure either. The narrative would consist of six major parts, and be based on this dominant conceptual perspective to which the units in their neighborhood would be subordinate — which is not the case.

The topographical and geographical signals point to the stages of the migration and its progression, however consistently or inconsistently these stages are ordered in the narrative. Their order of the migration's progression is not the conceptual matrix on which the structure of the narrative rests. Rather than being based on the stages of the migration themselves, the structure of the narrative appears to have been generated by the narrators' focus on such aspects by which the nature of the progressing migration, its stages and events, is interpreted in a qualified sense. For this interpreted history, the stages of the migration, and the localities and events therein provide only the foil.

Besides Moses, whose name pervades the entire narrative, the only others who are relevant are Aaron and Miriam (Aaron: units 4, 5, 8, 10, 11, 12, 14, 15 [Aaron's death], 23, 24, 26, and 31; Miriam: units 4, 14, and 24). The occurrences of Aaron and Miriam do not point to structural divisions. They belong first of all to their respective individual texts, and under different aspects, and to the major structural aspects only in as much as they play a role in those aspects that focus on the character of the migration and its events.

The long report about the second census of the Israelites in unit 24 (Num 25:19–26:65), after the first census, in 1:1-54, has played a major role in Olson's thesis of the two-part structure of the book of Numbers. Apart from the different two-part subdivision of the book submitted in this commentary, Olson's assumption of not more than two parts for the macrostructure of Numbers deserves confirmation. Also, whereas the two-part structure of Numbers does in this commentary not rest on the contradistinction of the two generations, Olson's argument appears to be on target in as much as it highlights the importance of — specifically theological — ideology, rather than of the material data, in the conceptual formation of narrative.

Although the findings in this commentary concur with the aspect of ideology in Olson's argument, its criteria for defining the two-part structure of Numbers rest on the two-part structure of the campaign narrative, rather than on the division of the "old" and the "new" generation, claimed to be ideologically definitive and demarcated by the two census reports. Indeed, the second census report appears in Lee's findings only within the second part of Numbers, 10:11–36:13, rather than as the signal for the two-part structure of the total book. Within that second part, Lee again identifies two subdivisions, which are also distinguished ideologically but not demarcated by the second census report.

The chronological data in the text are, likewise, not indicative of the macrostructure of Num 10:11–36:13. Some, such as Num 28:14; 33:38, do not count at all, while others at best support the real structural aspects. The datings in Num 1:1 and 10:11 — both with respect to the date of the exodus — support the distinction between the preparation and the execution of the campaign in the structure of the whole book of Numbers. Of the period of Israel's encampment at Sinai, they specifically allot the last nineteen days for the preparation of the impending campaign. The references in Num 13:23, 25 and 14:33, 34, within Lee's unit 5 (Num 13:1–14:45) belong to the larger concept of the forty years of the Exodus generation. In connection with this concept, the literary unit 13:1–14:45 plays a specific role, which is under its own aspects decisive — so Lee — for the two-part subdivision of the second part of Numbers. The references to the forty years in this unit do not represent the structural division as such. They belong to the general aspect, upon which the narrative elevates in this unit the specific reason for the separation of the two generations. That the chronological data refer only to the general aspect can, e.g., also be seen by the fact that they are not strictly unified in the text. Whereas the forty-year count begins in some passages with the exodus (Num 1:1; 10:11; 33:38 about Aaron's death), it begins, according to 13:25; 14:33, 34, with the wilderness time after the start of the campaign from Sinai, which time is understood as the forty-year period of judgment.

The macrostructure of Num 10:11–36:13 is generated by a number of related conceptual aspects in light of which the entire course of the narrated history is interpreted. These aspects provide the network upon and within which the individual units of the narrative, and their traditions, are organized and placed. They are theological in nature, and reveal the total narrative about the campaign as a theologized history.

According to this theologization, the campaign is, first of all, understood throughout from the perspective of the presence and role of Yahweh, as an epiphanic-revelatory presence in which the military and cultic sides go hand in hand and are often intertwined. As much as the narrative speaks about Israel's own role in that process, and lastly about Yahweh's reaction to this role of Israel, these aspects receive their meaning in light of the revelatory presence of Yahweh. Without that aspect, the total narrative and its structure would not be what they are.

The units 1, 5, 15, 17, 20, 21, 29, and also 19 and 31 focus on the military side. Following the report about its departure from Sinai in military formation, the reports about Israel's recurring military clashes with its enemies are not understood as isolated incidents, let alone as the goal of the campaign. They are considered as links in Israel's march toward the promised land. Rather than reflecting the aspect of Israel's relationship with each of these nations apart from its march, these reports reflect the chain of the obstacles that Israel encountered while being on its way to the goal of its campaign. Moreover, this chain of obstacles on the way to be met militarily is already anticipated at the outset in the military organization of the camp in Numbers 1–2 (3–4), the condition for Israel's departure from Sinai. It is well known that the images of these texts vary and came from different traditions. E.g., the war stories do not reflect the depiction of the camp order of Numbers 1–2 (3–4). Nevertheless, the conclusion is scarcely avoidable that they are to be read from the vantage point of that organization and departure: as actualizations of an epiphanic and hierocratically centered sanctuary campaign even as it was led by Moses.

In the picture of the epiphanic nature of the entire campaign, the units which focus on the never ceasing revelatory speeches of Yahweh are slightly even more numerous: 6, 7, 9, 12, 13, 26, 27, 32, 33, 34. See Lee, 134-35 and 136-236, and → Chapter 5 on the individual units. Diverse as these units are and dispersed as they occur, and occasionally connected with narratives about certain places and events, they too pervade the entire narrative and represent another important factor in the coherence and structure of Num 10:11–36:13. They point to the aspect of Yahweh's revelation which, having begun from Mount Sinai and continued from the sanctuary in the camp, extended throughout the entire course of the military campaign from its start at the Sinai camp to, and in, its encampment at the plains of Moab — ending there and being replaced by the instructions of Moses in Deuteronomy.

The narratives about instructions by speeches of Yahweh are attributed to the hands of the priestly writers, whereas the texts in Deuteronomy about the instructions of Moses are attributed to the writers of the deuteronomic-deuteronomistic school. The priestly writers emphasize the revelation of Yahweh; the deuteronomic-deuteronomistic school can, at least in the Pentateuch, do no more than emphasize the importance of the Mosaic instructions — and that with explicit acknowledgment of the priority of the Yahweh-revelation over their own claims. Next to other indicators, these different weightings, too, point to the priestly writers, especially of the Aaronide denomination, who controlled and produced the final formation of the Pentateuch.

Together with the instructions given from Sinai and the camp at Sinai, virtually all the Yahweh instructions said to have been given wherever and whenever during the campaign aim at Israel's anticipated permanent life in the promised land after its conquest, especially the land west of the Jordan, just as the texts about the campaign aim at the conquest itself of this land.

The narrative of Num 10:11–36:13 is pervaded by and rests on the concept of Israel's epiphanic military-cultic campaign. This concept is the background against which the specific criterion appears for the discernment of the two-part macrostructure of this narrative. This discernment comes into focus with Israel's reaction to the revelatory nature of its campaign, and lastly with Yahweh's response to Israel.

Israel repeatedly and in various ways fails to behave in accordance with the nature of the revelatory presence of Yahweh in its campaign, which is especially, and astonishingly consistently, narrated in the units 2, 3, 4, 5, 8, 10, 14, 18, 23, and also 29 and — though relative — 30. The narrative leaves no doubt about the gravity of this persistent failure of Israel. This failure is also said to have happened after the arrival and encampment in the plains of Moab, as stated in Num 22:1 (unit 22); see unit 23 and at least 29.

One might ask if the narrative of the campaign is not subdivided among the two aspects of the migration and the encampment in Moab, hence, between Num 10:11–21:35 and 22:1(introduced by the Balak-Balaam story)–36:13. If that were the case, however, the criterion for such a two-part subdivision would be the territorial aspect, regardless of the aspect of the nature of the campaign, of Israel's reaction to it, and of Yahweh's response to that reaction. Also, the aspect of the difference between the original generation and the one following it would lose its significance, because the original generation had not yet vanished by the time Israel arrived in Moab.

The decisive criterion for the macrostructure of the campaign narrative appears in the aspect of Yahweh's final reaction to Israel's failure to comply with Yahweh's presence. This response of Yahweh to Israel's failure consists of the decision which Yahweh made concerning the separation of the first from the second generation, at the juncture during the process of the campaign at which the decision was made, and, hence, at the place where this decision is narrated in the text. This criterion is conceptual, and highly theological in principle.

According to Lee, that juncture is located in Num 13:1–14:45 (unit 5). It signals the transition from part I. (Num 10:11–14:45), the end of which it represents, to part II. (Num 15:1–36:13). The decision of Yahweh in response to Israel's failure appears thereby as the reason for the two decisive aspects under which the total campaign is conceptualized in the narrative: the aspect of the failed campaign to enter the promised land (without delay) from the south (I.), and the aspect of the consequence: entrance into the promised land delayed by forty years (II.). That Yahweh's decision is by Lee considered to belong to the end of part I. is understandable. As much as it responds to the previous record, it stands at its end, just as it belongs to the specific unit in which the event is narrated that triggered the decision to end the conquest from the south; in addition, the decision happens before the consequence begins.

In some respects, the formulations in the structure presented by Lee should be changed. He defines Num 13:1–14:45 (in I.B.2.c.) as: "People's rebellion against Yahweh's leadership" — which is not more than how this story is often, and conventionally, described. However, quite apart from the fact that the story narrates not only the people's rebellion but also Yahweh's response, the reason for Lee's macrostructural division at this juncture of the narrative lies decisively in Yahweh's decision in response to the people's rebellion, not in that rebellion, and one like any of the other rebellions at that. Also, in light of the structural significance of this passage, it might be, or should be, given a higher signal in I. than that of a very subordinate part c.

Nevertheless, the aspect of Yahweh's decision is fundamental for the understanding of the campaign narrative. As much as one may speak about it as a saga of the campaign or migration of Israel, the narrative depends decisively on, and is structured by, the concept of the plan of Yahweh, his own will and decision, and their execution for the sake of his people Israel, rather than on a campaign by Israel with Yahweh's cooperation let alone without Yahweh. The narrative is a specifically conceptualized theological saga of the history of Yahweh's own campaign with his people Israel. Without this concept, it would not exist as it does. This concept is coherent with the basic concept on which the narrative of the entire Pentateuch rests.

This understanding is also reflected in the sub-sections A. (15:1–20:29) and B. (21:1–36:13) in part II. (15:1–36:13) of the macrostructure presented by Lee, when he speaks, in A., about the "Completion of Yahweh's punishment of all the Exodus generation: the death of the Exodus generation," and, in B., about the "Actualization of Yahweh's forgiveness of the Exodus generation: the call of the new generation as the new carrier of the divine land promise." One may wish that some of his formulations be adjusted, and also wonder if his two sub-sections, A. and B., divide this part of the narrative as well as possible, but his focus on the decisive role of Yahweh also in these sections of the narrative cannot be discounted. It is especially noteworthy that the report of the second census in Num 25:19–26:65 belongs according to Lee's structure to "Matters of the land proper: the goal of the new generation's campaign" (in II.B.2.b.), where it is under 1) a), "Introductory instructions," placed as the first of these instructions, (1) as the census "for the purpose of the distribution of the land," in contrast to the purpose of the first census: for the military campaign.

Genre

The narrative of Num 10:11–36:13 contains the second part of the two-part book of Numbers and belongs, together with the first part, to the basic genre SAGA of the whole book, particularly in the sense of the German word *Sage*. For explanation of the difference, see FOTL IIA, 171-72. For the discussion of SAGA, see the sections on Genre in → Chapters 1 and 2.

Generally, Saga/*Sage* is a long narrative in prose or poetry about the progression of events in human groups from the — often distant — past. While it can focus on many and changing events and aspects and be expressed in diverse forms, its cohesiveness consists basically in the organization of its sequentially ordered events. It is coherently composed by a guiding plot or theme. And it can be based upon a concept in the service of which a plot or theme is developed, by which it is controlled, and for the purpose of which the specifically narrated events are out of a larger pool of available memories and their own original shapes selected and even specifically shaped.

The presentation and discussion of the structure of Num 10:11–36:13 show that the second part of Numbers is conceptualized as a coherent literary work — about the execution of a prepared campaign, about the way of the Israelite community and its leader Moses from the wilderness of Sinai to the wilderness of Moab over the period of an entire generation, and that this work represents a theologically interpreted history of this campaign.

The essential theological aspects on which the conceptualization of this work rests are: Yahweh's presence, guidance, and plan throughout; Israel's failure; and Yahweh's response to the people's rebellion. The work is pervaded by the mythological and legendary components. But it is the human factor of Israel's failure in front of the revelatory presence, of the people's rebellion, which is basic to the work and without which it could not be what it is. The work is neither legend alone nor saga alone. In their comparison, it is more appropriate to consider the legendary component as an entirely plausible part of an overall saga than to break up the homogeneity of the legend genre by including in it the — quite unlegendary — components of the human characteristics in Saga. Num 10:11–36:13 is, therefore, the SAGA of the Campaign itself.

Setting

The question of the setting of Num 10:11–36:13 is confined to the setting of those writers to whom the essential structure of the second part of Numbers is attributable. They belong to the generations of priestly writers who are also behind Num 1:1–10:10, the Sinai pericope before Numbers, and in Genesis-Exodus before the Sinai pericope. For the discussion of setting in Numbers, see the sections on Setting in → Chapters 1 and 2. For the discussion of evidence of more than one priestly stratum, see the treatment of the individual units in → Chapters 3 and 5.

The assumption that the essential structure of Num 10:11–36:13 is attributable to the generations of the priestly writers — of the Aaronide denomination — does not mean that literary-historical distinctions in this material would be denied. It only means that they are not the primary objective of this commentary, and that there is sufficient evidence for justifying the primary focus on the priestly layer in its own right which is attributable to the essential structure of the extant text, even where, so it seems, it has become expanded by deuteronomistic additions. The application of structural interpretation to clearly distinguished, and commonly accepted, deuteronomistic portions of the text awaits further work.

However, the question of the adaptation of older traditions by the priestly writers, especially of the Yahwistic stratum J, is a different matter. In this respect, we have the literary-critical distinctions indicated by Professor Coats in his interpretations of the individual units of Num 11:1–36:13 in → Chapter 5.

We owe Dr. David Palmer, who, while still in his Ph.D. program, proceeded to what Coats, among other things, had not done and had become unable to do. Drawing from the overall macrostructures presented in Coats' previous volume, *Exodus 1–18* (FOTL IIA), he constructed the two major elements for the macrostructure for Num 11:1–36:13, of I. Food, enemy, spring (11:1–25:18), and II. Conquest traditions (25:19–36:13 [NRSV 26:1–36:16]). Following the system adopted from Coats, he also constructed the macrostructure, as it were, from Coats' total commentary of Num 11:1–36:13. Finally, he put together the macrostructures of P and J, as they would emerge from Coats' discussion of the individual units.

The authors and editors believe that the legacy of Coats' work, as far as it went, should be preserved for study and further discussion. However, the macrostructures reconstructed from Coats would have represented only a state of the development of his work. Since he had not included Num 10:11-36, and since he has not provided a discussion of any macrostructural interpretation, the editors have decided to present the reconstructions from his commentary as appendices to his commentary on the individual units in → Chapter 5.

Intention

The discussion of intention is a matter of interpretation that is, as always, especially in historical exegesis, beyond the reach of last definitiveness. One may even withdraw from the word "intention" and prefer instead a term such as "meaning" — as A. F. Campbell does in his FOTL commentary on 1 Samuel — in order to avoid pinning oneself down in the idea of a uni-directive purpose or function of a text. Interpretation of intention or meaning has to be circumspect.

Still, it should not be subjected to the priority of the subjective taste of — in our case — the readers. It should remain controlled by the boundaries of the text, by the explicitness of its structured content, and, as best as can be reconstructed hypothetically, by its conceptual undergirding which can even be detected as being operative in the text itself.

The discussion of the "intention" of Num 10:11–36:13 focuses on what pervades this block of the narrative as a conceptualized whole — rather than on each of its subunits — and on the exegetical insight that the text is itself the result of interpretative history-writing, in the form before us finally written by its writers some eight hundred years after the time about which it speaks — and about which they speak. It therefore represents their perspective and, to whatever extent we call it intention or meaning, their communication through their writing of its relevance for present and future readers. That this perspective is decisively theological in nature must be recognized at the outset.

First of all, their work about the Israelites' sanctuary campaign from Sinai to Moab under the leadership of Moses presupposes the entire Sinai pericope Exod 19:1–Num 10:10, the constitution of Israel as Yahweh's covenant community during its journey from Egypt to the promised land, and at its conclusion the preparation for the epiphanic military campaign towards that land itself, and in Num 10:11-36 even the campaign's ideal beginning. Num 10:11–36:13 narrates a history against the background of that presupposition, not a history in isolation from it. It is a history of the first journey to the land in its entire process. For the discussion of intention of the book of Numbers, → Chapter 1, Intention.

The Israel of the generation of Moses, the so-called wilderness generation, was ideally prepared for its movement toward the promised land — and it fails despite this preparation. The failure consists of the rebellion against Yahweh's plan, even to the extent of the attempt to nullify it (Numbers 13–14), and against Moses. It causes the failure to enter the promised land from the south, resulting in the death of the first generation in the wilderness but also the admonishment for the second generation not to repeat the rebellion of the first generation.

The failure of the Mosaic generation to enter the land is seen in two perspectives: The death of that generation is revealed as Yahweh's retribution for its failure to meet its election and vocation. This kind of retribution, or "punishment," is for this generation final; it is not remedial or corrective only. The writers are aware of more than a historical reminder that the generation of Moses did not succeed in entering the promised land. They are aware that a generation may have its time and, if failing, may end in failure, leaving the warning to the next generation not to repeat both the failure and its failing.

What prevails beyond any individual generation, however, beyond the precarious balance in any generation's time between final or remedial retribution, forgiveness, and exhortation and admonition, is that the covenant is not revoked and the promise remains unbroken throughout all generations. On this basis, the narrative contains ordinances designed for the life of Israel in the promised land after conquest and settlement — the land excluding the Transjordanian territories, in contrast to the Dtr program.

It is on this basis that the theological influence of the Aaronide priesthood appears in the foreground. It expands through additional ordinances what had already been established earlier in the Sinai revelation: the program for the life of the holy community in purity in the promised land. It envisions a hierocratically constituted community under that priesthood whose authority was established before the time in the land, before the monarchy and its authorizations. Indeed, the priesthood's authority was derived from Yahweh's own revealed instructions to Moses, not just from Moses' own testament. For these writers, the meaning also of their campaign story had — and has — to be transparent for their own time. Their story serves as the reminder of the past generations that perished in the wilderness, of their existence outside of the promised land, of the abiding promise for their own and their future generations, and of the expectation of compliance with the prescribed ordinances.

For a more extensive summary, cf. especially Lee's conclusion, 324-32. Cf. E. Blum, *Studien zur Komposition des Pentateuch* (BZAW 189; Berlin: W. de Gruyter, 1990), esp. 333-60.

Chapter 5

THE INDIVIDUAL UNITS
(NUMBERS 10:11–36:13)

Legend of the Ideal Beginning of the Epiphanic Campaign from the Wilderness of Sinai to the Wilderness of Paran (10:11-36)

Structure

I.	The start on the first day:	11-32
	A. Stated basically	11-12
	1. Calendric identification of the first day: year 2, month 2, day 20	11a
	2. The events on that day (in sequential perspective)	11b-12
	a. The epiphanic event: The cloud taken up from the tabernacle . . .	11b
	b. Israel's start from the Sinai wilderness "on their settings out"	12a
	c. The epiphanic event: The cloud settled down in Paran wilderness	12b
	B. Unfolding of I.A.2.b. (v. 12a): Departure "for the first time" as commanded	13-32
	1. The tribes under their leaders	13-28
	a. The condition for their original start: at Yahweh's command through Moses	13
	b. The order of the start of their march (based on Num 1; 2; 3; 7)	14-27
	1)-14) The tribes one after one, plus Gerson and Merari at 4) (v. 17), and Kohath at 8) (v. 21)	
	c. Concluding statement about the order of the march at the start	28
	2. Specific episode: Moses' twofold call on Hobab to join Israel (see below for amplification)	29-32

148

II. Summary about the campaign's first three days   33-36
   A. Statement of the campaign's basic structure   33-34
      1. Stated temporally: They set out . . . a three days' way   33a
      2. The two particular circumstances: the ark and the
         cloud   33b-34b
         a. The ark, starting before them by three days,
            to seek resting place   33b
         b. The cloud, over them by day   34a
         a.+b. As they were setting out from the camp
            (during these days), cf. v. 33a   34b
   B. Moses' twofold call on Yahweh for the role of the ark   35-36
      1. At the starting of the ark   35
         a. Introductory notice: the situation of the start of the ark   35a
         b. Moses' call for Yahweh's war (poetic formulation)   35b
      2. At the resting of the ark   36
         a. Introductory notice: the situation of the ark's
            (return to its) resting   36a
         b. Moses' call for Yahweh's return (poetic formulation)   36b

In as much as the reconstruction of the structure of the texts has played a role in the method of exegesis, the just presented structure of Num 10:11-36 differs from all structures of this text-unit discerned thus far.

The recognition of the text's structure does not rest on the identifiable divisions of its literary history, such as J and P and redactional parts. Nor does it rest on the list or sequence of the text's contents, notions, and connotations, or on typical stylistic characteristics such as chiasm or prose versus poetry, or on its plot and sub-plots however cohesively formulated or even coherently moving forward. While none of these factors may be neglected, the structure rests lastly on that aspect according to which the text appears as a conceptualized unit of meaning to which all the text's other indicators are subservient and within which the order of the relationship of the text's discernible parts can be understood.

The reason why Num 10:11-36 should be considered as a unit in its own right, which distinguishes it from the preceding and following texts, needs to be more specifically explained than is on record thus far.

1. As far as it belongs to larger text units, the passage has been considered as a subunit of 10:11–12:16 (cf., e.g., Milgrom, 76ff.; Harrison, 171ff.; Ashley, 190), 10:11–21:9 (cf. Gray, xxvii-xxviii), 10:11–22:1 (cf. Milgrom, 75; Seebass: "Zweiter Teil," 1ff.), 10:11–25:18 (cf. Olson, 34), 10:11–14:45 (cf. Lee, 322), 9:15–10:36 (cf. Noth, 72-80), 9:15–25:18 (cf. Budd, xvii), and 10:1-28 (cf. Levine, x). For the fuller synopsis on the part of Numbers assumed to begin with Num 10:11 and extending to its end in 36:13, cf. Lee, 333-36.

a. Regarding the question of the beginning of the unit in 10:11, Noth's assumption that a unit of Num 10:11-36 belongs to a larger unit — about "The Departure from Sinai," 72-80 — which already begins at Num 9:15 has found little support. This lack of support also affects Budd's proposal which says that the author's/editor's "work is on the whole well ordered, and falls into three major sections," and determines, like Noth, 9:15 as the beginning of the second section, "B. The journey — its setbacks and success (9:15–25:18)" (xvii).

However, the text distinguishes between aspects concerning departure and campaign in 9:15–10:10 and concerning the moment of the departure itself. The moment of the actual departure from Sinai is narrated only from 10:11 on, not yet in 9:15–10:10.

10:1-10, immediately before 10:11, about the command to make the silver trumpets and to use them "for summoning the congregation, and for breaking camp," presupposes the situation of the camp before its departure, not the moment of the departure itself. It points to the final act in the preparation for the departure and, not coincidentally, immediately before the departure's beginning. The literary position of this unit, immediately before the statement about the actual departure in 10:11, corresponds to the implicit conceptual aspect that the trumpets represent most immediately the specific materials in the preparation through which the breaking of the camp is signaled.

The position of 10:1-10, after 9:15-23, alone shows that 9:15-23 cannot be assumed as the beginning of the narrative of the moment of the departure. 9:15-23 is controlled by the aspect of the essential elements of the pattern according to which the campaign will take place once it will have begun.

Seebass, keeping 9:15–10:10 separate from 10:11-36, says the passage is one of those "in-between texts" that are often used by the Pentateuch-composition (IV/1, 6). His argument rests on redaction-critical observations but does not yet explain the position of the passage structurally, of whether this "in-between text" still belongs to the situation of the preparation or — extremely implausible — represents a unit about an "in-between situation" between preparation and departure.

Pointing to the final aspects and necessities in the preparation for the departure, in distinction to its execution, 9:15–10:10 represents the final part of the entire unit Num 1:1–10:10 about the preparation of the epiphanic campaign, which is followed by the entire narrative of the campaign's execution in 10:11–36:13, which itself sets 10:11 in with the dated departure from Sinai. The difference between preparation and execution in the twofold structure of Numbers is genre-typical.

According to Levine, x, the text about the beginning of the campaign in 10:11 is part of a unit "Part VII. Numbers 10:1-28: The Israelites on the March," within which vv. 1-10 and 11-28 are distinguished (301), and from which 9:15-23 is separate because it represents, after 9:1-14, one of the two subunits of "Part VI. Numbers 9: Two Matters of Cultic Significance."

However, it is more persuasive to consider 9:15-23 as belonging to 10:1-10, both concerned with the march, than to 9:1-15 which is concerned with cultic matters in the texts before, and also to distinguish between the Israelites still before the march in 10:1-10 and on the march in 10:11ff., rather than to take vv. 1-10 and 11ff. together under a — not existing — uniting aspect of "the Israelites on the march." The difference between the aspects of the preparation for and the beginning of the march, exactly in the text's transition from vv. 1-10 to 11ff., appears once again as fundamental.

b. Regarding the question of the end in Num 10:36 of a unit beginning in

10:11, 10:36 is by Harrison (171ff.), Ashley (190ff.), Seebass (2ff.), Lee (322), and also in this commentary, considered as the end of a structural unit 10:11-36.

By contrast, already Gray had separated 10:29-36 from vv. 11-28; Noth, while assigning 10:11-28 to P and vv. 29-36 to J, had still divided the subunits vv. 11-12, 13-28, 29-32, 33-34, and 35-36; Budd separated 10:11-28: "The Beginning of the Journey," from 10:29-36: "Hobab and the Ark" (109-16); Milgrom separated within his 10:11–12:16 the subunits 10:11-28: "The Order of the March"; 10:29-32: "Guidance in the Wilderness: Hobab"; 10:33-36: "Guidance in the Wilderness: the ARK"; and 11:1-3; 11:4-35(6) (75-93). Levine, after his "Part VII. Numbers 10:1-28: The Israelites on the March," assigned Num "10:29-32: Moses' Midianite Relations," and "10:33-36: The Song of the Ark," as two of four subunits of his "Part VIII: Numbers 10:29–12:16: Encounters and Experiences in the Sinai," 309-43. There is no agreement on whether or not 10:11-36 should be considered as a structural unit or why this should be so even among those who argue in its favor. In the following, the case will be made that 10:11-36 is a conceptual unit which is reflected in its structure presented above.

After demarcating 10:11-36 from the preceding narrative, the reasons must be shown for demarcating 11:1-3 from 10:11-36. 11:1-3, the passage about the people's complaint and its consequence, focuses on a particular incident in the wilderness (context: of Paran) after the just-begun campaign, in contrast to the focus in 10:11-36 on the basic pattern of the campaign itself, without a specific incident. Thus the kind of incident in 11:1-3 is unlike the Moses-Hobab encounter in 10:29-32.

Especially, 11:1-3 shows that the incident is started by the people, and their complaint, to which Yahweh's anger reacts, with fire. Both aspects directly contrast with the ideal picture of the relationship of Yahweh and Israel in 10:11-36 where Yahweh is shown to act, with the people reacting, and in perfect obedience. 11:1-3 is the first unit from which on the people's ongoing rebellion on the campaign is narrated, which relates the passage to the following narrative, again in contrast to the campaign's ideal beginning in 10:11-36. Seebass, 6, considers 10:11-36 in contrast to Numbers 13ff. It already contrasts with 11:1–12:16.

Also, 11:1-3 cannot be assumed to be an extension of the passage about the first three days of the campaign in 10:33-36. The text states in 11:3 that the name "Taberah" *(tab'ērâ)* came into existence through the naming of the place in response to the outbreak of Yahweh's fire, itself the reaction to the people's complaint. The text's knowledge of this name is at home in an etiological tradition according to which the name of this locality originated as the explanation for a revelatory act of Yahweh's judgment through a sudden destructive fire. The name has its origin exclusively in the theological tradition history of Israel's wilderness migration towards the promised land. The text does not presuppose that the place belonged to the localities in the geography of Paran that were topographically already identified and generally known before this incident. It does not imply that Israel aimed, and after three days arrived at Taberah, where then this unfortunate incident happened.

Fittingly, 10:33-36 indirectly confirms this picture. This passage neither says nor presupposes that the migration aimed, and after three days arrived, at Taberah, let alone a place Taberah that was previously and generally known. Considered from the vantage point of 11:1-3, 10:33-36 means that while a — suitable — resting place (in the desert of Paran, cf. v. 12b) had been sought out — and selected — by the ark, a place thus far unnamed (if not unknown, or: if known and named, in the narrative tradition not considered worth mentioning), that place received its name, Taberah, only after the tradition had begun to explain a fiery catastrophe in the camp as a judgment of Yahweh.

The two passages do not refer to the continuation of the ideal of the campaign as it had begun. They signal the break between the campaign's ideal beginning and the — beginning of the — breakdown of the ideal. They belong to separate parts in the larger structure of the narrative.

2. The structure within the unit 10:11-36 is not determined by those parts that have been distinguished from each other on literary/stylistic-tradition or redaction-critical grounds, such as the breaks *(Brüche)* after vv. 12, 28, 32, 34 (Seebass, 7), or Seebass' detailed ascription of vv. 11-12, 14-28a to Pg; 29-32 to J (adapted by J from an older tradition); 33-36 to the post-Dtr (33-34) and post-priestly Redaction (35-36, very ancient, perhaps Davidic), and of vv. 13 and 28a also to redactional hands (9-14).

It can be observed that the structure of this text is determined by a conceptual unity, to which the composition of the text's heterogeneous elements has remained subordinate. Its thought is transparent despite some disparities and tensions, and its order can be shown by explaining how the dominant and subordinate aspects in the parts of the text are related, especially at this place in the context of the larger narrative. Even so, as the intra-textual reading of the divers aspects of its parts attempts to allow for a more reasonable understanding of the conceptual coherence of the unit, and for the writers' own understanding of such coherence, one has to admit that such reading takes place in the face of the text's remaining stylistic unevenness.

Compared to its context, Num 10:11-36 represents an in-between unit, not for literary-critical but for substantive reasons. It narrates the beginning of Israel's campaign after the time of its sojourn at Sinai and before the events of the campaign from Taberah on. The events at — what in response to Yahweh's revelatory outbreak of fiery anger against Israel's murmuring became named — Taberah belong to the campaign's phase after its beginning. The aspect of its beginning, as indicated in the title above, is the prime aspect by which the unit is unified, and distinguished from its preceding and following contexts.

The particular conceptual aspects of this beginning have to be explained. This involves, lastly, the explanation of the difference between the statements about the events on the "first" day, v. 13, which under the influence of v. 11a is calendrically identified, and on the first "three days" mentioned twice in v. 33. This difference is accounted for in the two macro-structural parts shown above, I. (vv. 11-32) and II. (vv. 33-36). The two parts amount to a level of the text's organization which is greater and higher than the number and sequential order of its distinguishable smaller units of vv. 11-12, 13, 14-27, 28, 29-32, 33-34, and 35-36.

All these units are united in their statements about Israel's "setting out," as expressed by — forms of — the verb *nāsa‘* which occurs in each of them: vv. 12, 13, 14, 17, 18, 21, 22, 25, 28, 29, 33, 34, and 35. The unit may in its entirety be identified as the "setting out" narrative. However, since the "setting out" aspect expresses the denominator of the unity of this unit, it does not indicate the subdivisions within this unity, especially the primary subdivision above those subordinate to it.

The unit's aspect of the beginning of the campaign is connected to the aspect of the territorial change from the Wilderness of Sinai to the Wilderness of Paran, v. 12. "Sinai" (Num 10:12; 26:64; 33:15, 16) and "Paran" (Num 10:12; 12:16; 13:3, 26) are the terms for the campaign's territories, next to the territorial references to "the Wilderness of Zin" (Num 13:21; 20:1; 27:14) and "the Wilderness of Sin" (Num 33:11, 12). These territorial indicators belong to the larger aspects of the entire campaign narrative. They are clearly distinguished from the topographical indicators for the localities in these territories. Cf. Num 11:1-3, 4-35; 12:1-16; 13:1–14:45. For Kadesh, cf. 12:16; 13:26; 20:1, 14, 16, 22; 27:14.

10:11-36 has two topographical indicators: in 10:33a, "the mountain of Yahweh," and — indirectly — in 10:11b, "the Tabernacle of the Testimony." Both are for obvious reasons related to the respective places in the Sinai wilderness from which the departure took place. They are specifically related to the one and same aspect of the departure's beginning, even as the different subjects named in that beginning start from different places, in different ways, and in distinguished relation to each other: a) the cloud by being "lifted" *(na‘ălâ)* "from the tabernacle," v. 11b (cf. Num 9:15-23); b) the Israelites by "setting out from the mountain of Yahweh," v. 33a, and — as the syntax in vv. 11b-12 makes clear — c) the three sequential steps in the movements of first, cloud, v. 11b; second, Israel, v. 12a; and third, cloud, v. 12b. The statements about these three sequential steps in vv. 11b-12a involve several programmatic distinctions. When speaking about the cloud the text refers to both its being lifted and its "settling down" *(šākan)* in contrast to saying about Israel only that "it set out" without saying likewise that, following the cloud, Israel, too, settled down. While the text focuses on the cloud as the decisive carrier of the whole movement, it focuses only on Israel's setting out. This focus is supported by the aspect by which Israel's setting out is caused, following — and confined by — the cloud's own ascendance and descendance. It is subordinate to the aspect of the epiphanic event of the rise, the transmigration and settling down of the cloud. And while vv. 11-12 speak about this order of the departure on only the first day, one has to imply that this order is understood as the permanent order of the entire campaign.

The aspect that the start of the cloud — not only initially but regularly — is likewise considered as the cause for the start of the Israelites is not compromised by the statement in v. 34 that "the cloud of Yahweh was over them by day, whenever they set out from the camp." On the contrary, v. 34 reinforces the text's emphasis on the epiphanic nature of the campaign. It points not only to the function of the cloud for each of the Israelites' de- and encampments, but also to its presence over them during their march. As it prompts Israel's setting out by its own setting out, and Israel's settling down by its own settling down, so is Israel's march happening, regularly, under the cloud's forward motion over them.

When compared to the aspect of departure, which is explicitly stated throughout the unit, all other aspects about the departure signaled in the unit — of geography and topography, of the cloud and the Israelites, and also of the ark (vv. 33b, 35) — are narrated throughout with regard to that departure as their primary, basic, vantage point. This vantage point is common to them; they are connoted and subordinate to it; they serve it. Each of them points out a specifically clarifying aspect, and those aspects are complementary despite their obvious heterogeneity. However, none of them indicates as such the perspective by which the macrostructure of this text is determined — as long as one fails to account for the fact that the text speaks not only about the departure in the strict sense, i.e., in only the terms of the cloud's "being lifted," of Israel's "setting out" and the ark's "setting out," and of their setting out "from the Wilderness of Sinai," v. 12a, and "from the mountain of Yahweh," v. 33b. For it also speaks about aspects that go beyond the aspect of the start proper of the departure common to all, in terms of locality, moment, condition, and order of the very start.

Verse 12b says that the cloud settled down "in the Wilderness of Paran"; v. 34 complements: the cloud was over them by day "as they were setting out" — i.e., whenever they were setting out — "from the camp." This means that the cloud was over them after it had set out itself, and it did so continuously beyond the day of — and the days after each — departure.

Verses 35-36 speak about the return and resting of the ark, and as a regular pattern as well, and not about its "setting out" only, and only for its initial departure. Also, the ark was setting out before them "a three days' way, to seek out a resting place for them," v. 33b, just as the Israelites set out "a three days' way," v. 33a. Both statements point to the aspect of the departure beyond the initial decampment.

The aspect of a regular type of event beyond the initial departure is also addressed in v. 21b. The Kohathites carry the sacred objects — during, not only at the beginning of the, and each, march — while the tabernacle has to be set up — by the Gershonites and Merarites, vv. 17-20 — "before their," i.e., the Kohathites', "arrival," which presupposes the ever new dismantling, transport, and re-erection of the tabernacle at each new location after its initial dismantling and departure.

The macrostructure of the unit Num 10:11-36 is therefore determined by two aspects which extend over all other indicators of the text, and to which all those indicators are subordinate: by the distinction between the initial events at, and the following events of the first extension in, Israel's departure from the Wilderness of Sinai. The text distinguishes between the beginning and the immediate continuation of that beginning in Israel's departure from Sinai.

For this distinction, two signals stand clearly out. One is the territorial, and the other — the decisive one — is the temporal signal. Territorially, the passages that refer to or imply the territory beyond the location of the tabernacle and the mountain of Yahweh at the Sinai wilderness, weigh indirectly, cf. vv. 21, 33-34, 35-36, and also v. 31. Directly, and programmatically, however, v. 12b says that the cloud settled down "in the Wilderness of Paran." After the cloud is taken up from the tabernacle — in the Wilderness of Sinai — the Wilderness of Paran is the first location of arrival in the cloud's migratory transition. More specifically, rather than focusing on the movement itself, the text focuses on the two locations, the point of departure and the point of arrival, by which the first stage of the migratory campaign is marked.

This stage is identified calendrically as having taken place on "the twentieth day of the month" of the second month of the second year, v. 11a, on that one day, the first day of the campaign. Syntactically, all sentences in vv. 11b, 12a, and 12b depend on v. 11a. And their contents are said to have taken place on that "twentieth" day, including the cloud's settling down "in the Wilderness of Paran." The calendric aspect in vv. 11-12 for Israel's departure from Sinai belongs to the fundamental understanding of the Sinai narrative in the priestly tradition and for the redaction of the extant text.

The focus on days is also twice attested in v. 33a-b in the statements about Israel's and the ark's "three days' march." With respect to the one day in v. 11a, the two statements about three days in v. 33 point to the aspect of the extension of the beginning of the departure from Sinai from its first day to its first three days and, hence, to the distinction between the events on the first day and those on the first three days. Once this distinction is recognized, it becomes clear that the events said to belong to the regular pattern of the march, set on the first three days and not confined to the events of the first day, are — virtually as it should be — narrated at the end of the unit, in vv. 33-36, after the narrative of the events said to have taken place on the first day, in vv. 11-32. The distinction between the events on the first day and the basic pattern of the events on the first three days signals the decisive aspect for the twofold superstructure of Num 10:11-36: I., The start on the first day, vv. 11-32, and II., Summary about the campaign's first three days, vv. 33-36.

Although the aspect of the summary in vv. 33-36 is sufficiently clear, the relationship of the smaller units that now appear as subunits of the first part (vv. 11-32) needs further explanation.

As presented in the → Structure above, part I. (vv. 11-32) about the start on the first day consists of two sub-parts: A. (vv. 11-12), which speaks about this start basically, and B. (vv. 13-32), which specifically unfolds the section of I.A.2.b. (v. 12a), about the Israelites' start from the Sinai wilderness. The view of this twofold structure of vv. 11-32 differs from the view of several sequentially set elements of the text that have been identified literary-critically. While those elements (vv. 11-12, 13, 14-27, 28, 29-32) are still accounted for in the presented structure, they appear stratified on super- and subordinate levels in a narrative that is systemically conceptualized from the vantage point of Israel's start on the first day, basically, and then with regard to its specific aspects.

In the basic statement, A. (vv. 11-12), the sentence about the calendric identification of the day of the departure, 1. (v. 11a) introduces and controls the three following sentences under the unified aspect of the three events on that day: 2.a., then 2.b., then 2.c. (vv. 11b-12). Temporally these events are expressed, and meant, to have happened consecutively, the second and third following, respectively, the one preceding it; further, the second event, Israel's departure, does not only temporally follow that of the cloud, it depends on and is logically subordinate to the cloud's departure. From the local aspect, both the first and second event are said to take place at the location of the departure, whereas the third aspect speaks about the locality of arrival alone. Despite the aspect of the sequence of three events, the twofold focus on departure and arrival — of the cloud! — is decisive conceptually. It is the transition of the cloud, and not from one to the next locality but from one territory to the next, on the twentieth day. Within this transition, on the same day, Israel does nothing more than set out.

The focus on the cloud's transition from desert to desert, from one territory to the other rather than from one location to another, implies the text's knowledge that Paran includes more than one locality. By not referring to or implying any specific, known, locality throughout vv. 11-36, not even the one that became known *post eventum,* the text focuses on Paran and leaves room for the march in Paran from unnamed to unnamed locality, certainly on its first day and during its first three days as well.

Despite the syntactical order of vv. 11-12, which calls for the understanding of vv. 11b-12 in the sense of the events on the one, the twentieth, day, two phrases may be read to contradict this understanding. They may be read to refer to more than the "twentieth day" defined by v. 11a.

One of the phrases in v. 12a is *lĕmasʿêhem* ("by stages," RSV/NRSV; "on their journeys," i.e., their "journey in stages," Milgrom, 76; literally: "at/on/for/ or: according to their settings out"). The phrase "settings out" in the plural form expresses more than one setting out. It may be read to refer to all their settings out which, though begun at Sinai, involve more than the first one to the calendric date of which v. 12a is restricted syntactically. However, it may also be read to mean that they set out — on that day for the first time — in accordance with the kind of all their following settings out, especially by following each ascension of the cloud. The latter reading is preferred here. It respects the restricted aspect demanded by the syntax. The function of the phrase is connoted by the verb, "and they set out," which refers to the step following the first — not each and every — lifting of the cloud from the tabernacle — on that specific day — v. 11b, and which is said to have taken place before the cloud came to rest in the Wilderness of Paran.

The other ambiguity arises from the statement in v. 12b which says that the cloud came to rest "in the Wilderness of Paran." The text means that the cloud, being lifted from the tabernacle — in the Sinai wilderness — (and having left that wilderness), settled on that same first day in the other territory of the Wilderness of Paran. How can the cloud move from one wilderness to another in one day? One may study the perspectives of the various texts and traditions, and the resulting maps of the boundaries and proximities of these territories, as is done in commentaries. However, one would have to explain why the departure of the cloud from the Wilderness of Sinai, and from the time at Sinai, and the completion of this departure by its descent in the Wilderness of Paran on one and the same day should, in and for the text's epiphanic vision, be impossible or unreasonable. To account for the rationality of the text's epiphanic vision is exegetically preferable to a rationalizing query about the possibility or impossibility of — the cloud's! — transition from one territory to another.

In the context of vv. 11-12, the start of the Israelites had only to be stated basically. In B.1. (vv. 13-28), about the departure of the tribes under their leaders, the text unfolds this basically stated start specifically. In this entire subunit, the section of vv. 14-27, about the order of the fourteen successively starting tribal and subtribal entities, is framed by two statements concerning the picture of departure basic for all, including an introductory statement in v. 13 and a concluding statement in v. 28.

According to the introduction, they set out "at the beginning" *(bāri'šōnâ)*, which at least implies, if not directly clarifies, that their previously stated start on the twentieth day was the first of all their following starts. They set out "at Yahweh's command (mediated) through Moses," which emphasizes, in another revelatory connotation and in distinction to the revelatory role of the cloud and the ark, that the specific cause setting the Israelites in motion, at least at this beginning, was Yahweh's own command — revealed to and mediated — through Moses. Indeed Moses is said to have only been the mediator, not the commander, let alone the originator of the command to break camp at Sinai. Both references, the one to the "beginning" and the other about "Yahweh's command," clearly focus on the uniqueness of the first setting out of the Israelites from their encampment at Sinai, in distinction to all following ones. Cf. Seebass, 9: "Hervorhebung des *ersten* Aufbruchs."

Unit B.1.b. (vv. 14-27) narrates in the stereotyped forms of fourteen successive verses the fourteen consecutive "settings out" of fourteen groups of the Israelites into the linear formation of their campaign march. Although the text focuses on the specific situation in which the groups fall into this linear formation, it nevertheless depicts their sequential order as the result of an orderly transition from the order of the quadrangular encampment of the twelve tribes around the tabernacle and its Levitic subgroups. Cf. Numbers 2; 3; 7. The linear formation of the campaign march is at its start from Sinai portrayed as the application of the clearly systemic order of the encamped tribes for the purpose of that march. Conceptually, the order of the march is derived from, and subordinate to, the order of the encampment.

Thus, each tribe, led by its named leader, starts within one of four entities of three tribes per entity (vv. 14-16, 18-20, 22-24, and 25-27), with the entities proceeding clockwise from the east (cf. Num 2:3, 10, 18, and 25). The first tribe leading the start of each entity (v. 14, Judah; v. 18, Reuben; v. 22, Ephraim; v. 25, Dan) is the one encamped between the two tribes flanking it; further, it is only said which of the two comes first, after the leader, but not whether from the left or the right of the leader. They fall into line according to their sequence given in Numbers 2.

From the Levites, the Gershonites and Merarites, as the carriers of the tabernacle understandably combined, and the Kohathites, as the carriers of the sacred objects, represent the two groups who, in addition to the twelve tribes, account for the marching order of fourteen entities. The carriers of the tabernacle start and march thereby in fourth place (v. 17) after the first entity led by Judah (vv. 14-16). The carriers of the sacred objects start and march in the eighth place (v. 21) after the second entity from the southern group led by Reuben (vv. 18-20) and before the three tribes from the western group (vv. 22-24). The last group is the three tribes from the northern entity (vv. 25-27). As a point of strategy, the protection of the rear of the campaign appears to be of particular concern.

The text's vision of the departure from Sinai is confined to the body of the military units of the Israelites. Although it pays no attention to the un-counted mass of all other Israelites, it does refer in v. 17 to the initial disassemblement of the tabernacle and to it being carried when the Gershonites and the Merarites set out. Likewise, it says that "the Kohathites set out carrying the sacred objects, and they [i.e., the Gershonites and Merarites, cf. Milgrom, 77] had set up the tabernacle until they [i.e., the Kohathites] arrived" (v. 21). This vision exceeds by far any rational perception of the execution of the logis-tics of such a mammoth operation during the first and each of the following two days. Cf. Seebass's correct marginal note about the impossibility of executing the text's vision in real logistics, 14. The subscription v. 28 sums up the depar-tures of the Israelite tribal entities as in the order just reported.

The subunit I.B.2. (vv. 29-32) requires a more detailed examination. The short episode of Moses' twofold approach to Hobab in vv. 29-32 is a unit in its own right, clearly distinct within its context. After the concluding summary about the departure of the Israelites in v. 28, it sets v. 29 in with a speech of Mo-ses to Hobab. And after the end of Moses' approach to Hobab in v. 32, the text returns in v. 33 to its further summary about the departure of the Israelites.

Although the episode starts and ends abruptly, without explicit connec-tion to its preceding and following contexts, it is not placed *between* two units; nor is it the first part of a twofold unit, of vv. 29-32 + vv. 33-36, which would conclude a unit of vv. 11-28. The role of Moses in vv. 29-32 is different from his role for the Israelites in v. 13 and vv. 35-36, and is absent in vv. 33-34. The episode is by literary composition directly added to vv. 11-28, and stands as the concluding part of the legend about the departure of the twelve tribes on the first day, I. (vv. 11-32), in demarcation from the conclusion of the entire legend about the first three days in II. (vv. 33-36).

The text of the episode makes it clear that it belongs to this and no other place in the narrative. Immediately after vv. 13-28, it links the specific aspect of Moses' approach to Hobab to the same day on which Israel departs. Moses starts saying: "Setting out we are . . . ," v. 29, which should be read to mean: now, and: as we are setting out I am inviting you — now — to set out with us — this day. The temporal signals already indicate that the invitation belongs to the same moment of the first day of Israel's setting out that was indicated in vv. 11 and 13. Moreover, the logic in the text's picture of the situation is also persua-sive. For it to imply that the invitation may have been given at a moment differ-ent from that of the first day, a moment either before this day or after it, or irre-spective of the aspect of its moment, would mean that one should expect a reference to such a different aspect, indeed a different text, which is not the case.

The occurrence of Moses' approach to Hobab suggests that the episode is considered as an important specific addition to the legend about the start of the Israelites on the first day of their departure from Sinai. Hobab is thereby neither a part of the indivisible corporate Israelite entity nor of its indivisible start. He cannot be commanded by Moses — as are the tribes — and is not obligated to join Israel. He is invited to join, free not to join, and, for a second time even beseeched to join — he alone and no one else from outside the Israelite community!

The structure of this unit is as follows. (For its place within vv. 11-36, see above):

2. Specific episode: Moses' twofold call on Hobab to go with the Israelites	29-32
a. Moses' first call	29-30
1) The call	29
a) Narrative introduction	$29a\alpha_1$
b) Speech	$29a\alpha_2$-b
(1) Statement of the situation	$29a\alpha_2$-β
(a) we are setting out for the place (*māqôm*)	$29a\alpha_2$
(b) of which Yahweh has said *('āmar):* I will give it to you (pl.)	$29a\beta$
(2) The call [prepared by (1)]	29b
(a) Call proper: Come with us	$29b\alpha_1$
(b) Moses' promise to Hobab: we will treat you well *(ṭôb)*	$29b\alpha_2$-β
α. Promise proper	$29b\alpha_2$
β. Reason: Yahweh has spoken *(dibber)* good *(ṭôb)* to Israel	$29b\beta$
2) Hobab's negative answer	30
a) Narrative introduction	$30a\alpha$
b) Non-acceptance	$30a\beta$-b
(1) I will not go with you	$30a\beta$
(2) To my land and my kindred I will go	30b
b. Moses' second call	31-32
1) Narrative introduction	$31a\alpha_1$
2) Speech	$31a\alpha_2$-32
a) Entreaty not to leave	$31a\alpha_2$-b
(1) Entreaty proper: do not leave us	$31a\alpha_2$-β
(2) Reason: Knowledge of camps and scouting	31b
b) Promise (v. 29b essentially repeated)	32

The text appears as an episode within the larger narrative of vv. 11-36. The episode is a concisely composed narrative unit in the form of an approach of one person to another. The choice of this form is, however, generated by the writers' primary focus on the two identified individuals, Moses and Hobab. They are not considered replaceable by others. Specifically, the focus is on Moses as the one who approaches Hobab, and on the content of what Moses has to say. Without this message and the encounter of the two persons, the text could not be what it is. Moses and Hobab, the content of their exchange, and composition are intrinsic to the text, and must be interpreted together.

The narrative is a literary, i.e., written, composition of what it presents as an oral exchange. Its compressed structure is removed from the more elaborate forms of exchanges and also the more alternative kinds of expression in real oral situations. As it stands, the text suggests that the content of the exchange lasted no longer than it takes for the text to be read — and that in light of the far-reaching seriousness of what is under discussion. Although the text's picture of the oral situation is fictitious, it functions to make an ideological, in this case theological, point programmatically. It expresses the program of the writer(s), their historical time and their setting. Indeed, it gives the impression to be formed either to be recited verbatim or to function as a blueprint for, and at the same time controlling, the oral performance of the episode.

The label "dialog" for the unit is not accurate. It is better named a call narrative, or a narrative of a calling invitation. Moses addresses Hobab, who responds, whereupon Moses addresses him a second time — end of episode. The major focus shows that Moses has the initiative. He has the first and last word. Hobab is only the respondent, only once, and not a second time. Whatever Hobab finally does is left aside. It is of no concern to the text. The text's concern is to make clear that Moses, by calling on Hobab, repeatedly, to join them, did not fail his own part, personally and theologically. By this inviting call, Hobab is added to the Israelites who were departing "at Yahweh's command through Moses," v. 13. The text focuses primarily on this specific scene, and on Moses' role in it.

The structure shows the narrators' hand, their development of the exchange and its details. At the same time, their surface text points to presuppositions, either known or to be explored by the readers, without which what is said cannot be — more — fully understood. These presuppositions have to be explored together with the text.

The narrators state in 2.a.1)a) [v. 29aα_1]: "Moses said to Hobab son of Reuel the Midianite, Moses' father-in-law." Presupposed is who Hobab is, and Reuel, and "the Midianite," and that Moses has a father-in-law and who he is. The explanation for these presuppositions is not self-evident. It is necessary, however, so that we may know why the text is what it is.

Before challenging Hobab to "come with us," 2.a.1)b)(2)(a) [v. 29bα_1], Moses states to him the present situation of the Israelites with regard to two aspects: of their departure and of their goal. The goal is called here "the place" (hammāqôm). It is not a random but a definitive place, which is known on the basis of Yahweh's — past — promise by saying "I will give it to you." Presupposed is the knowledge of the origin of this promise to them, "you" (pl.), the knowledge of the territory of the place and also of what is meant by the expression "the place" which is — with one exception in Exod 23:20 — always called "the Land" (hā'āreṣ). Therefore they do not go to a place because they have to leave; they depart Sinai because they go to the place that is their destination because Yahweh has promised to give it to them. Hobab is informed about the theological program under which the moment of the Israelites' departure stands.

And to participate in this program by coming with them he is called [a.1)b)(2), v. 29b]. The call is followed by Moses' promise: Just as Yahweh has

declared good to Israel — in the place — so will the Israelites treat him well —
if he comes with them — to the place. Involved is the quality of their existence
in the place, not just its topography or geography. And involved is the certainty
of, not the hope for, the fulfillment of the two promises. The theology of promise, even in eschatology, does not belong to a theology of hope. Israel migrates
under the theology of promise of both the place and its goodness, and Moses
promises that the Israelites will do the same for Hobab if he goes with them to
the land. The offer for the call could not be more substantial. The text projects
the ideal.

Hobab decides not to accept. He says what he will not do: to go — with
them — to their place, and what he instead will do: go — to his land — and his
kindred. It is the only word he says in the exchange. In view of the alternative
— at the present place and moment — between going forward and being with
the Israelites in their place and returning to his own land and his kindred, he remains bound by his indigenousness. Is it his final decision? The text does not
say. Does it presuppose that he changed it or not? Why does it not clarify?

What Hobab had said meant that he would leave the Israelites. To which
Moses replies in the — jussive — form of an urgent entreaty: "Do not leave
us!" [2.b.2)a)(1), v. 31aα$_2$-β]. The transition from Hobab's answer to Moses'
entreaty is direct. But an additional aspect is introduced which — in addition to
its tension with vv. 33-36 — may in part also be in tension with Moses' first
call: "Go with us" and "do not leave us" are complements. However, whereas
Hobab was in the first call invited for his own sake, he is in the second call en-
treated for the sake of the Israelites. They need him for his knowledge of the
encampings and for being a scout for them, during their migration, not just for
their goal.

We may assume that the text presupposes that Hobab is even so meant to
go with the Israelites to their final destination, rather than implying that he
could still return to his own after completing his mission as their guide, and
without going with them all the way. Because it does not refer to the place of
the destination, v. 32 might be read to refer to good experience only during the
migration. Nevertheless, it is preferable to see in the promise of v. 32 a basic
repetition of the meaning expressed in the first promise, v. 29b.

The question remains why Moses asked Hobab a second time, now ur-
gently and with a different argument, and what the second argument has to do
with the first one. For an answer, one should stay as close to the text itself as
possible. Even if different literary strata should have been combined, not without creating tensions, their combination should have made sense to the writers.
They could scarcely have suggested that the attraction to Hobab in Moses' first
invitation was an enticing pretext for his real reason, the Israelites' own urgent
need for a guide — a need, however, which is neither in vv. 33-36 nor elsewhere confirmed. The most likely understanding of the composition of Moses'
two calls seems to be that he did what he himself could most possibly do. He
could attempt to persuade Hobab to go with them, under any circumstance to
the final destination promised to them. He could also reinforce this attempt by
his repeated promise that the Israelites themselves would extend their experience of goodness to him — certainly not only during the migration but also in

the final place — even as they are in need of his guidance in the wilderness. Why? Because Hobab was Moses' father-in-law. The text reveals an interest that is distinct, and isolated from everything else known about Moses' father-in-law, all the more as it focuses on Hobab alone with regard to its specific moment. It must be compared with those texts and their traditions.

Num 10:29-32 was added to the already existing P stratum or strata of vv. 11-28 because of the need for telling about Moses' approach to Hobab. This addition was achieved for a price: Hobab has no entry into and no exit from this unit, he is isolated within it. No father-in-law of Moses, however identified, is mentioned in the Sinai narrative from Exodus 19 on and in Numbers 11–36, or Deuteronomy for that matter. Moses' father-in-law appears in the specific unit Num 10:29-32 for the first, and only time — as Hobab.

It has been hypothesized that this unit is a fragment preserved from an older source, especially J, in which it would have had to be a part of a meaningful story. This hypothesis has a low degree of plausibility. We owe the existence of the unit in the extant biblical text, including its formulation, to the writers of this text. All we have is their text. If they did adapt an older text, we know neither its original formulation, nor its context, nor its reference to the place and moment of the exchange. We do not know what they did with it, whether they quoted or changed it, and why.

Why would they have not preserved more of such a story? Why would they eliminate elements of information that are indispensable for the important focus on this encounter, especially when one compares such a "Sinaitic" encounter, with Hobab, with the other, and different, pertinent traditions? The question for us is much more why the adaptors composed this text the way they did, regardless whether or not they used an older text, if this is at all what they did. More than anything else, the unit points to the writers' own hand.

In introducing "Hobab the son of Reuel the Midianite, Moses' father-in-law," Num 10:29-32 cannot be unaware that it chooses one of his identifications in the face of the other mentionings of Moses' father-in-law, either in the biblical texts or in the traditions. Also, it cannot have been unaware of the various aspects under which this father-in-law is referred to — his names; his identification as a priest; his land; his affiliation with Midian(ites) and Kenites — even as it introduces him as "the son of Reuel the Midianite." In the range of these biblical references and traditions, and in comparison with them, the particular meaning of Num 10:29-32 must be discerned.

One aspect thereby stands out. Regardless of his different identifications, the person related to Moses is in all pertinent texts defined through his particular family relationship with Moses as "Moses' father-in-law." Cf. Exod 2:16, 21; 4:18; 18:1, 2, 5, 6, 7, 8, 9, 10, 12, 14, 15, 17, 24, 27; Num 10:29; Judg 4:11; cf. 1:16. This notion is constitutive in all texts about the two persons together. The content of none of them could be what it is without the aspect of their family relationship. In Num 10:29-32, Moses said what he said to Hobab because Hobab was his father-in-law; he did not say it to his father-in-law because his name was Hobab (son of Reuel the Midianite).

However, Moses' father-in-law occurs in the framework of the Pentateuchal texts under three names that point to three different persons. He is

Reuel, the priest of Midian, Exod 2:16, 18; Jethro, also the priest of Midian, Exod 3:1; 4:18a, b; 18:1, 2, 5, 6, 9, 10, 12; and Hobab son of Reuel the Midianite, Num 10:29-32. The writers who put the Hobab episode into its present context could not have assumed three fathers-in-law of Moses. They must have had to contend with three mutually exclusive identifications of one and the same father-in-law of Moses. The texts indicate that the Reuel of Exodus 2 and the Jethro of Exodus 3; 4; 18 are different persons, and that neither is identical with the Hobab of Numbers 10. And the writers made no effort to connect or reconcile their Hobab with either the Reuel of Exodus 2 or the Jethro of Exodus 3; 4; 18. On the contrary.

Although not eliminating the Reuel of Exodus 2, he had for them become the father of their own version of the father-in-law of Moses, and was no longer "the priest of Midian" but "the Midianite," just as their Hobab is nowhere called a priest. For their Hobab and his father Reuel, priesthood does not apply. At the same time, they left behind Moses' father-in-law Jethro, also called "the priest of Midian," i.e., confined to the earlier text, Exodus 3–4; 18, before the Sinai pericope, and resolutely replaced him with their own Hobab. Indeed, Jethro had returned to his own land, and was gone, whereas Hobab appears in Num 10:29-32, disjointedly in terms of text and content, out of nowhere.

The meaning of the Moses-Hobab episode in Num 10:29-32 cannot be explained from the text and traditions of Exodus 2–18. It appears to be generated by the tradition about "Hobab the father-in-law of Moses" found in Judg 4:11; cf. 1:16: "the sons/descendants of a/the Kenite the father-in-law of Moses," implying the Hobab named in 4:11.

There is no alternative to concluding that the Hobab of Num 10:29 is the same as the Hobab of Judg 4:11; cf. 1:16. And the tradition has linked him in both cases as the father-in-law to Moses — whereby it may remain open whether one of the two passages depends on the other or is aware of the other or whether both rest on a common tradition independently.

Judg 1:16 focuses on the Kenites who are for the time of conquest and settlement — generations after the time of Moses and Hobab — said to have gone up "with the people of Judah . . . into the Wilderness of Judah . . . and then gone and settled with the Amalekites." These Kenites are said to be the descendants of — that ancestor — Hobab, himself known as a/the Kenite and especially as Moses' father-in-law. In this tradition, they are through their ancestor linked with Moses. Cf. Judg 4:11. The same linkage should also be presupposed, in reversed perspective, in Num 10:29 for Moses, his father-in-law Hobab, and the Kenites.

It seems that the text of Num 10:29-32 is generated by the interest that the lasting good relationship of the Judahites to the Kenites is more than merely the result of the loyalty of the Kenites to the Judahites or, for that matter, to the Israelites. It is even more than the result of the bonds of the family-relationship of their ancestor with Moses or of Moses with their ancestor. It is the result of the activation by Moses of this family relationship for a particular purpose. The enduring good relationship of the Judahites/Israelites to the Kenites in the land is rooted in a specific beginning: the initiative by Moses in which he attempted to integrate his father-in-law Hobab into the departure of the Israelites from Sinai for the ideal campaign toward the promised *māqôm,* for Hobab's — and his descendants'! — benefits along with those promised to the Israelites for that *māqôm.* The position for this episode chosen by the writers in their context is perfect.

With this focus, Num 10:29-32 wants to say something specific, compared to what the traditions have preserved about the relationship of the Israelites to the Kenites in the land. In distinction from the aspect of their corporate relationship, Num 10:29-32 looks at the encounter of the two decisive ancestral individuals at the particular juncture of the start from Sinai of the migration of the Israelites to the promised land. The history of the Kenites in their transition from their home territory to their movement with — not only the Judahites but — the Israelites into the promised land is rooted in Moses' invitation to Hobab to become part of the history of Yahweh's promise for, and gift of, the goodness of the land.

The focus on the ancestral patrons does not negate, dissolve, or suggest harmonizing the variety of the traditions about the Israelites and Kenites. It adds to them by centralizing — and theologizing in a specific way — their understanding. Thus, the Kenites lived in the southland in the neighborhood of the Amalekites, Judg 1:16. According to Num 24:20-21, Amalek is "to perish forever," but the Kenites' dwelling place is "secure" and their nest is "set in rocks." According to 1 Sam 15:1-6, the Kenites had to be protected from collateral destruction in Saul's war against the Amalekites. Here the reason is given: "you" — i.e., your ancestors — "showed *ḥesed*" (kindness; "unconditional friendliness," Stoebe, 285) as compared to hostility, a helpful stance toward/solidarity with all the people of Israel, when they came up out of Egypt," v. 6. The Kenites are not only safe, they are presently saved from the destruction of Amalek. Whereas 1 Sam 15:2-3 clearly remind of Exod 17:8-16, there is no record about the kindness of the Kenites when the Israelites came "up out of Egypt," especially in connection with the confrontation of Amalek and Israel. To refer to Exodus 18 for this sort of *ḥesed* is for more than one reason too farfetched.

Num 10:32 is not followed by a statement about what Hobab himself finally did. There is no evidence either way, if any was ever preserved in — a lost — tradition. Groundless speculation may distract from the fact that the question is for the text unimportant (for a recent discussion, with a different leaning, cf. E. Blum, 135-37). What is important is the fact of Kenites who had some ancient family relations with the Israelites, had been friendly with them on their way in the wilderness, and had joined especially the migration of Judah. This Judahite tradition was certainly Israeliticized, and already before the time of the text in Num 10:29-32.

What has been said leads to the preferable conclusion that this episode is not a fragment from an older source, but an episode ad hoc created and into its present place put either by the same priestly writers who are also responsible for the text Num 10:11-28, or by Dtr writers who added it to the priestly text. For them, the Hobab tradition does not belong to the tradition of priesthood in Moses' father-in-law's parentage. Their reference to the *māqôm* has only one parallel, in the also late passage Exod 23:20b as the word for the destination to which the angel *(mal'āk)* will lead the Israelites. (Gamberoni, 1118, who sees the term also in Gen 13:14-17 used for "the land," ignores that in Gen 13:14-15, Abraham is to look from the *māqôm,* "the place," where he stands — which is not the promised land — "northward and southward and eastward and westward; for all the land *(hā'āreṣ)* that you see I will give to you and your offspring forever." "The place" is here a place in the land, not the land itself.)

The episode of Num 10:29-32 is carried by the initiative of Moses. As much as this initiative is directly connected with the situation narrated in the context, Moses' role in the episode is different from the role he fulfills in 10:11-13a. The cloud lifted, v. 11; the Israelites set out according to (the tribal order of) their departure(s), v. 12a; [the cloud settled . . . , v. 12b]; and the Israelites set out at first "upon the mouth of Yahweh — by the hand of Moses," v. 13a. One may discern a conceptual discrepancy between the start of the Israelites prompted by the epiphany and their start prompted by the signal of Moses. But the two aspects are put together, suggesting a move to complement rather than exclude each other.

Thus, the Israelites set out — in their tribal order — prompted by and following the epiphanic event of the lifting of the cloud, vv. 11+12a — however, not automatically in reaction to the epiphanic revelation and especially not "at first." Their start was "at first" and from tribe to tribe actuated by "the hand (signal) of Moses,'" who — having received the command for this signal — acted "by the mouth of Yahweh," v. 13a.

While the epiphanic event actuates the start of the Israelites basically, their initial start in the order of the tribal units was specifically hand-signaled by Moses who, concurrently with the epiphany, had from Yahweh received the oral command to give the tribes the signal to start in their starting order. The epiphanic revelation for all and the word-revelation to Moses complement each other. Whereby in the "initial" start, Moses is the transmitter from a received divine word-event to his hand signal of it for the Israelites. On being the recipient of the mouth-to-mouth revelation by Yahweh (cf. also Num 12:8), he functions as the commander of the army.

By comparison, his role in vv. 29-32 is very different. He acts neither as commander of the army nor by virtue of transmitting a divinely ordained signal. He acts by his own initiative. Even so, he cannot summon Hobab to join them. He can only invite, lastly entreat, attempting to persuade. As Hobab's son-in-law, he has no authority over his father-in-law. Fittingly, the conditional promise he gives to Hobab is his own, not an inclusion of Hobab (and his descendants) into Yahweh's promise for the Israelites. But to grant this promise is in his authority. Hobab would be, as his descendants are, protected by the authority of the Mosaic promise. One does have to ask if this picture of Moses belongs more to the priestly or to the Dtr writers.

The unit Num 10:11-36 is concluded in part II. (vv. 33-36) by the summary narrative about the campaign's first three days. Heterogeneous aspects within the text and between the text and its preceding context are obvious. It is just as obvious that they are combined in a consciously constructed text with attention to detail as much as to its overall design.

The unit consists of two sub-parts, the narrative statement about the campaign's basic structure and nature, A. (vv. 33-34), and the statement about Moses' twofold call on Yahweh for the role of the ark, B. (vv. 35-36). The two parts have distinct, and different, foci. Part A. speaks about the Israelites — without

165

mentioning Moses — and both the ark and the cloud, whereas Part B., connecting onto the statement about the ark alone, in A.2.a. (v. 33b), speaks about the particular circumstance of Moses' role as the one who summons Yahweh at the occasions of the ark's setting out and returning.

The text of A. (vv. 33-34) depicts a particular order of the departure. First in 1. [v. 33a] (in logical consequence of what had been said before) they set out — from "the mountain *of Yahweh*" (not "the mountain *of God*," Exod 18:5; nor "the Wilderness of Sinai," Exod 19:1; Num 10:12; nor "Mount Sinai," Exod 19:16-25) — a three days' way. Next, in 2.a. (v. 33b), the ark of the covenant of *Yahweh* (not only "the ark" as in v. 35; nor only "the ark of Yahweh," but "the ark of the covenant of Yahweh") sets out before them a three days' way to find for them a rest, and in 2.b. [v. 34a], (at the same time) the cloud *of Yahweh* (not only "the cloud," as in vv. 11, 12) is above them by day. Lastly, a.+b. [v. 34b], (all) they were setting out from the camp (cf. "the mountain of Yahweh," v. 33a).

All three set out from the same place for three days (said twice, v. 33a-b), whereby the settings out of the ark and the cloud are envisioned in their respectively different functions which they have in relation to the daily march of the departing Israelites: The ark *sets out ahead of them,* to seek for them a rest (which is apparently mentioned first because of the primary aspect of the forward moving march led by the ark), during which the cloud is *above them by day.* Note the difference from vv. 11-12, where the cloud prompts the Israelites' departure rather than being a circumstance of it, and is also the subject determining the settling down, v. 12b, and where the ark is not mentioned at all, at best implied as among the sacred objects (v. 21). By contrast, the ark of Yahweh, in setting out and seeking out a rest appearing itself as an actant rather than being carried, functions, like the cloud, epiphanically.

The statement of vv. 33-34 is systematized from different and disparate elements and distinct when compared with its respective contexts. It amounts to a concise summary about the grandiose beginning of the Israelites' departure from their camp at the mountain of Yahweh under the twofold epiphanic guidance of the ark and the cloud of Yahweh during the first three days. The controlling aspect of the presence of Yahweh with the Israelites, at the mountain and on their departure, is thereby repeatedly expressed. This kind of departure could not have been more ideal.

Part B. (vv. 35-36) links up specifically with the previous statement about the ark of the covenant of Yahweh, yet in a turn of meaning that is not, at least not self-evidently, apparent in v. 33b. It connects the activity of Moses with the ark's own activity and its meaning. The short unit focuses on a specific concept in the history of the traditions of the ark, the tradition of the ark as Israel's sacred battle shrine, an originally genuine tradition that was integrated into the tradition of the ark of the covenant, as it is called in 1 Samuel 4–6; 2 Sam 6:1-20; also 1 Kgs 8:1-21. Cf. Ps 24:7-10. It narrates about two calls by Moses on Yahweh, in direct, 2nd pers. address, for his glorious epiphanic acts, one at the occasion of the departure of his ark into battle, and the other at the occasion of its — return to its — rest from battle. The calls have been characterized as "signal calls," *Signalworte* (Kutsch, 198; cf. Ps 68:2 [*NRSV* 1]; 138:1) reflecting 1 Sam 7:1-2; 2 Sam 6:2-15; but also Exod 17:15, 16; Jer 4:6. They signal the moments of the beginning and of the end of battle. The two particular occurrences for the calls, of the ark's departure into and its return from battle, are not only the causes but also the reasons for Moses' two calls on Yahweh.

The ark's exit and return prompt Moses' — presumed public — exclamations, and these exclamations are rooted in the certainty that in the material presence of the ark in battle, Yahweh is expected — and therefore called upon — to become in such battle and out of it himself epiphanically manifest. This certainty is the basis for Moses' call on Yahweh, or challenge, or even summons of Yahweh, cf. the impv. forms. The term "epiphany" refers thereby to Yahweh's revelation through his acts, as distinct from "theophany," which refers to the appearance of Yahweh personally.

The different contents of the calls are connected with the different moments of their exclamations. When the ark leaves the camp for battle, Yahweh is, in B.1.b. (v. 35b), summoned to "rise," so that his enemies are scattered and those who hate him flee. The enemies are Yahweh's own enemies, and are presumed to be terrified by the epiphanic experience of the fury of the God of Israel through the appearance of the ark. After which, when it — the ark — rested, Yahweh is, in B.2.b. (v. 36b), called to return . . . the multitudes of the thousands of Israel. Cf. Levine, 316-19, esp. 336.

The text in v. 36 is ambiguous. If the ark's resting means after battle but still before its return to camp, the call on Yahweh to "return" would work; if the ark's resting means after its return to the camp, the call for Yahweh's own return could mean, presupposing the distinction between ark and Yahweh, that Yahweh was being called to return at — the return of the ark to — its rest, just as he was called to rise when the ark was setting out from camp. Also, a translation saying that Yahweh return "to" the multitudes of Israel is syntactically not impossible (so Ashley, 192: "the verb *šub* followed by an accusative of direction is a relatively common feature"), but it meets with objections on substantive grounds, because it would mean that Israel's army was in the camp while Yahweh, and even the ark, were in battle. It is clear that the reference to the multitude of the thousands/or units of Israel adds another participant to the ark and Yahweh. The relation in which they stand especially to Yahweh, however, is unclear. E.g., NRSV: "Return, O LORD of the . . ."; Milgrom, 81: "Return, O LORD, you who are Israel's . . ."; Seebass, 4: "Kehre wieder, Jahwe: Unzahl der Tausende" [Return, Yahweh: no end of . . .]. The understanding that the multitude of the units of Israel appears as identical neither with Yahweh nor with the ark is preferable. It is implied to have been with the ark in battle. Likewise, Yahweh is called to return as the Yahweh of the multitude of Israel's units, when the ark returns to its rest. The reference to the multitude of the units of Israel is a hyperbole, reinforcing the legendary vision of the text, but it looks rational when considered in light of the numbers of the tribes of Israel's militia given in Numbers 2.

In its context, especially after vv. 11-32, the reference to Moses' call does not necessarily mean that Moses called on Yahweh for battle immediately at the beginning of the Israelites' departure from Sinai from the first day on. But it does mean that the march of the Israelites is from its beginning understood as an epiphanic military campaign — wherever and whenever battle will happen or not. Also, the text leaves no doubt that the contents of the two calls have the same common denominator: Yahweh's, the God of Israel's, battle on behalf of the Israelites, as he rises above Israel's ark into battle against his own enemies because they are Israel's enemies, and as he returns as the God of Israel's militia to rest with his ark. As he rises to and returns from battle, Yahweh does not migrate from location to location. He migrates with the Israelites' camp, from which he moves out and to which he returns. The common vantage point envisioned for both movements of the ark is thereby the camp, which is removed from the place of battle. And Moses is not envisioned as the leader in battle himself, but as the one who instead calls on Yahweh who moves into battle himself.

The signal words may have had their own tradition and original setting connected with Israel's battles. By being put into the context of Israel's departure from Sinai for the beginning of their migratory campaign, and by being pronounced by Moses, they received the status of Mosaic authority for all battles of Yahweh on Israel's behalf.

Genre

In as much as Num 10:11-36 is imbedded in the relevant aspects by which the whole book of Numbers is governed, it belongs to the overall genre of this book: the SAGA of Israel's Migratory Campaign, with its typical two-part literary structure of the preparation and the execution of this campaign. See the discussion of Genre in → Chapters 1 and 2.

In the two-part structure of the book of Numbers, Num 10:11-36 belongs to the second part, Num 10:11–36:13, about the execution of the campaign. Within this part, it is one of many and diverse units all of which are conceptually subordinate to the genre SAGA. For this classification, see the discussion of Genre in → Chapters 1 and 4.

As a unit in its own right, Num 10:11-36 repeats the typical components by which already the narrative about the organization of the campaign in Numbers 1–2 and 3–4 was constituted. But it is now structured from the perspective of the departure: the list of the tribes with their leaders; the four-by-three tribal units, envisioned in the linear order in which they set out (cf. the concluding statement v. 28), rather than in the quadrangular order of their encampment; and the places of the sanctuary (vv. 17, 21a) and its sacred objects (v. 21b) in that linear order.

The numbers of the tribal members of the militia are not listed again, as in the texts about the registration and induction of those registered into camp. Whatever the reasons are for leaving the numbers out in 10:11-28, it is clear that those setting out are meant to be the members of the militia, exclusive of all others who belong to the Israelite community. The setting out is that of a military campaign, literally carried out by the Israelite soldiers alone, while one has to imply that the accompanying masses of the rest of the population of the tribes are presupposed. They are presupposed but for the distinctive aspect of the operation they are not relevant.

In conjunction with the typology of the military campaign, the aspect of its sacral-cultic character is relevant in diverse aspects that, among other things, reveal the text's traditio-historical composite nature. Verses 17 and 21 are short but clear reminders of the presence of the sanctuary. Together with its appurtenances, the sanctuary constitutes the midst of the military camp. The encampment of the tribes is organized around it for its protection, and its entities are also in the center of the marching column. The text reflects the typology of the order of a sanctuary campaign.

The aspect in vv. 17, 21 of the sanctuary campaign is reinforced by the epiphanic aspect of the "cloud" which "lifted from over the tabernacle," to get the tribes setting out. From its very outset, the sanctuary campaign receives a clearly epiphanic quality. Cf. also v. 34, pointing beyond the cloud's original rise. Two epiphanic aspects are connoted with the ark: "The ark of the covenant of Yahweh" — the singular most important cultic object even without the sanctuary and its other objects — is in v. 33 said to be the agent itself of "going before them three days' journey, to seek out a resting place for them," while it, "the ark," is in vv. 35-36 understood as setting out for battle. Finally, Yahweh himself is — in actually theophanic language — called upon to rise as terror against Israel's enemies and to return to Israel's militia to rest with the ark.

The epiphanic campaign of the Israelites' militia is from its outset and in its territorial orientation predetermined by the campaign's objective: the march toward — and conquest of — the promised land. This understanding is clear from the entire context of the Patriarchal, the Exodus — Sinai — Wilderness and conquest and settlement texts in all their traditions. It is implied in 10:11-28, 33-36, and explicitly referred to as the goal in vv. 29-32. The campaign is transmigratory, understood to be a once and for all time, final transmigration from temporary territories to its final, long since preordained destination. In this regard, the campaign is unlike those military campaigns that involve the army's return to, after its departure from, its homeland.

In addition to the typical elements of the imagery of the campaign just listed, the position of Num 10:11-36, at the beginning of the narrative about the campaign's execution, points to the meaning or intention of this unit. It focuses on the nature of this very beginning of the campaign's execution, during the first day of the departure and the first three days of the territorial transition from the Wilderness of Sinai to the Wilderness of Paran. This nature was perfect, ideal. The preparation of the campaign carried over into its execution — for three days.

The idealization of the beginning, strongly reinforced by its references to its supernatural epiphanic nature, controls all other elements of the narrative. They point to the conscious concept of the legendary character of the narrated events, to the LEGEND of the ideal beginning of the epiphanic campaign of the Israelite militia from the Wilderness of Sinai to the Wilderness of Paran. For the discussion of LEGEND, see → Chapter 2, Genre.

Setting

This unit had its setting in the same generations of the priestly writers — of the Aaronide denomination — to which also the LEGEND of the preparation of the campaign in Num 1:1–10:10 belongs. For the discussion of this setting, see → Chapter 2, Setting.

The passage of vv. 29-32 is subordinate to the overall genre of the unit, and, unless it was created or in essence adopted by the priestly writers themselves, it was secondarily added to the priestly text, possibly by Dtr writers who had a particular interest in directing the focus on the relationship of the Israelites to the Kenites specifically on Moses and his invitation for his father-in-law to join the Israelites' destination — although Hobab had never to be liberated from slavery nor been in need of leaving his own homeland. The passage is subordinate to the legend of the entire unit, which is also apparent by the facts that Hobab is not reported to have followed Moses' invitation, to have served the Israelites as a guide, and that the guidance in the wilderness was instead provided by the cloud and the ark.

Intention

The unit intends to impress its readers with the message of how the Israelites, as a divinely organized and prepared militia setting out from Sinai on its course toward the — conquest of the — promised land under the guidance of Yahweh's revelatory signs, experienced an ideal beginning of its start. The vision of this beginning shines brightly; it serves as a beacon to which the immediately following story of Israel's own role in Num 11:1-3, and the end of the legend of the campaign, stand in sharp contrast.

Bibliography

T. A. Ashley, *The Book of Numbers* (NICOT; Grand Rapids: Eerdmans, 1993) 191-200; E. Blum, *Studien zur Komposition des Pentateuch* (BZAW 189; Berlin-New York: Walter de Gruyter, 1990) esp. 135-37; J. Gamberoni, *"māqôm,"* *TWAT* IV, 1113-24, esp. 1118; E. Kutsch, "Lade Jahwes," *RGG3*, vol. IV, 197-99; B. Levine, *Numbers 1–20* (AB 4A; New York/London: Doubleday, 1993) 316-19, 336; J. Milgrom, *Numbers,* (JPS; Philadephia/New York: Jewish Publication Society, 1990) 76-81; H. Seebass, *Numeri* (BKAT, IV/1ff.; Neukirchen: Neukirchener, 1993ff.) 1-19; T. Pola, *Die ursprüngliche Priesterschrift* (WMANT 70; Neukirchen: Neukirchener, 1995) 90-92.

The (Brief) Taberah Story (11:1-3)

Structure

I. Complication	1
II. Resolution	2
A. Moses' intercession	2a-bα
1. People appeal for aid *(ṣāʿaq)*	2a

2. Moses intercedes	2bα
B. Resolution of crisis	2bβ
III. Etiological Formula	3

This brief narrative has no itinerary formula to bind it into the larger context of wilderness traditions. It names a site as locale for its event. But that site is not picked up by the wilderness itinerary. Num 10:12 marks the new site for encampment following departure from Sinai as the Wilderness of Paran. But the intervening verses (10:13-36) concentrate on the departure from Sinai. Taberah, the site for this story, is not obviously in the Wilderness of Paran. Indeed, the Wilderness of Paran is not picked up again by the itinerary until Num 12:16. Num 33:16 suggests that an itinerary formula has fallen out of the series in Num 11:1. Thus, the structural problem lies in correlating Num 10:12 with Num 12:16, rather than suggesting that the itinerary elements in Num 11:35 and 12:16 are expansions of the series. The story is thus roughly connected to the preceding unit. It is important to note also that this story has no itinerary bridge with the following story. It is thus fully isolated in its context.

The story begins abruptly. No exposition sets the necessary conditions for narrating the story. There are no notes about the principals or their relationships. To the contrary, the story opens with a specification of the crisis almost as if in summary, as if employing formulaic language. The people complain (with no specification of content in their complaint) and God responds. In this case, contrary to other wilderness narratives, God's punishment for the people's complaint, not the privation posed by the wilderness, constitutes the crisis of the story. Then, as in other wilderness tales, the people appeal to Moses for help (so, the verb *ṣāʿaq*), Moses intercedes, and the Lord stays the punishment. In addition to the two principal elements of structure, an etiological appendix, built not on the intrinsic line of development in the story but only on a word play with the corresponding element in v. 1b, ends the story.

The story cannot be divided into more than one source. It derives totally from J. Behind the Yahwist, however, can be seen the lines of an earlier, local tradition. That tradition would have reported only a fire (of God) burning in the midst of the people (v. 1b) and its etiology for the place name (v. 3). The local tradition would then have been expanded into a tale with the characteristics of a murmuring story. Lines of the adaptation can be seen especially in the designation of crisis, not as an element in the wilderness provoking the murmuring, but as God's fire (→ Num 21:4-9). The people's cry for help *(ṣāʿaq)* thus does not appear here as a cry for aid in the face of natural crisis (→ Exod 14:10) but as a plea for relief from God's punishment.

Genre

The latest level of narrative in these verses is STORY, patterned after the MURMURING STORIES so widely spread in the wilderness theme (so, Exodus 14). If an earlier, local STORY can be seen, it would have been simply an ETIOLOGY.

171

Setting

The story belongs to a collection of wilderness stories, unified around the murmuring motif (so, Coats, *Rebellion*). The etiology would reflect a setting in local traditions about wilderness sites, perhaps preserved originally at the site itself.

Intention

The story would have expanded its antecedents in local tradition in order to connect with a larger complex of murmuring stories. Its intention is thus closely tied with the complex: to cast the fathers in the wilderness as rebels (see Exodus 14). The etiology intends to explain the place name by word play with a verb from the same root as the name, used in describing an event that occurred at the site.

Bibliography

B. S. Childs, "The Etiological Tale Re-examined," *VT* 24 (1974) 387-97; J. Fichtner, "Die etymologische Ätiologie in den Namengebungen der geschichtlichen Bücher des Alten Testament," *VT* 61 (1956) 372-96; V. Fritz, *Israel in der Wüste. Traditionsgeschichtliche Untersuchung der Wüstenüberlieferung des Jahwisten* (*MTS* 7; Marburg: Elwert, 1970); F. W. Golka, "The Aetiologies in the Old Testament," *VT* 26 (1976) 410-28; B. O. Long, *The Problem of Etiological Narrative in the Old Testament* (BZAW 108; Berlin: Töpelmann, 1968); H. Seebass, "Num XI, XII und die Hypothese des Jahwisten," *VT* 28 (1978) 214-23.

Annotation

The question needs particular attention why this concisely composed, complex but in itself complete, and highly theologized narrative was placed at this juncture in the total narrative, after Num 10:11-36 and before the following individual units. The question is not answered by reference to the facts that the aspect of the camp in 11:1b is connected with 10:31b-34b, and that the — fire — etiology of Taberah is integrated into the tradition of Moses the mediator and intercessor and even the one to whom "the place" owes its name Taberah. For these facts, the little unit could have been placed elsewhere. Just as the name Taberah is not connected with the names known in the itinerary of Numbers, so has "this story . . . no itinerary bridge with the following story," so Coats above.

However, the story appears to be placed at this juncture on the one hand because of the conceptual contrast between "the people's" (so for the first time in the book of Numbers, Levine, 319) murmuring, their unmotivated moaning after three days from Sinai (Seebass, 21), and the ideal conditions of the Israelites' departure from Sinai narrated in 10:11-36; and on the other hand as preparation for their immediately following more severe complaining. Moreover, the unit introduces the development of the narrative up to the large story Num 13:1–14:45. Although Num 13:1–14:45 narrates the failure — of the attempt — to conquer the promised land from the south (→ Chapter 4), Num 11:1-3 points to the beginning of the process of failure by pointing to the beginning of the — unmotivated — murmuring after, and in contrast to, the ideal start in 10:11-36. This understanding should be added to Coats's discussion above of the → Intention of the unit.

Rather than "tale," so originally Coats, the genre of the unit is more appropriately labeled as STORY. That it is concisely reduced to its most essential elements indicates that its present structure points much more to a product of writing, and to such a setting, than to a form of oral narrative. Indeed, the short structure of the loaded unit gives the impression of a kind of programmatic opening of the SAGA of the CAMPAIGN from this place and time on. Seebass's "Anekdote" would be fitting in the sense of a short account of an episode, except that the English "anecdote" refers usually to something biographical, an experience in the life of a person. See Coats's definitions of the units Num 15:32-36; 17:16-26 (*NRSV* 17:1-11); 25:1-18 as ANECDOTE.

The Quail Story (11:4-35)

Structure

I. Complication	4-15
A. Narration of crisis	4-6
1. Narrative: a faction of the people	4a
2. Speech: all the people	4b-6
a. Introduction: all the people	4bα
b. Speech	4bβ-6
1) Petition question	4bβ
2) Complaint	5-6
B. Parenthetical description of manna	7-9
C. Response to the crisis	10-15
1. Moses' response	10a
2. The Lord's response	10b
3. Moses' response to the Lord	11-15
a. Introduction: Moses to the Lord	11aα
b. Speech	11aβ-15
1) Complaint	11aβ-13
a) Complaint questions	11aβ-13a
b) Reason: citation of petition	13b
2) New petition	14-15
II. Resolution	16-34
A. Speech	16-20
1. Introduction: the Lord to Moses	16aα₁
2. Speech	16aα₂-20

        a. Instructions .... $16a\alpha_2$-17
           1) For gathering seventy elders .... $16a\alpha_2$-b
           2) Purpose: ordination 17
        b. Instructions 18-20
           1) Message commission formula .... $18a\alpha_1$
           2) Message .... $18a\alpha_2$-20
               a) Instructions for consecration ...... $18a\alpha_2$
               b) Purpose: to prepare for the Lord's gift ... $18a\alpha_3$-20
  B. Speech 21-22
    1. Introduction: Moses to the Lord .... $21a\alpha_1$
    2. Complaint .... $21a\alpha_2$-22
  C. Speech 23
    1. Introduction: the Lord to Moses .... $23a\alpha$
    2. Question .... $23a\beta$
    3. Event to establish knowledge 23b
  D. Execution of instructions for ordination 24-30
    1. Ordination of the seventy 24-25
    2. Eldad-Medad 26-29
        a. Exposition 26
        b. Speech 27
           1) Introduction: young man to Moses ... 27a
           2) Report of Eldad-Medad prophecy ... 27b
        c. Speech 28
           1) Introduction: Joshua to Moses 28a
           2) Request to stop unauthorized prophecy ... 28b
        d. Speech 29
           1) Introduction: Moses to Joshua ...... $29a\alpha$
           2) Saying .... $29a\beta$-b
    3. Conclusion 30
  E. Execution of instructions to feed Israel 31-34
    1. Description of the quail miracle 31-32
    2. Punishment for the rebels 33-34
        a. Statement of the punishment 33
        b. Etiology for the place name 34
III. Itinerary formula 35

The quail story begins without specification of place (cf. Num 11:1-3). No itinerary formula introduces the narration. The name of the site is designated in vv. 34-35. But the story itself is not tied into the structural pattern provided by the wilderness itinerary. Moreover, the story begins abruptly, with no exposition, no preparation for the crisis (vv. 4-6). These points suggest that the story relates to the context in a way not dictated by the wilderness itinerary chain.

The story comprises only two structural elements. The first reports the major crisis of the story and details responses to the crisis by various principals in the story. The second element then sets out the denouement of the plot. A final element provides an itinerary formula. But a problem in the continuity of the chain appears just at this point, for the itinerary formula jumps over the point of encampment from the previous itinerary element, Num 10:12 (cf. Coats, "Wilderness Itinerary").

The first element of structure has a double character. First, it notes that a faction within the people developed a strong craving. But no details about the craving can be seen. The word "craving" *(ta'ăwâ)* is picked up by the word play in the etiology in v. 34. But it plays no other structuring function in the pericope. Second, the text focuses greater attention on the cry of all the people. The nature of their cry is, however, unclear. It is not immediately obvious that the cry is the same event intended by the craving in v. 4a. Indeed, the question in v. 4b, "who will feed us meat?" is apparently neutral, simply an indirect petition or an expression of strong desire for meat without overtones of rebellion (cf. 2 Sam 15:4; 23:15; Isa 42:23; also the expression *mî yittēn* in Num 11:29 etc.). The elements of rebellion in the narrative appear only in the complaint in vv. 5-6, and there only implicitly. The nostalgia for Egypt anticipates the question more explicitly rejecting the exodus and Yahweh in v. 20.

The lengthy description of the manna in vv. 7-9 is parenthetical, picking up the catchword "manna" *(hammān)* in v. 6. The details of the description should be compared to Exod 16:13-15. But the distinction between the two stories comes sharply to the fore at just this point. In Exodus 16, the subject is primarily the gift of manna, with reference to a gift of meat incidental in the development of the plot (cf. vv. 8, 12, 13). In the Numbers story, the manna appears as an element of the wilderness diet too long unbroken by variety. The subject is not primarily manna but the gift of meat. The description of manna in vv. 7-9 thus emphasizes the monotony in diet by marking the regularity of the appearance of the manna.

The responses to the complaint in v. 10 are again complex. Moses' response begins as if his immediate goal is to handle the people's cry (v. 10a). But the narration quickly shifts from Moses to the Lord (v. 10b). And Moses then responds to the Lord's anger. The Moses speech in this element must be seen as a complaint. The series of questions, typical for such complaint (so, Ps 22:2), points to the people's petition for meat as the plight that provokes Moses. Indeed, the petition is cited now, not as an indirect question, but as an imperative directed immediately to Moses (v. 13). Verses 14-15 may involve a secondary addition to the speech, anticipating the seventy elders motif in vv. 16-17 (so, Noth). The focus of the complaint shifts here from the problems Moses faces in finding meat to the problems he faces in carrying responsibility for the entire people. The speech in vv. 16-17 clearly connects with vv. 14-15. Yet, vv. 14-15 need not be separated from the context as a separate motif. The burden Moses must carry may be nothing more than finding meat. The catchword "to carry" *(nāśā')* also appears in v. 12. Finally, the concluding petition, v. 15, gives Moses' complaint an air of rebellion against God himself and sets the stage for God's response in v. 23 (cf. Tiq Soph).

The seventy elders motif in vv. 16-17 and 24-30 cannot be separated from the quail story as an independent element. It appears here as a means for resolving the crisis posed by the people's request for meat. But it does seem to be clear that the motif is secondary in the scope of the story as a whole (so, Noth). The concern is not primarily for finding meat but for sharing Moses' responsibility (cf. Exodus 18). Indeed, the focus of the ordination lies not simply on administrative responsibility but on ecstatic prophecy, carried on as a result of contact with Moses' spirit. (For the contagious nature of ecstatic prophecy, cf. 1 Sam 19:18-24.) The motif thus represents a discrete development in the plot from the foundation reference to burden in vv. 14-15. The Eldad-Medad element in vv. 26-29 stands out structurally as a distinct sub-plot within the score of the story, structured with its own exposition and a series of short speeches. The focal point of structure falls on the final speech, a saying of Moses in v. 29. The entire section, vv. 24-30, must be understood structurally as execution of the instructions given to Moses in a Yahweh speech, vv. 16-17.

The instructions for consecrating the people, vv. 18-20, resume the major line of development within the plot. Structured under the heading of a message commission formula as a message Moses should give to his people, the instructions prepare the people to receive meat. This act, too, builds on the foundation laid by the Moses speech in vv. 11-15, including the reference to a burden. Thus, the resolution of the crisis in the narration moves in two distinct lines. The interpretation of the petition for meat in vv. 18-20 picks up the nostalgia for Egypt established in v. 5. But the negative element remains implicit. The question itself is a citation of the question in v. 4 (cf. MT, not the NRSV) and connotes nothing more than an indirect petition. The specification of response to the petition in vv. 18b-20 must be understood as favorable. God will grant what the people request. The negative implication of the response comes only through a (somewhat humorous) manipulation of the gift. The people will receive so much meat that they will become nauseous. Finally, v. 20b makes the negative tone of the request explicit by defining the act of the people as a rejection of Yahweh. But there the citation from the people has changed markedly. There is now no sign of their petition for meat. Now the citation embodies only the nostalgia for Egypt. Indeed, the question may be understood in the larger context of murmuring questions with their focus on a plan to return to Egypt, an anti-exodus motif (cf. Coats, *Rebellion;* Moran). The exchange between Moses and the Lord (vv. 21-23) only emphasizes the miraculous nature of the event to follow.

The narration in vv. 31-34 does not note that Moses gave the people the speech commissioned by God. Nor does it indicate that the instructions for consecration were explicitly carried out. It moves instead to a description of the event. Structurally, it stands nonetheless in position as execution of the instructions. Verses 31-32 make no reference to the negative character of the event. They note simply that an abundance of quail could be gathered by the people. Verse 33 introduces a negative element rather abruptly by noting that Yahweh sent a plague against the people while they were eating the meat. The plague must be seen as punishment for "rejecting the Lord." Yet, the tenuous relationship of negative elements to the basic structure of the story suggests that a story, originally structured to emphasize a positive relationship between people and Yahweh by showing how the Lord gave the people meat in response to their petition, has been reinterpreted as a negative story. A petition for meat with no necessary overtones of rebellion becomes an overt rejection of the Lord, coupled with a desire to return to Egypt and undo the exodus. And the favorable response to the petition has become an act of punishment against the rebellious people.

Verse 33 also serves structurally as a bridge from the story about the quail to the etiology in v. 34. The basis for the etiology is limited to v. 4a. But v. 33 provides an opening for understanding the etiology as a conclusion in the punishment for the rebels. The etiology thus presupposes the quail story in its negative form and suggests that its addition to the story occurred at a relatively late point in the history of the story. This point also suggests that the itinerary formula, v. 35, binding the story to Numbers 12 (cf. 12:16) is not intrinsic for the story itself. The itinerary system thus represents a late means for structuring several stories into a unified whole (see Coats, "Wilderness Itinerary").

The story derives entirely from J (see Noth). But it reveals several stages of growth behind the Yahwistic form. The most obvious element of growth is the motif of seventy elders and its justification for ecstatic prophecy. But in addition, the murmuring motif now hides a stage of the story that dealt only with divine aid for the people in the wilderness.

Genre

The quail narrative belongs to the genre category defined as STORY, parallel with other stories about Israel's life in the wilderness. Like Exod 16:1-36 etc. it involves a limited number of principals. Not one of the principal figures is exalted as a central hero, not even Moses. Rather, the plot focuses on events that bind all the principals together in the movement of interrelationships. It strangely has no exposition, suggesting a closer relationship with other tales in the series. The complication sets out the central core of the plot, with a sub-plot prepared through a Moses speech. Then the denouement moves to a new event. This pattern of movement in plot is typical for STORY. The STORY at all levels of its history maintains the same generic character.

A more narrowly defined genre category can be drawn from the contact the story has with other narrative units within the scope of the wilderness theme. The MURMURING STORY shares characteristic vocabulary with other murmuring stories (such as the question in v. 20). But in each case, the MURMURING STORY is dependent in structure on a prior aid story, a story that emphasizes God's leadership of his people through his gifts in the face of crises (→ Exodus 14). At that stage it would properly be classified as a story about God's aid, perhaps better as a part of a larger heroic SAGA. The seventy elders motif supports the heroic dimension since it emphasizes the importance of the spirit of Moses.

Formulas and stereotyped expressions include an indirect PETITION (vv. 5, 18) or a direct PETITION (v. 13), COMPLAINT QUESTIONS (vv. 11-12), ACCUSATION (v. 20), MESSAGE COMMISSION FORMULA (v. 18), ETIOLOGY FORMULA (v. 34), and an ITINERARY FORMULA (v. 35).

Setting

The latest stage for the unit carries the stamp of the murmuring tradition. It thus reflects the special interests of Jerusalem (Coats, *Rebellion*). The positive character of the story also belongs to the Yahwist's traditions. The form of the story with the seventy elders motif suggests the position of the story, not only in the wilderness theme, but in the Moses traditions as well. An earlier setting for the story, apart from its position in the wilderness theme or the Moses traditions, cannot yet be determined.

Intention

At its latest stage the unit contributes to the larger picture of the Israelites as rebels, rejecting Yahweh. It participates in the polemic designed to undercut election theology based on the exodus (so, Coats, *Rebellion*). The positive story contributes to a larger picture of the Israelites as faithful, depending totally on the Lord's aid to live in the face of dangers in the wilderness. Its intention is thus to emphasize divine aid for the fathers in the wilderness. The seventy elders motif has its own position in the structure of the story, thus its own intention. It functions to preserve the saying in v. 29 and establishes ecstatic prophecy as a part of Israel's inheritance from Moses. But it also emphasizes the heroic dimension of tradition about Moses. Moses' spirit was sufficient to endow seventy people with the power of ecstatic prophecy.

Bibliography

G. W. Coats, "The Wilderness Itinerary," *CBQ* 34 (1972) 135-52; G. I. Davies, "The Wilderness Itineraries: A Comparative Study," *Tyndale Bulletin* 25 (1974) 46-81; D. Jobling, "A Structural Analysis of Num 11 and 12," in *Seminar Papers* (Missoula: SBL, 1977) 171-204; D. Jobling, *The Sense of Biblical Narratives. Three Structural Analyses in the Old Testament* (JSOTSup 7; Sheffield: JSOT Press, 1978) 26-62; W. L. Moran, "The End of the Unholy War and the Anti-Exodus," *Bibl* 44 (1963) 333-42.

Addendum

B. D. Sommer, "Reflecting on Moses: The Redaction of Numbers 11," *JBL* 118 (1999) 601-24.

Aaron and Miriam Rebellion Story (12:1-16)

Text

Verse 6 in the MT is illegible. Read: "If there is a prophet of Yahweh among you." Compare Vulgate and Old Latin. LXX and Vulgate suggest that v. 16 should be structured with ch. 13. But see the comments below.

Structure

I. Complication	1-10
A. Narration of crisis	1-2a
1. Opening statement of opposition	1
2. Speech report	2a
a. Introduction: Miriam and Aaron	$2a\alpha_1$
b. Complaint questions	$2a\alpha_2$-$a\beta$
B. Response	2b-10
1. Narration of Yahweh's response	2b
2. Parenthetical description of Moses	3
3. Speech report	4a
a. Introduction: Yahweh to Moses, Aaron, Miriam	$4a\alpha$
b. Instructions for resolution of challenge	$4a\beta$
4. Execution of instructions	4b-5
5. Speech report	6-8
a. Introduction: Yahweh to Aaron and Miriam	$6a\alpha$
b. Speech	$6a\beta$-8
1) Call to attention	$6a\beta$
2) Message	6b-8
a) Motivation (legendary traits of Moses)	6b-8a
b) Accusation	8b
6. Punishment	9-10
II. Resolution	11-15
A. Speech report	11-12
1. Introduction: Aaron to Moses	11a
2. Intercession speech	11b-12
a. Petition formula	$11b\alpha_1$
b. Petition	$11b\alpha_2$-12
B. Speech report	13
1. Introduction: Moses to Yahweh	13a
2. Intercession speech	13b
C. Speech report	14
1. Introduction: Yahweh to Moses	14a
2. Instructions for healing	14b
D. Execution of instructions	15
III. Itinerary formula	16

The Aaron-Miriam story is structured into the larger complex of wilderness traditions by two itinerary formulas, 11:35 and 12:16. One might suggest that since itinerary formulas normally head a story, 11:35 more appropriately belongs with the Aaron-Miriam story, 12:16 with the following spy story (cf. LXX, Vulgate). But in both cases the itinerary formula is extrinsic to the story, serving only to bind one story with the next. It thus makes little difference whether the itinerary formula is cast in the structural analysis at the beginning or the ending of the story (so, Coats, "Wilderness Itinerary").

The formula in 12:16 notes Israel's departure from Hazeroth and arrival at the Wilderness of Paran. This note stands in conflict with Num 10:12 and points to a problem in the structure of the wilderness theme. The problem, however, is centered primarily in the movement noted by the wilderness chain of itineraries from Sinai to the first site of encampment (cf. Num 10:12; 11:1). It does not affect the structure of this particular pericope.

This narrative begins abruptly, with no exposition to set out the major conditions necessary for narrating the plot (→ Num 11:1-3; 4-35). This abrupt beginning sets the complication of plot in motion without preparing the audience for Miriam's position as a principal figure, much less for knowing what the problem with the Cushite wife might be. The structure of the story thus involves only two major elements, apart from the itinerary formula in v. 16: the complication (vv. 1-10) and the resolution (vv. 11-15).

The complication is itself complex. In the narration of crisis, the first element pinpoints a problem between Miriam-Aaron and Moses over the previously unknown Cushite wife. The problem involves primarily Miriam since the opening verb is feminine and Miriam is listed before Aaron (see the comments below on vv. 9-10, as well as other references to Aaron and Miriam with Aaron listed first). Moreover, the problem builds around a hostile relationship. (The prepositional *bêt* in *bĕmōšê*, v. 1, should be seen as an expression of hostility.) "Miriam (and Aaron) spoke against Moses because of the Cushite woman. . . ." Yet, the speech in v. 2, which might be a specification of the hostile confrontation (so, Num 14:3-4), has nothing to do with the Cushite woman. To the contrary, it challenges Moses' leadership as the sole spokesman of God's word. And the challenge (headed by a 2m. pl. verb) involves both Aaron and Miriam equally. The Cushite woman motif of the plot does not return until vv. 9-10.

The major section of response in vv. 2b-10 directs the Lord's wrath against Aaron and Miriam, limited to the challenge the two established against claims that the Lord speaks only through Moses (v. 2a). Both the parenthetical description of Moses in v. 3 and the speech in vv. 6-8 emphasize Moses' legendary position as a prophet vis-à-vis all challengers. Then, in light of that position, the Lord accuses Aaron and Miriam together of rebellion. The accusation would normally be posed in a positive sentence: "Why did you speak against my servant Moses?" The negative formulation here does not, however, violate the structural integrity of an accusation: "Why were you not afraid to speak against my servant Moses?"

Verses 9-10 then narrate the punishment for the rebellion: Leprosy infects the guilty. But remarkably the punishment involves only Miriam. Aaron appears in the verse. But the punishment has not infected him. Moreover, the denouement in vv. 11-15 casts Aaron as intercessor for Miriam, not as co-conspirator. Aaron's speech of intercession to Moses does describe the sin as "our sin" (see v. 11). But no explanation is offered for Aaron's exemption from the punishment. An obvious conclusion is that in this section of the narrative, the plot line has returned to the complaint about the Cushite wife and that the chief rebel is Miriam.

Aaron's petition to Moses, introduced by the petition formula (*bî 'ădōnî*) asks for removal of the punishment from Miriam. In the process, it assumes that the punishment was as bad as death. Moses then makes the intercession before the Lord (couched with the characteristic verb ṣāʿaq). And the Lord resolves the problem by providing Moses with instructions for Miriam's healing (rĕpāʾ; note the characteristic verb). The final element in the narration reports that the instructions were followed and Miriam's healing completed.

The story derives entirely from J, even in its present complex form. The final edition of the story places the focus of plot on an Aaron-Miriam rebellion against Moses. The structure is thus similar to the rebellion stories in 11:1-3; 4-34. Behind the rebellion story lies a tradition about a problem over a Cushite wife. The central section of that story has been obscured by the shift in attention from the challenge to Moses' legendary character as a prophet (see Num 11:24-30). Yet, some elements of structure at this stage remain clear. Miriam does not seem to be attacking Moses' position of leadership over all the people, but rather in some way his right to marry the Cushite woman. The challenge may then lie on the right to define the nature of the family (or tribal) group. Significantly, the attack results in leprosy for Miriam and her subsequent exclusion from the tribe. Moreover, Miriam's chances for reinstatement depend on her willingness to obey Moses' instructions. The focus of structure at this stage in the history of the story thus falls on Moses as tribal leader.

Genre

In its latest stage the Miriam-Aaron narrative is a STORY of REBELLION, similar in structure but not in content or tradition history to the MURMURING STORIES. Thus, the expression "to speak against" (wayĕdabbēr bĕ) in vv. 1 and 8 can be seen as synonymous for the expressions of murmuring (see Num 21:5). The point at issue is not the exodus, however, but Moses' position as a prophet (so, Num 11:24-30). Moreover, the elements of narration in vv. 3-8 show characteristics of LEGEND since Moses' traits as a prophet are elevated to the ideal toward which every prophet should strive (→ Numbers 22–24). A LEGEND about Moses the prophet stands in the immediate background of the story (so, Coats, "Legend").

The Cushite woman element moves in a distinct direction. The issue here is not so much Miriam's challenge, although the rebellion story has used the challenge as an opening to expand its own interests. Here the emphasis of structure falls on Miriam's challenge and its results. Her leprosy shows Moses to be not only the authority for the family, but also the one knowledgeable in the process for intercession and healing. The instructions for healing and the notation that the instructions were carefully followed suggest that the narrative at this level should be defined as a healing story (see Genesis 18; 2 Kings 5, 20, etc.). The absence of objection to obeying instructions does not invalidate this conclusion. Significantly, the instructions correspond to the stipulations for leprosy cases in Leviticus 13:4 (cf. also Lev 13:46; 14:8). The narrative thus becomes a case STORY for supporting the ritual since here the ritual derives not from tradition's requirement for handling leprosy, but from God's specification (cf. Num 15:32-36). Does the allusion to Miriam's condition as one like the dead suggest that healing involves restoration of victims near death or even, perhaps, resurrection from death?

Setting

At its latest stages, this story belongs with a larger collection of traditions centered in Moses, rather than the section of traditions concerned to describe divine aid and leadership for the people in the wilderness. The healing story also belongs in the larger scope of stories as a part of the Moses tradition. The original setting for the healing story remains obscure.

Intention

Legendary elements in the final stage of this story exalt Moses as the ideal prophet. An element of edification can thus be seen in the intention of the story. At this stage the tradition emphasizes Moses' legendary virtue, "meek" (*'ānāw*). This term does not suggest that Moses was submissive or deficient in spirit and courage. To the contrary, it suggests that Moses fulfills his duty with integrity (so, Coats, "Legend"). The healing story identifies an element in the function of the principal as hero (so, Coats, *Heroic Man*). An additional element of intention in the story at this level is to account for the trial period of exclusion from the camp for a (possible) victim of leprosy. The healing story moves from beyond that point to emphasize the importance of obedience to instructions in healing, and thus, obedience to Moses. In addition, the story fits into the basic system of rebellion stories centered in individual challenges to Moses' authority. The intention here, shared by all levels in the history of the story, is not to undercut election theology centered in the exodus, but to undergird the authority of Moses over his tribe as well as over all of his people.

Bibliography

G. W. Coats, "Humility and Honor: A Moses Legend in Numbers 12," in *Art and Meaning: Rhetoric in Biblical Literature* (ed. D. J. A. Clines, D. M. Gunn, A. J. Hauser; JSOT Monograph Series 19; Sheffield: JSOT Press, 1982) 97-107; idem, *Moses: Heroic Man and Man of God* (JSOTSup 57; Sheffield: JSOT Press, 1988).

Addendum

D. C. Hymes, "Numbers 12: Of Priests, Prophets, or 'None of the Above'," *AJBI* 24 (1998) 3-22.

Murmuring Story (13:1–14:45)

Structure

I. Spy report	13:1-33
A. Commission speech	1-2
1. Lord to Moses	1
2. Commission to send spies	2
B. Execution of commission	3-17a
1. General statement	3
2. Name list	4-16
a. Introduction	4a
b. Names	4b-15
c. Conclusion	16a
d. Gloss	16b
3. General statement	17a
C. Commission speech	17b-20a
1. Introduction: Moses to the spies	$17b\alpha_1$
2. Commission	$17b\alpha_2$-20a
D. Execution of instructions	20b-24
1. Foreshadowing	20b
2. Execution of the instructions	21-23
3. Etiology	24
E. Retort	25-33
1. Narrative description of return	25-26
2. Speech report	27-29
a. Spies to Moses	$27a\alpha$
b. Report	$27a\beta$-29
1) Positive	$27a\beta$-b
2) Negative	28-29
3. Narrative description	30a
4. Speech report	30b
a. Introduction: Caleb	$30b\alpha_1$
b. Speech: admonition to attack	$30b\alpha_2$-bβ
5. Speech report	31
a. Introduction: the other spies	$31a\alpha$
b. Speech: warning not to attack	$31a\beta$-b
6. Speech report	32-33
a. Introduction: spies to the people of Israel	32a
b. Speech: spy report	32b-33
1) The land: geared for war	$32b\alpha$
2) The people: great in stature	$32b\beta$
3) The Nephilim	33a
4) Self-description	33b
II. Complication	14:1-10a
A. Rebellion	1-4
1. General act	1

2. Rebellion speech   2-3
    a. Introduction: all the people against Moses and Aaron   2a-bα₁
    b. Speech   2bα₂-3
      1) Death wish   2bα₂-bβ
      2) Accusation   3
3. Rejection of Moses   4
    a. Introduction: the people to one another   4a
    b. Rejection of Moses   4b
B. Response to the rebellion   5-9
    1. Moses and Aaron   5
    2. Joshua and Caleb   6-9
      a. Introduction: Joshua and Caleb to people   6-7a
      b. Speech   7b-9
        1) Affirmation about the land   7b-8
        2) Admonition   9
C. Rebellion   10a
III. Resolution   14:10b-38
A. Theophany   10b
B. Dialogue   11-35
    1. Judgment speech   11-12
    2. Intercession   13-19
    3. Judgment speech   20-25
    4. Judgment speech   26-35
C. Execution of judgment   36-38
    1. Against spies   36-37
    2. For Joshua and Caleb   38
IV. Conclusion   14:39-45
A. Concluding observation   39
B. Battle report   40-45
    1. Intention   40
    2. Warning   41-43
    3. Results   44-45

The itinerary formula in 12:16 gives this pericope a place in the larger context constituted by the wilderness theme. The identification of place in 12:16b as the Wilderness of Paran connects with references to the same place for the events described in this pericope in 13:3 and 26.

The pattern controlling the structure of the pericope follows the paradigm established by a majority of the stories in the wilderness theme: introduction, complication, and resolution. This pattern is, however, complex because (a) it is more expansive than the brief scope of some stories, and (b) the position normally occupied by an exposition has been filled in this pericope by a larger, perhaps originally independent spy report. Yet, even though the spy report is in itself a distinct unit, with its own structural integrity and its own intention (→ 13:1-33), it has nonetheless been adapted by the storyteller as the beginning of this story. And indeed, as beginning, it meets the functions of an exposition for the whole unit.

The spy report itself, 13:1-33, does not develop a point of tension and thus the substance of a plot for a story. To be sure, there is some tension in the scope of the report by virtue of the conflicting statements about the land from the spies. Verses 27-29 highlight that conflict, followed by vv. 30-31 containing recommendations for action that mirror the conflict. The final speech in the element does not, however, resolve the tension. It simply leaves the point of issue between the two parties hanging. The structure of the spy report in itself cannot support a thesis that the report is the basis of a story within the larger story about the spies in the area of Hebron. And its depiction of tension without resolution points the audience beyond its own limits to the following elements of narrative. Indeed, the tension apparently reflects intentional adaptation of the report so that it can serve a function in the larger context. As it now stands, the report functions as a part of the larger whole, not as an independent unit. Perhaps an independent spy report lies behind the element, a part of the tradition's history. But in the present form of the story, the spy report simply introduces the larger unit.

As exposition for the larger pericope, 13:1-33 makes the following points: Moses establishes the entourage of spies for reconnaissance of the land of Canaan. The event thus looks forward to the conquest of Canaan and involves Moses in its purview. Moses' involvement gives expression to a contact with the larger motif about promise for possession of land. But the involvement here is not as participant in the act of giving the land, but rather as source of authority for the commission of the spies. It anticipates the conquest of the land. But it is not yet a tradition about the conquest.

Verses 1-2 provide formulation for this point by showing God's commission for Moses, instructions that detail the strategy for the spies. And the following elements constitute the obedience of Moses in carving out the commission. Two general statements of execution of the commission, vv. 3 and 17a, frame a name list. The body of the response to the divine commission is thus carried by the name list for the spies. The order of the list follows the stereotype of the names, with Ephraim and Manasseh replacing Levi and Joseph. It is interesting that Manasseh stands as a parenthetical gloss on Joseph, whose name still appears as a part of the list. (For the history of the list, → Genesis 49.) The gloss in v. 16b explains the name Hoshea, the son of Nun from v. 8, as Joshua and suggests by its position that the structure of the list is tight. The gloss does not interrupt the list at the point where the name Hoshea in fact appears. But the gloss does put special focus on Joshua, who is one of two heroes in the larger pericope. Another significant element in the list for the context of the spy story is the definition of Caleb as the representative of Judah (v. 6), for Caleb is the other hero for the larger pericope.

Verses 17b-20a then repeat the commission with the same point. But in this case, Moses commissions the spies for reconnaissance in Canaan. The general statement focuses on attributes of the native population (strong or weak, few or many) and of the land (good or bad, fortified or open, rich or poor, wood of what sort). The commission ends with a formula for encouraging the spies and instructions for producing evidence about the character of the land.

A brief section, vv. 20b-24, observes that the commission to the spies was carried out. Verse 20b anticipates the character of the spies' report concerning the land by observing that harvest for the grapes was in progress. The point looks forward to the account of the spies' report that the land was fertile, particularly to the account of the single cluster of grapes so large that two men had to carry it suspended on a pole between them (v. 23). Verses 21-22 report simply the location for the spying mission. Verse 22b would appear to be a simple addition of a datum about the place. Yet, the allusion to the descendants of Anak connects by implication with the giant cluster of grapes in v. 23. And the connection emphasizes two points: (1) The land was fertile. The fruit is incredibly large, and it supports large people. Both sign the evidence for fertility in the land. (2) The people are strong. Giants protect their land from grasshoppers. Verse 24 ends the description of the journey with a folk etiology. Because of the cluster of grapes, the spies call the place the Valley of the Cluster (nahal 'eškôl).

The weight of a spy report falls on the report produced by the mission. The spies return from their mission and make their report to Moses and the people (v. 26). The report has two forms: (a) The land flows with milk and honey (v. 27). It thus corresponds to the promised land from the tradition (→ Exod 3:8). The expression, a way to emphasize the fertility of the land, is a typical epithet for the land and thus points to the position of the tradition about the fertile land in popular lore. (b) The people are strong and large. The descendants of Anak are there. The cities are fortified. And the result is a self-description that constitutes a firm example of a frightened resignation. The spies name themselves grasshoppers (v. 33). The report is thus both good and bad.

This two-pronged report captures the structure of the conclusion in vv. 30-33. In v. 30 Caleb enjoins the people to attack, encouraging them about their ability to meet the enemy. The character of the conflict gains detail by the verb describing Caleb's positive efforts. "But Caleb quieted the people before Moses." The effort "before Moses" draws on the larger image of authority represented by Moses. The critical element lies in the act. "To quiet" (wayyahas) the people denotes the effort of Caleb to stay counter measures promoted by the negative report from the other spies (so, see the word in Neh 8:11). But the impact of the image for the unit highlights the conflict. The people must be threatening just at this point. And Caleb attempts to quell the anxiety that produces the threat (so, cf. Neh 8:11).

But v. 31 carries the counter-report, warning the people not to attack since they are not as strong as the Canaanites. Verses 32-33 conclude the spy report with a larger speech to the people from the negative point of view. The spies do not recommend that Israel not attack. They simply remind the people that the land is geared for war (see Coats, *Rebellion,* 141, on the phrase: "the land devours its inhabitants"). And the storyteller defines this report as evil (so, v. 32).

In the present form of the text, the spy report in 13:1-33 cannot be separated from the body of the story in 14:1-38. The unity between the two is solidified not only by the double-edge of the spy report, a factor that anticipates conflict and calls for some kind of resolution, but also by the foreshadowing that in fact confirms that this land is the land of promise. In the present form of the text, then, the spy report functions as the exposition for the larger murmuring tale.

14:1-10a expands the spy report into the substance of the murmuring tradition. There is no explicit connection between the negative report of the spies and the event described in this element. To be sure, the negative report and the split in the people of God it causes anticipate some kind of conflict. But the connections appear only by virtue of the juxtaposition of the two elements. Yet, the juxtaposition is effective. On the heels of the negative report from the spies, the element in vv. 1-4 pits the people of God in an overt act of rebellion, explicitly a rejection of Moses. And in the power of that rebellion, the storyteller's interpretation of the spy report as "evil" (13:32) gains effective completion.

Verse 1 describes the act of the people as a loud cry. "All the congregation raised [their voices]. They gave their voices and cried *(wayyibkû)* that night." The verb recalls the more general response of the people to wilderness life in Num 11:4. But in this case, the cry appears to be tantamount to rebellion. Indeed, v. 2 describes the same act with the murmuring verb, a word with obvious denotation for rebellion. The rebellion speech, v. 2b, confirms that conclusion. A death wish prefaces the accusation. As in other examples of the murmuring tradition, so here the death wish constitutes an assertion of anti-exodus polemic (see Exod 16:3; for a different construction of the same element, see Exod 14:12). The accusation in v. 3 defines the rebellion as an act directed against the Lord rather than against Moses or Aaron. Its weight as anti-exodus polemic is thus sharper. It carries an explicit expression in v. 3b: "Would it not be better for us to return to Egypt." The accusation against God then becomes an explicit rejection of Moses as the head of the people in a speech from the people, v. 4. A "captain" or "head" *(rō'š)* of the people refers to the position occupied by Moses. The speech calls for selection of a "head" who will lead the people back to Egypt.

The response of Moses and Aaron to the rebellion, v. 5, is on the surface problematic. Does it not depict the leaders as meek and submissive to the rebellious congregation? Yet, the context for the description carries the weight for interpretation. Moses and Aaron do not submit to the rebels. Joshua and Caleb intervene immediately (v. 6), blocking the connection between this description of Moses and Aaron and the obvious meaning of their act. Joshua and Caleb lament the tragedy of the rebellion (rend their clothes) and plead with the people not to rebel (v. 9). The basis for their plea is their conviction that God gives the land into Israel's hand. They have no need to fear the strongest enemy. In their appeal to the people, the land is defined again as "good." And the formula, "a land which flows with milk and honey," increases the weight of that appeal (v. 8). That traditional epithet for the land (cf. Exod 3:8, 17; 13:5) picks up the reference in 13:27 and ties the unit together. But the admonition rests not simply on the character of the land. Israel has no need to fear the enemy. And the reason is clear. "The Lord is with us. Do not fear them."

But the rebellion continues (v. 10a). Finally, the key to the action by Moses and Aaron appears. Verse 10b reports that "the Glory of the Lord appeared at the Tent of Meeting before all the Israelites." To fall on one's face, the act of Moses and Aaron described in v. 5, is an act that describes presentation of oneself before a superior, particularly, before God (so, Josh 5:14; 7:6; etc.). It anticipates the appearance of God to the rebellious people and shows the leaders' submission, not to the rebels, but to God.

Resolution of the murmuring crisis comes with the theophany in v. 10b. With the theophany is a judgment speech, vv. 11-12. The question in v. 11 is rhetorical. It sets up the judgment in v. 12. That judgment reveals God's impatience with the rebellious people and constitutes a severe increase of tension for the unit. God will execute the rebels and start over with Moses (v. 12). This judgment is the pinnacle, not only for the murmuring scene described in this pericope, but for the entire sequence of murmuring scenes beginning with Exod 14:11 (so, Coats, *Rebellion*).

The intercession speech in vv. 13-19 sounds an appeal to pardon the rebels in v. 19 on a reference to the loyalty *(ḥesed)* of God to his people and his record of past acts of forgiveness: ". . . according to the way you have carried this people from Egypt to here." The response is a new judgment speech. The people will not die immediately. But they will die in the wilderness. They will not enter the land. The intercession softens the immediate character of the judgment (→ Exodus 33). But the results of the rebellion deny the privilege of the promise to the wilderness generation. Yet, there is an exception. Caleb and Joshua will enter the land. They become, therefore, the *only* heirs to the promise. The rebellion in the wilderness forces the loss of the promise for all of the Israelites except Caleb and Joshua. Execution of this judgment demands the whole wilderness narrative. But a symbol of that execution comes in the execution of spies who brought an evil report, excluding Joshua and Caleb, and in the conclusion, vv. 39-45, reporting Israel's efforts to take the land in spite of the judgment. After the mourning over the judgment, the people declare their intention to take the land. Moses warns that the Lord will not accompany the raid. But the people attack anyway. And the Amalekites (→ Exod 17:14-16) and Canaanites win. The concluding reference to Hormah stands as a bitter irony in comparison to the reference to the same place in Num 21:3.

The structure in this unit may be clarified by reference to the sources that comprise the whole. The priestly source appears in 13:1-17a, 21, 25-26, 32-33; 14:1a, 2-3, 5-10, 26-38. The pattern of structure in these verses is as follows:

I. Spy report	13:1-17a
A. Commission speech	1-2
B. Execution of the commission by Moses	3-17a
II. Execution of the commission by the spies	21, 25-26, 32-33
A. Narration of the event	21
B. Narration of the return of the spies	25-26
C. Speech report	32-33
1. Introduction: spies to the people	32a
2. Report	32b-33
a. The land	32bα
b. The people	32bβ
c. The Nephilim	33a
d. Self-description	33b
III. Crisis	14:1a, 2-3, 5-10a

A. Narrative description	1a
B. Speech report	2-3
1. Introduction: all the people against Moses and Aaron	2a-bα₁
2. Rebellion speech	2bα₂-3
a. Death wish	2bα₂-bβ
b. Accusation	3
C. Response to the rebellion	5-10a
1. Moses and Aaron	5
2. Joshua and Caleb	6-9
3. Narrative conclusion	10a
IV. Resolution	10b, 26-38
A. Theophany	10b
B. Judgment speech	26-35
C. Execution of judgment	36-38

The priestly story follows the structural pattern noted for the final form of the text. Conflicting spy reports introduce the issues of obedience to God's command. In response to the conflict, the people reject Moses *and* Aaron, Joshua and Caleb, and launch a movement to return to Egypt. The issue is resolved when the glory of the Lord appears and renders judgment against the rebels. The patterns of the murmuring tradition dominate P here as in other parts of the wilderness tradition. Characteristic features of P in this structure include the details of the name list, the ritual self-presentation of Moses and Aaron before God by falling on their faces, the designation of the rebellion as an action directed against God rather than a political action directed against Moses and Aaron (for details, see Coats, *Rebellion*), and the coupling of Caleb and Joshua as the heroes of the spying mission. In addition, one might observe the structural doublets represented by 13:21 and 22, 14:1a and 1b, 20-25 and 26-35.

The name list in 13:4-16 carries in itself a stereotype from tradition. The structure of the list is as follows:

I. General statement	3
II. List	4-16
A. Reuben	4
B. Simeon	5
C. Judah	6
D. Issachar	7
E. Ephraim	8
F. Benjamin	9
G. Zebulun	10
H. Joseph-Manasseh	11
I. Dan	12
J. Asher	13
K. Naphtali	14
L. Gad	15
III. General statement	16a

IV. Gloss   16b

The gloss in v. 16b explains the name in v. 8 as Joshua, the representative of Ephraim. And the name in v. 6 is Caleb, the representative of Judah. The two spies who did not fall under the judgment of God for seditious reporting about the land are the representatives of Ephraim and Judah, the north and the south. The name list thus enables the priestly source to explain how the judgment of God could fall so heavily on the tribes of Israel and yet leave enough of the people to account for the Israel and the Judah of the day's tradition. Thus, the conflict in the tradition that promises rebellion in the wilderness is preserved by P. But it is significant that for P, the rebellion is not against Moses and Aaron simply, but rather it is against God. The particular character of rebellion apparent in the older sources becomes a theological issue for P. Rebellion is not simply a matter of political loyalty, a matter of obedience to the hero of the people. It is a matter of theological loyalty, obedience to the God who leads even Moses and Aaron.

One might observe, moreover, that the name list fits into the history of the tradition at that point where Levi is no longer a member of the list and Joseph has been split. To be sure, Joseph is a part of the list. But a gloss explains that Joseph is in fact Manasseh (v. 11). And Joshua himself represents Ephraim. The remaining names show some changes in order vis-à-vis other examples of the list (→ Genesis 49). But no significance in that variation emerges at this point.

The Yahwist appears in 13:17b-20, 22-24, 27-31, and 14:1b, 4, 11-25, 39-45. The pattern of structure in these verses is as follows:

I.	Spy report	13:17b-20, 22-24, 27-31
	A. Commission to the spies	13:17b-20
	B. Execution of the commission	22-24
	C. Report to the people	27-31
II.	Complication	14:1b, 4
	A. Rebellion	1b
	B. Rejection of Moses	4
III.	Resolution	11-25
	A. Judgment speech	11-12
	B. Intercession	13-19
	C. Judgment speech	20-25
IV.	Conclusion	14:39-45
	A. Concluding observation	39
	B. Battle report	40-45

The structure of the Yahwist corresponds to the structure still apparent in the priestly material, suggesting that the tradition carries the pattern. The priestly material may have simply borrowed both form and tradition from J. But even should that be the case, the point remains that the form is substantial for presentation of the tradition.

The spy report itself may reflect an even older stereotype, a standard structure for reporting the events of a journey to spy out a land under consideration for attack (so, Wagner). The traditional elements of this stereotyped form would include the commission with key verbs such as *hlk* (to go), *r'h* (to see) and, from P, *šlḥ* (to send), an account of the execution of the commission, and a report to the commissioning agent (→ Joshua 2). The spy report then serves the Yahwist as a means for depicting the split in the people. The leaders of the people, personified in the Yahwist only by Caleb, urge obedience to the admonition to attack. But the people reject the appeal, demand execution of Moses, and lay plans to return to Egypt. 14:1b describes the process as weeping, a parallel to murmuring and thus an act of rebellion. And for the Yahwist, weeping leads immediately to a decision to choose a captain (v. 4). This statement implies removing Moses as leader of the people. The event is thus open and hostile rebellion against Moses and, through him, against God.

The response to the rebellion comes first from the Lord himself. It is hostile and extreme. In 14:11, questions open the response. "How long will these people despise me? How long will they not believe in me in spite of the signs . . . ?" These questions are explicit accusations against Israel. Their focus describes the rebellion of the people as "despising God" (→ 2 Sam 12:14; Ps 74:10) and "not believing in God" (→ Exod 4:31). The accusations lead to judgment against the rebellious generation. Verse 12 asserts that the wilderness generation is rejected (→ Ps 78:67). And in its place Moses will become father of a new nation. The accusations thus encapsulate the rebellion tradition broadly based in the wilderness theme (so, Coats, *Rebellion*).

Moses then intercedes for the people (vv. 13-19), a typical element in the heroic structure of the Moses tradition. The intercession builds on an argument from the value of God's reputation. The Egyptians will hear and assume that God failed. Moreover, they will spread the word to the Canaanites, and no one will believe that God is able to keep his word (and thus, can we not conclude, no one will fear the Lord, a critical theme in the conquest traditions). Verses 17-18 expand the appeal by reference to a typical epithet for God (Exod 34:5-8), an epithet used in the context of intercession. The plea then gains its strongest statement in v. 18. Verse 20 notes that God apparently accepts Moses' plea. Yet, vv. 21-23 renew the judgment against the people. The rebels will not enter the land (so, especially, vv. 32-35). In the place of total rejection, however, Caleb will carry a new generation into the land, a new seed to inherit the promise. It is significant that for the Yahwist, Caleb is the new heir, for Caleb is the representative for Judah (so, 13:6). The other spies, excluded by the judgment that eliminates all except the Judean Caleb, die in a plague. Is this specific act of judgment not a portent of a judgment against all of Israel except Judah (so, Ps 78:67-68)?

The conclusion for J in vv. 39-45 simply confirms that the people of the wilderness generation cannot enter the land. And the reason is clear. For these people, excluding Caleb the Judean, the Lord is not present (v. 42). To the contrary, the people assume the power to initiate entry into the land and meet defeat. The Amalekites (→ Exod 17:14-16) and the Canaanites will win the day. Judgment against the rebels in the wilderness thus carries for the Yahwist a marked pro-Judean bias.

It is more difficult to reconstruct an earlier stage of this tradition that reported the spying event entirely in a positive frame, entirely as an act of God on behalf of his people. The spy tradition assumes from the beginning that the people acted, either out of a lack of faith or, in a positive frame, simply to prepare for the conquest. It may be that the tradition was originally quite positive, describing a divine commission for spying as preparation for conquest. But if that was the case, its details have been lost. Moreover, the topos, spy report, casts images of conquest for the unit (so, Wagner). But the tradition does not belong to the conquest theme as a part of the structure of the Hexateuch. To the contrary, the content of the pericope — failure at conquest, an act of disobedience to the Lord — constitutes grounds for keeping the Israelites in the wilderness until the rebels die. The unit, then, is a significant element in the larger structure of the wilderness theme, for J as well as all the later levels. The spy report itself may depict conquest images (so, Wagner). But in the structure of the Pentateuch/Hexateuch, the spy story is a part of the wilderness theme.

Genre

At all levels, the narrative is a STORY. To be sure, it is expansive, a theologically sensitive tradition. But even its most expansive stage reflects the functional structure of the STORY. One might ask if the redactional process that combined the priestly and Yahwistic versions produced a NOVELLA. In some sense, that conclusion is appropriate. But if it is sustained, the NOVELLA would be highly artificial. A NOVELLA would, under normal circumstances, be the creative production of an author. The redaction process that produced this combination is not the same kind of artistic creation. Genre definition is more valuable at the levels of the sources. For P and for J, the narrative is STORY. It describes an event in an arc of tension that features resolution of some kind of crisis. Losing sight of characterization even for Moses and Aaron or Caleb and Joshua, it now focuses on the split report and the ensuing rebellion. That is the subject of STORY.

In addition to the STORY, SPY REPORT is a genre of significance in the social structure of the ancient world (so, Wagner). It apparently functions as an instrument in preparing for holy war or even explicitly conquest (→ Joshua 2). The NAME LIST is not a genealogical pattern but rather an organizational list, designed to show the parts of the whole as organizational units sharing responsibility for the whole.

Setting

The spy story now has a setting in the literary construction of the larger saga. As a rebellion story, it contributes to the traditions about Moses. The same point applies for the literary sources. Perhaps at the basis of this level is a setting for the tradition in the royal court of Jerusalem, a part of the larger complex of traditions designed to confirm the validity of the Davidic kingship in contrast to the elements of Israel rejected by God in the wilderness. The spy story would reflect a popular setting for telling stories, not necessarily the conquest theme and its social (cultic) provenance. Indeed, content would suggest that the unit derives from the wilderness theme. The name list derives from institutions in Israel concerned with organization, such as the military interested in conscription of manpower (a draft) or the court interested in conscription of financial power (a tax).

Intention

At its latest stage, this story intends to describe an event in the wilderness that not only anticipates the conquest, but also draws the rebellion sequence to an end. The sequence depicts Israel's response to a situation in the wilderness as an act of rebellion against the authority of Moses or Moses and Aaron together. The rebellion event generally is overt, implying attack on the power and position of the leader. In the wilderness theme, the rebellion attacks the position of Moses or Moses and Aaron together, suggesting designs that will force the people to return to Egypt and thus to undo the exodus event. Implicit is the factor of divine election resident in the exodus. To return to Egypt is to forsake the election of God as his special people, a relationship established in the exodus event. The rebellion is thus clearly against God. In this text, the motif features an overt plan to replace Moses in order to return to Egypt. Moreover, in this text, God responds to the rebellion with an explicit act of rejection for the rebels and a plan to replace them with a new people. It is precisely in this context that the tradition depicts the center of the special tradition about Moses as hero, for Moses intercedes for the people who rebel against him.

The spy report is a genre that, in itself, functions for narrative description of events leading to war, especially to war with conquest as a goal ($\rightarrow$ Joshua 2). The report in this context thus shows the unit, and indeed, the sequence of rebellion stories, to be related to the conquest theme (so, Wagner). But it does not define the unit as in itself a conquest story. In fact, the unit accounts for the necessity Israel faced for remaining in the wilderness throughout the life period of the wilderness generation. That length of time was, in fact, punishment for the rebellion of the generation (so, Coats, *Rebellion*).

The name list is organizational, a description of a system in the body of the people that establishes patterns for conscription of a work force. It is not the same as a genealogical list.

Annotation

For the interpretation of the position and function of Num 13:1–14:45 in the macrostructure of Num 10:11–36:13, see the discussion in $\rightarrow$ Chapter 4, especially the interpretation by Lee.

Bibliography

W. Belts, *Die Kaleb-Traditionen im Alten Testament* (*BWANT* 98; Stuttgart: Kohlhammer, 1964); N. Lohfink, "Die Ursünden in der priesterlichen Geschichtserzählung," in *Die Zeit Jesu* (ed. G. Bornkamm, K. Rahner; Freiburg: Herder, 1970) 38-57; K. D. Sakenfeld, "The Problem of Divine Forgiveness in Num 14," *CBQ* 37 (1975) 317-30; S. Wagner, "Die Kundschaftergeschichten im Alten Testament," *ZAW* 76 (1964) 255-61.

Ordinance Speech (15:1-16)

Structure

I. Introduction: the Lord to Moses	1
II. Speech	2-16
A. Message commission formula	2a
B. Message	2b-16
1. Instructions for offerings with sacrifice	2b-10
a. Circumstances for sacrifice	2b-3
b. Definition of the offerings with a lamb	4-5
1) Cereal offering with oil	4
2) Drink	5
c. Definition of the offerings with a ram	6-7
1) Cereal offering with oil	6
2) Drink	7
d. Definition of the offerings with a bull	8-10
1) Cereal offering with oil	8-9
2) Drink	10
2. Concluding summary	11-16
a. Summary	11-12
1) Summary formula	$11a\alpha_1$
2) Qualification by participants	$11a\alpha_2$-12
b. Designation of jurisdiction	13-16
1) For natives	13
2) For stranger	14
3) One-law formula	15-16

The relationship between this unit and its context cannot readily be defined. The unit opens with a speech formula (v. 1). But the speech structure is artificial for the unit, employed only to give the content of the speech context within the Moses legal traditions of the wilderness theme. Moreover, the opening element of the message within the speech (vv. 2b-16) suggests that the conquest has not yet occurred, thus setting the unit properly at some point within the wilderness theme. But again, the device is artificial for the unit. The content of the speech presupposes life on the land, not life in the wilderness (so,

Noth). No closer tie to the wilderness setting can be found, unless it should be a vague structural and logical association with the following two units (→ 15:17-31; 32-36).

The speech itself opens with a message commission formula, addressing the stipulations for offerings with sacrifice through Moses to the people of Israel. The message has two principal structural elements: The first (vv. 2b-10) contains instructions for the offerings, while the second (vv. 11-16) summarizes those instructions with a designation of jurisdiction. The structure of the first element is defined by three different animals available for sacrifice by fire. But the structure of the element does not focus on instituting these animals as legitimate objects for sacrifice or the respective value of each animal (→ Leviticus 1). Rather, the institution of the sacrifice and its order are presupposed. The structure focuses instead on defining accompanying offerings, both cereal and drink, for each of the animals. A progression in quantity of the side offerings, increasing from the lamb to the bull, suggests the only element of ranging in the list of sacrificial animals and defines the structure of the verses. With the lamb, one-tenth (of an ephah) of fine meal should be mixed with one-fourth hin of oil and presented with one-fourth hin of wine. With the lamb, two-tenths of fine meal, mixed with one-third hin of oil, should be presented with one-third hin of wine. And with the bull three-tenths of fine meal should be mixed with one-half hin of oil, one-half hin of wine presented with it in the sacrifice. In the designation of these practices, a frustrating flux between personal address with second person verbs and suffixes and impersonal address with third person verbs and suffixes obscures the structure (cf. Noth). This variation should be understood in terms of the artificial, secondary presentation of the instructions as speech (→ Exodus 12).

The second major element in the speech summarizes the instructions (v. 11) with qualification of quantity by the number of animals prepared (→ Exod 16:16). Then a validation of authority the instructions carry over native and stranger alike follows. The validation formula designates the one law over both categories of population (→ Exod 12:43-49).

The unit reflects a tradition history that stands in line with Leviticus 1. In contrast to its antecedents, this text adds a drink offering as a part of the sacrificial procedure and designates both cereal and drink offerings as subordinate to the sacrifice by fire of an animal. Moreover, it makes no reference to fowl sacrifice as a part of the ritual for size offerings. And it fails to designate frankincense as a part of the formula for cereal offering (cf. Leviticus 2). Yet, it stands in the same tradition of priestly sacrifice by fire represented by Leviticus 1–2. It should be defined as an expansion over the priestly tradition in Leviticus 1–2, thus a part of a late growth in the priestly tradition of the Pentateuch (so, Noth).

Genre

Like other texts defining worship procedures, this unit develops its instructions in the guise of a SPEECH, a direct address. Contrary to some texts, this unit is not supported by a narrative that would make the speech guise obviously necessary. The introductory SPEECH FORMULA, indeed, the structural characteristic of the unit as SPEECH, may thus be considered secondary, a means for giving an ORDINANCE a context in a larger narrative complex (→ Exod 12:43-49). The genre of the unit should be defined as ORDINANCE. In its adapted structure as a SPEECH, the ORDINANCE loses its legislative character in order to become a rubric for worship. At that stage the genre shifts from ORDINANCE to RITUAL.

Setting

The literary setting for this unit, within the context of the priestly tradition, presupposes an address from priest to people. The setting would thus be worship, if not in the immediate act of worship, at least in preparation for the worship. As ordinance, however, the unit reflects tradition as a part of canon law, preserved by priests for public reference, not public address.

Intention

The intention of the ritual, as a part of address to the people, would be to direct the process of worship. As an ordinance, the text legislates the worship procedure. One should note in this unit that the legislation does not affect sacrifice of sheep, ram, or bull; rather, those sacrifices and the circumstances governing them are presupposed. The intention is to establish accompanying offerings of cereal and wine with the burnt sacrifice. The reasons for offering the two additional elements is not noted. There is no element of interpretation with the ordinance. The entire function of the unit is thus to establish the ritual.

Annotation

In order to preserve as much as advisable the original text in Coats's interpretation, the title of the unit Num 15:1-16 given by Coats as "Ordinance Speech" and certain formulations in his discussion pertinent to his focus indicated by his definition of this title have not been altered editorially. However, in order to point out methodological developments during the history of the FOTL project regarding the more correct presentation of the structure of text-units, the following needs to be said.

The title of this unit should be: "Report of an Ordinance Speech." The whole unit is a REPORT about a Yahweh speech, not a Yahweh speech, which is by Coats himself correctly indicated by his twofold structure: I. (v. 1) and II. (vv. 2-16). The Yahweh speech itself, vv. 2-16, is introduced by the, however patterned, report formula, which proves that the following speech is, so to say, quoted by the narrator. Without the transmission of the speech by the narrator, the speech would — strictly speaking — not exist. The entire part II. (vv. 2-16) depends on part I. (v. 1). To account for the identity of the text as a *report* — by a reporter/narrator — of a speech — by someone other than the narrator, or, to

196

account for the fact that the content of a speech, also a divine speech, is transmitted/communicated only through an intermediary reporter/narrator and not without such — in our case human — mediation, amounts to much more than technical remarks about redactors. Well-meaning Bible readers may violate their claim of reading the Bible literally by neglecting these introductory formulae. Lastly, attention to these reporting formulae and their forms is indispensable for the discussion of the genres of narratives. The question of their authors' and their own settings and intentions is thus altogether essential for comprehending the meaning of the texts.

What is said regarding the text-unit just discussed also applies to all other units defined by Coats without reference to their speech *report* nature: Num 15:17-31; 15:37-41; 17:27–18:32; 19:1-22; 25:19–26:65; 28:1–30:1; 30:2-17; 32:1-42; 33:1–35:34; esp. 33:50-56; 34:1-12; 34:13-15; 34:16-29; 35:1-8; 35:9-34.

Bibliography

D. J. McCarthy, "The Symbolism of Blood and Sacrifice," *JBL* 88 (1969) 166-76; idem, "Further Notes on the Symbolism of Blood and Sacrifice," *JBL* 92 (1973) 205-10; J. Milgrom, "Sin Offering or Purification Offering?" *VT* 21 (1971) 237-39; N. H. Snaith, "Sacrifices in the Old Testament," *VT* 7 (1957) 308-18; idem, "The Sin Offering and the Guilt Offering," *VT* 15 (1965) 73-80.

Ordinance Speech (15:17-31)*

Structure

I. Introduction: the Lord to Moses	17
II. Speech	18-31
A. Message commission formula	18a
B. Message	18b-31
1. Instructions for an offering	18b-21
a. Circumstances for an offering	18b-19a
b. Instructions	19b-21
2. Instructions for sin offering	22-31
a. Description of sin	22-23
b. Procedure for unwitting sin in congregation	24-26
1) Introductory formula	24aα
2) Instructions for sin offering	24aβ-25
3) Concluding designation of people	26
c. Procedure for unwitting sin in one person	27-29

*See Annotation to Num 15:1-16.

1) Introductory formula   27a
2) Instructions for sin offering   27b-28
3) One-law formula   29
d. Procedure for witting sin in one person   30-31
1) Judgment   30
   a) Accusation   30a
   b) Conclusion   30b
2) Judgment   31
   a) Accusation   31a
   b) Conclusion   31b

There is a structural similarity between this unit and the preceding one. Both begin as a speech addressed by the Lord to Moses. Both qualify the instructions they carry as a message addressed through Moses to Israel. And both indicate that the instructions in the speech are applicable for life in the land, not life in the wilderness. Moreover, the parallel with Leviticus 1–4 suggests a sequence of content with stipulation about the burnt offering followed by stipulations about sin offering. There is also a point of contact with the following unit, Num 15:32-36. That narrative provides a case study of the circumstances leading to the judgment required at the conclusion of this unit. The specification of locale in the following unit (v. 32) pinpoints this complex (perhaps also Num 15:1-16) as material suitable for inclusion in the wilderness theme of traditions. (For its inclusion here, see the comments on Numbers 16.)

This unit is structured as a speech. But the speech formula serves only as a bridge to the context in the wilderness theme. It is not an integral part of the unit. The speech itself begins with a message commission formula. Instructions for sacrificial procedure should be addressed through Moses to the people of Israel. The message has two principal elements. The first, vv. 18b-21, contains instructions for an offering as a part of the food produce of the land. The instructions are, however, somewhat problematic. Not only is the key word, "coarse meal" (*'ărisōtēkem*), obscure (so, Noth), but in addition the entire element contains marked duplications (cf. vv. 20, 21). This problem is not evidence for source duplication, however. It suggests simply that the instructions for the sacrifice have been put together haphazardly out of a loose collection of sayings or perhaps out of an obscure offering ceremony (cf. the only other occurrence of the word in Ezek 44:30). Such haphazard construction may reflect unfortunate transmission of the text. It may suggest that the evidence for determining what the offering might have involved is unfortunately preserved now only in part. But it also points to the relative subordinate function of this element in the overall shape of the unit. This element is not extraneous to the remaining portions of the speech (against Noth) but rather functions as a foil for the second element. The first element establishes an offering little known here or in other parts of the Old Testament. But any ordinance would have been adequate. It serves in the structure of the unit to set the stage for the second element.

The second element sets out regulations for sin offering, atonement for violating this or any other ordinance. These instructions divide into three groups. The first concerns an offering for unwitting sin in the entire congregation, including the stranger (cf. v. 26). The second concerns unwitting sin in an individual. In both cases, structure follows the same pattern, with the same results noted for proper observation of the sin offering. The only difference lies in definition of the sacrificial animal, a bull and a goat, both male, for the congregation, and a female goat for the individual. These instructions differ only slightly from the parallel in Leviticus 4, where only a bull is required for the congregation, and no reference to cereal and drink as side offerings appears. It is perhaps this point of contact that brings this speech unit into contact with Num 15:1-16.

One must ask what the relationship is between this speech and the speech in Leviticus 4, establishing procedure for the same unwitting sins. Indeed, the reference to the ordinance as a presupposed element in v. 24aβ *(kammišpāṭ)* suggests that the ordinance as ordinance is already known. The third element concerns the person who sins intentionally. And the pattern of structure for the element changes. Leviticus 5–6 suggests procedure for intentional sins, with the opening for atonement. This text does not set out ordinances for atonement for the intentional sinner. Rather, it sets out a pattern of judgment against the sinner. In two statements the element opens grounds for eliminating the guilty party from the people, whether that party be native or stranger. The first one construes a nominal sentence with *casus pendens* to define the accusation, then sets out a second sentence with the judgment. The second statement opens with a dependent causal *(kî)* clause, the accusation, then defines the judgment in the main clause. In both cases the judgment calls for cutting the guilty party away from the people. "The person who does anything with a high hand, whether he is native or a stranger, reviles the Lord. That person shall be cut off *(nikrĕtâ)* from among his people. Because he has despised the word of the Lord and has broken his commandment, that person shall be utterly cut off *(hikkārēt tikkārēt).* His iniquity shall be on him" (Num 15:30-31). The final judgment formula has a parallel in Lev 5:1 where, contrary to cases of sin offering where the sin of a person is forgiven *(ḥaṭṭā'),* the person who does not offer a sin sacrifice must bear his own iniquity *('ăwōnô).* The impact of that judgment is death (cf. Matt 27:25).

The unit is composite, but not as the result of compilation from several sources. Rather, several traditional ordinances have been compiled in a particular way to emphasize a particular point. The antecedents for this unit can be found in Leviticus 1–7. The unit thus relates to priestly tradition, most probably as a late expansion (so, Noth).

Genre

The unit is a composite of ordinances, based on stipulations for judgments or presupposing judgments already made. But the ordinances are subordinated by the structure of the unit to the judgment in the final element. The overriding genre definition for the unit should thus pick up the unit's character of JUDGMENT. The formulaic character of the final expression would emphasize this point.

Stereotyped expressions and formulas include the JUDGMENT FORMULA, "his iniquity shall be on him," and the emphasis of jurisdiction for this judgment for both natives and strangers. Finally, the SPEECH FORMULA introduces the unit with the typical explanation of speaker and addressee.

Setting

The artificial construction of the speech suggests a literary setting, perhaps originally in close conjunction with the following unit. The tradition that defines death for intentional violation of cultic ordinances must derive from a society controlled by cultic guidelines. This procedure suggests the period of Judaism following the Ezra-Nehemiah reforms when the identity of the people depended on obedience to cultic ordinance.

Intention

The ordinances collected in this unit intend to establish the sacrificial procedures they describe. Both the speech formula and the message commission formula cast the unit into a highly artificial context. But the primary intention of the unit is defined by the final element in the speech, a judgment of death for the person who intentionally violates these or any other cultic ordinances. The structure of the unit, contrasting ordinance for sacrifice as well as for atonement in unwitting sin with judgment for the intentional sinner, emphasizes the final element.

Bibliography

D. Kellerman, "Bemerkungen zum Sündopfergesetz in Num 15: 22ff." in *Wort und Geschichte* (ed. H. Gese, H. P. Rüger; Neukirchen-Vluyn: Neukirchener Verlag, 1973).

Anecdote: The Wood-Gathering Precedent (15:32-36)

Structure

I. Introductory report	32-34
A. Discovery of violation	32
B. Trial	33
C. Incarceration	34
II. Judgment speech	35
A. Introduction: the Lord to Moses	35aα
B. Instructions	35aβ-b
III. Execution of instructions	36

This unit is closely related to the preceding pericope (15:17-31) as a narrative illustration of a particular case subject to the judgment called for in instances of intentional violation of ordinances. It should be noted that the specific violation is not the issue. It makes no difference that the ordinance tradition in the preceding unit has nothing to do with the Sabbath. It makes no difference that the precise nature of the violation described in this unit cannot be determined, or at least must be deduced (cf. Weingreen). The connection lies in the intentional nature of the offense, both in the judgment for death in 15:30-31, and in the act of the wood-gatherer.

The narrative itself comprises three basic elements. The first contains a narration, recounting discovery of a man in flagrant violation of the Sabbath law, his arrest and subsequent incarceration pending judgment. It may be that the violation reflects an ancient law against kindling fire on the Sabbath (cf. Exod 35:3). In that case the act would anticipate the man's violations of the law; it does not constitute the violation itself (so, Weingreen). It may be that an extension in scope of the Sabbath law is reflected (so, Phillips). But whatever the precise nature of the violation, the point of the narration lies in the intentional nature of his act (so, Weingreen). The second element of the unit is a judgment speech from Yahweh. Significantly, no element of the narration notes that Moses sought the Lord in order to obtain the judgment. Rather, the narration moves from the report of arrest, trial, and incarceration directly to the Lord's judgment speech. The speech does not institute the Sabbath as a cultic ordinance. It presupposes the ordinance, with the violation a *fait accompli,* not an act calling for a new legislation. Rather, the speech pronounces judgment on the man, presumably on the basis of an ordinance already established. The structure of the unit thus paints a case of precedent for particular judgment, not a case calling for new law (against Noth). The relationship with the previous unit, with its stipulation calling for a death judgment, is thus clear. Moreover, the enigmatic, somewhat abrupt use of the Sabbath as the ordinance broken recalls the arbitrary use of an ordinance as an illustration for particular judgments in 15:17-31. The story here does not emphasize the Sabbath; it delineates what happens to a man when he intentionally violates the Sabbath or any other cultic ordinance.

The unit itself shows no marks of literary growth. It is whole as it now stands. Its dependency on the preceding unit suggests that it belongs to the same late stage of priestly traditions represented by vv. 17-31 (so Noth).

Genre

This unit cannot be classified as an ordinance or an etiology for an ordinance (against Noth). Rather, it is an ANECDOTE, a narrative that describes the particularities of an event from the past (Coats, "Anecdote"). But the anecdote relates to some previously established ordinance and sets a precedent for judgment in the event (cf. Lev 24:10-16).

The unit contains a stereotyped formula for DEATH SENTENCE in v. 35, a SPEECH FORMULA in v. 35.

Setting

The cultic control of social definition appears sharply developed here. Sabbath ordinance becomes a means by which identity could be established. The identity question lay in the hands of cultic officials, responsible for determining proper or improper observations of crucial ordinances. That setting, as in the preceding unit, reflects the cultic institution of the late postexilic period. That institution would apparently have a considerable amount of power to enforce the decisions reflected by the anecdote ($\rightarrow$ Ezek 10:1-5).

Intention

The story functions not as etiology but as an anecdote that recounts a particular event in order to establish the event and its consequences as a case precedent. The intention is not to account for the first observation of the Sabbath, but to establish legal, divine precedent for judgment when the age-old Sabbath ordinance should be violated. It is not legislation. It is judicial.

Bibliography

G. W. Coats, "Parable, Fable, and Anecdote: Storytelling in the Succession Narrative," *Int* 35 (1981) 368-82; A. Phillips, "The Case of the Wood-gatherer Reconsidered," *VT* 19 (1969) 125-28; J. Weingreen, "The Case of the Wood-gatherer (Numbers XV 32-36)," *VT* 16 (1966) 361-64.

Ordinance Speech for Vestment (15:37-41)*

Structure

I. Introduction: the Lord to Moses		37
II. Speech		38-41
A. Message commission formula		38aα
B. Message		38aβ-41
1. Instructions for making tassels		38aβ-b
2. Purpose		39-40
3. Concluding formulas		41
a. Exodus formula		41a
b. Self-revelation formula		41b

This unit is totally isolated in its context. It has no clear relationship with the preceding collection of ordinances and precedent traditions. Nor does it re-

*See Annotation to Num 15:1-16.

flect any point of contact with the following Dathan-Abiram-Korah story. Its isolation nevertheless points to this position in the wilderness theme and structural break in the progress of narration.

The unit is cast as a speech from the Lord to Moses. It begins with a speech formula, then continues with a message commission formula designed to transmit the message through Moses to the people. But the structural pattern is secondary, a means for incorporating the ordinance into the larger context of the Moses narration. It may well be this shift in structure that accounts for the variation from third person reference to the people in v. 38 to a second person plural address in vv. 39-41 (but cf. Deut 22:12).

The message comprises three parts. The first contains instructions for constructing the tassels. The tassels perhaps functioned originally as magical symbols (so, Noth). Similar tassels, even blue ones, served as garments of gods, kings, or other rulers, and even warriors (so, Bertman). If that practice from the larger culture reflects the same practice as the one described here, perhaps the point in common lies in a symbolic protective role. But even if some such symbolic function accounts for the original character of the tassels, the following elements of this speech have stripped away the magical quality, for the speech defines the purpose of the tassels as reminders for keeping the commandments. The ordinance is validated with an exodus formula and a self-revelation formula, reminding Israel that her ordinances are never very far removed from the crucial events of her history. Indeed, the event of prime importance, the exodus, becomes the provocation for Israel to keep the ordinance. For similar reminders → Num 17:5, 25.

The unity of the pericope cannot be challenged. No signs of literary growth appear. The antecedents for the tradition may be sought in the deuteronomic law, Deut 22:12, as well as in customs of the surrounding culture (so, Bertman). The unit should thus be attributed along with the others of this collection, to priestly tradition in a late period (so, Noth).

Genre

The SPEECH can be categorized as CULTIC ORDINANCE, although the character of the unit as SPEECH moves the statement to the position of ritual (cf. Exodus 12). The stereotyped formulas of the unit include not only the SPEECH FORMULA and the MESSAGE COMMISSION FORMULA in vv. 37-38, but the EXODUS FORMULA and the SELF-REVELATION FORMULA of v. 41.

Setting

The ordinance could live only in the cultic context concerned to preserve the tassel as a legitimate part of cultic vestment, even though its original significance may have been lost.

Intention

As ordinance, the speech functions as legislation. The tassel remains a part of cultic vestment, in all probability with a new explanation of the significance lifted out of Israel's peculiar theology. The exodus formula and the self-revelation formula provide authority to the call to obey the commandments in relationship to the tassel.

The speech formula and the message formula provide only a bridge relationship with the larger context. They tend to move the unit to function as immediate directions in the act of worship. But that appearance is artificial, derived only from the necessity to adjust the unit to the context.

Bibliography

S. Bertman, "Tasseled Garments in the Ancient East Mediterranean," *BA* 24 (1961) 119-28.

Rebellion Story: Dathan-Abiram-Korah
(16:1–17:5; *NRSV* 16:1-40)

Text

16:1 is problematic. The NRSV, "Now Korah . . . took . . . men," reconstructs the object, "men," without support from the manuscripts or the versions. The MT verb *(wayyiqqaḥ)*, has no clear object. Origen's Hexapla reads ὑπερηφανεύθη. This verb could be taken as a parallel to the verb in v. 2 *wayyāqumû*, since the verb *qûm* functions as a synonym of the murmuring-rebellion verbs. Gray observes the possibility that the verb is a corruption of an original *wayyāqom*. In his translation, however, he simply deletes the verb and leaves the sentence a fragment. If the verse is taken as exposition, the primary function would be to present data about the chief characters rather than opening the narration of events. As a parallel to v. 2, it would be structurally redundant. It seems most appropriate, then, to see the verse as the fragmented remains of the opening exposition. Moreover, vv. 2aβ-3b have no clear relationship with v. 2aα the beginning of the complication element in the plot structure. Cf. the *wāw* conjunction with *wa'ănāšîm*. This description of the two hundred fifty men can be considered also a part of the exposition.

Structure

I. Exposition	1-2
II. Complication	2-15
A. Narration of the crisis	2-3

        1. Act of rebellion (arose)   2
        2. Act of rebellion (assembled)   3
            a. Narration of the event   3aα₁
            b. Speech report   3aα₂-b
                1) Introduction: men to Moses and Aaron   3aα₂
                2) Accusation   3aα₃-b
    B. Response   4-15
        1. Narrative description of reaction   4
        2. Moses speech report   5-7
            a. Introduction: Moses to Korah and company   5aα
            b. Speech   5aβ-7
                1) Announcement of coming judgment   5aβ-b
                2) Instructions   6-7
        3. Moses speech report   8-11
            a. Introduction: Moses to Korah   8a
            b. Speech   8b-11
                1) Accusation   8-10
                2) Judgment: with abasement formula   11
        4. Narration of summons to Dathan-Abiram   12a
        5. Speech report   12b-14
            a. Introduction: Dathan and Abiram to Moses   12bα
            b. Speech   12bβ-14
                1) Refusal to execute instructions   12bβ
                2) Accusation   13-14
        6. Speech report   15
            a. Introduction: Moses to the Lord   15aα-aβ₁
            b. Speech   15aβ₂-b
                1) Petition for judgment   15aβ₂
                2) Self-defense   15b
III. Resolution   16-35
    A. Preparation for ordeal   16-27a
        1. Moses speech report   16-17
            a. Introduction: Moses to Korah   16aα
            b. Instructions for trial by ordeal   16aβ-17
        2. Execution of instructions   18-19
        3. Speech report   20-21
            a. Introduction: the Lord to Moses and Aaron   20
            b. Instructions for self-preservation   21
        4. Speech report   22
            a. Introduction: Moses and Aaron to the Lord   22aα
            b. Intercession for the remaining people   22aβ-b
        5. Speech report   23-24
            a. Introduction: the Lord to Moses and Aaron   23
            b. Instructions for preserving the people   24
        6. Execution of instructions by Moses   25-26
            a. Narrative description of action   25
            b. Speech report   26

        1) Introduction: Moses to the people   26aα

        2) Instructions for self-preservation   26aβ-b

    7. Execution of instructions by the people   27a

  B. Trial by ordeal   27b-35

    1. Narrative description of action   27b

    2. Speech report   28-30

      a. Introduction: Moses to Dathan-Abiram   28aα$_1$

      b. Speech   28aα$_2$-30

        1) Knowledge formula   28aα$_2$-b

        2) Evidence   29

        3) Contrary evidence   30a

        4) Knowledge formula   30b

    3. Narration of the event   31-35

      a. Description of the judgment   31-33

        1) Description of the ground opening   31

        2) Description of the earth opening   32-33

      b. Response of the people   34

      c. Destruction of the co-conspirators   35

IV. Conclusion   17:1-5 (*NRSV* 16:36-40)

  A. Speech report   1-3 (*NRSV* 36-38)

    1. Introduction: the Lord to Moses   1 (*NRSV* 36)

    2. Speech   2-3 (*NRSV* 37-38)

      a. Message commission formula: Moses to Eleazar

           2aα (*NRSV* 37aα)

      b. Message: instructions for preserving censers

           2aβ-3 (*NRSV* 37aβ-38)

  B. Execution of instructions   4-5 (*NRSV* 39-40)

The Dathan-Abiram-Korah story fits into the larger context of the Pentateuch without benefit of an itinerary formula. It is apparently controlled by the itinerary formula in Num 12:16, thus sharing the traditio-historical problem represented in the itinerary by the Wilderness of Paran (→ Num 10:12; 20:1). But the contact with the itinerary framework is a part of the final redaction of this material, contributing nothing to the story or even to careful bonds between this story and its context. Moreover, the legal collections in Numbers 15 and 17-19 isolate the story from the narrative sections of the wilderness traditions. The story thus reveals evidence of a peculiar relationship with the wilderness theme (→ The Framework, Chapter 3, FOTL IIA).

The story itself develops along a recognizable plot line from a fragmented exposition through presentation of complication to a resolution of the crisis. The final element, the conclusion, expands the resolution into an anticlimax, an element totally dependent on the major structure of the story, yet extrinsic to the story's plot. Structural problems within the scheme, such as the narration element in the middle of a series of speeches, v. 12a, or a structural duplication, v. 31//vv. 32-33, suggest that the story in its present shape is a compilation of two distinct sources.

Structure in the P account has the following scheme:

I. Exposition   1-2
II. Complication   3-11
   A. Rebellion narration   3
   B. Rebellion speeches   4-11
      1. Narrative description of action   4
      2. Speech report   5-7
         a. Introduction: Moses to Korah and company   5aα
         b. Speech   5aβ-7
            1) Announcement of coming judgment   5aβ-b
            2) Instructions   6-7
      3. Speech report   8-11
         a. Introduction: Moses to Korah   8a
         b. Speech   8b-11
            1) Accusation, with call to attention formula   8b-10
            2) Judgment, with abasement formula   11
III. Resolution   16-24, 27a, 32-35
   A. Preparation for ordeal   16-24, 27a
      1. Speech report   16-17
         a. Introduction: Moses to Korah   16aα
         b. Instructions for trial by ordeal   16aβ-17
      2. Execution of instructions   18-19
      3. Speech report   20-21
         a. Introduction: the Lord to Moses and Aaron   20
         b. Instructions for self-preservation   21
      4. Speech report   22
         a. Introduction: Moses and Aaron to the Lord   22aα
         b. Intercession for the remaining people   22aβ-b
      5. Speech report   23-24
         a. Introduction: the Lord to Moses and Aaron   23
         b. Instructions for preserving the people   24
      6. Execution of instructions   27a
   B. Narration of judgment event   32-35
IV. Conclusion   17:1-5 (NRSV 36-40)

The priestly story reflects the same basic structure now preserved in the final form of the text. A brief, fragmented exposition sets out the principal figures of the story. The complication sets Korah and his men against Moses and Aaron, in open rebellion against the authority of Moses and Aaron. Their accusation in v. 3 identifies the issue as a matter of sacred office (so, the claim for holiness, *qĕdōšîm,* for all the congregation), then poses the accusation question as an attack on Moses' appropriation of power in the sacred office. "Why do you exalt yourselves above the assembly of the Lord?" The response speech, vv. 5-7, sets up a resolution for the conflict in the context of a trial by ordeal. Each of the opposing parties is to present a sacrifice of incense; the implication is that the unauthorized faction will be consumed by the sacrificial fire (cf. Leviticus 10). The opening part of the speech again points to the sacred office as the issue (so, the technical term, "to bring near," *hiqrîb*). The speeches in vv. 8-

11 and 16-17 carry this struggle directly to the Levites and should be seen as a part of the secondary expansions in the priestly tradition represented also in 17:1-5 (cf. also v. 7b, perhaps a corruption in the text from vv. 3a and 8b). The narration of execution of instructions, vv. 18-19, is structured in P as sequence for the speech in vv. 16-17. In effect, it functions also as notation of instruction executed, the sequence for the speech in vv. 6-7. The instructions for judgment in vv. 18-19 suggest that all the people must die for the guilt of Korah. An intercession speech, followed with revised instructions for judgment, limits the punishment to the guilty. The instructions are carried out, and the stage is set for the trial. Verses 32-35 then narrate the destruction of the rebels. Korah and his family were swallowed by the earth, however, not consumed in fire. This motif must be seen as an element of tradition inherited by P. Only the supporting company of men were destroyed by fire. 17:1-5 (*NRSV* 16:36-40) is not simply an appendix, like 17:6-15. Rather, it extends the final element of the story by providing an anti-climax, instructions for preservation of the censers used in the trial as bronze overlay for the altar. The reason for the preservation lies in the holiness the censers achieved during the trial (so, Noth). But the preservation is given an additional function: The overlay will warn the congregation against all subsequent misappropriation of priestly duties.

The J story reveals a similar structure:

I. Exposition	1
II. Complication	12-15
III. Resolution	24-26, 27b, 28-31
A. Preparation for the trial	24-26, 27b
B. Narration of the judgment	28-31
1. Knowledge formula	28-30
2. Event	31

The structural duplication between the Dathan-Abiram story (J) and the Korah story (P) suggests that the two were not originally independent stories, combined in the process of redaction, but two versions of the same story (so, Coats, *Rebellion*). The Korah story reflects revisions of the Dathan-Abiram story for appropriation in disputes developed within priestly circles. Thus, the Dathan-Abiram story opens with an exposition noting genealogical data for the principals, then sets up the crisis as a challenge to Moses' authority (so, the accusation in vv. 12-14). But at this point the accusation does not involve a sacred office. It involves Moses' position of leadership in the exodus and thus anticipates the anti-exodus motifs of the murmuring tradition. Yet, it is not simply a part of the stereotyped murmuring pattern. Its roots must be seen in early traditions about opposition to Moses in the wilderness. The stereotyped murmuring motif perhaps draws on the patterns of this early tradition as a model for presenting its particular series of rebellion stories.

The third element in the structure of the Yahwistic story also parallels elements in P. Just as P reports a speech of the Lord in preparation for the trial, so J has a speech of the Lord concerned with preservation of the people when the rebels will be destroyed. The speech from Moses to Dathan-Abiram in vv. 28-

30 involves a knowledge formula, commonly a part of P. But in this case, the context of the formula focuses on the challenge to Moses' authority peculiar to J. And the duplication of the element in vv. 32-35, clearly a part of P, marks the section as J. The narration of the event itself in v. 31 is an exact doublet with v. 32, involving the same kind of punishment for the rebels. And in accord with the knowledge formula, the destruction of the rebels establishes Moses' authority to lead the people.

A comparison between the structures in J and P shows only three important differences. In P, the name of the chief rebel is Korah, not Dathan-Abiram. Korah has the support of two hundred and fifty men. And the anti-climax focus on the censers as bronze overlays finds no counterpart in J. In the first and last instances, the differences can be explained in terms of P's special interests or the special interests of secondary elements in P. The denigration of Korah as a rebel against Moses must reflect a polemic within the structure of priestly groups. The secondary addition to P in 17:1-5 (*NRSV* 16:36-40) again involves a concern over priestly office. Moreover, the company of two hundred and fifty men may not be peculiar to the Korahite level of the story. Ps 106:16-17 suggests that Dathan-Abiram had the support of a company of men. If that should be the case, then the stories would be identical in structure and tradition, suggesting successive stages in the history of the same tradition (so, Coats, *Rebellion*).

Genre

The latest stage in the history of this story has altered the context of the original plot line. But it did not break the genre that carried the tradition in the earlier stages. For both P and J, doubtlessly also for any earlier stages of the story as story, the narrative preserves the characteristics of STORY. The plot focuses on the events that define the relationships between the principal characters. Moreover, the pattern of the narration, picked up by the stories of rebellion stamped with the murmuring motif, categorizes the story as a REBELLION STORY. It is, indeed, this focus on rebellion in the J story that provides an opening for P to revise the story in accord with his own polemical interests.

Formulas and stereotyped expressions include an ACCUSATION (vv. 3, 8-10, 13-14), abasement formula (v. 11), PETITION for JUDGMENT (v. 15), SELF-DEFENSE SPEECH (v. 16), KNOWLEDGE FORMULA (vv. 28a, 30), MESSAGE COMMISSION FORMULA (17:2).

Setting

The latest stage of the story reflects a combination of the Korah story and the Dathan-Abiram story. The setting here is redactional. The Korah story itself was preserved in priestly groups interested particularly in polemical positions against the Korahite priestly guild. The secondary expansion of this story involves a polemic against the Levites, with Korah considered the chief of the levitical group. In both cases, the story has been adapted for use in internal struggles of the priesthood. The J story does not reveal evidence of concerns that reflect J's theology, as do the murmuring stories. Rather, J has preserved as a part of his narrative a story inherited from tradition. The story may trace its history to a period in the wilderness itself, a story that recounts opposition to Moses in the wilderness based on a kernel of fact. The story would then have been preserved as a part of the Moses traditions rather than as a part of the wilderness theme emphasizing God's aid for his people. But the overlap of the two structural elements can be seen here clearly. A more precise definition of setting for this tradition seems impossible to establish. (On the setting of the Moses traditions, see Coats, *Heroic Man and Man of God*).

Intention

The priestly Korah story develops the theme of rebellion against Moses' authority as a polemic against the Korahite people (and their descendants). Korah, the namesake for a specific group of priests, is cast as a traitor, thus undercutting the position of those priests who trace their lineage to the rebel. The expansion of the Korah story extends the polemic to the Levites. The reference to the overlay for the altar makes clear that the polemic favors the Aaronite priesthood. The intention of the polemic is to insure that no one other than an Aaronite can serve at the altar. The earlier story preserves a tradition about attack against Moses' authority in the wilderness without tying the attack to any recognizable institution. The genealogical data for Dathan-Abiram may reflect a conflict between Moses and the Reubenites, also accounting for the demise of the Reubenites at a rather early period in the history of Israel. But if that is the intention of the story, it remains rather obscure. Rather, the intention concentrates on establishing the legitimacy of Moses' authority. The knowledge formula particularly emphasizes that function. Moses is the Lord's man.

Bibliography

G. W. Coats, *Moses: Heroic Man and Man of God* (JSOTSup 57; Sheffield: JSOT Press, 1988); E. Gillischewski, "Die Geschichte von der 'Rotte Korah' Num 16," *Archiv für Orientforschung*, 3 (1926) 114-18; S. Lehming, "Versuch zu Num 16," *ZAW* 74 (1962) 291-321; J. Liver, "Korah, Dathan, and Abiram," in *Studies in the Bible* (ed. C. Rabin; Jerusalem: Magnes, 1961) 189-217.

Plague Story (17:6-15; *NRSV* 16:41-50)

Structure

I. Complication	17:6-10 (*NRSV* 16:41-45)
A. Speech report	17:6 (*NRSV* 16:41)

210

        1. Introduction: all the people against
           Moses and Aaron   6a (*NRSV* 41a)
        2. Accusation   6b (*NRSV* 41b)
    B. Response   17:7-10 (*NRSV* 16:42-45)
        1. Appearance of God   17:7 (*NRSV* 16:42)
        2. Narrative description of action   17:8 (*NRSV* 16:43)
        3. Speech report   17:9-10a (*NRSV* 16:44-45a)
          a. Introduction: the Lord to
             Moses (and Aaron)   17:9 (*NRSV* 16:44)
          b. Instructions for self-preservation   17:10a (*NRSV* 16:45a)
        4. Narration of intercession   17:10b (*NRSV* 16:45b)
  II. Resolution   17:11-13 (*NRSV* 16:46-48)
    A. Speech report   17:11 (*NRSV* 16:46)
         1. Introduction: Moses to Aaron   17:11aα₁ (*NRSV* 16:46aα₁)
        2. Instructions for atonement ritual 17:11aα₂-b (*NRSV* 16:46aα₂-b)
    B. Execution of instructions   17:12-13 (*NRSV* 16:47-48)
 III. Conclusion   17:14-15 (*NRSV* 16:49-50)
    A. Statistical observations   17:14 (*NRSV* 16:49)
    B. Concluding narration   17:15 (*NRSV* 16:50)

This plague story is dependent on the Korah story (P) in Num 16:1–17:5. Evidence for this conclusion can be found not only in common principals in the plot, a temporal bridge connecting the stories (so, v. 6: "on the morrow" [*mimmāḥŏrāt*]), an accusation in v. 6, and a summary reference to the Korah matter in v. 14, but also in structure and motif similarities. Yet, the story is not the same kind of extension from the Korah narrative that 17:1-5 represents. It cannot be evaluated as a structural appendix for the Korah story (against Noth). It is a distinct story with integrity in its own structure. It stands in sequence with the Korah story, as the accusation at the head of the unit shows. Indeed, the entire Korah story serves this unit as exposition. Yet, it is a distinct story.

The unit assumes an exposition, a structural element provided in the present form of the text by the Korah story. Then, two basic elements of structure plus a conclusion that functions as appendix to the plot line round out the unit. Element I establishes the crisis of the plot. The crisis narration begins with a murmuring formula, like the ones so common in narrative about Israel's rebellion in the wilderness (so, the technical term, "murmur," *wayyillōnû*). Moreover, like those formulas, but contrary to the Korah story, this story pits all of the people against Moses and Aaron. The reasons for the murmuring, expressed in the accusation, establish the connection between this story and Korah. The point of rebellion lies in the execution of the "people of the Lord." That this oblique allusion intends the Korah destruction is confirmed by the reference to the "Korah affair" in v. 14.

The response to the murmuring, 17:7-10 (*NRSV* 16:42-45) has marked parallels with the Korah story. The narration of God's appearance in v. 7 parallels 16:19. The Lord's instructions to Moses and Aaron for self-preservation in the face of the coming catastrophe, vv. 9-10a, parallel 16:21. And the narration of intercession in v. 10b parallels 16:22. The first element suggests that this story has been structured according to the model provided by the Korah story, but influenced in presentation by the murmuring tradition.

The resolution element depends on a Moses speech (without a counterpart from the Lord), giving instructions to Aaron for ritual procedure in bringing the Lord's punishment to a halt, for a plague had already begun. This structural element parallels the secondary addition to the Korah story preserved now in 17:1-5. In overall structure, however, its parallel can be more readily found in Num 21:4-9, for the crisis that prompts Moses' intercession and resolution in that story is not the privation of the wilderness but God's punishment for rebellion already committed. There is thus no positive antecedent for this negative murmuring story. The ritual process itself parallels the ritual as it develops in Numbers 21, insofar as the object is carried among the people to stop a plague. The closest ties in ritual codes appear in Lev 14:26, 31, etc., where a burnt offering with a pleasing odor is made for atonement. In Lev 16:11-14, a ritual process involving incense parallels to this one appears, although it is not offered in the midst of the people. And the process is set in the context of atonement.

The third element is an appendix on the plot structure with statistics for the dead, not only from the plague, but from the Korah affair as well. The two stories are thus closely linked (for statistics like these, → Exod 12:37). The final statement rounds off the narrative and prepares for the next story. The third element thus carries a bridging function for this story and its context.

With these observations, it is not hard to conclude that the story comes from P or secondary elements in P. The immediate background of the story is the priestly story of Korah and the murmuring tradition. And priestly concerns dominate the plot structure. It is not possible, moreover, to suggest that the story has roots in an oral tradition apart from Korah/Dathan-Abiram or the murmuring accounts.

Genre

The story is structured as a REBELLION STORY, parallel to the murmuring stories throughout the wilderness theme. Its closest parallel, Num 21:4-9, has etiological characteristics. But it contains no etiological formulas. Its etiological character is hypothesized from the role the primary object in the story played in subsequent tradition (→ Num 21:4-9). Here there are also no etiological formulas. There is no indication that the story was intended to function as etiology for an atonement ritual with censers. On the basis of the parallel with Numbers 21, however, something of that sort might be suggested as the character of the story.

Stereotyped refrains and formulas include the MURMURING/REBELLION FORMULA, the narrative description for intercession in v. 10b, and the description of the incense ritual, v. 11.

Setting

The priestly character of the story points to the priesthood as an institution interested in preserving this story. Its setting must be seen primarily as a part of P

212

or the secondary expansion in P. Whether the story ever had a life of its own outside its function in P seems doubtful. If that was the case, then the story would have no unique setting apart from the literary position in P.

Intention

The murmuring tradition has an inherent polemical function. If that polemic has been incorporated into this story along with the patterns of the murmuring motif, the function must be seen as an effort to exalt the position of the priest over rebels by demonstrating what happens to rebels and how the unfortunate fate of those rebels can be altered. The primary intention of the story, however, seems to lie in the establishment of a ritual of atonement, involving censers in a particular relationship with the congregation.

Almond Rod Anecdote (17:16-26; *NRSV* 17:1-11)

Structure

I. Instructions speech report	17:16-20 (*NRSV* 17:1-5)
A. Introduction: the Lord to Moses	16 (*NRSV* 1)
B. Speech	17-20 (*NRSV* 2-5)
1. Message commission formula	17aα$_1$ (*NRSV* 2aα$_1$)
2. Message	17aα$_2$-20 (*NRSV* 2aα$_2$-5)
a. Instructions concerning almond rods	17aα$_2$-19 (*NRSV* 2aα$_2$-4)
b. Purpose	20 (*NRSV* 5)
II. Execution of instructions	21-24 (*NRSV* 6-9)
A. Narration of the execution	21-22 (*NRSV* 6-7)
B. Results: the sign of the almond rod	23-24 (*NRSV* 8-9)
III. Conclusion	25-26 (*NRSV* 10-11)
A. Speech report	25 (*NRSV* 10)
1. Introduction: the Lord to Moses	25aα$_1$ (*NRSV* 10aα$_1$)
2. Speech	25aα$_2$-b (*NRSV* 10aα$_2$-b)
a. Instructions for preserving Aaron's rod	25aα$_2$-aβ (*NRSV* 10aα$_2$-aβ)
b. Reason	25b (*NRSV* 10b)
B. Execution of instructions	26 (*NRSV* 11)

These verses constitute a discrete unit, not simply an appendix on the Korah story in ch. 16 (against Noth). Moreover, they have no intrinsic relationship with the murmuring story in 12:1-15. The conclusion to the story in 17:15 rounds off the plot as it developed around Aaron's commission to halt the plague (→ Num 17:11-15). And the introductory formula in 17:16 marks the beginning of a new unit with its own particular function. Yet, the unit is not completely independent from the context. The oblique allusions to the murmurings (note the plural form *tělunnôt* in vv. 20, 25) and the people presuppose the larger skein of murmuring stories, not simply the Korah story. They depend on the skein, not on the internal patterns of the unit.

The structure in these verses comprises three principal elements: an instructions speech, narration of the execution of the instructions, and a specification of purpose for the event. Significantly, the unit cannot be analyzed in terms of plot structure. There is no exposition, no complication leading to a resolution of tension. Rather, the unit begins with a speech, directing Moses to a specific act. The speech opens with a message commission formula, suggesting that Moses should now address a message to the Israelites. But the message does not follow the expected sequence. Rather, the speech details the results expected from the instructions. Almond rods should be gathered from each of the tribes. Then further instructions about the rods set up a specification of the purpose of the act. The second element narrates Moses' execution of the instructions, with specification of the results. The results constitute the focal element of the unit, the sign (cf. v. 25 where the results of the act are designated as "sign"). The final elements contain a new speech, with instructions for preserving the sign, as well as its function vis-à-vis any rebels. Designation of the purpose fulfilled by the sprouted almond rod is a crucial, qualifying element of the unit (→ Exod 7:13 etc.).

These verses are literarily a unity, showing no clear signs of secondary growth. They belong to P or, perhaps more accurately, to a post-priestly expansion of the murmuring skein. It is significant that the tradition reflected by the unit is at a late stage of growth, alluding to groups of murmuring stories rather than to any one murmuring scene. Yet, perhaps the tradition preserves a memory of an older tradition about paraphernalia for established leaders in the community (→ Num 21:4-9).

Genre

The unit is a report, designed only to recount an event of general interest rather than to develop a plot around the event. As a report of an event from the wilderness period, it functions as ANECDOTE. The unit has, nevertheless, a specific structural pattern, similar to the individual sign elements in Exod 7:8–10:29. Here as there, the unit reports a speech from the Lord instructing the leader to perform a sign, a narrative element recounting the execution of the instructions and the results, and some specification of the purpose (or failure of purpose) in the sign. The antecedents for the sign anecdote may be sought in narrative accounts of magical acts (so, Fohrer).

The unit includes the stereotyped formulas, found commonly in narrative materials: MESSAGE COMMISSION FORMULA in v. 17, INSTRUCTIONS EXECUTED FORMULA in v. 26.

Setting

The struggles between priestly groups clearly dominate this unit, with the Levites elevated to a position of preeminence. Contrary to the secondary additions to the Korah story (Numbers 16), here Aaron is the head of the house of Levi. Thus, the setting for the unit must be seen in the postexilic struggles between priestly groups, specifically adapting tradition to the interests of the Levites.

Intention

The unit notes the importance of preserving the rod of Levi. Like the instructions for preserving the censers as bronze overlay for the altar, as well as the jar of manna and the bronze serpent, these instructions suggest a cultic preservation for the report.

One might inquire a step farther into the tradition history by exploring whether symbols of particular leadership play an important role in Israel's cultic life. Perhaps behind this late notice of preservation for the Aaron/Levi symbol lies an older tradition about paraphernalia that would witness the unique position of the ancestor in the tradition, and thus also attest to his authority.

Bibliography

G. Fohrer, *Überlieferung und Geschichte des Exodus: eine Analyse von Exod 1–15* (*BZAW* 91; Berlin: Töpelmann, 1964) 60-79

Collection of Priesthood Ordinances
(17:27–18:32; *NRSV* 17:12–18:32)*

Structure

I. Speech report	17:27-28 (*NRSV* 17:12-13)
A. Introduction: people of Israel to Moses	27a (*NRSV* 12a)
B. Lamentation speech	27b-28 (*NRSV* 12b-13)
II. Ordination speech	18:1-7
A. Introduction: the Lord to Aaron	1aα
B. Speech	1aβ-7
1. Designation of task as ordinances	1aβ-b
2. Designation of Levites' task	2-4
a. Service	2-3a
b. Warning	3b-4

*See Annotation to Num 15:1-16.

        3. Summary of priesthood task   5
           a. Service   5a
           b. Purpose of service   5b
        4. Designation of rift   6-7
           a. Levi   6
           b. Aaron   7
              1) Service   7a-bα
              2) Warning   7bβ
III. Wages speech   8-19
     A. Introduction: the Lord to Aaron   8aα
     B. Speech: list of salary specifications   8aβ-19
        1. Introduction   8aβ-b
        2. List   9-18
           a. Cereal, sin, guilt offerings   9-10
              1) Definition of wages in the offerings   9
              2) Qualification of place for eating   10a
              3) Qualification of persons eligible   10bα
              4) Proclamation formula   10bβ
           b. Wave offerings   11
              1) Definition of wages in the offerings   11a
              2) Qualification of persons eligible   11b
           c. Oil, wine, grain   12
           d. First ripe fruit   13
              1) Definition of wages in the offerings   13a
              2) Qualifications of persons eligible   13b
           e. Devoted things   14
           f. Everything opening the womb   15-18
              1) Definition of wages in the offering   15a
              2) Exceptions   15b
                 a) Human   15bα
                 b) Unclean animals   15bβ
              3) Redemption price   16
              4) Eligible sacrifices   17-18
                 a) Specification of sacrifices   17
                 b) Definition of wages in the sacrifice   18
        3. Conclusion   19
IV. Inheritance speech   18:20-24
    A. Introduction: the Lord to Aaron   20aα1
    B. Speech   20aα2-24
       1. Designation of Aaron's inheritance   20 aα2-b
       2. Designation of Levi's inheritance   21-24
          a. Inheritance definition   21
          b. Levi's function as priest   22-24
             1) Warning   22
             2) Service   23a
             3) Conclusion   23b-24
V. Ordinance speech   18:25-32

A. Introduction: the Lord to Moses 25
B. Speech 26-32
   1. Message commission formula 26aα
   2. Message: instructions for tithe 26aβ-29
     a. Specification of the tithe 26aβ-b
     b. Purpose 27
     c. Conclusion 28-29
   3. Message commission formula 30a
   4. Message 30b-32
     a. Specification of wages 30b-31
       1) Definition of wages 30b
       2) Qualification of place 31aα
       3) Qualification of persons eligible 31aβ
       4) Concluding formula 31b
     b. Pronouncement of innocence 32a
     c. Warning 32b

The ordinances collected within the confines of this unit were not originally formulated for this position in the Pentateuch, perhaps not even as constituents for this collection (so, Noth). The unit's position in the context depends on the secondary bridge provided by 17:27-28, not on intrinsic elements within the unit or the context. But the bridge is nevertheless effective. The speech in these two verses presupposes judgment from the murmuring episode in 17:16-26. Indeed, the complex of murmuring units, including 17:6-15, 17:1-5, and even the Korah tradition in 16:1-35, lies in the background of this story as it is defined by the bridge. Thus, the demise of Korah and his men at the entrance of the tent of meeting (16:19) accounts for the Israelites' concern to avoid trespassing the holy space of the sanctuary in 17:28 (for a different point of view, see Noth). And the promise that wrath would not break out against the Israelites *again ('ôd)* in 18:5 recalls the reference to the "wrath from Yahweh" in 17:11.

The collection comprises the bridge element and four distinct speeches. The bridge, element I, is composed of a series of lamentation cries in the face of potential death, a point that depends on the preceding Korah tradition (cf. Ps 31:13; 88:6; Job 10:18). It also provides a structural key for holding the loose collection of speeches in ch. 16 together as a unit. The focus of the speech in 17:27-28 falls on the dangers of death Israel would face if she should venture too close to the sanctuary. The ordinances collected under that headline, all of ch. 18, provide means for worship to continue without risking the death anticipated by the lamentation.

The next speech, element II in the collection, appears in some sense as an ordination speech. It is the first of four Yahweh speeches and defines duties for both Aaron and Levi. Yet, its function is quite distinct from the ordination speech in, for example, Exodus 28, its structural characteristics markedly different. There is no definition of the ordination rite, no formula for anointing oil. Rather, the specific function of the speech is to relate the duties of the priest (Aaron) and the Levites to the threat of death posed by the sanctuary. The opening designation of Aaron's task (18:1) defines Aaron's work with the expression "to bear the iniquity of the sanctuary," or "to bear the iniquity of your priesthood" *(tiś'û 'et-'ăwōn)*. The point of the expression is that the priest carries the iniquity of the worshippers in relationship to the sanctuary or as a part of his duties in the priesthood. He protects them from the consequences of "bearing iniquity." The expression itself designates one who is subject to death. Death does not necessarily follow; it can be averted if proper protection is available. But the threat of death is expressed by the term (so, Lev 19:8; Num 5:31; 15:31 etc.).

Levi is considered a part of the family of Aaron, but distinct and subordinate to the ordination of the priesthood. His task is to serve Aaron. But the significant point is that the designation of Levi's services concludes with a warning directed to both Levi and any other person, a stranger who might come too near (vv. 3b-4). Unauthorized encroachment of holy space, even by the Levites, brings death. That death can be avoided only by submitting to Aaron's sole right to function in the sanctuary.

The speech then moves to a summary statement of the priestly role (v. 5) including recognition that the priest protects the people from wrath like that described in Num 17:11. Finally, both Aaron and Levi are designated as gifts for the conduct of the sanctuary worship. A final warning again announces the consequence for any other person who violates the area. The structure of the second speech thus demonstrates the point of unity the speech carries with the lamentation in 17:27-28. The people's lamentation was well founded. But the threat motivates not only the lamentation of the people, but the ground for instituting the Aaronic priesthood with its corresponding levitic service.

The following speech, element III, develops an ordinance for a distinct but related cultic procedure, a definition of wages for the service rendered by Aaron. The speech is marked off from the preceding one by a renewed speech formula. The opening element defines the speech's purpose in designating Aaron's wages, then lists the sacrifices to be appropriated to the benefit of the priesthood. The list is enclosed by an introductory and concluding formula (vv. 8, 19). The entries are not constructed in parallel fashion. The first one defines the sacrifices as wages, designates the persons who can enjoy their benefits, and qualifies the place the sacrifices can be eaten. The concluding formula proclaims the character of the wages, the reason for excluding other population elements from eating it (cf. Exod 28:36; 29:34; 30:32, 37; 31:14, etc.). The second entry (so, also the fourth) defines wages in the sacrifice, then qualifies the persons eligible not only by reference to Aaron's family but also by reference to ritual cleanliness. But no other qualifications and no concluding formulas appear. The third and fifth entries have no qualifications at all. The fourth entry follows the pattern of the second, with the exception that no limitation is placed on persons eligible to eat the sacrifice except ritual purity. The sixth entry has the longest list of qualifications. After defining the wages in the sacrifice, the entry sets out exceptions in sacrificial objects with stipulations for redeeming those exceptions from the slaughter. The exceptions, the first born of man and unclean animals, may be controlled by a redemption price (not a substitute sacrifice, perhaps a sign of creeping capitalism). The entry concludes with a designation of eligible sacrificial animals, the process of sacrifice, and definition of

Aaron's wages. The conclusion (v. 19) designates the entire ordinance as a per-petual one *(ḥoq-ʿôlām)* and a covenant of salt *(běrît melaḥ)*. Both formulas have parallels, the first as a concluding formula for an ordinance (→ Exod 12:14, 17), the second as a seal of community communion (so, Noth; see Lev 2:13; 2 Chr 13:5). The point of connection with the context thus lies not so much in procedure for avoiding death from the sanctuary taboo, but in payment for priestly service to that end.

The fourth element, considerably shorter than the preceding speeches, designates Aaron's and Levi's inheritance within the scope of Israelite proce-dure. The point of contact with the initial definition of priestly responsibilities does not stand so obvious as with the speech in the third element. But signifi-cantly, the designation of inheritance for Levi is coupled with a warning about the sacred space and a new consideration of Levi's service. Otherwise, the speech observes the traditional exclusion of the priesthood from inheritance procedures, not only for Levi generally, but specifically for Aaron. Verse 20 de-fines Aaron's inheritance as Yahweh, v. 21 Levi's inheritance as the tithe. Verses 22-24 soon explain Levi's inheritance, first with the warning, then with a summary of Levi's duties. Significantly, the formula "to bear iniquity" (cf. 18:1) now appears in the description of Levi's service (18:23). The speech ends with a summarizing formula and a lengthy explanation of Levi's inheritance as a tithe from the people rather than as a portion of land.

The final speech, the fifth element, picks up the designation of tithes for Levi, thus following clearly from vv. 20-24. The speech has not only the speech formula to mark it off from the preceding one, but also the distinct messenger formulas. The first message (vv. 26aβ-29) establishes a required tithe of the tithe Levi should receive and designates the produce for Aaron. The second message (vv. 30b-32) defines the remainder of the tithe for Levi, notes no quali-fications of household members or place for consuming it, and pronounces Levi free from bearing sin *(wělōʾ-tiśʾû ʿālāyw ḥēṭěʾ)*. The formula here does not use the more common word, iniquity *(ʿāwōn)*. It is perhaps important to note in this change of the formula that the function does not fall on the danger involved in approaching too near to the sanctuary, but on the danger involved in contact with a secondary holy object. But the unifying theme of the collection is none-theless present. The speech ends with a general warning not to profane the holy things of Israel, lest the guilty die.

The collection of ordinances in this unit stands at the end of a long history of tradition. The ordinances have been appropriated out of earlier contexts, al-tered only in order to bend them to the unifying theme of the pericope, and placed in the appropriate slot. The background tradition history can be seen at various junctures, since the collection calls on various ordinance traditions. The designation of duties and wages for Aaron/Levi parallels Exodus 28 (see espe-cially vv. 40-43); Leviticus 22; Num 1:47-54; 3:5-51; 26:62; Deut 12:11-12; 14:28-29; 26:12. On the unique role of Levi as a tribe not eligible to participate in the inheritance proceedings of Israel, see Gunneweg. On the fatal character of holy space, → Lev 10:1-4; Numbers 16; 2 Sam 6:7. The unit as a collection thus reflects the late postexilic activity of priestly expansion noted in Numbers 16–17 (so, Noth).

Genre

The unit is a collection of five SPEECHES, each with its own genre identity. The first speech contains a series of lamentation cries. The second speech is an OR-DINANCE for establishing ordination of priesthood groups, both Aaronic and Levitic, although its character as a legislative instrument has been altered by a singular concern in this collection to show the priests' duty in protecting the people from the dangers of holy space during worship. The remaining three SPEECHES present ORDINANCES of various sorts, each adjusted in some way to the overarching concern for the unit. The third speech still reflects its character as a definition of wages for Aaron's priestly service. The fourth speech establishes wages for Levi (in lieu of an inheritance of land). And the final speech lays legislative claim to a tithe from Levi's wages.

Setting

At all junctures in the history of this collection, the work of priestly institutions can be seen. The final concern is to establish the priesthood's authority, particularly Aaron's authority over the process of worship. The power of death lies in the priest's hands in the event that his rights should be violated and points to the control of the priesthood at this point in the history of the tradition. At earlier junctures in the collection's history, the priesthood exerts its legislative power to establish wages, inheritance, indeed, prerogatives in worship for its membership.

Intention

In its final form, the unit is interpretative. It follows stories about death in the sacred precincts with stipulations for protection against such death through the priesthood. The primary intention of the elements in the unit is legislative. The elements establish priestly authority and wages in relationship to their work in the sanctuary territory.

The intention of the individual speeches in the collection can be described as follows: (1) 17:27-28 expresses lamentation in the face of death and anticipates the deadly threat posed by sacred objects and space. (2) 18:1-7 establishes the priestly duties of Levi/Aaron with recognition of a deadly threat in the process. (3) 18:8-19 defines wages for the priests. (4) 18:20-24 defines the inheritance for Aaron. (5) 18:25-32 establishes the tithe.

Bibliography

G. Berry, "Priests and Levites," *JBL* 42 (1923) 227-38; A. Cody, *A History of Old Testament Priesthood* (Rome: Pontifical Biblical Institute, 1969); G. Fohrer, *Überlieferung und Geschichte des Exodus: eine Analyse von Exod 1–15* (BZAW 91; Berlin: Töpelmann, 1964) 60-79; A. H. J. Gunneweg, *Leviten und Priester: Hauptlinien der Traditionsbildung und Geschichte des israelitisch-jüdischen Kultpersonals* (FRLANT 89; Göttingen: Vandenhoeck und Ruprecht, 1965); K. Möhlenbrink, "Die levitischen Überlieferungen des Alten Testaments," *ZAW* 52 (1934) 184-231; E. Nielsen, "The Levites in Ancient Israel," *ASTI* 3 (1964) 16-27.

Ordinance for Protective Cleansing (19:1-22)*

Structure

I. Introduction: the Lord to Moses and Aaron	1
II. Speech	2-22
A. Ordinance for making water of impurity	2-10
1. Introductory formula	2a
2. Ordinance	2b-10a
a. Message commission formula	2bα₁
b. Message	2bα₂-10a
1) Instructions for sacrifice	2bα₂-4
2) Instructions for burning	5-6
3) Designation of unclean status	7-10a
a) The priest	7
b) The one who burned the sacrifice	8
c) The one who gathered the ashes	9-10a
(1) Instructions for gathering ashes	9a
(2) Purpose for the ashes	9b
(3) Designation of unclean status	10a
3. Concluding formula	10b
B. Specific case	11-13
1. Designation of unclean status	11
2. Judgments on the basis of the cleansing ritual	12-13
a. Positive judgment	12a
b. Negative judgment	12b-13
1) Judgment for unclean status	12b
2) Death judgment	13a
3) Reason	13b
C. Specific case	14-20
1. Introductory formula	14a
2. Designation of unclean status	14b-16
3. Judgments on the basis of the cleansing ritual	17-20
a. Positive judgment	17-19
1) Instructions for ritual	17-19bβ₁
2) Judgment on the basis of the ritual	19bβ₂
b. Negative judgment	20

*See Annotation to Num 15:1-16.

	1) Judgment for death	20a
	2) Reason	20bα
	3) Judgment for unclean status	20bβ
D.	Concluding formula	21a
E.	Designation of unclean status	21b-22

The speech unit in this chapter is isolated within its context (so, Noth). Perhaps the single exception to this conclusion is the emphasis on the ritual described by this speech as a means for avoiding cultic death (execution) or as a means for establishing a judgment for cultic death. The isolation, however, comes to expression in the structural patterns of the speech. The ordinance established by the speech in vv. 2-10 controls judgments in specific cases described by vv. 11-20. A description of cases requiring specific judgments built on the ordinance distinguishes this speech from the speeches of the collection.

The unit begins with the traditional speech formula. The speech itself has three major elements, an ordinance calling for preservation of ashes for the water of impurity and two cases requiring implementation of the water in a cleansing ceremony. In addition, a concluding formula rounds off the unit; and an appendix of designations for unclean status, thus, persons who should use the ceremony for cleansing, trails the speech.

The first element begins with a formula designating the coming set of instructions as an ordinance, although the designation is made ambiguous by the double construction: "This is an ordinance of judgment" *(zō't ḥuqqat hattôrâ).* The ordinance following the formula opens with a message commission formula, then addresses the ordinance to the Israelites. But the structure of the ordinance is also ambiguous. It flows readily from a structure that might easily be identified as ordinance into elements of ritual and judicial character. The first series of instructions set out procedures that are commonly at home in a sacrifice ritual, although again the procedure is ambiguous. The slaughtering occurs not in a sanctuary, but outside it. It may be, then, that nothing more is involved than dedication of the animal, even in the blood rite (so, Noth). The burning process suggests a sacrifice by fire. But whether sacrifice or not, none of the instructions establish the event as a cultic ordinance, the goal of the unit. Rather, they describe the ritual for executing the animal. The instructions for burning the animal, clearly a distinct act apart from the slaughter and blood ritual itself, also elude ordinance status, remaining simply a description of procedure. Even the unique elements, instructions to add cedar-wood, hyssop, and scarlet stuff to the burning (cf. Lev 14:4-7), do not appear as anything more than ritual procedure. But at just the point in the development of the speech when the details of the ordinance would be expected, the structure breaks off with a designation of unclean status for those people involved in the ritual. And the designation is more judicial in character than legislative. The first two designations are to be expected; the personnel already described shall be unclean until evening. But a third member of the personnel is also included. And since his task in the process has not yet been defined, some detail of his role is given. One has the impression that this detail, now submerged in the context of ritual and judicial elements, constitutes the primary focus of legislation for the cleansing ritual. The ashes of the sacrifice are to be preserved for making the water of impurity. Yet, even here the ordinance is frustrated. No reference to the process for making the water is noted. No legislation for its function in the cult appears. An element of the speech that might at one time have been an ordinance for water of impurity has now been altered for other goals. It may well be that the easy interchange of goals and functions within the structure of this element accounts for the confusion in person and number for the addressee (→ Exodus 12–13). Finally, the concluding formula recalls at least an original function, if not the final function, of the unit as ordinance. The formula seems certainly to function as conclusion to the preceding element, rather than as introduction to the following element, since the following element is judicial (contrary to Noth). But the appendix, a collection of designations for unclean status, picks up the structural ambiguity characteristic for the entire element.

The second element defines circumstances calling for the use of the water of impurity. It opens with a designation for judgment concerning the unclean status of a person who touches the dead. Then it defines procedure for resolution of his position within the society. If he follows the ritual (as yet undefined in this unit), in the proper time he will be judged clean and eligible to return to society. If he does not, then he should be removed from the society, a point that clearly means his death. Significantly, in the lengthy description of the judgment, the designation of motivation for this judgment alludes to details of the ritual for the water of impurity not yet mentioned in the unit (v. 13b).

The third element of the speech again defines circumstances calling for the use of the water of impurity. The introductory formula (v. 14a) provides a definition of the function in this element of the speech, parallel to the ordinance formula. But significantly, it is not an ordinance formula, but a judgment formula *(zō't hattôrâ)*. Then, the speech follows the pattern of the second element with a designation for judgment concerning the unclean status of both persons and objects inside a tent (or house) that contains a dead person. Then, as in the second element, the speech designates judgments that must be made on the basis of obedience to the cleansing ritual. Significantly, in the section calling for positive judgment (vv. 17-19), specific details of the ceremony including the process for making the water of impurity are noted. Verse 20 follows the parallel from the second element by noting the circumstances for a negative judgment. The death judgment here, as in vv. 12b-13, is quite explicitly built on the failure of the person to follow the cleansing ritual (v. 13b). But contrary to v. 12b, the judgment for unclean status follows the death judgment.

The speech is a composite of legal, judicial, and ritual traditions. But its composite nature does not reflect literary-critical problems, but the process of tradition history. Secondary literary accretions to this text are few (against Noth). And no compilation of sources can be seen. The tradition history of the unit is difficult to trace. No other text in the OT outlines the ceremony established (cf. Num 31:23, a text that presupposes the ritual). Yet, here the ordinance quality of the text has been suppressed. The ceremony must have had some lengthy history in itself, not simply have been the fruit of an artificial composition. The direction of the history may retreat to a stage of magic, removed from direct control of the priesthood (so, in detail, Scheftelowitz). Thus, the person responsible for collecting the ashes of the burnt animal is designated as a clean person, but not as a priest. It is possible that the ritual process described in vv. 14 and 16, a seven-day process, stands in contrast to the process described in vv. 17-18, a process immediately effective (so, Noth). If that is the case, perhaps two different rituals have come together here. But lack of evidence makes it impossible to determine what those rituals might have been. Further inroads into the tradition history of this unit do not seem possible at this point. (For a more detailed tradition history, see the reconstruction by Scheftelowitz.)

Genre

A complex unit of material such as this one demands recognition of complex genre characteristics. The structural characteristics of the unit as it now stands suggest that it must be defined as a judicial statement, with elements of ritual supporting the process of decision making. But the governing formulas at the beginning and ending of the unit open the character of the unit as ordinance, suggesting that behind the present judicial unit lay a legislative unit. The legislative element is most prominent in the second element. Elements of that section do, however, retain their character as judicial.

Formulas abound in the speech. Not only do we have the common SPEECH FORMULA in v. 1a and the MESSENGER COMMISSION FORMULA in v. 2bα₁, but various specialized cultic formulas also appear. The designation for an ordinance in v. 2aβ is complicated by the addition of a second element in v. 2aα: *zō't ḥuqqat hattôrâ* (see also Num 31:21). The formula itself is more commonly found in relationship with only one noun, *tôrâ*. But no clear distinction in function can be seen. The formula serves as a DEFINITION FORMULA, an introduction or a conclusion to legal material (→ Exod 12:14). The concluding formula in v. 10b has the same character. The formula in v. 9 defines the water of impurity as a cultic ceremony (cf. Exod 12:11). The noun, *ḥaṭṭā't*, is not the beginning of a new sentence, a new formula (against Noth), but an apposition for *lĕmê niddâ,* indicating that the water of impurity is used for purification (cf. the use of the verb, *yithaṭṭā',* in exactly the same way in vv. 12, 20, as well as *ḥiṭṭĕ'ô* in v. 19 and the combination *śĕrēpat haḥaṭṭā't* in v. 17). The formula cannot be used to indicate the secondary nature of the sentence in the unit or the corresponding secondary nature of v. 17. Verse 13b again does not carry an expansion of the unit (against Noth), but a formula for JUDGMENT, similar to the formula in Num 15:31. The most common formula, a formula for JUDGMENT, is the priestly torah, vv. 15, 20.

Setting

A collection of ordinance and judicial tradition, defining circumstances for controlling cultic credentials and judgments to be made in order to eliminate those violating credential rules, can derive only from the cult, centered in the priest who wields the power to make such decisions. That kind of power doubtlessly reflects a period when Israel did not have a strong secular government, thus a time after the fall of the monarchy. This observation points to the setting of the unit as a theocratic power structure, the priesthood of the late postexilic period (→ Numbers 17–18).

Intention

As a whole the unit functions as a piece of judicial precedent, designed to define circumstances that demand particular kinds of decisions. Even the initial element of the speech avoids direct legislation of a cultic ceremony for cleansing. The second and third elements of the speech emphasize the judicial quality of the unit. Behind the present form of the unit lies a stage in the history of the tradition that intended legislation for a cleansing ceremony. And as is typical for legislative pieces, some degree of detail in ritual appears. The ritual elements, however, fit into the general function of the earlier layers as legislation.

Bibliography

J. Milgrom, "The Paradox of the Red Cow, (Num XIX)," *VT* 31 (1981) 62-72; I. Scheftelowitz, "Das Opfer der roten Kuh (Num 19)," *ZAW* 39 (1921) 113-23.

Meribah Spring Story (20:1-13)

Structure

I. Itinerary formula	1
II. Exposition	2a
III. Complication	2b-5
A. Crisis	2b-3a
1. Murmuring	2b
2. Etiology foundation	3a
B. Speech report	3b-5
1. Introduction: people to Moses	3bα
2. Speech	3bβ-5
a. Death wish	3bβ
b. Accusation	4-5
IV. Resolution	6-12
A. Narration of appeal to the Lord	6
B. Speech report	7-8
1. Introduction: the Lord to Moses	7
2. Speech	8
a. Instructions for the sign	8a
b. Results expected	8b

C. Execution of instructions 9-11
  1. Narration of first stage 9-10a
  2. Speech report 10b
    a. Introduction: Moses to the people 10bα₁
    b. Counter-accusation 10bα₂-bβ
  3. Narration of second stage 11
D. Speech report 12
  1. Introduction: the Lord to Moses and Aaron 12aα
  2. Judgment speech 12aβ-b
    a. Motivation 12aβ
    b. Sentence 12b
V. Concluding etiology 13

The literary context for this text lies not so much in the legal material in Numbers 17–19, not even in the literary sources in Numbers 16 (J/P) which are harmonious with this story, but rather in Numbers 13–14 (cf. especially Num 14:26-35). Judgment against the rebels in the wilderness, excluding them from the promised land, now extends to Moses and Aaron (v. 12). The redactional context is again controlled by an itinerary formula (v. 1). In this case, the context is obscure, for the itinerary does not include the normal notation about a departure site. Its context with previous itinerary formulas, its position in the wilderness chain, is thus difficult to determine. The note of arrival in the Wilderness of Zin, at Kadesh, should be considered a doublet of the second itinerary element from Num 12:16, a duplication of the chain reference to the Wilderness of Paran (so, Coats). Thus, all the tradition from Num 13:1 through Num 20:22 is structured in relationship to the same itinerary position. Significantly, there is no itinerary accommodation for the place name contained within the tradition. Both this story and its doublet in Exod 17:1-7 can be structured into their respective chain positions without concern to nullify the chain or eliminate the name from one of the stories.

The itinerary with this text centers on the arrival element in the normal itinerary construction. But it contains not only the note about arrival at Kadesh, in the Wilderness of Zin, but also a brief anecdote, a report of death and burial for Miriam. Lists commonly collect such anecdotal tradition (cf. Genesis 46; Numbers 26). This allusion, however, enhances a larger interest for showing the demise of the old generation in preparation for the conquest (cf. Num 14:20-23).

The story comprises three major units plus a final etiology for a place name. The first element, the itinerary, is thus not a part of the story itself, but a framework transition from the structure of the entire wilderness theme. The exposition (v. 2a) builds, at least in part, on the literary since it presupposes that the principals for the story are known. The word, "the congregation" *(hā'ēdâ)* picks up the itinerary reference to "the sons of Israel, all the congregation" *(běnē-yiśrā'ēl kol-hā'ēdâ)*. But in fact, the exposition sets out only the circumstances that call for the story's plot, perhaps suggesting the story's relationship with other, similar stories: "There was no water for the congregation." The exposition is thus parallel to other stories about the Lord's aid (cf. Exod 15:23;

17:1; perhaps also Exod 14:1-5a). The second element in the plot accounts for Israel's response to the physical circumstances of the wilderness life. Verse 2b constitutes a stereotyped narrative description for murmuring, for rebellion against leadership, while v. 3a parallels v. 2b with an introduction for legal process (so, the verb *wayyāreb*). The following speech clarifies the dispute. But it is structured more nearly in accord with v. 2b than v. 3a. Verse 3a thus functions only as a foundation for the etiology in v. 13. In the speech addressed by all the people to Moses and Aaron, the opening death wish illustrates the dire nature of the confrontation. The body of the speech then poses an accusation in the form of a question. The accusation does not call for provision of water as the context would seem to demand. Rather, it attacks Moses and Aaron for their work as leaders of the congregation. The first element in the accusation focuses on leadership in the wilderness and does not represent a point of unity with other murmuring stories. The second element, however, picks up the anti-exodus motif of the murmuring stories and shows the unity of this pericope with other texts in the murmuring tradition.

At this juncture in the story, the general structure for a trial story drops away. And the primary pattern of the story emerges with clarity, consistent with the exposition. Verse 6, a report of appeal from Moses and Aaron to the Lord, is structurally a transition from the complication to its resolution. The speech of the Lord, vv. 7-8, functions as instructions for executing a sign. It is significant, in light of the story's development in vv. 9-11, that the instructions specify that Moses should take his rod (Exod 7:6–10:29) to the site of the coming sign (cf. Exod 17:5). But then the rod drops out of the instructions in deference to a command to speak to the rock in order to effect the miracle (contrast Exod 17:6). The instructions conclude by setting out the character of the sign: "You shall bring water out of the rock for them; you shall give drink to the congregation and their cattle."

Verses 9-11 report execution of the instructions (especially, the formula element in v. 9b). Verses 9-10a report general preparation for the sign itself, in accord with Divine instructions. Verse 10b breaks the narration unit with a speech, addressed from Moses to the gathered people. He calls the people rebels, thus presupposing element III. The question in the speech is obscure. Its formulation corresponds to the instructions in v. 8b and cannot be considered a claim on Moses' part for more power than he rightfully possesses. It seems appropriate, although not altogether clear, to suggest that the question functions as a rebuke to the rebels, a counter-accusation, and thus accommodates this segment of the unit to the murmuring level of the pericope. The final stage in this element reports the sign's execution itself. Moses raises his rod, strikes the rock "twice" (note the emphasis on the act by the qualifying *pa'ămāyim*) and the water flows. The sign is complete.

Verse 12 then adds an enigmatic address to Moses and Aaron (with no counterpart in the Exodus 17 parallel). Because of their violation, described by this speech as a failure to sanctify the Lord in the eyes of the people, they will not be allowed into the promised land. The violation Moses and Aaron committed is not clearly defined by the verb *lĕhaqdîšēnî* ("to sanctify me"). But the structure of the unit leaves little doubt about the act. They were instructed to speak to the rock (contrary to Exod 17:5). But they did not. Moses struck the rock with his rod, not once, but twice (cf. Exod 17:6). And for that reason, both Moses and Aaron now stand with the condemned generation of wilderness people, excluded from the promised land (cf. Num 14:20-23).

The concluding etiology is extraneous to the development of plot in the story, both in the murmuring level and in the sign narration. Rather, it picks up the isolated reference to the people's act as a lawsuit in v. 3a (cf. *wayyāreb* in v. 3a and *rābû* in v. 13) and works out a word play as the explanation for the name Meribah. It may be that v. 12b, somewhat obscure in the total unit, is also a word play for the place name Kadesh (so, Noth).

The story derives from P, in contrast to the doublet in Exod 17:1-7. It has obviously altered the tradition it received from the past in order to incorporate the judgment against Moses and Aaron. Yet it preserves evidence of other stages in the tradition history of Meribah's spring. In its present form, it is dominated by the murmuring tradition. The people's response to the water crisis is an act of rebellion against the leadership Moses and Aaron have given the people. Again, P's peculiar appropriation of this tradition can be detected. Contrary to Exod 17:1-7, with focus on the anti-exodus element, P broadens the murmuring to include elements other than the accusation calling for a return to Egypt. Behind the murmuring stage lies a story focused on the Lord's gift of water in the face of wilderness privation. The story at this stage also belongs to a larger collection of tradition, thus accounting for the relatively incomplete exposition. The etiology picks up a tradition of legal process closely tied to the local site, the spring at Meribah.

Genre

The pericope is at all of its levels a STORY, a story designed to hold the attention of the audience by building tension toward a particular conclusion. The latest stage of this STORY is dominated by the murmuring tradition. But the story does not appear, even at this stage, as a STORY about a trial. Rather, the genre of the STORY, at both the murmuring stage and the aid stage, remains the same, a STORY about an event that can be defined as a sign (cf. Exod 7:6–10:20). The etiology builds on a word play constructed out of assonance between *wayyāreb* in v. 3a and *rābû — mĕrîbâ* in v. 13a. Verse 12b may play in the same kind of etiology on v. 1aβ (*wayyiqqādēš* in v. 13b; *bĕqādēš* in v. 1aβ).

Stereotyped expressions include the MURMURING accusations in vv. 4-5 and the narrative formula for INSTRUCTIONS EXECUTED in v. 9b.

Setting

The story reflects a crucial role in the literary framework of P; its latest, perhaps most crucial setting is literary. Both the murmuring and the more positive aid versions of the story derive from larger contexts and reflect the collective setting of the group (→ The Framework, Chapter 3, FOTL IIA). One must be cautious, however, in specifying the setting for the tradition, even for these levels, for setting in narrative material behind the more obvious literary framework is difficult to determine. Moreover, the etiology, perhaps obviously from a local setting interested in preserving tradition about the origin of the place name, is rather loosely connected with the sign narrative itself and does not provide a clear insight into setting. It would seem to be clear, nevertheless, that such tales as this one derive in some manner from popular settings, from the folk.

Intention

At its latest level, this story provides a structural key in the priestly source for excluding Moses and Aaron from entry into the promised land (→ Num 20:22-29; 27:12-23). Moses and Aaron are included with the rebels as people condemned to death before entry into the land. The story thus provides an interpretative tool for explaining a major feature in the development of the Pentateuchal narrative. As a part of the larger murmuring tradition, it contributes to the picture of Israel's rebellion in the wilderness, although not so explicitly over the exodus accusation. Thus, the intention for undercutting exodus election theology, present in the J doublet of the tradition, is not so apparent here. Its precise picture has now been extended to include a more general accusation against leadership. The story preserves its original genre as well as its original intention for presenting a gracious act of the Lord on behalf of his people in the wilderness. One of the most important consequences of such sign stories is to establish the authority of one (or two) in a position of leadership (cf. Num 17:16ff.).

Bibliography

E. Arden, "How Moses Failed God," *JBL* 76 (1957) 50-52; J. Gray, "The Desert Sojourn of the Hebrews and the Sinai Horeb Tradition," *VT* 4 (1954) 148-54; A. S. Kapelrud, "How Tradition Failed Moses," *JBL* 76 (1957) 242; S. Lehming, "Massa und Meriba," *ZAW* 73 (1961) 71-77; T. W. Mann, "Theological Reflections on the Denial of Moses," *JBL* 98 (1979) 481-94.

Negotiations Report (20:14-21)

Structure

I. Introduction		14a
II. Negotiations dialogue		14b-20
A. Speech report		14b-17
1. (Introduction: Moses to king of Edom)		(14a)
2. Speech		14b-17
a. Messenger formula		14bα

        b. Message   14bβ-17

- b. Message — 14bβ-17
  - 1) Recital — 14bβ-16
    - a) Introduction — 14bβ
    - b) Entry into Egypt — 15a
    - c) Exodus — 15b-16a
    - d) Wilderness — 16b
  - 2) Request — 17
    - a) Petition — $17a\alpha_1$
    - b) Qualifications — $17a\alpha_2$-b
- B. Speech report — 18
  - 1. Introduction: Edom — $18a\alpha$
  - 2. Speech — $18a\beta$-b
    - a. Refusal of petition — $18a\beta$
    - b. Warning — 18b
- C. Speech report — 19
  - 1. Introduction: people of Israel to Edom — $19a\alpha_1$
  - 2. Speech — $19a\alpha_2$-b
    - a. Petition — $19a\alpha_2$
    - b. Qualification — $19a\beta$
    - c. Petition — 19b
- D. Speech report — 20a
  - 1. Introduction: Edom — $20a\alpha_1$
  - 2. Speech: refusal of petition — $20a\alpha_2$-aβ
- E. Execution of warning against Israel — 20b
- III. Conclusion — 21

This unit is structured into the wilderness theme by means of an allusion to a particular itinerary site, Kadesh (v. 14). There is no itinerary formula here. But the allusion picks up the formula from 20:1 and clearly places this unit within its larger context. Moreover, the itinerary formula in 20:22, noting departure from Kadesh, completes the inclusion. Whether this unit was originally tied to Kadesh cannot be clearly determined (but, see v. 16b).

The structure of this unit builds around a series of speeches, with a final narration observing execution of a warning expressed in the second speech. Verse 21 is a conclusion to the entire speech series, a summary statement of the result effected by the negotiation process. The conclusion opens a possibility for a corresponding introduction. Unfortunately, v. 14a is ambiguous in the structure of the unit. It sets the introduction for the entire unit. As introduction, it marks the surroundings presupposed by the speech series; the speeches involve not a face-to-face encounter between two people, but exchanges of conversation carried on by messenger. But at the same time, v. 14a replaces the more common speech formula (cf. Num 21:21, including the stereotyped element from speech formulas, lē'mōr, missing from 20:14a).

The first speech is a carefully constructed request for permission to pass through occupied territory. It builds a case for the request by reciting the crucial events of the past. Structure in the recitation encompasses an introduction (cf. the word "adversity" [hattĕlā'â] with Exod 18:8) and specification of events covered by the introduction. The event series, structured by the traditional pattern of the credo, includes entry into Egypt, oppression and exodus, and brief allusion to the wilderness events at Kadesh. Structure and stereotyped language in the recital show that this element is controlled by traditional formulation (cf. Deut 26:5-9). The recital serves the speech as a polite warning to the addressee. If the request to follow is not granted, if new adversities befall Israel, then the Lord may send a new messenger to intervene. The request involves two major parts. First, a petition: "Let us pass through your land." Then, the speech notes qualifications that would govern the people should the petition be granted.

The second speech, Edom's response, denies the petition, coupling the denial with a counter warning. Edom will back up the denial with force. The third speech reformulates Israel's request. No foundation for the petition, no renewed warning, undergirds this element. It reveals nonetheless a structure similar to the first petition. The goal is stated; then qualifications on Israel's action are set out. And finally, the petition goal is renewed (with a shift from first person plural to first person singular). The series concludes in v. 20 with a repetition of Edom's refusal (v. 20a) and a narrative element reporting Edom's action to back up her initial warning.

The conclusion (v. 21) notes the general results of the negotiation series. Edom refused to allow Israel access to her territory. So Israel left Edom alone. There is no military confrontation (cf. in contrast Num 21:21-32). There is no conquest of land. The text reports that since the petition failed, Israel simply left.

Verses 19-20 cannot properly be considered a doublet of vv. 14-18 (against Noth). Rather, the renewed request and rejection of the request constitute simply structural emphasis on the negotiations process. Nor does the shift from plural to singular verb or suffix demand conclusions that secondary additions have violated the original unity of the pericope (so, Noth). Entirely from J with relatively consistent unity, this unit presupposes a continuation of the wilderness narration. There is no element in the tradition included here that reflects conquest interests. The people negotiate for passage and then continue their journey toward some other goal (against Noth; → The Framework, Chapter 3, FOTL IIA). The unit may nevertheless rest on an ancient tradition about Israel's confrontation with Edom, associated perhaps with the springs at Kadesh. Deut 2:1-18 shows that Edom, the territory of Esau, was not a part of the promised land, and thus this tradition is not a part of the conquest theme.

Genre

This unit has been incorporated into a narrative context by introduction and conclusion formulas, as well as the note that Edom enforced its warning. But it reflects no plot line characteristic of narrative stories. Rather, it simply reports what happened, according to the tradition, in the negotiations between Israel and Edom. The unit qualifies, then, as narrative report, the series of sequences in the report as a negotiation dialogue (→ Exod 7:6–10:29). The subject for negotiation is clearly established (cf. Num 21:21-32). The response is set out, failure in negotiations from Israel's perspective. But contrary to other negotiation reports, Israel did not respond with force. No signs, no battles extend this unit beyond its structural interests in negotiation. The genre for the unit is thus NE-GOTIATIONS REPORT. The process of exchange, indeed, the carefully worded petition, doubtlessly reflects the development of negotiation speeches in the active exchange of international politics.

Formulas and stereotyped expressions would include the messenger formula, v. 14bα, and, indeed, the messenger speech itself, a part of the process for political exchange.

Setting

The report reflects the interests of the literary redaction, both in the total scope of the Pentateuch and in the structure of J. Such negotiations reports belong essentially to political archives, political traditions. The negotiation process itself would reflect origin in the political exchange between two state leaders (or within the structure of state politics). The messenger process, widely known in the ancient world, would confirm that process.

Intention

The report intends to preserve tradition about Israel's encounters with Edom within the scope of the wilderness journey. The intention of the negotiations process would be to obtain concession from an opposing force (cf. Exod 7:6–10:29). It is important to note that the tradition preserves a memory of negotiations with Edom that fail, yet an experience with Edom that led to no conquest of territory.

Bibliography

J. R. Bartlett, "The Land of Seir and the Brotherhood of Edom," *JTS* 20 (1969) 1-20; idem, "The Rise and Fall of the Kingdom of Edom," *PEQ* 104 (1972) 26-37; idem, "The Brotherhood of Edom," *JSOT* (1977) 2-27; S. Mittman, "Num 20:14-21 — eine redaktionelle Kompilation," in *Wort und Geschichte* (ed. H. Gese, H. P. Rüger; Neukirchen-Vluyn: Neukirchener Verlag, 1973); W. A. Summer, "Israel's Encounters with Edom, Moab, Ammon, Sihon and Og According to the Deuteronomist," *VT* 18 (1968) 216-28.

Aaron Death Report (20:22-29)

Structure

I. Itinerary formula	22
II. Death announcement speech report	23-26
A. Introduction: the Lord to Moses and Aaron	23
B. Speech	24-26
1. Death judgment	24
a. Sentence against Aaron	24a
b. Reason	24b
2. Instructions for commissioning successor	25-26
a. Designation of place for the rite	25
b. Investiture	26a
c. Reason: announcement of Aaron's death	26b
III. Execution of instructions	27-28aα
IV. Death report	28aβ-29
A. Notice of Aaron's death	28aβ
B. Report	28b-29
1. Return to congregation	28b
2. Mourning	29

This brief unit is structured into the wilderness theme by means of a wilderness itinerary formula. The itinerary employs two stereotyped elements, a note of departure from Kadesh, the site for encampment in the previous itinerary element, and a note of arrival at Mt. Hor. The unit, at least in its present form, builds on that itinerary by defining explicitly the place for the following speech, not only by reference to the place name from the itinerary, but also by locating the place "on the border of the land of Edom." Both elements suggest a concern intrinsic to the structure of the unit for defining the place and suggest that the place identification is not simply dependent on the itinerary chain. It is possible that the place name and location in v. 23 are secondary, an addition to the unit designed to tie it more closely with the itinerary (so, Noth). But there are no clear structural indications that that conclusion obtains. It may be that correspondence between an original element of the tradition and one station in the wilderness chain opened a position in the wilderness theme at just this point for the Aaron death report.

The announcement of Aaron's death as an event impending before the whole people begins with a speech from the Lord addressed to both Moses and Aaron. Verse 24 proclaims a sentence of death against Aaron, and then sets out the reason for the sentence. The reason relates explicitly to the story in Num 20:1-13 (note v. 24b). But the judgment established against the entire people in Num 14:20-23 also lies in the background. None of the wilderness generation, with perhaps only one or two exceptions, may enter the promised land. The tradition about Aaron's death draws on the full range of murmuring stories in the wilderness collection. (I can see no reason to deny v. 24 to the basic structure of the unit, contrary to Noth. To be sure, the speech is addressed to both Moses and Aaron, and then refers to Aaron in third person. But that characteristic describes the entire unit. Rather, v. 24 seems to me to be crucial for the structure of the unit, pointing to the intrinsic focus of the pericope on Aaron's coming death.)

As a correlative element in the death sentence, the Lord instructs Moses to ordain Aaron's son, Eleazar, as successor in the priesthood. (One might compare 2 Kgs 2:1-18 where announcement of Elijah's imminent death leads to narration about Elijah's successor.) The commissioning instructions follow specific steps from designation of place to description of investiture rite. The rite involves removal of Aaron's official clothing as well as investiture for Eleazar with the same clothing. These instructions conclude with an explanation for the necessary change in office, again emphasizing the unit as an account of Aaron's approaching death. Significantly, the verb, *yē'āsēp,* functions regularly as a technical term in announcements of imminent death (cf. 2 Kgs 22:20). Normally, the verb would be associated with a preposition and noun: "He shall be *gathered* to his people" (cf. v. 24). In v. 26, however, the verb is employed in abstraction from other grammatical elements, fully in a technical connotation: "He shall be gathered!" And the impact of the verb is made explicit by the following phrase: "He shall die there."

The unit closes with two brief narrative elements. The first (vv. 27-28a) reports that instructions were fulfilled. The instructions at issue here can only be the rite for ordaining Eleazar in Aaron's place. But this stage is not of final importance for the unit. The text moves immediately to the second concluding element (vv. 28b-29). Here as a capstone of the unit, the text reports Aaron's death. Moses and Eleazar return to the people. Implicit in the element is a report to the people that Aaron was dead. And the people mourn Aaron's death. There is no reference to celebration for Eleazar's promotion. The structure of the unit recognizes succession of leadership as a crucial element. But it is only an element in a unit designed to report Aaron's death.

The death report derives from P, related to the story in Num 20:1-13 (so, Noth). I see no strong evidence for extensive secondary literary additions to the scope of the unit as it now stands. The only important development would be its incorporation into the wilderness theme through the itinerary formula, not originally a part of the tradition. The unit is related in some way to the tradition about Moses' death (so, especially Num 27:12-23 and Deut 34:1-12). It may well be that the Moses tradition served as an explicit model for this account. At least some traditional pattern for reporting the death of a leader and transition of power to a new leader seems to be at the basis of the unit. Whether the tradition here had a life independent of the Moses-Aaron tradition in Numbers 20 is not clear. Perhaps its association with Mt. Hor suggests such an independent origin (cf. Noth). Deut 10:6 associates Aaron's death, not with Mt. Hor, but with Moserah, thus complicating the picture (but cf. also the tradition about Moses' death, Num 27:12-13).

Genre

This unit should be categorized as a DEATH REPORT, not a report of commission, installation, or transfer of power. Tradition employed by the death report would call not only on technical language for death announcements like *yē'āsēp* (cf. 2 Kgs 22:20; Gen 49:29), but on ceremonial procedures such as a legal death sentence built on clear definition of cause, and an ordination ritual, particularly investiture for the new official coupled with divesting the predecessor of his official garments. The concluding elements of the unit again illustrate the function of this section as death report (→ Gen 49:33–50:3; 50:10-11).

Setting

In P the unit rounds out a structural unity with Num 20:1-13 and suggests that a close point of order exists between this tradition and Num 27:12-23. As a more ancient tradition, the Aaron death report preserves biographical and administrative interests peculiar to the priesthood, thus fully cultic in character. The details of the ordination rite as rite (in contrast to Num 27:12-23) would support this point.

Intention

The unit is designed primarily to report Aaron's death. It thus has a biographical function, set within the context of a larger scope of Aaronic tradition. There is no sign in the present form of the text of a heroic tradition about Aaron, with its conclusion in a heroic death report (contrast Deuteronomy 34). A corresponding intention is to report succession in the Aaronic priesthood by Eleazar. That pattern suggests some intention to establish a chain of succession for an Aaronic priesthood.

Hormah Etiology (21:1-3)

Structure

I. Report of defeat in the wilderness	1
II. Response	2-3a
A. Vow	2
B. Fulfillment	3a
1. By the Lord	3aα
2. By Israel	3aβ
III. Etiological formula	3b

The itinerary chain has no clear opening for this pericope. 20:22 places Israel at Mount Hor, the site of Aaron's death, while 21:4 reports departure from Mount Hor. Yet, the events described by this small unit do not assume location at Mount Hor or any other particular site in the itinerary chain. To the contrary, the reference to Israel in v. 1 assumes movement. The problem casts an impression of isolation for this pericope from the context that carries it.

The unit opens with a report about a military defeat for Israel. When the king of Arad heard that Israel was coming in his direction, he confronted them and in the process took some Israelites *(mimmenû)* as captives. It should be noted here that even though the victory for the king of Arad was limited — he took only *some* captives — the text records the event as a defeat for Israel. The response to the defeat involves both a record of a vow to the Lord as a commitment to undergird the request for victory over the enemy and a notice of fulfillment for the conditions of the vow. The condition embraced by Israel for victory over the enemy is utter destruction *(wĕhăḥăramtî)* of the cities that belonged to Arad. The notice of fulfillment for the vow employs both a reference to the Lord who gives victory (v. 3aα) and a reference to Israel's act in keeping her commitment to destroy *(wayyaḥărēm)* the cities. The element thus reports that the battle was won and the vow kept. The third element then builds on the catchword from the center of the pericope, *ḥrm,* for construction of an etiology for the place name, *ḥormâ,* "Hormah."

The unit as it now appears in the Pentateuch derives from J. It may draw on an older tradition, a battle report. Significantly, there is no leader of the army against the enemy. If an older battle report does lie behind the pericope, it would thus not be heroic in any manner, but rather a record of an event executed generally by the people.

Genre

The unit is an ETIOLOGY. It builds its structure with the key word demonstrated at critical points. And then it draws its etiological conclusion directly from the intrinsic lines of the narrative. It is not now a BATTLE REPORT. It is an ETIOLOGY.

Setting

The etiology derived from the literary, theological setting for the Yahwist. Victory at Hormah belongs to Israel's God, and thus the etiology reflects Israel's theology. If older tradition lies behind the literary construct provided by J, it would derive perhaps from local sources, memories attached directly to the place.

Intention

The etiology seeks to explain the origin of the name of the place by reference to the event effected there by Israel; indeed, the event functions as the basis for a word play as explanation of the name. But in addition to the etiological intention, there is also a theological intention, fundamental for the Yahwist: The Lord gives the enemy into the hand of his people.

236

Bibliography

G. W. Coats, "Conquest Traditions in the Wilderness Theme," *JBL* 95 (1976) 177-90; V. Fritz, "Arad in der biblischen Überlieferung und in der Liste Schoschenk I," *ZDPV* 91 (1975) 30-45; D. M. Gunn, "The 'Battle Report': Oral or Scribal Convention?" *JBL* 93 (1974) 513-18; M. Noth, "Num 21 als Glied der 'Hexateuch' Erzählung," *ZAW* 58 (1940/41) 161-89.

Fiery Serpents Story (21:4-9)

Structure

I. Itinerary formula	4a
II. Crisis	4b-6
A. General description	4b
B. Accusation	5
C. Punishment for rebellion	6
III. Resolution	7-8
A. Speech report	7a
1. Introduction: people to Moses	7aα_1
2. Repentance	7aα_2-aβ
a. Confession	7aα_2-aα_3
b. Petition	7aβ
B. Report of Moses' intercession	7b
C. Response to the intercession	8
1. Introduction: the Lord to Moses	8aα_1
2. Instructions for healing	8aα_2-b
IV. Conclusion: execution of the instructions	9

The itinerary formula in v. 4a defines the context for this pericope within the structure of the larger context, the wilderness theme. It is of significance that an adapted version of the itinerary formula appears here. The point of departure lists Mount Hor as the point of reference for the itinerary chain. And some direction for the journey fits the second position of the formula. Yet, in this position is no campsite, the natural second member of the formula. The position features a statement about the route for movement: "by the way of the Sea of Reeds, to go around the land of Edom." The event controlled by this adapted itinerary formula occurs with the people in motion, not at any one particular place. And that adapted form suggests that the unit effects Israel's experience more broadly than would be the case if its tradition were limited to one station in the itinerary list.

The crisis that provokes the plot of the pericope is not a single confrontation in the wilderness, such as an attack of an enemy or a challenge against Moses for food to meet the needs of the people. The verb that describes the event is "to be impatient," or better, "to be short." And the content of the people's short temper is an accusation that attacks both God and Moses for initiating the exodus, the typical element in the murmuring tradition: "Why have you brought us up out of Egypt to die in the wilderness?" The explanation for the accusation is general: no food, no water, and hostile responses to worthless food (manna?). In the pattern of the murmuring tradition, the accused would by necessity respond to the charges. The response comes from God alone, however. And it offers no defense against the charge. It simply notes that God attacks the rebels by means of fiery serpents *(hannĕḥāšîm haśśĕrāpîm)*. And the attack leads to the death of some of the people.

In typical fashion for the Moses traditions, Moses intercedes for the people. And God's response to the intercession provides instruction for Moses that will effect healing for those bitten by the serpents. To be sure, the people request help in meeting the crisis posed by the serpents. And the request contains both confession of sin in the rebellion against God and Moses and petition for help (v. 7a). But the focus of the unit falls on Moses' act. The act is prefaced by the intercession. But its focus is in the conclusion to the pericope, v. 9. Moses carries out God's instruction by constructing a bronze serpent *(nĕḥaš nĕḥōšet)* and setting it on a pole *(hannēs)*. And then, if anyone among the people suffered a bite from a serpent, that person would simply look at the bronze serpent in order to live. The healing process was thus effected by the serpent on a pole.

The tradition belongs to the Yahwist. But one should also be aware of the significant role the pericope plays for the Moses traditions. The bronze serpent belongs to Moses paraphernalia, perhaps the most significant part of that collection of symbols (see 2 Kgs 18:4). Indeed, there may be some connection between the bronze serpent *(nĕḥaš hannĕḥōšet)* and the rod *(maṭṭeh)* of Moses that becomes a serpent in Exod 4:3 *(nāḥāš)*. In Exod 7:10, the rod becomes a reptile *(ṭannîn),* as do the rods of the Egyptian magicians. But 7:15 alludes to the serpent as *nāḥāš.* At the center of the tradition about Moses, then, is the symbol of the serpent rod, the sign of Mosaic authority and, ever more, power to heal.

Genre

The unit employs the typical structure of the STORY. A problem in the wilderness provokes a crisis. Then, in response to the crisis, Moses, with the help of the Lord, acts to resolve the crisis. The unit is not an etiology. It does not carry structural signs of etiology. It is at the center of the Moses traditions as a STORY about an event of critical importance for the wilderness generation.

Setting

Even though the bronze serpent plays a role in the temple, rooted out of that place in an anti-Moses reformation (see 2 Kgs 18:4), the setting for this tale is not cultic, as if it might have had its origin and preservation in the temple. Some point in the history of the tradition doubtlessly did place the story in the cult as support for the cultic use of the object. Thus, the cult may be a secondary setting for the tradition. But the primary setting would be with the Moses tradition generally, among the folk who remembered Moses as their hero.

Intention

The story reports the event that accounts for the origins of the bronze serpent; it thus has an etiological dimension. But the primary intention of the tradition is to connect the bronze serpent with its healing role to Moses, the hero who heals his people. As a symbol, it stands for Moses' power to heal and authority to command obedience among the people.

Bibliography

K. R. Joines, "The Bronze Serpent in the Israelite Cult," *JBL* 87 (1968) 245-56; M. Noth, "Num 21 als Glied der 'Hexateuch' Erzählung," *ZAW* 58 (1939) 113-41; D. J. Wiseman, "Flying Serpents," *TB* 23 (1972) 108-10; W. Zimmerli, "Das Bilderverbot in der Geschichte des alten Israel. Goldenes Kalb, eherne Schlange, Mazzeba und Lade," in *Alttestamentliche Traditionsgeschichte und Theologie* (Munich: Kaiser, 1974).

Wilderness Itinerary (21:10-20)

Structure

I. First station	10
A. Departure	10a
B. Arrival	10b
II. Second station	11
A. Departure	11a
B. Arrival	11b
III. Third station	12
A. Departure	12a
B. Arrival	12b
IV. Fourth station	13-15
A. Departure	$13a\alpha_1$
B. Arrival	$13a\alpha_2$-b
1. Formula	$13a\alpha_2$-aβ
2. Gloss	13b
C. Book of the Wars of the Lord saying	14-15
V. Fifth station	16-18a
A. Departure	$16a\alpha$
B. Arrival	$16a\beta$-b
1. Formula	$16a\beta$
2. Gloss	16b

	C. Song	17-18a
VI.	Sixth station	18b
	A. Departure	18bα
	B. Arrival	18bβ
VII.	Seventh station	19a
	A. Departure	19aα
	B. Arrival	19aβ
VIII.	Eighth station	19b
	A. Departure	19bα
	B. Arrival	19bβ
IX.	Ninth station	20
	A. Departure	20aα$_1$
	B. Arrival	20aα$_2$-b

This unit is defined completely by the structure of the wilderness itinerary that controls the larger patterns of the wilderness theme. The first station in this list does not name the site from which Israel departed. The failure of the departure element does not, however, indicate a problem in the redaction of the wilderness theme. It recognizes that the previous itinerary formula in v. 4 listed the departure site for the Israelites, but it did not note the place of arrival. The break in the itinerary structure thus connects with the pattern of the itinerary from the previous pericope. The concluding itinerary element is not picked up explicitly by the following pericope, perhaps indicating some diverse character of the tradition embraced by the itinerary chain. In any case, the structure of this piece of itinerary simply connects to the pattern of the larger itinerary structure (see Coats, "Itinerary")

In successive stages, the itinerary lists nine stations in the wilderness journey, each with a two-part formula. The point of departure is generally marked by reference to a place name, but the departure site might be named with an indefinite pronoun, "from there" *(miššām),* as in vv. 13, 16. The distinctive elements for this simple list come in the fourth and fifth stations, vv. 13-18a. For both states, a gloss defines the point of arrival more exactly. In v. 13, the gloss explains that the location, simply a reference to the other side of the Arnon, serves as a boundary for Moab. Verse 16 explains the name of the place by reference to an oracle of Yahweh to Moses. Indeed, the oracle suggests a larger tradition, like the tradition associated with the place names of Marah or Meribah, a tradition no longer preserved. Moreover, for both sites, an additional element appears, a fragment of tradition now carried by the itinerary structure, but perhaps properly associated by tradition with the particular site. The first of these, vv. 14-15, is a saying, perhaps a closer definition of the site, perhaps a closer definition of the boundary with Moab. But of more importance is the allusion to the title of the book from which the saying comes: "Book of the Wars of the Lord." No other reference clarifies the nature of that book.

The second fragment of tradition carried by the itinerary is a SONG, vv. 17-18a. The fragment recognizes the excitement in the process of digging a well in the wilderness. The song addresses the well itself with a command to yield its water. The expression reflects the quasi-magical performance that inaugurates the well as a source of water. The magical dimension appears not only in the direct address in the song to the well: "Spring up, O well!" It appears also in the admonition to the workers to address the well: "Sing to it!" This magical dimension is enhanced by reference to the implements for the task, employed by nobles *(śārîm* and *nĕdîbê hāʿām)*. The reference to the nobles hardly means an identification of workers. It is rather an allusion to the authority behind the act of digging the well (so, Noth). It may be, however, that the song reflects nothing more than a working song, the chant of the workers urging the object of their work to reproduce its intended goal, celebrating in advance of completion of the task the fruits of their labor.

In its present form, this pericope reflects the latest redaction for the wilderness theme. But it preserves traditions that are older than Rjep. Both the saying and the song come from sources older than their context.

Genre

The unit as a whole is an ITINERARY, a list of sites in the wilderness that identify the wilderness journey. The ITINERARY would be related to (ROYAL) ANNALS, a means for organizing the military exploits of a king or some other leader of a people. The SAYING is simply a description of a geographical position, perhaps a traditional saying. But if it had any further identifying marks that would type it as an aphorism or some other type of expression, they have been lost. Perhaps the saying is in fact not complete as it stands. But reconstruction is futile. The SONG is a workman's song, a chant sung by the workers who dig wells.

Setting

The itinerary comes from military sources, a form used to organize battle reports and other items in the military archives. The saying is derived perhaps from the same source, a description of a particular place in the itinerary. The song derives from the situation that calls for work, in this case, work in digging a well. If the song reflects a quasi-magical structure, its setting would still be the work place, not a sanctuary.

Intention

The itinerary organizes tradition associated with an extended journey, perhaps military in focus (→ 21:21-31; 31:32-35). The saying describes a point in the itinerary. The song belongs especially to a site in the itinerary. But it is distinct, a worker's chant. Its intention may be described as quasi-magical, a means for soliciting obedience from the object of the work to the worker's wishes.

Bibliography

D. L. Christensen, "Num 21:14-15 and the Book of the Wars of Yahweh," *CBQ* 36 (1974) 359-60; G. W. Coats, "The Wilderness Itinerary," *CBQ* 34 (1972) 135-52; G. I. Davies, "The Wilderness Itineraries," *TB* 25 (1974) 46-81; M. Noth, "Num 21 als Glied der 'Hexateuch' Erzählung," *ZAW* 58 (1940/41) 161-89; J. T. Walsh, "From Egypt to Moab; a Source Critical Analysis of the Wilderness Itinerary," *CBQ* 39 (1977) 20-33.

Battle Report (21:21-31)

Structure

I. Speech report	21-22
A. Introduction: Israel to Sihon	21
B. Negotiations speech	22
1. Petition	$22a\alpha_1$
2. Self-imposed conditions	$22a\alpha_2\text{-}\alpha\beta$
3. Intention	22b
II. Response	23-30
A. Refusal by Sihon	$23a\alpha$
B. Battle report	$23a\beta\text{-}b$
C. Results	24-30
1. Defeat of Sihon	24a
2. Conquest of land	24b
3. Conquest of cities	25-30
a. General report	25
b. Heshbon	26-30
1) Identification of Heshbon	26
2) Song report	27-30
a) Introduction	$27a\alpha$
b) Song	$27a\beta\text{-}30$
(1) Liturgy for Heshbon	$27a\beta\text{-}28$
(a) Opening admonition	$27a\beta\text{-}b$
(b) Reason	28
(2) Woe oracle	29-30
(a) Woe formula	$29a\alpha$
(b) Description of defeat	$29a\beta\text{-}30$
III. Conclusion	31

No itinerary formula sets the pericope into the larger context of the wilderness theme. Identification of Heshbon, the central subject for the last elements in this unit, places the battle in Moab (vv. 26, 28, 29). That identification connects with the end of the itinerary chain, v. 20, thus giving the battle report the same kind of context provided by a single itinerary formula at the beginning of any unit (→ 20:1). But the context in the itinerary chain is even farther removed from the unit than normally is the case.

The battle report begins with a statement about formal negotiations between Israel and Sihon of the Amorites. Messengers deliver a carefully constructed appeal from Israel to Sihon. The appeal presents first the petition of Israel to pass through the land of Sihon (v. 22aα). In order to secure the petition, the second element in the speech sets out self-imposed conditions to be followed during the journey (v. 22aβ). The final stage of the speech elaborates the petition by naming the route for their trek and setting their goal: "until we have passed through your territory." Sihon's response to the petition, v. 23a, is negative. Indeed, in v. 23b, the report notes that he initiated the battle against Israel. The focus of the unit then falls on vv. 24-31, the account of the results of the battle. A general statement, v. 24a, reports that Israel slaughtered Sihon. Then, vv. 24b-30 observe the conquest and occupation of Sihon's territory. But again, the balance of structure suggests the focus of the unit. Verse 24b reports conquest of the land, vv. 25-30 conquest of the cities. Verse 25 contains a general statement of conquest of the cities, with Israel settling in their boundaries. Verses 26-30 then focus on Heshbon. Verse 26 identifies the city as the victim of an earlier battle when Sihon had displaced the king of Moab. Indeed, the song in vv. 27-30 celebrates the victory of Sihon, the Amorite, over the preceding king of Moab.

In the song, the invitation to a liturgy celebrating the victory at Heshbon remembers Sihon's attack on the Moabites and the ensuing process for rebuilding the city. The destruction of Heshbon described in v. 28 focuses on the demise of Moab. Moreover, the woe oracle in vv. 29-30 addresses Moab with its doom and recognizes Sihon as the beneficiary of the battle. Indeed, Sihon holds the captives as his spoil. And Sihon finishes the task by destroying three Moabite cities. The song, then, is a celebration of Sihon's victory at Heshbon. And the introduction to the song in v. 26 makes that point clear.

Yet, it is also clear that the song stands in contrast to the context. Verses 23-26 report a battle that goes against Sihon in favor of Israel. The song in vv. 27-30 celebrates a victory by the Amorite Sihon over the previous inhabitants of the city, the Moabites.

The battle report concludes in v. 31 with a notation of the results of Israel's conquest: "Thus Israel dwelt in the land of the Amorites." This item confirms the final stage in the history of the tradition. Sihon the Amorite displaced the Moabites from the city. Now the Israelites displace Sihon. Thus Israel can live in the land of the Amorites. This report derives from the older layers of the Pentateuch, perhaps from the Yahwist.

Genre

The unit as a whole is a BATTLE REPORT, noting the defeat of Sihon, occupation of his land and cities, and settlement in the territory. In addition, the Song of Sihon should be defined as a VICTORY SONG.

Setting

The battle report belongs to the folk tradition of Israel, the archives of the people who remember their history in terms of a particular victory. The song must belong particularly to the place it celebrates since it is contradictory to its context and its present Israelite environment.

Intention

The battle report celebrates the victory of Israel over Sihon, noting occupation of his territory. The song celebrates the victory of Sihon over the previous inhabitants, noting occupation of the conquered territory.

Bibliography

J. R. Bartlett, "The Conquest of Sihon's Kingdom: A Literary Re-examination," *JBL* 97 (1978) 347-51; idem, "Sihon and Og, Kings of the Amorites," *VT* 20 (1970) 257-77; D. M. Gunn, "The 'Battle Report': Oral or Scribal Convention?" *JBL* 93 (1974) 513-18; M. Noth, "Num 21 als Glied der 'Hexateuch' Erzählung," *ZAW* 58 (1940/1) 161-89; J. van Seters, "The Conquest of Sihon's Kingdom: A Literary Examination," *JBL* 91 (1972) 182-97; idem, "Once Again — the Conquest of Sihon's Kingdom," *JBL* 99 (1980) 117-19; W. A. Summer, "Israel's Encounters with Edom, Moab, Ammon, Sihon and Og According to the Deuteronomist," *VT* 18 (1968) 216-28.

Wilderness Itinerary (21:32-35)

Structure

I. First station	32
A. Spy report	32a
B. Futile report	32b
II. Second station	33-35
A. Itinerary station	33a
B. Battle report	33b-35
1. Battle	33b
2. Speech report	34
a. Introduction: the Lord to Moses	34aα₁
b. Salvation oracle	34aα₂-b
3. Results	35

The wilderness itinerary (→ 21:10-20) continues in these verses. Verse 32 assumes some particular wilderness station, although the verse itself does not make the connection explicit. In that report, the itinerary is like 21:21. One might consider the possibility that v. 31 functions not only as the conclusion for the preceding unit but also as the opening line for this unit, although the verb of v. 31, "dwelt" *(wayyēšeb),* is not a normal part of itinerary diction. Indeed, it stands in conflict with the general purposes of an itinerary unit (compare the rough relationship between vv. 31 and 33).

From the first station, Moses commissions spies to explore Jazer. No details of the spying mission appear. The notice leads immediately to a report that Israel took the villages of Jazer and removed its population. But again, no details in the report outline the significance of that victory, and no notice suggests that Israel settled in that land.

The second station of the itinerary notes movement to Bashan. And again, a battle report hangs on the itinerary station. The king of Bashan, Og, engages Israel in battle. Significantly, Og and Sihon represent a traditional pair (→ Num 32:33; Deut 1:4; 3:1-13; 4:46-47; 29:6; 31:4; Josh 12:2-4; 13:8-32; Neh 9:22; 1 Kgs 4:19; Ps 135:11; 136:19-20). The battle described in vv. 33-35 first by means of a simple battle report, v. 33b, then by a salvation oracle, v. 34, and finally by a statement concerning the victory, v. 35, leads through the announcement of the death of Og and his sons to a statement that Israel took possession of his land. The first element in that structure notes simply that the battle between Israel and Og was joined, initiated by Og. For Israel, it was a defensive war. The oracle of salvation begins with the formula for assistance with its admonition not to fear: "Do not fear him; for I have given him into your hand . . ." (→ Isa 41:14-16). Indeed, the salvation oracle, v. 34b, announces explicitly the results expected from the battle. And v. 35 reports that the results occurred as they were announced.

The unit derives from the older sources reporting events in the wilderness, doubtlessly from the Yahwist. The tradition is older than the literary creation of the Yahwist, as would be suggested by the traditional pairing of Sihon and Og.

Genre

The unit appears as a part of the larger wilderness itinerary scheme responsible for the shape of the wilderness theme (→ 21:10-20). In this particular example of the itinerary tradition, the character of the ITINERARY as a framework for BATTLE REPORTS, thus as a form of ANNALS for the military exploits of the people (compare the annals of the Babylonian and Assyrian kings), emerges more fully. Verse 34 can be defined as a SALVATION ORACLE, introduced by a SPEECH FORMULA. The element in vv. 33b-35 can be designated a BATTLE REPORT (so, Gunn).

Setting

The itinerary generally reflects the redactional setting responsible for putting the wilderness theme together. It doubtlessly derives from a redactional setting at that stage. Behind the redactional operation can be seen some signs of a military, perhaps a royal setting for such a system, the account of military exploits in a geographical sequence. The oracle of salvation would also reflect the military setting, an affirmation of God's favor for the military preparing for a battle.

Intention

The itinerary accounts for movement of Israel through the wilderness and assumes the larger framework for the wilderness theme (so, Coats, "Wilderness Itinerary"). As a framework, it serves the redaction by establishing a place for putting small items of tradition from the wilderness theme. Specifically, the itinerary notes the victory of Israel over Og, an Amorite king, and occupation of his territory.

Bibliography

G. W. Coats, "The Wilderness Itinerary," *CBQ* 34 (1972) 135-52; D. M. Gunn, "The 'Battle Report': Oral or Scribal Convention?" *JBL* 93 (1974) 513-18; J. van Seters, "The Conquest of Sihon's Kingdom: A Literary Examination," *JBL* 91 (1972) 182-97; idem, "Once Again — the Conquest of Sihon's Kingdom," *JBL* 99 (1980) 117-19.

Balaam Legend (22:1–24:25)

Structure

I.	Itinerary	22:1
II.	Exposition	22:2-6
	A. Report of circumstances	2
	B. Response	3-6
	1. Fear motif	3
	2. Speech report	4a
	a. Introduction: Moab to elders of Midian	$4a\alpha_1$
	b. Description of plight	$4a\alpha_2$-aβ
	3. Speech report	4b-6
	a. Introduction: Balak to Balaam	$4b$-$5b\alpha_1$
	b. Speech	$5b\alpha_2$-6
	1) Description of plight	$5b\alpha_2$-bβ
	2) Petition for aid	6
	a) Petition	$6a\alpha_1$
	b) Justification for the petition	$6a\alpha_2$
	c) Intention	$6a\beta$
	d) Justification for the intention	6b
III.	First panel for the legend	22:7-14

 A. Dispatch of elders from Moab and Midian 7
  1. Departure 7a
  2. Arrival 7b
 B. Speech report 8a
  1. Introduction: Balaam to the messengers 8aα₁
  2. Speech 8aα₂-αβ
   a. Instructions 8aα₂
   b. Goal: *the legendary motif* 8aβ
 C. Response by the elders 8b
 D. Dialogue 9-12
  1. Speech report 9
   a. God to Balaam 9a-bα₁
   b. Interrogation 9bα₂-bβ
  2. Speech report 10-11
   a. Balaam to God 10a
   b. Response 10b-11
    1) Description of Balak's act 10b
    2) Citation of Balak's invitation 11
  3. Speech report 12
   a. God to Balaam 12aα
   b. Instructions with reason for the act 12aβ-b
 E. Balaam's execution of the instructions 13-14
  1. Speech report 13
   a. Balaam to Balak's princes 13aα
   b. Refusal of invitation 13aβ-b
  2. Speech report 14
   a. Balak's princes to Balak 14a-bα
   b. Report of Balaam's refusal 14bβ
IV. Second panel for the legend 22:15-20
 A. Dispatch of princes 15-16a
  1. Departure 15
  2. Arrival 16a
 B. Speech report 16b-17
  1. Messengers to Balaam 16bα₁
  2. Message speech 16bα₂-17
   a. Messenger formula 16bα₂
   b. Message 16bβ-17
    1) Instructions 16bβ
    2) Reason for the instructions 17a
    3) Instructions 17b
 C. Speech report 18-19
  1. Balaam to the messengers 18aα
  2. Message 18aβ-19
   a. *Legendary motif* 18aβ-b
   b. Instructions 19
 D. Speech report 20
  1. God to Balaam 20aα-aβ₁

2. Speech — 20aβ₂-b

  a. Permission to go to Balak — 20aβ₂

  b. *Legendary motif* — 20b

V. Third panel for the legend — 22:21-40

A. Dispatch of princes from Moab with Balaam — 21

B. Fable — 22-35

  1. First scene — 22-23

    a. Report of confrontation — 22

      1) Lord's anger — 22aα

      2) Report about the Lord's messenger — 22αβ

      3) Balaam's position — 22b

    b. Description of the ass's act — 23a

      1) The ass *saw* — 23aα

      2) Response — 23aβ

    c. Balaam's response — 23b

  2. Second scene — 24-25

    a. Report of confrontation — 24

    b. Description of the ass's act — 25a

      1) The ass *saw* — 25aα₁

      2) Response — 25aα₂-aβ

    c. Balaam's response — 25b

  3. Third scene — 26-27

    a. Report of confrontation — 26

    b. Description of the ass's act — 27

      1) The ass *saw* — 27aα

      2) Response — 27αβ

    c. Balaam's response — 27b

  4. Fourth scene — 28-30

    a. Speech report — 28

      1) Introduction: ass to Balaam — 28aα₁

      2) Accusation — 28aα₂-b

    b. Speech report — 29

      1) Introduction: Balaam to the ass — 29aα

      2) Self-defense — 29aβ-b

    c. Speech report — 30a

      1) Introduction: ass to Balaam — 30aα₁

      2) Elaboration of accusation — 30aα₂-aβ

    d. Speech report — 30b

      1) Introduction: Balaam — 30bα

      2) Response to the accusation — 30bβ

  5. Fifth scene — 31-35a

    a. Report of resolution — 31

      1) The Lord opens Balaam's eyes: he *saw* — 31a

      2) Response — 31b

    b. Speech report — 32-33

      1) Introduction: angel to Balaam — 32aα

      2) Speech — 32aβ-33

          a) Accusation   32aβ
          b) Declaration of Balaam's sin   32b
          c) Explanation of the ass's act   33
             (1) The ass *saw*   33aα
             (2) The ass acted   33aβ
             (3) Results   33b
       c. Speech report   34
          1) Introduction: Balaam to the angel   34aα$_1$
          2) Speech   34aα$_2$-b
             a) Confession   34aα$_2$-aβ
             b) Commitment to turn back   34b
       d. Speech report   35a
          1) Introduction: angel to Balaam   35aα$_1$
          2) Speech   35aα$_2$-aβ
             a) Instructions to go   35aα$_2$
             b) *Legendary motif*   35aβ
    6. Conclusion to the fable   35b
  C. Conclusion to the panel for the legend   36-40
    1. Report of meeting   36
    2. Speech report   37
       a. Introduction: Balak to Balaam   37aα$_1$
       b. Accusation questions   37aα$_2$-b
    3. Speech report   38
       a. Introduction: Balaam to Balak   38aα$_1$
       b. Response to the accusation: *legendary motif*   38aα$_2$-b
    4. Conclusion   39-40
VI. Fourth panel for the legend   22:41–23:12
  A. Exposition   22:41
    1. Name of the place   41a
    2. View of the people   41b
  B. Description of sacrifice event   23:1-2
    1. Speech report   1
       a. Introduction: Balaam to Balak   1aα
       b. Instructions for altars and animals   1aβ-b
    2. Execution of the instructions   2a
    3. Report of the sacrifice   2b
  C. Speech report   3a
    1. Introduction: Balaam to Balak   3aα$_1$
    2. Speech   3aα$_2$-aβ
       a. Instructions for divination   3aα$_2$-aβ$_1$
       b. *Legendary motif*   3aβ$_2$
  D. Balaam-God confrontation   3b-4
    1. Narration of the event   3b-4a
    2. Speech report   4b
       a. Introduction: Balaam to God   4bα$_1$
       b. Report of instructions executed   4bα$_2$-bβ
  E. *Legendary motif*   5-6

1. *Motif*   5a
2. Speech report   5b
   a. Introduction: the Lord to Balaam $5b\alpha_1$
   b. Instructions for oracle: *legendary motif* $5b\alpha_2$-$b\beta$
3. Execution of instructions   6
F. Oracle   7-10
  1. Introduction: Balaam   7a
  2. Oracle   7b-10
   a. Report of past event   7b
   b. Rhetorical question   8
   c. Vision of the people   9
   d. Rhetorical question   10a
   e. Petition   10b
G. Conclusion   11-12
  1. Speech report   11
   a. Introduction: Balak to Balaam $11a\alpha$
   b. Accusation $11a\beta$-b
  2. Speech report   12
   a. Introduction: Balaam to Balak   12a
   b. *Legendary motif*   12b
VII. Fifth panel for the legend   23:13-26
  A. Speech report   13
   1. Introduction: Balak to Balaam $13a\alpha_1$
   2. Instructions for new effort for divination $13a\alpha_2$-b
  B. Execution of instructions   14
  C. Speech report   15
   1. Introduction: Balaam to Balak $15a\alpha$
   2. Instructions for divination $15a\beta$-b
  D. Speech report   16
   1. Introduction: God to Balaam $16a\alpha$
   2. Instructions for oracle $16a\beta$-b
  E. Execution of the instructions   17a
  F. Speech report   17b
   1. Introduction: Balak to Balaam $17b\alpha$
   2. Query $17b\beta$
  G. Oracle   18-24
   1. Introduction: Balaam   18a
   2. Oracle   18b-24
   a. Call to attention   18b
   b. Identification of God's character   19
   c. *Legendary motif*   20
   d. Blessing   21-24
  H. Conclusion   25-26
   1. Speech report   25
   a. Introduction: Balak to Balaam $25a\alpha$
   b. Instructions $25a\beta$-b
   2. Speech report   26

a. Introduction: Balaam to Balak	26a
b. Speech: *Legendary motif*	26b
VIII. Sixth panel for the legend	23:27–24:24
A. Speech report	23:27
1. Introduction: Balak to Balaam	27aα
2. Instructions for new effort	27aβ-b
B. Execution of instructions	28
C. Speech report	29
1. Introduction: Balaam to Balak	29aα
2. Instructions for divination	29aβ-b
D. Execution of instructions	30
E. Report of change in the pattern	24:1
F. Speech report	24:2-9
1. Introduction	2-3a
a. Circumstances for the oracle	2
b. Speech formula	3a
2. Oracle	3b-9
a. Introduction	3b-4
b. Definition of Israel	5-6
c. Fertility	7a
d. Position of the king	7b
e. Exodus	8a
f. Victory over the enemy	8b
g. Definition of Israel	9a
h. Blessing formula	9b
G. Conclusion	10-14
1. Balak's response	10a
2. Speech report	10b-11
a. Introduction: Balak to Balaam	10bα₁
b. Speech	10bα₂-11
1) Indictment	10bα₂
2) Judgment	11
3. Speech report	12-14
a. Introduction: Balaam to Balak	12a
b. Speech	12b-14
1) *Legendary motif*	12b-13
2) Conclusion	14a
3) Grounds for a new oracle	14b
H. Speech report	24:15-19
1. Introduction: Balaam	15a
2. Oracle	15b-19
a. Introduction	15b-16
b. Vision: star out of Jacob	17
c. Results	18-19
1) Victory over enemy	18
2) Power of Jacob	19
I. Speech report	20

        1. Introduction: Balaam about Amalek   20a
        2. Oracle: Destruction of Amalek   20b
  J. Speech report   21-22
        1. Introduction: Balaam about the Kenite   21a
        2. Oracle   21b-22
           a. For the Kenite   21b
           b. Against Kain   22a
           c. Accusation against Assyria   22b
  K. Speech report   23-24
        1. Introduction: Balaam   23a
        2. Oracle of doom   23b-24
           a. Complaint question   23b
           b. Judgment against Asshur and Eber   24a
           c. Announcement of destruction   24b
IX. Conclusion   24:25

The context for the pericope about Balaam is controlled by an itinerary formula, 22:1, although there is no place name for the first element in the formula. The context is thus rather loosely defined. The second element in the formula names the place for a new encampment as the plains of Moab, at Jericho. This identification also confuses the pattern of the itinerary chain since the Jericho traditions do not relate to this position in the larger narrative ($\rightarrow$ Josh 5:10-15). The itinerary location in Num 25:1 names the location for Israel's life at that point as Shittim ($\rightarrow$ 33:49). But Shittim is also in the vicinity of Jericho (so, Num 33:49-50; Josh 2:1; 3:1). The place name in 22:1 thus bends the itinerary tradition in order to accommodate the Balaam tradition at just this point in the narrative. And the itinerary suggests a certain isolation of this unit in its context. This isolation provides a critical insight into the tradition in the light of the reference to Balaam in Num 31:8.

The Balaam story itself begins in vv. 2-6 with an exposition, and then follows that point of departure with six distinct panels designed to depict essentially the same point in the Balaam tradition. A conclusion in 24:25 rounds off the picture of Balaam with a notation that each of the principals in the story went his own way. Although tension clearly develops over the course of these several panels, tension not only between the two principal characters but also between the two characters on the one hand and Israel on the other, the tension is not the focal element in the narration. Indeed, at the end of the unit, the tension remains unresolved. To the contrary, the focus in the structure of the unit highlights a particular element in the character of Balaam, a virtue that makes Balaam an ideal figure. Balaam was not an Israelite, yet he held a reputation as diviner, particularly as a prophet who could bless or curse a customer's enemy on command. Balaam, the foreign prophet, has an international reputation, known even outside the Old Testament (see Hoftijzer). But Balaam's virtue emphasized by this pericope is that he will proclaim only whatever word, blessing or curse, that Yahweh puts into his mouth. He cannot speak on demand from any customer. He can speak only the word as it comes to him from the Lord.

The circumstances that set up the situation for developing the narrative are defined in the exposition, 22:2-6. Verse 2 names the antagonists for the narration: Balak against Israel. Indeed, the verse defines the circumstance that makes the two parties antagonists. "Balak, the son of Zippor, saw all that Israel had done to the Amorites." The result of the opening events is defined in vv. 3-6. Verse 3 emphasizes the fear of the Moabites toward the Israelites by repeating the motif. In v. 3a, the Moabites show "great dread" *(wayyāgor)*. In v. 3b, the Moabites are "overcome with fear" *(wayyāqoṣ)*. This doublet should not be taken as evidence for source duplication. It simply emphasizes the fear motif. And that motif suggests a connection between this pericope and the conquest theme (so, Coats, "Conquest Traditions," 333, 334). Verse 4a describes the response of the Moabites. They lament to the elders of Midian that Israel threatens. The relationship between the Moabites, specifically Balak, the king of the Moabites, and the elders of Midian is not clear. In v. 7 the elders of Moab and the elders of Midian act in concert, as if the two people embrace a common plan to meet a common enemy. Again, the duplication does not suggest multiple sources, but rather a complexity in the history of the tradition. Perhaps the allusion to Midian here anticipates 25:6-18.

Verses 4b-6 round off the exposition by introducing the third party for the narration. Balak sends messengers to Balaam, the son of Beor. The verse defines Balaam as a distant foreigner. He lives in Pethor, near the River, in the land of Aram. The precise identity of the River (the Euphrates?) is not crucial for the pericope. The point is that Balaam lives in a distant land. The message for Balaam establishes the key for the development of the entire pericope: "Come, curse this people for me, because they are too mighty for me. Perhaps I will be able to defeat them and drive them from the land." The final element in the speech refers to Balaam's reputation. "I know that he whom you bless is blessed, and he whom you curse is cursed" (v. 6b). Balaam has the power to establish an effective blessing or curse. And obviously Balak assumes that Balaam will do that at his own discretion. If Balak asks, indeed, meets the price (so, v. 7) for the power of Balaam's word, he will obtain that power for resisting the Israelite invasion. Balaam is thus a diviner with an international reputation, a figure whose professional services could render power for the right price.

Balak's petition to Balaam for assistance repeats the severity of the threat he feels from the Israelites. The petition recognizes the power of Balaam's curse. If Balaam agrees to curse Israel, then Balak would have a chance against them. But the final line of the petition, v. 6b, picks up an element of tradition about Israel (→ Gen 12:3). Balak's citation uses the tradition as if it is a part of Balaam's reputation. But in fact, the tradition foreshadows Israel's fate, indeed, Balak's fate in the face of Balaam's work. The citation belongs to Israel.

In a series of panels, the goal of the pericope advances to the top position for the focus of the narrative. The first panel, 22:7-14, depicts Balak's messengers arriving before Balaam with the invitation to assist the Moabites. Balaam's pericope features the major motif for the unit: In v. 8, the story reports that Balaam did not accept or reject the invitation. To the contrary, his response shows his utter dependency on the word of Yahweh. "Lodge here tonight, and I will bring back word to you, just as the Lord speaks to me." It is important to note for the structure of the whole pericope that this process of inquiry from the

Lord is not treated negatively. Balaam's delay is not a process that requires bartering for a higher price or soliciting a special invitation. It is a process that requires exact inquiry by Balaam of the Lord. Moreover, it is not a deception of Balak's messengers, as if Balaam already knew what the Lord would do but sought to hide that knowledge from the messengers. Balaam makes a simple statement: "I will bring back word to you, just as the Lord speaks to me." The implication is clear. If the Lord tells Balaam to curse Israel, then Balaam would be quite willing to curse Israel. Balaam has no commitment to Israel. His only commitment is to the Lord. The purpose of the panel is to emphasize that fact (for other suggestions, see Wharton, 39).

Verses 9-12 contain the exchange between Balaam and God. The initial stage of the dialogue simply repeats what the narrative has already established. God asks Balaam for the identity of the messengers. Balaam responds by identifying the men as Balak's messengers and citing the message. God then denies Balaam the privilege of accepting the invitation. And the reason is clear: "You shall not go with them. You shall not curse the people, for they are blessed." Balaam then reports to the messengers. The messengers report to Balak. And the panel ends.

The second panel in the pericope, vv. 15-20, intensifies the terms of the first. Again, Balak sent messengers to Balaam. But in this case, there were more messengers than in the first panel. And these men were more prestigious. Moreover, the honor offered to Balaam by Balak now gains explicit reference, clearly an offer for unlimited honorarium. The response to the new offer, a depiction of character for Balaam, explicitly rejects the offer for higher honorarium. Verse 18 notes that even if the honorarium should be Balak's palace full of silver and gold, it would not affect the result of Balaam's work. The leitmotif then returns, Balaam's response to the messengers in v. 18b: "Though Balak were to give me his house full of silver and gold, I could not go beyond the command of the Lord my God to do less or more." Balaam will do whatever God gives him to do, regardless of the honorarium. In keeping with this assertion, he bids the men to wait the night and goes to inquire of the Lord. It should be clear that this renewal of the inquiry is not a violation of faith, an effort to find a way to accept a big honorarium despite the previous assertion of God that Israel was blessed. It is simply a repetition of the primary leitmotif. Balaam will say whatever God gives him to say. God said no to the first messengers. He might say yes to these messengers. Balaam assumes that God is free to change his mind. Thus, rather than assuming that God's answer is still no, Balaam pursues the process of inquiry again. God's answer is still no. God's answer to the inquiry in v. 20, however, marks a change in the divine decree. On this occasion, Balaam may accept the invitation. Verse 20b then repeats the leitmotif: "Only what I bid you, that shall you do." It should be clear here. The leitmotif is static. The character of the motif in the second panel is no different from the character of the motif in the first panel. The change that enables the story to proceed lies in God's direction for Balaam's response to the invitation, not in Balaam's desire to accept.

The third panel simply repeats the development in the negotiations from the second panel, in this case noting the return of Balak's messengers and

Balaam to Balak (v. 21). The pattern is completed by v. 35a, a notice that Balaam accompanied the messengers of Balak. Verses 36-40 bring this panel to its conclusion by reporting the meeting between Balaam and Balak. The meeting is hostile. In v. 37, Balak greets Balaam with an accusation about Balaam's refusal of the first envoy. And v. 38 carries Balaam's response to the accusation, a repetition of the leitmotif. "The word that God puts in my mouth, that must I speak." The conclusion in v. 39 places Balak and Balaam together. Verse 40 seems to imply that Balak and Balaam were not together since Balak informed Balaam and the princes by messenger that the sacrifice had been completed.

In the middle of this panel appears a distinct unit, vv. 22-35. The unit is disruptive for the context and assumes a quite distinct tradition about Balaam from the one that controls the larger pericope. In effect, the third panel of the Balaam story, 22:21-40, functions as an inclusion for the distinct unit, 22:22-35. In a series of scenes, the prophet-seer Balaam is confronted by an angry God. This anger, apparently directed against Balaam for his decision to accompany the messengers of Balak, stands in marked contradiction to the permission given by God for Balaam to join the expedition to Balak. A series of five distinct scenes, similar in structural function to the series of panels in the larger pericope, concludes in v. 35b with a notice that the larger narrative is picked up again. The scenes depict generally the ability of Balaam's animal to *see* more clearly than the famous *seer* can see. At no point in the entire pericope is Balaam named a seer. Yet, the tradition knows Balaam as seer (see the texts from Tell Deir 'Alla; Hackett). And the emphasis on the ability of the animal to see when Balaam cannot see cannot be accidental. The first three scenes set Balaam on his animal, in the process of a journey. Verse 22 notes the Lord's anger specifically because Balaam has joined the journey (no explicit reference to the messengers of Balak appears here). As an expression of his anger, the Lord blocks Balaam's path with the messenger. Unfortunately, Balaam cannot see the enemy, who threatens Balaam's life. But the animal can. And as a consequence, she leaves the path and enters a field. Balaam's response is violent. "Balaam struck the ass, to turn her into the road." The same transaction occurs in the second scene (vv. 24-25) and, with only slight modification, in the third scene (vv. 26-27). The fourth scene depicts the Lord's intervention on behalf of the animal. By his hand, the ass receives the power to talk and immediately addresses Balaam with an accusation. "What have I done to you that you have struck me these three times?" In typical fashion, the narration places no value on the fantastic element. It is no surprise to Balaam that the animal can speak. Rather, the weight of the scene falls on the accusation. The animal applies formal pressure to Balaam. And in keeping with formal procedures, Balaam must respond. He explains his action to the animal. "Because you made sport of me." Balaam, the seer, still does not know what the animal saw. The weight of the confrontation increases in v. 30a with an expansion of the accusation, drawing on precedent: "Am I not your ass, upon which you have ridden all your life long, to this day? Was I ever accustomed to do so to you?" Verse 30b has Balaam's simple response. And the scene ends with Balaam's own witness to the precedent serving as the evidence against him.

The final scene, vv. 31-35a, brings the exchange between the ass and the seer to its proper conclusion. The Lord opens the eyes of Balaam. And finally the seer can see. He submits to the Lord (v. 31b), but the Lord nevertheless confronts him with a new accusation. The first part of the accusation does in fact renew the charges from the accusation from the ass. But the new element in this speech plays on the ass's ability to *see* each of the three times she incurred Balaam's ire (v. 32). And the consequence of her action, made explicit in the Lord's accusation, was to save Balaam's life. Balaam's response, v. 34, is a confession of sin and a commitment for return to his home. The implication of the commitment is that now Balaam will not go to Balak, and that going to Balak provokes the Lord's anger and thus the confrontation with the messenger. Verse 35 completely reverses the pattern of the exchange. Having won Balaam's confession of sin, the Lord now agrees for Balaam to continue with Balak's messengers. This verse is obviously an adjustment in the tradition to accommodate the negative tradition about Balaam, the seer who could not see, with the positive tradition about the legendary Balaam who could speak only the word given him by the Lord. The two contradictory traditions about Balaam simply appear side by side in this panel without resolution of the contradiction (so, Coats, "The Way of Obedience").

The next panel in the narrative, 22:41–23:12, repeats many of the motifs developed in the first three panels. 22:41 in fact sets the stage, an exposition for the following narration. But the exposition does more than set the stage. The name of the place for the coming event also stipulates that Balaam could see the people from that vantage. To see the people at the magical moment of the curse or the blessing for the people would increase the power of the performative word (so, Noth, 182). Indeed, it is important to note that the story leaves Balaam free at this point to curse or bless as the Lord directs. That point dominates the speech of Balaam to Balak in 23:1. The ritual of sacrifice sets up the divination process. Verse 2 notes that Balak followed Balaam's instructions to the letter. Then, v. 3a, Balaam makes his point; "Stand beside your burnt offering, and I will go; perhaps the Lord will come to me, and whatever he shows me, I will tell you." The ritual is not a guarantee to effect a curse on Israel. But it is also not an automatic production of a blessing for Israel. Balaam will report whatever the Lord shows him. It is thus inappropriate to argue that Balaam attempts to deceive Balak since he already knows that the Lord will bless Israel. He does not know what the word will be. He must seek the word in the process of the ritual. At the point of the ritual, Balaam describes his act of sacrifice to God. And in return, the Lord places a word into Balaam's mouth.

The variation in this exchange between God *('ĕlōhîm)* and Lord (the Tetragrammaton) reflects a distinctive theology for the legendary patterns of the pericope. The legendary motif consistently uses the Tetragrammaton for its construction (thus, v. 5 vis-à-vis v. 4). The only exceptions to this pattern appear in 22:38 and 23:19-20.

Armed with the divine word, Balaam returns to Balak and presents the result of his inquiry, vv. 7-10. The oracle of Balaam is a distinct speech, perhaps older than the narrative that encircles it (so, Albright). Supported by two rhetorical questions to set the tone of the oracle (vv. 8, 10a) and a citation from Balak to mark the contrast with the oracle and its heavy use of the key expression "curse" *('ārûr)*, v. 9 defines the people of Israel. The verse accomplishes that goal with a preface noting the fact that Balaam had visual contact with Israel. The power of his word, whether blessing or curse, would thus be enriched. The definition then sets Israel apart from her neighbors. Israel is distinctive: "Lo, a people dwelling alone and not reckoning itself among the nations!" The rhetorical question following the assertion, v. 10a, contributes substantively to the definition. The point of the question is to affirm that Israel is numerous, although there is no explicit allusion to the promise for great posterity from the Abraham saga (→ Gen 12:1-3). The petition in v. 10b brings the definition to a conclusion by turning the power of the definition back to Balaam. Balaam asks that his death may be the death of the righteous *(yĕšārîm)* and thus asserts explicitly that the request calls for a death like whatever death Israel faces. The word *yāšār* defined Israel, not simply as numerous and thus blessed, but also as upright (1 Sam 29:6). The irony of this statement, created by the context, must not be lost. Balak has asked for a curse against Israel so that he could defeat his enemy. To announce the death of the enemy would be quite in keeping with Balak's request. Balaam announces "the death" of Balak's enemy. But the announcement glorifies the enemy by pronouncing them upright.

The panel concludes in vv. 11-12 with an accusation from Balak against Balaam's irony. Indeed, Balak makes the irony explicit: "I took you to curse my enemies, and behold you have done nothing but bless them." And Balaam's response to the accusation, v. 12, is the final assertion of the leitmotif for the panel, again using the Tetragrammaton: "Must I not take heed to speak what the LORD puts in my mouth?"

The fifth panel for the pericope, 23:13-26, again features the leitmotif prominently. The opening speech, v. 13, sets the stage for a new inquiry of God's word. Balak addresses Balaam with instructions to change location and try again. Again, a key element in the instructions is to find a place where Balaam can see the enemy. That factor apparently would increase the power of Balaam's curse. The end of the speech makes Balak's goal explicit. "Curse them for me from there." Verse 14 reports that the instructions were carried out. Verse 15 puts the divination initiative into Balaam's hand. But it is important just at this point to recognize that Balaam does not violate his character in his initiative for the divination. He tells Balak what to do during the process. But he promises only to meet the Lord, not to bring back a curse. The intentions of this part of the scene is not to deceive Balak by making him think that he will receive a curse when in fact Balaam knows that it will be a blessing. The scene presents Balaam as a prophet who must seek the Lord for his prophetic word, whether that word be curse or blessing.

The scene continues in v. 16 by emphasizing precisely the leitmotif at the center of the pericope. The Lord met Balaam, put the words into his mouth, and Balak's fate was sealed. The key in the process rests with the Lord, and Balaam's faithful devotion to the Lord simply facilitates the process. The word for Balak is not detailed at this point. The text reports only that the Lord put the word into Balaam's mouth. The Yahweh speech then instructs Balaam to return to Balak. Verse 17a reports that Balaam executed the instructions appropriately. And v. 17b carries a Balak speech, now loaded with a delightful irony. Balak asks: "What has the Lord spoken?" Balak himself now participates in the leit-motif.

The poetry of the oracle, vv. 18-24, may be older than the narrative (so, Albright). Yet, the poetry captures the same leitmotif that carried the structure of the prose. The point is particularly effective in v. 20: "I received a command to bless. He has blessed, and I cannot revoke it." The weight of this assertion rests on the power of the word, not simply on the character of the word as bless-ing. Whatever the character of the word, received by the speaker as a command, the speaker must simply give voice to it. Moreover, the poignancy of the motif is suggested in vv. 18-19 by drawing a contrast between God and human crea-tures. "God is not man." This contrast lies at the heart of the Yahwist's program (Genesis 1-11). But the point of the contrast rests on the authority of God's word: ". . . that he should lie . . . that he should change his mind." The word of God is effective. Therefore a prophet/diviner must obey the precise content of the word.

Verses 21-24 then express the content of the word. The general tone of the content establishes the contrast with the call of Balak to curse Israel and thus provides a contact between oracle and context. In v. 21a, the word reports no misfortune for Israel. Verse 22a refers this blessing to God's act in the exo-dus. Verse 23a then explicitly denies the power of any curse against Israel. And v. 24 defines the people by a simile, perhaps a reference to a totem animal (→ Gen 49:9-12). The simile itself establishes the power of Israel against its prey, perhaps an enemy that would seek God's curse to defeat God's own people. Verses 21b, 22b, and 23b then relate God's blessing for the people to a king in their midst. Verse 21b is explicit: "The shout of a king is among them." Verse 22b is ambiguous (→ 24:8); yet, royal power can be described with a similar expression (so, Ps 92:11). And finally, v. 23b refers to a significant act of God in Israel (→ Ps 68:29). The frame for the oracle, vv. 25-26, then marks the con-clusion for the panel. And again, the content derives from the leitmotif. In v. 26, a Balaam speech addresses Balak: "All that the Lord says, that I must do."

A new panel for the pericope begins in v. 27 with a speech from Balak, like the speech at the beginning of the preceding panel (so, 23:13). Again, the speech instructs Balaam to prepare another inquiry of God from another place. Verse 28 reports the execution of the instructions. Verse 29 then moves the scene forward with a Balaam speech to Balak, instructions for preparing the divination sacrifice. And v. 30 reports that Balak followed the instructions.

The development of the panel breaks the established pattern, however, in 24:1. For the preceding elements of the story, it is important that Balaam seek a word from the Lord at each turning point in his relationship with Balak. He does not assume that the Lord will say either curse or blessing. He asks. And the development of the unit emphasizes the virtue of Balaam, his commitment to seek the Lord's word and to obey it. Here, Balaam assumes the character of the word. 24:1 reports that Balaam did not work through the divination process but simply lifted his eyes, received the Spirit of God (not the Tetragrammaton), and delivered the next oracle. It is not appropriate to conclude that Balaam here learns for the first time that the Lord will bless Israel (against Budd). To the contrary, the point is simply that the pattern of the scenes, set by the previous panels, breaks here. The reason for the broken pattern is clearly stated. Balaam receives his answer from the Lord without the divination ritual. Now Balaam can *see:* "When Balaam *saw* that it pleased the Lord to bless Israel. . . ." Thus, Balaam gains what he did not have previously: the ability to see without assistance (contrast the story about the ass).

In the oracle, vv. 3b-4 refer to the Balaam context. The prophet falls under the power of God and discovers that his eyes are opened. In this allusion, again the opposite character of Balaam vis-à-vis the story about the seeing ass appears. Or perhaps in this element is a parallel to the ass story: The seer must fall under the power of God in order for his eyes to be open. The content of the oracle opens with a statement of wellbeing for Israel, like the statement in 23:21. But in content, the critical element involves an ascription of fertility to Israel through a simile. In this case, the simile uses plant parallels rather than animal totems. Yet, the results are the same: Israel prospers. And in this case, Israel prospers directly at the hands of the Lord (the Tetragrammaton). Moreover, v. 7 notes that this prosperity will include a king greater than Agag, a kingdom exalted. And the exalted kingdom rests on God's power in the exodus (v. 8). Indeed, the exodus event allusion connects with the simile about God's power also employed in 23:22. The point of the allusion is now clear. Israel, through the power of God (expressed through the power of the king?), will be victorious over all enemies (v. 8). And that assertion is confirmed by the animal simile, parallel to 23:22. Enemies cannot stand against the Lord who shows his power as effective as the horns of the wild ox.

The panel concludes in vv. 10-14 with Balak's hostile response to Balaam. His speech in v. 10, however, depicts the pathos of the irony that surrounds the whole story. Balak asked for a curse against Israel. But he got a blessing for Israel. And the result is an angry denial to Balaam for honor or honorarium. The scene concludes in vv. 13-14 with the final emphasis on the leitmotif. Balaam responds by assuring Balak that the honorarium makes no difference. "If Balak should give me his house full of silver and gold, I would not be able to go beyond the word of the Lord, to do either good or bad of my own will. What the Lord speaks, that will I speak."

This obvious ending now is expanded by three distinct oracles. In vv. 15-24, an oracle opens with an extended description of Balaam, the prophet whose eyes are uncovered by the power of God (contrast the story about the talking ass). The opening is like the refrain in vv. 3-4. Verse 3b parallels v. 15b; v. 4aα parallels v. 16aα. In this case, however, v. 16aβ introduces a new element: "who knows the knowledge of the Most High." The name for God, *'elyôn,* is a technical name that relates explicitly to God as he was known in Jerusalem (→ Gen 14:19). Moreover, the allusion in v. 17 to a star from Jacob, a scepter from Israel, is apparently a reference to the Davidic kingship whose seat of power was in the Jerusalem of *'elyôn* (so, Noth, 192). That power will destroy enemies like Moab, Edom, Seir. And the oracle concludes with an ascription of power to Jacob.

Verse 20 is an appendix, unrelated to the structure of the story about Balaam and Balak. It, too, contains an oracle, but the author of the oracle is undefined. In a simple couplet, the oracle pronounces destruction on Amalek, the opposite of the beginning enjoyed by Amalek (→ Exod 17:8-16).

Verse 21 is a second appendix, again an oracle pronounced without naming the author of the saying. The oracle is a blessing for the Kenite, establishing an enduring dwelling (→ 2 Sam 7:4-13), a home like a rock. Verse 22 shifts this collection from blessing to curse against Kain and Assyria. In fact, the curse stands as the opposite of the blessing in v. 21. In this case, Kain and Assyria receive implied or explicit instability. Verses 23-24 carry this collection of blessing and curse to another subject. Ships from Kittim will attack Assyria and Eber in order to bring destruction, thus functionally a curse. This collection of random blessings and curses, vv. 20-24, rounds off the tradition about Balaam by implying authorship for the collection by the famous seer. But that point can be seen only from the context. In fact, the blessings and curses here are floating, attributed to Balaam only to give them context and authority.

Verses 25 rounds off the Balaam tradition with a note that the antagonists went their respective ways. The story has ended.

It should be clear here that nothing in the formal analysis supports a conclusion that the Balaam unit can be divided into two or more parallel literary sources. The shift between divine names relates to the patterns of the leitmotif, not to diction patterns in the sources. To be sure, complexities in the tradition history can be seen. 22:22-35 contains a distinct story about Balaam with a different tradition from the one in the larger context (see Coats, "The Way of Obedience"). But the problem is a traditio-historical one, not a source-critical one. In the one tradition, Balaam appears a saint, a prophet who can do only what God tells him to do. In the other, Balaam is a sinner, a prophet who sells out his commitments for a high honorarium, only to have his efforts to curse Israel turned into blessings by the power of God (see Coats, "Sinner or Saint?"). The unit is functionally coherent. It belongs as a whole to the Yahwist.

Genre

As the Balaam pericope now stands, it is a LEGEND, constructed clearly from panel to panel in order to highlight the legendary virtue of the hero (so, Coats, "Sinner or Saint?"). The virtue is Balaam's commitment to report as his prophetic word only the word that the Lord gives him to say. As is typical for the genre, the depiction of the legendary virtue functions as edification for the audience of the story. All prophets should learn from the legendary Balaam that the first commitment in their roles as prophet is to report what they receive from the Lord. It should be noted here, in the light of typical observations about repetitions as signs of sources (see Budd, 257), that the genre typically involves repetitions of the leitmotif and thus of elements that carry the leitmotif. This type of repetition does not indicate the presence of multiple sources.

Behind the LEGEND may lie tradition about a foreign seer whose efforts to curse Israel were defeated by the Lord himself. At this level, the tradition would not have been cast as LEGEND. Perhaps one might hypothesize a tale, a SAGA, or even an anti-legend about the alien Balaam who could not win a victory over Israel (→ 31:8, 16). In all probability, the shift from a general name for God to the Tetragrammaton reflects a shift from the older anti-heroic narrative to the form of the LEGEND.

In addition, the distinct pericope about Balaam and his animal, 22:22-35, is a fable (but see Solomon). The FABLE is characterized not only by the talking animal, an element that does not qualify the unit as *Märchen* (against Scullion), but also by the design of the unit to show the foibles of the principal human figure. The ass who could see more clearly than the seer shows the seer to be incapable of seeing at the most crucial moment. And significantly, the structure of the fable emphasizes the act of seeing. It is correct to conclude, then, that especially in the light of observations about genre, the story about the ass cannot be taken as evidence for a different literary source (so, Budd, 258). It is a problem in the history of the tradition (so, Coats, "Way of Obedience").

The ORACLES of Balaam belong to the category of prophetic tribal ORACLES that define the character of the unit by reference to a totem animal or plant (→ Gen 49:17). But the ORACLES are more diverse than simply tribal totem SAYINGS. Negative ORACLES might in fact function as curse (so, 24:20), while positive ORACLES function as blessing (so, 24:15-19). These elements may suggest a particular form of tribal SAYING, the SAYING of a seer (so, Vetter).

Formulas and stereotyped expressions include the SPEECH FORMULA, a stereotyped formula for introducing the oracle of Balaam (23:11; → Gen 12:18), and the BLESSING/CURSE formula (24:9b; → Gen 12:3).

Setting

The legend belongs to the circles of Judean folk traditions, a story about how prophets should relate to the Lord, but in fact a story about the importance of kingship. At this level, the story is a part of the larger context of the Yahwist, indeed, the climax of the Yahwist source. It is clear, nonetheless, that Balaam tradition belonged to a larger circle than simply the Yahwistic, pro-Davidic, literary setting of the legend. The negative popular tradition, represented here by the fable, but also by every other reference to Balaam in both the OT and the NT, reflects a setting in Israelite prophetic circles, a foil designed to highlight the negative virtue of the prophet. As anti-legend, it would serve a prophetic circle by demonstrating the negative role for models of prophetic activity. The saying of the seer belongs more properly in the popular setting of the tribe/family.

Intention

At its latest level, the Balaam legend serves the Yahwistic source as a key for the divine appointment of kingship for Israel/Jacob. Indeed, the reference to the power base as "a star out of Jacob, a scepter out of Israel" sets the appeal to kingship within the context of Davidic structures. The end of the Yahwist shows God's assertion of his presence to protect his people from their enemies through David. And indeed, the name of God for this stage is *'elyôn,* the name of the God of Jerusalem. For the Yahwist, the whole structure of the narrative from creation and the Garden to the present focuses on God's gift to Israel: the king, the star from Jacob, the scepter from Israel. To be sure, non-Davidic terms appear here: Israel, Jacob. But they now fall under the shelter of *'elyôn*.

Moreover, the Yahwist suggests that by the power of the king, Jacob would exercise dominion over the enemies of God's people (24:17-19). That same point of exaltation is reflected in 24:7. The focus on David as the conclusion to the Yahwist's plan of history shows that God removes Israel's enemies (see also 24:9; 23:24). Yet, it is significant that 24:9 picks up the Yahwist's blessing for Israel in Gen 12:3. And the key to that blessing lay in Israel's intimacy with those who maintained intimacy with Israel by supportive relationships. The crux for the Yahwist is thus 24:9.

The intention of the fable is the opposite of the intention for the legend. The fable shows the weakness of the prophet, his willingness to go with the messengers of Balak, apparently only for the profit of the honorarium (see also every other reference to Balaam in both OT and NT). And the irony in this negative cast for Balaam is that the famous seer could not see as well as the ass.

The oracles from Balaam emphasize the blessing of God on Israel. Under God's care, Israel will prosper. And that prosperity comes specifically under the administration of David (24:17). Israel under David's blessing means restored intimacy. In contrast, the oracles also emphasize the curse on those who stand in strife with Israel. And that curse breaks the power of Israel's enemies (24:17b-18).

Bibliography

W. F. Albright, "The Oracles of Balaam," *JBL* 63 (1944) 207-53; D. L. Christensen, *Transformations of the War Oracle in Old Testament Prophecy* (Missoula: Scholars Press, 1975); George W. Coats, "Balaam: Sinner or Saint?" *BR* 18 (1973) 21-29; idem, "The Way of Obedience: Exegetical and Hermeneutical Perspectives on the Balaam Story," *Semeia* 24 (1982) 53-79; idem, "Conquest Traditions in the Wilderness Theme," *JBL* 95 (1976) 177-90; idem, "An Exposition of the Wilderness Traditions," *VT* 22 (1972) 288-95; J. Coppens, "Les Oracles de Bileam: Leur Origine Littéraire et leur Portée Prophétique," in *Mélanges Eugene Tisserant* I (Città del Vaticano: Bibliotheca Apostolica Vaticana, 1964); O. Eissfeldt, "Die Komposition der Bileam-Erzählung," *ZAW* 57 (1939) 212-41; idem, "Sinai Erzählung und Bileamsprüche," *HUCA* 32 (1961) 179-90; B. Gemser, "Der Stern aus Jacob (Num 24:17)," *ZAW* 2 (1925) 301-2; W. Gross, " 'Ein Zepter wird sich erheben aus Israel' (Num 24:17). Die messianische Hoffnung im Alten Testament," *BK* 17 (1962) 34-37; J. A. Hackett, *The Balaam Text from Deir 'Alla* (Chico, CA: Scholars, 1984); J. Hoftijzer, "The Prophet Balaam in a Sixth Century Aramaic Inscription," *BA* 39 (1976) 11-17; O. Loretz, "Die Herausführungsformel in Num 23:22 und 24:8," *UF* 7 (1975) 571-72; R. S. Mackensen, "The Present Literary Form of the Balaam Stories," *The Macdonald Presentation Volume* (Princeton: Books for Libraries, 1933); J. Mauchline, "The Balaam-Balak Songs and Saga," in *Studia Semitica et Orientalia* (ed. C. J. Mullo-Weir; Glasgow: University Oriental Society, 1945); S. Mowinckel, "Der Ursprung der Bileamsage," *ZAW* 48 (1930) 233-71; M. Noth, "Israelitische Stämme zwischen Ammon und Moab," *ZAW* 60 (1944) 11-57; L. M. von Pakozdy, "Theologische Redaktionsarbeit in der Bileam Perikope," *Von Ugarit nach Qumran* (ed. J. Hempel, L. Ross; *BZAW* 77; Berlin:

Töpelmann, 1958); G. von Rad, "Die Geschichte von Bileam," *Gottes Wirken in Israel* (Neukirchen: Neukirchener Verlag, 1974); idem, *God at Work in Israel* (tr. John Marks; Nashville; Abingdon, 1980) 36-39; L. Schmidt, "Die alttestamentliche Bileam-überlieferung," *BZ* 23 (1979) 234-61; K. Seyboldt, "Das Herrscherbild des Bileamorakels Num 24:15-19," *TZ* 29 (1973) 1-19; A. Tosato, "The Literary Structure of the First Two Poems of Balaam," *VT* 29 (1979) 98-106; D. Vetter, "Seherspruch und Segensschilderung. Ausdruckabsichten und sprachliche Verwirklichungen in den Bileam-Sprüchen von Numeri 23 und 24." *Theologische Versuche* 5 (1975) 11-31; J. A. Wharton, "The Command to Bless: An Exposition of Numbers 22:41–23:25," *Int* 13 (1959) 37-48.

Baal Peor Anecdote (25:1-18)

Structure

I. Report of the event	1-3a
A. General report	1
B. Nature of the event as apostasy	2
C. General report	3a
II. Results	3b-5
A. General report	3b
B. Speech report	4
1. Introduction: the Lord to Moses	$4a\alpha_1$
2. Instructions	$4a\alpha_2$-b
a. Execution of the leaders	$4a\alpha_2$-aβ
b. Goal	4b
C. Speech report	5
1. Introduction: Moses to the judges	5a
2. Instructions for execution of the guilty	5b
III. Report of the event	6
A. General report	$6a\alpha$
B. Location	$6a\beta$-b
1. Before Moses	$6a\beta_1$
2. Before the people at the Tent of Meeting	$6a\beta_2$-b
IV. Results	7-13
A. Specific report	7-8a
B. Results of the event	8b-9
1. Positive	8b
2. Negative	9
C. Speech report	10-13
1. Introduction: the Lord to Moses	10
2. Speech	11-13
a. References to the event	11
b. Act of ordination	12-13a
c. Reason	13b
V. Gloss	14-15

    A. Name of the guilty man   14

    B. Name of the Midianite woman   15

VI. Conclusion: speech report   16-18

    A. Introduction: the Lord to Moses   16

    B. Instructions   17-18

        1. Command   17

        2. Reason   18

The context for this unit derives from the reference to the location for the events described here as Shittim (v. 1). It is significant that neither at the beginning nor at the end does an itinerary formula bind this unit into the wilderness theme. This failure, plus the reference to Shittim (→ Numbers 22–24), suggests a closer contact between this unit and the conquest traditions (→ Numbers 22–24). In the light of this characteristic, it is important to notice the role of Moses. Moses speaks (v. 5); indeed, the Lord addresses Moses (v. 10). But the unit is not a Moses tradition.

The initial element in the unit reports an event from the life of the people, an event that occurred at Shittim. The event is described in general terms as "playing the harlot" *(liznôt)* with the daughters of Moab. Verse 2 defines that rather general verb as involvement with the sacrifices, sacred meals, and worship before the gods of the Moabites. The enticement comes from Moabite women, but no explicit reference to a sexual event appears here. The description remains general. Yet, specific or general, the act was apostasy from the Lord, and the Lord responds in anger (v. 3). He instructs Moses to hang the leaders of the people in order to divert the anger and by implication, the corresponding plague (v. 4). Moses then passes the instructions to the judges of the people (v. 5). "Slay each man his men who have yoked themselves to Baal Peor." Apostasy at the beginning of the entry into the land brings execution for the guilty. Loyalty to Yahweh is essential for inheriting the land.

Report of a new event appears in v. 6. The critical nature of the shift in the narration from the anecdote about apostasy at Baal Peor to this anecdote is marked by the Hebrew syntax. Not only does the sentence begin with the structural marker, *wĕhinnēh* (and behold), but also the sentence features inversion in word order and its corresponding construction of the verb as a participle. New principals appear: Phinehas, the son of Eleazar, the son of Aaron, sees an Israelite man and a Midianite woman enter a family dwelling, and the time for the event is also the time of mourning, apparently over the execution of the guilty at Baal Peor. If that connection is correct, then this event must be understood as a specific case of the apostasy at Baal Peor. And indeed, the introduction, v. 1, suggests that the apostasy involves the actions of the Israelites with Moabite women. The identity of the woman is nonetheless a problem. The foe for the event at Baal Peor was the daughters of Moab. Here the woman is a citizen of Midian. Would this shift between Moab and Midian not reflect the same traditio-historical problem as the one reflected in the identity of the elders who called Balaam to curse Israel (so, 22:3, 7)?

The focus of the element in v. 6 does not emerge, however, until the results of the event fall into place, vv. 7-13. Verses 7-8a report a response to this public event involving an Israelite man and a Midianite woman by one Phinehas. Immediately, the son of Eleazar, the son of Aaron the priest takes a weapon to the couple's inner room and kills them. No reference to a plague spreading among the people appears before the act. The previous element has called only for the execution of the leaders of the people. But the text makes the point explicit here that the act of Phinehas not only sanctifies the community but also wards off a plague. Verse 9 then specifies that the plague had already killed twenty-four thousand people.

The point in the element gains explicit formulation in vv. 10-13. Because Phinehas acted so quickly (out of jealousy for the Lord's jealousy), he saved the rest of the people from death by the plague. And that event becomes the foundation stone for making Phinehas and all of his descendants priests. The key phrase in this ordination ritual, "covenant of a perpetual priesthood" *(běrît kěhunnat 'ôlām),* indeed, the act of execution for the guilty, recalls the ordination of the Levites (→ Exod 32:25-29; 40:15) and suggests that at least one function of the perpetual priesthood was to forestall the wrath of God's holiness that surely would consume an unholy people if they had no protection. This process carries two technical terms: "Because he was *jealous* for his God *(qinnē' lē'lôhāyw)* and he *atoned* for the Israelites *(wayěkappēr 'al-běnê yiśrā'ēl)."* The priesthood requires fierce loyalty to God. But it atones for the violation of that loyalty by stopping God's anger. Verses 12-13a establish that reality by their performative word.

Verses 14-15 present information about the guilty parties without intrinsic demands for the information from the body of the unit. Then vv. 16-18 add an address to Moses that sanctifies the perpetual hostility between Israel and Midian. Significantly, two references in this element to the events at Peor tie these final elements into the opening account of apostasy at Peor.

The latest level in this unit expands an older anecdote about apostasy at Baal Peor with a second anecdote in order to make that account the foundation of an ordination tradition for the priesthood of Phinehas. This part of the unit reflects the interests of the priestly source, in all probability a late addition to P (so, Noth, 196). Verses 1-5 derive from the Yahwist. In itself, it is a complete unit, reporting the events of apostasy at Baal Peor, unencumbered with the details representing Phinehas as the hero of the events.

Genre

The unit as a whole maintains its character as an ANECDOTE, a report of a critical event. At this level, it may in fact reflect a tightly structured combination of traditions reporting the events: (1) the apostasy at Baal Peor, and (2) the ordination of Phinehas. The priestly account probably did not exist independently of the antecedents in the account of the apostasy at Baal Peor. The earlier account also appears to have been an ANECDOTE, a REPORT of an event intrinsic to the interest of the Yahwist.

Setting

The latest level of the tradition comes from the redaction of the Pentateuch as a whole, with its emphasis on the reflexive relationship between event (the apostasy) and law (leading to execution) and ritual (the atonement for the rest of the people). The interests of the priesthood doubtlessly assert some influence on the expanded form of the pericope. The oldest level shows the concern of the Yahwist to depict rebellion, indeed, rejection for Israel at key points in the traditions of the past (compare the Yahwist's emphasis on rebellion in the wilderness). A pre-Yahwistic account may have rested in the memory of the folk, a part of the storyteller's material.

Intention

At its latest stage, the unit accounts for the position of a particular facet within the structures of the Aaronic priesthood, similar in ordination if not identity to the Levites (→ Exod 32:25-29). The priestly expansion demonstrates the role of the priests in defending the people in the face of the holiness of God. The earlier level accounts for apostasy at the beginning of the conquest, thus for another event like the murmuring that accounts for a rejection of the earlier generations of God's people. Would this rejection not stand in sharp contrast to the emphasis on God's special gift to Israel in the person of a king, resident at the heart of the Balaam tradition in the preceding unit (→ 22:1–24:25).

Bibliography

G. Mendenhall, "The Incident at Beth Baal Peor," in *The Tenth Generation: The Origins of the Biblical Tradition* (Baltimore: Johns Hopkins Press, 1973) 105-21; S. C. Reiff, "What Enraged Phinehas? A Study of Numbers 25:8," *JBL* 90 (1971) 100-106.

Census/Conscription Report (25:19–26:65; NRSV 26:1-65)

Structure

I. Speech report   25:19–26:2
  A. Notation of time   25:19 (*NRSV* 26:1)
  B. Introduction: the Lord to Moses and Eleazar   26:1
  C. Instructions for census   2
II. Speech report   3-4a
  A. Introduction: Moses and Eleazar to the people   3
  B. Instructions for census   4a
III. Execution of instructions   4b-51
  A. Introduction to the census list   4b

B. Census list   5-50
  1. Reuben   5-11
    a. Introductory formula   5a
    b. List of Reuben's sons   5b-6
    c. Conclusion   7
    d. Sub-groups   8-11
      1) List of second generation   8
      2) List of third generation   9-11
        a) List proper   9a
        b) Report of their fate   9b-11
  2. Simon   12-14
    a. Introductory formula $12a\alpha$
    b. List of Simon's sons $12a\beta$-13
    c. Conclusion   14
  3. Gad   15-18
    a. Introductory formula $15a\alpha$
    b. List of Simeon's sons $15a\beta$-17
    c. Conclusion   18
  4. Judah   19-22
    a. Introductory formula $19a\alpha$
    b. List of Judah's sons $19a\beta$-b
      1) List proper $19\alpha\beta$
      2) Report of fate   19b
    c. Introductory formula $20a\alpha$
    d. List of Judah's sons $20a\beta$-b
    e. Sub-group: list of second generation   21
    f. Conclusion   22
  5. Issachar   23-25
    a. Introductory formula $23a\alpha$
    b. List of Issachar's sons $23a\beta$-24
    c. Conclusion   25
  6. Zebulun   26-27
    a. Introductory formula $26a\alpha$
    b. List of Zebulun's sons $26a\beta$-b
    c. Conclusion   27
  7. Joseph   28-37
    a. Introductory formula   28a
    b. List of Joseph's sons   28b
    c. Sub-groups   29-37
      1) Manasseh, son of Joseph   29-34
        a) Introductory formula $29a\alpha_1$
        b) List of Manasseh's sons $29a\alpha_2$
        c) Sub-groups $29a\beta$-33
          (1) Second generation: sons of Machir $29a\beta$
          (2) Third generation: sons of Gilead   29b-33
            (a) Introductory formula   29b
            (b) List   30-32

	(c) Sub-groups	33
	α. Introductory formula	33a
	β. List	33b
	d) Conclusion	34
	2) Ephraim, son of Joseph	35-37
	a) Introductory formula	35aα
	b) List of Ephraim's sons	35aβ-b
	c) Sub-group: sons of Shuthelah	36
	(1) Introductory formula	36a
	(2) List	36b
	d) Conclusion	37
	8. Benjamin	38-41
	a. Introductory formula	38aα$_1$
	b. List	38aα$_2$-39
	c. Sub-groups: sons of Bela	40
	1) Introductory formula	40aα
	2) List	40aβ-b
	d. Conclusion	41
	9. Dan	42-43
	a. Introductory formula	42aα
	b. List	42aβ
	c. Conclusion	42b-43
	1) For Dan	42b
	2) For sub-group	43
	10. Asher	44-47
	a. Introductory formula	44aα
	b. List	44aβ-46
	c. Conclusion	47
	11. Naphtali	48-50
	a. Introductory formula	48aα
	b. List	48aβ-49
	c. Conclusion	50
	C. Conclusion	51
IV.	Speech report	52-56
	A. Introduction: the Lord to Moses	52
	B. Speech	53-56
	1. Instructions for dividing land	53
	2. Principle for decisions	54-55
	a. Size of the tribe	54
	b. Lot	55
	3. Summary	56
V.	Levi	57-62
	A. Introductory formula	57aα
	B. List	57aβ-b
	C. Introductory formula	58aα$_1$
	D. List	58aα$_2$-aβ
	E. Sub-groups	58b-61

1. Kohath, father of Amran 58b-59
   a. Introductory formula 58b
   b. Wife of Amram 59
      1) Genealogical data for the wife 59a
      2) Birth of sons 59b
2. Aaron, son of Amram 60-61
   a. List of Aaron's sons 60
   b. Report of their fate 61
F. Conclusion 62
   1. Concluding formula 62a
   2. Explanations 62b
      a. Legal status of census 62bα
      b. Reasons 62bβ
VI. Conclusion 63-65
   A. General formula 63
   B. Comparison with earlier census 64-65
      1. Difference 64
      2. Reasons 65a-bα
      3. Exceptions 65bβ

The census list belongs to that group of units within the wilderness theme related in some manner to the conquest (→ The Framework, Chapter 3, FOTL IIA). The census, at least in the final form, looks forward to the division of the land as portions of inheritance for the tribes. It thus provides a structural pivot anticipating the legal problem in inheritance developed in Numbers 27, as well as traditions dealing with inheritance of land in the subsequent chapters of Numbers. One might note that none of the preceding units that concern the conquest traditions involve questions of inheritance.

The census is structured into the narrative context of the wilderness theme under the general pattern of instructions — execution of instructions. Thus, the unit opens with two speeches, one a Yahweh speech to Moses and Eleazar, the other a speech from Moses and Eleazar to the people, both calling for a new census of the people. The census then follows as an account of proper execution of the instructions. The second speech is problematic at just this point. It is apparently incomplete, composed now of only a fragment (4a). That fragment parallels v. 2aβ in the first speech and suggests that the structure of the second speech, perhaps originally elliptical, intended the same instructions as the first. Even without a reconstruction of the speech, its function is clear. Unfortunately, v. 4b is equally problematic. And its position in the overall unit is not so clear. The lead expression in this element normally serves as a narrative formula for describing proper execution of instructions. But it is incomplete (thus, compare Num 1:19). The second part of the formula, "the Israelites who came out of the land of Egypt," may be intended to complete the formula. But the content of the phrase, as well as its position at the head of the census list, suggests that it now functions as the list's introduction (thus, cf. Gen 46:8).

The census list is structured according to the division of the tribes, the traditional ordering of administrative groups (→ Genesis 46). As a part of that tradition, it reflects a typical problem. Levi is excluded from the list, ordered not only after the concluding formula in v. 51 (→ Exod 1:1-14) but also after an intervening speech designating the procedure for dividing the land. The normal procedure in lists excluding Levi is to replace Joseph with Manasseh and Ephraim. Variation on that procedure might call for subordination of Ephraim to Joseph and entry of Manasseh as an independent group (thus, Numbers 1). But here Manasseh and Ephraim are both subordinated under Joseph as a single structural entry in the list, leaving only *eleven* tribal categories. The subordination is accomplished by including the Ephraim/Manasseh entries within introductory and concluding formulas designating Joseph as the major category. Since the concluding Joseph formula has no reference to the total number in the group, the inclusion is weakened. It suggests that the original structure of the list built on Manasseh and Ephraim as elements in a twelve-fold pattern. The subordination in the list would thus anticipate vv. 57-62, the Levi entry, as a part of the census tradition (thus, cf. Exod 1:1-14, with its exclusion of Joseph).

Each tribal entry in the list builds on three elements: (1) a brief introduction designating the name of the tribe and the unit of counting controlled by families (see also Num 1:22), (2) the list of family names constructed regularly with the name plus genitive *lāmed* and the family name constructed with a genitive suffix (thus emphasizing the list as a collection of family units, not a register of all names represented by the list), and (3) a concluding formula containing a general designation of families, "these are the families of Simeon," and a number qualifying the collective membership represented by the entry. Entries for Simeon, Gad, Issachar, Zebulun, and Naphtali employ only these elements.

Several breaks in the basic pattern, however, extend the structure of the entry. Reuben, Judah, Joseph, Benjamin, Dan, and Asher incorporate genealogical data within the census structure by tracing the families represented by the entries to subsequent generations. In most of these instances, the structural function of the sub-group is to include an anecdote about some particular member of the subsequent generation (so, vv. 9b-11, 19b). In the Judah entry, introductory formula and list are repeated following the anecdote, and only at that point does the extension of the list to a second generation occur (v. 21). There is no anecdote at just this point. But the allusion to Perez and Zerah, with emphasis falling on Perez, must be related to the tradition preserved in Genesis 38. In the same manner, the Manasseh entry extends to the sixth generation, with a brief allusion to the daughters of Zelophehad. No anecdote appears. But the allusion should be related to Numbers 27. The break in the Joseph entry derives from the peculiar problem in the list tradition, noted in the discussion above. Finally, several breaks in the pattern, again extending the list to subsequent generations, have no recognizable ties to external traditions. These include Ephraim, Benjamin, Dan, and Asher. In the Dan entry, the problem is more complicated, since the concluding formula for Dan omits the census matter, and then repeats itself with the sub-group name as the formula lead. And at this point the number appears. In each of these cases, perhaps some tradition unknown to us but as well known to the past as Genesis 38 and Numbers 27 has been incorporated into the list. (For structural inclusion of anecdotes built on larger traditions, see Gen 46:8ff.)

The formula in v. 51 closes the census lists with a general list designation: "These are the numbers of the Israelites." The characteristic demonstrative, "these" *('ēlleh),* appears here but not in the introduction, v. 4b. The closing also features a specification of the total number encompassed by the list. The entry for Levi is separated from the list, not only by the concluding formula in v. 51 (cf. Exod 1:5), but also by the intervening speech in vv. 52-56. The speech defines the purpose of the primary census list, thus excluding Levi from that purpose. The entry for Levi reflects the same basic pattern of structure noted for each entry in the primary list, plus two types of expansion that break the pattern. The first break comes with a duplication of the introductory formula and family list (see the entry for Judah). The second introduces a series of sub-groups leading to an anecdote about the birth of Moses, Aaron, and Miriam (cf. Exod 6:20) and a second anecdote about Aaron's sons (cf. the emphasis on Aaron in the Exodus 6 list). Significantly, the introduction of sub-groups relates not to the family list associated with the second introductory formula, but to the family list in the first formula. The two expansions of the entry thus seem closely tied together.

The final element in the unit, vv. 63-65, contains a general formula for the conclusion of a name list, remarkably without a qualifying number, and an explicit point of comparison with the census list in Numbers 1. The point of comparison ties into the murmuring tradition in the wilderness theme by defining the present state of Israel's census as the result of punishment against the murmurers. The people are now poised at the edge of the land, ready to take their inheritance.

The census list as it now appears can be related to the priestly source (thus, Noth). Characteristics of this stage in the tradition history include designation of purpose in division of the land. The numbers in the concluding formulas may also be secondary in the history of the list (so, Noth). Yet, the number element has a consistent structural function in such lists not originally genealogical in character and more probably belongs to the primary structure of the unit (cf. Genesis 46; Exodus 1; Numbers 1). Any particular set of numbers may have been manipulated to fit new settings employing the list. The list tradition apparently draws from an early, premonarchical period (so, Noth, Mendenhall).

Genre

The unit in Numbers 26, incorporated by speech formulas into a larger narrative context, maintains its identity nonetheless as a CENSUS LIST, even to the final stage of its history. Perhaps the most characteristic element of structure in the CENSUS LIST, distinguishing the list from a genealogy, is the designation of the number of members represented by each census group. That the numbers qualify the entire group in the tribe, not any one of the class within the group, does not exclude the number from the census list as secondary (against Noth), but only points to the focus in the particular list. The numbers could have qualified each clan entry without altering the structure of the list in any way except length.

The genre of the list begins to take on characteristics of genealogy by the expansion of each entry into subsequent generations (so, see Genesis 46). But the expansions do not serve original functions in the CENSUS LIST, but rather open possibilities for including secondary anecdotes or allusions to anecdotes within the limits of the census.

Stereotyped formulas for introducing and concluding name lists define the junctures in the development of the list.

Setting

In the final form, this census list belongs to the special interests of the priestly source, marking a shift in structure to traditions explicitly concerned with legal problems involved in inheritance procedures on the land. Use of the list in just this fashion denotes its functional capacity in administrative settings. The administrative institution interested in lists of this sort was commonly military (so, Noth, Mendenhall), although economic interests could also be represented (so, Mendenhall, who excludes this alternative for Israel). Evidence in this list points to its origin in military circles (thus, the qualification of the census groups with the noun "host" (ṣābā') in v. 2; cf. also Num 1:3).

Intention

In its final stage, the census list in Numbers 26 describes the administrative units in Israel necessary for defining portions of inheritance in the land. It thus anticipates conquest traditions such as the ones found in the following units of Numbers. A census list normally would function as a definition of administrative divisions within a people, whether the specific purpose of the administration be taxation, military mobilization, or some other task. The mobilization quality of the tradition presented here can still be detected in v. 2 (cf. also Num 1:3). The shift in function from mobilization to land administration can perhaps be seen in the Levite entry, in contrast to its counterpart in Num 1:47-53. In the Numbers 1 parallel, explicit instructions forbid numbering the Levites because the peculiar duties of the Levites exclude military. In Num 26:57-62, the intention no longer lies on mobilization. Thus, the Levites are numbered. And the numbering reflects the new function of this list as an instrument for dividing the land. To limit the function of a census to military mobilization or taxation seems unnecessarily restrictive. The intention of a list generally should thus be defined broadly as definition of administrative units (cf. Genesis 46; Exodus 1).

Bibliography

G. E. Mendenhall, "The Census Lists of Numbers 1 and 26," *JBL* 77 (1958) 52-66; M. Noth, *Das System der zwölf Stämme Israels* (BWANT 4/1; Stuttgart: Kohlhammer, 1930).

Case Report, the Daughters of Zelophehad (27:1-11)

Structure

I. Introduction	1
A. Definition of topic	1aα₁
B. Identity of litigants	1aα₂-b
1. Genealogical data	1aα₂-aβ
2. Name list	1b
II. Speech report	2-4
A. Introduction	2
1. Daughters to Moses, Eleazar, leaders, congregation	2a
2. Place	2b
B. Speech	3-4
1. Declaration of father's legal status	3
a. Death report	3aα
b. Relationship with Korah	3aβ-b
2. Appeal	4
a. Crisis	4a
b. Request	4b
III. Transition: appeal to the Lord	5
IV. Speech report	6-11
A. Introduction: the Lord to Moses	6
B. Speech	7-11
1. Judgment about the appeal	7
2. Message commission formula	8a
3. Message	8b-11
a. Designation of inheritance sequence	8b-11a
b. Concluding formula	11b

This case report about the appeal of the daughters of Zelophehad follows the census list in Numbers 26 quite naturally since this unit defines more precisely the circumstances surrounding the legal process of inheritance, a process called for by the census (cf. Num 26:52-56). The case report thus shares in the complex problems posed by the conquest traditions within the scope of the wilderness theme (→ The Framework, Chapter 3, FOTL IIA). The report is separated, however, from the following two chapters by a marked shift in genre and loss of thematic unity. The impact of this point is to emphasize the unique position of the following two chapters in the collection of legal traditions represented by Numbers 26–36.

This unit comprises two major structural elements (II, IV), a transition between them (III), and a brief introduction (I). The introduction defines the subject of the unit with a technical term: "The daughters of Zelophehad . . . drew near" *(wattiqrabnâ)*. The same verb appears, again with technical connotations, in v. 5 (cf. also Num 36:1). The term means generally to approach the altar, the sanctuary, or any holy object (cf. Exod 12:48; Num 17:5). It can connote ordination of a priest (cf. Exod 29:4, 8, 10: 40:12, 14). In Num 27:1 the verb connotes presentation of a lawsuit, drawing near to the sanctuary in order to present a legal appeal (cf. Isa 5:19; 41:1). The remaining data about the subject of the verb, both the genealogical data and the name list, identify the litigants (cf. Num 26:29-33).

Verse 2 now stands as a part of the speech formula for the second element of the unit. But it functions more adequately as an elaboration of the introduction. To draw near for a lawsuit also means to stand before Moses, Eleazar, the leaders, and the congregation at the tent of meeting. The stage is set for a trial, a civil suit designed to determine the legitimacy of the daughters' claim for inheritance rights. In Num 36:1, an introduction contains a similar two-pronged definition of the appeal process.

Two major speeches present an appeal from an existing law (vv. 3-4) and the judgment in response to the appeal (vv. 6-11). The appeal speech comprises two major elements. The first (v. 3) defines the legal status of the father. The point of the definition is to claim that even though the father died in the wilderness, his death was not the result of legal punishment against the rebels of Korah's company ($\rightarrow$ Numbers 16). The implication is that had the father been executed with Korah, he would have forfeited his claim, and the claim of his estate, for inheritance in Israel (cf. Weingreen). The way is open, as a result of the father's legal record, for his estate to claim a share of the inheritance proceedings. The appeal itself, v. 4, presupposes a law, or at least an established practice for inheritance limiting the line of succession to male heirs (cf. Deut 21:15). The first part of the appeal states the legal problem. The father had no sons to establish proper inheritance lines. Thus, the family name, especially the family property, now stand under threat of extinction. The second part of the appeal, posed as a question, calls for recognition of a daughter's right to inherit when she has no brothers to insure the family property.

Verse 5 provides a transition between the appeal and divine judgment on the merits of the case. Significantly, this verse shows the special function of the verb "to bring near" *(wayyaqrēb)*. Introduced by a speech formula designating the judgment as divine, the speech opens with a declaration about the case: "The daughters of Zelophehad are right." Then an elaboration of the judgment, cast as a message to the Israelites generally, defines the line of succession in inheritance cases. The line of succession, minus the daughters in the family, doubtlessly represents the old procedure. The precedent for defining procedure in administration of previously established inheritance law is thus pronounced. The concluding formula, v. 11b, proclaims the new ruling as the prevailing principle, an addition to the law.

The case report in Numbers 27 derives from the priestly source (so, Noth). But the legal tradition preserved by the report doubtlessly antedates P. The outlines of inheritance principles appear already in Deuteronomy. And the basis for this appeal sets the process firmly in that tradition. Certainly, it would be reasonable to assume that the antecedents for the ruling lie in a period when possession of property might still be a live issue.

Genre

This unit is a CASE REPORT preserving a precedent establishing procedure in legal disputes over inheritance lines (cf. Lev 24:10-23; Num 9:6-14; 15:32-36; 36:1-12).

Setting

The literary setting for this case report belongs to the redactional interests of the priestly source. The unit deals with an issue involving a civil issue, not a cultic law. To be sure, the locale for resolving the case is defined as the tent of meeting, in the presence of Eleazar, the priest. The cultic element is thus preserved. But it is significant that the judges include more persons than the priest. Moses, the leaders, and the entire congregation are involved in the process, and Moses, not the priest, mediates the appeal to Yahweh. These elements suggest that the setting may have originally involved the legal institution represented by the convocation of the elders.

Intention

The unit is judicial, not legislative. It is important to remember that judicial proceedings become binding, thus developing the force of legislation. But the primary intention of the unit is to establish legal precedent on which previously existing law can be administered. It is significant, then, that the impact of the judgment lies not simply on the rights of the daughters, although the case of the daughters is just and provides the precedent. The judgment defines the entire line of succession applicable to all Israel. The specific intention of the unit, then, focuses on the line of succession in inheritance cases involving an estate with no legal male heirs, no sons of the dead patriarch. The daughters now have a right to be considered in the resolution of the estate. But significantly, if the dead man had no daughters, then the succession line runs entirely through male relatives of the patriarch.

Bibliography

N. H. Snaith, "The Daughters of Zelophehad," *VT* 16 (1966) 124-27; J. Weingreen, "The Case of the Daughters of Zelophehad," *VT* 16 (1966) 518-22.

Commission Report (27:12-23)

Structure

I. Speech report   12-14
  A. Introduction: the Lord to Moses   12aα
  B. Speech   12aβ-14
    1. Sentence of judgment   12αβ-13
    2. Reason   14
      a. Accusation   14a
      b. Gloss   14b
II. Speech report   15-17
  A. Introduction: Moses to the Lord   15
  B. Speech   16-17
    1. Request for successor   16
    2. Purpose   17
III. Commission speech report   18-21
  A. Introduction: the Lord to Moses   18aα₁
  B. Speech   18aα₂-21
    1. Instructions for commission   18aα₂-20
      a. Conversion rite   18aα₂-b
      b. Investiture   19-20
        1) Designation of place   19a
        2) Instructions for investiture 19b-20a
        3) Purpose   20b
    2. Description of successor's task   21
      a. Relationship with priest   21a
      b. Military responsibility   21b
IV. Execution of instructions   22-23

This unit has no clear relationship to its context. Indeed, the context necessitated shortening the unit, fundamentally altering the structural pattern. The parallel unit in Num 20:22-29 reports Aaron's death in conjunction with a commission for Aaron's successor. This unit begins in the same way with a judgment of death for Moses (vv. 12-14). But since the context maintains Moses as an active participant, the unit cannot report Moses' death at this point (so, Noth). The closest point of contact for the unit would be the Moses' death report in Deut 34:1-12.

Three major speeches, followed by a brief narrative account reporting that instructions in the third speech were faithfully executed, comprise the scope of this unit. The first speech, vv. 12-14, parallels Num 20:24 and announces a death sentence against Moses. It opens with instructions for Moses to go up into a mountain (cf. LXX, harmonizing this text with Deut 34:1) in order to view the land promised to his people. The instructions here reflect the judgment from Num 20:12 (cf. also Num 14:20-23) prohibiting Moses from entering the land. He can see the land promised to his people. But no more. The element parallels instructions to Moses and Aaron in Num 20:25, designating the scene of action as a mountaintop (so, Noth). And it probably presupposes Moses' death on a mountain, just as Aaron lies on a mountain (cf. Deut 34:1-12). This conclusion is confirmed by the judgment in vv. 13-14. The sentence in v. 13 designates the time: "When you have seen it. . . ." And the point is clear: "You shall be gathered *(wĕne'ĕsaptā)* to your people, just as Aaron your brother was gathered *(ne'ĕsap)*." The allusion recalls Num 20:24. Verse 14 establishes the case; the motivation for the judgment is the same as it was in Aaron's case (so, 20:24). Thus, the point of the first speech is that Moses must die.

Contrary to the Aaron parallel, here the Lord's instructions to Moses do not mention a successor. Rather, they break off with the death judgment. The second speech addresses a request of Moses to the Lord that a successor be appointed. The speech not only calls for an act of commission but designates the purpose of the call. Without a leader, the people would be like sheep without a shepherd (cf. 1 Kgs 22:17). The entire speech reflects the category of leadership requested as a category limited to military (so, Noth). The shift in structure at this point, in contrast to Num 20:22-29, points to subordination of the death sentence to the request for and installation of a new leader.

The third speech, the second Yahweh speech, parallels the second part of a single Yahweh speech in Num 20:25-26. It provides instructions for commissioning a successor for Moses, instructions to be carried out by Moses, the addressee. A new element in the rite, not mentioned in instructions for commissioning Eleazar, appears here. Moses is to lay his hands on the successor, an act that reflects contact with sacrificial ritual (cf. Num 8:10). In addition, the speech commissions an investiture rite parallel to Num 20:26. But the rite involves adorning Joshua, the appointed successor, with Moses' glory rather than his garment. Finally, the commission describes the successor's task, a task focused in the military with all other functions subordinate to the priest. MT has an ambiguous subject for the lead verb in v. 21: "He shall stand before Eleazar the priest and he (LXX reads "they") shall ask him for the judgment of the Urim before the Lord." If the subject should be the people rather than Joshua, then the focus of the verse falls simply on the task of the priest and is irrelevant to the context. The subject should be understood as Joshua.

The unit ends with a notation that commissioning instructions were carried out properly (// 20:27-28). Significantly, no notice of Moses' death appears, no report of the death to the people, although the development of the unit calls for such continuation. For what other reason would Moses relinquish his leadership? The unit simply breaks off before the line of narration is complete.

The priestly source claims this unit of material. Its similarity with Num 20:22-29 shows some type of relationship with the report of Aaron's death. It may be that the Aaron tradition was modeled on this unit, perhaps an original form of the Moses tradition that included a death report (→ Deuteronomy 34). It may be that the tradition lying behind this unit, including a death report, has been shaped by priestly redaction, not only to open the way for additional traditions involving Moses, but also in subordination of Moses' successor to the priest. Tradition history for this unit includes the doublet in Deut 32:48-52 and the death report in 34:1-12. Significantly, these two units of tradition are separated by Deuteronomy 33, the blessing of Moses, not an original part of either report.

Genre

In its present form, this unit is a REPORT about commissioning a successor for Moses. It may well be that an installation genre stands behind this element (see McCarthy). But if so, it does not directly affect the structure of the unit. An installation speech would be addressed to the successor. In this unit, as well as the parallel in Num 20:22-29, instructions for installation are addressed to the installing agency (cf. 1 Sam 16:12). The unit nevertheless reflects the basic function of a DEATH REPORT. Substantial in this genre is the JUDGMENT SPEECH, built on a DEATH SENTENCE and proper justification for it (→ Num 20:22-29). In addition, instructions for installing a successor as a guarantee for continued leadership are not foreign to the DEATH REPORT (against Noth; cf. 2 Kgs 2:1-18).

Setting

As a part of a larger literary context, this unit reflects the interests of the priestly source in completing the traditions of Moses' life, yet maintaining the opening for Moses in subsequent narratives. The tradition itself reflects the life-setting characteristic for the Moses heroic saga and its successors (→ The Exodus Saga, Chapter 1A, FOTL IIA, and The Framework, Chapter 3, FOTL IIA).

Intention

The unit in its present form reports the commission of Joshua as Moses' successor. But it is somewhat out of context since Joshua does not assume leadership within the scope of the immediate context. The original form of the tradition intended to report not only commission for a new leader in Moses' place, but also the death of Moses, the end of an era.

Bibliography

D. J. McCarthy, "An Installation Genre?" *JBL* 90 (1971) 31-41.

Ritual Calendar (28:1–30:1; *NRSV* 28:1–29:40)*

Structure

I. Speech report		28:1–29:39
A. Introduction: the Lord to Moses		28:1
B. Speech		28:2–29:39

*See Annotation to Num 15:1-16.

1. Message commission formula	28:2a
2. Message: sacrifice ordinance	28:2b
3. Message commission formula	28:3aα
4. Message	28:3αβ-29:39
a. Ordinary sacrifice ritual	3αβ-8
1) Sacrifice instructions	3αβ-7
a) Sacrificial objects	3αβ-b
b) Time clause	4
c) Cereal offering	5
d) Identification formula	6
e) Libation	7
2) Sacrifice instructions	8
a) Time clause	8a
b) Cereal offering	8bα₁
c) Libation	8bα₂
d) Identification	8bβ
b. Calendar for sacrifice	28:9–29:39
1) Sabbath	28:9-10
a) Calendar element	9aα
b) Sacrificial objects	9aβ
c) Identification formula	10a
d) Ordinary	10b
2) Beginning of the month	11-15
a) Calendar element	11a
b) Sacrifice list	11b-13a
c) Identification formula	13b
d) Libation	14a
e) Identification formula	14b
f) Sin offering	15a
g) Ordinary	15b
3) Passover	16
a) Calendar element	16a
b) Identification formula	16b
4) Unleavened bread	17-25
a) Calendar element	17aα
b) Identification	17αβ
c) Duration qualifications	17b-25
(1) General designation	17b
(2) First day	18-23a
(a) Calendar element	18aα
(b) Call to convocation	18aβ-b
(c) Sacrifice list	19-21
(d) Sin offering	22
(e) Ordinary	23a
(3) Daily stipulation	23b-24
(a) Distributive element	23b-24aα
(b) Identification formula	24αβ

        (c) Ordinary   24b

(c) Ordinary	24b
(4) Seventh day	25
(a) Calendar element	$25a\alpha$
(b) Call to convocation	$25a\beta$-b
5) First fruits	26-31
a) Calendar element	26a
b) Call to convocation	26b
c) Sacrifice list	27-29
d) Sin offering	30
e) Ordinary	31
(1) Ordinary sacrifice	$31a\alpha$
(2) Cereal	$31a\beta$
(3) Admonition to perfection	$31b\alpha$
(4) Libation	$31b\beta$
6) Trumpet day	29:1-6
a) Calendar element	$1a\alpha_1$
b) Call to convocation	$1a\alpha_2$-aβ
c) Identification formula	1b
d) Sacrifice list	2-4
e) Sin offering	5
f) Ordinary	6
7) Day of atonement	7-11
a) Calendar element	$7a\alpha_1$
b) Call to convocation	$7a\alpha_2$-b
c) Sacrifice list	8-10
d) Sin offering	11a
e) Ordinary	11b
8) Tabernacles	12-38
a) Calendar element	$12a\alpha_1$
b) Call to convocation	$12a\alpha_2$-aβ
c) Duration qualifications	12b-38
(1) General designations	12b
(2) First day	13-16
(a) Sacrificial list	13-15
(b) Sin offering	16a
(c) Ordinary	16b
(3) Second day	17-19
(a) Calendar element	$17a\alpha$
(b) Sacrifice list	$17a\beta$-18
(c) Sin offering	19a
(d) Ordinary	19b
(4) Third day	20-22
(a) Calendar element	$20a\alpha_1$
(b) Sacrifice list	$20a\alpha_2$-21
(c) Sin offering	22a
(d) Ordinary	22b
(5) Fourth day	23-25

(a) Calendar element	23aα$_1$
(b) Sacrifice list	23aα$_2$-24
(c) Sin offering	25a
(d) Ordinary	25b
(6) Fifth day	26-28
(a) Calendar element	26aα$_1$
(b) Sacrifice list	26aα$_2$-27
(c) Sin offering	28a
(d) Ordinary	28b
(7) Sixth day	29-31
(a) Calendar element	29aα$_1$
(b) Sacrifice list	29aα$_2$-30
(c) Sin offering	31a
(d) Ordinary	31b
(8) Seventh day	32-34
(a) Calendar element	32aα$_1$
(b) Sacrifice list	32aα$_2$-33
(c) Sin offering	34a
(d) Ordinary	34b
(9) Eighth day	35-38
(a) Calendar element	35aα
(b) Call to convocation	35aβ-b
(c) Sacrifice list	36-37
(d) Sin offering	38a
(e) Ordinary	38b
c. Conclusion summary	39
II. Conclusion: Execution of instructions	30:1 (*NRSV* 29:40)

This unit is fully isolated in its present context. Indeed, its position here stands in abrupt contrast to the report of commission for Joshua as Moses' successor in Num 27:12-23 since here Moses continues as the intermediary between the Lord and his people. Perhaps this continuation would account for the loss of death notice from the tradition in Num 27:12-23 (so, Noth). Moreover, no intrinsic connection between this text and the unit following this one can be determined. The most obvious point of unity lies in the overall structure of the chapters as Yahweh speeches to Moses. But that structure is secondary and late.

The overall structural pattern for the unit builds with two major elements. The one, a Yahweh speech, addresses Moses with instructions to transmit to the people. The other is a brief narration element to report that the instructions were faithfully carried out. This scheme reflects the procedure necessary for incorporating the unit into its Pentateuchal context. Moreover, the speech develops under the control of two distinct messages to be delivered to the people. In both cases, message commission formulas mark off the message Moses must deliver to the people. The first one has a rare formulation: "Command the people of Israel *(ṣaw 'et-bĕnê yiśrā'ēl)* and say to them . . ." (28:2a). The formula nevertheless functions in precisely the same way as the more common formulation. The second formula follows the more typical pattern, building on the verb *'āmar,* "you shall say to them. . . ."

The message following the headline of the first commission formula sets the key for the entire unit. Moses is to instruct the Israelites to make sacrifices at the appointed times *(běmô'ădô).* But no explicit details identify the sacrifices themselves as the focus of the unit. Rather, the general character of the sacrifice list provides a foundation for building the following intricate superstructure. It legislates a series of sacrifices; the following message designates the appointed times for carrying those sacrifices out (→ Intention).

Structure in the second message again builds on two principal elements, plus a concluding summary. The first element, vv. 28:3aβ-8, sets out the ritual for the ordinary (daily) sacrifice. Other sacrifices may accompany the ordinary (thus, the second major element in this message). The quality and quantity of those sacrifices would be defined by the particularities of the day. But the sacrifice presented in the ritual prescribed here must be offered each day. The term "continual burnt offering" *('ōlâ tāmîd)* designates this ordinary, daily sacrifice (cf. Exod 29:38-46; Ezek 46:13-15).

The ritual begins with an introduction to identify the general category of sacrifice. Then instructions for procedure follow, with stereotyped ritual formulations. The series includes designation of time, procedure in preparing a cereal offering as a side sacrifice, a declaration formula with the sacrifice named as the ordinary, and finally stipulations for a libation as an additional side offering. The ritual concludes (v. 8) with a summary of each step in the sacrificial procedure, applied to the second animal to be offered in the day's ritual as if the basic ritual applied only to the first. The order of ritual elements presented by the summary reverses the position for libation and declaration of the sacrifice name. Whether this change or the separation of cereal and drink offerings in vv. 3b-7 by the declaration formula indicates a secondary role for the drink offering cannot be determined (cf. Num 15:1-10).

The second major element in the message lists special occasions for sacrifice and designates the special sacrifices to accompany the ordinary on each day. It should be noted that the sequence in the list of special days does not follow a simple pattern, beginning at the first of the year and running through to its completion. Rather, three different systems for structuring a cultic year can be seen: One set of sacrifices occurs each week, one set each month, and one with the seasons once a year.

Structure in the entries for each special day follows a stereotyped pattern, although extensive variations in the pattern for any given day commonly appear. The pattern includes at least five basic elements, sharing points in common with the structure of the ritual for the ordinary sacrifice. This point alone suggests that the unit as a whole preserves a ritual calendar, with the ritual focused specifically on sacrifice. The five elements include: (1) *A calendar formula.* The controlling principle for the structure of the section, these formulas vary according to the position of the day they represent in one of the three systems for organizing a cultic year. For days identified primarily in terms of a week system, the formula designates the number of the day in the week or simply the day's name. For the day celebrating the monthly sacrifice, the formula designates the relationship of the day in the scope of the month to the other parts of the month. For an annual festival, the formula designates not only the number of the day in the month but also the number of the month in the year. The calendar element in this section of the unit should be distinguished functionally from the designation of time for the sacrifice in the ritual (28:4). The one pinpoints the exact time in any day for the sacrifice. The other identifies the day in one of the systems for organizing the year.

(2) *A sacrifice list.* The sacrifice list begins with a verbal formulation calling in general for a burnt offering. This introduction is similar in structure but not in function to the identification formula, noted below. It regularly designates the sacrifice as an offering "to the Lord." But the designation varies from a simple "burnt offering to the Lord" (*'ōlâ lĕyhwh*) to a fuller "burnt offering, an offering by fire, a pleasing odor to the Lord" (*'ōlâ 'iššēh rêaḥ nîḥōaḥ lĕyhwh*). No clear significance can be seen in the formula's variation. The principal sacrifice list in each entry includes a designation of the special sacrifices of the day, regularly involving a specific number of bulls, rams, and lambs. The most consistent formula involves some variation on one or two bulls, one ram, and seven lambs. This should be contrasted in content, but not in structure, to the ritual element for the ordinary requiring only two lambs. In addition to the animals, the list requires a cereal offering, identified regularly on the formula of three-tenths ephah flour mixed with oil for bulls, two-tenths ephah flour with oil for rams, and one-tenth ephah mixed with oil for lambs. The requirement for a cereal offering for the lambs sacrificed in the ordinary corresponds with this formula. Significantly, only one special day, the beginning of the month, specifies a libation as an additional side offering, with designation of amounts of wine: one-half hin of wine for each bull, one-third hin of wine for each ram, and one-fourth hin of wine for each lamb. The Sabbath calls for a libation but does not specify amounts, while the days in the Feast of Tabernacles call for libation in a generalized formula. With regard to the peculiar position for a drink offering see the discussion below for comment about shift from explicit description of the sin offerings to a generalizing formula.

(3) *Sin offering.* Each day's ritual includes a sin offering (except the Sabbath and shortened entries in the Feast of Tabernacles) as a distinct element from both the sacrifice list and the ordinary. The sacrifice list regularly concludes with stipulations for side offering, either by explicit instructions or by a stereotyped formula (so, 29:18, et al.). Following these stipulations, the regulation for a sin offering, an additional animal, appears. Yet, even though the sin offering appears regularly in each day's ritual, it should not be considered a part of the ordinary. This distinction is established by the characteristic preposition introducing the ordinary, either *'al* or *millĕbad*. The sin offering formula contains normally only two elements: (a) the number and name of the animal to be sacrificed, always constructed in the same way, "one male goat," and (b) an identification formula, "a sin offering to the Lord" (*lĕhaṭṭā't lĕyhwh*).

(4) *The ordinary.* Each day's ritual requires the sacrifice stipulated in 28:3-8. The formula calling for the ordinary is regularly controlled by prepositions, either *'al* or *millĕbad*. The technical name of the sacrifice established in

the ritual then appears (with a Niph'al verb on occasion — 28:15, 24). And a final description calls for one or both side offerings.

(5) *Identification formula.* The ritual designates the name of the special day, as in the ritual for the ordinary, with a declaration formula. "This is the burnt offering of the Sabbath in each Sabbath." In addition to these five regular elements, several entries include a call to assembly. The assembly functions as the occasion for sacrifice with the entire congregation present. And because of its sacred nature, all work during the period is prohibited.

The first entry in the calendar list calls for celebration on the Sabbath. The calendar element here does no more than name the day, with the implication that the sacrifice should occur on that day each week. The sacrifice list contains no introductory element; it begins immediately with a designation of the sacrificial animals — two lambs — plus cereal offering in accord with the general formula for lambs. The Sabbath entry thus stands outside the series of lists in all the other entries calling for bull-ram-lamb sacrifice. The identification formula declares the name of the sacrifice, while the ordinary calls for the continual burnt offering plus its required libation. No reference to a cereal offering with the ordinary appears, thus compounding the problematic character of the side offering requirements in the ordinary ritual.

The second entry designates celebration on the first of "your months." The calendar element thus defines the day in relationship to the scope of the month, presupposing by its formulation "your months" that the celebration is recurring, not unique to one particular month. The sacrifice list begins with a normal introductory element. The list itself follows the normal formula with no requirement for a libation through v. 13a. Verse 13b identifies the name of the sacrifice with a general formula: "This is a burnt offering, a pleasing odor, an offering by fire to the Lord." This formula is similar in content to the introduction for the sacrifice list, suggesting simply that the tradition knew a set stock of names for the sacrifices in this unit. Following the identification formula, the ritual calls for a libation, with explicit formulas for each type of animal. And a new identification formula defines the entire sacrifice for the day, markedly distinct in formulation from the first formula: "This is a burnt offering for the month in its month, for all the months of the year." The formulation here is parallel to the identification formula in the Sabbath calendar (v. 10a). Separation between the libation requirement and the other parts of the ritual again suggests that the libation element stands in a unique relationship to the total ritual. This entry concludes with a sin offering formula and the ordinary.

The third entry is abbreviated, composed of only two in the normal sequence of elements. First is the calendar element, a date formula that designates not only the number of the day within the scope of the month, but also the number of the month in the structure of the year. The second element is an identification of the day, constructed with the name of the day and the now typical designation of relationship to the Lord: "It is the Passover of the Lord" (*pesaḥ lěyhwh*). The same formula appears in Exod 12:11bβ. The abbreviated character of this entry is also emphasized by construction of the calendar element for the next entry in v. 17. The number of the day in the month is indicated. But the month is identified in relationship to the calendar element for the Passover. The abbreviation of the one entry and dependency in construction in the other doubtlessly reflect the peculiar history of Passover and Unleavened Bread (cf. Kraus, de Vaux). Yet, the Unleavened Bread entry cannot be treated in the structure of the unit simply as a continuation of the Passover. It stands as a distinct entry, separated from the Passover entry by its full structure (cf. the new calendar element) as well as its originally independent position in the cultic year.

The calendar element in the Unleavened Bread entry shows dependency on the preceding Passover entry. The identification formula normally following the calendar element has in this case been sharply reduced and stands now simply as one word: "Festival!" *(ḥag)*. An example of the longer formula can be found in Lev 23:6. The festival celebration opens a new kind of calendar entry, with celebration not on one day within the year but over the course of an entire week. The next point of structure is thus a designation of duration for the festival. Ritual within the week is then organized by the day in the week, with structure for each day following basically the same pattern as that noted for special days not structured into a week's celebration. Verses 18-23a define the ritual for the first day in the festival, then vv. 23b-24 require the same ritual on each day of the festival (cf. identification formula and the ordinary formula with a call for libation in v. 24). With the exception of the final day (v. 25) it is thus not necessary to specify ritual for each of the days of the festival.

The entry for the first day of the festival begins with a calendar element, simply a designation of the day's number within the structure of the week (cf. above, the discussion of different systems in calendar elements). A new ritual element follows. A call to convocation designates the day as holy *(miqrā'-qōdeš)*. And as a corollary all work on that day is prohibited. This element occurs primarily as a part of the ritual for holy days of festival weeks (cf. Exod 12:16; Lev 23:7, 21, et al.). But it can stand in unique relationship to a week (cf. Lev 23:3). Then regular elements of the sacrifice ritual appear. The sacrifice list begins with a standard introduction; then follow the name and number of animals required for the day. The cereal offering with its stereotyped formula for preparation is also a part of the list. But no reference to a libation can be detected. The formula for a sin offering adds a new element, an explicit intention for the offering as atonement: ". . . in order to atone for you" *(lĕkappēr 'ălêkem)*. The formula for the ordinary surprisingly calls for only the morning sacrifice; no rationale for excluding the evening sacrifice, as called for in the ordinary ritual, can be seen.

The festival ritual concludes in v. 25 with an abbreviated sequence for the last (seventh) day. The calendar element here contains only the number of the day in the week (cf. v. 18). Then follow a call to convocation and prohibition for work. The parallel with the first day is clear, even though shortened, so that the only function of this entry is to mark completion of the sequence with an enclosure construction.

The next major entry in the calendar fits into the general scheme of three annual festivals (cf. Exod 23:14; Deuteronomy 16; Leviticus 23). The calendar element is problematic, however. It contains only a name for the day, parallel to the calendar element in the Sabbath entry: "In the day of the first fruits. . . ."

Moreover, the calendar element supports a dependent clause: ". . . when you present a new grain cereal offering to the Lord in your weeks. . . ." This clause is similar in content, although not in syntactical construction, to the introduction normally expected in a sacrifice list (cf. v. 11). Here no sacrifice list follows. Rather, a call to convocation and its corresponding prohibition for work appear, elements normally reserved for a week's festival. And following these elements, the sacrifice list appears with its normal introduction. These problems may reflect stages in the history of this cultic event, one remembering the celebration as a special day (cf. Lev 23:12), the other moving the event into a week-long celebration (cf. the designation of the celebration as "your weeks," běšābu'ōtêkem). The sacrifice list follows the standard formulation, including explicit directions for mixing the cereal offering, but no reference to a libation. The sin offering formula includes the intention for atonement. The ordinary separates a requirement for the cereal offering from a notation for libation by means of a call to perfection.

The celebration ritual for the seventh month dominates ch. 29. Some evidence that these days of celebration originally belonged to one festival can still be detected (cf. the discussion below). But in the present structure of the chapter, the first day of the month and the tenth day of the month stand as independent entries in the calendar. This stage of the festival tradition thus reflects the isolation of these two days from the Tabernacles.

Ritual for the first day of the month begins with a calendar element, designating both the number of the day and the number of the month. Thus, an annual event lies at the basis of the ritual. The second element calls for a convocation, then its corresponding prohibition against work. Again, the element here presupposes position of the day in a larger framework of celebration. But the character of the calendar entry shifts from the longer festival framework to the particularities of a single day. Verse 1b provides a name for the celebration, with vv. 2-4 a sacrifice list in normal construction. The only variation lies in the requirement for one bull, not two as in the other days of the calendar. The sin offering appears, again with its intention specified in atonement. And the ordinary with some slight variation calls for the sacrifice with its cereal offering. Significantly, the ordinary formula now receives a new kind of ending: Both cereal and libation with the ordinary are stipulated by means of a general formula: ". . . according to their custom" (kĕmišpāṭām). And the formula ends with an identification of the sacrifice as a pleasing odor, an offering by fire to the Lord (cf. the introduction to the sacrifice list). This change again points to the unique position of the libation in the history of the ordinary sacrifice. But the structure of the entry follows the pattern attested at other positions for a single-day celebration, thus isolating the day from the larger context of convocation in a week's festival.

Verses 7-11 detail the ritual for the second major day in the fall festival. The calendar element designates the day by the number in the month, and the month by its number in the year. But here, like 28:17, the element shows dependency on the preceding entry with the demonstrative pronoun "this." The second day thus cannot be completely divorced from the pattern of an original festival holding all these events together (cf. 28:17). The next segment of the entry calls for a convocation on the tenth day and complements the call with a prohibition for work. As in the first day, so here the call for convocation presupposes the position of the day in a larger festival. The character of that day is specified by an addition to the convocation call, "you shall afflict yourselves" (→ Lev 23:27). This notation places the day in the category of the Day of Atonement festival, subsequently known in the cultic calendar as an independent celebration (cf. the ordinary element in the entry). In regular formulation the sacrifice list is introduced with general instructions to present a sacrifice, then with specifications for the sacrificial ritual. In this case only one bull qualifies as the first entry in the list, suggesting a pattern for the fall festival (cf. vv. 2, 36). The cereal offering, with specific formula for composition, concludes the list. Sin offering without atonement formula follows, but the ordinary formula denotes not only the burnt sacrifice with its cereal and libation offerings, but explicitly a sin offering for atonement *(ḥaṭṭa't hakkippurîm)*. The celebration in concluding formulas characterizes this ritual for the day of atonement.

The most extensive entry in the calendar list comes with the Feast of Tabernacles, beginning of the third major celebration day of the month. The calendar element designates the number of the day in the month as well as the number of the month, without reference to the demonstrative pronoun used to qualify dependency in multiple days of celebration. The calendar element is followed immediately by a call to convocation and its corresponding prohibition for work. The structure of the entry here, however, parallels 28:17-25 by designating the convocation as a part of a festival. The designation of festival functions in the entry as a duration clause, defining the scope of the celebration. At this point, however, a problem in structure appears. The parallel in 28:17 constructs the ritual for the first day of the festival immediately following the duration clause. Here a sacrifice list appears (vv. 13-15). Significantly, the sacrifice list doubles the requirement for rams and lambs and stipulates thirteen bulls. This pattern, with decreasing number for the bulls, characterizes each day of the seven-day celebration in the festival. Thus, the sacrifice list marks the beginning of the ritual for the first day of the series, even though the first day entry does not carry the normal calendar element. Moreover, the sacrifice list includes the cereal offering according to the stipulated formula. The final two entries in the first-day ritual correspond to the normal sin offering formula, as well as an ordinary formula including both cereal and libation. The second entry in the festival does employ a calendar element, specifying the day simply by its number in the week. No introduction to the sacrifice list marks the movement to the next element. The only item of note here is that the list follows the regular formula, with rams and lambs doubled in number and bulls designated at twelve. Both cereal and libation offerings are described in summary fashion "by their number, according to the custom." The sin offering formula corresponds to the regular pattern. And the ordinary includes both cereal and libation offerings. From this point through the seventh day of the festival, the entries follow exactly the same pattern (on v. 22, cf. Sam Pent, LXX, Syr, Vul). In contrast to the seventh day in the festival of Unleavened Bread, here the seventh day is not designated a convocation with prohibition of work. Rather, the system of days continues to an eighth day, breaking the festival scheme within the limits of a seven-day week. Yet, the entry for the eighth day stands markedly outside the pattern established throughout the scope of the seven-day series. The entry begins with the same kind of calendar element. But here the parallel breaks. The call for convocation establishes this day as the unique one, but a different formula for the call is employed (*'ăṣeret tihyeh lākem*). The call is followed, in regular fashion, by a prohibition for work. And the sacrifice list begins as it typically does. But the number of animals in the sacrifice list falls outside the system of the week by returning to requirements for one bull, one ram, and seven lambs (cf. 29:2, 8). Cereal and libation offerings follow in summary designation, while the sin offering formula and the ordinary appear without variation. Thus, while points of parallel between the ritual for this day and other days of sacrifice do appear, the day obviously stands outside the structure of the seven-day festival in the Feast of Tabernacles.

The speech presenting the ritual calendar through Moses to the people of Israel finally ends in v. 39 with a general formula calling for celebration on each of the named occasions, along with other independent sacrifices that may be called for by individual circumstances. 30:1 (*NRSV* 29:40) closes the pericope by noting that the instructions were properly executed.

The speech obviously presupposes a long tradition history. The most immediate antecedent for that tradition can be found in Leviticus 23. There is no evidence to suggest, at least on the basis of this text, that the calendar has been put together from two originally independent lists of sacrifices. The change in style marked by the shift in prepositions in the ordinary formula or by extending the calendar element to include subordinate elements, does not necessitate dividing the unit into two distinct literary sources. As a unit, the calendar is late, a part of P or, better, the secondary elements within P.

Genre

The Yahweh SPEECH in this unit comprises at least three distinct genres as elements in a larger administrative protocol. The first genre element is a CULTIC ORDINANCE, a law calling for particular kinds of sacrifice (28:2b). Since this law calls explicitly for sacrifice at determined times (*bĕmô'ădô*), administration of the law necessitates detailed specification of these times. The law thus provides the platform for developing an administrative document.

The second genre element is a RITUAL, specification of cultic acts necessary for a particular celebration (28:3aβ-8). The RITUAL sets out details for the continual burnt offering by noting the sacrifices that have to be offered, the times for the offering, and the side offerings that must accompany the sacrifices (cf. Kraus). Since the detail in this ritual is somewhat brief, with the order of acts confused by an IDENTIFICATION FORMULA, one might conclude that the RITUAL has lost its original intention for detailing the acts of the ceremony. If this is the case, perhaps the reason (or at least one of the reasons) for the loss lies in its service in a new context as a part of a larger genre.

The third genre element, and indeed, the element influencing the shape of the entire unit, is a cultic CALENDAR. The CALENDAR fixes the appointed time, duration, and names of the feasts that have to be celebrated *lĕyhwh*. In each step of the third genre element, the times for sacrifice are fixed, and a detailed list of the sacrifices required for that time is included. It should be noted that the genre, CALENDAR, could be used to organize any kind of tradition. In this case, the calendar specifies sacrifices for particular cult days, with accompanying rites. The CALENDAR can thus be specified as a sacrifice calendar, or perhaps more appropriately, a RITUAL CALENDAR since the sacrificial acts include not only the sacrifice list but accompanying acts as well. Moreover, since the other two genre elements are subordinate to the calendar structure, the entire administrative protocol, with ordinance and ritual as the platform for the calendar, can be understood as RITUAL CALENDAR (see Kraus, who notes the combination of ritual and calendar as a process of growth in the history of the two genres).

The unit abounds in stereotyped phrases and formulas. In addition to SPEECH FORMULAS and MESSAGE COMMISSION FORMULAS, the unit contains specifically cultic formulas: identification formulas, calendar formulas, calls to convocation, formulas for sin offering and the ordinary, and stereotyped sacrifice lists. For a complete discussion of these elements, → Leviticus 23.

Setting

This kind of administrative protocol presupposes a setting within the activity of temple personnel. The genre specifies cultic acts to be performed on particular days. As a part of the temple archives, the temple protocol would give the temple personnel immediate access to cultic specifications. Moreover, the cultic personnel would also have responsibility to inform the laity regularly of the special day's requirements. Thus, the setting for this unit must be seen within the active life of cultic personnel. The excessively high number of sacrificial animals, particularly in the Feast of Tabernacles, may suggest a process of idealization in composition of the protocol.

Intention

The primary intention of the unit is to provide an administrative document, functional as directions for carrying out sacrifices on particular days. The calendar designates those days and the list of sacrifices expected for each. In addition to the calendar function, the ritual for the continual burnt offering provides a single statement of details for a ritual act required for each of the calendar entries, suggesting emphasis in the administration protocol on the ordinary. Finally, the legislative element provides the official requirement underlying administrative protocol. Its function, legislative in character, is thus subordinate to the administrative function of the whole. One should note, nonetheless, that administrative protocol is not simply descriptive in character. It has an intrinsic prescriptive function.

Bibliography

D. F. Morgan, "The So-Called Cultic Calendars in the Pentateuch: A Morphological and Typological Study" (Diss., Claremont Graduate School, 1974); J. Morgenstern, "The Three Calendars of Ancient Israel," *HUCA* 1 (1924) 13-78; *HUCA* 3 (1926) 77-107.

Judicial Tradition concerning Vows
(30:2-17; *NRSV* 30:1-16)*

Structure

I. Speech report	2-16 (*NRSV* 1-15)
A. Introduction: Moses to the leaders of Israel	2a (*NRSV* 1a)
B. Speech	2b-16 (*NRSV* 1b-15)
1. Introduction formula	2b (*NRSV* 1b)
2. Stipulations	3-16 (*NRSV* 2-15)
a. Law for vows, bonds, oaths	3 (*NRSV* 2)
b. Qualifications involving women	4-13 (*NRSV* 3-12)
1) Women in father's house	4-6 (*NRSV* 3-5)
a) Definition of circumstances	4 (*NRSV* 3)
b) Qualification by father's action	5-6 (*NRSV* 4-5)
2) Married women	7-9 (*NRSV* 6-8)
a) Definition of circumstances	7 (*NRSV* 6)
b) Qualification by husband's action	8-9 (*NRSV* 7-8)
3) Widow, divorcée	10-13 (*NRSV* 9-12)
a) Definition of circumstances	10-11 (*NRSV* 9-10)
b) Qualification by guardian's action	12-13 (*NRSV* 11-12)
c. Summary of qualifications	14-16 (*NRSV* 13-15)
1) General summary	14 (*NRSV* 13)
2) Negative action	15 (*NRSV* 14)
3) Positive action	16 (*NRSV* 15)
II. Conclusion	17 (*NRSV* 16)

This unit is totally isolated in its larger Pentateuchal context, showing no intrinsic connections with either the preceding or the following material (so, Noth). It is structured into the larger context by means of a speech formula and a concluding formula defining the content of the speech. The speech formula designates the speaker as Moses, the addressee as the leaders of Israel. The unit thus shares in the structural problems represented by tradition attributed to Moses but ordered following the commission of Joshua in Num 27:12-23.

Following the speech formula, the unit organizes its tradition into four major elements, set under an introductory formula (v. 2b). The formula does nothing more than headline the content of the speech as a word given Moses by

*See Annotation to Num 15:1-16.

the Lord. Such a headline commonly appears as a part of a Yahweh speech addressed to Moses (cf. Exod 21:1). In this case, however, the movement of the speech has progressed to the next stage of transmission. Moreover, the formula identifies the following material as a word commanded by the Lord and thus corresponds with the conclusion in v. 17.

Verses 3 and 10 stipulate obedience to vows, bonds, or oaths. The vow particularly has economic connotations (Deut 12:11, 17, 26 +), although personal service (Gen 28:20; 31:13) or devotion of another member of one's family to special service (Judg 11:30-31; 1 Sam 1:11) can be involved. The other categories depend in some manner on the character of the vow. The bond appears only in this unit. An oath binds the author to fulfillment of its content, content that varies widely but commonly appears in parallel with a vow.

The first stipulation, v. 3, calls for obedience to vows, bonds, oaths from a man, or perhaps more broadly from a person (cf. Exod 12:3; Job 42:11; 1 Chr 16:3). The second, v. 10, designates the same unswerving loyalty to an oath expected from a widow or divorcée. In both cases legal requirement, whether by explicit legislation or by custom, calls for commitment to the spoken word. These elements are harmonious with the introduction formula and the general conclusion.

Verses 4-9 and 11-16 follow each of these legislative pieces with details for qualifications on the law. In the first case, qualifications for judgment fall within two categories: (1) a woman still under the authority of her father (vv. 4-6); and (2) a woman under the authority of another man (vv. 7-9), in most cases obviously a husband (cf. v. 7). The qualifications under these circumstances are formulated in essentially the same way, with only minor variations. The man in authority over the woman may choose to do nothing when he hears of the woman's vow. In that case, the vow will stand. If the man in authority so chooses, however, he can restrain the woman. In the first case, the positive action on the part of the man in restraining the woman results in cancellation of the woman's vow: "It shall not stand" *(lōʼ yāqûm).* Then follows a notation that the Lord will forgive the woman because of the man's action (cf. Noth). The second case does not parallel the first in noting the results of the man's action. Rather, the description of the man's action becomes a motivation for divine response, the only indication here that the vow will not stand. But despite this variation, the parallel between the two is apparent.

Verses 11-16 reflect parallel constructions with vv. 4-9. Yet, problems in the structure of this element hamper clear understanding of the text. First, the legislation element in v. 10 designates the subject of this element as widow or divorcée. Yet, as in the parallel in vv. 4-9, so here qualifications on the law can be established by the man who possesses authority over the woman. That man is designated as her husband *(ʼîšāh).* At least insofar as the final stage of this unit is concerned, however, the context calls for a broader understanding of the word. It is clear that a widow remained under the authority of her husband's house (→ Genesis 38). A divorcée apparently remained under the authority of her husband's house unless a bill of divorce and an explicit act sent her out of the house as evidence of her rejection (cf. Deut 24:1-4). Isa 54:6-7 presupposes that a wife may be rejected, yet still be subject to the authority of her husband (cf. also Judg 19:2-3; Hosea 2:4). Thus, it seems likely that the man in the development of the qualifications in vv. 11-16 should be interpreted as the person who maintains authority over the woman, quite in parallel to the circumstances described in vv. 4-9 (cf. the expression in v. 11, *bêt 'îšāh* // v. 4 *běbêt 'ābîhā*). If this position is defensible, then the structure of the unit as it now stands makes sense. The position of v. 10, immediately preceding these qualifications, requires that the qualifications apply for the widow and divorcée.

The qualifications on the woman's vows follow the same pattern as in vv. 4-9. Verse 11 defines the circumstances that open the qualifications. Then vv. 12-13 set out negative and positive actions for the man in authority over the woman. If he does nothing, then the vow stands. If he restrains her, the Lord will forgive her.

Verses 14-16 introduce a new element unparalleled in vv. 4-9. Verse 14 summarizes the qualifications procedure, noting that the power to establish or cancel the vow afflicting the woman lies in the hands of the man. The divorcée or widow clearly stands under impressive power in the hands of a guardian from her husband's family. Verses 15-16 add emphasis to the point. If the man is silent, then he establishes the vow against the woman. But if he objects, then he must bear the responsibility for her debt (see Noth).

The unit then concludes, as noted above, with a summarizing formula noting these positions to the laws given Moses by the Lord involving the relationships between a man and his wife or a father and his daughter.

It is possible to consider v. 10 a secondary intrusion into the original movement of the unit (so, Noth). In that case, the entire scope of the unit would shift, as demonstrated in the following outline:

a. Law for vows, bonds, oaths   3 (*NRSV* 2)
b. Qualifications in cases involving women   4-13 (*NRSV* 3-12)
  1) Women in father's house   4-6 (*NRSV* 3-5)
  2) Women newly given in marriage   7-9 (*NRSV* 6-8)
  3) Women already married   11-13 (*NRSV* 10-12)
c. Summary of qualifications   14-16 (*NRSV* 13-15)

This observation makes perhaps more sense out of the designation of the man in vv. 11-13. Moreover, it suggests particular attention to vows or rash words a woman might have made just before her marriage (vv. 7-9). And it eliminates the widow and divorcée entirely from consideration in the qualifications, a point that may stand more harmoniously with v. 10 than the qualifications in vv. 11-13. Yet, if such a tradition history has merit, it shows that for the present form of the text, great emphasis falls on the new element. What is the legal status in the community for widows and divorced women?

In its present form, the unit reflects legal collections from the priestly source. The immediate traditio-historical antecedents for the unit can be most clearly seen in stipulations concerning vows (→ Leviticus 27) or stipulations concerning divorce (→ Deuteronomy 24).

Genre

This Moses SPEECH presupposes stipulations in certain kinds of legal problems. The citation of legislation dealing with payment of vows is a genre element in the whole. But since it serves as a platform for providing qualifications for the law, it cannot fall easily into classifications of the laws themselves. The focus of the unit highlights the qualifications of the law. It presupposes the legislation. But it moves beyond legislative interests to stipulate directions for implementing the law. It must therefore be seen as judicial, instructions available for guidelines in returning decisions involving vows among women. The genre does not shift with the addition of v. 10.

Legal formulas, also in such a judicial category, include the declaration, "it shall stand," *yāqûm,* or "it shall not stand," *lō' yāqûm* (cf. Lev 27:14, 17; Deut 19:15; Isa 8:10).

Setting

In its final stage, the unit presupposes the larger structure of P, including the problems posed by the position of the commissioning of Joshua. In both stages of the unit itself, the text suggests a legal setting, civil or cultic in character, involving decisions concerning responsibility for fulfilling vows, bonds, or oaths.

Intention

The unit has basically a judicial intention. In its final form, it functions to establish the line of responsibility or absence of responsibility involved in vows made by people who were not fully liable for their own debts. The structure of the present text places special emphasis on the widow or divorced woman, emphasizing the power of male authority to determine legal responsibility facing the widow or divorced woman. Thus, a widow or divorced woman would not be able to commit a husband or the husband's house to undesirable distribution of property. Moreover, the vows defined as afflicting a woman suggest that the man in question maintained authority to enforce unfavorable debts the woman might have faced. In its original form, the judicial intention remains. But the focus on the widow or divorced woman shifts to the relationship between a daughter and her father or a man and his wife, as the conclusion suggests.

Report of Battle against Midian (31:1-54)

Structure

I. Speech report	1-2
A. Introduction: the Lord to Moses	1

    B. Speech   2

       1. Commission to fight the Midianites   2a

       2. Announcement of Moses' imminent death   2b

  II. Speech report   3-4

    A. Introduction: Moses to the people   3aα

    B. Speech   3aβ-4

       1. Instructions for preparation   3aβ-b

          a. Command for preparations   3aβ

          b. Purpose   3b

       2. Number for this draft   4

 III. Execution of instructions   5-11

    A. Draft   5

    B. War   6-11

       1. General description   6-7

       2. Details   8-10

          a. Kings killed   8a

          b. Balaam killed   8b

          c. Captives   9a

          d. Spoil   9b

          e. Cities destroyed   10

       3. General summary   11

 IV. Report to Moses   12-24

    A. Return to Moses and Eleazar   12-13

    B. Moses' response   14-20

       1. Description of Moses   14

       2. Speech report   15-20

          a. Introduction: Moses   15a

          b. Speech   15b-20

            1) Accusation against the army   15b

            2) Charges against the enemy   16

            3) Judgment   17-18

               a) Captives to be executed   17

               b) Captives to be kept alive   18

            4) Instructions for purification   19-20

    C. Speech report   21-24

       1. Introduction: Eleazer to men of war   21a

       2. Instructions for spoil   21b-24

          a. Introduction   21b

          b. Definitions   22-23

            1) Things that survive fire   22-23a

            2) Things that cannot survive fire   23b

          c. Purification ritual for people   24

            1) Washing ritual   24aα

            2) Declaration   24aβ

            3) Instructions for post-ritual status   24b

  V. Distribution of spoil   25-54

    A. Speech report   25-30

1. Introduction: the Lord to Moses   25
2. Instructions for distributing the spoil   26-30
     a. Inventory   26
     b. Division between warriors and congregation   27
     c. Levy for the sanctuary   28-30
         1) Introduction   28
         2) Distribution   29-30
             a) For Eleazar   29
             b) For the Levites   30
B. Execution of instructions   31-54
     1. General statement   31
     2. Inventory   32-40
     3. Distribution   41-54
         a. Description of Moses' act   41-47
         b. Response   48
         c. Speech report   49-50
             1) Introduction: Officers to Moses   49aα
             2) Speech   49aβ-50
                 a) Report on war casualties   49aβ-b
                 b) Atonement offering   50
         d. Conclusion   51-54
             1) General statement   51
             2) Inventory   52
             3) Gloss   53
             4) General statement   54

This pericope is isolated from the context that surrounds it. There are no itinerary formulas at the beginning or the end of the unit to give it position in the larger structures of the wilderness theme. Verse 12 does set the pericope in some relationship to the context by suggesting that the action described within its limits occurred in the plains of Moab by the Jordan at Jericho (→ 22:1). There is no narrative introduction that might expose the principal figures in a story or the circumstances that would create a plot. The unit begins *in medias res* with a speech formula and comprises a series of speeches with narrative elements interspersed in order to account for movement from one speech to another.

The first speech, vv. 1-2, combines two motifs: (1) The Lord commissions Moses to attack the Midianites. Indeed, the verb in the commission, "avenge" *(nĕqōm)*, plus the following noun from the same root *(niqmat)* in construct with "the Israelites," thus, "avenge the vengeance of the Israelites," suggests that the battle is retaliation for some previous atrocity by the Midianite enemy (→ 25:6-18). This anti-Midianite element stands in sharp contrast to the tradition about Moses' father-in-law (→ Exod 3:1-21; 18:1-27). (2) The speech also announces Moses' imminent death (→ 27:12-23; see also Deuteronomy 31; 34). But no further point is made of this element in the pericope. The allusion functions more directly to tie the pericope to the larger context that will call for an account of Moses' death (→ 27:12-23).

The second speech, vv. 3-4, demonstrates Moses' obedience to the command. He executes the instructions by instructing the people. Verse 3, set in the context of a speech formula to mark the element as Moses' address to the people, commands preparation for the war with Midian. And as in v. 2, this command reflects the hostile relationship with Midian as vengeance and shows the anticipated battle to be a holy war, a Yahweh war (see Smend). The speech closes with a specification of number for the draft that defines the army of the Lord.

Verses 5-11 describe the war. Verse 5 notes that the process of the draft was completed. Then vv. 6-11 detail the results of the war. A general description of the war in vv. 6-7 is complemented by a second general description in v 11. These verses frame the details of the battle. Verse 8 reports the enemy casualty list, including both the total number of enemy dead and a particular dead enemy — Balaam. The name, Balaam, suggests that from the point of view reflected by this report, Balaam was not an ideal prophet who spoke only the word of the Lord as blessing for Israel. Balaam was an enemy ($\rightarrow$ 22:22-35). The connection is vague. That it appears in an anti-Midianite text suggests that facet of the Balaam tradition that connects Balaam with the Midianite atrocity at Baal Peor ($\rightarrow$ 25:6-18). One facet of the negative Balaam tradition suggests that Balaam effected the seduction at Baal Peor, a point that is explicit in v. 16 of this pericope. It is important to note that no reference to Balaam appears in Numbers 25. Thus, again, a double edge to the Balaam/Baal Peor tradition appears. Part of the tradition makes no connection between the apostasy at Peor and Balaam, leaving Balaam free from the stigma of the negative tradition and open to the legendary status reflected in Numbers 22–24. The other part makes Balaam a sinner, guilty of enticing Israel into apostasy at Peor. Could that be the power of Balaam's curse against Israel, sought by Balak of Moab? Verses 9-10 then complete the element by noting the number of captives, the spoil, and the names of the enemy cities destroyed in the war. And v. 11 summarizes the element.

Verses 12-24 contain a report of the battle to Moses and a detailed account of the response of Moses to the news. The report, vv. 12-13, notes simply that the army brings the captives and spoil to Moses and Eleazar. Perhaps the reference place for Moses' camp at the plains of Moab by Jericho is an effort to tie the pericope to the itinerary. Moses responds to the report in anger (cf. Matt 21:12-13). The Moses speech in vv. 15-20 reflects the character of his anger through an accusation against the army, showing that the army had not properly carried out the duties of the ban against the enemy that belongs to a holy war, and an accusation against the enemy that justifies the war. The accusation against the enemy picks up that facet of the Balaam tradition that remembers Balaam as the initiator of the apostasy at Peor (so, v. 8). The conclusion of the Moses speech defines the judgment enacted by the Lord through Moses on the captives taken in the war (everyone except female virgins would be executed). And in response, the men of the war would undergo a purification process. Finally, the speech in vv. 21-24 carries instructions for taking spoil in the course of the war, then for the process of purification for the spoil and the people who were involved in the war ($\rightarrow$ 1 Samuel 15).

The final stage in the battle report, vv. 25-54, concerns distribution of the spoil. It is in effect the execution of instructions for completing the holy war. The speech in this section, vv. 25-30, carries the instructions for distributing the spoil. The execution of instructions follows in typical fashion, vv. 31-48. A report on casualties, vv. 49-50, leads finally to the conclusion in vv. 51-54. Again, in this element two general statements, vv. 51 and 54, frame an inventory of spoil and a gloss that explains the origin of the spoil.

The tradition in this narrative unit is late, a part of an addition to the priestly source that presupposes Numbers 25 (so, Noth, 229). It is remarkable, however, that some evidence appears here for tradition that parallels Midianite and Moabite elements as functional parts of the unit (contrast Noth, 229).

Genre

The narrative in this unit appears in a typical structure common for a BATTLE REPORT: (1) verbs of movement: "to go against" (*hāyâ 'al* [v. 3]), "to send" (*šlḥ* [vv. 4, 6]); (2) verbs of military activity: "to arm" (*hlṣ* [v. 3]), "to war against" (*ṣb'* [v. 7]); (3) verbs indicating outcome of the battle: "to slay" (*hrg* [vv. 7, 8]), "to take captive" (*šbh* [v. 9]), "to take booty" (*bzz* [v. 9]), "to burn" (*śrp* [v. 10]), "to take booty" (*lāqaḥ 'et-šālāl* [v. 11]); (4) concluding element indicating the extent of the war, in this case, a report to Moses (see Richter, van Seters, Gunn). Formulas and stereotyped expressions in the unit include the SPEECH FORMULA and patterns for reporting spoil.

Setting

The battle report is clearly set in the literary context of the late elements among the sources for the Pentateuch. In that capacity, it contributes to the growing narrative about conquest of land, particularly land in the Transjordan. That this tradition goes back to ancient sources is possible, a point that would assume that the battle report is not simply the product of the scribe but a form for oral communication of battle results as well as for preservation of battle tradition (see Gunn).

Intention

A BATTLE REPORT presents details of a conflict in order to show the outcome as a matter of public interest. In this case, the BATTLE REPORT registers Israelite victory over the Midianites as an event that demonstrates (1) the power of the Lord in war (Moses is of secondary importance here), and (2) fulfillment of the command to maintain a state of war with Midian (→ 25:16-18). The report lists spoil taken in the war but does not suggest that the territory of Midian was occupied by Israel. This is not a tradition that belongs to the conquest theme. It is a part of the theme of traditions about Israel's life in the wilderness.

Bibliography

D. M. Gunn, "The 'Battle Report': Oral or Scribal Convention?" *JBL* 93 (1974) 513-18; W. Richter, *Traditionsgeschichtliche Untersuchungen zum Richterbuch* (BBB 18; Bonn: Hanstein, 1966) 162-66; J. van Seters, "The Conquest of Sihon's Kingdom: A Literary Examination," *JBL* 91 (1972) 182-97; R. Smend, *Yahweh War and Tribal Confederation: Reflections upon Israel's Earliest History* (tr. M. G. Rogers; Nashville: Abingdon, 1970).

Negotiations Dialogue (32:1-42)*

Structure

I.	Description of the land of Gilead	1
II.	Dialogue	2-27
	A. Speech report	2-4
	1. Introduction: Gad and Reuben to Moses, Eleazar, leaders of the congregation	2
	2. Speech	3-4
	a. Description of the land	3-4a
	b. Warrant for appeal	4b
	B. Speech report	5
	1. Introduction: Gad and Reuben to Moses	5aα₁
	2. Appeal	5aα₂-b
	C. Speech report	6-15
	1. Introduction: Moses to Gad and Reuben	6a
	2. Speech	6b-15
	a. Accusation	6-7
	b. Precedent	8-13
	c. Accusation	14
	d. Judgment anticipated	15
	D. Speech report	16-19
	1. Introduction: Gad and Reuben to Moses	16aα
	2. Speech	16aβ-19
	a. Proposal for occupation	16aβ-b
	b. Condition	17a
	c. Proposal for occupation	17b
	d. Condition	18
	e. Proposal for occupation	19
	E. Speech report	20-24
	1. Introduction: Moses to Gad and Reuben	20a
	2. Speech	20b-24
	a. Condition	20b-22a

*See Annotation to Num 15:1-16.

	b. Agreement	22b
	c. Threat	23
	d. Agreement	24a
	e. Admonition	24b
F.	Speech report	25-27
	1. Introduction: Gad and Reuben to Moses	25a
	2. Speech	25b-27
	a. General commitment	25b
	b. Detailed commitment	26-27
III.	Report of the agreement	28-32
A.	General statement	28
B.	Speech report	29-30
	1. Introduction: Moses to Eleazar, Joshua, heads of the people	29aα₁
	2. Speech	29aα₂-30
	a. Conditions	29aα₂-aβ
	b. Result	29b
	c. Condition	30a
	d. Result	30b
C.	Speech report	31-32
	1. Introduction: Gad and Reuben to Moses	31a
	2. Speech	31b-32
	a. General commitment	31b
	b. Detail	32
IV.	Execution of the agreement	33-42
A.	General statement	33
B.	Details	34-42
	1. Land for Gad	34-36
	2. Land for Reuben	37-38
	3. Land for Manasseh	39-42
	a. Machir	39-40
	b. Jair	41
	c. Nobah	42

This unit is isolated from the larger unit, the wilderness theme, with its structure defined by the itinerary chain. There is no itinerary formula to secure the position of this unit within the context of the wilderness theme. The development of the unit presupposes that the people are poised on the edge of the Jordan, ready to move into Canaan (cf. v. 5). The point would suggest the same location in the itinerary as the one suggested for the preceding pericope (→ 31:1-54). But also that unit reflects isolation from the itinerary. Perhaps the "plains of Moab, beyond the Jordan, at Jericho" (22:1) is the point in the itinerary for collecting various traditions that have no firm position in the itinerary and no firm chronological anchor.

The opening setting exposes the principals for the unit and names the problem that creates the plan for the structure. The Reubenites and the Gadites (no reference to Manasseh) have an abundance of cattle. This point connects with the following description of the land. The land of Jazer and the land of Gilead are defined as a "place for cattle." The implication of the juxtaposition is clear: The cattle, so abundant for the Reubenites and the Gadites, belong in the land for cattle. Toward that end, the candidates approach Moses and Eleazer in order to petition for possession of the land as their inheritance.

To this point, the introduction functions as an exposition for a story. But the development of the unit exhibits the structure of dialogue, not a narration of events. The dialogue does in fact reflect a point of tension anticipating resolution in a clear moment of climax. Yet, the structure depends on a series of speeches designed to establish the resolution. It thus has the shape of a negotiations series rather than the shape of a tale or anecdote (→ Exodus 7–10).

The dialogue begins in vv. 2-5 with a double speech. The first speech, vv. 2-4, features Gad and Reuben before Moses. And the speech itself makes the point clearly noted for the audience by the introduction. (1) The land is a land for cattle. (2) Gad and Reuben have cattle. The second speech in this doublet, v. 5, builds on the implications of the first by making an explicit appeal. (1) Give the land to the obvious candidates. (2) Do not force them to cross the Jordan. The double speeches and, indeed, the double character of the content in speech and introduction do not suggest an artificial combination of sources. In both cases, the double construction functions to effect a strong presentation of the appeal to possess land in Transjordan.

The dialogue continues in vv. 6-15 with Moses' response. The response is hostile (→ 31:14). It opens in vv. 6-7 with an accusation against Gad and Reuben because their request would discourage the rest of the people from pursuing occupation of Canaan. Verses 8-13 then compare the request to the murmuring of the people at Kadesh-barnea (→ Numbers 13–14). And the accusation of this kind of sin is renewed in v. 14. Verse 15 makes the consequence of such sin explicit: "He will abandon them in the wilderness, and you will destroy all this people."

The speech in vv. 16-19 is designed to counter Moses' accusation. It asserts the intention of Gad and Reuben to settle in Transjordan by naming their plans for building structures. But it attaches those plans to a condition for occupation. Gad and Reuben will accompany the rest of Israel across the Jordan in order to secure land for them in Canaan. The condition is repeated in v. 18. And v. 19 repeats the intention of Gad and Reuben to occupy Transjordan. Moses' response, vv. 20-24, acknowledges the condition as the requisite for occupying Transjordan, thus establishing the right of the candidates to settle in the land of their choice. The agreement is bound by a threat, v. 23. Verse 24a repeats the agreement. And v. 24b admonishes the Reubenites and the Gadites to stand by their word. Verses 25-27 carry the agreement from Reuben and Gad, a short general statement that they will obey Moses followed by a detailed definition of the agreement. Families and flocks will remain in Transjordan. The men will follow the Lord into battle, obviously across the Jordan.

Verse 28 notes that Moses reported the agreement to Eleazar and Joshua, then to all of Israel. The speech in vv. 29-30 repeats the agreement and names the sanction should any fail to keep the conditions. And the speech in vv. 31-32 repeats the agreement from the Gadites and Reubenites. The negotiations have ended. The resolution of the petition is set. Verses 32-34 report that the conditions were met and that land for Gad, Reuben, and now the sons of Manasseh was defined.

Source identity for this dialogue about possession of land in Transjordan remains obscure. Noth suggests that some fragments of the Yahwist (vv. 1, 16, 39-42) appear in the midst of special tradition. That suggestion might explain why the principals in the major developments of the unit are limited to Reuben and Gad, with Manasseh entering the picture only in vv. 39-42. But the problem is a traditio-historical one, not a sign of source complications or form duplications. Indeed, the formal analysis shows no disunity in the pericope, no evidence for cutting vv. 1, 16, and 39-42 away as a distinct literary source (see Budd). The most likely conclusion is that the unit reflects special tradition added to the priestly redaction, if not a fundamental part of P.

Genre

The unit is not a story and cannot be classified as anecdote. It is in some sense a REPORT of negotiations since it shows how the Reubenites and Gadites (along with part of Manasseh) come into possession of land in Transjordan. But the REPORT has a particular character as a series of SPEECHES, a DIALOGUE. Moreover, the DIALOGUE reflects a particular kind of give and take, a process of negotiations over a specific point — the inheritance of land in Transjordan (→ Exodus 7–10). As would be expected, the series of SPEECHES relies on a careful use of SPEECH FORMULAS as a skeleton for arranging the order in the speeches.

Setting

The younger levels of the tradition show the work of the redactor, an effort to account for occupation in Transjordan as a final stage in the move from Egypt to Canaan. That setting is obviously literary in character. It demands its position as the product of careful organization. But the setting is also theologically sensitive. God gives the land through the decree of Moses (contrast Joshua 21). Older tradition doubtlessly shines through this text. Whether the Yahwist is involved remains moot. But surely some early effort to account for occupation in Transjordan can be assumed.

Intention

The negotiations series shows (1) that Reuben and Gad settled in Transjordan under the authority of Moses. Indeed, at some level the tradition includes Manasseh as one of the legitimate inhabitants of the Transjordan. The series also shows (2) that the settlement has divine approval, conditional only on the active participation of the Reubenites and Gadites in the conquest of the land on the other side of the Jordan (contrast Joshua 21).

Bibliography

A. Bergmann, "The Israelite Tribe of Half Manasseh," *JPOS* 16 (1936) 224-54; S. E. Loewenstamm, "The Relation of the Settlement of Gad and Reuben in Num 32:1-38: Its Background and Its Composition," *Tarbiz* 42 (1972) 12-26; J. Mauchline, "Gilead and Gilgal: Some Reflections on the Israelite Occupation of Palestine," *VT* 6 (1956) 19-33.

Wilderness Itinerary (33:1–35:34)

Structure

I. Introduction		33:1-2
A. Headline		1
B. Report of writing the record		2a
C. Headline		2b
II. Itinerary list		33:3–35:34
A. Rameses — Succoth		33:3-5
1. Itinerary formula: element a		3aα
2. Date formula		3aβ
3. Exodus anecdote		3b-5
a. Exodus report		3b
b. Report of Egyptian circumstances		4
1) Death of the first born		4a
2) Sign-judgments against Egyptian gods		4b
4. Itinerary formula		5
a. Element a: notice of departure from Rameses		5a
b. element b: notice of arrival at Succoth		5b
B. Succoth — 'Etham		6
1. Itinerary formula		6a-bα
a. Element a: notice of departure from Succoth		6a
b. Element b: notice of arrival at 'Etham		6bα
2. Geographical data		6bβ
C. 'Etham — Migdol		7
1. Itinerary formula: element a		7aα
2. Geographical data		7aβ
3. Itinerary formula: element b		7b
D. Haḥiroth — Marah		8
1. Itinerary formula: element a		8aα
2. Anecdote about the sea event and march		8aβ-bα
3. Itinerary formula: element b		8bβ
E. Marah — Elim		9
1. Itinerary formula: element a and b		9a
2. Geographical data		9bα
3. Itinerary formula: element b		9bβ
F. Elim — Reed Sea		10

1. Itinerary formula: element a	10a
2. Itinerary formula: element b	10b
G. Reed Sea — Wilderness of Sin	11
1. Itinerary formula: element a	11a
2. Itinerary formula: element b	11b
H. Wilderness of Sin — Dophkah	12
1. Itinerary formula: element a	12a
2. Itinerary formula: element b	12b
I. Dophkah — Alush	13
1. Itinerary formula: element a	13a
2. Itinerary formula: element b	13b
J. Alush — Rephidim	14
1. Itinerary formula: element a	14a
2. Itinerary formula: element b	14bα
3. Anecdote: no water to drink	14bβ
K. Rephidim — Wilderness of Sinai	15
1. Itinerary formula: element a	15a
2. Itinerary formula: element b	15b
L. Wilderness of Sinai — Kibroth-hattaavah	16
1. Itinerary formula: element a	16a
2. Itinerary formula: element b	16b
M. Kibroth-hattaavah — Ḥazeroth	17
1. Itinerary formula: element a	17a
2. Itinerary formula: element b	17b
N. Ḥazeroth — Rithmah	18
1. Itinerary formula: element a	18a
2. Itinerary formula: element b	18b
O. Rithmah — Rimmon-perez	19
1. Itinerary formula: element a	19a
2. Itinerary formula: element b	19b
P. Rimmon-perez — Libnah	20
1. Itinerary formula: element a	20a
2. Itinerary formula: element b	20b
Q. Libnah — Rissah	21
1. Itinerary formula: element a	21a
2. Itinerary formula: element b	21b
R. Rissah — Kehelathah	22
1. Itinerary formula: element a	22a
2. Itinerary formula: element b	22b
S. Kehelathah — Mt. Šepher	23
1. Itinerary formula: element a	23a
2. Itinerary formula: element b	23b
T. Mt. Šepher — Ḥaradah	24
1. Itinerary formula: element a	24a
2. Itinerary formula: element b	24b
U. Ḥaradah — Makheloth	25
1. Itinerary formula: element a	25a

2. Itinerary formula: element b		25b
V.	Makheloth — Taḥath	26
	1. Itinerary formula: element a	26a
	2. Itinerary formula: element b	26b
W.	Taḥath — Teraḥ	27
	1. Itinerary formula: element a	27a
	2. Itinerary formula: element b	27b
X.	Teraḥ — Mithkah	28
	1. Itinerary formula: element a	28a
	2. Itinerary formula: element b	28b
Y.	Mithkah — Ḥashmonah	29
	1. Itinerary formula: element a	29a
	2. Itinerary formula: element b	29b
Z.	Ḥashmonah — Moseroth	30
	1. Itinerary formula: element a	30a
	2. Itinerary formula: element b	30b
A'.	Moseroth — Bene-Jaʿakan	31
	1. Itinerary formula: element a	31a
	2. Itinerary formula: element b	31b
B'.	Bene-Jaʿakan — Ḥor Haggedgad	32
	1. Itinerary formula: element a	32a
	2. Itinerary formula: element b	32b
C'.	Ḥor Haggedgad — Joṭbatah	33
	1. Itinerary formula: element a	33a
	2. Itinerary formula: element b	33b
D'.	Joṭbatah — ʿAbronah	34
	1. Itinerary formula: element a	34a
	2. Itinerary formula: element b	34b
E'.	ʿAbronah — ʿEzion-geber	35
	1. Itinerary formula: element a	35a
	2. Itinerary formula: element b	35b
F'.	ʿEzion-geber — Wilderness of Zin (Kadesh)	36
	1. Itinerary formula: element a	36a
	2. Itinerary formula: element b	36bα
	3. Geographical gloss	36bβ
G'.	Kadesh — Mt. Hor	37-40
	1. Itinerary formula: element a	37a
	2. Itinerary formula: element b	37bα
	3. Geographical gloss	37bβ
	4. Anecdote: Aaron's death	38-39
	5. Political anecdote	40
H'.	Mt. Hor — Ṣalmonah	41
	1. Itinerary formula: element a	41a
	2. Itinerary formula: element b	41b
I'.	Ṣalmonah — Punon	42
	1. Itinerary formula: element a	42a
	2. Itinerary formula: element b	42b

J'. Punon — 'Oboth 43
   1. Itinerary formula: element a 43a
   2. Itinerary formula: element b 43b
K'. 'Oboth — 'Iye-ha'abarim 44
   1. Itinerary formula: element a 44a
   2. Itinerary formula: element b 44bα
   3. Geographical gloss 44bβ
L'. 'Iyim — Dibon-gad 45
   1. Itinerary formula: element a 45a
   2. Itinerary formula: element b 45b
M'. Dibon-gad — 'Almon-diblathaymah 46
   1. Itinerary formula: element a 46a
   2. Itinerary formula: element b 46b
N'. 'Almon-diblathaymah — Mountains of 'Abarim 47
   1. Itinerary formula: element a 47a
   2. Itinerary formula: element b 47bα
   3. Geographical gloss 47bβ
O'. Mountains of 'Abarim — Plains of Moab 33:48–35:34
   1. Itinerary formula: element a 48a
   2. Itinerary formula: element b 48b
   3. Itinerary formula: element b with gloss of
      geographical data 49
   4. Speech series 33:50–35:34
     a. Speech report 33:50-56
       1) The Lord to Moses, with reference to place 50
       2) Instructions for the conquest 51-56
     b. Speech report 34:1-12
       1) Introduction: the Lord to Moses 1
       2) Definition of land boundaries 2-12
     c. Speech report 34:13-15
       1) Introduction: Moses to Israelites 13a
       2) Explanation of inheritance 13b-15
     d. Speech report 34:16-29
       1) Introduction: the Lord to Moses 16
       2) Administration list 17-29
     e. Speech report 35:1-8
       1) Introduction 1
        a) The Lord to Moses 1aα
        b) Tie to the itinerary 1aβ-b
       2) Instructions for designating Levitical cities ... 2-8
     f. Speech report 9-34
       1) Introduction: the Lord to Moses 9
       2) Designation for cities of refuge 10-34

The unit in Numbers 33–35 stands at the end of the book of Numbers as a summary of the wilderness theme. In contrast, Numbers 36 relates directly to Num 27:1-11 as an appendix only to that particular legal tradition. The traditions contained in chs. 33-35 cannot be separated from the conquest theme. Yet here, as in chs. 21-32, the structure of the unit places such contact with conquest traditions, not as a structural element in the conquest theme, but as a concluding element in the wilderness theme (→ The Framework, Chapter 3, FOTL IIA). In the same manner the unit begins with traditions that cannot be separated from the exodus theme. Specifically, the itinerary list itself opens with an anecdote reporting the exodus event. But the exodus traditions serve to mark the beginning of the wilderness theme. One should note also the structural peculiarities involved by the position of the Sea event anecdote set, not at the beginning of the wilderness itinerary, but within its structure (→ Exodus 14). The impact of this organization is that exodus-wilderness-conquest cannot easily be divided into independent themes of tradition.

The unit comprises only two major parts: (I) an introduction, and (II) the itinerary list. The introduction functions primarily as a headline for the elements in the list. As is typical for lists, the headline begins with the demonstrative "these" ('ēlleh), then specifies the particular content of the list (cf. Exod 1:2-4). In this case, the headline is followed by a brief notation and a repetition of the headline. The anecdote observes that Moses had written the itinerary at the Lord's direction (cf. Exod 17:14; Deut 31:19). But the observation plays no essential role in the development of the unit (cf. Noth, who suggests that the observation is a secondary intrusion into the text). The repeated headline is shorter than the opening one, yet it follows the same pattern and functions as an inclusion for binding the anecdote into the introduction.

The itinerary list builds on a long series of itinerary formulas. Each formula contains at least (a) a notation of Israel's departure from a camping site, and (b) a notation of encampment at a new site (so, Coats). Contrary to the itinerary chain in Exodus and Numbers generally, here the list contains no incomplete entries. Like the itinerary chain, however, this list can pick up additional structural elements indiscriminately. Such expansion of the list with incidental data, in this case with geographical data or anecdotal tradition, seems typical, not only for the itinerary list (cf. annal itineraries with similar anecdotal expansions such as the annals of Sennacherib, the wilderness theme) but for lists generally (cf. Numbers 26). Such expansive tradition is included in an itinerary formula by splitting elements a and b in the formula with the additional data, or by enclosing the additional data with a repetition of one element from the itinerary formula.

The opening entry in the list provides a convenient illustration for such expansive structure. The entry begins with element a constructed in normal sequence. Then, rather than element b in the itinerary formula, the entry follows with a dating formula and anecdotal tradition about the exodus. Significantly, the dating formula places the exodus event of the day marked by cultic calendar tradition as the beginning of the Feast of Unleavened Bread, explicitly the day after the Passover. (Does this designation of the exodus following Passover not reflect the history of vacillation Israel experienced in specifying details about the exodus event?) Moreover, the anecdote itself reflects a double tradition. It reports first (v. 3) that Israel left with a high hand, a gesture of triumph before all the Egyptians (cf. Exod 14:8). That gesture must be associated in this case with the death of the first born (v. 4a). But the text also reports acts of judgment against Egypt's gods as a distinct event (v. 4b). This allusion picks up the sign in Exod 10:21-27. But the product of that sign, as for the sign cycle generally, was failure in Israel's design for an exodus. The significant point here is that these diverse traditions about the exodus have been combined in this anecdote into a single, relatively well unified allusion to the exodus event.

This expansion is then incorporated into the itinerary by a repetition of element a and a completion of the itinerary structure with element b. The incorporation could have been completed by introducing simply element b (thus, cf. v. 8). Repetition of element a reinforces the inclusion function (cf. also Num 20:1).

The opening entry corresponds in structure and function with the final entry, the longest entry in the series. This one begins with a complete itinerary formula, including an expansion to specify geographical details about the place name in element b: "They encamped on the plains of Moab, by the Jordan near Jericho." The entry then repeats element b with more expansive details about the encampment site. One might note here the chiastic structure in relationship with the opening entry of the itinerary list. Following the itinerary elements, a series of six speeches, 33:50–35:34, presupposes the setting provided by element b.* The first and the fifth speeches tie directly to the itinerary list by specifying in the speech formula that the speeches occurred in the plains of Moab. The second and sixth speeches contain instructions regarding details in Israel's activity expected after Israel crosses the Jordan, each keyed by a time clause (for more extensive discussion of these six speeches, see the articles below). The third and fourth speeches contain no explicit structural element to tie them into the itinerary list. The third speech is dependent not on the wilderness itinerary structure, as if six coordinated speeches conclude the process. To the contrary, it depends directly on the second speech, disrupting the parallel construction of the speech series. The fourth speech stands apart in structure from the others, thus establishing a structural pattern in the series according to the formula ABCA′B′. Nevertheless, all six speeches share an interest in division of the land and contribute to a general platform designed to prepare for the conquest theme. The final entry in the itinerary list places Israel on the border of the promised land, at the Jordan, ready to move into the conquest. It marks the end of the wilderness, at least at this point, not the beginning of the conquest. The outer limits of the wilderness itinerary link the wilderness theme closely with both the exodus and the conquest traditions. But they also function together as inclusion elements to distinguish the wilderness from the exodus and the conquest.

Other entries in the list have anecdotal expansions. The first is the formula Ḥaḥiroth — Marah. In this case the anecdote splits element a from element b without repetition of either. The anecdote contains only a report that Israel crossed the sea and marched three days into the wilderness to Marah. There is no reference to loss of enemy life in a confrontation. It thus stands at the end of a long history of tradition. Of more significance, the itinerary reports the sea event not in relationship to the exodus traditions, but as part of the wilderness life, in the middle of the itinerary removed by several stations from the exodus event.

* The items in this series are treated separately below.

A second anecdotal expansion appears in the Kadesh — Mt. Hor entry. The elements of the formula remain together, followed by a geographical expansion and then two distinct anecdotal traditions. The first reports Aaron's death; this point warns that the wilderness theme is approaching its end since the Aaronic tradition specifies the necessity for Aaron's death before entry into the land. The list significantly makes no allusion to Moses' death or the commission of Joshua. The second alludes to the tradition, contained in Num 21:1-3, about confrontation with the Canaanite Arad. The allusion coincides with a major structural demarcation in the wilderness theme (→ The Framework, Chapter 3, FOTL IIA) and again reflects the unifying character of the itinerary list.

A second kind of expansion in the itinerary list introduces geographical detail as more exact definition of a site in the itinerary formula. Thus, v. 6 identifies 'Etham as the site "on the edge of the wilderness." The 'Etham — Migdol entry (v. 7) contains compound data about the second site in the formula: "They turned back to Pi-Haḥiroth, which is east of Baʿal Zephon, and encamped before Migdol." Construction of element b makes Migdol the itinerary site, with the other data geographical expansion. Yet, the parallel in Exod 14:2 makes Haḥiroth the itinerary site, with the other data including Migdol as supporting information. This complexity explains the point of debarkation in the following entry, not as Migdol, but as Haḥiroth. The formula in v. 9 contains details about Elim, corresponding to Exod 15:27, but not tied directly to the tradition in Exod 15:22-26. Its only function, so far as present understanding of the tradition indicates, is to define more precisely characteristics of the site. This is not the case, however, in the geographical expansion in v. 14. The reference to "no water" as a characteristic of Rephidim must be understood as an allusion to the tradition preserved in Exod 17:1-7. Significantly, Num 20:2-13 contains the same tradition, yet ties it to a different itinerary slot. And no allusion to this doublet appears in the Numbers 33 itinerary list. The formula in v. 36 provides a connection between the Wilderness of Zin and Kadesh, a point necessary for undergirding element a in the following formula. The geographical data in vv. 37, 44, 47, 48, and 49, like the expansion in v. 6, simply locate the site.

The itinerary list corresponds basically with the itinerary chain used as a framework for structure in the wilderness theme (so, Coats, "Wilderness Itinerary"). In addition, this itinerary includes a number of sites not mentioned in the wilderness chain. There is no structural reason to eliminate any one of these additions as extraneous, disruptive elements in the itinerary tradition, unrelated to the substance of the wilderness traditions (so, Snaith against Noth for maintaining the Sea of Reeds as an entry in the itinerary list significantly distinct from the Sea event). In addition to incidental sites developed in the course of the itinerary list, the text reveals an extended section of itinerary with no counterpart in the Exodus-Numbers chain (on the relationship of Num 21:10-20 with this distinct itinerary tradition, see Noth, "Wallfahrtsweg"). This segment of the itinerary list may reflect a distinct itinerary tradition, incorporated into the wilderness list at a convenient juncture (so, Noth). The argument is, however, weak. The only evidence to support it is the absence of a parallel for the segment in Exodus and Numbers.

Evidence does not support reconstruction of the itinerary list based only on itinerary formulas, excluding the expansive elements (contrary to Noth). Distinct, originally independent material does appear here. This material can be seen not only in the anecdotal tradition and geographical details, but also in the speeches associated with the final entry. But these elements do not break the unity of the itinerary list. In its final form, the list reflects the redaction process unifying the entire wilderness theme (so, Coats, "Wilderness Itinerary"). And although different itinerary traditions may have grown together, reconstruction of any one of them in detail now seems overly hypothetical, if not impossible.

Genre

This unit may be categorized simply as an ITINERARY LIST. Even in its expanded structure, with inclusion of anecdotal tradition, the genre of the unit remains ITINERARY LIST. It is comparable to the ANNALS of the ancient Near East, constructed to report the deeds of the kings. Moreover, even the ANNALS, for example, the Annals of Sennacherib, can be more adequately understood as ITINERARY LIST expanded with a record of events. An ANNAL would more naturally be structured according to yearly sequence. Although yearly sequence appears in the ANNALS as DATING FORMULAS, the basic structure design derives from an itinerary sequence.

If the hypothetical itinerary tradition suggested by Noth is an adequate understanding of the material, its genre characteristics would not correspond to the itinerary described above. It would not provide a framework for records of events, but rather a route for a PILGRIMAGE. In that case, it would function as a ritual constructed according to an itinerary sequence (→ Joshua 6). This possibility suggests that "Itinerary List" in itself is not an adequate definition of the genre since the ITINERARY LIST could provide structure for several different types of tradition. In contrast to an itinerary ritual, the larger unit in Numbers 33–35 would function as a literary genre, an ITINERARY FRAMEWORK (so, the Annals of the Kings). The ITINERARY LIST in Num 21:10-20 exemplifies this genre.

Stereotyped formulas and expressions include the ITINERARY FORMULA (so, Coats, "Wilderness Itinerary"), DATE FORMULA (v. 3), the EXODUS FORMULA (see Childs), and typical SPEECH FORMULAS.

Setting

The unit derives from a redactional setting. Its composition reflects the concern of a redactor to organize the total expanse of wilderness traditions into a single theme. It is moreover in accord with the setting for such framework itineraries generally, for the genre served broadly in an archival setting, an institution concerned with organizing and preserving traditions about events from the past (so, especially the Annals of Sennacherib).

The hypothetical itinerary would reflect a distinct setting, a cultic process calling on the itinerary for direction in execution of a pilgrimage. It should be noted that the redactional setting for the framework itinerary must not be confused with the ritual setting for a pilgrimage itinerary.

Intention

The unit charts the limitation of the wilderness theme and highlights its scope with characteristic anecdotal tradition derived from the wilderness theme. Its function is organization, its goal, preservation of tradition about Israel's life from Egypt to the plains of Moab. The intention of the hypothetical ritual itinerary, however, would be to chart the route of the pilgrimage. The wilderness itinerary does not function as a chart of the Israelites' route through the wilderness. Rather, it serves simply as a framework for hanging distinct elements of tradition together in some recognizable order (thus, cf. Num 21:10-20, with its framework function for the "Song of Heshbon" and the "Song of the Well"). The itinerary in itself does not justify a suggestion that at some point in the history of the Israelite cult, a pilgrimage following the route from Egypt to the plains of Moab occurred. The itinerary here organizes the traditions that belong to the wilderness theme into a coherent whole.

Bibliography

A. Alt, "Die Wallfahrt von Sichem nach Bethel," in *In piam memoriam Alexander von Bulmerincq. Abhandlungen der Herder-Gesellschaft und des Herder-Instituts zu Riga 6/ 3* (Riga: Ernst Plates, 1938) 218-30; G. W. Coats, "The Wilderness Itinerary," *CBQ* 34 (1972) 135-52; G. I. Davies, "The Wilderness Itineraries," *Tyndale Bulletin* 25 (1974) 46-81; idem, "The Wilderness Itineraries and the Composition of the Pentateuch," *VT* 33 (1983) 1-13; idem, *The Way of the Wilderness* (Cambridge: University Press, 1979); M. J. Lagrange, "L'itinéraire des Israélites," *RB* 9 (1900) 63-86; M. Noth, "Der Wallfahrtsweg zum Sinai," *PJ* 36 (1940) 5-28; R. deVaux, "L'itinéraire des Israélites de Cades aux plaines de Moab," in *Hommages a André Dupont-Sommer* (Paris: Adrien-Maisonneuve, 1971) 331-42; J. T. Walsh, "From Egypt to Moab: A Source-Critical Analysis of the Wilderness Itinerary," *CBQ* 39 (1977) 1-19.

Instructions for Conquest (33:50-56)*

Structure

a. Speech report	50-56
1) Introduction	50
a) The Lord to Moses	50aα

*See Annotation to Num 15:1-16.

b) Tie to the itinerary   50aβ-b
2) Instructions for the conquest   51-56
  a) Message commission formula   51a
  b) Message   51b-56
    (1) Instructions for possessing land   51b-53
      (a) Time clause   51b
      (b) Instructions   52-53a
        α. For dispossessing inhabitants   52aα
        β. For destroying cultic paraphernalia   52aβ-b
        γ. For possessing land   53a
      (c) Motivation   53b
    (2) Instructions for inheriting land   54
    (3) Warning   55-56
      (a) Condition   55aα
      (b) Threat   55aβ-56

This speech is one of six speeches set within the framework of the last entry in the wilderness itinerary. The speech formula notes not only the identity of the speech as a Yahweh speech addressed to Moses, but also the geographical locale for the speech. And the localization ties the speech explicitly to the itinerary formula: "The Lord said to Moses in the plains of Moab by the Jordan at Jericho . . ." (cf. 33:48-49). Moreover, the speech sets the principal motif used for unifying all six speeches as a part of the final stage in the itinerary by laying stress on the land as an inheritance *(naḥălâ)*, a point resumed by the verb in v. 54.

The speech structure appears under the control of a message commission formula (v. 51a) with the body of the speech (vv. 51b-56) cast as a message commissioned by the Lord for delivery to the Israelites. The message builds on three principal elements. The first contains instructions for possession of the land. A time clause opens these instructions, marking the beginning of the conquest as the moment when Israel crosses the Jordan (v. 51b). The internal structure of the speech thus demonstrates that even though the focal interest in the speech lies in stipulating the process for the conquest, the speech itself stands not as a part of the conquest theme, but as preparation for the conquest. It is tied to a place on the east bank of the Jordan and thus conceived as a part of the final stage in the wilderness theme.

The instructions call for three specific acts: (1) dispossessing the current inhabitants of the land; (2) destruction of their cultic paraphernalia; and (3) possessing the land. Formulation of these three principal acts corresponds to peculiar interest in Dtr for dispossessing/destroying all the Canaanite predecessors on the land (cf. Exod 23:24, 33; 34:13; Deut 7:2, 5; 12:3). The instructions are then founded on a notation that the Lord has given the land to Israel (v. 53b). Formulation of this foundation element corresponds to the classic pattern of a land promise. Verse 54 returns to instruction. But the content of the instruction has now shifted from the process of possession to the process of division after possession is complete. Two methods of dividing the land are noted: (1) The land will be divided by lot according to the families or the tribes of the fathers, and (2) the land will be divided proportionally according to the size of the tribe. There is, however, no discrepancy in this double procedure, for proportional division will only emphasize divine control of the process through the lot. Both procedures can be harmoniously applied if one understands that the lot, directed by the Lord, will provide proportional partition of the land (cf. Noth).

Such instructions normally precede some indication that instructions were properly executed. In this case, it is not possible to note execution of the instructions since that kind of move would introduce the substance of the conquest theme. Instead, a warning appears, guaranteeing proper execution of the instructions at the proper time. The opening element of the warning defines the circumstances for the following threat: If Israel fails to execute the instructions to expel the Canaanites, then the threat will obtain. The threat itself is twofold: (1) The Canaanites left in the land will become a source of trouble for Israel. (2) The Lord will dispossess Israel.

There is no basis for making literary-critical distinctions within the structure of the speech. Verse 54 divides instructions for possessing the land and dispossessing the native population from a warning focused only on consequences for failing in the task of dispossessing the native population. But it should not thereby be seen as an intrusion (so, Noth). The entire unit reflects dependency on a late stage of tradition, just as the itinerary list as a whole.

The Yahweh speech is stamped by an overriding concern for the conquest. Its tradition history cannot be separated from similar tradition in Dtr requiring total expulsion of Canaanite predecessors. Yet, it is lifted out of its conquest focus and structured as a speech to Moses, a part of the wilderness theme. Its position establishes some link between wilderness and conquest.

Genre

The speech is an INSTRUCTIONS SPEECH, unsupported by a narrative framework. It is nevertheless not independent in its present context, having been hung on the framework provided by the wilderness itinerary. In a narrative framework, such a SPEECH would be followed by a note that in some way the instructions were faithfully carried out (or perhaps that they were not carried out). That element is replaced here by a warning, composed of a conditional clause and a threat. Such a warning would have the impact of a conditional curse.

Setting

The speech reflects the theological formulation about the conquest process, in all probability the literary-redactional process of Dtr, characterized by the necessity for removing all traces of Canaanite population, particularly Canaanite cults, since they would be a major threat to the stability of Israel's relationship with the Lord.

Intention

As a part of the itinerary list, the speech prepares for the conquest and thus establishes a connecting link between the wilderness theme and the conquest theme. The speech calls for explicit acts in the conquest, securing those acts by means of a conditional curse. This direction of the speech is the product of theological reflection on the process of the conquest and intends to undergird the sanctity of the Yahweh faith in the face of competition from Canaanite cultic attraction.

Bibliography

Y. Aharoni, "The Province List of Judah," *VT* 9 (1959) 225-46; M. Görg, "Zum 'Skorpionenpass' (Num 34:4: Josh 15:3)," *VT* 24 (1974) 508-9; Z. Kallai-Kleinmann, "The Town Lists of Judah, Simeon, Benjamin, and Dan," *VT* 8 (1958) 134-60; Z. Kallai, "The Boundaries of Canaan (Numbers 34; cf. Ezek 47:13-20) and the Land of Israel (Josh 13-19) in the Bible," *Eretz Israel* 12 (1975) 27-34; H. Weippert, "Das geographische System der Stämme Israels," *VT* 23 (1973) 76-89.

Definition of Boundaries (34:1-12)*

Structure

b. Speech report	1-12
1) Introduction: the Lord to Moses	1
2) Definition of land boundaries	2-12
a) Message commission formula	2aα
b) Message	2αβ-12
(1) Introduction	2aβ-b
(a) Time clause	2aβ
(b) Definition of the list	2b
(2) Boundary list	3-12a
(a) South	3-5
α. General description	3a
β. Boundary definition	3b-5
(b) West	6
α. Introductory formula	6aα
β. Boundary definition	6aβ
γ. Concluding formula	6b
(c) North	7-9
α. Introductory formula	7a
β. Boundary definition	7b-9a
γ. Concluding formula	9b
(d) East	10-12a

*See Annotation to Num 15:1-16.

α. Instructions: general description 10

β. Boundary definition 11-12a

(3) Conclusion 12b

The second speech in the series is structured in parallel to the first as a Yahweh speech to Moses. It employs not only the common speech formula (v. 1) but also a message commission formula constructed with the imperative of "command" *(ṣaw).* A *kî* conjunction follows the message commission formula and marks the beginning of the message, the basic substance of the speech. Moreover, the speech picks up the unifying motif for the speech series in v. 2b: "inheritance" *(bĕnaḥălâ).*

Three principal elements define basic structure in the message. The first element, an introduction (v. 2aβ-b), is in itself compound in structure. Its primary characteristic follows the standard pattern for introductory formulas preceding lists. The demonstrative pronoun is in this case singular rather than plural *(zōʾt).* But it fulfills the same function as the more typical *ʾēlleh.* Moreover, as in standard instructions with *ʾēlleh,* so here a definition of the list follows the demonstrative: "This is the land which shall fall to you as an inheritance, the land of Canaan according to its borders." The concluding formula, v. 12b, follows exactly the same pattern, thus defining the content of the list: "This [singular] shall be your land according to its borders all round." Again the key word dominates the formula: *ligbulōtêhā.* The same word appears in the introductory formula for the list, v. 2b. But perhaps of more significance is the exclusive character of the formula. The addressee is Israel, not simply nine and one-half tribes. But the boundary list excludes the Transjordan territory. And the formula emphasizes that exclusion by specifying the borders as complete *(sābîb).* The identity of the special land becomes an issue (→ Joshua 22).

In addition to its standard pattern as an introduction to a list, the opening formula contains a time clause (v. 2aβ). The primary role for this element, if not the only role, is to tie the speech to the structural position it occupies in the wilderness itinerary (compare the first and sixth speeches). The people have not yet crossed the border. They are now laying preparations for that move (so, 33:51). But in this case, no major instructions follow (but see vv. 7, 10). Thus, the element seems to function primarily as a key for tying the unit to its position in the wilderness itinerary, a part of the complex collection used by the itinerary to mark the final stage of the wilderness immediately preceding the conquest.

The boundary list divides into four major segments according to the four points of the compass. But the four sections do not parallel each other exactly in structure. The first, the south segment, opens with a general description of the boundary: "The south boundary shall be for you from the Wilderness of Zin to the edge of Edom." This description combines a specification of two points on the border with a boundary formula, used more widely without any additional elements: "[This] shall be your southern border." A boundary definition then makes the general description quite explicit, using major landmarks in the territory involved as the points of demarcation in the border. The second segment, the west, also begins with an introductory notation. But in this case, it is a simple headline: "The western border." A boundary definition follows, again marked by a single major landmark, the shore of the western sea. Finally, a concluding formula parallels the opening formula from the south entry: "This shall be for you a western border."

The north segment begins with a formula constructed just as the concluding formula in the previous entry: "This shall be for you a northern border." The border is then defined precisely by tracing its path along major natural landmarks. And a concluding formula duplicates the introductory formula. The east segment opens with a distinct formulation, instructions for laying out the border. But just as in the opening segment, so here a general description of the border appears, the object of the instructions. A precise boundary definition follows, with no concluding formula. The instructions here, as well as in vv. 7-8, break the general structural character of the unit as a list and accommodate the tradition to the larger characteristic of the unit as a speech.

The boundary tradition preserved in this list parallels Joshua 15 in particular details, but not in total structure. As in the other texts incorporated into the wilderness itinerary, so here the unit represents a late formulation, dependent on earlier tradition. Yet, the significant point of interest in this border tradition is that occupied territory in Transjordan is ruled out of the land Israel now prepares to inherit, out of the conquest theme. Verse 2b is especially important in just this light. No value judgment is expressed. But the opening time clause suggests that the appropriate beginning for occupation is marked by entry into Canaan, by crossing the Jordan. The firm designation of an eastern border, defined not only by natural landmarks above the Sea of Chinnereth but also along the Jordan to the Salt Sea, draws a vital distinction between the land of inheritance in Canaan and the land in Transjordan (→ 34:13-15; Joshua 22).

Genre

In its present form, the unit stands as a SPEECH of the Lord, a set of INSTRUCTIONS for defining the outer limits of the land to be occupied. The primary body of the unit, however, is a BOUNDARY LIST (cf. Joshua 15–16).

Setting

The unit derives immediately from a redactional setting, the work of organization in diverse traditions about the final stages preceding the conquest. This setting also shows signs of theological reflection since its presentation defines the outer limitations of the land to be occupied in the conquest. The redactional, theological stamp is perhaps the work of Dtr. As a boundary list, the unit reflects an archival setting, the product of official records (cf. Joshua 15–16).

Intention

The speech defines the outer limits of the land now available for inheritance, marking clear distinctions between this land as inheritance and the land that lies outside any of its borders. Implicit in the definition of these borders is a distinction between this land and the land occupied in Transjordan. Canaan constitutes the fulfillment of Israel's march from Egypt, the goal of the land promised to the patriarchs. As a boundary list, the unit simply defines the division between the land Israel is to occupy and the land outside its borders.

Bibliography

→ 33:50-56

Inheritance Explanation (34:13-15)*

Structure

c. Speech report	13-15
1) Introduction: Moses to the Israelites	13a
2) Speech: explanation for inheritance	13b-15
a) Normal inheritance procedure	13b
(1) Declaration of heritable land	13bα
(2) Eligible tribes	13bβ
b) Exceptional inheritance procedure	14-15
(1) Tribes involved	14
(2) Land involved	15

This speech, a Moses speech addressed to the Israelites rather than a Yahweh speech like the other five speeches in the series, is structured into the wilderness itinerary as one in a series of coordinated speeches. And it emphasizes the unifying motif — inheritance (cf. vv. 14-15). But in every other way, the speech breaks the parallel and ties directly to the preceding speech as an addendum (compare Numbers 36). No message commission formula designates this speech as divine in origin. Rather, it appears as the direct work of Moses. Following a typical speech formula, two elements of structure appear. The first, v. 13b, identifies the land open for inheritance by lot, as the Lord commanded, and designates the tribes who will be eligible for inheritance in the process. The second element of structure, vv. 14-15, then makes the distinction between the tribes inheriting land in Canaan and the tribes possessing land in Transjordan, implicit in 34:1-12, quite explicit. Moreover, the difference involves not only a designation of tribes involved, but also a distinction

*See Annotation to Num 15:1-16.

between heritable land in Canaan (v. 13b) and the land in Transjordan (v. 15). Whether implicit value judgment on the distinction can be seen cannot be determined with clarity.

This speech is dependent on the preceding one, thus sharing the late origin identified for that one. But the concern to distinguish the land in Canaan from the land in Transjordan may go back to an ancient polemic (→ Joshua 22). Noth does not recognize this speech as an element distinct from the following speech. This structural relationship does not, however, recognize the dependent quality of this speech on designation of boundaries in the land. There is no role of dependency on the administrative links contained in the following speeches.

Genre

This SPEECH is an interpretative gloss on the preceding SPEECH.

Setting

The speech derives entirely from a redactional context, showing the process of explicit theological reflection concerning the nature of the promised land.

Intention

The speech intends to explain the distinction, only implicit in the preceding speech, between the heritable land in Canaan and the land possessed by Reuben, Gad, and the half tribe of Manasseh in Transjordan. Implicit in the explanation is a value judgment on the land in Canaan vis-à-vis the land in Transjordan (→ Joshua 22).

Administrative Lists (34:16-29)*

Structure

d. Speech report	16-29
1) Introduction: the Lord to Moses	16
2) Administrative lists	17-29
a) Leadership list	17
(1) Introduction	17a
(2) List	17b
b) Instructions for choosing leaders	18-29
(1) Instructions	18

*See Annotation to Num 15:1-16.

(2) Leadership list   19-29
  (a) Introduction   19a
  (b) List   19b-28
    α. Judah   19b
      aa. Introduction   19bα
      bb. Name   19bβ
    β. Simeon   20
      aa. Introduction   20a
      bb. Name   20b
    γ. Benjamin   21
      aa. Introduction   21a
      bb. Name   21b
    δ. Dan   22
      aa. Introduction   22a
      bb. Name   22b
    ε. Joseph   23
      aa. Introduction   23aα
      bb. Manasseh   23aβ-b
        α) Introduction   23aβ
        β) Name   23b
    ζ. Ephraim   24
      aa. Introduction   24a
      bb. Name   24b
    η. Zebulun   25
      aa. Introduction   25a
      bb. Name   25b
    θ. Issachar   26
      aa. Introduction   26a
      bb. Name   26b
    ι. Asher   27
      aa. Introduction   27a
      bb. Name   27b
    κ. Naphtali   28
      aa. Introduction   28a
      bb. Name   28b
  (c) Conclusion   29

No explicit tie with the itinerary entry in 33:48-49 can be seen in this speech; yet, the structure of the speech series suggests that this speech should be seen as a middle element in parallel pattern ABCA'B'. Moreover, the content of the speech suggests a close relationship with the speech in 34:1-12 and its gloss in 34:13-15. The speech defines the persons who will represent each tribe in the process of dividing the heritable land in Canaan. And the unifying motif for the series in verbal form, *nhl,* appears in vv. 17, 18, 29.

The speech divides into two distinct administrative lists, separated by a brief instruction calling for selection of representatives from each tribe. The first list, v. 17, opens with a typical introductory formula. The characteristic demonstrative, *'ēlleh,* precedes a definition of the list: "These are the names of the men who shall divide the land to you for inheritance." The list contains only two names, Eleazar and Joshua, successors to Aaron and Moses, respectively. The list thus involves the principal leadership of the Israelites. No concluding formula marks the end of the list.

Verse 18 stipulates selection of representatives from each tribe as men responsible for dividing the land. The instructions thus move beyond the stipulations of the first list, noting the necessity for administrative officials under the authority of Eleazar and Joshua whose work will carry out the task of the principal leaders (cf. Num 11:16ff). Moreover, the instructions set the stage for the second name list, casting the list as an extension, a closer definition of the task called for in the instructions.

The second list follows the structural pattern of the first, introduced with a stereotyped formula for name lists. The opening demonstrative, *wĕ'ēlleh,* precedes a definition of the content in the list: "These are the names of the men." The ambiguous character of the definition presupposes dependency on the instructions in v. 18; the names belong to the men to be chosen as representatives in the task of dividing the land. In contrast to the first name list, the second also has a concluding formula, v. 29. Again a demonstrative introduces a formula to define the content of the list. The formula is, however, elliptical. In contrast to the opening formula in v. 17, quite specific in designating the content of the list, as "the names of the men who shall divide the land for you," this formula notes: "These are the ones whom the Lord commanded to divide the inheritance for the Israelites in the land of Canaan." It is clear, nonetheless, that the function of the concluding formula corresponds to the introductory formula with both of the name lists.

The second name list is structured according to the tribal list. Each entry designates the tribe by an introductory formula constructed as a genitive. The opening formula sets a convenient model: "From the tribe of Judah." In addition, all of the introductory formulas from v. 22 include the noun "leader" *(nāśî')* after the genitive bond. No clear reason for the change can be seen; the addition simply picks up the key word from the instructions in v. 18 and solidifies the bond between the name list and the presentation of the list as a part of the instructions to organize representatives from the tribes. Following the introductory formula is the representative's name, plus identification of his father: "Caleb, the son of Jephunneh."

The pattern of the list breaks with the tribe of Joseph. Immediately following the typical introductory formula for the Joseph entry, a second introductory formula designates a sub-entry for the tribe of Manasseh. This entry then follows the pattern standard for the entries in the primary structure of the list. Verse 24 returns to the regular construction of the name list. This entry for the tribe of Ephraim, a tribe related to the Joseph tribe, might be considered a sub-entry under the tribe of Joseph just like the Manasseh entry. Insofar as the tradition history of the name list is concerned, such subordination of the Ephraim entry would be in order. But no structural indication of that subordination appears. As a procedure for replacing Levi in the structure of the tribal list, Joseph is commonly replaced by two tribes, Ephraim and Manasseh. Commonly these two tribes can be ordered as subordinate entries under Joseph, leaving only an eleven-entry list at the primary level. In this case, however, the tribe of Ephraim has no evidence for such subordination.

Even with the division of Joseph into two entries, however, the list contains only ten tribes. This deviation in the tribe list reflects the speech's position as a part of tradition about inheritance in Canaan excluding the Transjordan territory. Reuben and Gad will have no representatives in the group responsible for dividing the land. The speech is thus tightly tied to the series, including 34:1-12 and its gloss in 34:13-15. Despite the relationship between the speech and its context, however, the speech in vv. 13-15 would not represent a gloss on this text. The gloss is concerned to explain the difference in inheriting land in Canaan and the land inherited in Transjordan. No indication of representatives from the two tribes and the half tribe can be seen there. The unity of the speeches thus does not suggest dependency between this speech and the gloss but points only to the implied distinctions in vv. 1-12 between the tribes and their land in Canaan vis-à-vis the tribes and their land in Transjordan (→ Joshua 22).

Unity between the speech here and the preceding speech, particularly vv. 1-12, marks this speech as late, adapted for this position in the redaction process that brought the wilderness itinerary with its incorporated traditions together. Tradition history background for this speech lies in the polemic against Transjordan occupation (→ Joshua 22).

Genre

The final form of the SPEECH defines the unit as a Yahweh SPEECH to Moses, specifying instructions for dividing the land among the tribes once the conquest should be completed. That speech is composed of two NAME LISTS. The first simply designates the responsible leadership. The second is subordinated to the instructions, thus stands as a part of directions to Moses that must be carried out in the process of the conquest. The primary genre category for that section is nonetheless NAME LIST.

Setting

The final form of the speech reflects redactional setting, particularly the process of theological reflection about the shape of the conquest tradition that led to exclusion of the Transjordan territory from the promised land. Name lists, including the specific content of these lists, doubtlessly reflect the archival concerns of official records.

Intention

Redaction, the process of theological reflection about major traditions, employs these name lists as further qualification in the description of the process for dividing the land. The tribes of Reuben and Gad (so also a half of Manasseh) fall outside the provisions for fulfilling the promise for a special land. Moreover, the lists set the stage for the conquest theme but do not introduce the theme. The wilderness theme thus maintains a firm root in the conquest traditions. Name lists function generally as administrative instruments, a means for organizing and preserving records.

Bibliography

M. Noth, *Das System der Zwölf Stämme Israels* (BWANT 4/1; Stuttgart: Kohlhammer, 1930).

Tariff for Levitical Cities, 35:1-8*

Structure

e. Speech report	35:1-8
1) Introduction	1
a) The Lord to Moses	1aα
b) Tie to the itinerary	1aβ-b
2) Instructions for providing Levitical cities	2-8
a) Instructions	2
(1) to provide cities	2a
(2) to provide pasture	2b
b) Declaration of purpose	3
(1) For the cities	3a
(2) For the pasture	3b
c) Definition	4-7
(1) Pasture	4-5
(a) General dimensions	4
(b) Instructions for establishing dimensions	5
α. Opening imperative	5aα$_1$
β. List	5aα$_2$-aβ
aa. East	5aα$_2$
bb. South	5aα$_3$
cc. West	5aβ$_1$
dd. North	5aβ$_2$
γ. Concluding formula	5b
(2) Cities	6
(a) General instructions	6aα
(b) Number of cities	6aβ-b
(3) Concluding summary	7
d) Selection procedure	8

*See Annotation to Num 15:1-16.

This speech follows the pattern for the speech series in the last entry for the wilderness itinerary. It begins with a speech formula, noting not only that the unit is a Yahweh speech to Moses but tying the speech directly to the itinerary entry: "The Lord spoke to Moses, in the plains of Moab by the Jordan near Jericho, saying. . . ." The speech thus parallels the first speech in the series and stands as A' in the parallel ABCA'B'. Moreover, the speech employs the unifying motif for the series in v. 2: "The inheritance of their possession" *(minnaḥălat 'ăḥuzzātām)*.

Contrary to the parallel pattern, however, this speech does not show a message commission formula or a time clause (so, compare the first, second, and sixth speeches). Rather, it opens in v. 2 with instructions to Moses, followed by a purpose clause: "Command the Israelites in order that they may give the Levites from the inheritance of their possession cities to dwell in." The construction nevertheless parallels speeches A, B, and B' by addressing Moses with specific instructions to be mediated to the Israelites. Indeed, the sentence carrying a command to Moses parallels the message commission formula in 34:2 (speech b), particularly in the opening refrain: "Command the Israelites." The only missing elements in this speech, preventing an exact parallel, are the end of the message commission formula and the time clause: ". . . and say to them, 'When you go into the land of Canaan. . . .'" One might compare also speech a, 33:51.

The speech comprises four major elements of structure. The first element constitutes instructions to Moses with a purpose clause, designating a requirement on the Israelites for providing cities, and their pasture, for the Levites (cf. Joshua 21). The two objects of the requirement, cities and their pasture, are designated here only by noun objects. But a parallel in the requirement, placing equal emphasis on both cities and pasture, is set up by repetition of the main verb. The second element, v. 3, is distinguished from the first by repetition of the cities/pasture parallel. This element functions to establish the purpose for the cities and their pasture.

The third element carries the major content of the speech, a definition in detail of the objects to be given to the Levites. Again, the parallel construction is apparent, although the order in the parallel has been reversed. The pasture is defined first, then designation of the cities. In the pasture section, precise description for defining the pasture in relation to the cities calls for one thousand cubits from the wall of the city measured all around (see Noth for comments about the artificial character of this description). The element remains description, however, with no directive calling for active execution of the instructions. The instructions appear only in v. 5. Here the dimensions are repeated, although the formula calls for two thousand cubits (LXX harmonizes v. 4 with this specification). And instead of casting the shape of the pasture as a simple circle around the city, the instructions stipulate measurement to each of the four directions. The element concludes in v. 5b with a formula like the formulas ending or beginning lists and recognizes that v. 5 casts instructions for measurement in the pasture as a list of the dimensions for the four directions.

Verse 6 provides precise information for defining the cities. The opening refrain repeats the requirement for providing levitical cities. Verse 6aβ duplicates the syntactical function of the first two words in v. 6aα, thus providing more precise definition of the cities than the general statement in v. 6aα. The emphasis of this precise definition falls not only on the qualification of the cities as cities of refuge *'ārê hammiqlāṭ,* but more directly on the number of the cities to be presented as cities of refuge. This point is confirmed by v. 6b, calling for additional cities according to number alone. A concluding summary in v. 7 returns to the order, cities/pasture, and specifies the total number of cities with pasture as the requirement the Israelites should provide for the Levites.

The final major element in the unit. v. 8, lays out the selection procedure according to size of the tribes. This element thus corresponds to the proportional designation for inheritance procedures in 33:54.

The speech is a literary unity, derived from older tradition but included as a part of very late material in the wilderness itinerary. Traditio-historical background for the unit can be seen in Joshua 21.

Genre

The unit is cast as a Yahweh SPEECH to Moses, thus sharing the larger context required as a portion of the wilderness itinerary. Its character here sets the unit into a narrative tradition similar to the anecdotal traditions preserved by the itinerary. Behind the wilderness itinerary context lies a unit that is primarily law, a tariff requiring proportional provision for the Levites. → Numbers 18.

Setting

The redactional setting for the unit reflects the process of theological organization of Israel's traditions, casting the end of the wilderness theme as a stage of preparation for the conquest. At the earlier level, the unit derives from a legislative setting, establishing requirements for providing sustenance for the Levites.

Intention

In the final form of the text, this speech shares with the general shape of the wilderness itinerary as a step in preparing for the conquest. It thus emphasizes the inheritance motif as the guideline for the final stages of the wilderness theme. The intention of the law is to provide a tariff on the Israelites as a cultic tax, like Numbers 18, but concerned not with food but with a place for the Levites to dwell and tend cattle. It envisions enclaves of Levites living in cities throughout all the tribes but set apart from other tribal cities as special accommodation for priestly figures. Whether it provides for levitical possession of this land is not altogether clear (see Noth).

Bibliography

A. G. Auld, *Joshua, Moses, and the Land* (Edinburgh: T. & T. Clark, 1980); M. Haran, "Studies in the Account of the Levitical Cities: I. Preliminary Considerations," *JBL* 80 (1961) 45-54; idem, "Studies in the Account of the Levitical Cities: II. Utopia and Historical Reality," *JBL* 80 (1961) 116-65.

Tariff for Cities of Refuge (35:9-34)*

Structure

f. Speech report	35:9-34
1) Introduction: the Lord to Moses	9
2) Speech	10-34
a) Message commission formula	10a
b) Message	10b-34
(1) Tariff for cities of refuge	10b-15
(a) Instructions	10b-11aα
α. Time clause	10b
β. Instructions proper	11aα
(b) Definitions of the cities	11aβ-15
α. First definition	11aβ-b
aa. Name	11aβ
bb. Purpose	11b
β. Second definition	12
aa. Name	12a
bb. Purpose	12b
γ. Third definition	13-15
aa. Number	13-15
α) Total number	13
β) Number according to locale	14
bb. Purpose	15
(2) Qualifications on law concerning violent death	16-28
(a) Legislation on murder	16-21
α. First case	16
aa. Conditions	16a
bb. Judgment	16b
β. Second case	17
aa. Conditions	17a
bb. Judgment	17b
γ. Third case	18-19
aa. Conditions	18a

*See Annotation to Num 15:1-16.

bb. Judgment	18b-19
δ. Fourth case	20-21
aa. Conditions	20-21aα
bb. Judgment	21aβ-b
(b) Legislation on manslaughter	22-25
α. Conditions	22-23
β. Judgment	24-25
(c) Legislation on breaking confinement	26-28
α. Conditions	26-27a
β. Judgment	27b-28
aa. Instructions for execution	27b
bb. Legal basis	28
(3) Conclusion	29
(4) Additional qualifications	30-34
(a) Ordinance for death sentences	30
α. Witnesses required	30a
β. Number	30b
(b) Prohibition against ransom	31-34
α. Against ransom for murderer	31
β. Against ransom for man-slayer	32-34
aa. Prohibition	32
bb. Reasons	33-34
α) Prohibition against pollution	33-34a
β) Reason	34b

This speech follows the structural parallel ABCA′B′ in the series of six speeches incorporated into the final entry of the wilderness itinerary as the B′ element. Like the second speech, it begins with a speech formula casting the unit as a Yahweh speech to Moses with no explicit tie to the itinerary entry. And like the second speech, it constructs the content of its tradition as a message, headed by a message commission formula and followed by a time clause. Yet, despite the obvious unity the speech holds with the series, a basic disunity with the other speeches in the series comes to light. The speech does not employ the unifying motif of the series, some kind of explicit emphasis on the land as Israel's inheritance. Rather, it relates directly to the fifth speech by catchword construction. In v. 6, the fifth speech designated six of the levitical cities as cities of refuge (*'ārê hammiqlāt*). This sixth speech begins with detailed instructions for establishing those cities (cf. *'ārê miqlāt* in v. 11). The traditional combination is also attested in Joshua 20–21, although the order is reversed. Moreover, the catchword construction in the unit itself accounts for a superficial unity in a speech that reveals basic lines of disunity (see the comments below on the relationship between vv. 10-15 and 16-28 or the relationship between 16-28 and 30-34). Thus, this speech is far more complex, far less unified than any of the other speeches in the series.

Four principal structural elements appear in the message section of the speech. The first carries instructions for establishing cities of refuge. Structure in this element is similar to the structure in the speech establishing the levitical cities (35:1-8). The first part of the elements of v. 11 contains the focal element of instructions for establishing the cities of refuge, built as a conclusion to the time clause in v. 10b. "When you cross the Jordan into the land of Canaan, then you shall establish cities for yourselves. . . ." The time clause thus defines the point of validation for the tariff appropriating cities from tribal inheritance for special purpose (compare the time clauses in speeches a. [33:50-56] and b. [34:1-12]). A series of definitions follows. Verse 11aβ-b establishes the name of the cities with a statement of purpose closely attached. The purpose statement designates the cities as refuge from the avenger for the manslayer who strikes a person in innocence. Verse 12 repeats the definition of the cities by name with additional information in the statement of purpose: "The cities shall be a refuge for you from the avenger, so that the man-slayer shall not be killed until he stands before the congregation for judgment." The definition process is repeated in vv. 13-15, at this point noting not the name but the number of cities required. The cities are defined by total number, then a designation of the number in Transjordan and in Canaan. An additional statement of purpose follows. These definitions serve to enforce precision in the initial statement of instructions in v. 11aα.

The second structural item, vv. 16-28, picks up from the instructions for establishing cities of refuge by means of catchword association (cf. the word *rōṣēaḥ*). Three distinct sections of legislation concerning a man who kills another man appear here. The first section, vv. 16-21, involves four cases of murder. In each case, a stipulation of conditions constructed as an *'ô* clause (on v. 18, cf. Sam Pent, LXX, some MSS) functions as a protasis for judgment in those cases. Duplications of the conditional clause with the conjunction *'ô* appear commonly (thus, cf. vv. 18, 20-21). The apodosis begins with a declaration formula: "He is a murderer" *(rōṣēaḥ hû').*

Then the sentence is established. "The murderer shall be killed" *(môt yûmat hārōṣēaḥ).* The third case adds the method of execution: "The avenger of blood shall kill the murderer. When he meets him, he shall kill him." The fourth case expands the conditions by adding a second *'im* clause. Then it reverses the order of sentence and declaration formula and finally spells out the means for execution. These laws are thus clearly formulated according to the structural style of casuistic statements.

The second section, vv. 22-25, sets out a single statement of legislation, again formulated in casuistic style. The subject here is not murder but manslaughter. The protasis, again constructed as an *'im* clause, compounds its pattern, like vv. 18 and 20-21, by adding a series of clauses with *'ô* conjunction. The apodosis in the formulation, vv. 24-25, sets out instructions for the judging congregation (cf. v. 12). The particularities of their judgment requires protection from the avenger for the manslayer, but punishment by confinement in the city of refuge until the death of the high priest is an alternative. The third section, vv. 26-28, is constructed in the same pattern, with an *'im* clause protasis setting out the conditions for judgment and the apodosis noting the proper judgment. In this case, however, the issue does not involve judgment on an act of murder or manslaughter, but judgment on a manslayer who breaks his confinement in the city of refuge before the prescribed time. The judgment recognizes the right of the avenger to kill the manslayer if he can find him outside the borders of the city. A declaratory formula pronounces the executor free of liability in the manslayer's death: "There shall be no blood on him." The basis for the judgment is thus detailed, confirming the intrinsic relationship between protasis and apodosis. The manslayer should remain in the city of refuge until the death of the high priest and only then go beyond the city to his own house. If he does not, he is subject to the just action of the avenger.

Verse 29 marks the conclusion of the laws, a formula that stands at the end of the section in vv. 16-28 but in the present text acts as a conclusion for vv. 10-15 as well. The formula thus suggests that all of vv. 10-28 must now be seen under the primary character of laws governing judgment in matters involving a violent death.

Verses 30-34 stand apart from the qualifications on the law in vv. 16-28, broken not only by the concluding formula in v. 29 but also by change in basic structure. The casuistically constructed laws in vv. 16-28 lapse in favor of statements constructed without conditions. The first statement regulates procedure in giving sentences of death by requiring eyewitnesses. The statement emphasizes the requirement, and then stipulates the number by calling for more than one eyewitness. The second statement is a prohibition against changing the judgment procedure on the basis of ransom. The process of justice has no right to soften the death penalty for a convicted murderer or to allow a convicted manslayer to leave the city of refuge before his time. Reasons for this position apply only to the second judgment. If a manslayer leaves his city of refuge, he will pollute the land. The reason is itself cast as a new prohibition, with a renewed reason for the prohibition established. The land should not be polluted because the Lord himself dwells in the midst of the people (note the formulaic construction: "I the Lord dwell in the midst of the Israelites"). This section appears to be constructed into the context, not on the basis of unity with the text as a whole, but on the basis of the catchword rōṣēaḥ in v. 30.

The unit is thus composite. The layers suggest at least the following stages of growth: (1) a collection of laws related to violent death; (2) a collection of laws concerning judgment on a man who kills another man; (3) tariff requirements establishing cities of refuge. The traditio-historical background of this speech can be seen in Joshua 20-21. Like the other speeches in the series, this speech as a whole should be identified as late priestly tradition, compiled as a part of the final redaction of the Pentateuch to serve as a platform for the conquest in the final stage of the wilderness itinerary.

Genre

At its final level of redaction, this SPEECH serves as one in a series of Yahweh SPEECHES incorporated like anecdotal tradition into the wilderness itinerary. It appears to be a collection of laws concerning judgments in cases involving violent death. Distinct collections of laws, constructed as casuistic or apodictic statements, make up this stage. It should be noted that the terms casuistic and apodictic are primarily structural terms rather than genre terms. The complexity of the collection can be seen by the combination of the two sections of laws without intermixing structural techniques. The earlier stage of the unit, to which the laws have been attached, is a tariff that requires establishment of the cities of refuge as a portion from the inheritance of each of the tribes (cf. Joshua 20). One should note here, contrary to the earlier speeches in the series, that no discrimination against the Transjordan tribes can be seen, unless the equal number of cities required from both Transjordan and Canaan suggests a heavier burden of taxation on the relatively smaller territory, in contradiction to the principle for selection of the cities in the previous speech.

Setting

The final stage of the speech is redactional, a part of the larger context of tradition marking the final stage of the wilderness theme in preparation for the conquest. The collection of laws reflects the judicial setting, calling for interpretation of the product from the legislative setting of the civil court. The tariff derives from civil administration of common life, marked as normally the case in the ancient world with the blessing of the cult.

Intention

The final stage of the speech belongs to the wilderness itinerary as a part of the platform used for preparing the conquest. The collection of laws preserves legal tradition designed to guide the court in administration of justice in cases involving violent death. The tariff establishes a means for protecting the manslayer from the traditional death by an avenger of the blood ($\rightarrow$ Gen 9:6).

Bibliography

A. G. Auld, "Cities of Refuge in Israelite Tradition," *JSOT* 10 (1978) 26-39.

Case Report: The Daughters of Zelophehad (36:1-12)

Structure

I. Introduction	1
A. Definition of theme	1a
1. Thematic verb	$1a\alpha_1$
2. Genealogical date for litigants	$1a\alpha_2$-aβ
B. Definition of theme	1b
II. Speech report	2-4
A. Introduction (heads of fathers' houses to Moses)	$2a\alpha_1$
B. Appeal speech	$2a\alpha_2$-4

       1. Precedent case   2aα₂-b

       2. Appeal: designation of legal crisis   3-4

  III. Judgment speech report   5-9

     A. Introduction: Moses to the Israelites   5a

     B. Speech   5b-9

       1. Judgment about the appeal   5b

       2. Message commission formula   6aα

       3. Message   6aβ-9

          a. Stipulation for marriage for daughters   6aβ-b

          b. Stipulation on inheritance   7

          c. General marriage instructions   8a

          d. Purpose   8b-9

  IV. Execution of instructions   10-12

The case report in this chapter appears as an appendix to the book of Numbers, but still within the context of traditions dealing with inheritance procedure and possession of the land. Specifically, it stands as an addendum to the case report in Num 27:1-11, a new qualification of the judgment built on the precedent case of the daughters of Zelophehad. As in Num 27:1-11, so here the unit comprises two major elements, again speeches of the litigants and the judge (without explicit transition between them), an introduction, and in this case, an element noting execution of the judgment. The introduction is structured in parallel to the first two verses of Numbers 27 (cf. especially 27:2). The verb of the opening verse defines the thematic unity of the pericope, again in parallel to Num 27:1: "They came near" *(wayyiqrĕbû).* And as in 27:1, so here, the remaining parts of the verse qualify the subject of the unit with explicit genealogical data: "The heads of the fathers of the families of the Gileadites, the son of Machir, son of Manasseh, from the families of the sons of Joseph, drew near." Verse 1a parallels 27:2 and shows the function of the second element in defining the general thematic unity of the pericope. The action of the litigants took place before Moses and the leaders, the heads of the fathers of the Israelites. The action involves legal process before designated judges.

The first speech parallels 27:2-4. It sets out the legal precedent for the appeal, explicitly the case report from 27:1-11. The point reflects a parallel also in 27:3. Then, on the basis of the legal precedent, it defines the corresponding legal crisis, paralleled in 27:4a. In effect, the rights of the daughters of Zelophehad are being challenged in court. Reference to the year of Jubilee in v. 4 is not clear, since in the Jubilee property should revert to its original owner. In this case the Jubilee seems to have no effect on the crisis concerning possession of land within the original tribal unit. The impact of the crisis is nonetheless clear. If a daughter who has inherited land from her father marries into another tribe, the original tribal possession of designated portions of land would be subverted. Significantly, no explicit appeal for judgment appears in the speech. The text apparently presupposes that the crisis described in vv. 2-4 implies the appeal.

The judgment speech begins with a speech formula designating Moses as speaker, but the origin of the speech lies in the Lord. The element thus parallels the Yahweh speech in 27:6-11 and presupposes an element of transition similar to 27:5. The first part of the judgment speech declares the lawsuit to be just (// 27:7). The term for defining the merits of the suit, *dōběrîm,* has its only clear parallel in such legal contexts as 27:7. Then the stipulations of the judgment develop under a message commission formula, as a message addressed specifically to the daughters of Zelophehad (v. 6aα//27:8a). The stipulations define not the succession of inheritance as it does in 27:1-11, but the necessity for maintaining heritable property within the original tribal group that established ownership. A daughter may marry whomsoever she chooses. But if she wants to inherit her father's property, she must marry within the clan.

The unit closes with a note that the daughters of Zelophehad married in accord with the divine judgment, thus preserving their property for the clan of the father's family.

The unit derives from the priestly source. But its antecedents set the traditions into older legal traditions, just as the unit in 27:1-11. The tradition history reflected by the basic precedent case would thus apply for the addendum to the basic case.

Genre

→ Num 27:1-11

Setting

→ Num 27:1-11

Intention

This unit, like Num 27:1-11, is judicial, not legislative. It intends to qualify an earlier decision reached in judicial process. The specific intention in contrast to the report in 27:1-11 is to limit the circumstances under which the original judgment can be applied. And the purpose for the limitation is to hold heritable property within the clan of the dead father.

Bibliography

→ Num 27:1-11

Conclusion Formula (36:13)

Structure

I. Introductory demonstrative	13aα₁
II. Definition of a unit	13aα₂-b
A. Major body of the unit	13aα₂
B. Qualifications	13aβ-b
1. Addressee	13aβ
a. Moses	13aβ₁
b. Message to the people	13aβ₂
2. Place	13b

This formula is built on a stereotyped pattern with an introductory demonstrative, "these" *('ēlleh),* and a specification of content in a major unit the formula modifies. The unit this formula controls is identified as laws and judgments *(hammiṣwôt wĕhammišpāṭîm).* More important for understanding the formula's structural function is the double qualification following the unit definition. The laws and judgments were delivered by the hand of Moses to the Israelites in the plains of Moab by the Jordan near Jericho. The formula thus represents an inclusion element with the last stage of the wilderness itinerary, Num 33:48-49, where the same definition of place occurs. A similar formulation of the place appears in 22:1. (22:1 has *mē'ēber lĕyardēn* instead of *'al yardēn* as 33:48-49 and 36:13 have.) On the importance of the structural unit, → 33:1–35:34.

The formula belongs to the latest stage in Pentateuchal redaction, related to the system represented by the wilderness itinerary.

Genre

The formula is a stereotyped unit formula, either CONCLUSION or INTRODUCTION, for legal collections.

Setting

The formula reflects a redactional process, specifically in the organization of the Pentateuch, generally in the organization for any legal collection.

Intention

The formula functions to mark off the outer limits of a collection, or any other type of unit, either at the beginning or the ending. In this case, it represents an inclusion element with Num 33:48-49, designating a major body of inheritance tradition at the end of the wilderness theme.

APPENDIX

Since Professor Coats had not provided a macrostructure of Num 10:11–36:13 for → Chapter 4 of this volume, research associate David Palmer hypothetically reconstructed such a structure, and also the macrostructures of J and P, from the elements of Coats's typescript on Num 11:1–36:13 by following Coats's work in Chapters 1B and 3 of his FOTL volume IIA on Exodus 1–18. Palmer's reconstruction makes it possible to recognize Coats's — presumable — understanding of the same structural pattern in the sagas before and after the Sinai narrative. It deserves interpretation and further study.

Macrostructure for Num 11:1–36:13

I. Food, enemy, spring	Num 11:1–25:18
A. Food	11:1-35
1. Taberah tale	1-3
2. The quail story	4-35
B. Enemy	12:1–19:22
1. Aaron and Miriam rebellion story	12:1-16
2. Murmuring tale	13:1–14:45
3. Ordinance speech	15:1-16
4. Ordinance speech	15:17-31
5. Anecdote: the wood-gathering precedent	15:32-36
6. Ordinance speech for vestment	15:37-41
7. Tale of rebellion: Dathan-Abiram-Korah	16:1–17:5 (*NRSV* 16:1-40)
8. Plague tale	17:6-15 (*NRSV* 16:41-50)
9. Almond rod anecdote	17:16-26 (*NRSV* 17:1-11)
10. Collection of priesthood ordinances	17:27–18:32 (*NRSV* 17:12–18:32)
11. Ordinance for protective cleansing	19:1-22
C. Spring: Meribah spring legend	20:1-13

    1. Itinerary formula 1
    2. Exposition 2a
    3. Complication 2b-5
    4. Resolution 6-12
    5. Concluding etiology 13
  D. Enemy 20:14–25:18
    1. Negotiations report 20:14-21
    2. Aaron death report 20:22-29
    3. Hormah etiology 21:1-3
    4. Fiery serpents tale 21:4-9
    5. Wilderness itinerary 21:10-20
    6. Battle report 21:21-31
    7. Wilderness itinerary 21:32-35
    8. Balaam legend 22:1–24:25
    9. Baal Peor anecdote 25:1-18
II. Conquest traditions .... 25:19–36:13 (*NRSV* 26:1–36:13)
  A. Census .... 25:19–26:65 (*NRSV* 26:1-65)
    1. Speech report 25:19–26:2
    2. Speech report 3-4a
    3. Execution of instructions 4b-51
    4. Speech report 52-56
    5. Levi 57-62
    6. Conclusion 63-65
  B. Case report: the daughters of Zelophehad 27:1-11
    1. Introduction 1
    2. Speech report 2-4
    3. Transition: appeal to the Lord 5
    4. Speech report 6-11
  C. Commission report 27:12-23
    1. Speech report 12-14
    2. Speech report 15-17
    3. Commission speech report 18-21
    4. Execution of instructions 22-23
  D. Ritual calendar .... 28:1–30:1 (*NRSV* 28:1–29:40)
    1. Speech report 28:1–29:39
    2. Conclusion: execution of instructions .... 30:1 (*NRSV* 29:40)
  E. Judicial tradition concerning vows .... 30:2-17 (*NRSV* 30:1-16)
    1. Speech report .... 2-16 (*NRSV* 1-15)
    2. Conclusion .... 17 (*NRSV* 16)
  F. Report of battle against Midian 31:1-54
    1. Speech report 1-2
    2. Speech report 3-4
    3. Execution of instructions 5-11
    4. Report to Moses 12-24
    5. Distribution of spoil 25-54
  G. Negotiations dialogue 32:1-42
    1. Description of the land of Gilead 1

2. Dialogue	2-27
3. Report of the agreement	28-32
4. Execution of the agreement	33-42
H. Wilderness itinerary	33:1–35:34
1. Introduction	33:1-2
2. Itinerary list	33:3–35:34
I. Case report: the daughters of Zelophehad	36:1-12
1. Introduction	1
2. Speech report	2-4
3. Judgment speech report	5-9
4. Execution of instructions	10-12
J. Conclusion formula	36:13
1. Introductory demonstrative	13aα_1
2. Definition of a unit	13aα_2-b

Addendum

The following detailed macrostructures for P and J, not provided by Coats, were reconstructed from his typescript for this volume (FOTL IV) and from the structural elements presented in his volume *Exodus 1–18* (FOTL IIA). These macrostructures for P and J are presented here for further study and interpretation.

Macrostructure for P in Num 11:1–36:13

I. Enemy, thirst	P references in Num 13:1–25:5
A. Enemy	P references in Num 13:1–19:22
1. Murmuring tale	13:1-17a, 21, 25-26, 32-33; 14:1a, 2-3, 5-10, 26-38
2. Ordinance speeches	15:1-31
3. Anecdote: the wood-gathering precedent	15:32-36
4. Ordinance speech for vestment	15:37-41
5. Tale of rebellion: Dathan-Abiram-Korah	16:1-11, 16-24, 27a, 32-35; 17:1-5 (*NRSV* 16:36-40)
6. Plague tale	17:6-15 (*NRSV* 16:41-50)
7. Almond rod anecdote	17:16-26 (*NRSV* 17:1-11)
8. Collection of priesthood ordinances	17:27–18:32 (*NRSV* 17:12–18:32)
9. Ordinance for protective cleansing	19:1-22
B. Thirst	20:1-29
1. Meribah spring legend	20:1-13
2. Aaron death report	20:22-29
II. Conquest traditions	25:6–36:13 (*NRSV* 26:1–36:13)
A. Baal Peor anecdote	25:6-18 (also J)

B. Census   25:19–26:65 (*NRSV* 26:1-65)
   1. Speech report   25:19–26:2
   2. Speech report   26:3-4a
   3. Execution of instructions   4b-51
   4. Speech report   52-56
   5. Levi   57-62
   6. Conclusion   63-65
C. Case report: the daughters of Zelophehad 27:1-11
   1. Introduction   1
   2. Speech report   2-4
   3. Transition: appeal to the Lord   5
   4. Speech report   6-11
D. Legend about Moses' successor   27:12-23
   1. Speech report   12-14
   2. Speech report   15-17
   3. Commission speech report   18-21
   4. Execution of instructions   22-23
E. Ritual calendar   28:1–30:1 (*NRSV* 28:1–29:40)
   1. Speech report   28:1–29:39
   2. Conclusion: execution of instructions 30:1 (*NRSV* 29:40)
F. Judicial tradition concerning vows   30:2-17 (*NRSV* 30:1-16)
   1. Speech report   2-16 (*NRSV* 1-15)
   2. Conclusion   17 (*NRSV* 16)
G. Report of battle against Midian   31:1-54
   1. Speech report   1-2
   2. Speech report   3-4
   3. Execution of instructions   5-11
   4. Report to Moses   12-24
   5. Distribution of spoil   25-54
H. Negotiations dialogue   32:1-42 (also J)
   1. Description of the land of Gilead   1
   2. Dialogue   2-27
   3. Report of the agreement   28-32
   4. Execution of the agreement   33-42
I. Wilderness itinerary   33:1–35:34
   1. Introduction   33:1-2
   2. Itinerary list   33:3–35:34
J. Case report: the daughters of Zelophehad 36:1-12
   1. Introduction   1
   2. Speech report   2-4
   3. Judgment speech report   5-9
   4. Execution of instructions   10-12
K. Conclusion formula   36:13

Macrostructure for J in Num 11:1–36:13

I. Heroic deeds — Num 11:1–12:16; J references from 13:17b–16:31 and 20:14–25:5

  A. Food — 11:1-35
    1. Taberah tale — 1-3
    2. The quail story — 4-35
  B. Enemy — 12:1-16; J references from 13:17b–16:31

    1. Aaron and Miriam rebellion story — 12:1-16
    2. Murmuring tale — 13:17b-20, 22-24, 27-31; 14:1b, 4, 11-25, 39-45
    3. Tale of rebellion: Dathan-Abiram-Korah — 16:1, 12-15, 24-26, 27b, 28-31
  C. Enemy — J references from 20:14–25:5
    1. Negotiations report — 20:14-21
    2. Hormah etiology — 21:1-3
    3. Fiery serpents tale — 21:4-9
    4. Battle report — 21:21-31
    5. Wilderness itinerary — 21:32-35
    6. Balaam legend — 22:1–24:25
    7. Baal Peor anecdote — 25:1-5
II. Conquest traditions — Num 32 (also P)

GLOSSARY

Genres

ACCOUNT (Rechenschaftsbericht). Referred to in Num 1:1–10:10. A particular kind of (→) report, an accounting report. FOTL IIA, 155.
  Cf. FOTL IX, 243; X, 291; XI, 426; XIII, 172.

ACCUSATION (Anklage). Num 11:20; 16:8-10. A speech alleging that someone has broken the law or otherwise done wrong. This speech form had its original setting in judicial practice, but was adapted by the prophets and could be used in a literary context. It may be addressed directly to the accused or refer to them in the 3rd pers. The simplest form of an accusation is a declaratory sentence (cf. 2 Sam 12:9b; Jer 29:21, 23) or accusing question (2 Sam 12:9a; Jer 22:15). A more developed form establishes a causal connection between the offense and its consequence (Exod 1:18; 5:14; 10:3ab; 18:14-23; 32:11, 21-24; cf. 1 Sam 15:23). FOTL XX, 105.
  Cf. FOTL IIA, 156; XI, 427; XIV, 243; XV 507; XVI 512; C. Westermann, *Basic Forms of Prophetic Speech* (tr. W. C. White; Philadelphia: Westminster, 1967) 142-48.

ADMINISTRATION OF IMPURE PERSONS (Verfügung über unreine Personen). Num 5:1-4. → Report.

ADMINISTRATIVE LIST (Administrative Liste). Num 34:17-29. → List, Register.

ADMONITION (Ermahnung gegen). Num 28:31bα. An attempt at dissuasion from doing something wrong or not doing what is right; a negative expression, such as: "do not forget," by which one party appeals to the mind either of an addressed (2nd pers.) or a third (3rd pers.) party in an attempt to dissuade those addressed or implied from wrong action or behavior.
  What would be done wrong may consist either of an improper act or behavior or of a failure to act or behave properly. In either case, the nature of the wrong is

337

predetermined by what appears to be disadvantageous, as, e.g., in wisdom reflection, as well as by the violation of established customs, positive ethical standards, laws, commands, prohibitions, and instructions.

While the various kinds of societal standards must by virtue of their intrinsic authority not be violated — even unconditionally — the admonition focuses on the danger of their violation which lies in the unsteadiness of the human mind, or psyche, and in its temptation, ability, or willingness to avoid doing what is right, necessary, decreed, or even apodictically commanded. The admonition aims at deactivating the negative potentials of the mind so as to overcome the obstacles in it by discouraging wrongdoing or not doing what is right. It does so by appealing to persons either directly or indirectly by way of explanatory or empirical argumentation. Like exhortation or parenesis, it is in principle motivating.

It is, however, no more than an attempt. Whether or not it will succeed is just as much open as the aims of exhortation, and as whether or not laws or directives are obeyed.

Admonition can be discerned by expressions of direct appeals at dissuasion, ad hominem, even in grammatical forms of prohibitives (as especially in the Wisdom literature; cf. Murphy, FOTL XIII, with reference to Bright), but also in additions to laws, prohibitions, commands, prophetic announcements, et al., which function as explanations to otherwise given interdicts.

The grammatical forms may, however, belong to the genre of prohibition or of admonition. The criterion for distinguishing their genre should be whether they focus on discouragement from the negative human attitude in action and behavior, as in admonition, or on the non-negotiable authority of what is said and regardless of the addressees' general psychological predisposition, as in prohibition. FOTL IIA 156-57.

→ Exhortation, see FOTL IIA, 161; → Parenesis, see FOTL IIA, 167-68; → Prohibition; → Command; → Order.

Cf. FOTL IX, 243; X, 291; XI, 427; XIII, 172; XVI, 513; XX 105.

ANECDOTE (Anekdote). Num 15:32-36; 17:16-26 [*NRSV* 17:1-11]; 25:1-18. A particular kind of (→) report that records an event or experience in the life of a person. Anecdote may also show a tendency toward storylike features, such as conversation and imaginative description. It is the private "biographical" focus, however, as distinct from "public" events recounted in many reports, that is characteristic of anecdote. Examples are 1 Kgs 9:10-14; 19:19-21. Societal setting and intention for anecdote would naturally vary according to circumstances and content. FOTL IX, 243; X, 291.

Cf. FOTL I, 317; XI, 427; XIII, 173.

ANNALS (Annalen). Num 21:10-20. Records for and from the archives of the royal court (Gen 14:1-24). FOTL I, 317.

Cf. FOTL IIA, 157; IX, 243-44; X, 292.

APPEAL (Anrufung, Berufung auf . . . , dringende Bitte). Num 27:4. Specifically, a call by one to another, mostly authoritative, party to justify or reconsider a decision or change a situation. → Complaint. Generally, an urgent call to incite a certain kind of conduct, but without the assumption of an obligation on the part of the addressee to respond to such a call (cf. Exod 5:15; 32:12-13; 33:18). FOTL IIA, 157.

→ Petition.

Cf. FOTL XI, 427; XVI, 515.

AVOWAL OF INNOCENCE (Unschuldsbeteuerung). Num 16:16. A statement in which one denies wrongdoing or even affirms good behavior. The setting can be legal, as when the avowal is aimed at an unjust accuser and before a judge, or it can be cultic, as the avowal in Psalms 7, 17, 26. Imitations of the avowal of innocence are found in Job (cf. 9:29-31; ch. 31). FOTL XIII, 173.

BATTLE REPORT (Schlachtbericht). Num 14:40-45; 21:21-31; 33b-35. A schematic recounting of a military encounter typically organized around the following elements: (a) the confrontation of forces, (b) the battle, (c) the consequences of battle, whether defeat or victory, usually with summarizing and characterizing statements. Examples are: Num 21:21-24; Josh 7:2-5; Judg 3:26-30; 8:10-12; 2 Sam 10:15-19. Often, the report will include a scene of consultation with priests for divine words of guidance (as in 1 Sam 23:2-4; 14:36-37; → report of oracular inquiry) or words of encouragement (e.g., Josh 8:1-2). We have little or no evidence for the typical societal settings for this report. All the examples in the OT are now integrated into larger narrative contexts of varied contents. FOTL IX 244; X, 293.

Cf. FOTL XI, 428; XIII, 173.

BLESSING (Segen, Segnung). (1) Num 6:22-27. → Blessing Wish.

(2) A speech, structured in either a subjunctive (imperative, cohortative, jussive) or indicative mood, designed to enhance the object of the blessing with the creative power of the performative word. FOTL I, 317.

(3) A pronouncement cast in either the imperative or indicative mode, designed to call down divine power through the spoken word. Blessing can be introduced or concluded with a formula employing the participle *bārûk,* "blessed," followed by the person who is to be blessed. Good examples are in Gen 24:60; Num 24:5-9. Blessing derives from a tribal ethos (so Gen 24:60; 27:27-29) but was also at home in organized cultic affairs (e.g., 1 Kgs 8:14). Blessings should be distinguished from beatitude (e.g., Ps 2:12; 1 Kgs 10:8), which acclaims blessings already deemed to have been received and becomes a type of didactic saying — as indeed some formulas with *bārûk* have become (e.g., Jer 17:7). Blessing is also different from praise speech (e.g., Ps 72:18; Exod 18:10), which, though beginning with a *bārûk* formula, always has God as its object, and so offers praise to *God* rather than invokes his blessing upon *people.* FOTL IX 245; X, 294.

(4) A pronouncement cast in either the imperative (cf. Gen 24:60) or the indicative (cf. Num 24:5-9), designated to release the inherent power of the spoken, performative word.

A blessing can be introduced or concluded by a formula employing the passive participle *bārûk,* followed by the object of the blessing (cf. Num 24:9). Those formulas setting Yahweh as the object of the blessing represent a development from the formula, but nonetheless are part of the history of this genre. FOTL XIII, 174.

Cf. FOTL XVI, 515-16.

BLESSING WISH (Segenswunsch). Num 6:22-24. The blessing wish ought to be distinguished from (→) prayer and (→) petition. It addresses but does not pray to or petition Israel. And it does not address Yahweh, which happens in prayers and petitions.

→ Blessing; → Prayer; → Petition.

BOUNDARY LIST (Liste der Grenzorte). Num 34:1-12 (cf. Josh 15–16). → List

CALENDAR (Kalender). → Cultic Calendar (Ritual Calendar).

CALL TO CONVOCATION (Ruf zur Versammlung). Num 28:1–30:1.

CAMPAIGN (Feldzug). Referring to Num 1–36. → Saga.

CASE LAW (kasuistisch formuliertes Gesetz). Num 5:5-10, 11-31; 6:1-21. A written expression, which prescribes the type of consequence assumed to be consistent with a described or identified type of action, the so-called case, and which presupposes that the prescription of such consequence is meant to function as a rightful basis for the actualization, implementation, or enforcement of the consequence in the law's application to individual situations of such types of actions. The application of a case law may happen through the parties directly involved in the case or through the active authoritative judicial intervention by a third party.

The case law is *case*-law because of its focus on and expression of the *connection of the two factors:* of (types of) consequence(s) for (types of) action(s); and it is case-*law* because of its *prescriptive determination* of the consequences for actions, and because of the presupposition that its prescriptiveness represents the justifiable basis for the actualization of the prescribed types in extra-judicial settlements or judicial proceedings.

Its character as *law* is thereby constituted by the logic that the authority of the prescribed consequences is intrinsic to the fact of their prescription, rather than, extrinsically, being constituted by an outside legislative or judicial authority or writers of laws. Also, its character as *law* is independent of whether or not such law is actually applied.

"Cases" of actions and their consequences are referred to typologically in the case laws, rather than in the sense of specific individual happenings or in the different form of reports or records about such happenings.

The expression of types of actions, and types of their consequences as well, rests — in part — on the societal tradition of the typical resolution of individual happenings in the past. From the vantage point of the extant law, however, its typological description of an action looks forward just as much to the types of such possible happenings in the future as does its prescription of the consequences for such an envisioned action. This means that if — in the future — a person will have committed such a kind of action, such and such will have to happen to her/him.

The forms of the expression of the so-called protasis, the expression of the action, vary. Their interpretation is subject to the history of the case laws and the settings of their writers, and also to the diverse assessments of their grammar and syntax. It is advisable to distinguish between forms of expression and conceptuality. The forms of expression vary. Common throughout all forms, however, is the concept of the connection of the two different aspects, of action and consequence, in one and the same case law.

The case law is distinguished from (→) prohibition and (→) command, which directly (2nd pers.) or indirectly (3rd pers.) prohibit or command a type of action, or a specific action, but without referring to the consequences for — basically — the violation of such a prohibition or command. The question is under discussion whether (→) prohibitions and (→) commands can also be laws. It seems that allowance must be made, that a prohibition may fall under the category of law if evidence exists that its violation will have legal consequences. A prohibition may not merely be an ethical imperative for what people should not do. It may be an intensified legal expression for what must not be done by anyone — precisely because of the presupposed and known inevitable legal consequences.

Visitors of Yellowstone Park have for years (tradition!) been addressed: "Do not approach bison or any wildlife," or: "Never approach or feed wildlife," or: "do not approach bears," which are prohibitions, or: "Keep a safe distance from all wildlife," which is a command. Further information says that "it is against *the law* (emphasis mine) to approach within 100 yards of bears or within 25 yards of other wildlife." Here, the prohibitions are considered as forms of law. On July 16, 2002, the *Los Angeles Times* reported: "Criminal charges were pending against a Yellowstone National Park visitor who was gored by a bison after he tried to get the animal to raise its head for a photograph, park officials said. No action will be taken against the bison. . . ." The man ignored the prohibition, a law, and for its violation faces criminal charges.

→ Legal Instruction; → Legal Prescription; → Legal Genres, FOTL IIB; → Liability for Guilt Law.

CASE REPORT (Einzelfallbericht). Num 27:1-11; 36:1-12. → Report

CATALOGUE (Katalog). (1) A list that enumerates items according to a systematic principle of classification. 1 Chr 6:39-66. FOTL XI, 428.

(2) Decisive for the form is the scholastic and systematizing character of the material. Thus, catalogue is not simply a random (→) list, a summary, or a (→) register, which orders items according to the needs of governmental control. Nor is it simply a form of record keeping. Catalogue results from a particular kind of intellectual activity that seeks to order reality into systematic and classifiable bodies of knowledge. It probably was created by scribes and/or priests. Examples of catalogue in the OT are Leviticus 11; Exod 25:3-7; Num 7:12-88. Texts that perhaps are based upon catalogues are Gen 6:19-21; 7:2-3, 8, 9; 1 Kgs

7:40b-44, 48-50. For ancient Near Eastern examples, cf. *ANET,* 205 (catalogue of gods), 276 (catalogue of tributes), 328-29 (catalogue of execrations). FOTL IX 245-46; X, 295.

CENSUS LIST (Zensusliste). See → Conscription. Also → List; → Catalogue.
　　Cf. FOTL I, 318 (List); IIA, 158; IX, 245-46 (Catalogue); XI, 428 (Census Roll).

COLLECTION (Sammlung). Num 17:27–18:32 [*NRSV* 17:12–18:32]. A general term describing any combination of genres. Thus, a collection of sayings would be a combination of individual tribal sayings organized according to the traditional list of the twelve tribes. FOTL I, 317.
　　→ Catalogue; → List.
　　Cf. FOTL IIA, 158.

COMMAND (positiver Befehl, Gebot). Num 1:50-53; 2:2-31; 5:1-3(4), 12a; 8:6-19, 26b; 9:1-4 (cf. Exod 5:7b, 8-9, 11, 18; 13:2aα, 5, 10, 11-12). An authoritative positive expression by one party that directs either an addressed (2nd pers.) or a third (3rd pers.) party to what is unconditionally expressed without regard to the psychological disposition of those directed, and which is to be complied with immediately. By directing only positively what must be done, the command alone does not address a possibly or actually prohibited opposite — whether or not such an opposite is implied or presupposed.
　　The command may refer to a single act or an ongoing activity. It may or may not be accompanied by an explanation, and it may stand alone or be in a series.
　　The authority of the command rests either in the official authority of the person giving it or in the force of its content by virtue of its custom, or law, or an immediate necessity, represented by the commanding person. FOTL IIA, 158.
　　→ Order; → Prohibition; → Parenesis, see FOTL IIA, 167-68; → Admonition; → Exhortation, see FOTL IIA, 161.
　　Cf. FOTL XI, 429; XIII, 174; XVI 516.

COMMISSION (Beauftragung, Sendung). Num 6:23a-26. An authoritative charge given by a superior to a subordinate. In Exod 3:1–4:18; 6:2b-8, 10-11; 7:2-5, the commissioning authority is the deity. FOTL IIA, 158.
　　Cf. FOTL IX, 246; X, 295-96; XI, 429; XVI, 516-17.

COMMISSION REPORT (Sendungsbericht). Num 27:12-23. A narrative characterized by the genre of (→) report. FOTL IIA, 159.
　　→ Account.

COMMISSION SPEECH (Sendungsrede). Num 13:1-2. The part in a (→) commission report in which the commissioning speech is quoted verbatim. FOTL IIA, 159.

COMPLAINT (Klage als Beschwerde, Beschwerde-Klage). Num 11:11-13; cf. Exod 2:23aβ-b; 5:22-23. A statement which describes personal or communal distress, often addressed to God with a plea for deliverance (Job 3; Hab 1:2-4; etc.). The description of the distress is characterized by vivid language (cf. the so-called confession of Jeremiah, 12:1ff., etc.), and by the use of the question "why?" (Gen 47:15). In contrast to lament, the complaint presupposes a reversible calamity or injustice that it desires to be changed. FOTL XIII, 174.

Cf. FOTL IIA, 159; XI, 429; XIV, 246, and XV, 513-14 (Complaint Element); XVI, 518; XXII, 628-29.

COMPLIANCE REPORT (Einwilligungsbericht). Num 1:17-19, 48-50. → Report.

CONFESSION OF SIN (Sündenbekenntnis). Num 22:34. A direct expression of guilt, the most widespread formulation of which is "I have erred" *(ḥāṭā'tî)* in Exod 9:27; 10:16; Deut 1:41; Josh 7:20; Judg 10:10, 15; 1 Sam 7:6; 12:10; 15:30; 2 Sam 12:13; 19:21 [*NRSV* 20]; 24:10, 17; 2 Kgs 18:14; Isa 42:24; Jer 3:25; 8:14; 14:7, 20; Mic 7:9; Ps 41:5 [*NRSV* 4]; 51:6 [*NRSV* 4]; 106:6; Job 7:20; 33:27; Lam 5:16; Dan 9:5, 11, 15; Neh 1:6; 6:13. Confessions are used in both individual and corporate contexts and reflect diverse situations and contents.

In Israel and the ancient Near East, as in other cultures, one's guilt was considered a possible cause for all kinds of calamities. Therefore (→) complaints and thanksgivings, in properly diagnosed situations, allow room for a formal confession of sin (cf. Psalm 51). In accordance with ritual language and practice, it includes only a generalized admission of fault without reference to specific sins (2 Sam 12:13; 24:17; Ps 25:7; 38:6, 19 [*NRSV* 5, 18]; 40:13 [*NRSV* 12]; 69:6 [*NRSV* 5]). If one's guilt is not involved in the suffering experienced, there will be a vehement protestation of innocence instead. After the exile, communal confession plays a very important role in synagogue worship (cf. Psalm 106; Nehemiah 9; Ezra 9; Daniel 9). In earlier times confession of sin was certainly tied to sin offerings (Leviticus 4–5; 1 Kgs 8:31ff.). In both cases, it was intended to pacify the wrath of God and prepare for expiation and new blessings from the deity. FOTL XIV, 247; XV, 514-15.

→ Confession of Guilt, see FOTL IIA, 159.

CONSCRIPTION (Registrierung, Musterung zum Wehrdienst). Num 1:1-54; 26:5-50. The setting of the mandatory enlistment/registration of men for military service.

The two indicated texts are (→) reports of conscription. The setting of the reporters/writers of the two texts is different — and distant — from the setting of the persons involved in the conscriptions themselves. However, as the form of their narrative, report, reflects their perception of — an ideal of — actual conscriptions in real societal life, the genre of (→) report of conscription points beyond its literary setting to the original generic setting of the event of conscription itself.

The customary definition of Num 1:1-54; 26:5-50 as (→) census list (also by Coats) is misleading. The texts neither speak about nor mean kinds of census, such as in terms of the head-count of a total population or of persons for taxation. They exclusively refer to the conditions for the society-wide — written — registration of all draftable males from twenty years on who are able to go out to war, including those also registered to go out but without being part of the fighting force, cf. 1:48-54.

The conscription is conceptualized as a systematized process. It begins with the command for it by the highest authority, who also decrees the basic instructions for organization and the appointment of the supreme and tribal leaders. The command is followed by the compliance of the leaders, which involves the organization of the registration of the individual names of the draftable males, the progressive summing up of the head-count from the members of the families to the clans to the tribes and up to the total count of — in this case — the congregation of Israel.

The conscription is the pre-stage for the induction, or draft, of the registered into camp, and for the (→) mobilization for the actual beginning of their military campaign.

Cf. → Muster Roll, FOTL XI, 432.

CULTIC CALENDAR (Kult-kalender). Num 28:1–30:1 [*NRSV* 29:40]. A calendar that sets the dates of required petitionary and thanksgiving feasts. For the most part, such calendars emerge from an agricultural economy and connect the changes of the seasons to their appropriate religious rituals. Early texts mention a yearly pilgrimage to a regional shrine, which has seasonal connotations (1 Sam 1:3). Systematization developed later with three yearly "appearances" before Yahweh (Exod 23:14, 17; 34:23), and the dates were more precisely marked (Exod 23:15-16; Deut 16:1-15; Lev 23:23-44). These calendars are lists of commandments, in the imperative tone, directed to the male community. Older Canaanite prototypes give only the names of months and seasons, presupposing the ritual knowledge necessary for each ritual. FOTL XIV, 247; XV, 516.

CULTIC INQUIRY → Oracular Inquiry.

CULTIC LAW (Kultgesetz). Num 5:11-31; 6:1-21; 28:1–30:1. Law concerning matters of the institutionalized cult.
→ Case Law; → Legal Instruction; → Legal Prescription; → Prescription; → Procedural Law.

CULTIC ORDINANCE (Kultische Verordnung). Num 8:1-4; 15:1-16, 17-31, 37-41; 17:27[*NRSV* 17:12]–18:32; 19:1-22; 28:1–30:1 [*NRSV* 29:40]. An official order structured according to a system for the practice of cultic customs or rituals. FOTL IIA, 159.
→ Ordinance.

DEATH PENALTY LAW (Todesstrafegesetz). Num 1:51. → Case Law.

DEATH REPORT (Todesbericht). Num 20:22-29. A (→) report about the death of a person, cf. Exod 1:6; Deuteronomy 34. FOTL IIA, 159.
Cf. FOTL XI, 429.

DEATH SENTENCE (Todesurteil). Num 27:12-23. → Death Penalty Law.

DEDICATION GIFT, REPORT OF (Einweihungsgabe, Bericht von). → Free-will Gift, Report of.

DIALOGUE (Dialog, Zwiegespräch). Num 9:6b-8. A combination of speeches, each in response to the other, with the pattern of response significant for special types of dialogue (Exod 2:7-8, 18-20; 3:4-6; 4:2; 5:1-5; 8:4-7; 10:24-26; 18:14-18; 32:21-24). This structure determines the genre. FOTL IIA, 160.
  Cf. FOTL I, 317; XIII, 175; XVI, 518.

DIVINE ORACLE (Gottesurteil). Num 9:1-14. → Oracle.

EPOS (Epos). Num 1:1–36:13. Only referred to for comparison with → Saga.

ETIOLOGY (Ätiologie). Num 13:24; 21:1-3. A narrative designed in its basic structure to support some kind of explanation for a situation or name that exists at the time of the storyteller. It builds a connection between a saying in the body of the genre and a conclusion that provides the explanation. Sometimes it is a simple wordplay (Gen 32:2-3; Exod 2:10b; 4:24-26; 12:26-27a, 39; 15:23; 16:31; 17:7, 15-16; 18:3, 4). FOTL I, 318.
  Cf. FOTL IIA, 160-61; IX, 248-49; X, 299; XI, 430; XIX, 349.

FABLE (Fabel). Num 1:1–36:13. Only referred to for comparison with → Saga.

FAIRY TALE (Märchen). Num 1:1–36:13. Only referred to for comparison with → Saga.

FREE-WILL GIFT, REPORT OF (Freiwilligkeitsgabe, -gelübde, Bericht von). Num 7:10-88. A particular type of gift that is given at someone's own free decision and initiative. A one-time event for a particular, one-time occasion. Nevertheless, it appears to be given in recognition of particular needs. It may be for the cult, but is not cultic in nature.

It is distinguished from sacrifices, tax, obligatory regular support for ongoing institutional operations, and vows in which the offerers determine the kind and amount of their gifts themselves.

The OT contains the tradition of references to the technical term for this type, *nĕdābâ*, and to the fact of their being expected or taking place, and also of narratives in reporting form about such events whether these can be historically confirmed or represent an idealized pattern abstracted from the reality of actual events.

The recognition of a genre of free-will reports rests on the tradition's attestation of the settings of particular free-will events, on its conceptual specifications (whether technically identified as *nĕdābâ* or — as in Numbers 7 — not), and on the, even idealized, perception of its elements that are, however variably, constitutive for the genre of such reports.

While certain parts of Num 7:1-89 are scarcely elements of the (→) report genre, others, especially in vv. 10-88(9), are, such as the naming of the contributing individuals, the identified kinds and numbers of the gifts and their summary, all recorded in (→) catalogue form.

Connoted to the genre of free-will gift is the explicit reference to the function of this gift, of *ḥănukkâ* in the sense of an initiatory gift, a gift for the initiation of the use of the altar rather than in the sense of a dedicatory gift, a gift for the cultic event of the altar's dedication. See also Milgrom, *Numbers,* 53-54.

GENEALOGY (Stammbaum, Genealogie). Num 3:1-4; cf. Exod 6:14-25. Builds on a system of enumeration rather than narration. It is more nearly akin to (→) list, but can incorporate (→) story in its scope. It derives ultimately from tribal circles as a means for the history and validation of tribal units. Linear Genealogy (Gen 4:1-26; 5:1-32; 11:10-32; 22:20-24; 25:1-6). Segmented Genealogy (Gen 10:1-32; 25:12-16; 36:9-14). FOTL I, 318.
　　Cf. FOTL IIA, 161-62; IX, 249-50; X, 300-301; XI, 430.

HISTORY (Geschichtsschreibung). Num 1:1–36:13. Only referred to for comparison with → Saga.
　　Cf. FOTL I, 318; IX, 250-51; XI, 431; XIX, 349-50; XX, 110-11.

INDICTMENT (Anklage). Num 24:10b. → Indictment Speech.
　　Cf. FOTL IIA, 163.

INDICTMENT SPEECH (Anklagerede, Anklageerhebung). Num 24:10b. One of the (→) trial genres. The indictment speech is a component of the trial speech. It is a statement formally handed down by a judicial authority charging a person with committing an act punishable under the provisions of the law. It is presented either on approval of an accusation or in its own right.

Because of the particular structure of Israel's and Judah's judicial systems, the judicial authorities who issue an indictment may function as both accuser and judge, such as a king or a trial judge (cf. 1 Sam 15:17-19; 22:12; 1 Kgs 2:42-43; 18:17; 22:18). Other officials may also bring an indictment against someone before a judicial authority (cf. Jer 36:20; 2 Sam 19:22).

A modified form of the indictment speech can also be employed in prophetic literature as the accusation or the reason for punishment in the (→) prophetic judgment speech (Isa 8:6; Jer 11:9-10; Mic 3:9-11), the (→) prophetic announcement of punishment against an individual (Amos 7:17; Jer 23:1), and the (→) prophetic announcement of punishment against the people (Isa 30:12; Hos 2:7-8). FOTL XVI, 521-22.
　　Cf. FOTL IIA, 163; IX, 251; X, 302; XI, 431; XX, 111.

INITIATION GIFT, REPORT OF (Einführungsgabe, Bericht von) → Free-Will Gift, Report of.

INSTALLATION REPORT (Installierungs-, Einsetzungsbericht). Num 8:5-22. A sub-type of the genre (→) report. It presupposes, and particularly focuses on, the societal setting of the practice of official installations of groups or persons into specific functions. A report about a typical societal practice must be distinguished from the settings of that practice.

As a (→) report about an event, it differs from legal or cultic (→) prescription or (→) instruction for institutional permanence. Also, its individual structure depends on the narrator's particular interest, in Num 8:5-22 on the installation of the Levites through a ritual of dedication by which they are transferred from Israel to Yahweh for the clerical work at the sanctuary (Milgrom, *Studies,* 145-46). The report is particularly remote from the setting of the reporters as it speaks about the first-time Sinaitic event of this installation, whereby the short (→) compliance report is dominated by the extensive narrative about Yahweh's command.

INSTRUCTION (Instruktion, Unterweisung). Num 6:2b-20, 22-27; 8:23-26; 10:1-10; 11:16-17, 18-20; 15:2b-10; 15:18b-21, 22-31 (cf. Exod 4:3aα, 4a, 6aα, 7aα; 14:2; 16:13-30). A writing or discourse, chiefly in imperative mode, that offers guidance to an individual or group by setting forth particular values or prescribing rules of conduct. Instruction typically tends to deal with universals: broad values, traditional rules for conduct, or aphoristic knowledge drawn from wide experience. The setting and occasions of use for instructions were probably created by persons of some official or aristocratic standing, such as lawgiver, priest, prophet, scribe, wisdom teacher, or even king. In Egypt, the best examples derive from scribes who formulated didactic works to summarize accepted knowledge or, in some cases, produced instruction in the guise of an after-the-fact testament from a king to his successor, with propagandistic overtones (*ANET,* 414-19; more generally, see M. Lichtheim, *Ancient Egyptian Literature* [3 vols.; Berkeley: University of California, 1973-81] 1:58-80). Similarly, the clearest examples from the OT are in the didactic literature (e.g. Proverbs 1–9; 22:17–24:22). Prophetic examples tend to be employed for persuasive purposes, and they become somewhat more specific by focusing on the wisdom of continued adherence to Yahweh, who promises to defend Zion and the Davidic house, and on the opportunities for national restoration presented to Judah by Yahweh's bringing about catastrophe (e.g., Isa 8:16–9:6 [*NRSV* 7]; 28:1–33:24). FOTL XVI, 522.

→ Priestly Daat.

Cf. FOTL IIA, 163-64; IX, 251; X, 302-3; XI, 431; XIII, 177; XIV, 251; XV 523-24; XXII, 631.

INTERCESSION (Fürbitte). Num 12:11-13. If one person pleads the case of other persons we call this procedure intercession. Moses and Jeremiah are pictured as interceders (Exod 32:11-13; Num 12:11-13; Jer 14:11-14). This role has become proverbial for Moses and Samuel (Jer 15:1). The prayers spoken to God are intercessions as well. They contain invocation and (→) petition. Since the psalms do not narrate interceding procedure we have to evaluate prayer texts as to their interceding quality (cf. Psalms 20; 21). FOTL XIV, 251.

Cf. FOTL XV, 524.

ITINERARY (Wegverzeichnis, Itinerar). Num 21:10-20, 32-35. A formal structure of (→) accounts or (→) reports, which relate movement by stages. Itinerary often includes special formulas, noting the point of departure ("set out from so-and-so") and/or the point of arrival in a journey ("encamped at so-and-so" or "came to so-and-so"), and thus may serve as a literary skeleton for larger collections of varied material (e.g., Exod 15:22, 27; 16:1; 17:1–18:27; 19:1–Num 10:10; 1 Kgs 19:1-18). If the itinerary appears with little or no narrative materials between the stages of movement, it should be understood as a type of (→) list, as e.g., Num 33:5-37, 41-49. FOTL IX, 251-52; X, 303.

Cf. FOTL I, 318; IIA, 164.

ITINERARY INSTRUCTION (Itinerarinstruktion) → Itinerary; → Instruction.

ITINERARY LIST (Itinerarliste). Num 33:1–35:34. → Itinerary; → List.

JOURNEY (Reisebericht). Num 1:1–36:13. Only referred to for comparison with → Saga.

JUDGMENT SPEECH (Gerichtswort). Num 14:11-12, 20-25, 26-35; 15:35 (cf. Exod 32:9-10). → Trial Genres.

LAW ABOUT TRIAL BY ORDEAL (Gesetz über einen Gottesurteilsprozeß). Num 5:5-10.
→ Legal Instruction; → Trial Genres; → Legal Genres, FOTL IIB.

LEGAL INSTRUCTION (Rechtsbelehrung). Num 5:5-10, 11-31; 6:1-21; 8:23-26.
→ Instruction; → Ordeal; → Legal Genres, FOTL IIB.

LEGAL PRESCRIPTION (Rechtsvorschrift). Num 5:5-10; 6:3-8; 8:6-13, 25a-26a; et al. The contents prescribed in (→) legal instruction. In as much as they are legal, rather than moral or ethical, they are expressed in the forms of substantive or procedural (→) case law, and of those (→) prohibitions and (→) commands that can be identified as referring to institutionally adjudicable (→) prescriptions. They aim at permanence.
→ Prescription; → Legal Genres, FOTL IIB.

LEGAL PRONOUNCEMENT (Rechtsverkündigung). Report of Yahweh Pronouncement, as in Num 5:1-3, 5-10, 11-31; 6:1-21; 9:9-14; et al.

LEGEND (Legende). Num 1:1–10:10; 10:11-36; 22:1–24:25. A narrative essentially concerned with the wonderful and miraculous events or persons in the real world. It claims belief in the wonderful dimensions in such events or persons, and aims at edification (Gen 22:1-19; 39–41; Exodus 12–16; 17:8-16). FOTL IIA, 164.
Cf. FOTL I, 318; IX, 252; X, 304; XI, 432; XIII, 177; XVI, 523-24; XX 111-12.

LIABILITY FOR GUILT LAW (Schuldverpflichtungsgesetz). Num 5:5-10. A particular category in (→) case law, according to which the nature of a typical kind of consequence, namely, of guilt-obligation, *'āšām,* for the violation of a correspondingly typical kind of responsibility is prescribed. In Num 5:5-10, the kind of the guilt-obligation is (→) restitution, prescribed in view of different conditions.

LIST (Liste). Num 18:9-18. A written document that consists of the line, or lines, of collected names of persons or objects. In a rudimentary form, such a collection is not determined by a systematized order of the names within it but by an aspect by which they belong together as a group regardless of their relation to each other. This group aspect may or may not be head- or sub-lined in a text (Exod 6:14b-25).

List is a literary macrostructure that is particularly representative of the ancient science of lists *(Listenwissenschaft).* However, since virtually all known lists are also governed by various types of systemization, the specific genre of any list depends on the specific type of its systemization and its purpose. A series may originally be written or oral. → Name List (Gen 35:22b-26; 36:15-19, 40-43; 46:8-27). FOTL IIA, 164.

→ Genealogy; → Catalogue; → Register.

Cf. FOTL I, 318; IX, 253; X, 305; XI, 432; XIX, 350; XX, 112.

LITURGICAL PROCEDURE (Gottesdienstliches Verfahren). Num 8:1-3. The order of steps in a liturgical event.

Cf. FOTL XI, 432; XIV, 252; XV, 525.

MARCH (Marsch). Num 1:1–36:13. Referred to as a particular expression for the people's and also the theophanic movement (→ theophanic march) in the (→) saga of the (→) campaign.

MESSAGE (Botschaft). Num 12:6b-8; 15:2b-16; 18:25-29, 30-32. The content of a communication, typically a (→) speech, sent from one subject to another by a third party, designed to deliver information or instruction for some particular goal (Exod 3:16b-22; 7:2bβ; 12:3aβb-11). FOTL I, 318.

Cf. FOTL IIA, 165.

MIGRATION (Migration). Num 1:1–36:13. Referred to with respect to the basic characteristic of a people's movement in the (→) saga of their (→) campaign, and with respect to the specifically transmigratory nature of a migration, their definitive, once and for all time departure from their original to their — intended or actual — arrival in their new location.

MOBILIZATION (Mobilmachung). Num 2:1-34. The activation of the conscripted/registered males — not for their military training but for setting them up for the start of a planned military campaign, cf. Num 10:11-28. It is in an ideal form conceived to happen through the induction of the draftees into the military encampment according to their already established tribal and subtribal units, and the placement of these units under their respective banners and identified tribal leaders according to the order issued by the highest authority. This order is based on the determination of the relationship of four times three tribal units, and on the aspect of all tribes facing the sanctuary, the center of the camp.

The focus on the genre of the mobilization itself differs from the genre of the writers' ($\rightarrow$) report about such a mobilization. It rests on the writers' perception of how the mobilization of militias does, or ideally should, take place in actual societal settings. And while their ($\rightarrow$) report does not fail to briefly note the ($\rightarrow$) compliance with the ($\rightarrow$) command for the mobilization, it focuses in this case virtually totally on the perceived setting of the ($\rightarrow$) command itself by the highest authority for the mobilization and its encampment order, rather than on the setting of the encampment procedure executing the ($\rightarrow$) command. As a ($\rightarrow$) report, it is specifically a report about the command for a mobilization.

MURMURING STORY $\rightarrow$ Rebellion Story.

MYTH (Mythus). Num 1:1–36:13. Referred to only for comparison with $\rightarrow$ Saga.

NAME LIST (Namensliste). Num 13:4-16. A ($\rightarrow$) list of proper names of persons, cities, or countries. It is based on and organized according to a certain unifying aspect that is normally defined in its superscription.

The aspects vary. They may be related to ($\rightarrow$) genealogy, ($\rightarrow$) lists of heroes or officials, or ($\rightarrow$) census for labor, taxes, and particularly the military registration of the adult male population, etc. The lists belong to administrative settings. First Chronicles has sixty-one name lists and 2 Chronicles has thirteen name lists (cf. Gen 46:8-27; Exod 1:2-4). FOTL IIA, 165.

$\rightarrow$ Onomasticon

Cf. FOTL XI, 432.

NARRATIVE (Erzählung). Exod 13:17–Deut 34:12. Not a genre. The oral or written text in which any and all sorts of happenings, of actions, events, thoughts, speeches, or experiences are narrated.

At least form-critically, narrative includes all texts which are determined by narrative style, i.e., the verbal forms of the sentences and their connectedness throughout a text — as distinguished from those kinds of texts which either describe permanent conditions or define attitudes or express ($\rightarrow$) commands, ($\rightarrow$) prohibitions, ($\rightarrow$) admonitions, exhortations, and even laws and prophetic announcements in which narrative style is also used.

A narrative may therefore consist of one sentence that narrates, e.g., that a person did or does or will or may do something, or that something did, does, will or may happen. Mostly, it consists of smaller or larger units whose parts are either also of narrative character or governed by their narrative unit, and narrated sequentially. The sequentially narrated parts are related under the perspective of the forward movement of what is narrated. The forward movement may be seen as a sequence of the narrated events in terms of time or, e.g., of causality. It may be presented in the form of a unilinear sequence, or in a form of two or more sequences that happen simultaneously or at different times.

A narrative may be long or short, refer to past or present or future events, and to real or imagined things. It may be told for any purpose and with or without much detail. The narrative encompasses classes of narratives and genres of such classes. It is constitutive for the narrative character of all classes of narrative and their genres, but not for the character of those classes themselves and of their genres. What is class and genre specific within narrative is determined by its own, respectively pertinent, criteria. The term must, therefore, not be mixed with terms for particular narrative genres such as (→) story, (→) account, (→) report, (→) legend, etc.

In German, the use of the term *Erzählung* must distinguish between its meanings of narrative (as above), i.e., a narrated text *(das Erzählte),* and the act of narrating *(das Erzählen),* and especially of (→) story (Gunkel's *Sagen der Genesis* are not legends but stories, hence translated as *The Stories of Genesis* [tr. J. J. Scullion; ed. W. R. Scott; Vallejo, Calif.: BIBAL, 1994], and so are Westermann's *Arten der Erzählung in der Genesis* [cf. the English translation: "Types of Narrative in Genesis," in *The Promises to the Fathers* (tr. D. E. Green; Philadelphia: Fortress, 1980), 1-94]. FOTL IIA, 165-66.

Cf. FOTL XIII, 179; XVI, 525; XX, 114.

NEGOTIATION (Verhandlung). Num 20:14-21; 32:1-42. An exchange of (→) speeches moving toward agreement or disagreement and focused on a particular issue (1 Chr 21:20-25; 2 Chr 2:3-16). FOTL XI, 432.

Cf. FOTL IIA, 166.

NEGOTIATION DIALOGUE (Verhandlungsdialog). Num 32:1-42. → Dialogue; → Negotiation.

NEGOTIATIONS REPORT (Verhandlungsbericht). Num 20:14-21. → Report, → Negotiation.

NOVELLA (Novelle). Num 13:1–14:45. A long prose (→) narrative produced by a literary artisan for his or her own particular purposes.

The structure depends on the ability of the author to develop suspense and resolve it in particular directions. Toward that end, sub-plots and interweaving motifs provide depth to the major plot line. Even in the major plot, multiple structures can facilitate a wider range of goals than would normally be the case in traditional narrative. Moreover, characterization can develop subtle tones. Thus the entire piece gives the reader a total impression of event as a complex and subtle process. Figures in the process are subordinated to the crucial character of the process itself.

Setting for the novella lies in the literary activity of the author, who may draw on traditional (→) narratives with settings in various institutions. However, the qualifying characteristic of the novella is the unique shape given to the subject matter by the author. In that sense, the novella is not simply a stage in the history of typical traditional material, but an original creation (cf. Genesis 37–47). FOTL XIII, 179-80.

Cf. FOTL I, 319; XVI, 525; XX, 114.

OFFICIAL REPORT (Amtlicher Bericht). See Num 13:1–14:45. The representation of the transmittal of information or a message by a person duly authorized and sent forth, such as a military envoy or royal messenger. Official report amounts to a narrative sequence which recounts (a) the commissioning of a messenger, (b) the going forth and reception of the messenger, (c) the message, directly quoted, (d) the recipient's reaction. In the interests of narrative economy or special effects, some of these elements may be omitted, expanded, or abbreviated. In most cases, the message from one party to another is quoted, and so to be distinguished from (→) report, which simply narrates in 3rd pers. style, *for the reader,* the simple course of an event. Examples of official report are 2 Sam 11:18-25; 18:19–19:1 [*NRSV* 18:33]; Josh 2:1, 23-24. Fragments of, or allusions to, official report may be seen in 1 Kgs 20:2-3, 5-6, 32. Cf. 1 Kgs 5:15-16. FOTL IX, 253-54; X, 305-6.

→ Spy Report; → Report.
Cf. FOTL XI, 432.

ONOMASTICON (Namensliste). Num 1:1–36:13. A list of the names of localities. Referred to with regard to the question of the macrostructure of the book of Numbers.

→ List; → Name List.

ORACLE (Orakel, Gottesrede, -bescheid). Num 9:10-14; 23:18-24. A communication from the deity, often through an intermediary such as priest or prophet, especially in response to an inquiry (→ oracular inquiry). The OT also describes oracles as unsolicited. In all cases, the structure and content vary; oracles have to do with, e.g., salvation, healing, punishment, judgment, promise, encouragement, and warning. Some oracles commission a prophet to his lifelong vocation, and frequently the prophet's speeches are presented as God's own words, hence as oracle. Settings and intentions vary, according to content and circumstances. Some clue as to solicited oracles comes from (→) reports which mention dreams, prophets, priests, as involved in procedures for obtaining divine communication (cf. Exod 11:4b-8a; 1 Sam 28:6; Num 22:7-12, 19-20; Josh 7:6-15; 1 Kgs 20:13-14; 22:5-6, 15-17; Ezek 20:1-8). FOTL IX, 254; X, 306.

Cf. FOTL I, 319; IIA, 166-67; XI, 432; XV, 528; XVI, 526; XIX, 350; XX, 115; XXII, 633-34.

ORACLE OF SALVATION (Heilsorakel, Heilsspruch, Heilsankündigung). Num 21:34; 24:15-24. A divine assurance of grace, expressed formally by a priest or other officiant in Israelite worship. The existence of such a liturgical practice has become a matter of debate in OT scholarship. J. Begrich postulated this form (usually initiated by the formula "do not fear"; → assurance formula, see FOTL XIV, 258; also → reassurance formula, FOTL XVI, 547), principally on the strength of its occurrences in Second Isaiah (Isa 41:14; 43:1; 44:2; etc.; accepted by Gunkel; Westermann; Kraus; Schoors; et al.). R. Kilian has contested the existence of such a form in the agenda of individual complaint. Frequent usage of the formula, however, would also indicate fixed cultic habits, and individual complaint must be seen in its communal setting, as Kilian himself demands. Consequently, Ps 35:3 asks for a divine response to be articulated in the worship situation (cf. also the different types of salvation oracles in Ps 12:6 [*NRSV* 5];

91:2-8, 9-13; 121:3-4). Salvation oracles, then, do not have to be assumed to explain a psychological change from distress to exuberant joy, but they can be regarded as potential ingredients of petitionary liturgy, similar to the "assurance of grace" or "words of assurance" following confession in Christian worship. See FOTL XIV, 253; XV, 528, for references.

Cf. FOTL I, 319; IIA, 167; XVI, 526.

ORACULAR INQUIRY (Einholung eines Gottesbescheids). Num 9:8. A report telling and receiving an (→) oracle.

Cf. FOTL IX, 254-55; XI, 433; XIX, 350.

ORDEAL (Gottesurteil). Num 5:11-31. → Trial Genres; → Law about Trial by Ordeal.

ORDER (Anordnung, Befehl). Num 1:49-50 (cf. Exod 5:7; 12:20, 46-47). A particular form of expression in which a (→) command and a (→) prohibition are juxtaposed in antithetical parallelism. This type of expression intends to make certain that what is commanded is clarified and reinforced by the explicit addition of its prohibited opposite. Conversely, it intends to make certain that what is prohibited is clarified and reinforced by the explicit addition of its commanded opposite. This terminological specification for order is used for the sake of differentiating among different types of generic expressions. FOTL IIA, 167.

→ Command; → Prohibition; → Parenesis, see FOTL IIA, 167-68; → Admonition; → Exhortation, see FOTL IIA, 161.

Cf. FOTL IX, 255; X, 307; XI, 433; XIII, 180; XVI, 526; XXII, 634.

ORDINANCE (Verordnung). Num 19:1-22. A rule prescribing authoritatively what is to be done. As a broad legal category, ordinance includes many specific types and fields of laws (e.g., → cultic ordinances, festival ordinances, etc.), but an ordaining authority is normally the common element. (Cf. Exod 12:1-28, 43-51; 13:1-16). FOTL XIX, 351.

Cf. FOTL IIA, 167.

ORDINANCE SPEECH REPORT (Bericht der Rede einer Verordnung). Num 15:1-16, 17-31, 37-41; 17:27[*NSRV* 17:12]–18:32; 19:1-22.

→ Ordinance; → Cultic Law; → Case Law.

ORGANIZATION OF THE SANCTUARY, REPORT OF THE (Bericht von der Organisation des Heiligtums). Numbers 3–4. There is insufficient evidence for claiming that this (→) narrative, even in its reporting style, represents an exemplary structure for a genre of (→) reports about the organization of sanctuaries. This narrative seems to be shaped by the writers' vision of the singular event of the organization of the service personnel for the Sinaitic sanctuary, as a part of their total narrative about the preparation for the sanctuary's epiphanic (→) campaign.

One should hypothesize, however, that a genre of (→) reports about such organizations, including systems of the recruitment of work forces for public projects and including the organizations of service personnel for them, existed in the settings of central administrations throughout history, including Israel's own ancient administrative settings. Cf. (→) lists as a rudimentary form of such reporting or accounting. The narrative in Numbers 3–4 may be considered as an exceptional case in light of the tradition in this background.

Also, the question of the genre of (→) reports about such undertakings, and their own settings, must be distinguished from the aspect of the settings of such undertakings themselves and the structures of their own developments that are beyond doubt typical historical and societal realities of their own kind, whether recorded or not. While narratives reflect the settings of the narrators or writers or reporters or recorders and their perspectives, interests, and intentions, they provide as such no proof for the settings of the events themselves; proof, especially for how things "really" happened, would have to be provided by evidence from outside, and independent of, the texts.

Cf. → Lists, FOTL I, 318; IX, 253; XI, 432; XIX, 350; XX, 112.

Passover, Law/Statute of (Passahsatzung, -gesetz). Num 9:1-14, esp. vv. 12b, 14aβ. A reference in narrative texts (of → reports or → instructions) about the Passover to a genre called therein *ḥuqqat happesaḥ,* "the law of Passover." The texts vary, as do the specific instructions. The tradition is explicit about this law as a genre relating to the setting of the practice of the Passover and its order.

Passover Report (Passahfestbericht). Num 9:1-14. → Passover, Law/Statute of; → Report.

Petition (Bitte, Bittrede, Bittschrift, Petition). Num 11:5, 13, 18; 21:22aα. A request or plea from one person to another asking for some definite response. The petition may occur in contexts that express ordinary, day-to-day situations. In such cases the structure of the petition includes both the basis for the petition and the petition proper, expressed directly or indirectly (e.g., Gen 18:3-4; 23:4; Exod 32:12b-13; 1 Kgs 2:15-17; 5:17-20[*NSRV* 3-6]). The petition also occurs as the central element of all (→) complaints, in which the suppliant asks for divine help. It is usually formulated in the imperative, but the jussive, imperfect, and cohortative are also employed to express the suppliant's "wish." FOTL XVI, 527.

Cf. FOTL IIA, 168; IX, 255; XI, 433; XIV, 254; XV, 529; XX, 116.

Pilgrimage (Wallfahrt). Num 1:1–36:13. Only referred to for comparison with → Saga of a → Campaign.

Praise Speech (Lobrede). Num 6:22-27. Only referred to for comparison with → Hymn.

→ Hymn, FOTL I, 318; XI, 431; XIII, 176-77; XIV, 249; XV, 520.

Prayer (Gebet). Num 11:1-3, 4-35; 12:1-16; 16:1–17:5; 20:1-13; 21:4-9. Any communication of a person toward his or her God. It is a direct address to God in the 2nd pers. sg., and it encompasses a wide variety of expression, motivation, purpose, and societal setting. Thus, prayer may take a number of different literary forms or genres depending on content, intention, and setting. Besides the book of Psalms, which contains in effect many cultic prayers, we find mention of prayer in narrative contexts, e.g., Gen 24:10-14; 2 Kgs 20:3; Gen 18:23-32. FOTL IX, 255; X, 308.

Cf. FOTL IIA, 168; XI, 433; XVI, 527; XX, 116-17.

PRESCRIPTION (Vorschrift). Num 8:6-13, 25a-26a; et al. → Legal Prescription.

PRIESTLY DAʿAT (Priesterliches Berufswissen). Num 10:1-10. A genre of specifically professional knowledge for priests for the execution of their priestly functions and duties. The content of the Daʿat is normally contained in (→) reports of (Yahweh's pronouncement or instruction of) (→) legal prescription. Cf. Rendtorff, Gesetze; Leviticus, BKAT III, on chapters 1–7.

PRIESTLY DECISION (Priesterliche Entscheidung). Num 9:1-14. Only referred to for comparison to → Oracular Inquiry.

PRIESTLY TORAH (Priesterliche Tora). (1) Num 18:15, 20.

(2) An authoritative instructional form, postulated by J. Begrich, from which prophetic (→) instruction (prophetic torah) is believed to have developed. The priestly form seems to have focused on instruction concerning cultic purity, i.e., proper separations between clean and unclean and between holy and profane. Priestly torah was given by a priest in response to a question about such matters. Haggai 2:11-13 demonstrates both this teaching aspect of the priestly office and prophetic utilization of the form. The instruction could take various shapes, and these were often employed by prophets: a command or prohibition (Isa 1:11; Ezek 45:8b-9; Amos 5:5a), a statement of Yahweh's desire (Amos 5:21-22), the determination of a judgment (Isa 1:13), or a description of consequences (Amos 4:5). FOTL XVI, 527-28.

(3) Authoritative instruction given by priests in response to a question. The word *tôrâ* designates a pointing of the way and seems to have centered in instruction about proper separations, i.e., between clean and unclean, holy and profane. Haggai 2:11-13 demonstrates both this teaching aspect of the priestly office and prophetic utilization of it. The instruction could take various shapes, and these were often imitated by prophets: a command or prohibition (Isa 1:13; Ezek 45:8b-9; Amos 5:5a), a statement of Yahweh's desire (Isa 1:11; Amos 5:21f.), the determination of a judgment (Isa 1:13), or a description of consequences (Amos 4:5). Many of the prophetic imitations are of a polemic and parodying character. FOTL XIX, 351.

Cf. FOTL XXII, 634-35.

PROCEDURAL LAW (Verfahrensrecht, -gesetz, -vorschrift). Num 5:11-31; 6:1-21. (→) Legal prescription for the correct procedure in cases pertaining to the domain of law. Procedures are prescribed for types of judicial cases in court, as in the trial by ordeal in Num 5:11-31 (→ trial genres), and for legally, including

cult-legally, binding cases outside court proceedings, as in Num 6:1-21. Regarding (→) liturgical procedure, cf. Num 8:1-3.
→ Legal Genres, FOTL IIB.

PROCESSION (Prozession). Num 1:1–36:13. Only referred to for comparison with → Saga of a → Campaign.

PROCLAMATION OF LAW (Rechtsproklamation). Num 5:5-10. → Legal Pronouncement.

PROFESSIONAL INSTRUCTION FOR PRIESTS (Instruktion für Priester). Num 10:1-10. Instruction for the knowledge of the priests concerning their professional duties.
→ Priestly Daat.

PROHIBITION (Verbot). Num 1:49 (cf. Exod 5:7a; 12:15b, 16, 19, 43b, 45, 48b; 13:3b, 7b). An authoritative negative expression by one party that directs either an addressed (2nd pers.) or a third (3rd pers.) party not to do what is unconditionally expressed, without regard to the psychological disposition of those directed. By directing only negatively what must not be done, the prohibition alone does not address a possibly or actually commanded opposite, whether or not such an opposite is implied or presupposed. The prohibition may refer to a single act or an ongoing activity. It may or may not be accompanied by an explanation, and it may stand alone or be in a series. The authority of the prohibition rests either in the subjective authority of the person giving it, or in the force of its content by virtue of its custom, or law, or an immediate necessity, represented by the prohibiting person. FOTL IIA, 168.
→ Order; → Command; → Parenesis, see FOTL IIA, 167-68; → Admonition; → Exhortation, see FOTL IIA, 161.
Cf. FOTL XI, 433; XIII, 180; XIV, 254-55; XV, 531-32; XVI, 528; XIX, 351.

PRONOUNCEMENT OF LAW (Gesetzesverkündigung). Num 5:5-10. → Legal Pronouncement.

PROTOCOL (Protokoll). Num 1:1-54; 3:1–4:49. An administrative record or (→) register of data or events written for official documentation. The two units in Numbers referred to reflect the tradition of this genre.
Cf. also, however, FOTL XI, 434.

REBELLION STORY (Auflehnungs-, Rebellionserzählung). Num 12:1-16; 16:1–17:5[*NSRV* 16:40]; 21:4-9; also: → Murmuring Story (Murrenerzählung). Num 13:1–14:45; 17:6-15[*NRSV* 16:41-50], 16-26 (*NRSV* 17:1-11); 20:1-13. According to Coats, not a genre, but a characteristic motif in the Pentateuchal Exodus-Wilderness (→) Stories or (→) Sagas or (→) Legends.
In Coats's interpretation, the term "rebellion" appears to be distinguished from the term "murmuring" in that the former refers to a more aggressive, compared to a more defensive, complaining meaning of the latter.

Cf. Exod 15:22-27; 16:1-16; 17:1-7 in FOTL IIA.

REGISTER (Register). Num 31:32-47. An (→) administrative list, or even a book, which records for official purposes items or persons according to the means by which they are subject to administration by institutions or corporate bodies. The purpose of a register is to record and document the basis on which persons or items can be administered. Depending on the content, the forms of a register vary. OT texts either based on a register, or themselves a register, list citizens for labor recruitment (Nehemiah 3), or for military service (Num 1:17-47); officials to administer the state (1 Kgs 4:2-6, 7-19; Num 1:5-16); or booty for support of religious shrines (Num 31:32-47). Cf. references to making registers in Num 1:2-4; 2 Samuel 24. Parallels appear frequently in Mesopotamian and Egyptian (→) royal inscriptions designed to commemorate the king and his deeds (e.g., *ANET,* 242-43, 249, 260-61, 278-79). Register originated with the scribal classes whose jobs included keeping administrative records of a centralized state. If such activity did not actually begin with the monarchy, it surely grew enormously with the consolidation of the Israelite state. FOTL IX, 258-59.

Cf. FOTL I, 319; X, 311; XI, 434; XIII, 181.

REPORT (Report, Bericht). Num 1:1-47 (48-54); 2:1-34; 3:1–4:49; 7:1-89; 8:1-4, 5-22; 9:1-14, 15-23; 13:1-33. A particular kind of oral or written communication, based on (→) narrative form, through which one party relates to or for another party the content of an event and its course. The report may or may not contain an explicit affirmation by the reporting party — e.g., by a formula of affirmation or even an oath — that the report is factual, accurate, and true, and corresponds in part or as a whole to the course of the reported events. Whether a report actually corresponds to an event is not decided by the use of this genre. As is the case with all rhetoric, the report may be slanted or even be perjury.

This understanding of a report in the actual setting of a communication event needs to be distinguished from the function of this genre in the larger literary works of the OT such as (→) saga and history writing. In these works the choice of this genre functions as their own device for the portrayal of the nature of a communication by one party to another. The question of such a report's factuality, accuracy, and truth for the readers of those (→) sagas and histories does not depend on the use of this genre for the literary and rhetorical purposes of these works, but on the question of the meaning of these works themselves for their readers.

Next to reports in historical literature about events such as specific military campaigns, the genre is most ostentatiously employed in narratives of authoritative divine speech, especially about the laws in the Pentateuch and about divine pronouncements in the prophetic literature. Introducing a speech by nothing more than a short report formula, the narrator claims the following speech to be the quotation of a received divine speech that must be taken verbatim and without apology by the speaking authority or its mediator or messenger, as in (→) account. FOTL IIA, 170.

Cf. FOTL I, 319; IIA, 170; IX, 259; X, 312; XI, 434; XIII, 181; XVI, 536; XIX, 354; XXII, 645-46.

Request (Bitte, höfliche Aufforderung). Num 20:17. → Appeal.

Response (Antwort, Erwiderung). Num 9:9-14. There are various types, including response to accusation (Exod 1:19) and to summons (Exod 5:22-23). FOTL IIA, 170.

Restitution, Law of (Zurückerstattungs-, Entschädigungsgesetz). Num 5:5-10. See → Liability for Guilt Law; → Case Law.

Ritual (Ritual). Num 28:1–30:1 [*NRSV* 29:40]. The specific steps or acts necessary for a cultic procedure. → Ritual Instruction.

Ritual Calendar (Ritualkalender). Num 28:1–30:1 [*NRSV* 29:40]. → Cultic Calendar.

Ritual Instructions (Ritualinstruktionen). Num 5:11-31; 6:1-21; 15:1-16, 17-31, 37-41; 19:1-22; 28:1–30:1 [*NRSV* 29:40]. A series of compact directions prescribing individual actions inherent in the course of a cultic ceremony. The pattern known from Leviticus 1–7 is used in Ezek 43:18-27; 45:18-20; and 46:1-3, 12. While a formulaic heading or subscription, e.g., "this is . . ." or "these . . . are," often appears, the essential content of this genre is a series of stereotypical directions about presenting, killing, sprinkling, etc. The directions may be given in 2nd masc. sg. or 3rd masc. sg., but at bottom they express an impersonal "whoever." Some actions may be open to laity and others only to priests. It is difficult to determine the setting of such material, but it has been thought to lack enough detail for the liturgical training of the priests themselves, and therefore possibly to reflect the public instruction of the laity by priests. FOTL XIX, 355.
    → Instruction.

Ritual Law (Ritualrecht). → Ritual Instructions; → Case Law; → Procedural Law.

Saga (Sage). Num 1:1–36:13. A long, prose, traditional (→) narrative having an episodic structure developed around stereotyped themes or objects. It may include narratives that represent distinct genres in themselves. The episodes narrate deeds or virtues from the past insofar as they contribute to the composition of the present narrator's world.
    The book of Numbers reflects a people's saga of a divinely ordained campaign migration that was guided by the people's divinely chosen leader.

Types of sagas previously defined are:
    (1) Primeval Saga (Ursage). A narrative account of the beginning of time, the time that produced the world as it is from an original ideal world. Episodic series. (Yahwist's version, Genesis 1–11).
    (2) Family Saga (Familiensage). A narrative account of the events that compose the past of a family unit, exemplified primarily by the affairs of the patriar-

chal head of the family. Episodic series. (Yahwist's version of the Abraham Saga, Genesis 12–26).

(3) HEROIC SAGA (Heldensage). A narrative account of the events that compose the past of a people's leader who, by virtue of his identification with his people, made it possible for them to endure. Episodic units. (Yahwist's version of the Moses Saga). FOTL I, 319.

Cf. FOTL IX, 260; X, 313-14; XI, 435.

Annotation: In Old Testament form criticism, the technical use of the word *saga* in English has been controversial, because the word refers originally to the medieval Icelandic/Nordic tradition of prose narratives and only secondarily to any narrative or legend of heroic exploits.

It is difficult to exclude the secondary use of the term in English because the subject especially of heroic saga occurs not only in Nordic but also in English literature, e.g., in the heroic poem *Beowulf,* the "highest achievement of Old English literature" (*Encyclopaedia Britannica,* 13th ed., Ready Reference I, 989). Cf. also the *Legend of King Arthur,* called "legend" because of the wonders and marvels of the hero Arthur and his heroic band.

These prose narratives or poetic epics rest on oral tradition. They represent historical fiction, imaginative reconstruction of the past. And as far as they focus on heroic persons, aspects of other characters, sites, and events may be verified even if the hero her- or himself is historically uncorroborated.

In German, the word *Saga* is distinguished from the word *Sage,* but in such a way that the word *Saga* refers to the Nordic sagas specifically, whereas *Sage* is primarily defined by the nature and perspective of its narrated subject and only secondarily by its ethnic or territorial origin. From the eighteenth century on, *Sage* has been the standard term of folklorists for a particular type of prose narrative. Resting on elements of traditional oral folklore, these narratives are told about events and persons of the distant past as a matter of history. They are amplified by fantasy in such a way that the connection to events with known historical data, localities, and general circumstances, and especially the references to the heroic persons, may or may not be historically verifiable. Especially the named heroes may only be otherwise personifications of character types or roles of unverifiable persons.

Although the substantive characteristics of *Sage* are also found in English literature, just as in other ethnic literatures, there has been no adequate translation for it in English. In light of the lack of such a translation, the use of the word *saga* for the Moses narratives seems defensible — for Coats in FOTL I and IIA — as long as it is understood that the portrait of the decisive life of a person of the past — especially when heightened to heroic proportion among and for her/his people and their history — refers to its Israelite rather than a Nordic, Germanic, or any other origin and worldview.

Finally, the long saga, often consisting of sagas combined as a sequence or cycle, needs to be distinguished from the short, local, or migratory saga. FOTL IIA, 171-72.

SANCTUARY LEGEND (Heiligtumslegende). Num 1:1–10:10. Only referred to for comparison with the genre of Legends about Sanctuaries. → Legend.

SAYING (Spruch). Num 21:14-15, 31. This term is used in a neutral sense to indicate a one-line or two-line (sometimes more) unit, such as can most readily be seen in the collections that make up the book of Proverbs.

Saying is not a form-critical term in itself, but it can describe such form-critical genres as wisdom saying and proverb.

A saying can be described as experiential or observational when it merely registers a fact; any didactic character it has derives from the context (as in Proverbs 10ff.). When the saying inculcates a value, it is properly didactic (→ wisdom saying). FOTL XIII, 181.

The saying associated with the (→) itinerary is simply a description of a geographical position in an itinerary. Any identifying marks that would type it as an aphorism or some other type of expression have been lost. The saying, like the (→) itinerary, may have derived from military sources.

Cf. FOTL XI, 435 (→ Repudiation Saying); FOTL XIII (→ "Better" Saying, 173; → Biography, 173-74; and → Numerical Saying, 180).

SELF-DEFENSE SPEECH (Selbstverteidigungsrede). Num 16:16. → Avowal of Innocence.

SONG (Gesang, Lied). Num 21:17-18a, 27b-30. Poetic composition performed by an individual or group (Gen 4:23-24; Exod 15:1-21). FOTL I, 320; IIA, 172.
→ Boast, FOTL IX, 245.
Cf. FOTL XIII, 182; XVI, 539.

SONG REPORT (Bericht eines Liedes). Num 21:27-30. → Report.

SPEECH (Rede). Num 5:5-19; 11:4b, 16-30; 15:18-31. A general term describing any oral communication enacted by one of the principals of a pericope. More detailed definition of speech is desirable. For example, a speech may be an (→) oath (see FOTL I, 319), an (→) oracle, an (→) accusation, etc. FOTL I, 320; IIA, 172.
Cf. FOTL XIII, 182; XVI, 539.

SPEECH REPORT (Bericht einer Rede). Num 12:2b, 4a, 6-8; 16:12b-14, 20-21 (cf. Exod 7:26-29 [*NRSV* 8:1-4]; 8:1 [*NRSV* 5], 4 [*NRSV* 8], 5 [*NRSV* 9], 6-7 [*NRSV* 10-11]). → Report. FOTL IIA, 172.

SPY REPORT (Kundschafterbericht). Num 13:1-33. → Official Report; → Report.

STORY (eine erzählte Geschichte). Num 11:1-3, 4-35; 12:1-16; 13:1–14:45; 16:1–17:5 [*NRSV* 16:1-40]; 20:1-13; 21:4-9. A self-contained, relatively short narrative about an event the nature of which is perceived to belong to common experience, and the content of which is of special importance and interest for a community related to it and may even be a part of that community's life. It focuses on its content and its information, education, even instructive but also aesthetic relevance. It is in principle not free of questions concerning the specific veracity of its historical and factual origin. But it is free to be shaped by narrative artistry. FOTL IIA, 172.

→ Account; → Anecdote; → Legend; → Fable, see FOTL I, 318; → Märchen, see FOTL XIII, 178; → Report.

Cf. FOTL IX, 261-62; X, 315; XI, 435; XIII, 182-83; XIX, 357; XX, 117-18; XXII, 648.

SUBSTANTIVE LAW (Inhaltsbezogenes Gesetz). Num 6:1-21. The kind of (→) legal prescription by which the contents of rights are described.

→ Procedural Law; → Legal Genres, FOTL IIB.

SUMMARY STORY/REPORT (Summarische Form einer Geschichte oder eines Reports). Num 15:11-12; cf. Exod 1:1-14; 2:23-25; 4:19-23; 12:37-42; 13:17-22. A narratological device for condensing potentially fully developed stories or reports into a summary of short, prismatic, and essential elements. The elements can be generically diverse. Characteristic for this kind of summary is the incorporation of the elements into a narrative pattern through which they appear as successive stages of events or conditions.

This form does not represent an independent genre but is a particular form of (→) story or (→) report. It is positioned at certain junctures of larger narrative contexts where it functions as a transition from developed narratives that precede it to those that follow it. The purpose of its transitional function is to move the larger narrative effectively forward.

The difference between story and report in such summaries is relative. It depends on whether one or another characteristic in a summary is dominant. FOTL IIA, 172-73.

THEOPHANIC MARCH (Theophanisch gesehener Marsch). Num 9:15-23. A people's march envisioned as led by the march of the theophany itself. → Legend; → Campaign.

→ Theophany, see FOTL IX, 263; XI, 436; XIV, 255; XV, 533; XVI, 541; XIX, 358; XX, 119.

TORAH (Instruction). Num 5:11-31, esp. v. 29. → Instruction; → Legal Instruction.

Cf. FOTL, I, 320.

TRANSMIGRATION (Transmigration). Num 1:1–36:13. Referred to as a specific characteristic of the movement of a people in the (→) saga of their (→) campaign. → Migration.

TRAVEL (Reise). Num 1:1–36:13. Referred to only for comparison with → Saga of a → Campaign.

TRIAL GENRES (Prozessgattungen, Gerichtsreden). Num 5:11-31. A collective term for generic elements related to legal procedure and the context of the law court. The setting may be the jurisdiction of the civil courts held at the gates of a city (cf. Ruth 4:1-12), the sacral jurisdiction of the sanctuaries (Joshua 7; Jeremiah 26), or the royal court (2 Sam 12:1-6; 1 Kgs 3:16-28). Trial genres and formulas appear in many situations of daily life; they are especially prevalent in the prophets, where they appear to have had some influence on the prophetic announcements of punishment, the (→) prophetic judgment speech, and prophetic forms of (→) instruction.

One characteristic prophetic form of the trial genre is the so-called trial speech, often identified as the "*rîb*-pattern" or the "(covenant) lawsuit" form. Examples appear in Isaiah 1; Jeremiah 2; Hosea 4; Micah 6; and various other texts, especially in Deutero-Isaiah. The term *rîb* means "controversy" and can refer to a legal case brought by one party against another; in the case of the prophets, it typically refers to Yahweh's case against Israel for violation of the terms of the covenant between Yahweh and Israel (cf. Isa 3:13; Jer 2:9; Hos 4:1; Mic 6:1-2). Characteristic elements might include a (→) call to attention (Isa 1:2; Hos 4:1; Mic 6:1-2); an appeal for a legal proceeding (Isa 1:18-20); an (→) accusation (Isa 1:2-20; 3:12-15; Hos 4:4-8; Jer 2:5-34); rhetorical questions (Isa 1:5, 12; 3:15; Jer 2:5, 14, 31-32); and, finally, an (→) announcement of judgment (Jer 2:35-37; Hos 4:4-10) or some form of (→) instruction in proper behavior (Isa 1:10-17; Mic 6:6-8). FOTL XVI, 541-42.

A particular type of trial for which the procedure is prescribed in Num 5:11-31 is the trial by ordeal. An ordeal is the deity's revelatory decision through the course of set procedures prescribed for such — critically important — judicial cases that cannot be solved through proof obtainable in regular trial proceedings. Behind the prescription of such procedures stand institutional authorities, and the procedure itself is in Num 5:11-31 said to be carried out under the control and the participation of a priest. → Procedural Law.

Cf. FOTL IIA, 173-74; XI, 436.

TRIP (Ausflug). Num 1:1–36:13. Only referred to for comparison with → Saga of a → Campaign.

VICTORY SONG (Siegeslied). Num 21:27-30. May be interpreted as hymn of praise or communal thanksgiving song. Not visible in this song are those short chants that the women sang whenever their men came back home from battle (1 Sam 18:7; Exod 15:21). From these primitive chants developed artistic poems narrating the course of events and extolling the heroes (cf. Judges 5; Exod 15:1-18; Psalm 68). FOTL XIV, 257; XV, 537.
→ Song

WANDERING (Wanderung). Num 1:1–36:13. Only referred to for comparison with → Saga of a → Campaign.

WOE ORACLE (Weheruf). Num 21:29-30. A genre that is used in the prophetic literature to criticize particular actions or attitudes of people, and sometimes to announce punishment upon them. Woe oracles are found as individual units (Isa 1:4; 3:11; 10:5) or in a series (Isa 5:8-24).

The typical woe oracle has two parts: (a) the exclamation *hôy* ("woe") followed by a participle denoting the criticized action, or a noun characterizing people in a negative way, and (b) a continuation with a variety of forms, including threats (Isa 5:9, 13-14, 24; 28:2-8), accusations (Ezek 13:3-9, 18-19), or rhetorical questions (Isa 10:3-4; Amos 6:2). This genre was likely adopted by the prophets from wisdom circles (Gerstenberger, Wolff, Whedbee); according to Westermann it is a milder form of curse. FOTL XIII, 184-85.

Cf. FOTL XVI, 543; XIX, 358/9; XXII, 649.

Formulae

ACCUSATION FORMULA (Anklage-). Num 11:20; 16:3, 8, 10-14. Typically begins with the interrogative particle *lāmmâ* "Why have you done this thing?" or *mah zō't 'āśît* "What have you done?" The formula is constructed in the 2nd pers. as a direct challenge to some previous act (Gen 3:13; 4:6, 10; 12:18-19a; 16:5a; 20:9; 26:9a, 10; 29:25b; 31:26-28a; 31:30, 36b-37aα; 42:1b; 43:6; 44:4-5, 15). FOTL I, 320.

Cf. FOTL IIA, 174-75.

BLESSING FORMULA (Segens-). Num 6:24-26; 24:9b (cf. Exod 18:11). Introduced with the verb "to bless" *(bārak)* and constructed with imperatives (Gen 1:28; 8:17b; 9:1-2, 26-27; 12:2-3; 27:29; 28:3-4; 32:30b [*NRSV* 29b]; 43:14, 29; 48:15, 16, 20). An utterance that expresses the wish for good will or (divine) favor toward another. In some cases, as in the blessings formally given to one's children, the words are believed to set into motion what they call for. A very old blessing of the congregation is preserved in Num 6:24, "Yahweh may keep you" *(yĕbārekkā yhwh wĕyišmĕrekā);* cf. Gen 28:3; Ps 121:7. This formula was originally used in greetings but then came to be used in cultic proceedings. Later, the passive form "blessed be you" *(bārûk 'attâ;* cf. Deut 7:14; 28:3-6; 1 Sam 15:13; Ps 115:15) apparently became more frequent. In the Psalms the *bārûk* wish is mostly used as an expression of praise directed to Yahweh (Ps 18:47 [*NRSV* 46]; 28:6; 31:22 [*NRSV* 21]; 41:14 [*NRSV* 13]; 66:20; 68:20-36 [*NRSV* 19-35]; 72:18-19; 89:53 [*NRSV* 52]; 106:48; 119:12; 124:6; 135:21; 144:1). FOTL XIV, 258-59.

Cf. FOTL I, 320; IIA, 175; XI, 437; XV, 539-40.

CALL TO ATTENTION FORMULA (Lehreröffnungs-, Aufforderung zum Hören) Num 16:8; 20:10; cf. Exod 3:4. This formula was developed from the short invitation, "Listen" (Gen 37:6; 1 Sam 22:7), which could be used by anyone who wished to open a conversation. It is also a formula that opens a public presentation or address and intends to attract the attention of the hearers to the speech that follows. The constituent elements include: (a) an invitation to listen — "listen," "hearken," "hear me" (1 Chr 28:2; 2 Chr 13:4; 15:2; 20:15, 20); (b) mention of the addressee(s) (Gen 46:2a), and (c) an indication of what is to be heard. This call would be used by, e.g., a singer (Judg 5:3), a wisdom teacher (Prov 7:24), or an official envoy (2 Kgs 18:28-29). It is frequently found in the prophetic literature in various forms, and is often expanded by relative clauses (Amos 3:1; Hos 4:1; Mic 6:1; Isa 1:10; Ezek 6:3; cf. 2 Kgs 7:1ab). It is also found in cultic (→) exhortation, see FOTL IIA, 161, and (→) instruction (Ps 34:3, 12 [*NRSV* 2, 11]; 49:2 [*NRSV* 1]; 50:7; 81:9 [*NRSV* 8]). FOTL IIA, 175-76.

Cf. FOTL I, 320; X, 319: XI, 428, 437; XIV, 259; XV, 540; XVI, 544; XIX, 359.

COMMISSION FORMULA (Sendungs-, Auftrags-). Num 6:23a-b; 13:1-2. The essential part of an authoritative charge to a messenger or emissary to deliver a message on behalf of the sender. The standard wording is "Go and say to PN" plus the identification of the addressee. The (→) messenger formula and (→) message then normally follow. Examples appear in Gen 32:5; 1 Kgs 14:7a; 2 Kgs 18:19; 19:6; Isa 7:3-4; 35:4; 37:6; 38:4-5; Ezek 3:1b, 4b, and 11a. FOTL XVI, 545.

Cf. FOTL X, 320 (Commissioning Formula).

COMPLAINT QUESTION (Beschwerde Frage). Num 11:11-12; 12:2. One of the many elements of the (→) complaint, often with accusing tone and content.

Cf. FOTL XIV, 246; XV, 513.

CONCLUSION FORMULA (Abschluß-). Num 9:10b, 21a; 26:62a; 27:11b; 34:6b, 9b; 36:13. Signals the conclusion of a unit and the juncture between texts.

CONVEYANCE COMMAND FORMULA (Formel für den Befehl zur Übermittlung eines Auftrags). Num 6:2a. The formula expresses the command to the recipient of a (→) message to convey the message to a third party.

DATING FORMULA (Datierungs-). Num 1:1; 9:1; 10:11; 33:3aβ; Exod 12:2, 14; 19:1; Deut 1:3. Cf. also Exod 12:41, 51; 13:3-4. The calendrically formulated expression, basically, of the month, day, and year of a number of events during Israel's migration in the wilderness, whereby each event is dated with reference to the date of Israel's departure from Egypt.

DEATH SENTENCE FORMULA (Todesurteils-). Num 15:35aβ-b. Basically expressed by *môt yûmat,* "he shall be put to death." Mostly in authoritative legal prescriptions, the formula for the death penalty to be imposed upon a person who commits a defined capital crime. Cf. Gen 26:11; Exod 19:12; 21:12, 15, 16, 17, 29; 22:18; 28:35; 31:14, 15; 35:2; Lev 15:31; 16:2, 13; 20:2, 9, 10, 11, 12, 13, 15, 20, 21, 27; 24:15, 16; 27:29; Num 3:10b, 38; 18:3, 7; 35:16, 17, 18, 21, 31; Deut 13:6; 17:6; Josh 1:18; Judg 6:31; 21:5; 1 Sam 14:39, 44; 2 Sam 19:22 (cf. 12:14); 1 Kgs 2:24, 42.

→ Legal Genres, FOTL IIB.

DECLARATORY FORMULA (Deklaratorische Formel). Num 9:13aβ, 13bα, β. A concise, formulaic expression by which a certain act or condition is authoritatively defined and/or (dis)qualified and the kind of its consequences determined.

The specific forms of the declaratory expressions depend on the different factors that are subject to definition, (dis)qualification, and determination.

DEFINITION FORMULA (Definitions-). Num 19:2aa, 10b; 31:12. An introductory or concluding statement that defines the typical nature of a case in legal materials.

ETIOLOGICAL FORMULA (Ätiologische-). Num 11:34; 20:13a; 21:13b. Cf. Gen 2:23; 4:25; 16:13-14; 19:22, 37, 38; 21:31; 26:20b, 21b, 22aβ, 22b, 33; 28:16-17; 31:48-49; 32:3b, 31, 32-33 [NRSV 2b, 30, 31-32]; 38:29b, 30; 50:11; Exod 2:10b; 15:23b. FOTL I, 321; IIA, 176.
→ Etiology.

EXODUS FORMULA (Exodus-). Num 15:41a; 33:3b-5. A form of the typical expressions that are centered in the Exodus tradition. Most distinct is the formula for Yahweh's self-identification: "I am Yahweh, your God, who brought you out of the land of Egypt."

HOLINESS FORMULA (Heiligkeits-). Num 3:13. → Self-Revelation Formula.

IDENTIFICATION FORMULA (Identifizierungs-). Num 28:6, 8b, 10a, 13b, 14b, 16b, 17aβ, 24aβ; 29:1b. The designation of a ritual, whether a sacrifice or a festival.

INSTRUCTIONS EXECUTED FORMULA (Instruktionsausführungs-). Num 12:4b-5; 17:26[NSRV 11]; 20:9b; 30:1. A type of expression that states the execution of a given instruction or command. → Instruction.
Cf. FOTL IX, 251; XI, 431; XIII, 177; XIV/1, 251.

INTERCESSION FORMULA (Fürbitte-). Num 17:10b.

INTRODUCTION FORMULA (Einleitungs-). Num 2:1; 15:24a, 27a; 21 times in Numbers 26; Num 30:2b; 34:7a. Functions to introduce a new narrative unit, e.g., "It was in those days . . ." (Exod 2:11, 23; Judg 19:1; 1 Sam 28:1).
Cf. FOTL I, 321 (Introductory Formula); IIA, 177.

INTRODUCTORY SPEECH REPORT FORMULA (Einleitungs — für den Bericht einer Rede). Num 5:1, 11; 6:1, 22; 8:1, 5, 23. → Introduction Formula.

ITINERARY FORMULA (Itinerar-). The formula is composed of two parts: a notice of departure from one site and a notice of arrival at another (Num 11:35; 12:16; 20:1, 22; 21:4a, 10, 11, 12, 13, 16, 18b, 19, 20; 22:1; 33:3aα, 5, 6abα, 7aα, 7b, 8bβ, etc., throughout 33:1–35:34. Cf. Gen 12:8-9; 13:1, 3, 18; 20:1; 26:17, 22aα, 23; 28:10; 33:18; 35:16a, 21; 46:la, 5-7; Exod 12:37a; 13:20; 15:22a, 27; 16:1; 17:1a-bα; 19:2. FOTL I, 321; IIA, 177.
→ Itinerary.

JUDGMENT FORMULA (Gerichts-, Urteils-). Num 5:27-31; 15:30-31; 19:13b, 15, 20. From the deity to the addressee. Typically employs some statement of indictment as the foundation for a sentence as divine judgment (Gen 2:17; 3:14-15; 6:5, 13; 7:1-4, 11-12, 17-21; 11:8; 20:3). FOTL I, 321.

KNOWLEDGE FORMULA (Kenntnis-). Num 16:28a, 30b. Cf. Exod 6:7b-8; 7:5, 17; 8:10, 18b [*NRSV* 22b]; 9:14, 15, 29; 10:2; 11:7b; 14:4aβ, 18; 16:6b, 8b, 12. → Recognition Formula in FOTL IX, 265; X, 323; XIX, 362: A formula that expresses that humans will recognize the identity of Yahweh in their own experience of divine actions. Its main elements are: You/they shall know — that I am Yahweh. FOTL IIA, 177.
　　Cf. FOTL I, 321.

MESSAGE/MESSENGER FORMULA (Botschafts-/Boten-). Num 15:2a, 18a, 38aα; 17:2aα, 17aα; 18:26aα; 19:2bα; 20:14bα; 22:16bα; 27:8a; 28:2a; 33:51a; 34:2aα; 35:10a; 36:6aα. Part of the speech commissioned by the sender for delivery to the recipient. It is an introduction to the (→) message and functions to identify the sender for the recipient, if not also to claim the authority of the sender for the (→) message (Gen 32:5bβ-6 [*NRSV* 4bβ-5]; 45:9; 24:30). This introduction is a stereotyped 2nd pers. expression marking the (→) message's commission (Gen 50:17; Exod 3:15, 16a; 7:2abα, 15-16aα, 19; 8:5, 16; 9:1, 13; 11:2, 3aα; 16:9, 12; 19:3; 1 Sam 18:25; 2 Sam 7:8; 11:25; 1 Kgs 12:10; 2 Kgs 22:18; Jer 23:35, 37; 27:4; 37:7; 45:4; Ezek 33:27; 1 Chr 17:4; 2 Chr 10:10). FOTL IIA, 177.
　　Cf. FOTL I, 321; IX, 265; X, 322; XI, 438; XVI, 546; XIX, 361; XXII, 650.

MESSAGE COMMISSION FORMULA (Botensendungs-, Botenbeauftragungs-). Num 11:18; 15:2a, 18a, 38aα; 17:2aα, 17aα; 18:26aα, 30a; 19:2b; 27:8a; 28:2a, 3aα; 33:51a; 34:2aα; 35:10a. Addresses the messenger directly with the (→) commission to act for the sender as bearer of a (→) message (Gen 32:4-5bα [*NRSV* 3-4bα]; 44:4; 45:17, 18; 46:34; 50:4). FOTL I, 321.
　　Cf. FOTL IIA, 177.

MURMURING/REBELLION FORMULA (Murren-, Auflehnungs-, Rebellions-). Num 14:2, 27, 29, 36; 16:11; 17:6 [*NRSV* 16:41]; 20:4-5; Exod 15:24; 16:2, 7, 8; 17:3. The formula, especially expressed by the verb *lûn,* "to murmur, rebel," characteristically disqualifies Israel's rebellion against Moses and Yahweh in the wilderness narratives.
　　→ Rebellion.

ONE LAW FORMULA (Ein einziges Gesetz für alle-). Num 15:29. It expresses the validity of a judgment for both natives and strangers.

PETITION FORMULA (Petitions-). Num 11:5, 13, 18; 12:11b; 16:15. A form of typical expressions in (→) petitions, the central element of (→) complaints. FOTL XV, 529.
　　Cf. FOTL IX, 255; XI, 433; XIV/1, 254; XV/2, 529; XX, 116.

PROCLAMATION FORMULA (Proklamations-). Num 18:10bβ. The formula "it is/shall be holy" — to you — is one of the expressions in an authoritative (→) proclamation or (→) decree for the force of law of the subject to which it refers. FOTL XX, 108, 117.

SALVATION ORACLE FORMULA (Heilsorakel-). Num 21:34. Typically the introduction to an (→) oracle of salvation.
Cf. FOTL I, 319; XIV, 253; XV, 528; XVI, 526.

SELF-ABASEMENT FORMULA (Selbsterniedrigungs-, Selbstdemütigungs-). Num 16:11. A formula that makes the speaker less significant or worthy because he measures himself over against some greater or more notable person or being (Gen 18:27; Exod 3:11; 16:7, 8; 1 Chr 17:16). FOTL XI, 439.
Cf. FOTL I, 322; IIA, 177.

SELF-REVELATION FORMULA (Selbstoffenbarungs-, Selbstenthüllungs-). Num 15:41. Constructed with the 1st pers. pronoun "I" (*'ānî*) plus a proper noun, especially a name (Gen 15:1b, 7; 17:1bα; 24:24; 26:24; 27:19; 28:13aβ; 31:13a; 35:11-12; 45:3, 4; 46:3-4; Exod 3:6a; 6:2bβ). FOTL I, 322; IIA, 178.
→ Identification Formula

SPEECH FORMULA (Redeformel). Num 15:1, 17, 35aα, 37; 18:1; 19:1; 21:34; 23:3a, 11. A broad general term to indicate a formal marker of a (→) speech. Speech formulas may employ any verb or noun that indicates speech, especially the verbs *'āmar,* "to say," *dibber,* "to speak," and *'ānâ,* "to answer," or nouns such as *dābār,* "word," and *nĕ'um,* "utterance." Specific genre types are included, such as the (→) messenger formula, the oracular formula, and the prophetic word formula. FOTL XVI, 547.
Cf. FOTL I, 322.

STATUTORY LAW FORMULA (Gesetzes-satzungs Formel). Num 10:8b. A formula belonging and referring to the foundational nature of a law and its instruction or pronouncement.

SUMMARIZING FORMULA (Zusammenfassungs-). Num 15:11a; 26:56; 29:39; 35:7; 36:13. Rather than formulaic, a type of statement by which previously made statements of various sorts are briefly summarized.
Cf. FOTL I, 322; IX, 262.

WOE FORMULA (Wehe-). Num 21:29aα. The introduction to the (→) woe oracle, exclaimed by *'ôy* or *hôy.* FOTL XVI, 543.